PRAISE FOR *T*...   ...*RY*
OF THE NEW T...   ...*RCH*

"This unique volume is full of documentation as well, showing the care that went into it. For pastors and all others interested in the unfolding of the New Testament, this book is a treasure to mine."
—Darrell Bock, Executive Director for Cultural Engagement Hendricks Center Senior Research Professor of New Testament Studies

"With great erudition, Frank Viola has provided readers with a wonderful resource. It would be an understatement to say the breadth of research involved in this project is 'impressive.' Highly recommended."
—Michael Licona, Ph.D., Professor of New Testament Studies, Houston Christian University

"Frank Viola performs an invaluable service for Christians today by centering this book on the story of the early church, what he calls "the community of the King." The result is a highly readable (and well-researched) story of the New Testament church, a genuinely accessible biography of the church, that congregations and classrooms will find indispensable."
—Joel B. Green, Senior Professor of New Testament Interpretation, Fuller Theological Seminary

"In this fascinating volume Frank Viola seeks to write a narrative history of the early church by examining the New Testament documents within their respective historical and chronological contexts. His conclusions are plausible and consistently interesting and insightful. This is an excellent resource for those seeking to understand authentic Christianity by listening to its earliest voices."
—Mark L. Strauss, Ph.D., University Professor of New Testament, Bethel Seminary

"In one volume Frank Viola has recast the entire New Testament as a single readable narrative, but as supported by scholarly notation of the highest order. This single book is for the general reader, the pastor, and the academic. *The Untold Story of the New Testament Church* is an amazing accomplishment. I know of no book like it. Highly recommended."
—Paul Barnett, Ph.D., New Testament Scholar and Lecturer Emeritus, Moore College, Sydney; teaching fellow at Regent College, Vancouver

"This is an enormously helpful survey of the history of the roughly thirty years from the ministry of Jesus to the end of the apostolic period, replete with comments on the significance of historical events for the faith of Jesus followers and with comments on secondary literature."
—Eckhard Schnabel, Mary F. Rockefeller Emeritus Distinguished Professor of New Testament Studies at Gordon-Conwell Theological Seminary

THE
UNTOLD
STORY

OF THE
New Testament Church

THE
UNTOLD
STORY

OF THE
New Testament Church

REVISED AND EXPANDED

FRANK VIOLA

DESTINY IMAGE® PUBLISHERS, INC.
PO Box 310, Shippensburg, PA 17257-0310

"Publishing cutting-edge prophetic resources to supernaturally empower the body of Christ"

This book and all other Destiny Image and Destiny Image Fiction books are available at Christian bookstores and distributors worldwide.

For more information on foreign distributors, call 717-532-3040.
Or reach us on the Internet: www.destinyimage.com

ISBN 13 TP: 978-0-7684-6162-6
ISBN 13 EBook: 978-0-7684-6163-3

For Worldwide Distribution, Printed in the USA

1 2 3 4 5 6 / 28 27 26 25

With deepest love and appreciation,
to the kindest woman I've ever known,
my mother—Jeanette.

CONTENTS

FOREWORD

CONTEXT IS ONE of the most crucial resources for properly understanding the New Testament. The God of the Bible is not a God of isolated verses without their context. History testifies that taking verses out of context has led to all kinds of beliefs and practices that are unbiblical. Too often we take short-cuts to understanding the Bible by quoting random verses or assuming that others who taught us have understood them correctly.

After one begins reading the New Testament a book at a time, one quickly recognizes that verses isolated from their context nearly always mean something different when read in context. But we cannot, in fact, pretend to make sense of most verses without reading their context. In fact, the method of isolating verses from their context disrespects the authority of Scripture.

That people so often read the Bible out of context is not because it comes naturally to us, but because we have been taught the wrong way by others' examples. It is important that we not get so wrapped up in the details of the text (or worse yet, the point for which we wish to use it) that we miss the larger picture of the context. If we ignore context, we will almost always misunderstand what we read in the Bible. Context, coupled with background information, is the most critical key to biblical interpretation. In my academic work and commentaries, I've consistently emphasized this principle as foundational for sound biblical exegesis.

In *The Untold Story of the New Testament Church: Revised and Expanded*, Frank Viola brings context and background together, inviting us on a captivating journey through the birth and growth of the first-century church. With a reputation for captivating prose and heartfelt storytelling, Viola brings his unique perspective to reconstruct the events from Matthew to Revelation. *The Untold Story* offers a plausible chronological narrative that reveals the grand tapestry of God's kingdom plan and brings the characters of the story to life.

The book expertly weaves the framework of Acts with the epistles, tracing the early church's evolution from Pentecost to Patmos. The narrative takes you through pivotal locations such as Jerusalem, Antioch, Greece, Ephesus, and Rome, allowing you to experience Paul's letters—as well as the other epistles—within the context of the early church's history.

While the heart of the story begins at Pentecost, *The Untold Story* ensures that Jesus remains the central figure, illustrating how the church grows from and around Him.

The book is designed for accessibility. Readers can easily navigate through the main text and delve into the footnotes for deeper insights. Viola draws on a wealth of evangelical scholarship, consulting the best resources from the past and present, making this work both informative and engaging.

Whether you're a seasoned Christian or a curious newcomer, this book will transform your understanding of the New Testament. It's not just a history lesson; it's an invitation to see yourself as part of this ongoing story—a story that began two thousand years ago and continues to shape our world today. Prepare to be enlightened, inspired, and challenged as you embark on this extraordinary journey through the cradle of Christianity and the profound impact of Jesus in this unique book.

Craig S. Keener
F. M. and Ada Thompson Professor of Biblical Studies
Asbury Theological Seminary

READ THIS FIRST

Of course, one can always read some kind of meaning into a verse of Scripture. But those who understand that the books of the New Testament were written to specific people, in specific places, nearly two thousand years ago, know that this is not a good idea. If the New Testament texts were written to make sense to people in the first century, then we must try to put ourselves into their places to determine what the writers of the New Testament intended their readers to understand by what they wrote. If we try to make sense of the Bible with no knowledge of the people who wrote it, those who read it, and the society in which they lived, we will be inclined to read into the Scriptures our own society's values and ideas. This would be a major mistake since our culture is very different from that of the ancient Romans.[1]

IN THE FOLLOWING PAGES, I have set out to present the unfolding drama of the New Testament church in chronological order. Reconstructing the first-century story chronologically is not only a herculean effort; it's an impossible one. This is true not just for me but for every person who attempts such a task, including the best scholars and historians. The reason is simple. *None of us were there.*

The information we have about the first-century church is limited. But we have enough solid data about the ancient world that a plausible reconstruction can be created.[2] By "New Testament church," I'm referring collectively to the Christian communities we find in the twenty-seven books that comprise our New Testament.[3] A large portion of the

---

1. James Jeffers, *The Greco-Roman World of the New Testament Era: Exploring the Background of Early Christianity* (Downers Grove, IL: InterVarsity Press, 1999), 11.

2. I write the book I wish existed but cannot find because it doesn't exist. I'm unaware of a book that (1) tells the entire story of the primitive church from Pentecost to Patmos in an easy-to-read format, (2) that's nonfiction, and (3) that's historically plausible and heavily documented using the best scholarship available.

3. The term "New Testament" was created in the second century. The phrase is a translation from the Latin *Novum Testamentum*, and according to many sources, it was first coined by Tertullian (*An Answer to the Jews*). Melito of Sardis is credited with coining the term "Old Testament" (*From the Book of Extracts*). Note that I'm referring specifically to the phrase "New Testament," not "New Covenant." New Covenant (*kaine diatheke*) occurs in the Greek New Testament in the narratives of the Last Supper and in Hebrews 8.

New Testament drama is based on the narrative of Luke's two-volume work known as Luke-Acts.[4]

Luke's first volume, the Gospel of Luke, narrates the story of Jesus during "the days of His flesh"[5]—while He was incarnated in human form—from Galilee to Jerusalem.[6] Luke's second volume, the Acts of the Apostles, narrates the continuing story of Jesus—now in the Spirit working through His body (the church)[7]—from Jerusalem to Rome.[8] To put it in

4. Witherington argues that Luke and Acts are "a two-volume historiographical work." Ben Witherington III, *The Acts of the Apostles: A Socio-Rhetorical Commentary* (Grand Rapids, MI: Eerdmans, 1998), 15-39. See also Colin Hemer, *The Book of Acts in the Setting of Hellenistic History* (Winona Lake, IN: Eisenbrauns, 1990), chaps. 1-3. Keener agrees adding that Acts is an authentic historical monograph. It's both accurate and detailed in its travel journal aspects, and the "we" portions attest to its legitimacy. Craig Keener, "Lessons on Acts," Sessions 1 and 2 (Seedbed, unpublished video series, undated). Luke-Acts makes up almost one-third of the New Testament. Ben Witherington III, *Invitation to the New Testament: First Things*, second edition (New York, NY: Oxford University Press, 2017), 105. For a discussion on Luke-Acts in the context of Jewish and Greek historiography, see Gregory Sterling, *Shaping the Past to Define the Present: Luke-Acts and Apologetic Historiography* (Grand Rapids, MI: Eerdmans, 2023); Ben Witherington III, ed., *History, Literature and Society in the Book of Acts* (New York, NY: Cambridge University Press, 1996), chap. 3. A good overview of Luke-Acts, including purpose, historicity, and themes, can be found in Michael Bird, *A Bird's-Eye View of Luke and Acts: Context, Story, and Themes* (Downers Grove, IL: InterVarsity Press, 2023).

5. This phrase comes from Hebrews 5:7, NKJV.

6. The Gospel of Luke and the book of Acts each cover a period of a little over thirty years. (The book of Luke likely covers 4 B.C. to A.D. 30, while Acts covers A.D. 30 to A.D. 62.) Both volumes are about the same length. Ancient historiographers in the Greek tradition tried to keep the volumes of a historical series the same size and proportion. Interestingly, the last 23 percent of Luke's Gospel chronicles the events leading to Jesus' trials and death, while the last 24 percent of Acts chronicles the events leading to Paul's trials and imprisonment. For details, see Wayne Meeks, ed., *Library of Early Christianity* (Philadelphia: Westminster Press, 1987), 8:77-115. The prologues in both volumes indicate that the documents were intended to be first-century histories. Bruce Malina and John Pilch, *Social-Science Commentary on the Book of Acts* (Minneapolis, MN: Fortress Press, 2008), 6. For a careful examination of the structure of the Gospel of Luke and the book of Acts, see Craig Keener, *Acts: An Exegetical Commentary* (Grand Rapids, MI: Baker Academic, 2012), 1:550-581.

7. Even though "church" is a poor translation of ekklesia, I'm intentionally using it in this book at times since it's universally known. I hope my use of the term throughout the story will recapture its original meaning.

8. In the Gospel of Luke, the story moves *toward* Jerusalem. In Acts, the story moves *away* from Jerusalem. Luke Timothy Johnson, *The Gospel of Luke*: Sacra Pagina (Collegeville, MN: Liturgical Press, 1991), 14-15. I agree with those scholars who make the case that Acts (as well as the Gospel of Luke) is historically accurate. Ancient historiographies were not only meant to document historical events; they were also designed to teach

Luke's words, the Gospel of Luke presents what Jesus *began* to do and teach in His mortal body, while Acts presents what Jesus *continued* to do and teach through His spiritual body, the ekklesia.[9]

> *The first book I wrote, Theophilus, concerned all that Jesus began both to do and to teach....*
> *(Acts 1:1)*[10]

Luke's second volume (Acts) satisfies the promise of the first volume (Luke). The "light for revelation to the nations" is fulfilled,[11] and the gospel of Jesus Christ spreads from Jerusalem to the ends of the earth.[12] *The Untold Story of the New Testament Church* is unique

---

moral, theological, or political lessons. In Acts, Luke teaches about how God empowered His apostles and His ekklesia to penetrate all cultural and social barriers to bring the gospel of the kingdom to the nations and establish kingdom communities. Ancient historical works like Acts were written differently from how history is written today. "Dr. Craig Keener on the Historicity of the Book of Acts," video interview, Seedbed, January 23, 2013; "Lessons on Acts," Session 3. For details on the historical reliability of Acts, see Colin Hemer, *The Book of Acts in the Setting of Hellenistic History*; Martin Hengel, *Acts and the History of Earliest Christianity* (Minneapolis, MN: Fortress Press, 1980); John Stott, *The Message of Acts: The Spirit, the Church & the World* (Downers Grove, IL: InterVarsity Press, 1990), 21-37; Craig Keener, *Acts*, 1:3-220; *The Historical Jesus of the Gospels* (Grand Rapids, MI: Eerdmans, 2009), chaps. 6-8. For a detailed exploration of the apologetics and purpose of Acts, see Craig Keener, *Acts*, 1:435-458; F.F. Bruce, *A Mind for What Matters: Collected Essays* (Grand Rapids, MI: Eerdmans, 1990), chap. 11.

9. The ekklesia (church) is the body of Christ. Ephesians 1:22-23. Luke and Acts are known as "parallel" works. This means the wording and events in Acts parallel the wording and events in Luke. Some examples: Jesus was anointed with the Spirit in Luke; the ekklesia was anointed with the Spirit in Acts. Jesus had three trials in Luke; Paul had three trials in Acts, etc. See Craig Keener, "Lessons on Acts," Session 3.

10. Scripture quotes are from the World English Bible (WEB). There are different versions of this edition. Quotes in this book have been taken from the version that appeared on biblegateway.com, accessed July 2023. The WEB version was selected because it's an excellent translation. It also contains textual notes that shed light on the Greek text. For instance, "brothers" can often be translated "brothers and sisters." While a perfect translation of the New Testament doesn't exist, the WEB is among the best.

11. Luke 2:32.

12. Acts 1:8; 13:46-47; 26:16-18. Paul Barnett, *Paul: Missionary of Jesus* (Grand Rapids, MI: Eerdmans, 2008), 203, 209. For a detailed analysis of the Jewish-Christian mission from Jerusalem to Rome, see Eckhard Schnabel, *Early Christian Mission* (Downers Grove, IL: InterVarsity Press, 2004), 1:730-910. As we shall later see, the phrase "the end of the earth" in Greek and Roman literature referred to Spain (meaning, the

in that it uses the rest of the New Testament to inform the drama in Acts, a drama Luke deliberately abridged. It also weaves into the story the best scholarship to date on day-to-day life for the common person living in the first century. The result is a free-flowing narrative that puts you in the center of the story—a story that has at its core the kingdom of God breaking into the earth. The words of one scholar capture the essence of this work:

> *As we read on, we find that the story of the early church in the Acts of the Apostles is also incomplete and needs to be complemented by information from Paul's letters.... I believe many readers will be surprised at the wealth of solid historical information to be found within the New Testament and the degree to which the New Testament story can be reconstructed.*[13]

This book guides the reader through the New Testament letters in sequential order, providing the historical background for each. As such, it is a cross between a narrative commentary and a Bible handbook. One would think the story of the first-century Christians would be common knowledge among those who read and study the Bible. But that's not the case. In my experience and observation, the majority of pastors, Bible teachers, and seminary students are unaware of many important details in this wonderful saga.

The reason has to do with how ministers are trained today. In many seminaries, there's a fundamental disconnect between church history and the New Testament epistles. The seminary student typically studies the events mentioned in the book of Acts in a "church history" course, and the same student learns to exegete (interpret and expound) the letters of the New Testament in a "New Testament studies" class.[14] The result: What God has

end of the world in the west). Eckhard Schnabel, *Jesus in Jerusalem: The Last Days* (Grand Rapids, MI: Eerdmans, 2018), 394-395.

13. Paul Barnett, *Bethlehem to Patmos: The New Testament Story* (Sydney: Hodder & Stoughton Australia, 1989), 10-11.

14. An example of New Testament exegesis can be found in N. Clayton Croy's excellent book, *Prima Scriptura: An Introduction to New Testament Interpretation* (Grand Rapids, MI: Baker Academic, 2011) and N.T. Wright's, *Interpreting Scripture: Essays on the Bible and Hermeneutics* (Grand Rapids, MI: Zondervan, 2020). A related matter is how "biblical studies" and "systematic theology" have been separated. For the discussion, see C. Kavin Rowe, *Method, Context, and Meaning in New Testament Studies* (Grand Rapids, MI: Eerdmans, 2024), 36-58.

joined together, man has put asunder.[15] The free-flowing story that harmonizes the narrative in Acts with the New Testament letters is rarely connected.[16]

A valuable skill that seminary provides is the ability to exegete Scripture. In this regard, seminary students who major in New Testament studies become masters at analyzing the individual books of Matthew through Revelation. They are like ecologists who study the composition of a tree. They're trained to uncover the bark, examine the sap, inspect the roots, and dissect the leaves. But by and large, they miss the drama for the details and are blinded from seeing the larger shape of the forest.[17]

Once we step back and survey the entire forest, however, we can see how each tree came into being and its relationship to the other trees. Learning the heart-pounding saga of the New Testament church provides this broader perspective—a perspective that provides insight into the meaning of the New Testament writings. My intention in this book is to expand our horizons so we can see the story differently—to view it from new perspectives and fresh angles, putting the pieces together in illuminating ways. Grasping what the New Testament is trying to communicate will never happen by applying a fresh coat of paint or adding new furniture to old rooms. What's required is building new foundations that challenge the old and escort us into new vistas. This is what I have attempted to do in these pages.

The book is divided into five sections, each representing a specific "motion" God has taken to fulfill His magnificent obsession, which the New Testament calls "the eternal

15. In the words of Jeffrey Weima, "the human authors are ultimately only the secondary authors of Scripture; they are inspired by the primary author, the Holy Spirit, and because there is only the one and same Holy Spirit speaking through various secondary human authors, He (the Holy Spirit) gives a fundamental unity to the whole of the Bible; thus, we can and ought to 'compare Scripture with Scripture,' that is, use one portion of God's word (such as the New Testament letters) to shed light on another portion of God's word (such as the book of Acts)." Personal correspondence with Jeffrey Weima, 12/28/23.

16. Throughout the book of Acts, Luke clearly has gaps in his narrative. Like other historiographies, he compresses and abridges many of the stories he rehearses. But often, the gaps can be filled in from the epistles. Craig Keener, *Acts: An Exegetical Commentary* (Grand Rapids, MI: Baker Academic, 2014), 3:2295; David Bauer, *The Book of Acts as Story: A Narrative-Critical Study* (Grand Rapids, MI: Baker Academic, 2021), 7-10.

17. For a fuller explanation of this problem, see Ben Witherington III, *Paul's Narrative Thought World: The Tapestry and Tragedy of Triumph* (Louisville, KY: Westminster John Knox Press, 1994), 1-5.

purpose."[18] I build the story around the theme of the explosive gospel of the kingdom of God,[19] the subject of my landmark work *Insurgence: Reclaiming the Gospel of the Kingdom.*[20]

A Word About the Sources

Whenever I give talks in conferences and churches on the explosive story of the New Testament church, at least one person throws up their hand and asks, "Where are you getting all this information from?" For this reason, I've been extremely careful to document all the sources I've used in compiling the story. This includes biblical references. It should be noted that in the world of New Testament scholarship, everything is disputable. There is no such thing as 100 percent "scholarly consensus." All of it is up for debate.[21] In fact, scholars dispute the date and origin of every New Testament book. Therefore, when Bible commentators attempt to reconstruct the historical background of a New Testament book, they make countless hypothetical reconstructions and educated conjectures based on the available evidence.

Their views are derived from what they consider to be solid evidence, but how they interpret it often results from their own presuppositions and theological leanings. As a result, they often disagree with the details of other scholars' conclusions. For this reason, I've cited numerous scholarly and historical sources that either *inform* or *confirm* what makes the most sense to me when I read the New Testament in light of the available historical

---

18. Ephesians 3:11, ESV. For a detailed discussion of the eternal purpose of God, see my book *From Eternity to Here: Rediscovering the Ageless Purpose of God* (Colorado Springs, CO: David C. Cook, 2009). I give further details in the premium master class *Exquisite Passion: A Deeper Journey into God's Eternal Purpose* at thedeeperchristianlife.com/classes. See also frankviola.org/eternalpurpose for all my work on God's timeless purpose.

19. The kingdom of God is at the heart of God's eternal purpose and thus cannot be separated from it.

20. Frank Viola, *Insurgence: Reclaiming the Gospel of the Kingdom* (Grand Rapids, MI: Baker, 2018). If you haven't read that book yet, I encourage you to do so after you read *The Untold Story*. It explains the high-voltage gospel that Jesus, Paul, and the other apostolic workers preached and how it differs from what's often proclaimed today. I also give further details on the gospel of the kingdom in the master class *Everlasting Domain: Restoring the Kingdom Message* at thedeeperchristianlife.com/classes. The eternal purpose and the kingdom of God cannot be separated.

21. Just because I cite a book by a scholar to support a certain point does not mean I agree with everything contained in that particular book or what the scholar has said elsewhere.

data. In the words of one of my historical advisors, the book you hold in your hands is a "plausible reconstruction" of the first-century church since a reconstruction that's certain at every point is impossible.[22]

What is more, I've sought to write a plausible narrative that's also *readable*–almost like a novel. Every part of the book is either certain, likely, plausible, or at least possible. The footnotes provide biblical support, historical sources, reasoning for my conclusions, and debated points among scholars.

I was happy to test my theories against numerous scholars, being corrected by some while challenging others. Often, my instincts on how I connected the dots were confirmed. To my initial surprise, virtually every scholar I read or with whom I dialogued speculates generously about the details of what took place in the first century. Consequently, the person who demands "proof" to buttress every detail in the story will be sadly disappointed. The best we can do is piece together the available evidence and create plausible scenarios to make sense of the narrative.[23]

In that regard, when one sets out to reconstruct the New Testament drama, the question is never, "Can you prove your scenario?" Instead, the question is always, "Is this scenario historically plausible or at least possible?"[24] To the objection that I am "jumping to

22. New Testament scholar Craig Keener gave me this terminology, calling the book a "plausible reconstruction" of the primitive church after reviewing the first draft. Personal correspondence with Craig Keener, 12/4/23.

23. This is why there is tremendous debate among scholars over the details of every book in the New Testament. For example, all of Paul's letters are in dispute except Romans, 1 and 2 Corinthians, Galatians, Philippians, 1 Thessalonians, and Philemon. Bruce Longenecker, *In Stone and Story: Early Christianity in the Roman World* (Grand Rapids, MI: Baker Academic, 2020), 33; Lars Kierspel, *Charts on the Life, Letters, and Theology of Paul* (Grand Rapids, MI: Kregel Academic, 2012), 79. Throughout this book, I side with those scholars who believe the entire "Pauline canon" (Romans to Philemon) was authored by Paul of Tarsus. See David Capes, Rodney Reeves, and E. Randolph Richards, *Rediscovering Paul: An Introduction to His World, Letters and Theology*, second edition (Downers Grove, IL: InterVarsity Press, 2017), 7-10.

24. Incidentally, I agree with those scholars who believe the Gospels and the book of Acts are authentic and historically reliable. For details, see F.F. Bruce, *The New Testament Documents: Are They Reliable?* (Grand Rapids, MI: Eerdmans, 1943); Michael Licona, *Jesus, Contradicted: Why the Gospels Tell the Same Story Differently* (Grand Rapids, MI: Zondervan, 2024); Craig Blomberg, *Historical Reliability of the Gospels,* second edition (Downers Grove, IL: InterVarsity Press, 2007); N.T. Wright and Michael Bird, *The New Testament in Its World: An Introduction to the History, Literature, and Theology of the First Christians* (Grand Rapids, MI: Zondervan, 2019), chaps. 1-4, 35-36; J.B. Lightfoot, *The Acts of the Apostles* (Downers Grove, IL: InterVarsity Press, 2014), 53ff.; Richard Bauckham, *Jesus and the Eyewitnesses: The Gospels as Eyewitness Testimony*, second

conclusions" in the book, it would be more accurate to say that I'm carefully walking to my conclusions with at least one respected scholar leading or confirming every step.

A Word About the Footnotes and Boxes

Since this work is written for a popular audience rather than an academic one, I've presented the story as simply as I could without bogging down the narrative with academic minutia. At the same time, scholars and those academically inclined will find my perspectives supported in the footnotes. Sometimes I've used footnotes to add further details that help illuminate the main narrative. At other times, I reference a book, podcast episode, or article where I've expanded a particular subject in more detail. I also liberally reference the works of others who expand on topics I only briefly discuss. (If I didn't take this approach, this book would be at least 5,000 pages long, which means no human would read it.[25])

There's no reason to be overwhelmed by the footnotes. I chose to use them instead of endnotes because I want readers to understand how I'm connecting the dots. I also wanted to add further details to parts of the story, some of which are fascinating but too granular

---

edition (Grand Rapids, MI: Eerdmans, 2017); Darrell Bock, *Acts: Baker Exegetical Commentary on the New Testament* (Grand Rapids, MI: Baker Academic, 2007), 6-20; James D.G. Dunn, *Jesus, Paul, and the Gospels* (Grand Rapids, MI: Eerdmans, 2011), chap. 1; Darrell Bock and Robert Webb, *Key Events in the Life of the Historical Jesus* (Grand Rapids, MI: Baker Academic, 2002); Craig Keener, *Christobiography: Memory, History, and the Reliability of the Gospels* (Grand Rapids, MI: Eerdmans, 2019). According to Luke 24, women were witnesses to the resurrection of Jesus. This attests to the credibility of the author and the story. No ancient author would have fabricated such an account. Under Roman and Jewish law, the testimony of women was essentially discounted. Craig Keener, "Lessons on Acts," Session 3; Holly Carey, *Women Who Do: Female Disciples in the Gospels* (Grand Rapids, MI: Eerdmans, 2023), 40. For a discussion on how the New Testament came to be written and recognized, see Ben Witherington III, *The New Testament Story*, 3-105; *Invitation to the New Testament*, 433-451; *Sola Scriptura: Scripture's Final Authority in the Modern World* (Waco, TX: Baylor University Press, 2023); F.F. Bruce, *The Canon of Scripture* (Downers Grove, IL: InterVarsity Press, 1988), 117-334; Benjamin Laird, *Creating the Canon: Composition, Controversy, and the Authority of the New Testament* (Downers Grove, IL: InterVarsity Press, 2023), chaps. 4-8; Susan Lim, *Light of the Word: How Knowing the History of the Bible Illuminates Our Faith* (Downers Grove, IL: InterVarsity Press, 2023); Michael Shepherd, *An Introduction to the Making and Meaning of the Bible* (Grand Rapids, MI: Eerdmans, 2024).

25. Many scholars get into the weeds on the subjects they treat. Others not only examine every weed; they investigate the microorganisms in the soil! Craig Keener's magisterial four-volume commentary on Acts is an example, standing at over 4,400 pages.

to insert into the main text.[26] *Therefore, if you aren't used to reading heavily documented books, ignore the footnotes.* You can always go back for a second read and peruse them. Additionally, you can consult the notes whenever you encounter a question or need clarification while reading the primary text. (The notes also help prevent misunderstandings and incorrect assumptions.)

To further aid the readability of the main narrative, I've placed more comprehensive information about each New Testament book, Paul's apostolic journeys, and the sociological conditions of the first century in gray boxes throughout the chapters. The boxes shed further light on the narrative. I've also added all the New Testament epistles in what many scholars regard as their proper chronological sequence within the story.[27] Chapter and verse notations have been removed to best reflect how the letters sounded to their original audiences. As one scholar put it,

> *It is high time, in any editions that wish to facilitate rather than impede readers' understanding of the New Testament writings, for not only verse divisions...but also the conventional chapter divisions to disappear completely from the text and to be placed as inconspicuously as possible in the margins.*[28]

As you can see in the bibliography, my research is both varied and far-reaching. However, I've relied most heavily on several highly respected scholars. For the chronological sequence and dating of each New Testament event, I've largely followed the chronologies in the works of F.F. Bruce and Ben Witherington III.[29] Regarding the dating of each

---

26. You can think of the book you hold in your hands as an entire seminary library on New Testament studies and early church history condensed into a readable narrative and put under one cover.

27. The Gospels, Acts, and Revelation do not appear in this book. Adding the text of these volumes would take up far too much space. But their content is summarized later in the story. Since this book is designed to unlock the epistles, it's necessary that they appear in their entirety in the appropriate locations.

28. Hermann von Soden, quoted in Christopher Smith, *The Beauty Behind the Mask: Rediscovering the Books of the Bible* (Toronto: Clements Publishing, 2007), 75.

29. Bruce's chronology can be found in his two books: F.F. Bruce, *Paul: Apostle of the Heart Set Free* (Grand Rapids, MI: Eerdmans, 1977) and *The Book of the Acts*, revised edition, NICNT (Grand Rapids, MI: Eerdmans, 1988). For Witherington's chronology, see his *Invitation to the New Testament*, 161-172; *The New Testament Story* (Grand Rapids, MI: Eerdmans, 2004), 273-274; *The Acts of the Apostles*, 81-86. I've also consulted Alan Bandy's chronology in *An Illustrated Guide to the Apostle Paul: His Life, Ministry, and Missionary Journeys*

New Testament epistle, I've sometimes followed the research in Jonathan Bernier's *Rethinking the Dates of the New Testament*, adding additional conclusions by other scholars.[30] Distances between cities are mostly based on the *Lexham Geographic Commentary on Acts through Revelation*.[31]

Beyond the names that appear in the Acknowledgments at the end of the book, I am indebted to Craig Keener,[32] David deSilva,[33] Jeffrey Weima,[34] Alan Bandy,[35] and Paul Barnett.[36] All of them served as my historical advisors for this project.[37] Each one kindly offered suggestions, corrections, improvements, clarifications, and additions. My

---

(Grand Rapids, MI: Baker Books, 2021), 18-19. For Witherington's fuller discussion on chronology, see *The Paul Quest: The Renewed Search for the Jew of Tarsus* (Downers Grove, IL: InterVarsity Press, 1998), 304-331. For a detailed conversation on dating and the disputes over New Testament chronology, see James D.G. Dunn, *Beginning from Jerusalem* (Grand Rapids, MI: Eerdmans, 2009), 497-512; Robert Jewett, *A Chronology of Paul's Life* (Minneapolis, MN: Fortress Press, 1979), chap. 1; Craig Blomberg and Darlene Seal, *From Pentecost to Patmos* (Nashville, TN: B&H Academic, 2021), 24-28; David Capes, et al., *Rediscovering Paul*, 78-81. N.T. Wright's chronological table differs slightly from the above works. N.T. Wright, *Paul: A Biography* (New York, NY: HarperOne, 2018), 433-434. See also F.F. Bruce, *A Mind for What Matters*, chap. 9.

30. Jonathan Bernier, *Rethinking the Dates of the New Testament: The Evidence for Early Composition* (Grand Rapids, MI: Baker Academic, 2022). Bernier's book is an upgrade of John A.T. Robinson's *Redating the New Testament* (London: SCM Press, 1976). Keep in mind that dating the New Testament documents, "especially of the Gospels is to some degree a matter of conjecture." Personal correspondence with Craig Keener, 12/4/23.

31. Barry Beitzel, ed., *Lexham Geographic Commentary on Acts through Revelation* (Bellingham, WA: Lexham Press, 2019). Distances between cities is another area where scholars and historians diverge.

32. Craig S. Keener is F. M. and Ada Thompson Professor of Biblical Studies at Asbury Theological Seminary. He's widely regarded to be one of the world's foremost experts on New Testament background.

33. David A. deSilva is the Trustees' Distinguished Professor of New Testament and Greek at Ashland Theological Seminary.

34. Jeffrey A. D. Weima is professor of New Testament at Calvin Theological Seminary in Grand Rapids, Michigan.

35. Alan S. Bandy, PhD, is the Robert Hamblin Chair of Biblical Exposition Professor of New Testament and Greek at New Orleans Baptist Theological Seminary.

36. Paul Barnett, AM, is a world-renowned ancient historian and New Testament scholar. He is currently a lecturer emeritus at Moore College in Sydney, Australia, and a teaching fellow at Regent College in Vancouver, Canada.

37. Ben Witherington was also helpful through lengthy email correspondences that spanned many years. While I have significant disagreements with Witherington on certain aspects of ecclesiology, his understanding of New Testament chronology and various aspects of first-century history is exceptional.

sentiments regarding the book's balance of academically rigorous research with popularly accessible prose are expressed perfectly by one well-respected scholar's description of one of his own works:

> *This is not a technical book, nor a popular one either...the former are too linguistically daunting for most readers, while the latter are too particular in their emphasis...I have written this for those who find themselves caught in the middle.*[38]

A Word About How the Book Is Organized

Following "Decoding the New Testament" and "A Note about Words and Definitions"—which are critical to understanding this book—I begin the story with a Prologue and the first motion (or divine movement) that began before time, when God conceived His eternal purpose. That brief chapter is followed by several short chapters on the life and ministry of Jesus. Since *The Untold Story of the New Testament Church* focuses on the story from Pentecost to Patmos,[39] the chapters on Jesus in Nazareth and Galilee are intentionally brief. They are designed to lay specific groundwork that will reappear later in the story.

The meat of the book begins at Pentecost in A.D. 30. Following that, we go to Antioch of Syria where Paul (also called "Saul" by Luke) is sent out to begin his apostolic ministry. That's when the book hits its stride and we watch the incredible drama of the New Testament epistles unfold. The book ends with Patmos and how the first apostles of Jesus served and died for their Lord. That section is followed by the coming of the King to earth and the eternal future that God has prepared for all who love Him.

Finally, after the Epilogue, more chapters follow that expand some of the key themes in the book. While these chapters do not continue the narrative, they are vital for reflections, insights, and takeaways.

---

38. Robert Banks, *Paul's Idea of Community: Spirit and Culture in the Early House Churches* (Grand Rapids, MI: Baker Academic, 2020), xi.

39. While the main focus of this narrative begins at Pentecost and ends at Patmos, I begin the story before time, through Israel's history, and then through Bethlehem and Nazareth. I then extend the story after the death of the apostles, into the present time and eternity future.

Mirror-Reading Biblical Texts

Many of the conclusions I draw in this narrative are derived from a method commonly referred to as "mirror-reading." Mirror-reading is the process of reconstructing the historical situation of a New Testament letter by reading the author's response within the letter and then inferring the situation to which he was responding. In the words of F.F. Bruce, when reading the New Testament letters, "We are in a position of people listening to one end of a telephone conversation; we have to infer what is being said at the other end in order to reconstruct the situation for ourselves."[40] The idea is that the author's response reveals or "mirrors" the specific situation he addresses.[41] Emphasizing the importance of this approach, other scholars have put it this way:

> *The first thing one must try to do with any of the Epistles is to form a tentative but informed reconstruction of the situation to which the author is speaking. What was going on in Corinth that caused Paul to write 1 Corinthians? How does he come to learn of their situation? What kind of relationship and former contacts has he had with them? What attitudes do they and he reflect in this letter? These are the kinds of questions to which you want answers.*[42]

One writer aptly states, "In order to begin interpreting the biblical text, we must understand its context in the world from which it came."[43] I firmly agree. Without a thorough and accurate understanding of the context of a biblical text, we risk misinterpreting it:

40. F.F. Bruce, *Answers to Questions* (Grand Rapids, MI: Zondervan, 1973), 93.

41. For a discussion on mirror-reading, see E.P. Sanders, *Paul: The Apostle's Life, Letters, and Thought* (Minneapolis, MN: Fortress Press, 2015), 165; Moisés Silva, *Explorations in Exegetical Method: Galatians As a Test Case* (Grand Rapids, MI: Baker, 1996). When speaking about Paul's letters, Sanders rightly argues that they were "real letters" rather than "academic essays" (169). Depending on how one uses it, "mirror-reading can become very speculative [so] scholars today warn that this should be used with caution." Personal correspondence with Craig Keener, 12/4/23. Knowing this to be the case, I've used mirror-reading throughout this book with extreme care. I agree with Weima who says, "While scholars today are often critical about it [mirror-reading], it nevertheless is an approach that, when used properly, can be used to reconstruct historical contexts confidently." Personal correspondence with Jeffrey Weima, 12/28/23.

42. Gordon Fee and Douglas Stuart, *How to Read the Bible for All Its Worth:* fourth edition (Grand Rapids, MI: Zondervan, 2014), 61.

43. Sherri Brown and Francis Moloney, *Interpreting the Gospel and Letters of John: An Introduction* (Grand Rapids, MI: Zondervan, 2017), 33.

When we read the New Testament through our modern cultural and theological lenses, we bring all kinds of convictions, constraints, and contexts to the text that were not there for the authors and first audiences.[44]

Let me illustrate how mirror-reading works.[45] Consider this text in Philippians 4:2:

I exhort Euodia, and I exhort Syntyche, to think the same way in the Lord.

Mirror-reading enables us to conclude that two women in the church were in conflict with one another. Paul's appeal that they "think the same way" informs this interpretation.[46] Richard Horsley and Neil Asher Silberman sum up the argument this way:

Although the Pauline letters have been adopted as separate "books" of the New Testament and have been interpreted for centuries as timeless theological essays, we must remember that each letter (and, in some cases, specific passages within the individual letters) was composed in a particular historical context.[47]

---

44. Personal correspondence with David deSilva, 3/23/22.

45. James D.G. Dunn describes the importance of mirror-reading when he notes, "We will not really be able to understand the 'why' of a line of argument or of a particular emphasis without having some awareness of the arguments being thus countered." James D.G. Dunn, *The Theology of Paul the Apostle* (Grand Rapids, MI: Eerdmans, 1998), 17. John Barclay sketches out the benefits and pitfalls of mirror-reading in "Mirror-Reading a Polemical Letter: Galatians as a Test Case," *JSNT* 31 (1987): 73-93. While I agree with Barclay's points overall, I think he overstates some of the pitfalls. For example, I don't question Paul's motivations nor the reliability of his sources when he describes his opponents. Neither do I believe Paul was creating a straw man fallacy (which is what his detractors did). To my mind, one of the benefits of understanding "the story" and grasping the whole sweep of the New Testament narrative is that it helps us understand Paul, his opponents, and the other New Testament writers. See Jeffrey Weima, *1-2 Thessalonians: Baker Exegetical Commentary on the New Testament* (Grand Rapids, MI: Baker Academic, 2014), 129-130.

46. In the next verse (4:3), Paul calls on someone else in the ekklesia to help the women resolve their discord. Bruce Winter discusses this more broadly in *Seek the Welfare of the City: Christians as Benefactors and Citizens* (Grand Rapids, MI: Eerdmans, 1994), 98-100.

47. Understanding historical context is essential for comprehending Paul's letters. The task of the scholar is to reconstruct. Richard Horsley and Neil Asher Silberman, *The Message and the Kingdom: How Jesus and Paul Ignited a Revolution and Transformed the Ancient World* (New York, NY: Grosset/Putnam, 1997), 147.

Understanding Ekklesia

Whenever you come across the phrase "kingdom community" or "assembly" in this volume, I'm using it as a substitute for the Greek word "ekklesia,"[48] which is typically translated "church" in most versions of the New Testament. (Some Bible versions accurately translate "ekklesia" as "assembly" or "congregation."[49])

Unfortunately, the term "church" has evolved (or devolved) to mean a denomination, a building, or a religious service.[50] But in the New Testament, the word referred to something entirely different. An ekklesia was an assembly of Jesus-followers.[51] Specifically, an ekklesia referred to the assembled people who were part of the kingdom of God in a locality; hence, I use the phrase "kingdom community" or "assembly" to describe "church."[52]

48. While *ekklesia* is a Greek word and technically should be italicized as I have done here, it's become common vocabulary in Christian circles. So going forward, it will not be italicized.

49. The translation used throughout this book (WEB) translates ekklesia as "assembly." So does the Literal Standard Version, Young's Literal Translation, the Darby Translation, et al.

50. The word "ekklesia" is used 114 times in the New Testament. James D.G. Dunn, *Jesus, Paul, and the Gospels*, 165. It's used sixty-two times in Paul's letters, three in Matthew, twenty-three in Acts, six in the non-Pauline epistles, and twenty times in Revelation. Gerald Hawthorne and Ralph Martin, eds., *Dictionary of Paul and His Letters* (Downers Grove, IL: InterVarsity Press, 2009), 124.

51. Robert Banks, *Paul's Idea of Community*, 25-28; James D.G. Dunn, *Beginning from Jerusalem*, 599-601; *Jesus, Paul, and the Gospels*, 166-167; Gerald Hawthorne, et al., eds., *Dictionary of Paul and His Letters*, 123-124; Douglas Mangum, ed., "Assembly," *Lexham Theological Wordbook*, Logos edition (Bellingham, WA: Lexham Press, 2014). "An *ekklesia* was a meeting or assembly." It was used to describe "a local congregation of Christians and never a building." J.D. Douglas and N. Hillyer, eds., *New Bible Dictionary*, second edition (Downers Grove, IL: InterVarsity Press, 1982), 205. According to Wayne Meeks, the term "ekklesia" was borrowed from the political assembly in Greek cities. In the ekklesia of God, "there is no temple, no priest, no sacrifice, except Jesus himself." Wayne Meeks, ed., *Library of Early Christianity* (Philadelphia, PA: Westminster Press, 1985-1988), 2:138.

52. Throughout the New Testament, "ekklesia" is relegated to a church in a city while "ekklesias" is relegated to a group of churches in a province. Examples: "the assembly which was in Jerusalem" (Acts 8:1; 11:22); "the assemblies throughout all Judea, Galilee, and Samaria" (Acts 9:31); "He went through Syria and Cilicia, strengthening the assemblies" (Acts 15:41). Watchman Nee makes a compelling case for this observation (one ekklesia per city) in his marvelous book, *The Normal Christian Church Life* (Anaheim, CA: Living Stream Ministry, 1980), chaps. 4-5. (Note that the best translations of Acts 9:31 are in the WEB, BLB, LSV, KJV, and NKJV, all of which have the plural "ekklesias.") For the differences between a city and a province in the Roman Empire, see Gary Burge, Lynn Cohick, and Gene Green, *The New Testament in Antiquity: A Survey of the New Testament Within Its Cultural Contexts* (Grand Rapids, MI: Zondervan, 1995), 95-97; Richard

My Hope

For the first twenty years of my Christian life, I never heard anyone reconstruct the story of the first-century church. I heard countless talks on the epistles and the book of Acts, but I hadn't come across a single person who put it all together into a seamless drama. Only later did I discover a few people who attempted this kind of work.[53] Yet even today, it's exotically rare. It is for this reason that I've entitled this book *The Untold Story*.[54] The story is certainly present in the New Testament, but it's rarely told.

The aim of this book, therefore, is to create a working model of the first-century church by weaving together the best available scholarship in the fields of history, New Testament studies, geography, archaeology, and sociology—putting all of it together under one cover. My goal in doing this is three-fold:

1. To help God's people better understand the New Testament so they can avoid misinterpreting and misapplying it.
2. To grip them by the power of the story so they can be transformed by its explosive message.
3. To help them appreciate the genius of God's work within the narrative and discern the principles that govern the advancement of His kingdom today.

Note that this book is *not* to be interpreted as an apologetic for any particular form of church, whether house church, organic church, simple church, missional church, traditional church, industrial church, institutional church, liturgical church, etc.[55] Neither is it a

---

Longenecker, ed., *Community Formation in the Early Church and in the Church Today* (Peabody, MA: Hendrickson, 2002), 74-80; Clinton Arnold, ed., *Zondervan Illustrated Bible Backgrounds Commentary* (Grand Rapids, MI: Zondervan, 2002), 2b:37.

53. See the "Acknowledgments" for an explanation.

54. I credit the late James Rutz for giving me the title. When I first began writing the book in the early 2000s, I had a working title. But during a phone conversation with James, he bluntly told me "The Untold Story of the New Testament Church is far better," and I agreed. Also, I'm using the term "church" in the title as a collective word to refer to the entire body of Christ in the New Testament.

55. The normative gathering for the assemblies in the first century was the house, not any specially designated structure. James D.G. Dunn, *Beginning from Jerusalem*, 601-606. For details on the social location of the first-century ekklesia, see Robert Banks, *Paul's Idea of Community*; Frank Viola, *Reimagining Church: Pursuing the Dream of Organic Christianity* (Colorado Springs, CO: David C. Cook, 2008), chap. 4; Roger Gehring,

defense of any particular theological camp, whether Charismatic, Pentecostal, Reformed, Wesleyan, Baptist, Progressive, etc. The way the early Christians gathered and the focus of their faith are made plain in the story, but the reader is left to decide how to apply the ramifications.

One last thing: This book serves as an introduction to a much larger project that I've been working on for years. Since 2005, I've been holding conferences that present Paul's epistles in a novel way. Those conference messages have been converted into audio master classes that take a 3D, right-brained approach to the epistles. That is, they present the drama behind each letter using what scholars call "narrative exegesis."[56] If you find this book helpful, you will gain further insight by listening to the master classes.[57]

My hope in penning this volume is that the Lord would use it to give His people a new and exciting glimpse into the New Testament story, which is really *His* story of how the living God continues to bring His heavenly kingdom to planet Earth. And more amazing: that story is also *your* story.

House Church and Mission: The Importance of Household Structures in Early Christianity (Peabody, MA: Hendrickson, 2004). However, this doesn't mean that any modern group of believers meeting in a house automatically qualifies as an ekklesia in the New Testament sense. Likewise, it doesn't mean that a congregation gathering in a dedicated building cannot be an ekklesia.

56. Walter Hollenweger is credited with the term. I call it "biblical narrative." My books, *God's Favorite Place on Earth* (Colorado Springs, CO: David C. Cook, 2013), and *The Day I Met Jesus: The Revealing Diaries of Five Women from the Gospels* (Grand Rapids, MI: Baker, 2015), written with Mary DeMuth, use this approach. Robert Banks gives an example of his own in *Paul's Idea of Community*, 173ff.

57. These master classes are part of my premium training resource, The Deeper Christian Life Network, found at thedeeperchristianlife.com/classes.

DECODING THE NEW TESTAMENT

The arrangement of the letters of Paul in the New Testament is in general that of their length. When we rearrange them into their chronological order, fitting them as far as possible into their life-setting within the record of the Acts of the Apostles, they begin to yield up more of their treasure; they become self-explanatory, to a greater extent than when this background is ignored.[1]

HAVE YOU EVER READ your Bible without understanding what you were reading? Have you ever read any of Paul's letters and wondered,

What did Paul mean when he penned this verse? Who was this letter written to specifically? What were the people to whom he was writing like? How did they live? Where was Paul when he wrote the letter, and what was he feeling? What events prompted him to pen the epistle in the first place?

Have you ever read the book of Acts and the rest of the New Testament and thought to yourself,

When exactly did these events take place? At what point in this riveting drama did Paul, Peter, James, John, and Jude pen their letters? And how do all the books in the New Testament fit together? What special historical events were also occurring during the days of Peter, Paul, and John? And what influence did those events have on the early church?

These were the questions that provoked this book. What's contained in these pages, therefore, is a chronological, socio-historical synopsis of the entire New Testament, the value of which is priceless.

First, understanding the story of the New Testament church will give you a whole new understanding of each New Testament letter—an understanding that is rich, illuminating,

---

1. G.C.D. Howley in "The Letters of Paul," *New International Bible Commentary* (Grand Rapids, MI: Zondervan, 1979), 1095.

and exciting. No longer will you see the epistles as sterile, complicated reads. Instead, they'll turn into flesh and blood voices that are part of a heart-racing saga. To use F.F. Bruce's analogy about mirror-reading from the previous chapter, you'll begin to understand both sides of the phone conversation.

Second, understanding the story will help you see "the big picture" that undergirds the events that followed the birth of the church and its subsequent growth. This "big picture" has at its center an unbroken pattern of God's work. The theme of God's kingdom moving "from eternity to here" is the unifying thread that runs throughout the entire Bible, from Genesis to Revelation. Reading this book, therefore, will not only help you better understand your New Testament, it will also give you a fresh, clear-eyed look at the immensity of God's eternal purpose.

Third, understanding the story will supply you with the proper historical context that will equip you to *accurately* apply Scripture to your life. Many Christians routinely take verses out of context and misapply them to their daily living.[2] But seeing the Scripture in its proper historical context will safeguard you from making this frequent mistake. As one scholar aptly put it, "In order to speak with confidence of 'the beginning of the New Testament story,' we must first examine the biblical passages in their historical context."[3]

Fourth, understanding the story will radically alter how you study the Bible as well as how you interact during group Bible studies. Have you ever had this experience? You're sitting in a circle in someone's home, listening to everyone's subjective reading of a biblical text. Someone says, "I think Paul meant [xyz] in that verse. That's what I get out of it." Another responds, "What the deuce!? That text has nothing to do with that. What's wrong with you? Did you take hermeneutics with satan or something?"[4] Your chest tightens, and you conclude that you're sitting in the presence of a full-blown SYI[5] session. Perhaps you've been there before, maybe one too many times. If so, this book should help with that problem—a lot.

2. I speak from firsthand experience, having done this often as a young believer.

3. Paul Barnett, *Bethlehem to Patmos*, 14.

4. Hermeneutics is the process of biblical interpretation. My scenario is exaggerated, of course, as it's an attempt at humorizing the way Christians sometimes harshly treat one another over differences of biblical interpretation.

5. SYI = share your ignorance.

Combating the Proof-Texting Method

One of the immediate benefits of understanding the story of the New Testament church is that it will deliver you from the "cut-and-paste" approach to Bible study that dominates evangelical thinking today. The "cut-and-paste" approach is the all-too-common practice of coming to the New Testament with scissors and glue,[6] clipping and pasting together disjointed sentences (verses) from books that were written decades apart to different audiences. This "cut-and-paste" approach has spawned all sorts of spiritual hazards.

One hazard is the misguided practice of "proof-texting," a technique employed to win theological arguments and build floatable doctrines.[7] Proof-texting is the lamentable innovation of privileging certain biblical texts that support a certain theology while ignoring context and other texts that present a contrary view. Today, many Christians behave as if the mere citation of some random, de contextualized verse ends all discussion on virtually every subject.[8]

You take one text, find some remote metaphorical connection with another text, and voilà, an ironclad doctrine is born! But this is an insipid approach to understanding the Bible. While it is great for reading one's own biases into the text,[9] it's horrible for understanding the original intent of the biblical authors. It has been rightly said that a person can prove *anything* by taking Bible verses out of context and lashing them together. Permit

6. I'm speaking metaphorically.

7. Nuance is important here. Citing or referencing a group of scriptural texts to support a point or spiritual truth is not proof-texting, *as long as* those texts are applied within the context of the biblical narrative. Paul and Jesus cited texts often, but they didn't lift them out of their local contexts and misapply them. Proof-texting only occurs when isolated verses, removed from their historical context, are cited to prove a point. The tendency to proof-text where the "plain sense" of a verse is assumed as the final inconvertible proof of a given doctrinal position is tragic. Consequently, "the Bible says it, I believe it, so that settles it" becomes a pathetic conversation stopper.

8. In this regard, many Christians suffer from what I call AVS (Acute Versification Syndrome). This is a cognitive condition characterized by an inability to comprehend biblical texts holistically. Those who suffer from this "malady" exhibit a tendency to isolate individual verses, divorcing them from their broader narrative and thematic context. Such people understand the New Testament in terms of sentences rather than story. (My friend Len Sweet calls it "versitis.") This book offers a cure.

9. The technical term for interpreting a text through one's presuppositions, agendas, or biases is called "eisegesis." By contrast, "exegesis" is the legitimate interpretation of a text that reads it in light of what the original authors intended to convey.

me to use an outrageous example. What follows is how a person can biblically "prove" that it is God's will that people commit suicide. All one has to do is lift two verses out of their historical setting and paste them together:

He [Judas] threw down the pieces of silver in the sanctuary and departed. Then he went away and hanged himself. (Matthew 27:5)

Then Jesus said to him, "Go and do likewise." (Luke 10:37b)

While this is a preposterous example, it demonstrates how the "cut-and-paste" approach works. Because the New Testament didn't fall out of heaven with red letters and maps in the back, but rather arose out of real historical situations, proof-texting is not only a dead-end street; it's dangerous. When you read Paul, Peter, John, etc., you're reading someone else's mail. Consequently, when Paul writes to the assembly in Corinth about lawsuits, what he says shouldn't automatically be applied to every potential situation involving civil cases. Context must be taken into consideration.

Without context, we'll routinely misunderstand and misapply Scripture, making certain issues binding that are no longer in force and vice versa. As a result, Christians have managed to build doctrines and invent practices that have fragmented the body of Christ into thousands of denominations, movements, and organizations, many of which have been at war with one another for generations. David deSilva sums up the necessity of a contextual understanding in order to accurately interpret Scripture saying,

If we are to hear the texts correctly, we must apply ourselves to understand the culture out of which and to which they spoke. We need to recognize the cultural cues the authors have woven into their strategies and instructions. This enterprise prevents potential misreading of the texts.... Without taking some care to recover the culture of the first-century Greco-Roman writers and addresses, we will simply read the texts from the perspective of our cultural norms and codes. Negatively, then, this task is essential as a check against our impositions of our own cultural, theological and social contexts onto the text.[10]

10. David deSilva, *Honor, Patronage, Kinship & Purity: Unlocking New Testament Culture* (Downers Grove, IL: InterVarsity Press, 2000), 18. (A newer edition was published in 2022.) See also Bruce Malina, *The New Testament World: Insights from Cultural Anthropology* (Louisville, KY: Westminster John Knox Press, 2001), 24.

Getting the Sequence Right

Another obstacle to accurately understanding Scripture has to do with the way our current Bibles are arranged. The books that make up our New Testament are grossly out of sequence, making it easy for us to "lose the story" as we read. Chronologically, Romans doesn't follow Acts, and 1 Corinthians wasn't written after Romans. The same is true for the rest of the New Testament epistles.

Reading the books of the New Testament out of their chronological sequence is like listening to an audiobook on shuffle where the chapters are heard out of order.[11] Understanding the chronological sequence of each New Testament book and the socio-historical setting that undergirds it is a powerful remedy for misunderstanding and misapplication.

One may wonder why the New Testament was arranged in its current manner. The answer is that when the New Testament canon was compiled during the second century, Paul's epistles were arranged according to length rather than according to the time periods in which they were penned.[12] To add to the problem, chapter divisions were inserted in the year 1227, and verse divisions were added in 1551.[13] These artificial divisions have made the "proof-texting" method of Bible reading almost a default setting. Christopher Smith explains one of the reasons why chapter-verse divisions prevent us from understanding the meaning of a text:

---

11. For details on this problem, see my article, "Reapproaching the New Testament: The Bible Is Not a Jigsaw Puzzle," at frankviola.org/jigsaw.pdf.

12. Jerome Murphy-O'Connor, *Paul the Letter-Writer: His World, His Options, His Skills* (Collegeville, MN: The Liturgical Press, 1995), 120-130; F.F. Bruce, *The Message of the New Testament* (Grand Rapids, MI: Eerdmans, 1973), 23. The exception to the order of descending length is Galatians, which is a hair shorter than Ephesians. (Some believe this is due to a scribal gloss.) Also, Hebrews does not appear to be Pauline, so it was not part of the Pauline corpus. In addition, the compiler couldn't have organized the letters chronologically because none of Paul's letters had dates on them, and there was no precedent for alphabetical ordering. Jerome Murphy-O'Connor, *Paul the Letter-Writer*, 121.

13. Christopher Smith, *The Beauty Behind the Mask*, 15; *After Chapters & Verses* (Colorado Springs, CO: Biblica Publishing, 2010), chaps. 1-2. While I personally have no issue with chapters and verses for the purpose of locating specific sentences in the Bible, the invention has created the problems I discuss in this book.

Anyone who has been reading the Bible for even a short time has no doubt noticed many individual examples of how verse divisions can break up sentences and phrases that belong together, or else combine those that should be kept separate.[14]

At the end of the day, we simply cannot ignore historical context when reading the Bible—that is, if we want to understand what we're reading accurately. In the words of David Barr,

We [must] make the basic assumption that an author was trying to communicate something meaningful to the audience for which he or she wrote. This approach attempts to discover who wrote the text, when it was written, and what issues it was intended to address in its own time. Only when we grasp the historical situation of both author and audience can we hope to understand the message communicated.[15]

I don't pretend to have created the ultimate guide to the New Testament or promise something that only God Himself can deliver. As one scholar writes of his own work,

This book makes no claim to be the last word on the subject of the New Testament story; others will tell it differently. My aim is to show that there is a story to be told, based on solid data, and to tell it as simply as I can.[16]

That last sentence is precisely what I have sought to accomplish in this book. And I pray it serves you well. Beyond everything else I've said in this chapter, I hope that as you watch the spellbinding saga of the New Testament church dance before your eyes, it will revolutionize your Christian life as well as your relationship with the Lord.

---

14. Christopher Smith, *The Beauty Behind the Mask*, 27. In that book, Smith provides a deep dive into how the man-made chapter-verse divisions in the Bible have kept us from understanding the message that Scripture seeks to convey.

15. David Barr, *An Introduction: New Testament Story* (New York, NY: Wadsworth Publishing Company, 1995), 6.

16. Paul Barnett, *Bethlehem to Patmos*, 12.

A NOTE ABOUT WORDS AND DEFINITIONS

CHURCH

"Assembly," "the body of Christ," "kingdom community," "believing community," "Jesus community," "community of believers," "ekklesia," and even "church" are all used as synonyms to refer to a local group of Jesus-followers who are meeting under the headship and kingship of Jesus Christ in a given locality.

CHRISTIANS

"Converts," "disciples," "believers," "followers of Jesus," "Christ-followers," "Jesus-followers," and "Christians" are all used as synonyms to refer to those who have entrusted their lives to Jesus of Nazareth, giving their believing allegiance to Him.[1]

THE GOSPEL

"The gospel," "the gospel of the kingdom," "the gospel of Christ," "the gospel of liberty," "the gospel of grace," and "preaching Christ" are all used as synonyms for the explosive message that Jesus and the apostles unleashed on the world.[2]

1. After we come to Acts 11 in our story (when the believers were first called "Christians"), I will sometimes use "Christians" as a synonym for believers/disciples. For the history of the term "Christian," see James D.G. Dunn, *The Acts of the Apostles* (Grand Rapids, MI: Eerdmans, 2016), 1. The word "disciple/disciples" is used thirty times in Acts (WEB). Some key verses that support the idea that all true converts (those who believed in Jesus) were called "disciples" are Acts 6:1-2, 7; 11:26; 14:21-22; 18:23, ESV. Compare with Acts 2:44; 4:4; 5:14; 15:5; 17:12; 19:18, ESV. Interestingly, the term "disciple/disciples" is only used in the Gospels and Acts. The word never appears in Paul's epistles.

2. The term "gospel" comes from the Old English word "godspell," and it means "good news" or "good story." F.F. Bruce, *The Defense of the Gospel in the New Testament* (Grand Rapids, MI: Eerdmans, 1977), 1. In my book *Insurgence*, I explain how and why these terms all refer to the same message. The New Testament knows only one gospel, but different terms emphasize aspects of it.

CONVERSION

Today, when a person is converted to Christ, phrases like "they were won to the Lord," "they came to Christ," "they received Jesus," "they trusted Christ," etc., are often used to describe the experience. While I have no problem with any of these phrases, in this volume we will mostly stay with how conversions were described in the book of Acts. Those phrases are:

- They were saved (2:21, 47; 11:14; 16:31, ESV)
- They were added to the Lord (5:14; 11:24, ESV)
- They were added to the ekklesia (2:41, NLT; 2:47, ESV)
- They believed (4:4, 32; 13:12, 48; 14:1, 23; 16:31; 17:12, 34; 18:27; 19:2, 18; 21:20, ESV)
- They believed in the Lord (9:42; 10:43; 11:17; 18:8, ESV)
- They received the word of God (2:41; 11:1; 17:11, ESV)
- They became obedient to the faith (6:7, ESV)[3]
- They were baptized (2:41; 8:12, 38; 9:18; 16:15, 33; 18:8; 19:5, ESV)
- They turned to the Lord (9:35; 11:21, ESV)
- They were persuaded or convinced (17:4; 18:4; 26:28; 28:23, ESV)[4]

3. The Greek word translated "faith" also includes the idea of loyalty. "Believing obedience" is another way to communicate the idea. N.T. Wright, *Paul: A Biography*, 412.

4. In the opening of Acts 17, Luke uses six words to describe the work of evangelism and the result. Those words are "reasoned," "explaining," "demonstrating," "proclaim," "persuaded," and "joined." They are all present in this text: "Paul, as was his custom, went in to them, and for three Sabbath days *reasoned* with them from the Scriptures, *explaining* and *demonstrating* that the Christ had to suffer and rise again from the dead, and saying, 'This Jesus, whom I *proclaim* to you, is the Christ.' Some of them were *persuaded* and *joined* Paul and Silas, of the devout Greeks a great multitude, and not a few of the chief women" (Acts 17:2-4, italics mine).

PROLOGUE

…in hope of eternal life, which God, who can't lie, promised before time began….
(Titus 1:2)

I ASSUME YOU HAVE READ the New Testament, perhaps more than once. Imagine that your dream is to *see* the drama that's recorded from Matthew through Revelation unfold in 4K Ultra HD color and *hear* it in surround sound.[1] Now imagine again. A time machine has just been created, and you are chosen to go back to any era you want. In line with your dream, you choose first-century Palestine (Israel).[2] This is better than a recording, because you get to watch the complete pulse-pounding narrative unfold live and in person until the nail-biting end.

Because you will be there.[3]

Well, your wish has been granted. We are now ready to begin our journey. Find a comfortable place to sit. I now introduce you to the most remarkable story in the world, the untold story of the New Testament church. The story doesn't begin in Bethlehem, or Nazareth, or Jerusalem. It begins in the dateless past.

---

1. You may be reading this book when 4K HD televisions and surround sound have been outshined by better technology. So feel free to insert the newest and best picture quality and audio sound into my example.

2. Ancient "Palestine" is the term used by historians and scholars to refer to what is now current-day Israel. In today's geopolitics, some regard the term "Palestine" as siding with Palestinians against the Israelis, and the term "Israel" as the reverse. But this is an incorrect assumption. I am not using the terms in this way. Like most Christian historians and scholars, I'm using Palestine as the equivalent of Judea and Galilee. Some scholars add Samaria as well. According to Craig Keener, "Some say Rome named the region 'Palestine' only in the second century, but Josephus already notes it as a Greek name for the territory." Personal correspondence with Craig Keener, 12/4/23. In the words of deSilva, "The term 'Israel,' a fitting designation in the monarchical period, is no longer a geographic designation during the Greek and Roman periods, though it still occurs as an ideological one… [Palestine] precisely refers to the specific regions of Idumea, Judea, Galilee, and Perea as appropriate." Personal correspondence with David deSilva, 1/12/24.

3. It is for this reason that I use the present tense throughout this book. I'm seeking to bring you, the reader, into the narrative as if you were watching it unfold in real time.

CHAPTER 1

THE FIRST MOTION: THE KINGDOM IN ETERNITY PAST

This was according to the eternal purpose that he has realized in Christ Jesus our Lord…. (Ephesians 3:11, ESV)

IT IS A TIME before time, before atoms or angels. Nothing exists except God: The eternal Father, the eternal Son, and the eternal Spirit.[1] And God is *All*. The divine community of Father, Son, and Spirit dwells in the heavenly realm.[2] God is King of this realm. His will is done there; His reign holds sway. Both His kingly rule and His realm are known as "the kingdom of God" or "the kingdom of heaven." Within the Godhead,[3] there is unbroken fellowship. The eternal Father and the eternal Son commune with each other through the

---

1. For a detailed discussion of what Jesus Christ did before creation in His preincarnate state, including all the pertinent biblical references, see Leonard Sweet and Frank Viola, *Jesus: A Theography* (Nashville, TN: Thomas Nelson, 2012), chap. 1.

2. Also called "heaven," "the heavens," "heavenly places," and "the heavenlies."

3. I realize that some who are reading this book have been taught that God is not triune. The "Godhead" is the biblical and theological term for the triune unity and oneness of Father, Son, and Spirit. See Romans 1:20 and Colossians 2:9 in the NKJV. For a discussion on the triune nature of God, see "Rediscovering the Triune Nature of God" at frankviola.org/triune. In my books, *Reimagining Church* and *Finding Organic Church: A Comprehensive Guide to Starting and Sustaining Authentic Christian Communities* (Colorado Springs, CO: David C. Cook, 2009), I argue that the Christian life, the ekklesia, and God's mission all flow out of the eternal communion between Father and Son through the Spirit. If you disagree with the orthodox concept that God is communal and triune, don't allow this detail to hinder you from benefiting from the story unfolded in this book. Agreeing with the details of God's nature is not necessary to appreciate the narrative and be helped by it. This is not a book about theology. It's a narrative that presents the New Testament story from the Gospels to Revelation.

eternal Spirit. And within the fellowship of the triune God, there is a holy exchange of life, love, and glory.[4]

A council is held, and God conceives a plan.[5] He shrouds the plan in a mystery, and He hides it in His Son. The plan will be disclosed at an appointed time. A man named Paul of Tarsus will emerge in history, and he will call this timeless plan "the eternal purpose"[6] and "the mystery."[7] What is this matchless plan? It is this: In eternity past, the Godhead purposed to expand their fellowship to a people not yet created.[8]

The Almighty desired to birth a community on earth that would reflect the divine community in heaven. In other words, God desired to bring His kingdom, which is in the heavenly realm, to earth.[9] That kingdom will begin with a community of fallen humans who possess His divine life, and it will eventually fill the created universe. God, who sees the end from the beginning, takes the first step in carrying out His grand purpose. Within the eternal Son are hidden ones whom the Father has chosen to be part of His ordained

---

4. For a detailed discussion on the divine community that circulates within the Godhead, see Leonardo Boff, *Trinity and Society* (Maryknoll, NY: Orbis Books, 1986); Stanley Grenz, *Created for Community: Connecting Christian Belief with Christian Living* (Grand Rapids, MI: Baker Books, 1998); *Rediscovering the Triune God: The Trinity in Contemporary Theology* (Minneapolis, MN: Fortress Press, 2004); Gilbert Bilezikian, *Community 101: Reclaiming the Local Church as Community of Oneness* (Grand Rapids, MI: Zondervan, 1997); Catherine LaCugna, *God for Us: The Trinity and Christian Life* (San Francisco, CA: HarperSanFrancisco, 1991); Roderick Leupp, *Knowing the Name of God: A Trinitarian Tapestry of Grace, Faith and Community* (Downers Grove, IL: InterVarsity Press, 1996); Jürgen Moltmann, *History and the Triune God* (New York, NY: Crossroad, 1992); Ted Peters, *God as Trinity: Relationality and Temporality in Divine Life* (Louisville, KY: Westminster Press, 1993); Thomas Torrance, *The Christian Doctrine of God: One Being, Three Persons* (Edinburgh: T & T Clark, 1996).

5. Ephesians 1:11. The plan takes place before time, which theologians often call "eternity past."

6. Also called "the purpose of the ages." Ephesians 3:11; Romans 8:28; 2 Timothy 1:9.

7. Ephesians 1:9; 3:3-9; Colossians 1:26; 2:2; Romans 16:25, NIV.

8. 1 John 1:3; 1 Corinthians 1:9; 2 Corinthians 13:14. For a scholarly discussion on the union between Christ and the believer, see Clive Bowsher, *Life in the Son: Exploring Participation and Union with Christ in John's Gospel and Letters* (Downers Grove, IL: InterVarsity Press, 2023). In that work, Bowsher discusses "the participation and the in-one-anotherness of God and believers, and the connections of these to the life of the age to come" (4).

9. Matthew 6:10.

kingdom community—the holy assembly of His people.[10] The names of these hidden ones whom He has chosen are written in an eternal volume called "the Book of Life."[11]

In the incomprehensible councils of the living God, the eternal Son—who will later be depicted by the creation of a lamb—is slain in eternity past.[12] And God completes all things before He creates all things.[13] The eternal purpose provokes the Almighty to create a physical universe, and He integrates into His creation pictures, symbols, and allusions of His Son and of the future community that will express His image and exercise His authority visibly.[14] The timeless purpose of God contains four remarkable aspects: obtaining a bride for the Son, a house for the Father, a body for the Son, and a family for the Father, all through the activity of the eternal Spirit.[15]

God decides to choose a man (Abraham) and a people for Himself who will descend from that man—the nation of Israel. Israel's entire life and history will prefigure the spiritual community that will one day display God's nature and reign on the earth.[16] The nation of Israel will be destined to be a kingdom on earth that expresses God's rule—a rule that holds full sway in the heavenly realm.[17] The Almighty promises to bless the whole world through Israel and bring His heavenly kingdom on earth through Abraham's seed.[18] All of this is planned in the everlasting councils within the eternal God before space, time, and creation.

10. Ephesians 1:4.

11. Revelation 17:8; 20:12; 21:27. References to the Book of Life in the Old Testament are sparse, but they do exist. See Exodus 32:32-33; Psalm 69:28; Daniel 12:1. Jesus also referred to it in Luke 10:20.

12. Acts 2:23; 1 Peter 1:19-20; Revelation 13:8, NKJV.

13. Hebrews 4:3.

14. For a theological explanation based in Scripture demonstrating that the Son of God is the eternal reality of the elements in the created order such as the lamb, the sun, the moon, the stars, the fish, the birds, water, and Adam himself, see Leonard Sweet and Frank Viola, *Jesus: A Theography*, chaps. 1-3.

15. These themes are traced from Genesis to Revelation in the Christ is All podcast, episode #35, "The Eternal Purpose" at frankviola.org/thechristisallpodcast as well as in my book *From Eternity to Here*.

16. Acts 7:38; Romans 2:28-29; 1 Corinthians 10:1ff.; Galatians 6:16; Colossians 2:16ff.; Hebrews 10:1ff.

17. Exodus 19:6. The call for Israel to become a kingdom of priests is fulfilled in the New Testament ekklesia (1 Peter 2:9; Revelation 1:6; 5:10).

18. For a spoken message that traces the seed from Genesis to Revelation, showing how it typifies Christ as the true seed of God, see Frank Viola, "A Tale of Two Seeds" on the Christ is All podcast, episode #154 at frankviola.org/thechristisallpodcast.

CHAPTER 2

THE SECOND MOTION: THE KING IS SENT TO EARTH

But when the fullness of the time came, God sent out his Son, born to a woman, born under the law…. (Galatians 4:4)

THE APPOINTED TIME has arrived. God the Father sends His much-loved Son from the heavenly realm to planet Earth. Divinity takes on humanity, and the eternal Son steps out of the heavenly realm through the portal of a young woman named Mary. Mary's womb becomes the passage through which the living God becomes incarnate.[1] He is born in the city of David—Bethlehem—and given the name "Jesus," which means "God saves."[2] Jesus will become the embodiment of all the symbols embedded in creation. He will also fulfill all that Adam and the nation of Israel were tasked to do, but failed.[3] Namely, He will bear God's image and exercise His authority, eventually multiplying both on the earth.[4]

1. Aside from being part of the eternal Godhead, Jesus is the self-knowledge of God enfleshed (John 1:1, 14, 18). As such, He is the mirror image of the invisible God (Colossians 1:15; Hebrews 1:3).

2. Matthew 1:21. More literally, the name "Jesus" (Aramaic, *Yeshua*; Greek *Iesous*) means "God is salvation." Craig Keener, *The IVP Bible Background Commentary: New Testament*, second edition (Downers Grove, IL: InterVarsity Press, 2014), 48. The best scholarship estimates that Jesus was born between 6 and 4 B.C. Darrell Bock, *Studying the Historical Jesus* (Grand Rapids, MI: Baker Academic), 2002, 71. "Jesus was born shortly before Herod's death in 4 B.C.E." Wayne Meeks, ed., *Library of Early Christianity*, 2:24. "Jesus' birth would have been no later than March/April 4 B.C." Joel Green, Jeannine Brown, and Nicholas Perrin, eds., *Dictionary of Jesus and the Gospels*, second edition (Downers Grove, IL: InterVarsity Press, 2013), 134. See also Richard Horsley, et al., *The Message and the Kingdom*, 16, 233; Walter Elwell and Philip Wesley Comfort, eds., *Tyndale Bible Dictionary*, Logos edition (Wheaton, IL: Tyndale, 2001), 1104.

3. Hosea 11:1; Matthew 2:15; Colossians 2:16-17; Hebrews chapters 6 through 10. Adam and Israel failed through disobedience while Jesus perfectly fulfilled the task through obedience to His Father.

4. The Adamic commission is found in Genesis 1:26-28. It's then repeated in Genesis 9:1-7; 12:1-3; Exodus 1:7, etc. Essentially, the commission was to rule and carry God's image, and watch your diet! I provide

Jesus, the eternal Son, will embody God's original intention. He is the promised Christ,[5] the Anointed One, the Messiah of Israel who is destined to be Lord of the world.[6] For this reason, He is born with a price on His head. "He represents the dangerous alternative, the possibility of a different empire, a different power, a different glory, a different peace" from that of Rome.[7] Jesus comes to earth to manifest and fulfill God's eternal purpose for humankind; namely, to bring the kingdom of the heavens to the planet. He does this by establishing the community that the Godhead purposed in the timeless past—"the community of the King."[8] This community will possess the King's nature and authority, and it will be known as the ekklesia or assembly of the living God.

---

details in "Vantage Point: The Story We Haven't Heard" on the Christ is All podcast, episodes #18 and #19 at frankviola.org/thechristisallpodcast.

5. "Christ" is the Greek word for "Messiah." N.T. Wright, *Acts for Everyone: Part One* (Louisville, KY: Westminster John Knox Press, 2008), 178.

6. The term "Messiah" refers to a person chosen by God to be His vice-regent on behalf of His people. Bruce Malina and John Pilch, *Social-Science Commentary on the Letters of Paul* (Minneapolis, MN: Fortress Press, 2006), 33. According to Isaiah 9, 11, and 42, when the Messiah comes, He will be the sovereign Lord over the entire world. According to Psalm 2 and 72, Israel's true King, the final seed of David, will rule from sea to sea, and everyone—Jew and Gentile alike—will bow to His authority. In short, the Messiahship of Jesus is a royal Messiahship, which means He is Israel's true King and at the same time Lord of the world. Richard Horsley, ed., *Paul and Politics: Ekklesia, Israel, Imperium, Interpretation* (Harrisburg, PA: Trinity Press International, 2000), 169; N.T. Wright, *Paul: In Fresh Perspective* (Minneapolis, MN: Fortress Press, 2009), 43, 69. For details on the term "Messiah," see George Ladd, *A Theology of the New Testament,* revised edition (Grand Rapids, MI: Eerdmans, 1993), chap. 10.

7. N.T. Wright, "The Most Dangerous Baby: How an Infant in a Cow Shed Overturns the Brute Force of Caesar," *Christianity Today*, December 6, 1996.

8. I credit Howard Snyder for this term. Howard Snyder, *The Community of the King* (Downers Grove, IL: InterVarsity Press, 1977).

CHAPTER 3

THE NAZARETH CHRONICLE[1]

… and [He] came and lived in a city called Nazareth; that it might be fulfilled which was spoken through the prophets that he will be called a Nazarene. (Matthew 2:23)

JESUS IS RAISED in the insignificant town of Nazareth.[2] Consequently, He will be called "Jesus of Nazareth."[3] In Nazareth, He has ongoing fellowship with His Father. It's the same fellowship He knew in eternity past as the eternal Son. Only now He enjoys it as a human being. Jesus lives under His Father's reign. While some of His peers move to Jerusalem as young boys to receive formal theological training as rabbis,[4] scribes, or priests, Jesus does not. God the Father prepares His Son for His ministry as a blue-collar worker, a day laborer, a working-class hero in an artisan's shop.[5] He becomes a craftsman, working

1. Since the main focus of this book is the retelling of the story of the primitive church from Pentecost to Patmos, this chapter on Nazareth is intentionally short. But it lays out a number of key threads that run throughout the rest of the narrative. For details on the life of Jesus in Nazareth, see Leonard Sweet and Frank Viola, *Jesus: A Theography,* chaps. 4 through 6.

2. John 1:46. "Some might call Nazareth 'a dinky little' town." Personal correspondence with Craig Keener, 12/4/23. The population of Nazareth was fewer than 400. Scott Korb, *Life in Year One: What the World Was Like in First-Century Palestine* (New York, NY: Riverhead, 2010), 70.

3. Matthew 26:71; Mark 1:24; 10:47. For details on Jesus' birth and boyhood, see Paul Barnett, *Jesus & the Rise of Early Christianity: A History of New Testament Times* (Downers Grove, IL: InterVarsity Press, 1999), chap. 5.

4. Rabbi means "great one" or "master." Personal correspondence with Ben Witherington III, 12/18/11. During the time of Jesus, "rabbi" was a polite title meaning "teacher." Anyone could be a rabbi, and the position was voluntary. Personal correspondence with Amy-Jill Levine and Joseph Sievers, 3/8/22. According to Barnett, Jesus was an "unusual and unorthodox rabbi, whose activities defy neat classification." In all four Gospels, Jesus is called a "rabbi" and its likely synonym "teacher." Paul Barnett, *Finding the Historical Christ* (Grand Rapids, MI: Eerdmans, 2009), 100.

5. For details on the Lord's earthly occupation, see Leonard Sweet and Frank Viola, *Jesus: A Theography,* chap. 6.

with wood and stone.[6] He lives on earth for thirty years before His ministry begins. And the eternal fellowship that existed within the Godhead continues unbroken in the life of the Son of God.[7] The communion Jesus knew in eternity past simply moved from the heavens to the earth. It shifted from the divine key to the human key, but the song remained the same.

Jesus is the human face of God. He perfectly expresses the Father in visible form.[8] He is also the embodiment of God's kingdom in human flesh.[9] Ever since His birth in Bethlehem, where there was no guest room for Him, Jesus is rejected in all quarters. He's

6. Mark 6:3. According to Alan Bandy, the word translated "carpenter" in the Gospels may be better understood as a "stone worker" or "stone mason." Personal correspondence with Bandy, 11/27/23. Rabbis expected fathers to train their sons by age thirteen in their own trade or have someone else apprentice them for a different trade. Jesus, and later, Paul of Tarsus, were no exceptions. Craig Keener, *Acts*, 3:2729. Most scholars believe Jesus could read (based on Luke 4). Personal correspondence with Dr. Michael Brown, 4/7/23.

7. John 14:10, NIV; Luke 4:1, NIV. For details on the phrase, "Son of God," see George Ladd, *A Theology of the New Testament,* chap. 12.

8. John 1:18, NLT; 14:9, ESV. N.T. Wright, *The Challenge of Jesus: Rediscovering Who Jesus Was and Is* (Downers Grove, IL: InterVarsity Press, 1999), 16. Jesus is "Immanuel," God with us (Matthew 1:23), and the divine and eternal Logos made flesh (John 1:1, 14). For a discussion on how Jesus stands apart from other deities and divine figures, see Michael Bird, *Jesus Among the Gods: Early Christology in the Greco-Roman World* (Waco, TX: Baylor University Press, 2022), chap. 5.

9. Luke 17:21, ESV; Matthew 12:28. The kingdom is incarnated in Jesus and "burst on the world with all the suddenness of an invasion." Michael Green, *Evangelism: Learning from the Past* (Grand Rapids, MI: Eerdmans, 2023), 1. For details on the historical Jesus, including His self-identity, see David deSilva, *An Introduction to the New Testament: Contexts, Methods & Ministry Formation*, second edition (Downers Grove, IL: InterVarsity Press, 2018), 151-173; N.T. Wright and Michael Bird, *The New Testament in Its World*, chaps. 8-10. In his book *Jesus the Messiah: An Illustrated Life of Christ* (Grand Rapids, MI: Zondervan, 1972), Donald Guthrie does a wonderful job tracing the story of Jesus from beginning to end. This is the companion volume to Guthrie's *The Apostles* (Grand Rapids, MI: Zondervan, 1975). In *A Shorter Life of Christ* (Grand Rapids, MI: Zondervan, 1970), Guthrie provides an account of the background, sources, and historical outline of the life of Jesus. For a discussion of the glorious person of Jesus Christ as the last Adam, the image of God, the offspring of Abraham, Lord of the world, and the appropriate subject of human worship and exaltation, see Thomas Schreiner, *Paul, Apostle of God's Glory in Christ: A Pauline Theology*, second edition (Downers Grove, IL: InterVarsity Press, 2020), chap. 7.

repudiated in His own hometown of Nazareth.[10] He's dismissed in Samaria.[11] He's spurned in Jerusalem.[12] Ironically, the Son of God can find no place to "lay His head" on the very earth He created.[13] There is only one exception: a little village barely two miles from Jerusalem called Bethany. In Bethany, Jesus of Nazareth is received, honored, loved, and given His rightful place. For this reason, Bethany becomes His favorite place on earth.[14]

10. Luke 4:14-30.

11. "In Luke 9, He is dismissed in Samaria, but in John 4, He's embraced in Sychar (in Samaria). He's more received in Capernaum, though not as much as He should have been (Matthew 11:23; Luke 10:15)." Personal correspondence with Craig Keener, 12/4/23.

12. Luke 13:34-35.

13. Matthew 8:20. "He came into the very world he created, but the world didn't recognize him" (John 1:10, NLT).

14. I make a scriptural case for this point in my book *God's Favorite Place on Earth*.

CHAPTER 4

THE GALILEAN CHRONICLE[1]

A.D. 28 – A.D. 30[2]

Now after John was put in prison, Jesus came to Galilee, preaching the gospel of the kingdom of God, and saying, "The time is fulfilled, and the kingdom of God is at hand. Repent, and believe in the gospel." (Mark 1:14-15, NKJV)

A PROPHET CALLED "John the Baptist" is the promised "voice crying in the wilderness," the forerunner to the promised Anointed One.[3] John is preparing the nation of Israel for the ministry of its Messiah.[4] The prophet is the first human to preach the life-altering gospel of the kingdom.[5] His message is a frontal assault on the complacency of elite

---

1. Like the last chapter, this treatment of Jesus in Galilee is brief since my focus is the primitive church from Pentecost to Patmos. However, there are threads in this chapter that are expanded throughout the rest of the narrative. For details on the life of Jesus in Galilee, see Leonard Sweet and Frank Viola, *Jesus: A Theography*, chaps. 7-12; Paul Barnett, *Jesus & the Rise of Early Christianity*, chap. 6.

2. F.F. Bruce, *Paul: Apostle of the Heart Set Free*, 475.

3. For an excellent survey of John the Baptist, see Joel Green, et al., eds., *Dictionary of Jesus and the Gospels*, 436-444.

4. Isaiah 40:3; John 1:23. For a discussion on the Messianic problem and mission, see George Ladd, *A Theology of the New Testament*, chaps. 13-14.

5. The gospel of the kingdom is rooted in Isaiah 52:7. John's ministry was prophesied about in Isaiah 40:3, 9. In my book *Insurgence* and on the supplemental Insurgence podcast, I make a biblical case for the continuity of John's gospel of the kingdom, Jesus' gospel, and the apostolic gospel. They are all the same message with minor distinctions.

religious institutions.[6] John lives similarly to a Nazirite.[7] He's been dwelling in the wilderness since he was a young man, wearing unusual garb, never drinking wine, and never knowing the love of a woman.[8] Jesus is related to John by blood.[9]

John the Baptist is an exotic sight to behold. So much so that the people of Israel travel to the wilderness in droves just to see and hear him.[10] His outward appearance represents his radical message of forsaking the world for the sake of God's kingdom.[11] The prophet is a torch on fire. His blistering message of repentance blasts everything that moves. John proclaims the imminent arrival of the true King of Israel and His everlasting kingdom.[12] He baptizes those who receive his message and repent of their sins.

6. C.H. Dodd, *The Founder of Christianity* (New York, NY: The Macmillan Company, 1970), 149. Jesus echoed and expanded John's message, adding a positive announcement that the new temple God was building existed for all nations, not just for Israel.

7. "Like Samuel and Samson, two other sons of previously infertile mothers and two other men associated with the Nazirite tradition, John will be, in today's parlance, *intoxicated* not by wine but *by the Spirit*." Amy-Jill Levine and Ben Witherington III, *The Gospel of Luke*, NCBC (New York, NY: Cambridge University Press, 2018), 30. The Nazirite (also spelled "Nazarite") vow was an oath a person who was not part of the priestly order took. It is found in Numbers 6:1-21. Men and women could take the vow. The person was set apart to the Lord for a set period of time. They abstained from wine (and other intoxicating substances), they would not eat anything obtained from the grapevine, and they would not cut their hair or go where there was a dead person, including deceased family members. For details, see Jacob Milgrom, *Numbers: The Traditional Hebrew Text with the New JPS Translation*, The JPS Torah Commentary (Philadelphia, PA: The Jewish Publication Society, 1990), 44-46. Although the Gospels do not allege that John never cut his hair, some scholars believe John took the Nazirite vow because he never drank wine or strong drink. And he was a Nazirite for life (Luke 1:15). However, it cannot be proven that he took the vow. See Joan Taylor, *John the Baptist Within Second Temple Judaism: A Historical Study* (London: SPCK, 1997).

8. Some believe John had spent some time as an Essene and part of the Qumran community, while others do not. For the debate, see Joan Taylor, *John the Baptist Within Second Temple Judaism*, chap. 1. If John had ever been an Essene, he broke with the community before he began his own unique ministry.

9. Based on Luke 1:36, some commentators believe Mary and Elizabeth were first cousins, which would make Jesus and John second cousins. Regardless of the specific relationship, Luke 1:36 (ESV) states that Elizabeth (John's mother) is Mary's "relative."

10. Mark 1:1-8.

11. These features also characterize John to be an Elijah figure.

12. For details on the kingdom proclamation of John and Jesus, along with their mission, see Eckhard Schnabel, *New Testament Theology* (Grand Rapids, MI: Baker Academic, 2023), 71-260.

In His earthly life, Jesus replays the story of Israel. As a child, He is brought out of Egypt.[13] At age thirty, He is baptized and launches His remarkable ministry.[14] (Thirty is the age when Israel's priests began their liturgical service.[15] It was also the age of David when he was crowned king.[16]) John baptizes Jesus in the Jordan River. The Holy Spirit descends upon Jesus in the form of a dove, and the voice of the Father breaks through the earthly realm announcing, "This is my beloved Son, with whom I am well pleased."[17]

The Father's dramatic declaration that Jesus is God's much-loved Son, with whom He's totally delighted, publicly communicates that Jesus is Israel's promised Messiah.[18] Through His baptism, Jesus is manifested to Israel as the Promised One who will end their long exile and restore the Davidic kingdom. (Jewish kings were anointed when they were installed into their office. The dove descending upon Jesus, therefore, is His anointing for kingship. Israel crossed the Jordan River to get into the new land, marking their exodus from Egypt. John's act of baptizing Jesus in the Jordan River signals that the new Exodus is underway.[19])

After He is baptized, the Spirit of God leads Jesus into the wilderness to be tempted by the devil for forty days. This is a replay of Israel's temptation in the wilderness for forty years. However, where Israel failed, Jesus—the new Israel—is victorious. John the Baptist regards himself as a "friend of the bridegroom," and presents Jesus as the true bridegroom to God's people.[20] Anointed by the Spirit and having resisted the devil's temptations in the

13. Hosea 11:1 quoted in Matthew 2:14-15.

14. Luke 3:23. For a detailed discussion on John the Baptist and Jesus' baptism and temptation, see James D.G. Dunn, *Jesus Remembered* (Grand Rapids, MI: Eerdmans, 2003), chap. 11.

15. Numbers 4:3. You can think of a Jewish priest as a butcher with blood up to his waist. He was responsible for the temple sacrifices. David deSilva adds, "On a busy day, the court of the priests looked more like a slaughterhouse than a sanctuary." Personal correspondence with deSilva, 2/2/24.

16. 2 Samuel 5:4.

17. Matthew 3:17.

18. The Jews understood that the Messiah was also called "the king of the Jews," as well as "the Son of God." Jesus, as the Messiah and Son of God, claimed His royal title, meaning He was Israel's true King. N.T. Wright, *The Early Christian Letters for Everyone* (Louisville, KY: Westminster John Knox Press, 2011), 132.

19. Craig Keener, *The Gospel of Matthew: A Socio-Rhetorical Commentary* (Grand Rapids, MI: Eerdmans, 2009), 116-117.

20. John 3:29. For a fine survey of how the Gospels present Jesus as the bridegroom, see Joel Green, et al., eds., *Dictionary of Jesus and the Gospels*, 95-97.

wilderness, Jesus begins His ministry in Galilee by proclaiming the mind-blowing gospel of the kingdom.[21] His message can be summed up as follows:[22]

The time has finally come. The big day that God's people have been longing for has arrived. The era that God promised is here. The heavenly kingdom of the Almighty is arriving; it's breaking into the earth. Repent—realign your life—and entrust your believing allegiance to Me.[23] Forsake this world and all that it offers and follow Me.[24] And you will receive My life now and in the future.[25]

In Jesus of Nazareth, the God of Israel is acting in a new way and fulfilling His promise of ultimate redemption and salvation. Jesus is not proclaiming a new philosophy or good advice. He is preaching good *news*—a royal heralding that something new is afoot, a new king

21. For a detailed look at Galilee during the time of Jesus, along with the other cities and villages He visited during His earthly ministry, see Barry Beitzel, ed., *Lexham Geographic Commentary on the Gospels* (Bellingham, WA: Lexham Press, 2017); Richard Horsley, *Galilee: History, Politics, People* (Valley Forge, PA: Trinity Press International, 1995); Richard Horsley, et al., *The Message and the Kingdom*, chap. 2; Gary Burge, et al., *The New Testament in Antiquity*, 61. Dunn is right when he says, "Jesus' message was simple but revolutionary. He *radicalized* the claim of God…." James D.G. Dunn, *Unity and Diversity in the New Testament: An Inquiry into the Character of Earliest Christianity* (Philadelphia, PA: Westminster Press, 1977), 16. Despite the aversion between Galileans and the professional elites of the cities, "Jesus won the secret approval of persons in high places." Edwin Judge, *The Social Pattern of the Christian Groups in the First Century* (London: The Tyndale Press, 1960), 54.

22. This quote is my own paraphrase of the heart of Jesus' message.

23. For a fuller description on the challenge of God's kingdom, see N.T. Wright, *The Challenge of Jesus*, chap. 2; Craig Keener, *The Historical Jesus of the Gospels*, chap. 14; Frank Viola, *Insurgence*, parts 3 and 4.

24. The demand of Jesus to forsake all and follow Him included a person's relationship to money. For a discussion on Jesus' attitudes toward wealth and possessions, see Thomas Schmidt, *Hostility to Wealth in the Synoptics* (Sheffield: JSOT Press, 1987) and Michael Bird, *A Bird's-Eye View of Luke and Acts*, chap. 10.

25. Throughout the Gospels, the kingdom is revealed as already but not yet. In Matthew, the idea that the kingdom is present is predominant. In John, the person of Christ is predominant. In Acts, both Christ and the kingdom come together and are united. Preaching the kingdom and preaching Christ are different ways of saying the same thing. For details on the proclamation of the kingdom of God in Jesus' ministry, see James D.G. Dunn, *Jesus Remembered*, chaps. 12-14.

has entered the world. Jesus proclaims His kingdom message[26] in the synagogues.[27] He shares it along roadsides, He declares it in the open air, and He preaches it on hills and plains.[28]

All that the Old Testament Scriptures foretold serves as prologue for the ministry of Jesus.[29] The royal cliffhanger with which the Hebrew Scriptures ended has now reached its climax. The explosive message of Jesus that the kingdom of God is arriving fulfills Israel's entire story.[30]

"The time is fulfilled!" he said; "God's kingdom is arriving! Turn back, and believe the good news!" (Mark 1:15, KNT)[31]

"Repent!" he would say. "The kingdom of heaven is arriving!" (Matthew 4:17, KNT)

There is revolution in those words.

But he said to them, "I must preach the good news of God's Kingdom to the other cities also. For this reason I have been sent." (Luke 4:43)

26. In the Gospels, there are ninety unique references to the kingdom of God (eight-five in the Synoptic Gospels and five in John's Gospel, appearing in three verses). Adding Acts and the epistles, the kingdom of God is mentioned over thirty more times. The gospel of the kingdom was the central message of Jesus and the apostles who followed Him.

27. Synagogues were the education and community centers of the time. For details, see Craig Keener, *The Gospel of Matthew*, 156-159; Richard Longenecker, ed., *Community Formation in the Early Church and in the Church Today*, chap. 2. For a fine survey on the synagogue in Jesus' day, see Joel Green, et al., eds., *Dictionary of Jesus and the Gospels*, 903-910.

28. Jesus spoke mainly to the peasant class (around 90 percent of the population) which was comprised of manual and agricultural laborers who lived in rural areas including villages, small towns, hamlets, and the countryside. Jesus rarely went to the large cities (Jerusalem is one exception). Marcus Borg, *Evolution of the Word: The New Testament in the Order the Books Were Written* (New York, NY: HarperOne, 2012), 17.

29. The phrase "Old Testament" doesn't appear in the New Testament. Jews called their Bible "the Torah, the Prophets, and the Writings." Scholars call this the "Hebrew Bible" or "Hebrew Scriptures," even though part of them was written in Aramaic. John Goldingay, *Reading Jesus's Bible: How the New Testament Helps Us Understand the Old Testament* (Grand Rapids, MI: Eerdmans, 2017), 1.

30. Most first-century Jews believed they would automatically enter the kingdom and be saved because they were descendants of Abraham. But Jesus turned this idea on its head. Craig Keener, *The Gospel of Matthew*, 250.

31. N.T. Wright, *The Kingdom New Testament* (New York, NY: HarperOne, 2011), 67.

Jesus preaches the politically subversive gospel of the kingdom throughout Galilee[32] and later in Judea and Samaria. He bears God's image and exercises His authority through healings, casting out demons,[33] the supernatural feeding of the poor, and the formation of a new community.[34] Jesus reaches out to the oppressed and marginalized, breaking Jewish custom by having table fellowship (shared meals)[35] with those dismissed as "sinners."[36] These are all signs that the kingdom of God has broken into the earth.[37]

Jesus is unlike the other rabbis. When He speaks, people are awestruck. He doesn't use footnotes like the other teachers of the day.[38] He speaks in parables, aphorisms, riddles, and one-liners.[39] Through His parables, Jesus explains that God's kingdom isn't like what

---

32. To their shame, the cities and villages in Galilee where Jesus worked most extensively—Capernaum, Chorazin, and Bethsaida—appeared to have rejected Him and His message. Amy-Jill Levine and Ben Witherington III, *The Gospel of Luke*, 222. Nevertheless, He still had a large following among Galileans and Judeans, which speaks of widespread acceptance and accolades. Personal correspondence with David deSilva, 1/18/24.

33. Richard Horsley, *Jesus and Empire: The Kingdom of God and the New World Disorder* (Minneapolis, MN: Fortress Press, 2003), 77. The miraculous deeds of Jesus demonstrated the kingdom, revealing God's desire for wholeness, healing, and justice. Michael Green, *Evangelism*, 5ff.

34. The miraculous deeds in Jesus' ministry and that of the apostles after Him weren't simply alterations in the natural order; they were evidences that the new creation had broken into the earth. N.T. Wright, *Paul: A Biography*, 122.

35. For an informative survey of table fellowship in the Gospels, see Joel Green, et al., eds., *Dictionary of Jesus and the Gospels*, 925-931.

36. According to some scholars, the "elites" and "rich" were primarily the "sinners and tax collectors" with whom Jesus affiliated. This is one of the issues that the Pharisees had with Jesus. To their minds, Jesus was associating with the ancient equivalents of drug dealers, loan sharks, and contract killers. Personal correspondence with Amy-Jill Levine and Joseph Sievers, 3/8/22. For details on the controversial table fellowship of Jesus and its authenticity, see Darrell Bock, et al., *Key Events in the Life of the Historical Jesus*, chap. 6.

37. For an insightful discussion of the meaning of Jesus' mission and message, see T. Austin-Sparks, *The Mission, the Meaning, and the Message of Jesus Christ* (Tulsa, OK: Emmanuel Church), chaps. 1-4.

38. In other words, He didn't laboriously cite the opinions of earlier sages. Personal correspondence with David deSilva, 1/18/24.

39. For details, see Ben Witherington III, *Jesus the Sage: The Pilgrimage of Wisdom* (Minneapolis, MN: Fortress Press, 2000). While Jesus primarily spoke Aramaic, the common language in Galilee (and Judea) at the time, His teachings have been preserved predominantly in Greek, with only a few brief exceptions in the original language. Michael Licona, *Jesus, Contradicted*, 112. Jesus likely knew Hebrew as well, and He could have known some Greek since Galilean craftspeople were expected to know enough of the language to do business with non-Jews. David deSilva, *An Introduction to the New Testament*, 768.

anyone imagined or expected.[40] The wisdom He unveils through His parables reaches back from before the creation of the world, when God planned to bring His heavenly kingdom on earth and give it to those whom He chose.

...that it might be fulfilled which was spoken through the prophet, saying, "I will open my mouth in parables; I will utter things hidden from the foundation of the world." (Matthew 13:35)[41]

Then the King will tell those on his right hand, "Come, blessed of my Father, inherit the Kingdom prepared for you from the foundation of the world...." (Matthew 25:34)

Jesus speaks with authority and regularly contradicts enshrined religious traditions.[42] This causes the people to marvel and the religious leaders to be consumed with jealousy.[43] Early in His ministry, He selects twelve men to be on the ground floor of a new community.[44]

40. The region Jesus belonged to was "notoriously backward" by modern standards. He and His followers weren't in step with the sophisticated elites of the cities. The populace mistrusted those in power. Jesus spoke His parables to this audience. Through His parables, He unveiled that the kingdom of God was coming in and through His ministry, but the kingdom didn't resemble what any Israelite had anticipated. N.T. Wright, *The Challenge of Jesus*, 48ff. For the discussion among scholars on how Jesus communicated the kingdom message through His parables, see Klyne Snodgrass, *Stories with Intent: A Comprehensive Guide to the Parables of Jesus*, second edition (Grand Rapids, MI: Eerdmans, 2018) and Craig Blomberg, *Interpreting the Parables*, second edition (Downers Grove, IL: InterVarsity Press, 2012).

41. The phrase "from the foundation of the world" can be translated "since the foundation of the world." The decision as to who would inherit the kingdom of God "predates the creation of the world." R.T. France, *The Gospel of Matthew*, NICNT (Grand Rapids, MI: Eerdmans, 2007), 963.

42. Matthew 7:29. See also C.H. Dodd, *The Founder of Christianity*, 47. Again, Jesus didn't quote the authorities who preceded Him. He instead prefaced what He taught by the words, "Truly, truly I tell you." This practice was unprecedented at the time. Michael Green, *Evangelism*, 3.

43. Mark 1:22, 27-28; Luke 7:16; Matthew 21:37-39; 27:18, ESV.

44. The Twelve, as Luke refers to them, were only a fraction of Jesus' students. Robert Hutchinson, *The Dawn of Christianity: How God Used Simple Fishermen, Soldiers, and Prostitutes to Transform the World* (Nashville, TN: Nelson Books, 2017), 7. Jesus had around seven women and a family in Bethany who learned from Him. He also had at least seventy (or seventy-two) other disciples (Luke 10). For a summary of each of the twelve disciples of Jesus, see David and Pat Alexander, eds., *Handbook to the Bible*, fifth edition (Grand Rapids, MI: Zondervan, 2009), 557-558.

By choosing twelve, He replicates the twelve tribes of Israel.[45] The message is unmistakable: God is starting over. The new Exodus is here. But again, it doesn't look like anything Israel thought or expected. Jesus is the fulfillment of Israel's hopes, promises, and longings.[46] He is creating a new Israel, a new corporate people—the family of God. This new community begins with the Jewish people, but it will eventually extend to the Gentiles.[47] And it will embody and reflect the community of the Godhead.

Jesus calls the Twelve[48] to live with Him for a little over three years.[49] He trains them to take His place after He leaves the earth. The Twelve are called to proclaim the titanic gospel of the kingdom and take it throughout the world. They are also called

45. For a detailed discussion on the mission of the Twelve, including their geographical outreach, see Eckhard Schnabel, *Early Christian Mission*, 1:263-315. Craig Keener believes most of the Twelve were in their mid-teens when Jesus chose them. Peter, however, may have been the oldest (perhaps eighteen years old) because he had a family. In the Greek world, tertiary training began in the mid-teens. The most educated scribes in the Sanhedrin may have started their training at age ten. Jewish people emphasized education more than most cultures. A person entered adulthood at puberty. Personal correspondence with Craig Keener, 8/27/11. Jewish primary education began around six to ten years of age, and it was home-centered. Secondary education began around the ages of ten to thirteen, with boys continuing their studies into their mid-to-late teens, often training for vocations such as that of a scribe. They would attach themselves to a rabbi. Personal correspondence with Joel Green, 10/5/11.

46. For details on the hope of Israel and its fulfillment in Jesus, see N.T. Wright, *The New Testament and the People of God* (Minneapolis, MN: Fortress Press, 1992), chap. 10.

47. For a comprehensive survey of Jesus' mission to the Gentiles, see Schnabel, *Early Christian Mission*, 1:327-382. Later, Jesus would call Saul/Paul of Tarsus to be the chief apostle to the Gentiles. For the phrase, "the apostle to the Gentiles," see Galatians 2:8, NLT.

48. The Gospel writers use "the Twelve" as shorthand for the twelve disciples. See Matthew 26:14; Mark 6:7; Luke 9:1; John 20:24; Acts 6:2. Paul also uses this shorthand phrase (1 Corinthians 15:5).

49. Mark 3:13-14. Scholars who calculate at least three Passovers during Jesus' public ministry in the Gospel of John estimate that "Jesus' public ministry would have been over three years in length." Joel Green, et al., eds., *Dictionary of Jesus and the Gospels*, second edition (Downers Grove, IL: InterVarsity Press, 2013), 135. In this regard, I agree with Bock who says, "For me, three-and-a-half years makes the most sense." Personal correspondence with Darrell Bock, 2/3/24. Strauss agrees and follows the longer chronology also. Mark Strauss, *Four Portraits, One Jesus* (Grand Rapids, MI: Zondervan, 2020), 495.

to raise up kingdom communities, the outstanding fruit of that gospel.[50] The twelve men are:[51]

- Peter (also called Simon, Simeon, and Cephas)[52]
- Andrew, brother of Peter
- Bartholomew (who may have also been called Nathanael)
- James, son of Zebedee
- James, son of Alphaeus (also called "James the Less")[53]
- John, son of Zebedee[54]
- Judas Iscariot
- Judas (also called Lebbaeus, Jude, and Thaddaeus)
- Matthew (also called Levi)[55]
- Philip

50. Central to the gospel of the kingdom is the proclamation that Jesus of Nazareth is Lord of the world. The *kerygma* is the apostolic proclamation (preaching) that Jesus is Lord (*kurios*). For details, see C.H. Dodd, *The Apostolic Preaching and Its Developments: Three Lectures with an Eschatology and History* (New York, NY: Harper and Row, 1964). As we will see throughout the story, the gospel was designed to produce ekklesias, kingdom communities that bear God's image and exercise His authority.

51. Matthew 10:2-4; Mark 3:14-19; Luke 6:13-16.

52. John 1:42; 2 Peter 1:1. Peter (*Petros*) in Greek and Cephas in Aramaic means "rock." This was the nickname Jesus gave to Simon (the Hebrew form of his name is Simeon). Ben Witherington III, *A Week in the Fall of Jerusalem* (Downers Grove, IL: InterVarsity Press, 2017), 111.

53. Or "James the Younger." A number of scholars identify James, son of Alphaeus (Matthew 10:3 and Acts 1:13) with James the Less (Mark 15:40). J.D. Douglas, et al., eds., *New Bible Dictionary*, 549.

54. James and John, the sons of Zebedee, are brothers. Jesus will nickname them "Sons of Thunder." Mark 3:17.

55. Keener wonders whether he may have been the brother of James (son of Alphaeus) since in Mark 2:14, Levi is son of Alphaeus, and Alphaeus was not a common Jewish name. Personal correspondence with Craig Keener, 12/4/23.

- Simon the Zealot[56] (also called Simon the Kananean)[57]
- Thomas (also called Didymus)[58]

For three years, Jesus brings the Twelve into the same experience He knew in Nazareth.[59] Just as Jesus communed with His Father, the Twelve learn to commune with Jesus. And just as Jesus learned to hear the voice of the Father, the Twelve learn to hear the voice of the Son.[60] *What the eternal Father is to Jesus, Jesus is to the Twelve.* In this way, the Twelve become the primitive embryo of the community of the King—the ekklesia of God—that will one day fill the earth.

Jesus is the alternative to Roman imperial rule,[61] and His disciples will form the seed of the alternative family He is creating.[62] As such, the Twelve have informal gatherings where

56. The Zealots were a Jewish revolutionary group who violently opposed Roman rule over Palestine. This militant wing of the Jewish independence movement took the lead in the revolt against Rome in A.D. 66. Another group committed to violent resistance was called the Sicarii (or dagger-men). They were a splinter group of the Zealots. James D.G. Dunn, *The Acts of the Apostles*, 290. The Sicarii would conceal daggers under their clothes, mingle with multitudes at festivals, and stab their enemies unnoticed. Lars Kierspel, *Charts on the Life, Letters, and Theology of Paul*, 24.

57. Or "Kananite"—the word does not mean "Canaanite" as some translations render it. The word is "Kananean" which is the Aramaic word rendered into Greek as *Zêlôtês* (zealous one). Personal correspondence with Craig Keener, 12/4/23.

58. For a comparative chart displaying how the Twelve are named in all four Gospels, see *The NKJV Study Bible,* third edition (Nashville, TN: Thomas Nelson, 2018), 1469.

59. Elsewhere, I sketch out this pattern from Jesus to the Twelve to the apostolic workers who followed them (Paul, etc.). Frank Viola, *Finding Organic Church*, 15-92.

60. Jesus passed on the same relationship He had with His Father to His disciples. It wasn't a "pyramid scheme," it was the passage of divine life. What the Father is to Jesus, Jesus is to all who follow Him and possess His life by the Holy Spirit.

61. Richard Horsley, *Jesus and Empire*, 126-128. For details on the historical setting of Jesus' life and ministry, see Gerd Theissen, *The Shadow of the Galilean: The Quest of the Historical Jesus in Narrative Form* (Philadelphia, PA: Fortress Press, 1987).

62. Joseph Hellerman, *When the Church Was a Family: Recapturing Jesus' Vision for Authentic Christian Community* (Nashville, TN: B&H Publishing, 2009), chaps. 3-7; N.T. Wright, *Jesus and the Victory of God* (Minneapolis, MN: Fortress Press, 1996), 398-403. According to Hellerman, the values of this "alternative family" are affection, loyalty, the sharing of possessions, and unity. For details on Jesus' unique perspective of family, see Joseph Hellerman, *The Ancient Church as Family* (Minneapolis, MN: Fortress Press, 2001), 69ff. Also see David deSilva, *Honor, Patronage, Kinship & Purity*, chaps. 5-6. "The concept of church as the family of God became the social model and affected the way Christians related to each other." Roger Gehring, *House Church*

Jesus is Lord. Christ is the central object of their attention, worship, and fellowship (shared life). This embryonic community also includes women, a radical move on the part of Jesus since women have been summarily dismissed by virtually every rabbi before Him.[63] Jesus teaches the Twelve—and the women—how to care for one another without erecting social structures that divide based on gender, background, education, title, position, or talent.

But Jesus summoned them, and said, "You know that the rulers of the nations lord it over them, and their great ones exercise authority over them. It shall not be so among you; but whoever desires to become great among you shall be your servant...." (Matthew 20:25-26)

But you are not to be called "Rabbi," for one is your teacher, the Christ, and all of you are brothers. Call no man on the earth your father, for one is your Father, he who is in heaven. Neither be called masters, for one is your master, the Christ. (Matthew 23:8-10)

Jesus and this embryonic community are the newly constituted Israel of God, the people through whom the whole world will be blessed and the kingdom of God will find visible expression.[64] According to the Hebrew prophets, the God of Israel promised to establish

---

and Mission, 293. Gehring adds that the home meeting allowed the ekklesia to "maintain a family-like atmosphere and practice brotherly love in a very personal and concrete way" (117).

63. For examples of how Jesus elevated women, see Kenneth Bailey, *Jesus Through Middle Eastern Eyes: Cultural Studies in the Gospels* (Downers Grove, IL: InterVarsity Press, 2008), chaps. 14-20; Nijay Gupta, *Tell Her Story: How Women Led, Taught, and Ministered in the Early Church* (Downers Grove, IL: InterVarsity Press, 2023), chap. 4; Barbara Reid, *Choosing The Better Part?: Women in the Gospel of Luke* (Collegeville, MN: Liturgical Press, 1996); Holly Carey, *Women Who Do*; Michael Bird, *A Bird's-Eye View of Luke and Acts*, chap. 9; Frank Viola and Mary DeMuth, *The Day I Met Jesus*. Not counting Mary and Martha of Bethany, the Gospel authors mention seven women who were prominent during Jesus' earthly ministry. Eckhard Schnabel, *Jesus in Jerusalem*, 46-47. Women in the first-century Roman world were second-class citizens, sometimes having no better status than a slave. Normally, women ran the household while men worked and ran businesses. There were exceptions, however, as we shall see later in the story. John Byron, *A Week in the Life of a Slave* (Downers Grove, IL: InterVarsity Press, 2019), 31. For a summary of how Jesus viewed women, see Frank Viola, "God's View of a Woman," at frankviola.org/godsview.

64. One of the main outcomes of the entire life and ministry of Jesus was the birth of the ekklesia, a new society that saw itself as "the people of God," fulfilling Israel's distinctive vocation. The ekklesia is the *new* Israel constituted by a *new* covenant. The aim of Jesus' mission was the integration of a new Israel as the true people of God. C.H. Dodd, *The Founder of Christianity*, 99, 139.

His sovereign rule over Israel and the whole world. Jesus and His new community of disciples embody this intention. Israel's God is becoming King in and through Jesus of Nazareth.[65] The God of Abraham, Isaac, and Jacob is now present in human form.

The fulfillment of Israel's story is found in the story of the Messiah.[66] Consequently, Jesus embodies all the feasts of Israel, including the feast of Tabernacles where He is depicted as the real living water.[67] Christ is launching God's renewed people,[68] and His kingly rule is good news for sinners, especially the poor and oppressed.[69] At the same time, the gospel that Jesus preaches clashes with the kingdom of Caesar and the pagan gods of money, sex, and power.[70]

The kingdom of God is not *from* this world.[71] But it is *for* the world.[72] Through the voices of the prophets,[73] God promised that His Messiah would accomplish the following:

65. N.T. Wright develops this theme in detail in his book *How God Became King: The Forgotten Story of the Gospels* (New York, NY: HarperOne, 2012). The Davidic covenant also features prominently in the Gospels as a basis for the kingship of Jesus.

66. Jesus, as the Messiah, is the "inclusive representative" of Israel. He is the "true Israel." C.H. Dodd, *The Founder of Christianity*, 106. According to N.T. Wright, "Israel's king sums up his people in himself; what is true of him is true of them." Quoted in Richard Horsley, ed., *Paul and Politics*, 166.

67. John 7:37-39. For biblical references demonstrating that Jesus is the fulfillment of all of Israel's feasts, see Leonard Sweet and Frank Viola, *Jesus: A Theography*, 292-294.

68. The Gospel writers deeply connect Jesus with Israel's story. This is why the New Testament authors cite the Old Testament over 300 times. The Gospels reframe Israel's story as the Jesus story. This is the Holy Spirit's intent; hence, why all Scripture points to Christ (John 5:39).

69. James D.G. Dunn, *Jesus, Paul, and the Gospels*, 98-102.

70. The four Gospels reveal the new reality of Jesus and His mission of launching God's kingdom. In Jesus, the living God has become King of the entire cosmos. For details, see the Insurgence podcast, episode #23, "A Clash Between Kingdoms" at frankviola.org/insurgencepodcast. Caesar, as the guardian of the state, was believed to supply justice and peace to the world. For this reason, Caesar was hailed as the trusted savior and lord of the world, a belief challenged by the apostles who proclaimed Jesus as the true Lord and Savior. Richard Horsley, ed., *Paul and Politics*, 168.

71. John 18:36, NET.

72. Jesus taught that the kingdom was already but not yet (having a dual dimension). For a list of supporting texts, see "The Kingdom Present and Future," insurgencebook.com/PresentFuture.pdf. While Jesus often talked about the future aspect of the kingdom, He did not believe it would take place during His earthly life. While it was a popular viewpoint in the past, both liberal and conservative scholars today reject the idea that Jesus thought the world would end during His earthly lifetime. Robert Hutchinson, *The Dawn of Christianity*, 17.

73. "The voices of the prophets" is a phrase from Acts 13:27, NKJV.

- He would return to Zion (i.e., Jerusalem).

- He would dwell in His holy temple again.

- He would cleanse the temple.[74]

- He would renew the covenant He made with His people.

- He would liberate His people from bondage.

- He would restore His image and His authority in the earth.

- He would set up the Davidic kingdom once again, and it would be a kingdom with no end.

Just as Adam was placed into a Garden-paradise, Israel was brought into a Garden-paradise, the land of Canaan.[75] Jesus, the Son of God, represents and fulfills Israel's commission as well as Adam's.[76] That is, He bears the visible image of the invisible God and exercises His authority in the world. For this reason, Jesus is called the last Adam,[77] the second Man,[78] and the Son of man.[79]

74. The only person who had greater authority in the temple than the Jewish high priest was the Messiah. N.T. Wright, *Matthew for Everyone: Part Two* (Louisville, KY: Westminster John Knox Press, 2004), 75. Therefore, Jesus' act of cleansing the temple demonstrated that He was the promised Christ.

75. For details on this theme, see G.K. Beale, *The Temple and the Church's Mission: A Biblical Theology of the Dwelling Place of God* (Downers Grove, IL: InterVarsity Press, 2004).

76. To proclaim that Jesus is the "Son of God" is to announce that He is the anointed King (Messiah) who will reign on David's throne. Clinton Arnold, ed., *Zondervan Illustrated Bible Backgrounds Commentary*, 2b:79; Richard Longenecker, *Luke-Acts*, revised edition, EBC (Grand Rapids, MI: Zondervan, 2007), 860.

77. 1 Corinthians 15:45.

78. 1 Corinthians 15:47.

79. Matthew 8:20; Mark 2:10; Luke 12:40. "Son of man" was Jesus' favorite self-designation. It's found in the Gospels over eighty times. Leon Morris, *Luke: An Introduction and Commentary*, revised edition, TNTC (Grand Rapids, MI: Eerdmans, 1988), 130. According to Michael Bird, *ben adam* can be translated literally as "son of Adam." Therefore, a son of man/Adam means "human being." Michael Bird, "The 'Son of Man': Six Interesting Facts about a Disputed Title," published in TheNIVBible.com, undated. "Son of man" can operate as a Hebrew term for "human being." N.T. Wright and Michael Bird, *The New Testament in Its World*, 222. For this reason, "the Son of man" can be translated, "the true human." For more details on the phrase "Son of Man," see George Ladd, *A Theology of the New Testament*, chap. 11.

In the Old Testament, *life* represents living in the land of Canaan while *death* represents exile from the land. Jesus is ending Israel's long exile, bringing life out of death.[80] He also represents the Garden of Eden, the tree of life, and the land of Canaan.[81] In His person, Jesus joins heaven (God's space) and earth (the space of humans). He is the reality of the temple, the place where heaven and earth overlap.[82]

A great deal of the Lord's ministry occurs in Capernaum, in and around the home of Peter.[83] The house of Mary, in the village of Bethany, serves as the counterpart to the house of Peter in Capernaum.[84] The houses of Peter (in Capernaum) and Mary (in Bethany) represent the dwelling place of the ekklesia in primitive form, the cradle of the early church. Both houses become homes for the new family of God.[85]

80. N.T. Wright, *The Challenge of Jesus*, 39-43, 52-53. All four Gospels introduce the public ministry of Jesus by citing Isaiah 40:3-5. John the Baptist was the voice crying in the wilderness who presented the Messiah and His agenda. For details on Jesus' mission to Israel, see Eckhard Schnabel, *Early Christian Mission*, 1:207-262.

81. I have supported and developed these points in *From Eternity to Here* and *Jesus: A Theography*. See also the references in the next note.

82. The ancient Jews believed that heaven and earth met in the temple (which reflected the Garden). The early Christians believed that heaven and earth met in Jesus. N.T. Wright, *Revelation for Everyone*, advanced reader copy (Louisville, KY: Westminster John Knox Press, 2011), 3. This is why John refers to Jesus as both the tabernacle and the temple (John 1:14, YLT; John 2:19-22). For details, see G.K. Beale, *God Dwells Among Us: Expanding Eden to the Ends of the Earth* (Downers Grove, IL: InterVarsity Press, 2014); Edward Klink III, *The Beginning and End of All Things: A Biblical Theology of Creation and New Creation* (Downers Grove, IL: InterVarsity Press, 2023); Gary Anderson, *That I May Dwell among Them: Incarnation and Atonement in the Tabernacle Narrative* (Grand Rapids, MI: Eerdmans, 2023); N.T. Wright, *How God Became King*, 101-104.

83. According to Weima, "the majority of Jesus' ministry took place in 'the evangelical triangle'—the three nearby villages of Capernaum, Bethsaida, and Chorizim—located in the north-west corner of the Sea of Galilee." Personal correspondence with Jeffrey Weima, 12/28/23. The population of Capernaum, a fishing village on the Sea of Galilee, was 600 to 1200. Scott Korb, *Life in Year One*, 70. Gaining the head of a household (Peter) and his entire household as a base of the mission became a pattern that continued throughout the story, passed down to the apostles and ultimately Paul of Tarsus. Roger Gehring, *House Church and Mission*, 35-47. For a chronology of Jesus' ministry, see Mark Strauss, *Four Portraits, One Jesus*, chap. 13.

84. Roger Gehring, *House Church and Mission*, 43-46.

85. Roger Gehring, *House Church and Mission*, 47.

Throughout His ministry, Jesus is opposed by the religious leaders of the day; namely, the Pharisees,[86] Sadducees,[87] chief priests,[88] and

86. There were two main religious parties in first-century Israel: the Pharisees and Sadducees. The contemporaries of the Pharisees regarded them to be the people most devoted to God, and they regarded the scribes who were associated with them as the Bible experts. Craig Keener, *The Gospel of Matthew*, 547. Pharisees embraced all of the Old Testament and believed in spirits, angels, the soul, and the resurrection. They were the sectarian purists, obsessed with strict legalism, especially in respect to Jewish dietary laws and ceremonial cleanliness. There were over 6,000 Pharisees in Judea and Galilee. Craig Keener, "Lessons on Acts," Session 12. According to Luke, the Pharisees loved money (Luke 16:14). They were "the separated ones" who lived pious lives. Richard Longenecker, *Luke-Acts*, 799. As the guardians of the traditions of their forebears, the Pharisees were made up mostly of artisans and merchants from the middle and lower urban classes, though they clearly had priests among their number (Josephus himself claims to have been one). In ancient Jewish writings, they were discussed more than any other Jewish sect in antiquity; they are mentioned far more frequently in the New Testament than other Jewish groups. Darrell Bock, *Studying the Historical Jesus*, 133-134; F.F. Bruce, *Paul: Apostle of the Heart Set Free*, 44-50; David Rhoads, *Israel in Revolution 6-74 C.E.: A Political History Based on the Writings of Josephus* (Minneapolis, MN: Fortress Press, 1976), 32ff. In Matthew 21:28 through 22:14 along with chapter 23, Jesus levels a scathing denunciation of the Pharisees, scribes, and chief priests. Also: Richard Horsley, *The Pharisees and the Temple-State of Judea* (Eugene, OR: Cascade Books, 2022).

87. As part of the aristocracy, the Sadducees were the most powerful group in Judaism. They controlled the temple establishment. They denied the existence of spirits, angels, the soul, the afterlife, and the resurrection. They only observed the Law of Moses (the first five books of the Old Testament) and did not honor the traditions of the Pharisees. The Sadducees had their hands on the levers of political power. They were "the establishment" of the day. Sadducees were found among the wealthy landowners and aristocratic high priestly families. They did not survive the destruction of Jerusalem in A.D. 70 and none of their writings survived (unless one counts Ben Sira as coming from them). N.T. Wright, *Luke for Everyone* (Louisville, KY: Westminster John Knox Press, 2004), 313-314. The term "Sadducee" may have come from the name Zadok, a leading priest during the days of David and Solomon. James VanderKam, *An Introduction to Early Judaism*, 192-193; N.T. Wright, *Acts for Everyone: Part One*, 207. Since their writings didn't survive, all we know about them comes from their critics. For further details on the difference between the Pharisees and Sadducees, see Ben Witherington III, *Invitation to the New Testament*, 24; Eckhard Schnabel, *Jesus in Jerusalem*, 71-76; Matthew Novenson, *Paul, Then and Now* (Grand Rapids, MI: Eerdmans, 2022), 31-39; Daniel Harrington, *The Gospel of Matthew, Sacra Pagina* (Collegeville, MN: Liturgical Press, 1991), 322-323; Joseph Sievers and Amy-Jill Levine, *The Pharisees* (Grand Rapids, MI: Eerdmans, 2021). Pharisees believed in a combination of free will and fate, while Sadducees believed only in free will. Pharisees in both Judea and Galilee were popular among the masses, while the Sadducees were based in Jerusalem and lacked popular support. Personal correspondence with Amy-Jill Levine and Joseph Sievers, 3/8/22.

88. The chief priests managed the functions of the temple and may have included temple officers such as treasurer and captain of the people. They were members of the high-priestly family who served in the

scribes.[89] And they will eventually succeed in putting Him to death.[90] But what will emerge from Christ's execution will astonish everyone.

Sanhedrin. Most of them were probably Sadducees. Some of them wielded political power and influence. Herbert Lockyer, ed., *Nelson's Illustrated Bible Dictionary* (Nashville, TN: Thomas Nelson, 1986), 873; J.D. Douglas, et al., eds., *New Bible Dictionary*, 971-972.

89. The scribes were a trained class of writers (in a world where few people could write). Many scribes were legal experts, and they are often named alongside the Pharisees in the Gospels (Matthew 5:20; 12:38). N.T. Wright, *Matthew for Everyone: Part One* (Louisville, KY: Westminster John Knox Press, 2004), 220; J.D. Douglas, et al., eds., *New Bible Dictionary*, 1078-1079. One could think of the scribes as the professional scholars in the first century who interpreted the Law, as well as copied and wrote sections of it. The Pharisees and the Sadducees both had scribes, and there were scribes who sided with no particular sect. Calvin Roetzel, *The World That Shaped the New Testament*, 41-49.

90. On the one hand, Jesus was an observant Jew. On the other, He refused to conform to the traditions of the elders, which was the source of many of His conflicts with the Pharisees. The scribes and Pharisees were "the self-appointed arbiters of all matters of religious law and practice." R.T. France, *The Gospel of Matthew*, 854. Where Jesus was concerned, the religious leaders were driven by self-righteous fury.

CHAPTER 5

THE HINGE PIN OF THE DRAMA: CALVARY

A.D. 30

For I delivered to you first of all that which I also received: that Christ died for our sins according to the Scriptures, that he was buried, that he was raised on the third day according to the Scriptures, and that he appeared to Cephas, then to the twelve. Then he appeared to over five hundred brothers at once, most of whom remain until now, but some have also fallen asleep. (1 Corinthians 15:3-6)

Spring 30

It is four days before the Passover festival.[1] Each Israelite family has secured a lamb without blemish or defect. The lambs are set aside for four days of preparation.[2] Jesus of Nazareth, the spotless Lamb of God, enters the city of Jerusalem.[3] Up until the very end, Jesus lives

---

1. The Passover feast (festival) is described in Exodus chapters 12 and 13. For details on the festival, see Gary Burge, *Jesus and the Jewish Festivals: Uncover the Ancient Culture, Discover Hidden Meanings* (Grand Rapids, MI: Zondervan, 2012), chap. 3.

2. During the Passover festival, the city of Jerusalem grew from 30,000 to 100,000 people. Gary Burge, *Jesus and the Jewish Festivals*, 55. Witherington estimates it rose to 180,000 to 200,000 during feast time. Ben Witherington III, *The Acts of the Apostles*, 156. Bruce raises the normal population up to 50,000. F.F. Bruce, *Paul: Apostle of the Heart Set Free*, 30.

3. Matthew 21:1ff.; Mark 11:1ff.; John 12:1ff.

as a revolutionary.[4] Soon, He will be put to death through a state-sponsored execution,[5] and He will die the death of an insurgent.[6] In this regard, Jesus will establish His kingdom in solidarity with brutalized victims, for He chooses His own death instead of killing His enemies.[7]

Through His death, however, something dramatic will happen in the spiritual realm. Jesus will solve the entire problem of fallen humanity, the earth's corruption, and satan's rebellion.[8] He will destroy the power of sin, the world system,[9] the enmity produced by the Mosaic Law,[10] the wall that divides Jew[11] and Gentile, as well as the entire kingdom of darkness. He will also forgive the sins of the world by dying *for* us, *as* us, and *instead of* us. His pierced side will be the womb from which the bride of Christ will be born. The bride—the community of God's people—will soon make her appearance.[12]

4. For details on how Jesus Christ was a revolutionary and an insurgent, see "A Second Glance at the Savior: Jesus, the Revolutionary" at frankviola.org/revolutionary.

5. The trials of Jesus are beyond the scope of this book. For a helpful survey of each trial and their significance, see Paul Barnett, *The Trials of Jesus: Evidence, Conclusions, and Aftermath* (Grand Rapids, MI: Eerdmans, 2024).

6. Barabbas and the two men crucified with Jesus were each called a *lēstēs*, which means insurgent, insurrectionist, or revolutionary—a person who agitates with political motives. Mark 15:7, BSB (Berean Standard Bible) uses "insurrectionist." John 18:40 and Mark 15:27, NLT use "revolutionaries."

7. Matthew 26:52-53. Note that Jesus wasn't a revolutionary in the sense of military insurrectionists who employed violence. Craig Keener, *The Historical Jesus of the Gospels*, 10-11.

8. Romans chapters 5 through 8; Galatians 6:14; Colossians 1:20; 2:14-15; Ephesians 2:14-16; Hebrews 2:14-15. For a discussion on the death of Jesus and its spiritual significance, see Eckhard Schnabel, *Jesus in Jerusalem*, 385-389.

9. The "world" as used in passages like John 12:31, 1 Corinthians 2:12, Ephesians 2:2, and 1 John 2:15 refers to a system. Therefore, theologians often refer to it as "the world system." For details, see Frank Viola, *Insurgence*, 239-296.

10. Ephesians 2:15, NKJV. In this context, "enmity" refers to the hostility, division, and animosity between Jews and Gentiles.

11. The terms "Jew" and "Jews" are not derogatory words. The New Testament uses them in abundance, some 191 times (WEB version). For example, see Acts 2:5; 10:28; 13:43; Romans 2:10; Galatians 3:28, etc. The same is true for the terms Gentile/Greek, which are used seventy-five times in the New Testament. Every New Testament scholar mentioned in the bibliography uses these terms (Jew and Gentile) in a non-derogatory way.

12. This theme is sketched out in detail in my books *From Eternity to Here*, Part 1 and *Jesus: A Theography*, chaps. 13 and 15. All the brides found in the Hebrew Scriptures foreshadowed the bride of Christ. The bride is also the body of Christ, the house of God, and the family of God. These are the four dimensions of God's

The kingdom of God will be established by the innocent dying in place of the guilty. In this way, the death of Jesus will become the ultimate expression of God's love for the good world that He created.

Friday, April 7[13]
A.D. 30

From noon to 3 p.m., the cries of sacrificial lambs fill Jerusalem as they are slaughtered for the Passover feast. At the same time, Jesus—the *consummate* Lamb—is crucified outside the walls of Jerusalem in a location known as Calvary (in Latin) and Golgotha (in Hebrew).[14]

---

eternal purpose. For the story of the bride from Genesis to Revelation, see the Christ is All podcast, episode #43, "Who is This Woman? God's Ultimate Passion" at frankviola.org/thechristisallpodcast.

13. According to Schnabel, "Nisan 14 falls on a Friday on only two dates, A.D. 30 (April 7) and A.D. 33 (April 3). Given our earlier considerations, this leaves A.D. 30 as the year of Jesus' crucifixion." Eckhard Schnabel, *Jesus in Jerusalem*, 140. (Schnabel offers more details on pages 139-140.) After putting forth the evidence, Riesner writes, "The fourteenth of Nissan (7 April) of the year A.D. 30 is, apparently in the opinion of the majority of contemporary scholars as well, far and away the most likely date of the crucifixion of Jesus." Rainer Riesner, *Paul's Early Period: Chronology, Mission Strategy, Theology* (Grand Rapids, MI: Eerdmans, 1997), 58. (Riesner offers more details on pages 48-58.) See also Joel Green, et al., eds., *Dictionary of Jesus and the Gospels*, 177-178. Some scholars prefer April 3 of A.D. 33 as more accurate. Others believe Christ was crucified on a Wednesday or Thursday. Harold Hoehner, *Chronological Aspects of the Life of Christ* (Grand Rapids, MI: Zondervan, 1977). Bock and Jewett favor A.D. 33 as well. Darrell Bock, *Studying the Historical Jesus*, 75-77; Robert Jewett, *A Chronology of Paul's Life*, 29. However, I have been convinced by the scholars who date the Lord's death at A.D. 30. Ben Witherington III, *The Acts of the Apostles*, 78; N.T. Wright, *The New Testament and the People of God*, 355; Bruce Longenecker, *In Stone and Story*, 35; James D.G. Dunn, *Beginning from Jerusalem*, 501. According to Witherington, "I agree with John Meier on this [that it cannot be A.D. 33]. It is too late, and in fact makes Luke wrong about the age of Jesus when he ministered, even if we calculate a three-year ministry." Personal correspondence with Ben Witherington III, 4/15/99. For a timeline on the events leading up to and after the crucifixion of Jesus, see Eckhard Schnabel, *Jesus in Jerusalem*, 139-151.

14. Matthew 26:2; John 19:17; 1 Corinthians 5:7; 1 Peter 1:19; Hebrews 9:14. The brutality of a Roman crucifixion is beyond imagination. For the political circumstances that led to Jesus' death, see Robert Hutchinson, *The Dawn of Christianity*, 23-24. (Hutchinson sheds new light on the trials of Jesus in chap. 10.) For details on Jesus' last week and His crucifixion, see James D.G. Dunn, *Jesus Remembered*, chap. 17; Craig Keener, *The Historical Jesus of the Gospels*, chap. 21; N.T. Wright and Michael Bird, *The New Testament in Its World*, chap. 11. While the magnitude of Jesus' death is beyond the parameters of this book, we can summarize by saying that in Jesus' death all the forces of evil, pride, tyranny, oppression, and wickedness rushed in

As Jesus breathes His last breath, an earthquake shakes Jerusalem and the curtain (veil) that encloses the Most Holy Place in the temple is torn in two from top to bottom.[15] This signifies that the way to commune with the living God has now been opened and made available for all humans to experience.[16] Following Christ's death, Joseph of Arimathea, a wealthy member of the Sanhedrin and a disciple of Jesus, places the body of Christ in an unused tomb.[17]

Sunday, April 9
A.D. 30

The feast of the Sheaf of Firstfruits has arrived. An Israelite walks into a field and locates the first ripened stalk of barley that has sprung up. The blade signals that a harvest is coming. The Israelite gathers enough stalks to create a sheaf, which is pulled out of the ground and handed to a Jewish priest. The priest waves the barley sheaf in the temple before the living God.[18] At the same moment, the Lord Jesus Christ breaks out of the tomb as the firstfruits of all who will rise from the dead.[19] Jesus was put into the earth as a single grain

---

to do their worst to the kingdom-bearer, Jesus. Christ took the full force of it all onto Himself and defeated it forever. N.T. Wright, Lecture 3, The Soularize Conference (Bahamas, October 25-27, 2007). For a further elaboration on the spiritual significance of the cross of Christ, see T. Austin-Sparks, *The Centrality and Universality of the Cross* (Bethesda, MD: Testimony Book Ministry, 1988).

15. Matthew 27:50-51; Mark 15:37-38.

16. Hebrews 10:19-20. It may also signify the desacralization of the temple prior to its destruction, which Jesus had been foregrounding in Mark 11 and Mark 13 (and the parallels). Personal correspondence with David deSilva, 1/18/24. Historically, God dwelt on top of the ark of the covenant in the Most Holy Place. During his lifetime, Moses had access to God in this inner tent of the tabernacle (Exodus 25:22ff.). Thereafter, the only person who was allowed to penetrate the curtain (veil) that enclosed the Most Holy Place was the high priest. He did so once a year. When Jesus died, He made a way for all of God's people to enter the Most Holy Place (spiritually speaking) to have fellowship with God the Father.

17. Matthew 27:57-60; Mark 15:42-47; Luke 23:50-53; John 19:41-42.

18. The process is described in Kevin Connor, *The Feasts of Israel* (Portland, OR: Bible Temple, 1980), 29.

19. Leviticus 23:10ff.; 1 Corinthians 15:20, 23. For details on the resurrection of Jesus, see James D.G. Dunn, *Jesus Remembered*, chap. 18; Craig Keener, *The Historical Jesus of the Gospels*, chap. 22 and appx. 8; N.T. Wright and Michael Bird, *The New Testament in Its World*, chaps. 12-14; N.T. Wright, *The Resurrection of the Son of God* (Minneapolis, MN: Fortress Press, 2003).

of wheat. But as daylight breaks into morning, He rises as a new grain that has freshly sprouted, with many others to follow.

Jesus answered them, "The time has come for the Son of Man to be glorified. Most certainly I tell you, unless a grain of wheat falls into the earth and dies, it remains by itself alone. But if it dies, it bears much fruit." (John 12:23-24)

The God of Abraham, Isaac, and Jacob raises the lifeless body of Jesus from the dead.[20] Christ's resurrection fulfills Israel's story, creating a new people, a new nation, and a new humanity.[21] The risen Christ has ended Israel's long exile. But that's not all. By His resurrection, Jesus has been vindicated as the Jewish Messiah and, therefore, the rightful Lord of the world.[22] (A crucified and risen Messiah was not something Israel imagined, even though it was predicted in the Hebrew Scriptures.[23]) After His resurrection, Jesus meets

20. The New Testament is explicit and emphatic that the one true God (the Father) raised Jesus from the dead. 1 Corinthians 6:14; Ephesians 1:20; 2 Corinthians 4:14; Romans 8:11; Acts 2:24, 32; 3:15; 4:10; 5:30; 10:40; 13:30; 17:31; Galatians 1:1; Hebrews 13:20.

21. According to some scholars, Jesus' resurrection occurred on Nisan 16. Eckhard Schnabel, *Jesus in Jerusalem*, 149. For details on the resurrection of Jesus from a scholarly perspective, see Craig Evans and N.T. Wright, *Jesus, the Final Days: What Really Happened* (Louisville, KY: Westminster John Knox Press, 2009; N.T. Wright, *Jesus and the Victory of God*; Paul Copan and Ronald Tacelli, eds., *Jesus' Resurrection: Fact or Figment?: A Debate Between William Lane Craig & Gerd Ludemann* (Downers Grove, IL: InterVarsity Press), 2000; Eckhard Schnabel, *Jesus in Jerusalem*, 389-392. For a helpful take on the spiritual significance of the resurrection of Jesus, see N.T. Wright, *The Challenge of Jesus*, chap. 6; T. Austin-Sparks, *The Horizon of Christ* (Tulsa, OK: Emmanuel Church, 2012), chap. 7; *The Octave of Redemption* (Tulsa, OK: Emmanuel Church, 2000), chap. 3; *The Great Transition from One Humanity to Another* (Tulsa, OK: Emmanuel Church, 1982), chap. 6.

22. N.T. Wright, *Pauline Perspectives: Essays on Paul, 1978-2013* (Minneapolis, MN: Fortress Press, 2013), 242ff.

23. N.T. Wright develops this idea in detail in *Simply Jesus: A New Vision of Who He Was, What He Did, and Why He Matters* (New York, NY: HarperOne, 2011). See also Leonard Sweet and Frank Viola, *Jesus: A Theography*; G.K. Beale and D.A. Carson's *Commentary on the New Testament: Use of the Old Testament* (Grand Rapids, MI: Baker Academic, 2007) and Matthias Henze and David Lincicum, eds., *Israel's Scriptures in Early Christian Writings: The Use of the Old Testament in the New* (Grand Rapids, MI: Eerdmans, 2023). The Old Testament (or Hebrew Scriptures) has also been called the "First Testament." The "First Testament" tells the story in which Jesus of Nazareth is the climax. John Goldingay, *Reading Jesus's Bible*, 5.

with His disciples and breathes the Holy Spirit into them.[24] Jesus Christ now indwells His disciples by the Spirit, just as God the Father indwelt Jesus by the same Spirit.[25]

The new creation has begun. The culture of heaven has extended to earth. The age to come has been inaugurated.[26] Jesus remains in the human realm for forty days, intermittently appearing to His first followers.[27] He also appears to 500 of His disciples at one time.[28] And whenever He appears, He speaks to them about the kingdom.[29] The disciples ask Jesus if this is the time when He will restore the kingdom to Israel.[30] Jesus offers an interesting response:

> *...It isn't for you to know times or seasons which the Father has set within his own authority. But you will receive power when the Holy Spirit has come upon you. You will be witnesses to me in Jerusalem, in all Judea and Samaria, and to the uttermost parts of the earth. (Acts 1:7-8)*[31]

These words are a coded *yes*, but not in the way the disciples expected.[32] Jesus was saying that His first followers will be authorized with God's power to display the kingdom of God on earth. And that display is what the restoration of Israel will look like. After the forty days end, Jesus meets with His first followers on the Mount of Olives, overlooking the city

---

24. John 20:21-22. Judas was missing from this scene, since he killed himself, so the disciples at this point numbered eleven.

25. Romans 8:11, NKJV. According to the New Testament, the Father, the Spirit, and Christ all indwell the believer. 1 John 4:12-16; Ephesians 3:17; Romans 8:10; Galatians 2:19-20; 2 Timothy 1:14.

26. In Jewish thought, the resurrection marked the beginning of the age to come. In Paul and the other writers of the New Testament, the age to come had arrived in the present with the resurrection of Jesus. Thomas Schreiner, *Paul, Apostle of God's Glory in Christ*, 506.

27. Acts 13:31. For a helpful explanation of the forty days, see T. Austin-Sparks, *The Octave of Redemption*, chap. 4.

28. 1 Corinthians 15:4-7, ESV. Verse 6 of the NIV says "at the same time." According to Lightfoot, the appearance to 500 most likely took place in Galilee. J.B. Lightfoot, *The Acts of the Apostles*, 178.

29. Acts 1:3.

30. Acts 1:6.

31. According to Jewish expectation, the restoration of Israel's fortunes and blessings would be marked by a renewed activity of God's Spirit, which was withheld since the final prophets. Jesus, however, had something different in mind from their expectations. Richard Longenecker, *Luke-Acts*, 718.

32. The disciples were still thinking in nationalistic terms.

of Jerusalem below. He sends them out to preach the heart-stirring gospel of the kingdom and establish kingdom communities. But He commands them to wait in Jerusalem until their sending is activated. The Holy Spirit of promise[33] will empower and equip them for their ministry.[34]

May 19
A.D. 30

From the little village of Bethany—the only place on earth where Christ was fully received—Jesus disappears into a cloud and ascends into the heavens.[35] As the disciples gaze into the sky, two men clothed in white instruct them that Jesus will return in the same way as they saw Him exit into the heavens.[36] Jesus is now installed as Lord of the world and eternal King, sharing the throne with God the Father. Seated at the Father's right hand,[37] Jesus enters His present-day ministry as great high priest, chief shepherd, heavenly bridegroom, author and finisher of our faith, builder of ekklesia, head of the church, and Lord of the world.[38]

Immediately after Jesus vanishes, the disciples walk a Sabbath day's journey from the Mount of Olives to the city of Jerusalem.[39] They are accompanied by over one hundred

33. Acts 1:4; 2:33; Ephesians 1:13.

34. Luke 24:49; Acts 1:1-12. According to Acts 1:4-8, Jesus' mandate to witness to His resurrection was given to the apostles who would act in the power of the Spirit. This idea is developed throughout the book of Acts. Richard Longenecker, *Luke-Acts*, 714-715.

35. Luke 24:50ff. According to Alan Bandy, it's possible Jesus led the disciples to the outskirts of Bethany, but within 2,000 cubits of Jerusalem on the Mount of Olives. Personal correspondence with Bandy, 11/27/23. One of the main theological points of the ascension is that heaven and earth are now fully joined in Jesus, and He is now in charge of the world. Jesus is running the show by working through His body, the ekklesia, which will be given birth at Pentecost. N.T. Wright, Lecture 1, The Soularize Conference.

36. Acts 1:10-11.

37. Jesus' exaltation at the Father's right hand was His enthronement as Lord of heaven and earth. Romans 8:34; Ephesians 1:20; Colossians 3:1; Hebrews 1:3; 8:1; 10:12; 12:2; 1 Peter 3:22.

38. For details on the present-day ministry of Christ, based on the relevant biblical texts, see Frank Viola, *Jesus Now: Unveiling the Present-Day Ministry of Christ* (Colorado Springs, CO: David C. Cook, 2014).

39. Acts 1:9-15.

other followers of Jesus.[40] Christ is now the crucified, risen, ascended, enthroned Lord of glory. His work on Calvary has paved the way for His kingdom community—the assembly that will express His nature and exercise His reign—to be established on the earth.

...on this rock I will build my assembly, and the gates of Hades will not prevail against it. (Matthew 16:18)[41]

In His resurrection and ascension, Jesus becomes the head of a new people chosen by God from before the foundation of the world.[42] This renewed group of people forms a new kingdom. This kingdom will ultimately include both Jews and Gentiles, uniting them as members of the same alternative family.[43] It will be a new humanity, a new race.[44] Throughout the New Testament, this renewed people are called the house of God, the bride of Christ, the family of God, and the body of Christ. The ekklesia is the ultimate passion of God's heart, an alternative civilization led by a new emperor (Jesus) who leads a new empire (God's kingdom) on planet Earth.[45]

40. This calculation is based on removing the Twelve (minus Judas) from the 120. Luke says, "the company of persons was in all about 120" (Acts 1:15, ESV).

41. In line with many other scholars, I do not connect this statement to Peter's exclusive role in the church (the Catholic view). My conversation partner and I offer an explanation in episode #113 of the Insurgence podcast, "On This Rock I Will Build My Church," at frankviola.org/insurgencepodcast.

42. Ephesians 1:4. Other texts that shed light on God's calling and activity before creation are John 17:24; Titus 1:2; Revelation 13:8; 17:8.

43. The ekklesia of the first century was a surrogate family that took precedence over one's physical family, and it was more important than the individual members. In addition, loyalty to God was understood in terms of loyalty to God's family, the ekklesia. Joseph Hellerman, *When the Church Was a Family*, 64, 112-113; *The Ancient Church as Family*, chaps 1-2, 7.

44. Ephesians 2:15, NIV; Galatians 6:15, ESV. Notably, 1 Corinthians 10:32 includes three different human groups: Jews, Gentiles, and the ekklesia. The second-century Christians referred to themselves as "the third race" as well as the "new race." See F.F. Bruce, *The Epistles to the Colossians, to Philemon, and to the Ephesians*, NICNT (Grand Rapids, MI: Eerdmans, 1984), 296; Martin Hengel and Anna Maria Schwemer, *Paul Between Damascus and Antioch: The Unknown Years* (Louisville, KY: Westminster John Knox Press, 1997), 285. For the scholarly debate over this concept, see N.T. Wright, *Paul and the Faithfulness of God* (Minneapolis, MN: Fortress Press, 2013), 2:1443ff.

45. The New Testament presents Jesus as "the real emperor of the world" and the "head of an anti-imperial international alternative society." Richard Horsley, *Jesus and Empire*, 134. This alternative society is the ekklesia.

This new alternative society will be "deeply, but not openly, subversive,"[46] and it will bear God's image and exercise His authority. From the beginning, God's intention has been that this community multiply worldwide, just as His original intent was for the Garden of Eden to spread around the globe.[47]

46. James D.G. Dunn, *Beginning from Jerusalem*, 555.

47. This point is explained biblically in Frank Viola, "Vantage Point: The Story We Haven't Heard," the Christ is All podcast, episodes #18 and #19 at frankviola.org/thechristisallpodcast.

CHAPTER 6

THE THIRD MOTION: THE COMMUNITY OF THE KING IS BORN

His intent was that now, through the church, the manifold wisdom of God should be made known to the rulers and authorities in the heavenly realms…. (Ephesians 3:10, NIV)

THE CHURCH—the assembly—is the community that God has carried in His heart from before time.[1] This community embodies and displays the kingdom of God that resides in the heavens. God's eternal purpose of expanding the divine fellowship that eternally flows within the Godhead finds its fulfillment in and through the assembly.[2] With the birth of the assembly, the kingdom of heaven—which was "at hand" during Jesus' earthly ministry—is about to break further into the planet.

…your kingdom come…on earth as it is in heaven. (Matthew 6:10)

In the following pages, you will read the story of *how* and *where* this colony from heaven—the kingdom of God—makes its appearance in human history. You will also uncover how God, in the person of Jesus, fully became King of the world.

---

1. Ephesians 1:4. For a superb discussion on the significance of the ekklesia in God's eyes, see T. Austin-Sparks, *God's Spiritual House: A Classic Study of the Ministry of Jesus Christ in the Church* (Shippensburg, PA: MercyPlace, 2001).
2. Ephesians 3:9-11.

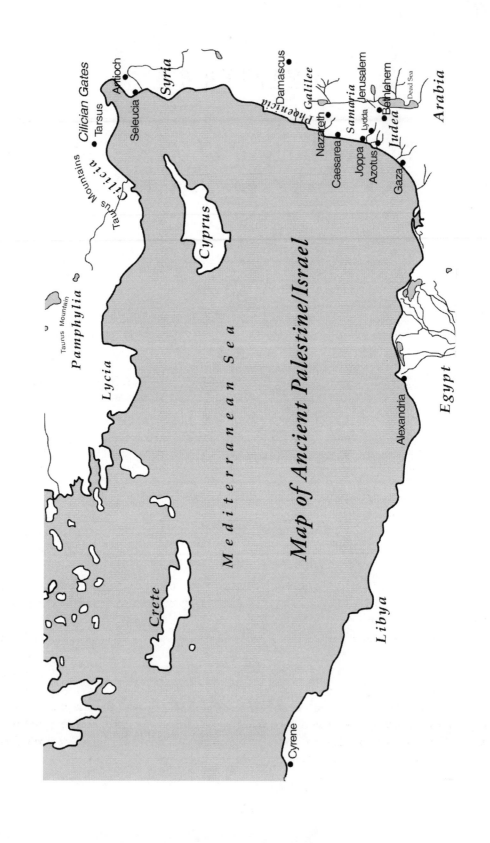

Map of Ancient Palestine/Israel

CHAPTER 7

THE JERUSALEM CHRONICLE

A.D. 30 – 41

With great power, the apostles gave their testimony of the resurrection of the Lord Jesus. Great grace was on them all. For neither was there among them any who lacked, for as many as were owners of lands or houses sold them, and brought the proceeds of the things that were sold, and laid them at the apostles' feet, and distribution was made to each, according as anyone had need. (Acts 4:33-35)

IN THE UPPER ROOM of a private house in Jerusalem, approximately 120 Jewish disciples of Jesus hold a prayer meeting.[1] (The home may belong to Mary, John Mark's mother.[2])

---

1. Clinton Arnold, ed., *Zondervan Illustrated Bible Backgrounds Commentary*, 2b:11. Early Christian tradition identified this home as the "Cenacle." According to Craig Keener, "the Cenacle is the traditional site and where tourists visit today. I tend to affirm tradition since it's often deeply rooted in facts." Personal correspondence with Keener, 12/4/23.

2. This may be the same house mentioned in Acts 12:12. F.F. Bruce, *The Pauline Circle* (Grand Rapids, MI: Eerdmans, 1985), 74; Eckhard Schnabel, *Early Christian Mission*, 1:406. Schnabel says "it was located on the southwest hill in close proximity to the Essene quarter" (406). It's probably the same house in which Jesus kept the Passover meal on the eve before His death (Mark 14:15ff.). For a discussion on the location of the "last supper," see Eckhard Schnabel, *Jesus in Jerusalem*, 118-121. The size of the house, which accommodated over one hundred disciples, indicates that Mark's mother was a woman of some means. Wayne Meeks, *The First Urban Christians: The Social World of the Apostle Paul* (New Haven, CT: Yale University Press, 1983), 60-61. Some scholars, like Gehring, believe the upper (upstairs) room belonged to James, the Lord's brother, not to Mary. Roger Gehring, *House Church and Mission*, 70-72. Finger disagrees, believing that the home belonged to a wealthy sympathizer of Jesus' mission. Reta Halteman Finger, *Of Widows and Meals: Communal Meals in the Book of Acts* (Grand Rapids, MI: Eerdmans, 2007), 119.

The Twelve have been living in this house.[3] Therefore, the first eleven followers of Jesus are present,[4] along with Mary, the mother of Jesus, the brothers of Jesus (James, Jude, Joseph, and Simon),[5] and the women who have been following Christ throughout His earthly ministry.[6]

Peter speaks to the group and convinces them that someone must replace Judas Iscariot.[7] Judas committed suicide after betraying Jesus. Joseph (also known as Barsabbas and Justus) and Matthias are nominated to replace him.[8] These men are selected because they have been with Jesus from the beginning of His ministry, and they are witnesses to His resurrection.[9] The eleven disciples ask God to select the right man, and they cast lots.[10] The lot falls to Matthias, who is added to the first followers of Jesus, a group that continues to be called "the Twelve."[11]

3. Acts 1:12-13. It's possible, though not certain, that some of the 120 were also living together in this house.

4. The twelve disciples, minus Judas (Acts 1:12-15).

5. See Matthew 13:55 and Mark 6:3 in the Douay-Rheims Bible. Some translations render "Jude" as "Judas." Both represent the Hebrew-Aramaic "Judah." Acts 1:14 also mentions Jesus' natural "brothers" (ESV).

6. Luke features the wider group of women who followed Jesus closely beyond the Twelve. Richard Bauckham, *Jesus and the Eyewitnesses*, 129ff.

7. In his argument, Peter appeals to the prophetic words in the Hebrew Scriptures regarding Judas (Acts 1:15-22).

8. Matthias means "gift of God," and Barsabbas means "son of Sabbath." Darrell Bock, *Acts*, 88. According to tradition, Matthias and Joseph Barsabbas were among the seventy (or seventy-two) whom Jesus sent out during His earthly ministry (Luke 10:1ff.). Eusebius, *The History of the Church*, 1.12; 2.1. While his proper name was Joseph, his Roman (Latin) name was Justus. Clinton Arnold, ed., *Zondervan Illustrated Bible Backgrounds Commentary*, 2b:14. The necessity for replacing Judas is supported by Psalm 109:8. For the twelve-fold witness of the apostles, see Richard Longenecker, *Luke-Acts*, 728.

9. Acts 1:21-22. The phrase in Acts 1:21 stating these men were with Jesus from the beginning as the Lord "went in and out among us" is a Semitic idiom, meaning unhindered and familiar fellowship. Richard Longenecker, *Luke-Acts*, 728.

10. Casting lots was a Hebrew custom to obtain the Lord's mind on a matter (Proverbs 16:33). It involved the use of stones, sticks, or other objects that were thrown or drawn from a container to make a decision or choice. It was believed that God would guide the outcome of the lot to reveal His will. After the Spirit was poured out on the day of Pentecost, however, we never see the early Christians casting lots to discern God's mind.

11. Acts 1:16-26; 6:2.

Sunday, May 29[12]
A.D. 30

It is the day of Pentecost, the Greek name for the Jewish Festival of Weeks.[13] Hebrew-speaking Jews, Greek-speaking Jews, and proselytes[14] from across the Roman Empire stream into the city of Jerusalem to celebrate Pentecost. This multinational gathering is comprised of Parthians, Medes, and Elamites; residents of Mesopotamia, Judea, Cappadocia, Pontus, Asia, Phrygia, Pamphylia, Egypt, and the parts of Libya near Cyrene.[15] Also included are Jewish visitors from Rome.[16]

12. The Berkeley Bible dates Pentecost on Sunday, May 29, A.D. 30. This calculation makes sense if Jesus died on April 7. Gerrit Verkuyl, *The Berkeley Bible* (Grand Rapids, MI: Zondervan, 1945), 288. Ben Witherington III confirms the date as likely. Personal correspondence with Witherington, 6/21/22. Schnabel dates the day of Pentecost in Acts 2 on May 27, A.D. 30. Eckhard Schnabel, *Early Christian Mission*, 1:398. Ramsay puts it at May 26, A.D. 30. William Ramsay, *St. Paul the Traveler and Roman Citizen*, revised and updated version, edited by Mark Wilson (Grand Rapids, MI: Kregel, 2001), 288. According to Witherington, however, the problem with this calculation is that Pentecost is fifty days after the end of Passover, not the beginning of it. Personal correspondence with Witherington, 9/7/22. For details on the history of the day of Pentecost, see F.F. Bruce, *The Book of the Acts*, 49-50. Pentecost means "fiftieth" in Greek. It falls on the fiftieth day after the first day following the Sabbath during the feast of Unleavened Bread, which coincides with Passover. Robert Hutchinson, *The Dawn of Christianity*, 135.

13. The Pentecost festival is also known as "the feast of weeks." Darrell Bock, *Acts*, 95. For details on Jesus and the Jewish festivals, see Gary Burge, *Jesus and the Jewish Festivals*.

14. Proselytes were Gentiles who converted to Judaism. Strict Judeans not only required converts to be circumcised, but also to purify themselves from Gentile impurities through proselyte baptism (ritual washing). Craig Keener, *1 Peter: A Commentary* (Grand Rapids, MI: Baker Academic, 2021), 280. For details, see Bruce Winter, et al., eds., *The Book of Acts in Its First Century Setting*, vol. 5 (Grand Rapids, MI: Eerdmans, 1996), chap. 3; Craig Evans and Stanley Porter, eds., *Dictionary of New Testament Background* (Downers Grove, IL: InterVarsity Press, 2000), 835-847.

15. Acts 2:9-11, NIV. For a helpful table listing all the countries mentioned with their local dialects, see Clinton Arnold, ed., *Zondervan Illustrated Bible Backgrounds Commentary*, 2b:17.

16. Acts 2:10. It's quite possible that among those included in "the visitors from Rome" were Priscilla and her husband Aquila. Personal correspondence with Ben Witherington III, 1/28/22.

Sharpening the Focus: The Roman Empire is presently enjoying the *Pax Romana* ("Roman peace") that Emperor Augustus[17] established from Spain to the Black Sea, and Egypt to the English Channel.[18] For the most part, life in the empire is secure and trade is safe. There are between fifty million and one hundred million people living in the empire.[19] As many as twelve million are slaves,[20] and around seven million are free Roman citizens.[21]

Slaves often aren't regarded as humans. Roman law reinforces this idea. However, there are a number of factors that mitigate the disadvantages of being a slave in the first century compared to some other eras. Unlike antebellum slavery in the United States, slavery isn't based on race or class.[22] Later, Paul of Tarsus will seek to reform the existing household structure, which includes slaves, within the Christian communities.[23]

17. Augustus ruled from 27 B.C. to A.D. 14.

18. For details on the historical, social, and religious realities in the Roman Empire, see Eckhard Schnabel, *Early Christian Mission*, 1:557-652.

19. Schnabel estimates sixty million. Eckhard Schnabel, *Early Christian Mission*, 1:4. For other figures, see M. Cary, *A History of Rome: Down to the Reign of Constantine*, second edition (London: The Macmillan Company, 1954), 507; Darrell Bock, *Studying the Historical Jesus*, 109. "It's impossible to have precise figures." Personal correspondence with Eckhard Schnabel, 8/25/23. For a breakdown on the population by city and region, see Schnabel, *Early Christian Mission*, 1:558-560.

20. Joel Green and Lee Martin McDonald, *The World of the New Testament* (Grand Rapids, MI: Baker, 2013), 170-171. Penal slavery was designed to punish those who committed crimes. John Byron, *A Week in the Life of a Slave*, 65.

21. Darrell Bock, *Acts*, 43. Some estimate that 50 percent of the major cities in the Roman Empire were made up of slaves. Ben Witherington III, *A Week in the Fall of Jerusalem*, 147. With respect to Italy, there were an estimated two million slaves out of a population of six million. For the entire empire, 500,000 new slaves were needed every year to replace those who were freed, had run away or died. Reta Halteman Finger, *Roman House Churches for Today: A Practical Guide for Small Groups* (Grand Rapids, MI: Eerdmans, 2007), 31.

22. For details, see Ben Witherington III, *A Week in the Fall of Jerusalem*, 147-148.

23. John Byron, *A Week in the Life of a Slave*, 97; Ben Witherington III, *The Letters to Philemon, the Colossians, and the Ephesians: A Socio-Rhetorical Commentary on the Captivity Letters* (Grand Rapids, MI: Eerdmans, 2007), 27; *A Week in the Fall of Jerusalem*, 72-73. For details on the household community in the first century (*oikonomia*), see Edwin Judge, *The Social Pattern of the Christian Groups in the First Century*, chap. 3.

The Roman Empire runs on slave labor. It's essentially a slave society.[24] Slaves have few legal rights and are viewed as the personal property of their masters. Some wealthy Romans, including the emperor, are known to own as many as 20,000 slaves.[25] Slaves owned by Roman citizens can become citizens themselves after they are emancipated. Some former slaves learn a skill during their servitude that enables them to operate a business.[26] In the empire, slaves can be manumitted (freed) at age thirty.[27] Female slaves can be manumitted earlier for the purposes of marriage.[28] The elite despise both active slaves and former slaves.[29]

Slaves are not distinguished by any physical or educational differences from the general population. Most are used in manufacturing and household maintenance.[30] The most common ways people become slaves are through lost wars, piracy, and failing to pay personal debts. Children of slaves remain slaves, and even free children are sometimes sold into slavery, especially females.[31] Marriage is forbidden to slaves

24. Richard Horsley, ed., *Paul and Politics*, 110ff.; Ben Witherington III, *New Testament History: A Narrative Account* (Grand Rapids, MI: Baker, 2003), 321.

25. For details on the slave market in ancient Rome, see Alberto Angela, *A Day in the Life of Ancient Rome* (New York, NY: Europa Editions, 2009), 179-194. In addition, Keener has a comprehensive excursus on ancient slavery in Craig Keener, *Acts,* 3:1906-1942.

26. John Byron, *A Week in the Life of a Slave*, 48.

27. Urban and domestic slaves could expect emancipation by age thirty, provided they met certain legal requirements. They were also eligible to become Roman citizens if their master was a citizen. John Byron, *A Week in the Life of a Slave*, 71. A substantial number of slaves were manumitted before their thirtieth birthday. James D.G. Dunn, *Beginning from Jerusalem*, 630-631.

28. David Balch and Carolyn Osiek, *Early Christian Families in Context: An Interdisciplinary Dialogue* (Grand Rapids, MI: Eerdmans, 2003), 261.

29. The stigma of slavery wasn't always removed, even after emancipation. John Byron, *A Week in the Life of a Slave*, 81.

30. For details on slavery in the ancient Greco-Roman world, see David deSilva, *Honor, Patronage, Kinship & Purity*, 190-193; P.R.C. Weaver, *Familia Caesaris: A Social Study of the Emperor's Freedmen and Slaves* (Cambridge: Cambridge University Press, 1972), 97-104.

31. For details on the household and slavery in the Roman Empire, see Bruce Longenecker, *In Stone and Story*, chap. 15.

because they cannot form a legal relationship.[32] Jews practice slavery in the same way that Gentiles do. Slavery is just as acceptable to Jews as to non-Jews.[33]

"Freedpersons" (or "Freedmen") consist of former slaves who don't possess full rights as citizens.[34] Most of them are extremely poor, having less security than they did in their previous lives as slaves.[35] However, it is possible for freedmen to advance in wealth.[36]

The empire functions through "trickle-up" economics. Money flows to the elite, with little for those with lesser means.[37] Possibly 3 percent are part of the social elite. Few people—perhaps one-tenth of 1 percent—in the Roman Empire are part of the wealthy senatorial class.[38] Most belong to the poor plebeian class.[39] Eighty to 90 percent live at just about the necessary level to sustain life.[40] Around 90 percent of the empire's workers are involved in farming and herding.[41] More than half the population is dependent on the regular distribution of free grain.[42]

32. John Byron, *A Week in the Life of a Slave*, 62.

33. See Josephus, *The Antiquities of the Jews*, 18.21; Philo, *That Every Good Person is Free*, 12. Both sources point out that the Jewish community called the "Essenes" didn't own slaves. In general, the Greeks weren't enslavers of Jews like the Romans were. Personal correspondence with Ben Witherington III, 1/8/22.

34. Most Bible translations use "freedmen" in Acts 6:9. The NLT uses "freed slaves."

35. For details on the status of freedpersons ("freedmen"), see Craig Keener, *Acts*, 2:1304-1306 and John Byron, *A Week in the Life of a Slave*, 104.

36. Wayne Meeks, *The First Urban Christians*, 73.

37. Darrell Bock, *Studying the Historical Jesus*, 121. For a description of how money was used during the time of Jesus and in the first century, see David and Pat Alexander, eds., *Handbook to the Bible*, 566-567.

38. The senatorial class was the elite of the elite. A tiny proportion (about 3 percent) of a city population was rich, and there was no middle class. James D.G. Dunn, *Beginning from Jerusalem*, 632.

39. One scholar estimates that 3 percent of the population made up the wealthy, 7 percent made up the upper middle class, 22 percent made up the lower middle class, 40 percent made up the subsistent poor, and 28 percent was made up of the desperately poor. David Capes, et al., *Rediscovering Paul*, 14; Steven Friesen, "Poverty in Pauline Studies: Beyond the So-Called New Consensus," *JSNT* 26 (2004): 323-361.

40. Holly Beers, *A Week in the Life of a Greco-Roman Woman* (Downers Grove, IL: InterVarsity Press, 2019), 31.

41. James Jeffers, *The Greco-Roman World of the New Testament Era*, 20. For further details on the economy in the empire, see Wayne Meeks, ed., *Library of Early Christianity*, 2:63-81; Richard Horsley, *Jesus and Empire*, 25.

42. Grain was the most precious commodity in the ancient world, necessary for survival, especially in light of the frequent famines. Ben Witherington III, *Invitation to the New Testament*, 28.

About 10 percent of the empire's population lives in the city. The rest live in the countryside.[43] The average person doesn't travel. They don't have the means, money, or freedom, so countless people never visit another city all their lives. Only well-to-do people can travel.[44] The normal diet of a lower-class person in the first century is legumes, vegetables, grains (like barley, millet, and wheat), olives, olive oil, vinegar, wine, turnips, and onions. Meat is eaten on rare and special occasions. Higher class folks consume meat and fish more frequently.[45]

Most people rise at about sunrise to begin their day.[46] Sometimes the wealthy eat a meal after dusk. They typically present the food on a low table in the dining room (the *triclinium*) of a house, placing cushions around the table.[47] They use an oil lamp for light. The meal sometimes contains fresh bread, fruit, olives, and fish stew. Bowls filled with cold water are passed around for washing. Red wine is drunk from carved stoned cups.[48]

In the Roman colonies, the towns are built according to the pattern of Rome (more on that later). In short, they are dirty, smelly, and unsafe. Because of these conditions, many people are racked with disease and malnutrition. In the ancient world, life expectancy averages between nineteen and twenty years. The infant mortality rate is 466.9 per 1,000. About 25 percent of babies do not survive their first year. Three of every ten Jewish children die before the age of eighteen. The number is higher among the Gentiles.[49]

If a person reaches age five, the expectancy rises to age forty.[50] (Of all humans born in the empire, half die before age five.[51]) More specifically, the average life expectancy

---

43. For a discussion on how the social stratification of society was mirrored in the city, countryside, and villages, see Reta Halteman Finger, *Of Widows and Meals*, 104ff.

44. Personal correspondence with Jeffrey Weima, 2/10/22.

45. Holly Beers, *A Week in the Life of a Greco-Roman Woman*, 50; personal correspondence with Ben Witherington III, 1/21/04.

46. Craig Keener, *The IVP Bible Background Commentary: New Testament*, 272.

47. When we get to the Corinthian story, I will explain more about how the Romans and Greeks dined.

48. Gary Burge, *A Week in the Life of a Roman Centurion*, 143-145.

49. Calvin Roetzel, *The World That Shaped the New Testament*, 100.

50. Darrell Bock, *Studying the Historical Jesus*, 116.

51. Personal correspondence with Mark Philip Reasoner, 6/24/99.

for a male in the empire is forty years old. Women don't live as long. Their lifespans are closer to thirty years.[52] The life expectancy of Jewish men is about twenty-nine years.[53]

Women usually marry between the ages of twelve and fifteen while Jewish men marry around age eighteen. Gentile men marry in their twenties or thirties.[54] The Greeks and Romans are extremely tolerant of male sex outside of marriage.[55] Adultery is widespread, and married men are expected to have mistresses.[56] Unmarried

52. Holly Beers, *A Week in the Life of a Greco-Roman Woman*, 18. According to Keener, the life expectancy in the ancient world was about forty. Craig Keener, *The IVP Bible Background Commentary: New Testament*, 141. More specifically, people lived thirty-five to forty years. Craig Keener, *1 Peter*, 373. Elderly people were respected in the Mediterranean world due to their perceived wisdom. If infant mortality is added to the mix, the average life span was between twenty and thirty years. Those who lived above the age of sixty were rare. John Barclay, *Pauline Churches and Diaspora Jews* (Grand Rapids, MI: Eerdmans, 2016), 259; Tim Parkin, *Demography and Roman Society* (Baltimore, MD: Johns Hopkins University Press, 1992), 92, 144. Less than half the population of the empire reached age twenty-five, and "hardly five percent reached fifty." Rainer Riesner, *Paul's Early Period*, 383. For details on how women lived in the world of the New Testament, see Susan Hylen, *Finding Phoebe: What New Testament Women Were Really Like* (Grand Rapids, MI: Eerdmans, 2023) and Nijay Gupta, *Tell Her Story*, chap. 1.

53. Scott Korb, *Life in Year One*, 192.

54. Darrell Bock, *Studying the Historical Jesus*, 117; John Barclay, *Pauline Churches and Diaspora Jews*, 260. According to Weima, men in their mid-twenties would typically marry young women barely in their teens. Neither would have met beforehand. Consequently, married men were expected to have sex with other women. Jeffrey Weima, *1-2 Thessalonians*, 261-262. Finger says Jewish men married between ages sixteen and seventeen. Reta Halteman Finger, *Of Widows and Meals*, 154. Other scholars report that women more commonly married in their early twenties while men commonly married in their late twenties. Nijay Gupta, *Tell Her Story*, 38. Some historians present lower numbers, suggesting that twelve-year-old girls were deemed ready to marry, and boys were deemed ready at age fourteen. Augustus penalized men who were still single at age twenty-five and women at age twenty. Lewis Lord, "The Year One," *U.S. News & World Report*, January 8, 2001, 40.

55. Jeffrey Weima, *1-2 Thessalonians*, 261.

56. Jeffrey Weima, *1-2 Thessalonians*, 262-263; Clinton Arnold, ed., *Zondervan Illustrated Bible Backgrounds Commentary* (Grand Rapids, MI: Zondervan, 2002), 3:419. See also Bruce Longenecker and Todd Still, *Thinking Through Paul: A Survey of His Life, Letters and Theology* (Grand Rapids, MI: Zondervan, 2014), 63. According to Keener, a specific kind of adultery (i.e., a wife's unfaithfulness to her husband and a man's seduction of a married woman) was disapproved of in all ancient Mediterranean cultures. Craig Keener, *Acts*, 3:2275. Adultery was sometimes called "wife stealing," and it was viewed as immoral by many. But it

men below the age of thirty commonly have sex with prostitutes, slaves, and other males.[57] The wife's function is to manage the household and give her husband legitimate children and heirs.[58]

Brothels are common in the Roman Empire, appearing in almost every city. Dinner parties ending with sexual play with prostitutes is typical.[59] Erotic art, pottery, and poetry are normal features in Roman life.[60] Most marriages are arranged by the parents, and they usually remain within the broader family or clan.[61] Birth control is rarely practiced.[62] Between 10 and 20 percent of mothers die due to complications related to childbirth.[63]

Baby girls are sometimes "exposed" (abandoned in remote places to die) if their parents are too poor to care for them.[64] Daughters are considered a financial liability and giving birth to a boy is much preferred. Because birth control isn't effective

---

was widespread among the Roman elite. Adultery was also punished by Roman law. Craig Keener and John Walton, *NIV Cultural Backgrounds Study Bible* (Grand Rapids, MI: Zondervan, 2016), 1990-1991.

57. Craig Keener, *The IVP Bible Background Commentary: New Testament*, 587.

58. Bruce Longenecker, *In Stone and Story*, 203-204; F.F. Bruce, *1 & 2 Thessalonians*, WBC (Waco, TX: Word Books, 1982), 82.

59. Even though Jews forbade the practice of prostitution and Jewish teachers resented it as a primarily Gentile practice, it still existed in Jerusalem during the Second Temple period among Jewish women and men. Many Gentiles viewed prostitution as shameful and hurtful, but they saw it as a better outlet for passion than adultery. Craig Keener, *The Gospel of Matthew*, 508.

60. Gary Burge, *A Week in the Life of a Roman Centurion*, 78.

61. Arranged marriages (by parents) was the normal practice in both Jewish and pagan communities. Personal correspondence with Jeff Weima, 10/5/23. "This tended to be truer in Jewish contexts, whereas in Roman contexts the linking of different families through marriage was considered a good strategy." Personal correspondence with David deSilva, 1/18/24. See also deSilva, *Honor, Patronage, Kinship & Purity*, 174-178. For details on kinship and marriage in the ancient world, see Bruce Malina, *The New Testament World*, chap. 5.

62. For a summary of marriage and family in the Roman world, see James Papandrea, *A Week in the Life of Rome* (Downers Grove, IL: InterVarsity Press, 2019), 32-35.

63. Holly Beers, *A Week in the Life of a Greco-Roman Woman*, 18.

64. Preborn and newborn life was considered disposable in the Greco-Roman world. For a discussion on infant exposure, see James Papandrea, *A Week in the Life of Rome*, 56; Holly Beers, *A Week in the Life of a Greco-Roman Woman*, 13-14.

and abortion is dangerous, exposing newborn infants is common. In cases when the infants are found, they are usually raised to be slaves or prostitutes.[65]

The two most popular institutions in the first century are the baths and the gymnasium, where activity is done in the nude. Some Jews are so embarrassed about their circumcision (widely viewed as a barbaric act)[66] that they undergo surgery to hide their circumcision. Most conservative Jews, however, do not participate much in the baths and the gymnasiums."[67]

In the Roman world of the first century, the *group* is more important than the *individual*, the *family* more important than the *person*, and siblings take priority over spouses.[68] Households, rather than nuclear families, are the primary social unit.[69]

65. John Byron, *A Week in the Life of a Slave*, 66. Even though some high-class prostitutes became wealthy, prostitution was usually provoked by economic needs and often slavery. Craig Keener, *The Gospel of Matthew*, 509.

66. Circumcision was "largely regarded as a barbaric mutilation of the human form." David deSilva, *Letter to the Galatians,* NICNT, Logos edition (Grand Rapids, MI: Eerdmans, 2018), 17. Romans even saw it as a form of castration. Ben Witherington III, *Grace in Galatia: A Commentary on Paul's Letter to the Galatians* (Grand Rapids, MI: Eerdmans, 1998), 374.

67. Personal correspondence with Jeffrey Weima, 2/12/22. For a discussion of epispasm (the operation that removes a person's circumcision), see Bruce Winter, *Seek the Welfare of the City*, 147-152. When a person bathed in a public Roman bath, it would be known if they were circumcised or not, since bathing was done in the nude. Virtually all social classes went to the bath houses. For a discussion on Roman baths, see James Papandrea, *A Week in the Life of Rome*, 60-62. For details on Roman attire, see Alberto Angela, *A Day in the Life of Ancient Rome*, 273-292. Jewish males invited harsh criticism if they participated in the gymnasium (which meant being naked) due to their circumcised state. N.T. Wright, *Paul: A Biography*, 86.

68. Joseph Hellerman, *When the Church Was a Family*, 13-52; *The Ancient Church as Family*, 214ff.; Bruce Malina, *The New Testament World*, chap. 2. This was especially true among the Jews. Also, Hebrew thought saw humans as a totality while Greek thought saw humans as separate individuals. Hebrew life was lived in "a social totality of religion and justice." James Barr, *The Semantics of Biblical Language* (London: Oxford University, 1961), 13.

69. Reta Halteman Finger, *Of Widows and Meals*, 51. In the first century, households were made up of family members, servants, slaves, stewards, and friends. The family was regarded as the most important institution in the Hellenistic world. Calvin Roetzel, *The World That Shaped the New Testament*, 97; Douglas Campbell, *Paul: An Apostle's Journey* (Grand Rapids, MI: Eerdmans, 2018), 49. "Early Christianity was basically a 'household' movement first in that it sought after the conversion of heads of households, whose dependents would follow them into the new faith." David deSilva, *Honor, Patronage, Kinship & Purity*, 226-229. It was also a household movement in that it depended on the generosity of householders to accommodate the meetings

Privacy is rare. Most people live their lives on the streets, sidewalks, and squares.[70]

The entire first-century world is constructed on a culture of honor and shame. This culture explains all sorts of behaviors for both Jews and Gentiles.[71] The patronage system, where wealthy individuals fund or support the less fortunate, is endemic to Greco-Roman society.[72] Patriarchy, the system of male power and domination, controls the Roman world.

Common stereotypes for women include that they are overly emotional, simple-minded, overly passionate, backstabbing, and given to gossip.[73] Women do not have any significant inherent value. They are regarded as inferior to men. Other than producing heirs, the only value a woman has is if she links herself with other people.

---

of the ekklesia. For details on household and communal Judaism in Galilean cities, towns, and villages, see James Riley Strange, *Excavating the Land of Jesus: How Archaeologists Study the People of the Gospels* (Grand Rapids, MI: Eerdmans, 2023), 120ff. For an overview of Hellenism and the Hellenistic world, see *The SBL Study Bible* (New York, NY: HarperOne, 2023), 1327-1334.

70. Wayne Meeks, *The First Urban Christians*, 29. For details on ancient society life in Palestine, see Wayne Meeks, ed., *Library of Early Christianity*, 2:82-107.

71. It was rare for people to view themselves as private individuals. Therefore, public shaming was quite effective. Gary Burge, *A Week in the Life of a Roman Centurion* (Downers Grove, IL: InterVarsity Press, 2015), 63; Bruce Malina, *The New Testament World*, chap. 1. According to David deSilva, "Hebrews 10:32-34 provides a great window into the array of shaming techniques available to and applied by their neighbors: verbal assaults, physical affronts, economic embargo, manipulation of the legal system against undesirables. 1 Peter suggests some common venues for physical affront. For example, Christian slaves in the homes of non-Christian masters. On occasion the extreme deviancy-control technique of murder or execution could be applied." Personal correspondence with deSilva, 3/23/22. For a detailed discussion on the honor and shame culture that dominated the first century, see David deSilva, *Honor, Patronage, Kinship & Purity*, chaps. 1-2. In his book, deSilva shows that the vocabulary of the New Testament (examples being *glory*, *praise*, *reproach*, *scorn*, et al.) all point to the honor-shame culture and mindset (27-28, 43-93).

72. For details on how patronage worked in the first-century world of unbelievers as well as in the family of Jesus-followers, see David deSilva, *Honor, Patronage, Kinship & Purity*, chaps. 3-4. For more on what life was like in first-century Palestine, including the use of money, home life, food, baths, health, religion, respect, war, and death, see Scott Korb, *Life in Year One*, chaps. 1-10. For more on the cultural and social environment of the first Christians, see David deSilva, *An Introduction to the New Testament*, chaps. 2-3; N.T. Wright and Michael Bird, *The New Testament in Its World*, chaps. 5-7.

73. Nijay Gupta, *Tell Her Story*, 30-34.

Thus, she can gain respect if or when she marries.[74] While women cannot hold political office or vote, women of high class can be benefactors to men. They can also own property and engage in business, the most common being food production, crafts, hairdressing, nannying, and wet nursing.[75]

It is 9:00 a.m. on the day of Pentecost.[76] A priest has prepared two loaves of leavened bread. He pours oil on the loaves and slips them into an oven to be baked.[77] At the same moment, God's Spirit descends into the upper room where the 120 are staying. The Spirit of the Lord enters the room with the noise of a rushing, mighty windstorm.[78] The Spirit fills the 120 with God's presence and power.[79]

74. Holly Carey, *Women Who Do*, 26-27.

75. Nijay Gupta, *Tell Her Story*, 35, 39-43. According to Susan Hylen, women owned one-third of all property in the empire. When a woman's father died, she would be legally independent. Marriage didn't change her independent status. Most women owned some property. They were also in charge of the household. Jewish women behaved similarly to Greek and Roman women. For the most part, they owned property, ran businesses, were leaders in communities, and valued norms of modesty. That said, it was regarded as virtuous for a woman to defer to a man and to remain silent among people of higher status. But this didn't eliminate them from taking on leadership roles. Personal correspondence with Susan Hylen, 6/5/23. For further details on life in the first-century Greco-Roman world and the historical background of the New Testament era, see James Jeffers, *The Greco-Roman World of the New Testament Era*; Peter Garnsey and Richard Saller, *The Roman Empire: Economy, Society and Culture*, second edition (Oakland, CA: University of California, 2014).

76. Acts 2:15.

77. Leviticus 23:15-17.

78. According to Weima, "There was no actual wind, only the sound of something like a mighty wind; similarly, there was no actual fire, only the sight of something like tongues of fire. Luke is trying to describe supernatural events in language that his readers can understand." Personal correspondence with Jeffrey Weima, 12/28/23.

79. With Matthias replacing Judas, Luke continues to call the first followers of Jesus "the Twelve" (Acts 6:2). While the majority of the Twelve were already filled *inwardly* by the Spirit when Christ was resurrected, they were now empowered by the Spirit *outwardly*. The other 108 disciples received both the inward filling and the outward empowering at the same time.

Tongues of fire appear on the heads of those in the upper room, and they speak in languages they've never learned.[80] As a result, those visiting Jerusalem from around the empire hear God magnified in their own language and dialect.[81] The crowd is both amazed and perplexed that Galileans can speak in other languages and dialects.[82]

What is happening marks the reversal of what took place at Babel.[83] In Babel, human languages divided people, but in the new reality of God's kingdom, all people and nations are united into one family. The strange miracle is also a grand sign that God is inaugurating His new temple. Just as the fire fell on the temple of old when it was dedicated and God's glory filled it, fire falls upon the disciples in the upper room and the Spirit of God fills them.[84]

80. Acts 2:1-12. The fire powerfully symbolized cleansing and purification. James D.G. Dunn, *The Acts of the Apostles*, 23. In 1 Kings 8 and Isaiah 6, the Lord's presence filled the temple and the house was filled with smoke. Pentecost revealed that the ekklesia was the new temple where heaven and earth overlap (as was the case with the physical temple).

81. For a discussion on the imagery of wind and fire in the Pentecost account, see Leland Ryken, James Wilhoit, and Tremper Longman III, eds., *Dictionary of Biblical Imagery* (Downers Grove, IL: InterVarsity Press, 1998), 634.

82. "They were all amazed and marveled, saying to one another, 'Behold, aren't all these who speak Galileans?'" (Acts 2:7). The majority of Jesus-followers at this stage were Galileans. Clinton Arnold, ed., *Zondervan Illustrated Bible Backgrounds Commentary*, 2b:16. Consequently, the majority of the 120 were undoubtedly Galileans too. Eckhard Schnabel, *Acts: Zondervan Exegetical Commentary on the New Testament* (Grand Rapids, MI: Zondervan, 2012), 117. Galileans were simple country folks, not typically highly educated, so hearing them speak fluently in such an array of languages was astounding to those who were in Jerusalem from all four points of the compass. Personal correspondence with Alan Bandy, 12/6/23. How did the crowd know they were Galileans? Either their accent gave them away or the audience knew them as Jesus' followers from Galilee. Either way, the crowd was surprised by their diverse linguistic ability. Darrell Bock, *Acts,* 101-102.

83. In Acts 2:3, the same Greek word used for "divided" tongues (ESV) is used in Deuteronomy 32:8 (when God "divided" humankind) in the Septuagint (the Greek version of the Old Testament). Also, in Acts 2:6, the word "bewildered" (ESV) is the same Greek word used in Genesis 11:7 ("confuse" their language) in the Septuagint. In addition, the nations mentioned in Acts 2 correlate with the Table of Nations listed in Genesis 10, only their names have been updated. At Babel, fallen men tried to achieve unity and God confused them by scrambling their languages. At Pentecost, God united His people. They spoke in many languages yet they understood each other. Michael Heiser, *The Unseen Realm: Recovering the Supernatural Worldview of the Bible* (Bellingham, WA: Lexham Press, 2015), 298-302; Frank Viola, *Insurgence*, 358-359. In his massive Acts commentary, Keener provides a comprehensive discussion on the biblical allusions presented in Acts 2:1-12. Craig Keener, *Acts,* 1:801-806, 840-853.

84. 2 Chronicles 7:1-3; Acts 2:3-4.

Significantly, the day of Pentecost is also a commemoration of Moses' giving of the Law.[85] God had formerly promised through the prophet Jeremiah that He would make a new covenant and write His laws directly on the hearts of His people.[86] The message is clear: God is building His new temple, a new covenant is being sealed, and Jesus is the new Moses.

A Kingdom Community Is Born in Jerusalem

With the Holy Spirit's arrival, Jesus Christ—the head of the ekklesia—baptizes 120 Jews into His body, and the first kingdom community is born on earth.[87] There is now an assembly of people that possesses God's indwelling life through the Holy Spirit. This assembly begins to bear God's image and exercise His authority in Jerusalem. The flame has been lit, and Jesus finds tangible expression in the city. Spiritually speaking, one of the leavened loaves has been baked. This points to the Jewish part of Christ's body.

Ten years will pass, and the Holy Spirit will baptize the first Gentiles into the same body. The two oil-covered loaves, slipped into an oven on the day of Pentecost, will find fulfillment. The Jew and Gentile will be baptized into one body, constituting a new spiritual community.[88]

For in one Spirit we were all baptized into one body, whether Jews or Greeks, whether bond or free; and were all given to drink into one Spirit. (1 Corinthians 12:13)

The noise from the upper room provokes a crowd of Jews standing outside the house to investigate. What they see leaves them bewildered, and some question what the strange phenomenon means. Others accuse the 120 of inebriation. Peter, surrounded by the other

85. According to Jewish tradition, the Law was supernaturally uttered from Sinai in the seventy languages of the nations of the world. Craig Keener, *Acts*, 1:807ff. "Pentecost was already a covenant renewal celebration, but there is some debate about when it became a commemoration of the giving of the Law, since that tradition first appears in later rabbis." Personal correspondence with Craig Keener, 12/4/23.

86. Jeremiah 31:31-33.

87. According to Matthew 3:11 and 1 Corinthians 12:13, it is Jesus who baptizes people with the Holy Spirit into His body.

88. Ephesians 2:11-19.

apostles, stands in the midst of a crowded Jerusalem[89] and boldly proclaims that Jesus of Nazareth is the Christ, the promised Messiah. He exhorts everyone to repent and be baptized into the name of Jesus.[90] Three thousand Jews respond, being "stabbed to the heart" by Peter's piercing words.[91] The apostles baptize the new converts in the nearby pools in Bethesda and Siloam.[92] The believers, freshly baptized in water, are immediately added to the newly formed ekklesia. The fellowship of the divine community has now broadened from twelve, to 120, to 3,000.[93]

Strikingly, the first instinct of the new Christ-followers is to meet together and to do so constantly.[94] The Holy Spirit is like a magnet that draws those He indwells together. Now, the Galilean experience of informal gatherings with Jesus Christ as head is brought to Jerusalem by the Twelve, and it is reproduced among 3,000 people.[95]

89. Acts 2:14. The eleven other apostles stood up with Peter, lending their full support.

90. While Jesus proclaimed the kingdom, the apostles proclaimed Jesus as Lord, King, and Christ, which is another way of describing the kingdom. James D.G. Dunn points out that the preaching messages in Acts hardly ever mention the ministry of Jesus on earth (*Unity and Diversity in the New Testament*, 17). For a highly detailed examination of the speeches in Acts, see Craig Keener, *Acts*, 1:258-319. For a fuller treatment of how the Jerusalem apostles proclaimed the gospel of Jesus, see Eckhard Schnabel, *New Testament Theology*, 263-330.

91. Reta Halteman Finger, *Of Widows and Meals*, 223.

92. Ben Witherington III, *The Acts of the Apostles*, 156. It's possible they were baptized in the ritual baths within the walls of the temple. There were six large pools in Jerusalem (four more other than the Sheep's pool in Bethesda and Solomon's pool in Siloam). Clinton Arnold, ed., *Zondervan Illustrated Bible Backgrounds Commentary*, 2b:20. The large pools of Bethesda were very close, just outside the north side of the temple mount. The pool of Siloam was located farther away to the south of the temple mount. Personal correspondence with Jeffrey Weima, 12/28/23.

93. Acts 2:41.

94. Acts 2:42, 46-47. As more ekklesias were planted throughout the Roman Empire, the believers appeared to have had at least one of their regular church meetings on Sunday, likely chosen to commemorate the resurrection of Jesus (Acts 20:7; 1 Corinthians 16:2). Wayne Meeks, *The First Urban Christians*, 143. However, they would have other meetings in addition to the "first day of the week" gathering (e.g., Hebrews 3:13; Acts 2:46).

95. Acts 2:41-47. Gehring suggests this calculates to approximately 150 households following Jesus at this time. Roger Gehring, *House Church and Mission*, 87.

Then those who gladly received his word were baptized. There were added that day about three thousand souls. They continued steadfastly in the apostles' teaching and fellowship, in the breaking of bread, and prayer. (Acts 2:41-42)

Those in the new Jesus community devote themselves to the teaching of the apostles, sharing common meals, praying together, and enjoying fellowship.[96] As will be the case with all future ekklesias, the church in Jerusalem is "held together by the fact that all its members shared the experience of the presence of the Risen Lord."[97] When Jesus was with the Twelve and the women, He interacted with them *externally*. But now He has come in the Spirit and lives within them *internally*, just as He promised.[98]

The Twelve perform signs and wonders throughout the city. The ekklesia—and the city—watch in awe as they behold God's consuming fire made visible in the form of healings and miracles.[99] Many of the Jews who visited Jerusalem for the feast of Pentecost and believed in Jesus choose to remain in the city because it cradles the only kingdom community on the planet. Astonishingly, they leave their houses, quit their jobs, and settle in Jerusalem. To accommodate them all, the believers sell their possessions and pool their resources to care for each other.[100]

96. Acts 2:42. For details, see Eckhard Schnabel, *Early Christian Mission*, 1:406-416ff. "Fellowshipping" doesn't mean casual conversation that includes a potluck. Fellowship (*koinonia*) refers to the shared life and participation of the Holy Spirit among the members of the body of Christ. It's what Dietrich Bonhoeffer called "life together." The phrase "breaking bread" likely points to common meals. However, those meals probably included the Lord's Supper. In the first century, the Lord's Supper was taken as a full meal. It was called the communion (*koinonia*), the thanksgiving meal (*eucharisto*), the Lord's Supper (or meal), and the love (*agape*) feast. Tom Wright, *The Meal Jesus Gave Us: Understanding Holy Communion* (Louisville, KY: Westminster John Knox Press, 1999), 35-36; Ben Witherington III, *Making a Meal of It: Rethinking the Theology of the Lord's Supper* (Waco, TX: Baylor University Press, 2007), 53-62, 88. For the "breaking bread" custom in ancient Palestine, see Reta Halteman Finger, *Of Widows and Meals*, 229.

97. Hans Leitzmann, *A History of the Early Church* (London: Lutterworth Press, 1961), 1:64.

98. See John chaps. 14, 15, and 16.

99. Acts 2:43.

100. Living communally was not a practice of the other ekklesias founded later in the story. It was a unique experience of the Jerusalem church to meet an unusual need. Thousands of new converts without homes or jobs had just moved to the city, rendering them poor. Therefore, selling all and sharing their resources was the motivation of the new believers during this season in Jerusalem. Darrell Bock, *Acts*, 153. At the same time, the spiritual instinct of the body of Christ is *always* to care for its own and live detached from wealth and possessions, just as Jesus taught (Matthew 6:19-21, 24; Luke 12:32-34; 14:33).

The ekklesia in Jerusalem is a microcosm of the city. It includes rich and poor as well as a substantial number of Jews who speak only Greek, only Aramaic, or both Aramaic and Greek. Those who speak mostly Greek are called "Hellenists," and those who speak mostly Aramaic as their mother tongue are called "Hebrews."[101]

Sharpening the Focus: Approximately eight million Jews live in the empire.[102] Only a quarter to one-third live in Israel.[103] The much larger group living outside Palestine[104] is called the Dispersion or "Diaspora."[105]

Approximately six million Jews live in the Diaspora.[106] In some Diaspora cities, Jews might make up 10 to 15 percent of the total population.[107] Around 90 percent of those inhabiting Palestine live under harsh economic conditions.[108] They work all day

101. N.T. Wright, *Acts for Everyone: Part One*, 98-99. According to Keener, most Jews in Palestine were bilingual, and Greek was probably the first language for many Jews who lived in Jerusalem. "Hellenists," therefore, were Greek-speaking Diaspora Jews opposed to "Hebrews" who were bilingual natives of Judea and Galilee. Craig Keener, *The IVP Bible Background Commentary: New Testament*, 334. For details on the Hellenists, see Ben Witherington III, *The Acts of the Apostles*, 240-247. For a careful examination of the entire narrative found in Acts 2, see Craig Keener, *Acts*, 1:862-1038. For a clear summary of the makeup of the church in Jerusalem, including its constituency, theology, and mission, see Richard Longenecker, *Paul, Apostle of Liberty*, second edition (Grand Rapids, MI: Eerdmans, 2015), 247-263.

102. Eckhard Schnabel, *Early Christian Mission*, 1:122. Other historians estimate seven million or less, even as low as one million (but the latter figure is unlikely). Victor Tcherikover, *Hellenistic Civilization and the Jews* (Grand Rapids, MI: Baker Academic, 1999), 292-293, 504-505, note 86.

103. Darrell Bock, *Studying the Historical Jesus*, 109.

104. See previous note on the use of "Palestine" in this book.

105. The Diaspora refers to the Jews who were dispersed into Gentile nations. It is also known as the "Dispersion" (or scattering) that began in 586 B.C. John Drane, *Early Christians*, 19.

106. Wayne Meeks, *The First Urban Christians*, 34. One scholar states that Jews comprised 20 percent of the population in the Roman Empire. Richard Plummer and John Mark Terry, *Paul's Missionary Methods: In His Time and Ours* (Downers Grove, IL: InterVarsity Press, 2012), 24. Other scholars estimate there were between two and seven million Jews in the Diaspora. Eckhard Schnabel, *Early Christian Mission*, 1:122.

107. Large cities like Alexandria would be a little higher. Wayne Meeks, *The First Urban Christians*, 34. For details on Jewish identity and life in the Diaspora, see John Barclay, *Jews in the Mediterranean Diaspora: From Alexander to Trajan (323 BCE – 117 CE)* (Edinburgh: T & T Clark, 1996), chap. 14.

108. For a detailed discussion on the historical and social realities of first-century Palestine, see Eckhard Schnabel, *Early Christian Mission*, 1:178-206.

to earn enough money to buy food for dinner. They often remain hungry.[109] Education is mostly for the elite. At a young age, Jewish males are taught to read and write, since they are expected to study the Torah.[110]

Because the Jews have "strange" beliefs (they serve only one God) and "odd" practices (keeping the Sabbath holy, circumcision, avoiding pork, refusing to participate in the common practices of infanticide and exposure),[111] they are despised by most Romans and Greeks.[112]

Many Romans and Greeks view circumcision as mutilation,[113] the Sabbath as a cloak for laziness, and Jewish dietary laws as foolishness. The fact that the Jews don't eat a readily accessible and enjoyable meat (pork) is perceived as a senseless rejection of nature's bounty.[114] So Jews are widely mocked for not consuming it.[115]

The majority of Diaspora Jews observe Old Testament food laws. It's a significant mark of their distinctive identity.[116] These restrictions around food, its preparation, and its separation from anything related to idolatry, however, also tend to restrict social interaction with non-Jews. This leads to hostility toward Jews as antisocial. The Jews are viewed as having hostility toward everyone who isn't a Jew.[117] They are

109. Reta Halteman Finger, *Of Widows and Meals*, 156. Nearly everyone was poor in the first century. There was no middle class as there is today. Finger, *Of Widows and Meals*, 255, 277.

110. N.T. Wright, *Paul: A Biography*, 425.

111. Post-birth exposure and infanticide were the main forms of birth control in the ancient world among Greco-Romans. The common practice of infant exposure was completely foreign to the Jews. Scott Korb, *Life in Year One*, 83; Wayne Meeks, ed., *Library of Early Christianity*, 2:84.

112. The Greeks and Romans regarded the Jews as lazy because they didn't work on the Sabbath. Personal correspondence with Jeffrey Weima on 5/11/23.

113. James D.G. Dunn, *Beginning from Jerusalem*, 439. Some Jews believed that circumcision reduced lust. N.T. Wright, *Paul: A Biography*, 139. For the two forms of circumcision in antiquity, see E.P. Sanders, *Paul: The Apostle's Life, Letters, and Thought*, 460ff. For details on the centrality of circumcision in Judaism, see Craig Keener, *Acts*, 3:2215-2222.

114. 4 Maccabees 5:8-9; N.T. Wright, *Paul: A Biography*, 86.

115. Craig Keener, *Romans: A New Covenant Commentary*, NCCS (Eugene, OR: Cascade Books, 2009), 161.

116. Personal correspondence with Jeffrey Weima, 2/12/22.

117. According to the Roman historian Tacitus, the Jews felt hostility and hatred toward all other people. Jeffrey Weima, *1-2 Thessalonians*, 173. This view was widely held among Gentiles.

also regarded to be atheists since they deny the existence of the gods and only affirm the reality of their own God. Their refusal to craft any image or statue of their God is also an oddity in a world full of idols.[118] In addition, they refuse to participate in the imperial cult.[119] Despite all of this, Judaism is tolerated and protected under Roman law.[120]

Jerusalem is the epicenter of the Jewish faith. The city is less than one square mile.[121] The normal population is estimated between 30,000 and 60,000.[122] Multiple

118. On ancient anti-Judaism and Jewish responses to Gentile criticism, see David deSilva, *An Introduction to the New Testament*, 70-75. According to Weima, the most offensive thing about Jews was that they worshipped only one God. The fact that the one God of the Jews could *not* be seen in any image or form meant (to the pagan mind) that He simply did not exist. Christians would also be commonly accused of atheism for their denial of their neighbors' gods. Personal correspondence with Jeffrey Weima, 12/28/23. See also N.T. Wright, *Paul: A Biography*, 87; Michael Smith, *From Christ to Constantine* (Downers Grove, IL: InterVarsity Press, 1973), 25.

119. David Capes, et al., *Rediscovering Paul*, 46. The imperial cult (more accurately described as "imperial cults") is also known as the "imperial divine honors." For a detailed reconstruction of the imperial cult/divine honors in the first century and how they influenced the early followers of Jesus, see D. Clint Burnett, *Paul and Imperial Divine Honors: Christ, Caesar, and the Gospel* (Grand Rapids, MI: Eerdmans, 2024).

120. Interestingly, many Jews in the Diaspora were Hellenized. One scholar noted that the Jews in the Diaspora were virtually indistinguishable from Gentiles, except when they were observed in the synagogue or at home. Rodney Stark, *Cities of God* (San Francisco, CA: Harper Collins, 2006), 78. Some Jewish athletes even attempted to reverse their circumcision so they wouldn't be harassed in the gymnasiums and could compete in the athletic games. Ben Witherington III, *The Acts of the Apostles*, 210-213. The imperial cult was part of the Roman religions, cults, and associations. James Aageson, *After Paul: The Apostle's Legacy in Early Christianity* (Waco, TX: Baylor University Press, 2023), 117. According to Weima, "The Jews under Herod the Great took advantage of his close relationship with the Roman Caesars in order to work out a special arrangement by which they could offer sacrifices not *to* the Roman state and emperor (which would make them guilty of idolatry), but *on behalf of* the Roman state and emperor to their own God, thereby avoiding the charge that they were anti-Roman or engaged in subversive activity." Personal correspondence with Jeffrey Weima, 12/28/23.

121. Lee Levine, *Jerusalem: Portrait of the City in the Second Temple Period* (Philadelphia, PA: Jewish Publication Society, 2002), 343.

122. Bruce estimates 40,000 to 60,000 Jews lived in the city during the first century. F.F. Bruce, *Paul: Apostle of the Heart Set Free*, 30. Burge estimates 30,000. Gary Burge, *Jesus and the Jewish Festivals*, 55. Other scholars estimate different numbers. Finger presents evidence from numerous scholars on the sizes, ranging from 20,000 within the city walls to 10,000 outside them, and up to 400,000 during the feasts. See Reta

synagogues exist in the city.[123] It is the most distinguished city in the East. It's called the metropolis, the "mother city," by Judeans around the world.[124] Most people living in the city are Jewish. During the Pentecost celebration, the city swells to between 180,000 and 200,000 people.[125] The city is composed of the very rich, the destitute, craftsmen, and merchants.[126] The New Testament uses the phrase "going up" when it describes traveling to Jerusalem. The city is approximately 2,500 feet above sea level.[127]

Halteman Finger, *Of Widows and Meals,* 110-113. Other historians estimate the normal living population to be 100,000 rising to one million during feast times. Paul Barnett, *The Birth of Christianity: The First Twenty Years* (Grand Rapids, MI: Eerdmans, 2005), 19. Note that "there is virtually no direct evidence for the populations of ancient cities, so scholars have been forced to fall back on the assortment of evidence provided by extant textual sources and archaeological material." J.W. Hanson, *An Urban Geography of the Roman World, 100 BC to AD 300* (Oxford: Archaeopress, 2016), 49.

123. There is debate over the number of synagogues in Jerusalem during the first century. Some believe it was hundreds. E.M. Meyers, "Synagogue: Introductory Survey," in David Noel Freedman, ed., *The Anchor Yale Bible Dictionary*; Roger Gehring, *House Church and Mission*, 89, n. 152; Martin Hengel, *The Pre-Christian Paul* (Philadelphia, PA: Trinity Press International, 1991), 119, n. 160. Others believe these numbers are greatly exaggerated. Personal correspondence with David deSilva, 1/18/24. According to Keener, "the Theodotus inscription plainly attests a pre-70 synagogue in Jerusalem, and it is hardly likely that we have by chance the mention of the *only* pre-70 synagogue there. The New Testament mentions *synagogues* there (Mark 12:39; Acts 22:19; 24:12; 26:11). Just as we should not weigh too much on the later rabbis, neither should we limit the number of synagogues based on our extremely limited sample of archaeological evidence from pre-70 Jerusalem." Personal correspondence with Craig Keener, 1/26/24. Regarding size, some large synagogues in Palestine could hold about 300 people, though many of those excavated would have had a much smaller capacity. Craig Keener, *Acts: An Exegetical Commentary* (Grand Rapids, MI: Baker Academic, 2013), 2:2043.

124. Craig Keener, "Lessons on Acts," Session 24. For details on ancient Judea, see David deSilva, *Judea Under Greek and Roman Rule* (New York, NY: Oxford University Press, 2024); Paul Barnett, *Jesus & the Rise of Early Christianity*, chap. 7.

125. Ben Witherington III, *The Acts of the Apostles*, 156. Scholars vary on the numbers. Bock says the city swelled between 55,000 and 200,000 during the feast. Darrell Bock, *Acts*, 146. Other estimates range from 100,000-400,000. Reta Halteman Finger, *Of Widows and Meals*, 111-112; Gary Burge, *Jesus and the Jewish Festivals*, 55. Others note that "estimates range as high as 125,000, but today many think 10,000 is more likely." Craig Keener, *The Gospel of John: A Commentary* (Peabody, MA: Hendrickson, 2003), 2:861, n. 228.

126. For a discussion on the housing in Jerusalem, see Reta Halteman Finger, *Of Widows and Meals*, 117-120. For details on the typical Israelite house in the first century, see Eckhard Schnabel, *Early Christian Mission*, 1:299.

127. Michael Dumper, *Jerusalem Unbound: Geography, History, and the Future of the Holy City* (New York, NY: Columbia University Press, 2014), 146. Some sources say 2,300 feet. This is why a person always "goes up"

Most residents only speak and understand Aramaic.[128] Ten to 20 percent of the population speaks Greek.[129] Some are bilingual, and Greek is their second language. Others speak only Greek. Merchants learn Greek for business purposes.[130]

The Romans have a military presence in Jerusalem in the Antonia Fortress.[131] Since Judea came under direct Roman administration in A.D. 6, Roman auxiliaries (drawn mostly from the populations of Samaria and Caesarea) are the principal police force in Jerusalem.[132] In the small towns, Jewish families sometimes live in a single room.

---

to Jerusalem, no matter where they are located. Otto F.A. Meinardus, *St. Paul in Ephesus and the Cities of Galatia and Cyprus* (Athens, Greece: Lycabettus Press, 1973), 66. Nazareth was about 1,000 feet above sea level. George Adam Smith, *The Historical Geography of the Holy Land*, ninth edition (New York, NY: A.C. Armstrong and Son, 1902), 418, n. 1.

128. Personal correspondence with Darrell Bock, 3/14/24. "Palestinian Aramaic was the language in most common use among first-century Jews born and domiciled in Palestine, with Biblical Hebrew known by some, and Mishnaic Hebrew used as a spoken medium by others. Knowledge of Latin was fairly limited, whereas Greek was widely understood and used, the amount varying according to locality, social and educational background, and mobility." Greg Horsley, *New Documents Illustrating Early Christianity*, vol. 5 (Liverpool: Liverpool University Press, 1007), 19ff. "Hebrew and Aramaic are both Semitic languages that are extremely similar to each other in terms of the formation of letters and grammar. By New Testament times, Aramaic was widely spoken and used not just in Palestine, but in other surrounding near-Eastern people groups. So the common language of the people was Aramaic, but they could understand the Hebrew that would have been part of their reading of Scripture." Personal correspondence with Jeffrey Weima, 3/14/24. Aramaic was the language of the Persian empire, which Jews learned while in exile. Hebrew is a sister language to Aramaic, much like Spanish and Portuguese are close, but not identical. Personal correspondence with Ben Witherington III, 2/12/04. The Diaspora synagogues would have used Greek.

129. Bruce Winter, et al., eds., *The Book of Acts in Its First Century Setting*, 4:230-231. According to Schnabel's research, between 10 and 15 percent of Jerusalem's population in the first century spoke Greek as their native language. Eckhard Schnabel, *Early Christian Mission*, 1:201.

130. In the fifth century, and presumably during the first century, the four primary languages in Palestine were Latin, Greek, Aramaic, and Hebrew. Latin, however, wasn't spoken much in the region. Wayne Meeks, ed., *Library of Early Christianity*, 2:87. For further details on first-century Jerusalem, see P.W.L. Walker, ed., *Jerusalem Past and Present in the Purposes of God*, second edition (Grand Rapids, MI: Baker, 1994).

131. According to Weima, "The Romans have a military garrison housed in the Antonia Fortress (named after the famous Roman general Marc Antony) which is situated on the northwest corner of the temple mount, thereby allowing the Roman authorities to keep a close eye on the center of Judaism—the temple—and any suspicious activity that might take place there." Personal correspondence with Jeffrey Weima, 12/28/23.

132. Personal correspondence with David deSilva, 1/18/24.

Some extended families sleep in one bedroom. However, most have separate bedrooms for the couples and the children. Ovens are necessary in the home. Bread is baked often for the entire family.[133] In fact, bread makes up around 70 percent of the calories a person consumes in a normal day. Galileans consume around 550 pounds of grain per capita annually.[134]

Galilee, a region in northern Palestine/Israel, is where Jesus spent the majority of His life. It covers the area west of the Jordan River valley and the Sea of Galilee. While predominantly Jewish, Galilee has a minority Gentile population of Greeks, Phoenicians, Syrians and others due to its location along trade routes. The largest city in Galilee is Sepphoris, about four miles northwest of Nazareth where Jesus grew up. It has a mixed Jewish, Greek, and Syrian population.

Rarely does a Jewish person remain unmarried. Parents arrange the marriages of their children, and a person in Galilee could not spend time alone with their intended spouse until after the wedding.[135] Many Galileans own small houses and work in fields and crafts. Others are peasants who work the estates of landowners, who often aren't present.[136]

Kingdom Life Begins in Jerusalem
A.D. 30 – 31

Each day, the Twelve teach the multitudes of converts at Solomon's porch (also called Solomon's colonnade or portico). This structure is a sizeable area located along the eastern wall of the court of the Gentiles in Herod's temple.[137] It is simply a large open porch with

133. Wayne Meeks, ed., *Library of Early Christianity*, 2:84; Ben Witherington III, *A Week in the Fall of Jerusalem*, 46-47.

134. Scott Korb, *Life in Year One*, 83.

135. Craig Keener, *The Gospel of Matthew*, 471.

136. Craig Keener, *The Gospel of Matthew*, 482. For further details on first-century Judaism and life in the Greco-Roman world, see N.T. Wright, *The New Testament and the People of God*, chaps. 6-7.

137. Solomon's portico extended over 300 yards. Clinton Arnold, ed., *Zondervan Illustrated Bible Backgrounds Commentary*, 2b:27. Herod the Great (37-4 B.C.) ruled for thirty-three years thanks to the support of

a roof over it.[138] In Solomon's porch, the assembly in Jerusalem hears the apostles minister God's word. The apostles have lived with the Son of God for a little over three years; consequently, their preaching and teaching is nothing other than Jesus Christ.

That which was from the beginning, that which we have heard, that which we have seen with our eyes, that which we saw, and our hands touched, concerning the Word of life (and the life was revealed, and we have seen, and testify, and declare to you the life, the eternal life, which was with the Father, and was revealed to us); that which we have seen and heard we declare to you, that you also may have fellowship with us. Yes, and our fellowship is with the Father, and with his Son, Jesus Christ. (1 John 1:1-3)

Daily, the believers meet in homes throughout the city.[139] New converts are made regularly and added to the ekklesia.[140] At this point, the believing community in Jerusalem is finding favor with the Jews of the city.[141]

---

the Romans. Herod reconstructed the temple of Jerusalem beginning in 20 B.C. Gary Burge, et al., *The New Testament in Antiquity*, 37-41. David deSilva adds, "Renovations to the sanctuary were completed within two years; major work to the retaining walls, courtyards, and porticoes was largely completed within another ten years. Maintenance and repair of damage caused by subsidences, however, kept construction active through A.D. 63." Personal correspondence with deSilva, 1/18/24.

138. It could also be described as a large, covered walkway. "It had two rows of columns, while the colonnade on the south side (known as the Royal Portico) had four rows." Josephus, *The Jewish War*, 5.5.1; *The Antiquities of the Jews*, 15.11.5; 20.9.7. Solomon's portico is the scene of the following texts: John 10:23; Acts 3:11; 5:12). See also John Barry, et al., "Solomon's Portico," *The Lexham Bible Dictionary*, Logos edition (Bellingham, WA: Lexham Press, 2016). For a full-color diagram of Herod's temple, see David and Pat Alexander, eds., *Handbook to the Bible*, 532-533.

139. Private homes were the normative meeting place for Jesus-followers during the first three centuries of the ekklesia's existence. The wealthier members of the ekklesia in Jerusalem opened their homes for the believers to gather. Clinton Arnold, ed., *Zondervan Illustrated Bible Backgrounds Commentary*, 2b:22-23.

140. Again, the conversion experience is also referred to as being "added to the Lord" and "added to the ekklesia" (Acts 2:47; 5:14; 11:24, NKJV).

141. Acts 2:46-47. This will not last, however.

Demonstrations of God's Healing Power

It is 3:00 p.m., the Jewish hour of prayer.[142] Peter and John head toward the temple to participate in the Hebrew prayer service. As they approach the sacred building, they meet a disabled man who has been unable to walk since birth. The man is over forty years old.[143] Every day, he begs beside the temple gate, also called "the Beautiful Gate." (This is probably one of the gates in the Court of Women. It's exceptionally ornate and grand, covered with silver, gold, and remarkable Corinthian bronze.[144])

As Peter and John are ready to enter the temple, the disabled man asks them for money. Peter and John cannot meet his request because they're flat broke. But they do something better. They heal him in the name of Jesus. Astounded, the man jumps to his feet and joins the two apostles as they enter the temple courts. With his newly healed legs, he cannot help but leap up and down while praising God.

The people recognize this man, and as they see him walking, they gawk with shock. In wonder and amazement, they rush into Solomon's colonnade where the man stands with Peter and John. Taking advantage of his immensely interested audience, Peter preaches that Jesus, in whose name the formerly lame[145] man was healed, is the promised Christ.[146] Some of the priests, temple guards, and Sadducees hear Peter and John declaring Jesus and His resurrection.[147]

Since the Sadducees completely reject the belief of resurrection, they're disturbed by the message the two apostles proclaim. Consequently, the Sadducees, priests, and captain

142. Acts 3:1. Clinton Arnold, ed., *Zondervan Illustrated Bible Backgrounds Commentary*, 2b:25.

143. Acts 4:22.

144. Clinton Arnold, ed., *Zondervan Illustrated Bible Backgrounds Commentary*, 2b:25-26.

145. Virtually every Bible translation of Acts 3:2 uses the word "lame" to describe the man's condition, meaning he was unable to walk.

146. This narrative is based on Acts 3.

147. Acts 4:1 makes clear that John was also involved in the preaching. According to Levine and Sievers, the priests weren't religious leaders like the Pharisees, Sadducees, and scribes. Priests didn't lead the "religion" of Judaism; they were merely in charge of the temple. They didn't determine daily practice or belief. Personal correspondence with Amy-Jill Levine and Joseph Sievers, 3/8/22. At the same time, the degree of overlap between the priestly caste and the constituency of each of these three other groups was quite strong. Personal correspondence with David deSilva, 1/18/24. Some of the poorest priests were Pharisees. The upper-class priests were Sadducees. Craig Keener, "Lessons on Acts," Session 14.

of the guard immediately seize Peter and John[148] and throw them in jail for the evening.[149] But many who heard them preach are converted to Christ. At this point, the Jerusalem ekklesia has rapidly grown to 5,000 men.[150] Counting women and children, the believers number at least 10,000.[151]

The next day, Peter and John are brought before the Sanhedrin for questioning. The Sanhedrin is the Senate and Supreme Court for the Jewish nation. The council contains seventy members along with the high priest, who presides over the procedures.[152] The Sanhedrin is both religious and political, and most of its members are from the Sadducee party.[153] Annas, the ex-high priest, is present. (Annas' son-in-law, Caiaphas, currently occupies

148. According to Weima, "The Sadducees were a priestly party—a party made up of those who serve in the temple and thus they were naturally mentioned in the same breath as the priests and the temple guards. This is their 'turf' that the Jesus movement was invading. As the priestly party, their power base was the temple. So it was the destruction of the temple, more than the destruction of the city, that resulted in the demise of their party. By contrast the power base of the Pharisees was the Torah (Law), and that was not destroyed in A.D. 70, so the Pharisees live on beyond the Jewish revolt." Personal correspondence with Jeffrey Weima, 12/28/23.

149. Acts 4:3. The context suggests they were taken to the prison of the Sanhedrin which was located below the western wall of the temple mount. Personal correspondence with Eckhard Schnabel, 8/25/23.

150. Acts 4:4. The term used clearly indicates only the men were counted in this number. Clinton Arnold, ed., *Zondervan Illustrated Bible Backgrounds Commentary*, 2b:30.

151. Luke points out the consistent growth of the Jerusalem church throughout Acts. On Pentecost, the birthday of the assembly, 3,000 were converted (Acts 2:41). Not long after, it swelled to 5,000 men (Acts 4:4, ESV). The church now had a "multitude" of believers (Acts 4:32, NKJV). Afterward, the ekklesia grew from a "multitude" to "multitudes" (Acts 5:14, ESV). In a short time following, the number of believers multiplied greatly (Acts 6:7, ESV). With the persecution under Saul, the Jerusalem assembly dissolved. But years later it grew to "myriads" (Acts 21:20, BLB).

152. The Greek word for "Sanhedrin" means "council." Ben Witherington III, *New Testament History*, 148. The Sanhedrin contained the rulers, elders, and teachers of the Law. *The NIV Study Bible* (Grand Rapids, MI: Zondervan, 2020), 1902. The high priest was present and in charge when the Sanhedrin in Jerusalem tried cases. According to the Mishnah, the Sanhedrin consisted of seventy-one members. James VanderKam, *An Introduction to Early Judaism*, second edition (Grand Rapids, MI: Eerdmans, 2022), 189. For details on the Sanhedrin, the high priests, and Sadducees, see Craig Keener, *The Gospel of Matthew*, 613-616; Joel Green, et al., eds., *Dictionary of Jesus and the Gospels*, 836-840.

153. Ben Witherington III, *New Testament History*, 149. Even though Sadducees made up the majority, Pharisees formed "a substantial element in the Sanhedrin," though it's probable that they were represented mainly among the scribes rather than the elders. R.T. France, *The Gospel of Matthew*, 819.

the office of high priest.[154]) The Sanhedrin demands that Peter and John tell them by what power they performed the miracle. Filled with the Holy Spirit, Peter and John boldly proclaim Jesus of Nazareth as the Christ whose power healed the lame man. Peter then accuses the Sanhedrin of crucifying Jesus and adds that God raised Him from the dead.

Peter and John's courage astonishes the members of the Sanhedrin, and they note that the two apostles had been with Jesus. Peter and John are unlearned and ignorant men,[155] without formal religious training, yet they speak with the same authority for which Jesus was known. (This observation reveals that Jesus taught with boldness, despite the fact that He too had no formal religious training.) With the healed man standing in their midst, the Sanhedrin cannot deny the miracle. So the leaders send Peter and John out of the council chamber and confer among themselves.

The members of the Sanhedrin fear that if they don't stop the apostles from speaking in the name of Jesus, the movement will spread. But they cannot discount the miracle, so they decide to forbid Peter and John from speaking in the name of Jesus. Calling the two apostles back into the chamber, the council gives them their command. Peter and John reply saying,

Which is right in God's eyes: to listen to you, or to him? You be the judges! As for us, we cannot help speaking about what we have seen and heard. (Acts 4:19-20, NIV)[156]

154. Caiaphas' reign extended from A.D. 18-36. In this period, the high priest no longer achieved his office by bloodline, but by appointment. The high priest of Jesus' day was appointed by Pilate.

155. Acts 4:13. The text refers to the fact that the apostles were unschooled, uneducated, and untrained. It does not mean they couldn't read. The Jewish authorities assumed incorrectly that the Galilean fishermen were rural country bumpkins. Craig Keener, "Lessons on Acts," Session 12. According to Witherington and deSilva, most Galileans knew some Greek, which Jesus would have used when He went to the regions around Gerasa, Tyre, and Sidon. Aramaic would have been their more common, everyday language. Personal correspondence with Ben Witherington III, 5/22/18 and David deSilva, 1/18/24. According to Bruce Longenecker, "Jesus had at least an elementary reading ability" which was common for being raised in a Judean home. It's unlikely that Peter and John had anything beyond a basic form of literacy. They could read but may not have been able to write. Bruce Longenecker, *In Stone and Story*, 150-151; Clinton Arnold, ed., *Zondervan Illustrated Bible Backgrounds Commentary*, 2b:32.

156. Look closely at 1 John 1:1-3 (NIV) for the same wording— "which we have heard, which we have seen…what we have seen and heard."

The Sanhedrin threatens the two apostles further, but still ends up releasing them because the members don't know how to punish the men without inciting a riot. Upon their release, Peter and John immediately report to the Jerusalem ekklesia all that occurred. The assembly prays, asking God to bless the apostles with boldness and continue to grant them His miraculous power in the name of Jesus. While they are touching heaven's throne in prayer, the Holy Spirit descends powerfully and fills the entire building, shaking its foundations. The Spirit fills the apostles, and they continue to preach Jesus Christ boldly, despite the Sanhedrin's command.

The Twelve bear witness to Christ's resurrection with great power.[157] The ekklesia in Jerusalem is unified in heart and soul, and the believers hold everything in common—so much so that not a single person among them has any lack.[158] From time to time, those who own land and property sell them, handing their money to the Twelve to distribute to those in need.[159] One such man is Joseph, a native from the island of Cyprus and a Levite.[160] Joseph voluntarily sells his land and brings the income to the apostles.[161]

Joseph is a good man, full of the Holy Spirit and overflowing with faith.[162] He's also an encourager. Consequently, the apostles nickname him "Barnabas," which means "son of encouragement" or "son of exhortation."[163] He is a man of "rare quality," known to

157. Many signs and wonders were done among the people through the hands of the apostles. Acts 5:12, NKJV.

158. The believers didn't abandon their possessions all at once but sold their goods as the needs arose and shared the profits with the assembly. Their detachment to material things and their generosity to those in need was taken directly from the teachings and example of Jesus (Mark 10:21; Matthew 19:24, etc.). John Drane, *Early Christians*, 69.

159. Acts 4:34-35.

160. A Levite was a member of the priestly Hebrew tribe of Levi. Levites were assigned to lesser ceremonial offices under the Levitical priests in the family of Aaron.

161. The "land" or "field" that belonged to Joseph refers to medium-sized estates or larger. Unlike what is prescribed in the Law, the Levites during this time could own land. Joseph's gift was likely large because he probably had a vineyard on Cyprus that provided the wine used in the Jerusalem temple. Personal correspondence with Alan Bandy, 12/6/23.

162. Acts 11:24.

163. Acts 4:36, NIV. "Joseph" is his original name. F.F. Bruce, *The Pauline Circle*, 16. "Son of Exhortation" may be a better translation. Clinton Arnold, ed., *Zondervan Illustrated Bible Backgrounds Commentary*, 2b:35. Barnabas appears to be a relative of Mary, the mother of John Mark. Personal correspondence with Alan Bandy, 12/6/23.

"promote and sustain warm and constructive personal relations."[164] He is also a man of reasonable financial means.[165]

Persecution Begins
A.D. 31 – 33

A married couple in the Jerusalem assembly, Ananias and Sapphira, sell some property and give a portion of the proceeds to the ekklesia. Regrettably, they lie to the apostles about the amount because they want to keep some of the profits for themselves. God, however, supernaturally reveals their deception to Peter who unveils their sin. Peter tells the couple they have lied to God rather than to men. Within three hours of one another, Ananias and his wife Sapphira fall to the ground dead.[166]

The young men carry their bodies out and bury them, one after the other. As a result, great fear grips the ekklesia in Jerusalem and all who hear about the unusual events.[167] The Twelve perform many signs and wonders as they continue to preach Christ and His kingdom in Solomon's colonnade. While the people in the city highly regard the apostles, they are hesitant to join them, recalling the fate that befell Ananias and Sapphira.[168] (The apostles do not leave Jerusalem yet. And at this point, no one except the apostles has preached the gospel.)

The believers continue to meet regularly in Solomon's colonnade. Crowds of people from the city and neighboring villages bring their sick and demon-possessed friends and family into the streets. They place them on beds and mats so the apostles can heal and deliver them. Remarkably, each sick person is healed. In fact, some in the crowd believe the

---

164. James D.G. Dunn, *The Acts of the Apostles*, 60.

165. Wayne Meeks, *The First Urban Christians*, 61. He was also from a well-to-do family. Alan Bandy, *An Illustrated Guide to the Apostle Paul*, 40.

166. The problem wasn't that they wanted to keep some of the money. The problem was that they tried to deceive the ekklesia. Personal correspondence with Alan Bandy, 12/6/23.

167. This tragic story is told in Acts 5:1-11.

168. Acts 5:12-13.

mere passing of Peter's shadow will heal them.[169] Multitudes of men and women believe in Jesus as a result.

The high priest and his friends (who are Sadducees) react to these events with violent jealousy. Motivated by envy, they arrest the apostles and put them in jail. But in the evening, an angel delivers them from the cell.[170] The angel tells the apostles to go back into the temple court and resume preaching "the words of this life"[171]—the new life in Jesus, which is God's life come to earth. The apostles obey the angel and enter the temple court at daybreak. They continue to preach Jesus as life.

When the Sanhedrin receives the news, the captain of the temple guard and his officers re-arrest the apostles. They bring them before the Sanhedrin to be interrogated. But Peter and the other apostles answer that they must obey God rather than man. Now furious, the Sanhedrin plots to put the apostles to death. But Gamaliel, an expert in religious law and the most influential Pharisaic teacher of the day, persuades the council to leave the men alone.[172]

Instead of killing them, the council has the apostles flogged. Thus, the "forty lashes minus one" are inflicted upon the apostles.[173] (Flogging is a savage, brutal experience. Victims are tied to a pillar by their hands and whipped on the bare back and chest. The whip used for the beating is called a scourge.[174]) Following the vicious beating, the Sanhedrin

169. It's not clear from the text (Acts 5:15) if people were actually healed by Peter's shadow or if the people just believed his shadow would heal them. Both Jewish and Hellenistic folklore held that a person's shadow could contain spiritual power. For details, see Clinton Arnold, ed., *Zondervan Illustrated Bible Backgrounds Commentary*, 2b:38.

170. The Sanhedrin had a space of incarceration in the temple or below it. Clinton Arnold, ed., *Zondervan Illustrated Bible Backgrounds Commentary*, 2b:39.

171. Acts 5:19-20

172. Acts 5:34-39. Rabbi Gamaliel was highly honored as the greatest educator of the time. He was also the head of his own school in the tradition of Hillel. A Jew by the name of Saul of Tarsus was one of his pupils (Acts 22:3). Clinton Arnold, ed., *Zondervan Illustrated Bible Backgrounds Commentary*, 2b:41, 223. In Acts 5:37, Gamaliel mentions Judas the Galilean, the man who incited the people to revolt. The rise of Judas occurred in A.D. 6. F.F. Bruce, *Paul: Apostle of the Heart Set Free*, 109. For the background on Judas, see David Rhoads, *Israel in Revolution 6-74 C.E.*, 47ff. Gamaliel himself was either the son or grandson of Hillel. Richard Longenecker, *Luke-Acts*, 796.

173. This was the normal punishment handed out by Jewish courts (Deuteronomy 25:2-4).

174. The flogging was so savage that people were known to die from it. I. Howard Marshall, *Acts: An Introduction and Commentary*, TNTC (Grand Rapids, MI: Eerdmans, 1980), 123-124. The minister of the

commands the apostles not to speak in the name of Jesus. Afterward, they release them. The apostles leave the presence of the Sanhedrin bloodied and bruised. But they are also rejoicing because they were counted worthy to suffer for the Lord's name.

Blessed are those who have been persecuted for righteousness' sake, for theirs is the Kingdom of Heaven. Blessed are you when people reproach you, persecute you, and say all kinds of evil against you falsely, for my sake. Rejoice, and be exceedingly glad, for great is your reward in heaven. For that is how they persecuted the prophets who were before you. (Matthew 5:10-12)

Despite the savage beating they just took, the Twelve fearlessly continue to preach and teach Jesus Christ in the temple court and in the homes of the believers.[175] The predictive warning Jesus issued before His death and resurrection prepared and emboldened them to continue.

But beware of men, for they will deliver you up to councils, and in their synagogues they will scourge you. Yes, and you will be brought before governors and kings for my sake, for a testimony to them and to the nations. But when they deliver you up, don't be anxious how or what you will say, for it will be given you in that hour what you will say. For it is not you who speak, but the Spirit of your Father who speaks in you. (Matthew 10:17-20)

Conflict in Jerusalem

As the assembly in Jerusalem increases in number, the Greek-speaking (Hellenistic) Jews begin complaining about the Hebraic (Hebrew) Jews.[176] Each day, food is distributed to the

---

synagogue would stand on a raised stone inflicting the blows with all his might using a redoubled calf strap, to which two other straps were attached. Thirteen blows were delivered to the chest and twenty-six to the back. Paul Barnett, *The Second Epistle to the Corinthians,* 542, also n. 13. For more details on the brutality of Jewish floggings, see F.F. Bruce, *1 and 2 Corinthians* (London: Marshall, Morgan and Scott, 1971), 242; Clinton Arnold, ed., *Zondervan Illustrated Bible Backgrounds Commentary*, 2b:43.

175. Acts 5:12-42.

176. The Hellenistic Jews spoke Greek and embraced Greco-Roman culture and customs. The Hebraic Jews spoke Aramaic or Hebrew and were reluctant to adopt the Hellenistic practices that were making inroads into Jewish society. Personal correspondence with Jeffrey Weima, 12/28/23. The Hellenistic Jews

needy members of the assembly. But the Hellenistic Jews feel that their widows are continuously neglected. Thus, the ekklesia in Jerusalem faces its first internal crisis. To solve the problem, the Twelve gather the whole ekklesia together. They explain that they cannot devote time to the issue, since their hands are full ministering the word of God.

Therefore, they instruct the believing community to choose seven men from among them to oversee the food distribution. The men must be spiritual (full of the Holy Spirit) and practical (full of wisdom). The ekklesia is pleased with the idea, and they select seven men—all Hellenistic Jews.[177] They are:

- Stephen[178]
- Prochorus
- Parmenas
- Nicolaus[179]
- Timon
- Nicanor
- Philip

The ekklesia presents the seven men to the Twelve, and the apostles lay hands on them with prayer.[180] The word of God advances, and the believing community in Jerusalem

---

were born outside of Palestine; most Hebraic Jews were born in Palestine. In short, Hellenistic Jews sought to build bridges with Greek culture. David deSilva, *The Letter to the Galatians,* 17. For a detailed analysis of the Hellenistic Jewish believers in Jerusalem, see Eckhard Schnabel, *Early Christian Mission,* 1:653-669. For a full survey on the difference between the Hellenistic Jews and the Hebraic Jews, see Craig Keener, *Acts,* 2:1254-1259.

177. In designating seven Hellenistic Jews to handle the food distribution, the church gave authority to the party that had been experiencing discrimination. Craig Keener, "Lessons on Acts," Session 14.

178. Stephen is described as a man full of wisdom, faith, and the Holy Spirit (Acts 6:3, 5). All the names in this list reflect the spelling of the WEB.

179. Nicolaus was from Antioch (Acts 6:5). He was a Gentile who converted to Judaism (a proselyte). James D.G. Dunn, *The Acts of the Apostles,* 83. According to ancient church tradition, he later founded the Nicolaitan party condemned in Revelation 2:6, 15. Irenaeus, *Against Heresies,* 1.26.3; Eusebius, *The History of the Church,* 3.29. But according to some scholars like Weima, this association is highly unlikely. Personal correspondence with Jeffrey Weima, 12/28/23.

180. Acts 6:5-6. James D.G. Dunn, *The Acts of the Apostles,* 83.

greatly increases. A large company of Jewish priests are converted and added to the assembly also.[181]

Stephen Shines and Is Martyred

Stephen, one of the "seven" who helps with the food distribution, begins preaching Christ in the city. He also performs miraculous signs, confirming his message. Outside the Twelve, Stephen is the first person in the assembly to show evidence of being called to God's work.[182] He frequents one of the synagogues in the city—the synagogue of the Freedmen.[183] There, he debates the Hellenistic Jews who attend. (The synagogue of the Freedmen is frequented by Jews from Cyrene, Alexandria, Asia, and Cilicia.) Saul of Tarsus hears Stephen preach a radical message[184]—a message that declares God is uncontrollable and cannot be manipulated or confined to the temple. The Almighty's true dwelling place is not human-made.[185]

181. Acts 6:1-7. Already, the number of only men who were Jesus-followers was kicking up to 5,000. The movement to follow Jesus was getting larger and could not be ignored. Craig Keener, "Lessons on Acts," Session 12.

182. This is demonstrated by his ability to preach with power and exhibit God's supernatural power. If Stephen had lived, he may have proven to be an apostle who planted ekklesias or at least an evangelist like Philip. See Ephesians 4:11ff.

183. Clinton Arnold, ed., *Zondervan Illustrated Bible Backgrounds Commentary*, 2b:49. Some older translations render it the synagogue of the "Libertines." Some freedpersons eventually became wealthy and influential. However, most remained poor and had less security than in their previous lives as slaves. Synagogues had multiple functions: they served religious, judicial, social, educational, and political roles. Calvin Roetzel, *The World That Shaped the New Testament*, 94ff. On the origins of synagogues, see Ben Witherington III, *The Acts of the Apostles*, 255-257.

184. It's possible that Saul attended the synagogue of the Freedmen, but we cannot be certain. I agree with Barnett who states that Saul "was present on that occasion." Therefore, Saul heard Stephen's words which made an impression on him. Stephen's words would later be reflected in his post-conversion ministry. Paul Barnett, *Bethlehem to Patmos,* 147-149.

185. According to Barnett, embedded in Stephen's message is the idea that God's mission to the nations will go out from Jerusalem and its temple rather than in the opposite direction. See Paul Barnett, *Paul: Missionary of Jesus*, 53. His message (which some have called a "defense") is the longest recorded discourse in the book of Acts. Stott writes that Stephen's speech "was not so much a self-defense as a testimony to Christ." John Stott, *The Message of Acts,* 141. For details, see Ben Witherington III, *The Acts of the Apostles*, 259-274; Eckhard Schnabel, *Acts*, 385-388.

The Hellenistic Jews argue with Stephen, but they cannot stand up to his wisdom or the Spirit by which he speaks. So they secretly persuade some of the people to falsely accuse him of blaspheming against God's temple and the Law of Moses. Although false, this charge causes a violent stir in the synagogue, and Stephen is seized by the elders and teachers of the Law. He is tried before the Sanhedrin on the charge that he is preaching that Jesus of Nazareth would destroy the temple.[186] As the charges are brought, the members of the court stare intently at Stephen. But despite their hostility, they perceive his face to be like an angel—aglow as though he is standing in the presence of God.[187]

The high priest asks Stephen if the charges are true, and Stephen responds with a lengthy speech.[188] He provides a survey of the Old Testament narrative in which he magnifies Jesus as the climax of the story. Jesus, Stephen confidently declares, is the promised Christ.

At the end of his speech, Stephen rebukes the Jewish leaders for murdering the Messiah and disobeying God's Law.[189] The Sanhedrin seethes with such fury that they grind their teeth at him. Stephen looks up to the heavens and sees Jesus standing at the right hand of God the Father.[190] Christ is cheering Stephen on, waiting to receive him as a victor.[191] When the Jews hear Stephen say he sees Jesus, they cover their ears, scream at the top of their lungs, and drag Stephen out of the city. In a mad rage, they brutally stone him to death.[192]

186. This was a false charge. Matthew 26:59-61; Acts 6:11-14.

187. Acts 6:15. According to Darrell Bock, this description probably represents a striking brightness on Stephen's face, since angels are described as bright. (The angels at the tomb of Jesus are said to have been wearing bright white.) Personal correspondence with Darrell Bock, 7/14/23. Witherington agrees. See Ben Witherington III, *The Acts of the Apostles,* 259.

188. You can find Stephen's speech in Acts 7:2-53. This presumably took place in A.D. 31 or 32. Eckhard Schnabel, *Acts,* 329.

189. He calls them "stiff-necked," a term God used for His people in the Old Testament (Acts 7:51; Exodus 33:3-5, NIV). Clinton Arnold, ed., *Zondervan Illustrated Bible Backgrounds Commentary,* 2b:57.

190. For other examples of this kind of visionary experience, see Ezekiel 1:1, John 1:51, and Genesis 28:12.

191. Acts 7:55. Throughout the New Testament, Jesus is always described as *sitting* at God's right hand. But in this text, He is *standing.*

192. Acts 7:54-58. The Sanhedrin was allowed to pronounce and execute the death sentence in only one case—offenses against the sanctity of the temple. When Judea became a Roman province in A.D. 6, the jurisdiction for capital offenses was reserved for the Roman governor, except in this one case. F.F. Bruce, *Paul: Apostle of the Heart Set Free,* 68. When Jesus was brought to trial before the same court, an attempt was made to convict Him on the charge of speaking against the temple. Had that attempt succeeded, it would not have been necessary to refer Jesus' case to Pilate. Mark 14:57ff.; Acts 6:14. According to Witherington, the events described in Acts 3 to

As the rocks crush Stephen's body, he prays, "Lord Jesus, receive my spirit."[193] He falls to his knees and adds, "Do not hold this sin against them."[194] Stephen dies a brutal, unjust death. Godly men bury him and mourn his loss.[195] Stephen is the first martyr for Jesus Christ. The earliest firebrand beyond the Twelve is now gone, but his tribe will rapidly increase.

The Ekklesia Is Transplanted Throughout Palestine

Saul of Tarsus is a young man, almost thirty years old.[196] He's a well-known Pharisee who witnessed Stephen's death.[197] In fact, Saul guarded the clothes of Stephen's executioners, showing his full support for the brutal slaying.[198]

Acts 7 took place between A.D. 30 and 33. Ben Witherington III, *The Acts of the Apostles*, 81. For a discussion on the rabbinic regulations for stoning, see Clinton Arnold, ed., *Zondervan Illustrated Bible Backgrounds Commentary*, 2b:60. The execution of Stephen was illegal. Craig Keener, "Lessons on Acts," Session 15.

193. These words contain echoes of Jesus' last words to His Father (Luke 23:46).

194. Stephen exhibited the forgiving spirit of Christ when Jesus was also unjustly slain (Luke 23:34). For comparisons between Jesus and Stephen, see Ben Witherington III, *The Acts of the Apostles*, 276.

195. The narrative you've just read is based on Acts 6:8–7:60; 8:2. Dying without a burial was a huge dishonor. A person who buried a criminal risked their life, so it was an act of courage to bury criminals. Public mourning for a condemned criminal was prohibited. According to Keener, the followers of Jesus took a risk by burying Stephen. Craig Keener, "Lessons on Acts," Session 15.

196. Acts 7:58, ESV. Saul is described as a "young man." Saul's age is based on the math. If Saul was born in A.D. 5 and converted in A.D. 33 or 34, as Witherington suggests, that made him almost thirty at Stephen's stoning. Ben Witherington III, *Invitation to the New Testament*, 161-162. Alan Bandy states that a "young man" (*neaniou*) referred to a man between the ages of twenty-five and thirty-five. We will follow Luke's narrative by calling him by his Roman name "Paul" later in our story.

197. It's also possible that Saul was Stephen's prosecutor at his trial. Alan Bandy, *An Illustrated Guide to the Apostle Paul*, 17; Paul Barnett, *Paul: Missionary of Jesus*, 24. Some further details on the Pharisees: They were concerned with interpreting and applying the Law of Moses in daily life. They were "an unofficial but powerful Jewish pressure group." N.T. Wright, *Acts for Everyone: Part One*, 204. They were chiefly concerned with how to be a loyal Jew amid pagan oppression and unfaithful Jews. Purity, then, was the seal of that concern. N.T. Wright, *Paul and the Faithfulness of God* (Minneapolis, MN: Fortress Press, 2013), 1:83. The Pharisees were mostly a lay-led group during this era. N.T. Wright, *Luke for Everyone*, 312. Because the people did not have access to the Scriptures, they relied on the Pharisees and Sadducees. But most of the populace followed the teachings of the Pharisees. Mark Fairchild, "The Last Apostle," documentary film.

198. Although Saul wasn't directly involved in Stephen's stoning, according to a reasonable reading of Acts 26:10, he "took actions and cooperated with efforts that led to the death of various Christians." Ben Witherington III, *The Acts of the Apostles*, 670.

Saul acts as a commissioner for the Sanhedrin and begins to ravage the ekklesia in Jerusalem. The chief priests give him authority to bind the believers, those who call on the name of Jesus.[199] As a result, Saul invades their home meetings and drags the women and men to prison.[200]

But Saul ravaged the assembly, entering into every house and dragged both men and women off to prison. (Acts 8:3)

Saul/Paul would later rehearse his conduct when writing to the Christians in Galatia:

For you have heard of my way of living in time past in the Jews' religion, how that beyond measure I persecuted the assembly of God and ravaged it. (Galatians 1:13)

To escape the persecution, the ekklesia in Jerusalem disperses throughout Judea, Samaria, and Galilee. Some even flee as far as Damascus, Syria—a city 130 miles north of Jerusalem.[201] The Twelve stay behind in Jerusalem and go into hiding.[202] The believers who scatter throughout Palestine begin to share the gospel in their new locales.[203] And for the first time, the gospel is being proclaimed outside the city of Jerusalem.

199. Acts 9:14. Followers of Jesus were recognized as those who called on the name of the Lord (Acts 2:21; 1 Corinthians 1:2; 2 Timothy 2:22).

200. For details on how Saul tried to destroy the new faith, see Martin Hengel, *The Pre-Christian Paul*, 71-72. Weima observes, "Paul's references later in life to his pre-Christian perspective as one who was 'zealous' and 'full of zeal' [Philippians 3:6] reveal that he saw himself as following in the footsteps of Phinehas in the Old Testament who was full of zeal for the Lord when he put a spear between an Israelite man and a Moabite woman, and this violent action atoned for the sins of God's nation. Saul was a religious revolutionary who not surprisingly would go anywhere and do anything to hunt down Jesus-followers." Personal correspondence with Jeffrey Weima, 12/28/23.

201. Barry Beitzel, *Lexham Geographic Commentary on Acts through Revelation*, 226-227. Due to the problematic nature of travel, it would have taken anyone from Jerusalem up to a week to make this trip, unless the person was in a rush. For a detailed discussion on the transregional mission of the Jewish believers from Jerusalem (transplantation and migration), see Eckhard Schnabel, *Early Christian Mission*, 1:670-701.

202. Keener notes that most of the apostles didn't leave Jerusalem for a long time. They were still there in A.D. 48, which "may reflect their devotion to establishing Jerusalem first," which was the starting point of the Lord's commission. Craig Keener, *Acts*, 3:2223.

203. Acts 8:4. The vast majority of the 5,000 men in the ekklesia (not counting the women) fled Jerusalem. This means that perhaps up to 10,000 believers left the city. Clinton Arnold, ed., *Zondervan Illustrated Bible Backgrounds Commentary*, 2b:61.

As a result, new ekklesias are transplanted all over Palestine. The community of the King—the assembly of the living God—has now migrated from Jerusalem to Judea, Galilee, and Samaria. The flame of God's Spirit spreads, and Jesus Christ and His kingdom are now expressed beyond the holy city.

Sharpening the Focus: Named after King Saul of Israel,[204] Saul of Tarsus was born a Hebrew of the tribe of Benjamin.[205] His birth took place around A.D. 5 in the Cilician city of Tarsus.[206] Tarsus is one of the major centers of Hellenistic culture.[207] It's a university town with a large population.[208] It's also the principal city of Cilicia, described as a "metropolis," and "the greatest of all the cities of Cilicia."[209]

Tarsus has a rich past, witnessing the romantic first meeting of Antony and Cleopatra. Additionally, it's a prosperous city, renowned for its material products, particularly linen (made from the flax that grows in the city's fertile plain) and *cilicium* (which serves as a protective covering made of goat's hair).[210] Saul was born a Roman

204. Otto F.A. Meinardus, *St. Paul in Ephesus*, iii.

205. For details on the names "Saul" and "Paul," see David Capes, et al., *Rediscovering Paul*, 41.

206. Paul Barnett, *Paul: Missionary of Jesus*, 5, 25; Alan Bandy, *An Illustrated Guide to the Apostle Paul*, 17; Ben Witherington puts Saul's birth between A.D. 5 and 10. Ben Witherington III, *Invitation to the New Testament*, 161; N.T. Wright, *Paul: A Biography*, 175. Many scholars believe Saul couldn't have been born before A.D. 4. Walter Elwell and Barry Beitzel, "Paul, The Apostle" in *Baker Encyclopedia of the Bible*, Logos edition (Grand Rapids, MI: Baker Book House, 1988), vol. 2:1621. For further details on Tarsus, see Mark Wilson, *Biblical Turkey: A Guide to the Jewish and Christian Sites of Asia Minor*, revised edition (Istanbul: Ege, 2020), 120-122.

207. For the pagan and philosophical influences on Saul that he picked up in Tarsus, see Martin Hengel, et al., *Paul Between Damascus and Antioch*, 167-171.

208. Martin Hengel, et al., *Paul Between Damascus and Antioch*, 35. Tarsus may have had up to 75,000 inhabitants during Saul's time. Anthony Thiselton, *Discovering Romans: Content, Interpretation, Reception* (Grand Rapids, MI: Eerdmans, 2016), 62. For details on Saul's immersion into the Hellenistic world, see F.F. Bruce, *Paul: Apostle of the Heart Set Free*, 126-133.

209. Ben Witherington III, ed., *History, Literature and Society in the Book of Acts*, 271. The eastern part of Cilicia was known for its fertile plains and was called "Smooth" while the western part was called "Rough," due to its mountains. Mark Wilson, *Biblical Turkey*, 53.

210. F.F. Bruce, *Paul: Apostle of the Heart Set Free*, 35.

citizen,[211] but we don't have any clues as to how his family acquired Roman citizenship. Regardless, his status as a Roman citizen places Saul among the social elite of Tarsus.[212]

Roman citizens have three names: a forename (*praenomen*), a family name (*nomen gentile*), and an additional name (*cognomen*).[213] "Saul" is his Jewish name; "Paul" is his additional Roman name (*cognomen*).[214] (We don't know his other two names.[215]) As an adolescent, probably aged thirteen or fourteen, Saul relocated to Jerusalem to receive his Hebrew training.[216] He grew up in the holy

211. Acts 22:27ff. Bruce gives a detailed sketch of Saul's upbringing in *Paul: Apostle of the Heart Set Free*, 32-61. See also Ben Witherington III, ed., *History, Literature and Society in the Book of Acts*, 276-278.

212. Much of this information comes from F.F. Bruce, *Paul: Apostle of the Heart Set Free*, 33-38. Roman citizens frequently assumed the family name of their patrons. For details on Saul's origins and citizenship, see Martin Hengel, *The Pre-Christian Paul*, chap. 1.

213. Clinton Arnold, ed., *Zondervan Illustrated Bible Backgrounds Commentary*, 2b:122.

214. The name Paul (*Paulus*) means "little" or "small" in Latin. Alan Bandy, *An Illustrated Guide to the Apostle Paul*, 21.

215. Eckhard Schnabel, *Paul the Missionary: Realities, Strategies, and Methods* (Downers Grove, IL: InterVarsity Press, 2008), 42; F.F. Bruce, *Paul: Apostle of the Heart Set Free*, 38; Paul Barnett, *Paul: Missionary of Jesus*, 205-207. According to tradition, Saul was bald, small in size, had eyebrows that met, and a hooked nose. Sometimes he appeared as a man, other times he had the face of an angel. William Ramsay, *St. Paul the Traveler and Roman Citizen*, 46.

216. While it's impossible to know for certain, I agree with Witherington who asserts that Saul was raised in Jerusalem (not Tarsus) at a young age. Ben Witherington III, *The Acts of the Apostles*, 669. See also Darrell Bock, *Acts*, 659, 714. It is also possible that Saul was brought to Jerusalem at age twelve, which would have been around A.D. 17. Paul Barnett, *Paul: Missionary of Jesus*, 27. According to Keener, Saul may have begun to learn the Law around his fifth year and other Pharisaic traditions around his tenth year. He then pursued training to teach the Law around age thirteen. He would have finished his training no later than age twenty. Craig Keener, *The IVP Bible Background Commentary: New Testament*, 396. Saul's training included an intimate knowledge of the Scriptures, various methods of exegesis, and Hellenistic education filtered through a conservative Pharisaic mindset. "According to the tractate *Avot* in the Mishnah, one began studying the Torah at five, the Mishnah at ten, and the Talmud at fifteen. Saul's study seems to have been of a more advanced sort." Personal correspondence with James Claire VanderKam on 6/26/22. "Saul spent his early childhood in Tarsus before moving to Jerusalem for study in his teen years sometime around A.D. 15-17." Alan Bandy, *An Illustrated Guide to the Apostle Paul*, 22. For details on Saul as a Greco-Roman Jew as well as a Jewish Christian (later), see Ben Witherington III, *Conflict and Community in Corinth: A Socio-Rhetorical Commentary on*

city.[217] Given the excellent education Paul evidently received, his parents were probably well-to-do.[218] He has at least one sister.[219] Saul is well-educated, speaking Aramaic, Hebrew, Greek, and possibly some Latin.[220] He was mentored by the greatest teacher of his day, Gamaliel.[221]

---

1 and 2 Corinthians (Grand Rapids, MI: Eerdmans, 1995), 1-5. For further details on Saul's upbringing and education in Tarsus and Jerusalem, see Martin Hengel, *The Pre-Christian Paul*, chaps. 2-3.

217. While the Greek word in Acts 22:3 can also mean "educated," virtually all translations render it "brought up," "raised," or "grew up" in this city, meaning Jerusalem. For about half of Saul's life, however, he lived as a Diaspora Jew. John Barclay, *Jews in the Mediterranean Diaspora*, 381. For more on Saul's origins, see William Ramsay, *St. Paul the Traveler and Roman Citizen*, chap. 2.

218. Eckhard Schnabel, *Paul the Missionary*, 43-45. Weima agrees saying, "There is strong evidence that Saul was, in fact, born into a wealthy family—both his Roman citizenship (achieved by birth from his father) and his training at the 'Harvard' school of Judaism—at the feet of Gamaliel, the renowned rabbinical teacher, point to this." Personal correspondence with Jeffrey Weima, 12/28/23. Other scholars, however, think the idea that Saul came from an affluent background is a myth. See Bruce Longenecker, et al., *Thinking Through Paul*, 26, n. 12. According to Jerome, Saul's parents were from Gischala in Galilee, a Jewish town about twenty-five miles north of Nazareth, where Saul was born. The family was later deported to Tarsus. For commentary on this tradition, see Mark Fairchild, "Paul's Pre-Christian Zealot Associations: A Re-examination of Gal. 1:14 and Acts 22:3," *NTS* 45:514-532; Matthew Novenson, *Paul Then and Now*, 42-44.

219. Saul's nephew is mentioned in Acts 23:16. He also has some other relatives (Romans 16:7, 11, 21). Otto F.A. Meinardus, *St. Paul in Greece* (Athens, Greece: Lycabettus Press, 1972), 2. Saul may have stayed with his sister on his first visit to Jerusalem as a follower of Jesus. Richard Longenecker, *Luke-Acts*, 863.

220. Ben Witherington III, *Invitation to the New Testament*, 176-177. Saul probably learned to read and write Greek in Tarsus. Alan Bandy, *An Illustrated Guide to the Apostle Paul*, 22. Luke depicts him as being fluent in Aramaic and Greek. Paul Barnett, *Paul: Missionary of Jesus*, 41. Saul was a remarkably gifted child, speaking fluent Hebrew, Aramaic, and Greek, and speaking and writing at great speed. N.T. Wright, *Paul: A Biography*, 15-16. Saul had no need to speak Latin in the vast majority of places where he ministered, since Greek was the *lingua franca*. Personal correspondence with Ben Witherington III, 6/26/05.

221. Acts 22:3. The Talmud claims that Gamaliel's school had 500 young men who studied the Torah and another 500 who studied Greek (*b. Bava Qamma* 83a). But this number is regarded as a gross exaggeration by some scholars. Personal correspondence with David deSilva, 1/18/24; Paul Barnett, *Paul: Missionary of Jesus*, 35. When Gamaliel died, it was said that "the glory of the Torah ceased, and purity and 'separateness' died." (*m. Sotah* 9:15). Gamaliel was a Pharisaic moderate and a Jerusalem aristocrat. He was probably the most elite Pharisee of the time. Craig Keener, "Lessons on Acts," Sessions 13 and 31.

Saul was trained to be a hard-lined, fanatical Jew—a Pharisee. In this capacity, he was far more zealous than his peers.[222] (To contemporize his schooling and credentials, we can say that Saul graduated from the "Harvard" school of Judaism. This serves him well when he later begins preaching in the synagogues throughout the Diaspora.[223])

Although Gamaliel was a moderate Hillelite, Saul became a more radical Shammaite.[224] The Shammaites made up the majority of the Pharisees.[225] They were stricter toward the Gentiles than the Hillelites, the more liberal sect. Since Saul is a Pharisee, he was likely married at one time. Later, however, he will find himself single.[226]

All Jewish rabbis work for a living, so they were expected to learn a skill to support themselves.[227] Saul's trade is that of a tentmaker. This means that he repairs tents and

222. Galatians 1:14; Philippians 3:4-6. F.F. Bruce, *Paul: Apostle of the Heart Set Free*, 41-44. The Pharisees were Jesus' primary enemies. They eventually came to dominate the Jewish world after A.D. 70. N.T. Wright and Michael Bird, *The New Testament in Its World*, 124. Zeal meant more than having a passion for God. It meant a willingness to use violence to defend the Torah. Clinton Arnold, ed., *Zondervan Illustrated Bible Backgrounds Commentary*, 2b:223.

223. Jeffrey Weima, *1-2 Thessalonians*, 27.

224. Craig Keener, "Lessons on Acts," Session 24. For details, see Paul Barnett, *Paul: Missionary of Jesus*, 46ff.; John Drane, *Paul: An Illustrated Documentary on the Life and Writings of a Key Figure in the Beginnings of Christianity* (San Francisco, CA: Harper and Row, 1976), 16-17; N.T. Wright, *Paul: A Biography*, 35-36.

225. This was true before A.D. 70. Craig Keener, "Lessons on Acts," Session 24.

226. Bruce Longenecker, et al., *Thinking Through Paul*, 27. Most orthodox Jews married and did so quite young. Paul Barnett, *A Short Book about Paul: The Servant of Jesus* (Eugene, OR: Cascade Books, 2019), 21. If Saul was married, we aren't sure if his wife asked to be divorced or if she died. But he was clearly single when he wrote 1 Corinthians (1 Corinthians 7:8; 9:5-6). It's possible that Saul's wife decided to end the marriage after his conversion to Jesus. He spoke about "the loss of all things" for Christ (Philippians 3:7-8), which could have included his former wife. He also wrote about an unbelieving wife who leaves her husband (1 Corinthians 7:15). From reading his epistles, he clearly understood marital relationships, so it's reasonable to assume he was married at one time. Yet he also had the gift of celibacy (1 Corinthians 7:7). F.F. Bruce affirms the probability that the apostle was once married, and his wife left him when he became a follower of Jesus. F.F. Bruce, *Paul: Apostle of the Heart Set Free*, 270. Wright also notes this scenario is a possibility along with a few other options. N.T. Wright, *Paul: A Biography*, 81.

227. This was true of the Pharisees. Most refused to teach for money, so they learned a trade. Douglas Campbell, *Paul: An Apostle's Journey*, 70; Ronald Hock, *The Social Context of Paul's Ministry: Tentmaking and Apostleship* (Philadelphia, PA: Fortress Press, 1980).

makes other leather products.[228] Therefore, it's more accurate to call him a leather-worker.[229] During his travels, Saul probably carried a small bag of cutting tools—particularly, an awl (a pointed tool for making holes in leather), and a sharpening stone. Saul's manual labor is important because it will serve as a model to God's people of freely offering ministry while laboring hard to make a living without burdening anyone.[230]

Philip the Evangelist

Philip, one of the "seven," travels to Samaria and preaches the revolutionary gospel of the kingdom to a city in the region.[231] His preaching is confirmed by miraculous signs, heal-

228. Gerald Hawthorne, et al., eds., *Dictionary of Paul and His Letters*, 926-927; F.F. Bruce, *The Pauline Circle*, 45; Jeffrey Weima, *1-2 Thessalonians*, 30, 150; N.T. Wright, *Acts for Everyone: Part Two* (Louisville, KY: Westminster John Knox Press, 2008), 97.

229. Jeffrey Weima, *1-2 Thessalonians*, 150; Martin Hengel, *The Pre-Christian Paul*, 112, n. 114. Some scholars believe Saul probably learned his trade from his father as a boy. Bruce Longenecker, et al., *Thinking Through Paul*, 26. Paul's occupation is referred to in relation to his visit to Corinth (Acts 18:3). This is probably because leather products, like tents for visitors to the city who came to see the spring games, awnings for marketplace retailers, and sails for merchant ships, were common needs in Corinth. James D.G. Dunn, *Beginning from Jerusalem*, 696, n. 194. Leatherworkers were generally known for making sun awnings to protect customers from the scorching heat. Eckhard Schnabel, *Acts*, 756-757; N.T. Wright, *Paul: A Biography*, 15; Craig Keener, *Acts*, 3:2732-2736.

230. Jeffrey Weima, *1-2 Thessalonians*, 150. For more on the life and ministry of Saul/Paul, see E.P. Sanders, *Paul: The Apostle's Life, Letters, and Thought*, chap. 2; Mark Galli, ed., "Paul and His Times," *Christian History* 47, 1995. For further details on Saul's life in Tarsus and Jerusalem, including his apostolic call and self-understanding, see Eckhard Schnabel, *Early Christian Mission* (Downers Grove, IL: InterVarsity Press, 2004), 2:923-982; William Ramsay, *St. Paul the Traveler and Roman Citizen*, chap. 2; N.T. Wright and Michael Bird, *The New Testament in Its World*, chaps. 15-16; David deSilva, *An Introduction to the New Testament*, 409-426.

231. The city could have been Shechem, one of the main cities in Samaria. *The ESV Study Bible* (Wheaton, IL: Crossway Bibles, 2008), 2096; John Stott, *The Message of Acts*, 148. Dunn believes the city was Sebaste. James D.G. Dunn, *The Acts of the Apostles*, 108. Witherington points out that Luke didn't feel naming the city was important, so we can't be sure which one it was. Ben Witherington III, *The Acts of the Apostles*, 282.

ings, and the casting out of demons. Philip is the second person who preaches the gospel outside the Twelve.[232] (Stephen was the first.)

Philip's ministry of deliverance brings great joy to the city. He baptizes both women and men who respond to the kingdom message.[233] Given the long history of hostility between Jews and Samaritans, the event is revolutionary. Jews who have held Samaritans at arm's length now receive them into fellowship on equal footing.[234] A kingdom community is born in Samaria![235]

The apostles in Jerusalem receive a report about the conversions in Samaria, so they send Peter and John to help establish the new kingdom community.[236] When they arrive,

232. The book of Acts calls Philip an evangelist (Acts 21:8), which is a gift in the body of Christ, marked by proclaiming the gospel with boldness. The term "evangelist" is also used in Ephesians 4:11 and 2 Timothy 4:5.

233. In Acts 8:12, BSB, the translation says Philip preached "the gospel of the kingdom of God." Water baptism was the normative custom of those who believed in Christ in the first century, the initial step of conversion-initiation. When people were baptized, they were completely breaking ties with the world system and ending their loyalty oath with Caesar. For the biblical argument, see my article, "Rethinking Water Baptism," at insurgencebook.com/waterbaptism.pdf. Baptism was most likely done by immersion. The house impluvium was too shallow; therefore, other water sources like monumental fountains, public baths, and rivers were used. Vincent Branick, *The House Church in the Writings of Paul*, 112-113; personal correspondence with Jeffrey Weima, 3/9/22.

234. Clinton Arnold, ed., *Zondervan Illustrated Bible Backgrounds Commentary*, 2b:64, 66. Jews despised Samaritans. The origin of the Samaritans traces back to the Assyrian invasion of Israel in the eighth century B.C. Some of the Israelites were taken into Assyrian exile, and the Samaritans were the result of intermarriage between Assyrians and Jews. Consequently, they were considered "half-breeds." The religious differences they had with Jews only heightened the animosity. Bruce Longenecker, *The Lost Letters of Pergamum* (Grand Rapids, MI: Baker Academic, 2003), 94.

235. According to Acts 8:12, Peter preached the good news of the kingdom (NASB, NIV, ESV, NRSV, WEB). Other translations say he preached "the gospel of the kingdom," which is the same thing (Berean Standard Bible, Majority Standard Bible, etc.). Jesus had sown the seed of the gospel in Samaria almost a decade beforehand, a scandalous act given the way Jews viewed Samaritans (John 4:1-42). Philip now reaped the harvest from those seeds. I can imagine the Samaritan woman listening to Philip preach and being on the ground floor of the new ekklesia.

236. While they certainly went to "investigate" the situation, there's good reason to believe they did more than that. Philip wasn't an apostle (he was an evangelist), so Peter and John came to Samaria to lay the foundation for the ekklesia, which is what apostolic workers do. (For a full examination of the function of the apostolic ministry, see Frank Viola, *Finding Organic Church*, Part 1.) The word of Jesus to the Twelve in Acts 1:8 began to find fulfillment. The apostles were His witnesses in Judea, Samaria, and the utmost parts of the

Peter and John lay hands on the new converts and they are baptized with the Holy Spirit. Simon Magus[237]—a well-known and highly acclaimed sorcerer from Samaria—is also baptized. Simon offers money to the two apostles in exchange for the ability to impart the Spirit to people.[238] Peter rebukes Simon and exposes his wicked heart.[239] Filled with dread, Simon asks Peter to pray that God will not judge him.[240]

Peter and John return to Jerusalem, preaching the gospel in many Samaritan villages along the way.[241] Meanwhile, Philip remains in Samaria, but an angel appears to him and instructs him to head south to the desert road that leads from Jerusalem to Gaza. Philip responds, and on his way, he meets an Ethiopian eunuch[242] who is a Gentile worshipper of the God of Israel.[243]

The eunuch is the official treasurer for "the Candace," queen of Ethiopia.[244] The eunuch is heading home from Jerusalem, where he had just visited to worship. The Holy Spirit

world. Some scholars have argued that Acts 1:8 is the proper framework by which to understand the book of Acts. See David Bauer, *The Book of Acts as Story*, 51ff.

237. Simon is known as Simon the Sorcerer, Simon Magus, and Simon of Gitta.

238. For more on Simon Magus, see Eusebius, *The History of the Church*, 2.13-14; Josephus, *The Antiquities of the Jews*, 20.7; Clinton Arnold, ed., *Zondervan Illustrated Bible Backgrounds Commentary*, 2b:65. Sorcerers/magicians in that day were frauds. They deceived people into thinking they had supernatural powers. Mark Fairchild, "The Last Apostle," documentary film.

239. Peter told Simon he was full of bitter poison, captive to sin. Acts 8:23. Clinton Arnold, ed., *Zondervan Illustrated Bible Backgrounds Commentary*, 2b:67.

240. Luke doesn't report whether Peter prayed for Simon.

241. Acts 8:25.

242. A eunuch was a man who had been castrated or emasculated so he might fulfill official duties, generally involving close contact with women of the royal household without threatening the legitimacy of the royal line or having the distraction (or temptation) of other women. As a eunuch, this man was permanently on the fringes of the Jewish religion, excluded from participation in the Jewish assembly. Ben Witherington III, *The Acts of the Apostles*, 296; James D.G. Dunn, *The Acts of the Apostles*, 114. For details on Philip's encounter with the Ethiopian, see Clinton Arnold, ed., *Zondervan Illustrated Bible Backgrounds Commentary*, 2b:68-73. The "Ethiopia" in Acts 8 refers to Nubia, now in Sudan. David Bauer, *The Book of Acts as Story*, 137.

243. In other words, the eunuch was probably a God-fearer (or proselyte). *The NIV Study Bible*, 1911. Both Witherington and Arnold favor this idea, while Stott favors the idea that he was Jewish (by birth or conversion). Compare Ben Witherington III, *The Acts of the Apostles*, 280, 297; Clinton Arnold, ed., *Zondervan Illustrated Bible Backgrounds Commentary*, 2b:70; John Stott, *The Message of Acts*, 160.

244. "The Candace" was a title, not a personal name. Personal correspondence with Craig Keener, 12/14/23. If the eunuch traveled at the normal rate of about twenty-five miles a day, the trip to Jerusalem

tells Philip to approach the chariot where the Ethiopian is reading Isaiah 53 out loud.[245] The evangelist engages the eunuch and shares Christ with him. The eunuch believes, and Philip baptizes him.[246] As soon as the eunuch emerges out of the water, the Holy Spirit snatches Philip away to Azotus—the old Philistine city of Ashdod, about twenty miles up the coast from Gaza.[247]

The eunuch returns to Ethiopia radiating with the joy of salvation.[248] From Azotus, Philip preaches the gospel from town to town until he arrives in Caesarea (also called Caesarea Maritima or Caesarea-by-the-Sea).[249] The evangelist will reside in Caesarea for the

would have taken him anywhere from forty-eight to sixty days one way, if he made no stops along the way. Clinton Arnold, ed., *Zondervan Illustrated Bible Backgrounds Commentary*, 2b:69.

245. In the first century, reading was almost always done aloud. Ben Witherington III, *The Acts of the Apostles*, 297; *Letters and Homilies for Hellenized Christians: A Socio-Rhetorical Commentary on Titus, 1-2 Timothy and 1-3 John* (Downers Grove, IL: InterVarsity Press, 2006), 1:410. Hence, Paul's letters were written to be read out loud. According to Nicholas Elder, silent reading was also known and practiced in the first century; therefore, vocalized reading wasn't the exclusive method. Nicholas Elder, *Gospel Media: Reading, Writing, and Circulating Jesus Traditions* (Grand Rapids, MI: Eerdmans, 2024), chap. 1.

246. Acts 8:36-38. It's plausible to conclude that Philip instructed the eunuch that baptism was an expression of conversion-initiation, just as Peter did at Pentecost (Acts 2:38) and Philip himself probably did in Samaria (Acts 8:12). Richard Longenecker, *Luke-Acts*, 847. The fact that the eunuch asked to be baptized in Acts 8:36 confirms this. (I credit James D.G. Dunn for the term "conversion-initiation.") Some scholars believe the Wadi El-Hesi, a seasonal river located between Hebron and Gaza in modern-day Israel/Palestine, is the most likely candidate for where this pivotal baptism of the Ethiopian eunuch occurred.

247. Warren Wiersbe, *BE DYNAMIC: Acts 1-12*, The "Be" Commentary (Colorado Springs, CO: David C. Cook, 2010), 126 (digital version).

248. According to Irenaeus, the eunuch brought the gospel to his own people in the regions of Ethiopia. Irenaeus, *Against Heresies*, 3.12.8-10. However, there is no evidence of an ekklesia in Ethiopia in the first century. Ben Witherington III, *The Acts of the Apostles*, 301. Note that individual conversions do not always result in the formation of an ekklesia. An ekklesia is a local community of dedicated Jesus-followers who gather regularly to worship, support one another, and share in life's experiences.

249. Caesarea Maritima is sixty-four miles from Jerusalem. This city is not to be confused with Caesarea Philippi. The Jews didn't care much for Caesarea, as it was only built to serve Rome's purposes. For a good description of Caesarea Maritima, see Gary Burge, *A Week in the Life of a Roman Centurion*, 66-76. Caesarea was built by Herod the Great between 20 and 9 B.C. F.F. Bruce, *Paul: Apostle of the Heart Set Free*, 354. Herod constructed this port city as a tribute to his new Roman patron, Caesar Augustus. The city was named after Augustus, and a grand temple was built within it. This temple contained cult statues of Augustus himself and the personified, deified Rome (Roma), serving as a focal point for their worship. The city was also where Paul would later be placed under house arrest for two years under the Roman governors Felix and then Festus. Personal correspondence with Jeffrey Weima, 12/28/23.

next twenty years.[250] He will remain faithful to the Lord, raising his daughters and preaching the gospel of the kingdom.

Jesus Christ Appears to Saul
A.D. 33 – 37[251]

Back in Jerusalem, Saul hunts the followers of Jesus and roots them out from wherever they have dispersed. He threatens to murder every disciple of Christ, receiving permission from the high priest to search for them, even in the far away synagogues of Damascus, Syria.[252] Saul plots to arrest the Jesus-followers (both women and men) and bring them back to Jerusalem as prisoners. One of his methods for securing the verdict of capital punishment is to lure them to blaspheme.[253]

It is noon. Saul and several companions are traveling to Damascus. Suddenly, the Lord Jesus Christ appears to him in a blinding light from heaven.[254] The light is so bright Saul and his companions fall to the ground.[255] Jesus speaks to Saul and asks Him in the Hebrew

---

250. Acts 8:5-40. Like the house of Cornelius, also in Caesarea, Philip's home served as another residence where the ekklesia in that locality gathered. Roger Gehring, *House Church and Mission*, 106-108.

251. The first eight chapters of the book of Acts cover the years A.D. 30 to 33, approximately. Ben Witherington III, *The New Testament Story*, 273.

252. A large Jewish colony existed in Damascus. An estimated 10,000 to 18,000 Jews were massacred in the city in A.D. 66. Greek was the dominant language of the city in Paul's day, with Aramaic spoken by those in the Jewish community. F.F. Bruce, *Paul: Apostle of the Heart Set Free*, 77. For more on the synagogues in Damascus, as well as the Jewish community in Damascus, see Martin Hengel, et al., *Paul Between Damascus and Antioch*, 50-61.

253. Acts 9:1-2; 22:5ff.; 26:9ff.; 1 Corinthians 15:9; Galatians 1:13; Philippians 3:6; 1 Timothy 1:13. Clinton Arnold, ed., *Zondervan Illustrated Bible Backgrounds Commentary*, 2b:248.

254. Jewett dates Saul's conversion occurring between August and October of A.D. 34. Robert Jewett, *A Chronology of Paul's Life*, 99. Other scholars agree on the A.D. 34 date. Paul Barnett, *Paul: Missionary of Jesus*, 211; David Capes, et al., *Rediscovering Paul*, 78. Witherington dates his conversion in A.D. 33 or 34. Ben Witherington III, *Invitation to the New Testament*, 162. Bruce dates it in A.D. 33. F.F. Bruce, *Paul: Apostle of the Heart Set Free*, 17, 475. I side with those scholars who date Saul's conversion at A.D. 34.

255. According to Keener, "Saul is on the way, and he ends up in the way. He meets the leader of the Way head on." Acts 9:2-3, ESV. Craig Keener, "Lessons on Acts," Session 17.

tongue, "Saul, Saul, why are you persecuting Me?"[256] Saul responds asking, "Who are you, Lord?" The Lord replies:

> *...I am Jesus, whom you are persecuting. But arise, and stand on your feet, for I have appeared to you for this purpose: to appoint you a servant and a witness both of the things which you have seen, and of the things which I will reveal to you; delivering you from the people, and from the Gentiles, to whom I send you, to open their eyes, that they may turn from darkness to light and from the power of Satan to God, that they may receive remission of sins and an inheritance among those who are sanctified by faith in me. (Acts 26:15-18)*[257]

Fear-stricken, Saul's companions see a light and hear a voice, but they cannot decipher what is said. And they see no one.[258] As Saul rises to his feet, he discovers he is blind. So Saul's companions lead him by the hand into Damascus. This is a pregnant moment in history. Saul follows a long line of people who have had the glorious privilege of seeing the resurrected Christ. Saul, however, feels that witnessing the risen Jesus is like experiencing an untimely birth.

256. Acts 9:4, NKJV. The NKJV also adds this statement from Jesus, "It is hard for you to kick against the goads" (Acts 9:5). This was a common phrase in the Greek world to mean opposition to a deity. Richard Longenecker, *Paul, Apostle of Liberty*, 91. A goad is a long stick with a sharp pointed end used to prod animals yoked to a wagon. Clinton Arnold, ed., *Zondervan Illustrated Bible Backgrounds Commentary*, 2b:248. We don't know if Saul ever saw or heard Jesus before this encounter, but he obviously heard *about* Him since Saul was persecuting Christ-followers. Paul Barnett, *Paul: Missionary of Jesus*, 5.

257. In Galatians and Romans, Paul describes his ministry and mission as being primarily to the Gentiles. Wayne Meeks, *The First Urban Christians*, 81. Paul knew the Greco-Roman world well. He knew the mystery religions and the traditional gods. He also knew Greek philosophy. He was immersed in the culture and was bilingual, speaking Hebrew and Greek (and Aramaic, of course). These are some of the reasons why God used him as an apostle to the Gentiles. Mark Fairchild, "The Last Apostle," documentary film. According to Acts 26:16, Jesus appointed Paul to be a servant. This expression harkens back to Isaiah 42:1-7. While Jesus fulfilled this prophecy, Paul continued it. Jesus also promised to protect Paul, which He did, despite the afflictions he suffered (Acts 26:17).

258. Saul's conversion is rehearsed three times in Acts (chaps. 9, 22, and 26). Luke uses such repetitions to underscore their significance. David Bauer, *The Book of Acts as Story*, 46. For a side-by-side comparison of Paul's conversion accounts in Acts, see Ben Witherington III, *The Acts of the Apostles*, 305. See also Martin Hengel, et al., *Paul Between Damascus and Antioch*, 38-43.

THE UNTOLD STORY OF THE NEW TESTAMENT CHURCH

...that he was buried, that he was raised on the third day according to the Scriptures, and that he appeared to Cephas, then to the twelve. Then he appeared to over five hundred brothers at once, most of whom remain until now, but some have also fallen asleep. Then he appeared to James, then to all the apostles, and last of all, as to the child born at the wrong time, he appeared to me also. (1 Corinthians 15:4-8)[259]

Saul remains blind for three days, during which time he neither eats nor drinks. A kingdom community of Jesus-followers exists in Damascus, and Ananias is a faithful man in the assembly.[260] He is fully devoted to God, and the other believers in the church speak well of him.[261] Jesus speaks to Ananias in a vision and instructs him to find Saul in the house of Judas on Straight Street. Knowing who Saul is (a persecutor of the disciples), Ananias voices his doubts about Saul.

The Lord reassures Ananias that Saul is a chosen instrument who will bring salvation to the Gentiles and their kings, as well as to the people of Israel. He will also suffer greatly for the name of Jesus.[262] The Lord tells Ananias that Saul will be praying.[263]

Ananias obeys and finds Saul. After they meet, Ananias lays his hands on the Pharisee and confirms his call to go to the Gentiles.[264] When Ananias lays hands on him, Saul's sight is instantly restored, and he is filled with the Holy Spirit. Ananias baptizes Saul in water, and Saul resumes eating and drinking.[265] He regains his strength and stays with the ekklesia in Damascus for a short time. Immediately, Saul begins preaching in the synagogues

259. In this passage, Saul invokes a violent image of "a Caesarian section, in which a baby is ripped from the woman, born before it was ready." N.T. Wright, *The Challenge of Jesus*, 141.

260. Ananias was probably a Jewish believer of Damascus rather than a refugee from Judea. F.F. Bruce, *The Pauline Circle*, 11.

261. For details on how Damascus turned out to be a major turning point in Saul's life, see Martin Hengel, et al., *Paul Between Damascus and Antioch*, chap. 2.

262. Acts 9:15-16.

263. Acts 9:11. Saul/Paul was a man of prayer (Acts 16:25; 20:36; 22:17). Richard Longenecker, *Luke-Acts*, 856.

264. Galatians 1:12, 15ff.; Acts 26:15-18.

265. Acts 9:17-18; Acts 22:12-16. See also F.F. Bruce, *The Pauline Circle*, 13.

that Jesus is the promised Christ.[266] Those who hear him are astounded, for they know he recently persecuted the disciples of Jesus.[267]

Saul grows more powerful in his preaching. He baffles the Jews by skillfully demonstrating from the Hebrew Scriptures that Jesus is the Messiah. But not long after, he vanishes to Arabia for a time.[268]

...I went away into Arabia. Then I returned to Damascus. Then after three years I went up to Jerusalem to visit Peter, and stayed with him fifteen days. (Galatians 1:17-18)

In the Arabian Desert, God prepares Saul for his special calling. Following the pattern of Elijah who went to Mount Sinai, Saul communes with God in the desert.[269] Through

266. Acts 9:3-22; 26:20.

267. "Astonished," "baffled," and "confounded" are other terms describing the reaction of those who heard Saul preach. Richard Longenecker, *Luke-Acts*, 860.

268. In the book of Acts, there is a gap in the narrative of Saul's activities described in Acts 9:17-30. His journey to Arabia, mentioned in Galatians, likely occurred sometime within that narrative.

269. This probably took place between A.D. 34 and 37. Ben Witherington III, *The New Testament Story*, 273. A number of scholars believe Arabia doesn't refer to the sandy desert, but to the Nabataean kingdom and its cities (Petra, Gerasa, Bostra, etc.). Jerome Murphy-O'Connor, *Paul: His Story* (Oxford: Oxford University Press, 2004), 25. But Saul may have gone into the Arabian Desert to commune with God in the vicinity of Horeb, the mount of God. While Bruce concedes that some scholars hold this view, he thinks Saul preached during this time. F.F. Bruce, *Paul: Apostle of the Heart Set Free*, 81. N.T. Wright believes Saul went to Mount Sinai following the pattern of Elijah, and he did *not* preach while there. N.T. Wright, "Paul, Arabia, and Elijah (Galatians 1:17)," *JBL* 115, 683-692; *Paul: A Biography*, 62-66. According to Wright, Saul's trip to Arabia contained "very obvious echoes of the Elijah story in Galatians 1, which demonstrates that he went off to Sinai—or that region—not to evangelise but to do urgent business with God." Personal correspondence with N.T. Wright, 7/25/16. I side with Wright on this. Regarding how much time Saul spent in Arabia, some scholars believe it was most of the three years. Others believe it was much shorter. See Wayne Meeks, *The First Urban Christians*, 40. Jerome Murphy-O'Connor, *Paul: His Story*, 26; Grant Osborne, *Galatians: Verse by Verse*, Logos edition (Bellingham, WA; Lexham Press, 2017), 39; Alan Bandy, *An Illustrated Guide to the Apostle Paul*, 37. For a discussion on Saul's "unknown years" from A.D. 34 to 47, see Paul Barnett, *Paul: Missionary of Jesus*, 77ff. Witherington says it was "surely Syrian Arabia." Ben Witherington III, *The Acts of the Apostles*, 323. See also Martin Hengel, et al., *Paul Between Damascus and Antioch*, chap. 4, for another reconstruction. Hengel states that Saul stayed in Arabia (the Nabataean kingdom) eighteen months to two years (127). Interestingly, Nabataean Arabia includes Sinai. Personal correspondence with Craig Keener, 7/14/16. Paul mentions his trip to Arabia in Galatians chapter 1, because he wanted to emphasize that he received his gospel directly from Jesus before he met with the apostles in Jerusalem. Alan Bandy, *An Illustrated Guide to the Apostle*

divine revelation, Jesus gives Saul further light on his calling and commission.[270] Consequently, Saul learns to read the Scriptures in a new light, the light of Christ. He returns to Damascus and resumes preaching in the synagogues. As a result, the Jews plot to kill him, but Saul learns about their murderous plan.[271] The governor under King Aretas has the gates of the city guarded so he cannot escape.[272]

Saul shares the evil plot with the disciples in Damascus, and they lower him out of a window by a basket during the night. This smuggling act allows him to flee Damascus safely.[273] Saul travels south to Jerusalem to meet Peter. The ekklesia there is afraid of him, doubting the genuineness of his conversion. Barnabas, however, believes Saul's faith in Jesus is authentic. He takes a risk and sets up a private meeting to introduce Saul to Peter and James.[274]

Barnabas shares Saul's dramatic conversion with Peter, and the apostle is convinced.[275] So Saul stays with Peter for fifteen days.[276] He also meets James (the Lord's half-brother).[277]

Paul, 35-36. By contrast, Craig Keener doesn't see a reason to suppose that Saul went all the way to Sinai. Personal correspondence with Keener, 7/15/16. (Keener has a long excursus on Nabataea in Craig Keener, *Acts*, 2:1676-1683.) See also Barry Beitzel, *Lexham Geographic Commentary on Acts through Revelation*, 230-232. It's my belief that Saul first went to Nabataea and then journeyed to Mount Sinai. See Douglas Moo, *Galatians: Baker Exegetical Commentary on the New Testament* (Grand Rapids, MI: Baker Academic, 2013), 106-107.

270. Galatians 1:11-18. Saul made clear that his gospel was given to him before he had contact with any of the twelve apostles.

271. Saul was head and shoulders above his peers, and he became a prominent leader in Judaism. He believed the Jesus-followers were infidels desecrating the Torah, thus he made efforts to exterminate the faith. But after he was converted, he was viewed as a traitor by the Jews, and that's why they sought to kill him. Mark Fairchild, "The Last Apostle," documentary film.

272. 2 Corinthians 11:32. King Aretas was king of the Nabataean Arabs. Saul may have done some preaching to the Nabataeans at the end of his stay in Arabia since the governor under Aretas—the leader of the Nabataean community—showed hostility toward him and began hunting him down. It seems both the governor and the Jews in Damascus plotted to arrest Saul. But when he describes the event in 2 Corinthians 11:32, he avoids accusing his own people (as was his custom). See also F.F. Bruce, *Paul: Apostle of the Heart Set Free*, 81-82.

273. Acts 9:23-25; 2 Corinthians 11:32-33.

274. N.T. Wright, *Paul: A Biography*, 67.

275. Acts 9:26-27.

276. Galatians 1:18-19. Two weeks of hospitality was no short time. For details on Saul as Peter's guest, see Martin Hengel, et al., *Paul Between Damascus and Antioch*, 144-150.

277. That this James (also called "James the Just") was the half-brother of Jesus has wide attestation. J.B. Lightfoot, *The Acts of the Apostles*, 194-195. (He is said to be the Lord's "half-brother" because Jesus did not

During the visit, Peter and James tell Saul about Jesus' earthly life and teachings.[278] Later, Saul/Paul will cite some of Jesus' words in his epistles.[279] While in Jerusalem, Saul boldly preaches Christ in the synagogues. But the Hellenistic Jews are enraged, so they seek to kill him.[280]

One day, Saul visits the temple to pray, and the Lord appears to him in a trance.[281] Jesus tells him to leave the city because the Jews will not receive his testimony. The Lord also tells Saul that He will be sending him far away to the Gentiles.[282] As a result, the believers bring Saul to Caesarea Maritima, sixty-four miles northwest of Jerusalem.[283] And they send him by ship to Tarsus, his hometown in Cilicia.[284] At this time, Saul begins traveling throughout the regions of Syria and Cilicia.[285]

---

have an earthly biological father.) Peter and James were regarded as "apostles." It appears that Saul did not meet with any other apostles during this time.

278. Among the many things that Peter and James spoke to Saul concerning Jesus, they told him how and when Jesus appeared to them after His resurrection (1 Corinthians 15:4-7).

279. For a list of sayings by Jesus echoed in Paul's letters (the Pauline corpus), see Gerald Hawthorne, et al., eds., *Dictionary of Paul and His Letters*, 480ff.; Paul Barnett, *From Jerusalem to Illyricum: Earliest Christianity through the Eyes of Paul* (Eugene, OR: Cascade Books, 2022), 146-148; *A Short Book about Paul*, 60-65.

280. Acts 9:26-31.

281. Acts 22:17-21. This is the third recorded vision that Paul received. The first was his encounter with Jesus mentioned in Acts 9 and 26. The second was the vision he received regarding Ananias (Acts 9:12).

282. Acts 9:29; 22:17-21. F.F. Bruce, *Paul: Apostle of the Heart Set Free*, 94.

283. Barry Beitzel, *Lexham Geographic Commentary on Acts through Revelation*, 206.

284. Acts 9:30. Witherington believes this took place in A.D. 37 and lasted through A.D. 46. Ben Witherington III, *The Acts of the Apostles*, 82, 368. We know very little about this decade. One of the reasons why the Jerusalem church sent Saul to Cilicia was because he was too hot to handle, due to his past persecution of the churches in Judea. There was a great deal of animus against him. Personal correspondence with Ben Witherington III, 7/18/16. During this time in Cilicia, Saul may have been disinherited from his family and suffered the loss of all things (Philippians 3:8). R. Kent Hughes, *Acts: The Church Afire*, PTW, Logos edition (Wheaton, IL: Crossway Books, 1996), 161. For information on the Jewish community in Tarsus and Saul's reason for visiting there, see Martin Hengel, et al., *Paul Between Damascus and Antioch*, 158-161. The water around Cilicia was beautiful. But there were pirates all through the region, and piracy was active there, including on the coast. So Saul was relating to people in Cilicia who were oppressed by pirates who robbed people. Mark Fairchild, "The Last Apostle," documentary film.

285. Paul makes mention of this trip in Galatians 1:21. F.F. Bruce, *Paul: Apostle of the Heart Set Free*, 94. The time he spent in these regions may have lasted anywhere from five to ten years. According to Fairchild, Saul was in Cilicia for seven to nine years. Personal correspondence with Mark Fairchild, 8/4/23. While Saul may have tried to evangelize all seventeen cities in Cilicia, three cities would have been likely candidates:

With the exception of Jerusalem, the kingdom communities in Judea have never seen Saul's face. But they receive word that "the man who formerly persecuted us is now preaching the faith he once tried to destroy."[286] The ekklesias glorify God for the incredible news.[287] Saul's conversion ends the persecution, and the churches in Judea, Galilee, and Samaria enjoy peace and spiritual prosperity for a time.[288] Some of the apostles leave Jerusalem and begin traveling to establish the new assemblies in these regions.[289] The brothers of Jesus, Jude included, also begin to travel.[290]

Tarsus, Adana, and Mopsuestia. Joel Green, et al., *The World of the New Testament*, 496-498. Witherington has Peter traveling through these same regions in the 40s, evangelizing them, then possibly heading to Pontus. It's likely that some of Paul's five beatings at the hands of the Jews (2 Corinthians 11:24) occurred during this time period in the synagogues of Syria-Cilicia. Paul Barnett, *Bethlehem to Patmos*, 166.

286. Galatians 1:23, NIV. We read about "the ekklesias in Cilicia" in Acts 15:23, 41. Some scholars believe Saul planted churches in Cilicia during his "Silent Years." However, others think the churches in Cilicia were planted in much the same way that the ekklesias in other areas were established by those who dispersed from the Jerusalem church during the persecution in connection with Stephen (see Acts 11:19-21). Saul likely preached, but there is no evidence that he raised up any ekklesias in these areas. One scholar confirms saying, "there is no evidence that a single congregation was started by him [Saul] during those years." R.C.H. Lenski, *The Interpretation of the Acts of the Apostles*, Logos edition (Minneapolis, MN: Augsburg Publishing House, 1961), 456. According to Longenecker, the people in these regions were probably converted through the witness of the assembly in Syrian Antioch. Richard Longenecker, *The Ministry and Message of Paul* (Grand Rapids, MI: Zondervan, 1971), 61. While Saul certainly began preaching the gospel immediately following his conversion, he had no experience in raising up ekklesias until he came to Syrian Antioch where he experienced ekklesia life firsthand with Barnabas. (Preaching the gospel and seeing conversions is not the same as founding a living, breathing ekklesia that lives as a shared-life community.) More on that later.

287. Galatians 1:22-24.

288. The only mention of Galilee in Acts is Acts 9:31. In the NKJV, "churches" are mentioned. According to Barnett, as a result of the events that took place in Acts 8:4, "it's reasonable to suppose that many of the original hearers of Jesus were drawn into the churches in Galilee through unnamed 'Hebrew' preachers." Paul Barnett, *The Birth of Christianity: The First Twenty Years* (Grand Rapids, MI: Eerdmans, 2005), 99. Peter would later visit these churches.

289. According to Acts 8:1-4, ekklesias were transplanted throughout Judea, Samaria, and Galilee (Acts 9:31, NKJV). The apostles visited these new assemblies, laying foundations for each.

290. 1 Corinthians 9:5. The wording in this text ("take along") reveals that the Lord's brothers, as well as some of the other apostles, traveled for ministry with their wives. "Have we no right to take along a wife who is a believer, even as the rest of the apostles, and the brothers of the Lord, and Cephas?" *The NIV Study Bible*, 2013.

Peter Travels Throughout Judea
A.D. 37 – 39

On March 16, A.D. 37, Emperor Tiberius dies and is succeeded by Gaius (nicknamed Caligula or "Little Boots").[291] Peter makes a general tour of the believing communities in western Judea.[292] He visits the ekklesia in Lydda and heals a paralyzed man named Aeneas who has been bedridden for eight years. The assembly in Lydda grows as a result.

Peter then visits Joppa, a town about ten miles northwest of Lydda and thirty-four miles northwest of Jerusalem.[293] While there, he raises a respected sister in Christ named Tabitha (also known as Dorcas) from the dead.[294] The assembly in Joppa grows as a result.[295] Peter remains in Joppa for a long time, residing with Simon the tanner[296] who lives in a house near the Mediterranean.[297]

291. F.F. Bruce, *The Book of the Acts*, 232; Jerome Murphy-O'Connor, *Paul: His Story*, 31; Ben Witherington III, *The Acts of the Apostles*, 81. About the same time (A.D. 36 or 37), Pilate was removed from office. F.F. Bruce, *The Book of the Acts*, 159.

292. Witherington believes Peter followed up with the Diaspora Jews who converted to Christ at Pentecost, traveling to their home regions. In 1 Peter 1:1, Pontus and Cappadocia are mentioned (compare with Acts 2:9-11). Ben Witherington III, *Letters and Homilies for Hellenized Christians: A Socio-Rhetorical Commentary on 1-2 Peter* (Downers Grove, IL: InterVarsity Press, 2007), 2:39.

293. Barry Beitzel, *Lexham Geographic Commentary on Acts through Revelation*, 238. For a detailed analysis of Peter's apostolic work, see Eckhard Schnabel, *Early Christian Mission*, 1:702-728.

294. "Tabitha" is Aramaic, and her name in Greek is "Dorcas." She was a female disciple, a person of "some status and importance in the Joppa Christian community." Ben Witherington III, *The Acts of the Apostles*, 331.

295. Acts 9:32-42.

296. Acts 9:43. Jews were often suspicious of tanners, frequently scorning them. Eckhard Schnabel, *Acts*, 470-471.

297. Acts 10:6.

A.D. 40[298]

Cornelius, a Roman centurion,[299] dwells in the predominantly Gentile city of Caesarea Maritima.[300] Cornelius is a "God-fearer."[301] He is also a man of prayer and benevolence. At 3:00 p.m. in the afternoon, Cornelius receives a vision of an angel instructing him to invite a man named Peter to his home. The next day at noon, Peter prays on his rooftop.[302]

298. Ben Witherington III, *The Acts of the Apostles,* 347ff.; Clinton Arnold, ed., *Zondervan Illustrated Bible Backgrounds Commentary,* 2b:85. It's also possible that the Peter/Cornelius story took place in A.D. 39. Either way, the dramatic story took place about a decade after Jesus rose from the dead.

299. The Roman army was organized into twenty-eight legions that made up a force of 300,000 professional soldiers. Each legion contained about 5,000 men segmented into cohorts. The cohorts (about ten in number) each had approximately 480 men that were divided into six centuries, each century consisting of about eighty men. A centurion led each century. Gary Burge, *A Week in the Life of a Roman Centurion,* 12. Therefore, most centurions oversaw roughly eighty men (instead of the traditional one hundred). Centurions were the backbone of the Roman army. Craig Keener, et al., *NIV Cultural Backgrounds Study Bible,* 1624. For a diagram of the organization of the Roman military, see Gary Burge, *A Week in the Life of a Roman Centurion,* 23.

300. The population of Caesarea was about 50,000. For more details on the city, see Clinton Arnold, ed., *Zondervan Illustrated Bible Backgrounds Commentary*, 2b:86-89. It was often referred to as Caesarea Palestine (or Caesarea Maritima) to distinguish it from Caesarea Philippi.

301. God-fearers were Gentile adherents to Judaism who worshipped the God of Israel. They were not full-fledged converts, meaning they typically did not follow the entire Law of Moses nor undergo circumcision. They simply moved from polytheism to monotheism and regularly attended the synagogue. Ben Witherington III, *The Acts of the Apostles,* 341-344; *New Testament History,* 208-209; Jeffrey Weima, *1-2 Thessalonians,* 28. One of the reasons for this is that some Gentiles were "dissatisfied with the moral laxity and the intellectual absurdity of polytheism," so they were attracted to the high morality that marked Judaism. Leon Morris, *The First and Second Epistles to the Thessalonians,* revised edition, NICNT (Grand Rapids, MI: Eerdmans, 1991), 4. Some scholars believe there was a concerted Jewish effort to convert Gentiles to Judaism, but recent evidence suggests that such efforts were not widespread. Richard Plummer, et al., *Paul's Missionary Methods,* 25; Colin Hemer, *The Book of Acts in the Setting of Hellenistic History,* appx. 2. For further details on God-fearers, see Bruce Winter, et al., eds., *The Book of Acts in Its First Century Setting,* vol. 5, chaps. 4 and 7; Craig Evans, et al., eds., *Dictionary of New Testament Background,* 835-847. Most people in the first century were polytheistic. They believed the Jews were obnoxious and narrow because they believed in only one God. But the early Jesus-followers were even more narrow, proclaiming that Jesus was the only way to salvation. Craig Keener, "Lessons on Acts," Session 12.

302. Normal homes in Palestine had an outside staircase that went up to the roof where a person would go to be alone. It's possible that the roof had an awning which would protect one from the heat. Ben Witherington III, *The Acts of the Apostles,* 349.

He becomes hungry and falls into a trance where he sees a vision of a sheet falling from heaven.

The sheet contains unclean animals. Peter hears a voice saying, "Rise up, kill, and eat…. What God has cleansed do not call unclean."[303] The vision occurs three times. (The meaning of the vision is that God has included the Gentiles in the saving work of Christ and the sanctifying work of the Spirit.) Shortly after the vision ends, three men whom Cornelius sent arrive at Peter's gate. They explain why they are visiting him, and Peter invites them to be his guests for the evening.

The next day, Peter, the men Cornelius sent, and six other men from the assembly in Joppa head out to Caesarea Maritima to meet Cornelius. The trip from Joppa to Caesarea, a distance of thirty-three miles, typically takes about two days.[304]

A Kingdom Community Is Planted in Caesarea

In Rome, Emperor Gaius (Caligula) gives orders to set up a statue of himself in the temple in Jerusalem.[305] His decree is counteracted, and it doesn't come to pass.[306] But Paul will later allude to it in one of his letters.[307] Peter arrives in Caesarea, welcomed by Cornelius and his household. A large group of Gentiles is present. After exchanging stories about how God brought Peter and Cornelius together, Peter preaches Jesus Christ. (Among other

---

303. Acts 10:13, 15. In Judaism, there was a Messianic expectation that when the Messiah came, all the animals once declared unclean would be pronounced clean. Clinton Arnold, ed., *Zondervan Illustrated Bible Backgrounds Commentary*, 2b:93. In Mark 7:15-16, Jesus declared that all foods were clean. Craig Keener, "Lessons on Acts," Session 19.

304. Barry Beitzel, *Lexham Geographic Commentary on Acts through Revelation*, 202.

305. This took place in A.D. 40. F.F. Bruce, *New Testament History* (New York, NY: Doubleday, 1983), 309. Gaius (Caligula) was murdered suddenly in A.D. 41. N.T. Wright, *Paul for Everyone: Galatians and Thessalonians* (Louisville, KY: Westminster John Knox Press, 2004), 147-148.

306. According to Weima, "Local Roman officials realized how provocative this act would be to the Jews, likely causing a revolt, so they purposely delayed action on completing the decree of Caligula." Personal correspondence with Jeffrey Weima, 12/28/23.

307. F.F. Bruce, *Paul: Apostle of the Heart Set Free*, 232-233. In 2 Thessalonians, Paul predicts that another leader would actually pull off what Gaius planned (2 Thessalonians 2:4).

things, Mark's Gospel is an expanded version of Peter's message.[308]) While Peter preaches, the Gentiles believe in Jesus. The Spirit of God falls on them all, and they begin speaking in other languages ("tongues"). This stuns the Jewish men accompanying Peter. They didn't expect God to give His Spirit to unwashed, heathen Gentiles. Peter has all the believing Gentiles baptized in water, and they are now part of the body of Christ.[309]

The flame has now spread from Jew to Gentile. The "unclean" are now part of the Spirit-baptized community—the ekklesia. They have been added to the family of God where the difference between Jew and Gentile no longer exists in Christ.[310] This kingdom community is the "one new humanity," a new creation on planet Earth.[311] The idea that Jew and Gentile could share the same life of the risen Christ and live together as a family is both profound and shocking. The long-standing division and hostility between Gentiles and Jews (in both directions) is greater than any other cultural or social division in the ancient world.[312]

After the first Gentile ekklesia is born in Caesarea, the new converts beg Peter to stay with them a little longer.[313] Peter and his companions comply, and they eat with the new Gentile converts.[314] But back in Jerusalem, some of the priests who have believed on Jesus[315] along with many believing Pharisees begin to form what Paul will later call "the

308. Mark's Gospel follows the outline of Peter's message in Acts 10:34-43. Early church tradition claims that Mark received most of his account about Jesus from Peter. More on this later.

309. We can assume that Cornelius' household was baptized (Acts 10:47-48; 11:14). Roman soldiers weren't permitted to have legal families, but they could have concubines, biological children, and slaves. Ben Witherington III, *Matthew, Smyth & Helwys Bible Commentary* (Macon, GA: Smyth & Helwys Publishing, 2006), 182. According to deSilva, "Cornelius appears to have been stationed for the long haul in Caesarea over the auxiliary troops that were raised from the local (Gentile) population and were permanently stationed there. I would think his having a family of procreation there (legal or otherwise) quite likely." Personal correspondence with David deSilva, 1/18/24.

310. Galatians 3:28; Colossians 3:11; Ephesians 2:11-17.

311. Colossians 3:11, Ephesians 2:11-16. Jesus and His followers constituted a new family that rivaled a person's natural family. Joseph Hellerman, *When the Church Was a Family*, 53-75.

312. N.T. Wright, *Paul: A Biography*, 86.

313. The narrative you just read is based on Acts 10; 11:5-16.

314. Acts 11:3. Jews regarded drinking the wine of a Gentile or eating their food as unclean. Yet Peter did just that! Craig Keener, "Lessons on Acts," Session 19.

315. Acts 6:7.

circumcision party."³¹⁶ This party is made up of strict ("hardline") Jewish Christians who are zealous for the Law of Moses. They fiercely believe that no social or spiritual fellowship should exist between the circumcised and the uncircumcised.³¹⁷ They insist that Gentiles are spiritually unclean and must be circumcised and follow the Law in order to become part of the people of God.³¹⁸

The news that Gentiles have received the gospel in Caesarea spreads like wildfire throughout Judea. But when the ekklesia in Jerusalem hears about it, some in the assembly become alarmed and infuriated. The Law of Moses prohibits the fraternization of Jew and Gentile. From childhood, Jews have been taught never to eat with or touch an unclean Gentile. So in the eyes of hardline Jews, Peter's act of eating with Gentiles is a repulsive breach of loyalty to God's covenant.

When Peter returns to the Jerusalem assembly, the circumcision party reproves him for fellowshipping with unclean Gentiles.³¹⁹ Peter boldly responds by rehearsing the vision he received from the Lord. He explains what took place on his visit to Caesarea—how God

316. The "circumcision party" is derived from the wording of Acts 15:5, ESV. The phrase is explicitly used in Acts 11:2 (ESV, CSB); Galatians 2:12 (ESV; NASB). While some translations don't use the word "party," it is clear that a specific group of Jewish Christ-followers believed that Gentiles must be circumcised in order to receive salvation. F.F. Bruce, *The Book of the Acts*, 220. Barnett gives a good description of their origin and activity in *Bethlehem to Patmos*, 176-177. He also points out that the Jerusalem-based countermission (the circumcision party) was made up of Pharisees. Acts 15:5 explicitly refers to believers among the Pharisees; Acts 21:20 suggests this as well, though other Jews could also be "zealous for the Law." Paul Barnett, *Paul: Missionary of Jesus*, 196. See also Eckhard Schnabel, *Early Christian Mission*, 2:1025; Clinton Arnold, ed., *Zondervan Illustrated Bible Backgrounds Commentary*, 2b:216. Given their background and upbringing, it's plausible to assume that this group was also made up of some of the Jewish priests who converted. F.F. Bruce explains the origin of this group and what they ended up doing in *The Defense of the Gospel in the New Testament*, 70ff.

317. Jews used the term "uncircumcised" as code for Gentiles. Personal correspondence with Gary Burge, 7/12/22.

318. For a devout Jew to eat with a Gentile was to become spiritually defiled. Most (if not all) of the meat accessible outside Jerusalem had been used in pagan sacrifices. Jews believed that Gentiles hatefully sought to pollute Jews with unclean meat and drink. Jerome Murphy-O'Connor, *Paul: His Story*, 43. In addition, for the Jews, "circumcision symbolizes the cutting away of pleasures and the passions of the flesh." David deSilva, *Letter to the Galatians,* 19.

319. "When Peter had come up to Jerusalem, those who were of the circumcision contended with him" (Acts 11:2).

supernaturally spoke to both him and Cornelius. He narrates how the Spirit of God fell on the Gentiles while he spoke to them. Peter tells them,

If then God gave to them the same gift as us, when we believed in the Lord Jesus Christ, who was I, that I could withstand God? (Acts 11:17)

When Peter's fellow Jewish Christians hear his explanation, they stop arguing and glorify God saying, "Then God has also granted to the Gentiles repentance to life!"[320] Back in Alexandria (Egypt), a horrible tempest of hostility breaks out against the Jewish residents of the city. Many Jews are tortured and killed in their synagogues and homes, and their businesses are destroyed.[321] The violence spills over into other Gentile cities in Palestine and Syria that have large Jewish populations. Despite the violence, an ekklesia will soon be born in Antioch of Syria. And it will include both Jews and Gentiles.[322]

320. Acts 11:18.

321. This violent rage against Jews occurred between A.D. 38 and 40. Clinton Arnold, ed., *Zondervan Illustrated Bible Backgrounds Commentary*, 2b:104. Much of this took place when Caligula insisted he be worshipped as a god. Philo of Alexandria left a grisly account in his treatise "Against Flaccus," an accusation against the Roman governor of Alexandria.

322. For a further sketch of Peter's ministry in Palestine, see Paul Barnett, *Jesus & the Rise of Early Christianity*, chap. 12.

CHAPTER 8

THE ANTIOCH CHRONICLE

A.D. 41 – 47

But there were some of them, men of Cyprus and Cyrene, who, when they had come to Antioch, spoke to the Hellenists, preaching the Lord Jesus. The hand of the Lord was with them, and a great number believed and turned to the Lord. (Acts 11:20-21)

January 24[1]
A.D. 41

Emperor Gaius (Caligula) is assassinated, and Claudius takes his place as leader of the Roman world.[2] Some of the disciples who previously dispersed throughout Palestine make their way as far as Phoenicia and Cyprus.[3] They spread the gospel to Jews only (mostly Hellenistic Jews). A number of them from Cyprus and Cyrene reach Antioch, the capital city of the Roman province of Syria.

---

1. Nigel Rodgers, *Roman Empire* (New York, NY: Metro Books, 2008), 72; D. Clint Burnett, *Paul and Imperial Divine Honors*, 234.
2. Anthony Barrett, *Caligula: The Corruption of Power* (London: B.T. Batsford, 1989), xiv; Michael Grant, *History of Rome* (New York, NY: Scribner's, 1979), 280-283; Nigel Rodgers, *Roman Empire*, 68.
3. Acts 11:19-20. By "dispersed" disciples, I'm referring to the dispersion from the persecution in Acts 8. Also, with the mention of Joseph/Barnabas in Acts 4, it's possible the gospel made it to Cyprus much earlier. Personal correspondence with Alan Bandy, 12/6/23. F.F. Bruce discusses the significance of this event in *The Book of the Acts*, 225.

Sharpening the Focus: Antioch of Syria is located on the Orontes River and sits 391 miles north of Jerusalem.[4] For this reason, it's often called "Antioch on the Orontes."[5] Antioch is the third largest city in the Roman Empire.[6] The city is known as "Antioch the beautiful," "the third city of the empire," and "the Pearl of the East."[7]

The city is the center of political, military, and commercial communication between Rome and the Persian frontier.[8] It's a wealthy city—the only one that contains streetlights.[9] Antioch's main east-west street is paved with polished stone, and there are colonnades on both sides. The population of Antioch is estimated to be about 500,000.[10]

4. Barry Beitzel, *Lexham Geographic Commentary on Acts through Revelation*, 333. The trip could have taken up to twenty-five days by foot. Some historians believe the distance between Antioch and Jerusalem was 250 miles. Ben Witherington III, *New Testament History*, 245; Darrell Bock, *Acts*, 495. Others say it was about 300 miles away while some scholars say it was about 425 miles north. Craig Keener, Joseph Dodson, and Caryn Reeder, *Journeys of the Apostle Paul*, 27. The straight-line distance between Antioch of Syria and Jerusalem is approximately 313 miles. The actual travel distance by land would be longer due to the earth's curvature and the need to follow existing roads and terrains. So the actual travel distance could be 20-30% longer, potentially putting it closer to 400 miles. The actual routes that one would travel to get from Jerusalem to Antioch also accounts for the discrepancies.

5. Clyde Fant and Mitchell Reddish, *A Guide to Biblical Sites in Greece and Turkey* (Oxford: Oxford University Press, 2003), 143-148.

6. Josephus, *The Jewish War,* 3.29; F.F. Bruce, *Paul: Apostle of the Heart Set Free*, 130; Ben Witherington III, *New Testament History*, 224. Rome was the largest having a population of about one million. Alexandria was second with an estimated population of 500,000 to 700,000. Darrell Bock, *Studying the Historical Jesus*, 109, n. 8. Antioch was third. For details on population and size estimates for the major cities in the Roman Empire, see J.W. Hanson, *An Urban Geography of the Roman World, 100 BC to AD 300*, chap. 4.

7. Gary Burge, et al., *The New Testament in Antiquity*, 236.

8. "Antioch was a cosmopolitan city, where Jew and Gentile, Greek and barbarian rubbed shoulders, where Mediterranean civilization met the Syrian desert...." F.F. Bruce, *The Book of the Acts*, 228.

9. E.S. Bouchier, *A Short History of Antioch: 300 BC-AD 1268* (London: Blackwell, 1921), 154. See also Jørgen Christensen-Ernst, *Antioch on the Orontes: A History and a Guide* (Lanham, MD: Hamilton Books, 2012).

10. Ben Witherington III, *New Testament History*, 224; Darrell Bock, *Studying the Historical Jesus*, 109, n. 8. Some scholars estimate it had between 150,000 and 600,000 inhabitants in the first century. J.W. Hanson, *An Urban Geography of the Roman World, 100 BC to AD 300*, 67. Rainer Riesner, *Paul's Early Period*, 111; M.C. Pacwa, "Antioch of Syria" (Place) in D.N. Freedman, ed., *The Anchor Yale Bible Dictionary*, Logos edition (New York, NY: Doubleday, 1992); Magnus Zetterholm, *The Formation of Christianity in Antioch: A Social-Scientific Approach to the Separation Between Judaism and Christianity* (New York, NY: Routledge, 2003), 28.

The Jewish population is large and vigorous, standing between 22,000 and 40,000.[11]

The city is comprised of merchants and artisans, most of whom live at a subsistence level. Like most ancient regions, the bulk of the population lives in villages as peasant farmers (90 percent). The rest, who are elites, merchants, and artisans (10 percent), live in the city.[12] Antioch has a reputation of being highly immoral. So much so that it was accused of defiling other parts of the empire.[13]

The city is typical of all Greco-Roman[14] cities of the first century. It's a pesthole of infectious disease. Sickness is highly visible on the streets. Swollen eyes, skin rashes, and lost limbs are readily seen in public. In fact, most deaths in Antioch are caused by infectious diseases.[15] The average family lives in filthy, crowded quarters. At least half of all children die at birth or during infancy.[16] They aren't considered human until they walk and talk. Most children lose one parent before reaching maturity.[17] Like all

11. Magnus Zetterholm, *The Formation of Christianity in Antioch*, 37-38; Eckhard Schnabel, *Paul the Missionary*, 71. Some scholars estimate the Jewish population of the city as high as 65,000. Richard Horsley, et al., *The Message and the Kingdom*, 127; Rainer Riesner, *Paul's Early Period*, 111. For details on the Jews in Syria during this time, see John Barclay, *Jews in the Mediterranean Diaspora*, 242-258; Bruce Winter, et al., eds., *The Book of Acts in Its First Century Setting*, vol. 5, chap. 8.

12. For a description of the social stratification of advanced agrarian societies, including rulers, governors, merchants, priests, peasants, artisans, unclean, degraded, and expendables, see Ben Witherington III, ed., *History, Literature and Society in the Book of Acts*, 256-267; Bruce Malina, *The New Testament World*, chap. 3.

13. Clinton Arnold, ed., *Zondervan Illustrated Bible Backgrounds Commentary*, 2b:100.

14. The term "Greco-Roman" is based on the fact that Alexander the Great (a Greek) brought cultural and political reform ("Hellenism") to his conquered subjects. While the Romans controlled the economic resources of the Mediterranean world, the Greeks captured their mind and culture. David Capes, et al., *Rediscovering Paul*, 34-36.

15. Magnus Zetterholm, *The Formation of Christianity in Antioch*, 29.

16. Rodney Stark, *The Rise of Christianity: How the Obscure, Marginal Jesus Movement Became the Dominant Force in the Western World in a Few Centuries* (San Francisco, CA: Harper Collins, 1997), 160-161. Keener points out that an estimated half of all children died before age ten. Craig Keener, *1 Peter*, 373.

17. Rodney Stark, *The Rise of Christianity*, 160-161.

parts of the empire, people clean themselves with olive oil and a scraping tool (not soap).[18] They also use a stick holding a wet sponge on the tip for toilet paper.[19]

The city was largely populated through immigration since it was founded in the third century B.C. Thus, it's peopled by strangers. Ethnic antagonism breeds hatred and fear. The problem is worsened by the constant influx of foreigners. Crime is rampant, and the streets are unsafe at night. Not a few residents are homeless.[20] Syrian Antioch is filled with misery, danger, despair, fear, and hatred.

The Christian movement will bring a new culture, capable of making life in Greco-Roman cities far more tolerable. The Greco-Roman world depends largely on the contributions of generous-minded benefactors. They pay for the public works. Well-to-do Christ-followers are taught to seek the welfare of their neighbors and fellow citizens.[21] They also use their homes to serve the believers for corporate meetings, worship, prayer, instruction, the Lord's Supper, etc.[22] The kingdom community of Jesus Christ—the ekklesia—will bring joy, hope, charity, a sense of family, and social solidarity to such cruel conditions. In the years to come, Syrian Antioch will become the cradle of Gentile Christianity.

A Kingdom Community Is Planted in Antioch of Syria

Some of the more adventurous believers from Cyprus[23] and Cyrene[24] make a radical decision to begin preaching the gospel to the Gentiles.[25] Among these believers is a Jewish

18. For the many uses of olive oil in the first century, see James Riley Strange, *Excavating the Land of Jesus*, 111ff.
19. Lewis Lord, "The Year One," 41.
20. Rodney Stark, *The Rise of Christianity*, 160-161.
21. Bruce Winter, *Seek the Welfare of the City*, 26ff., 39ff.
22. Roger Gehring, *House Church and Mission*, 226.
23. It's difficult to determine the population of Cyprus. Certainly, the Jewish population was outnumbered. The number of Jews, as compared with Gentiles, was always small in the Diaspora. That was also true for Alexandria, the city with the largest Jewish population outside of Palestine. Personal correspondence with Mark Fairchild, 8/23/23.
24. Cyrene had a large Jewish population. Craig Keener, "Lessons on Acts," Session 21.
25. F.F. Bruce, *The Pauline Circle*, 17.

Cypriot named Mnason.[26] The Lord blesses these daring disciples as they carry out their mission, and a great number of Greeks believe the gospel. As a result of their preaching, an assembly of Jesus Christ gathers in Antioch of Syria. The flame of God's Spirit has spread within the Gentile world.

The ekklesia in Antioch quickly becomes a multiethnic community full of pure, dyed-in-the-wool Gentiles who are free from the rituals of the Law of Moses.[27] They are basking in the love of Jesus Christ and His Spirit alongside converts from the Jewish community. News of the Lord's work travels to Jerusalem. In response, the Jerusalem church sends Barnabas, who is originally from Cyprus. The church has great confidence in Barnabas, and they select him to supervise and direct the gospel advancement in Syrian Antioch.

When Barnabas arrives in Antioch, he's overjoyed by the flourishing growth of the assembly. God is doing an amazing work among the Gentiles. True to his name, Barnabas encourages the new kingdom community to continue learning Christ's teachings and share in the life of the Spirit.[28] Saul of Tarsus continues to reside in Cilicia. While there, he has a profound spiritual encounter with the resurrected Christ.[29]

I know a man in Christ who was caught up into the third heaven fourteen years ago–whether in the body, I don't know, or whether out of the body, I don't know; God knows. I know such a man (whether in the body, or outside of the body, I don't know; God knows), how he was

26. Mnason is the man Paul and his companions lodged with after arriving in Jerusalem (Acts 21:16). "Like Barnabas, he [Mnason] was a Jewish Cypriot." J.D. Douglas, et al., eds., *New Bible Dictionary*, 786. He may have been converted by Paul during his first apostolic journey into Cyprus or even earlier by Barnabas. Ben Witherington III, *The Acts of the Apostles*, 635.

27. By this statement, I'm referring to the fact that the Gentiles in Antioch were not observing circumcision, the Jewish dietary laws, and other Jewish rituals specified in the Law. This fact became a problem for some of the Jews in Jerusalem. More on that later.

28. Acts 11:19-24. Craig Keener guesses that the church in Antioch may have contained as many as 1,500 people in A.D. 50, but an estimate of hundreds seems safe. Personal correspondence with Craig Keener, 7/14/16.

29. Witherington dates the vision in A.D. 42 (or 41). Ben Witherington III, *The Acts of the Apostles*, 83. Bruce dates it at A.D. 42 (or 43) in Cilicia. F.F. Bruce, *Paul: Apostle of the Heart Set Free*, 134-135. If Paul wrote 2 Corinthians in A.D. 56, which I assert, this encounter would have occurred around A.D. 42 (see 2 Corinthians 12:2, "fourteen years ago").

caught up into Paradise, and heard unspeakable words, which it is not lawful for a man to utter. (2 Corinthians 12:2-4)

The encounter is so striking that Paul is not sure if he is taken out of his body. All he knows is that he ascends to the third heaven, also known as Paradise—the space where God and angels dwell.[30] While in the third heaven, Paul hears utterances that mortals are forbidden to divulge.[31]

The Coming Famine
A.D. 44

During the Judean reign of King Agrippa I (the grandson of Herod the Great), some prophets from the ekklesia in Jerusalem pay a visit to the assembly in Antioch.[32] One of the prophets is Agabus, who prophesies of a great famine that will encompass the entire Roman world.[33] This isn't happy news for anyone, especially not for the Jerusalem ekklesia, which already struggles with poverty. Beneath the weight of such an extensive famine, the church will be devastated.

Upon hearing news about the impoverished Jerusalem assembly and the coming famine, the believers in Antioch organize a collection of money to help relieve their brothers and sisters in Judea. Each person gives according to his or her ability, in proportion to their prosperity.[34]

30. The first heaven is the sky that contains the visible clouds. The second heaven is the atmosphere beyond the clouds. The third heaven is the invisible spiritual realm where God and His celestial beings dwell. Paul calls it "Paradise" in 2 Corinthians 12:4, NASB.

31. 2 Corinthians 12:1-4.

32. Herod Agrippa was brought up in Rome and was friends with the imperial family. James D.G. Dunn, *The Acts of the Apostles*, 161.

33. The famine eventually took place under the reign of Claudius. It's probably the same severe famine that came to Judea between A.D. 46-47. James D.G. Dunn, *The Acts of the Apostles*, 157; Martin Hengel, *Acts and the History of Earliest Christianity*, 111; N.T. Wright, *Paul: A Biography*, 94. According to Witherington, Agabus' prophecy was uttered in A.D. 44. Ben Witherington III, *The Acts of the Apostles*, 82.

34. Acts 11:27-29.

James Is Martyred
April 44

During the season of Unleavened Bread, King Agrippa seeks to gain favor with the Jewish leaders just as Pontius Pilate did before him. Since many of the Jews in Jerusalem are starting to hate the Christians, Agrippa imprisons James (the son of Zebedee and brother of John, the apostle). To further please the Jewish leaders, Agrippa has James beheaded, making him the first of the Twelve to be martyred.[35]

The fact that James is executed by the secular power suggests that the new "sect" of Jesus-followers is now a political threat.[36] James' execution satisfies the Jews, so Herod takes Peter into custody to garner even greater favor with the people.[37] To secure his plan for a public trial and likely execution, Herod holds Peter captive until after Passover. Four squads of four men guard the apostle during various watches of the night. The believers in Jerusalem gather to pray fervently for Peter's release.

The Lord answers their prayers and sends an angel to deliver Peter from prison.[38] Now free, Peter heads to the house of Mary (John Mark's mother), a common meeting place for the assembly. When Peter arrives, a large group of disciples are praying in the home's upper room.[39] A disciple named Rhoda answers Peter's knock at the door.[40] She is overjoyed at the sound of Peter's voice, so she runs to tell the other disciples that he is at the

35. Eusebius records the tradition that the guard who oversaw James in prison was so impressed with his testimony that he professed to be a Christian and was beheaded along with him. Eusebius, *The History of the Church*, 2.9. The year this likely occurred was also A.D. 44. Ben Witherington III, *Invitation to the New Testament*, 280.

36. James D.G. Dunn, *The Acts of the Apostles*, 162.

37. Acts 12:3.

38. For details on how this miracle took place, see Clinton Arnold, ed., *Zondervan Illustrated Bible Backgrounds Commentary*, 2b:111. For instance, the angel didn't nudge or tap Peter out of sleep. He struck him, which suggests a strong blow (Acts 12:7). Peter may have been a heavy sleeper!

39. Acts 12:12-13. The church was praying constantly for Peter (Acts 12:5). Mary, mother of Mark and sister-in-law to Barnabas, was wealthy enough to own this large home. Reta Halteman Finger, *Of Widows and Meals*, 133.

40. Rhoda means "rose." The Greek word used in Acts 12:13 could indicate that Rhoda was a slave in the household. Personal correspondence with David deSilva, 1/18/24.

door, forgetting in her excitement to let him in. Everyone stares at Rhoda in disbelief and concludes she is out of her mind.[41]

While she argues her case, Peter keeps knocking. Eventually, the disciples let him in. When they see his face, they're astonished. The apostle tells them about the miracle of his release and asks them to report it to James (the Lord's half-brother) along with the rest of the ekklesia. Before dawn, Peter leaves Jerusalem.[42] The next morning, Herod learns that Peter has escaped and orders another execution—that of the guards responsible for watching the apostle![43] Herod leaves Jerusalem and travels to the coastal port of Caesarea Maritima. There, he tries to put out a few political fires with the people of Tyre and Sidon. Despite the renewed persecution against the disciples of Jesus in Jerusalem, the ekklesia continues to grow.[44]

August 1
A.D. 44

Draped in a silver royal robe, glittering spectacularly beneath the sun's rays, Herod Agrippa delivers an oration to the people of Caesarea. As he speaks, the public is awed and exclaims, "You are more than a mortal. You are a god!" Instead of rebuking the people for their idolatry, Herod preens beneath their impious flattery. Immediately, the angel of the Lord strikes him with pain. The king complains of intestinal cramps and is hustled inside,

41. Rhoda's testimony was probably dismissed due to the cultural mindset of the day. According to Jewish teaching, the testimony of a woman was considered as reliable as that of a thief. Roman law also discounted the testimony of women. Yet ironically, women were the first ones God chose to witness to the resurrected Christ. Craig Keener, "Lessons on Acts," Session 21.

42. Peter's exit from Jerusalem can be dated at A.D. 44. James D.G. Dunn, *The Acts of the Apostles*, 164; Eckhard Schnabel, *Paul the Missionary*, 30-31. Peter showed up in Jerusalem again briefly when he met with Paul (Galatians 1:18) and also at the Jerusalem council (Acts 15).

43. According to Weima, "It was common in that day for the guards or jailers who allowed a prisoner to escape under their watch to receive the same penalty that their prisoner was about to face." Personal correspondence with Jeffrey Weima, 12/28/23.

44. The word of God also continued to spread and flourish (Acts 12:24).

away from the adoring crowds. He suffers stomach pains for five days until he dies.[45] Herod is eaten from within by intestinal worms.[46]

The Antiochian Believers
A.D. 45 – 46[47]

A massive influx of Gentiles joins the Antioch church. The ekklesia has grown so large that Barnabas can no longer care for the community on his own. Considering the matter, he recalls that Saul speaks Greek (since he hails from the Hellenistic city of Tarsus). He also remembers how the Lord specifically called Saul to minister to the Gentiles. So without delay, Barnabas heads to Tarsus to hunt for Saul. After searching the city, he locates Saul

---

45. This description blends the account given by Jewish historian, Josephus, with Luke's account. See Josephus, *The Antiquities of the Jews*, 19.343-352 and Acts 12:20-23. Some scholars believe Herod's death was caused by peritonitis or poison. James D.G. Dunn, *The Acts of the Apostles*, 167. If so, the angel used it as the mechanism for his demise. Witherington believes Herod was stricken on August 1, A.D. 44. Ben Witherington III, *The Acts of the Apostles*, 389. Luke is a rhetorical historian, so he was interested in placing his story of the early church within the context of secular historical events. Ben Witherington III, *The Acts of the Apostles*, 367.

46. Acts 12:23 and Eusebius, *The History of the Church*, 2.10. The preceding narrative comes from Acts 12:1-23. The first twelve chapters of Acts are dominated by Peter's ministry. Herod Agrippa's death marks the end of the first part of Luke's account. With Peter leaving Jerusalem, the focus shifts to Paul's apostolic ministry, which makes up the second half of Acts (beginning in Acts 13). James D.G. Dunn, *The Acts of the Apostles*, 159, 165. The book of Acts makes plain that Paul was Luke's hero. William Ramsay, *St. Paul the Traveler and Roman Citizen*, 28. For a highly detailed treatment of how Luke depicts Paul throughout Acts, see Craig Keener, *Acts*, 1:220-257. According to some scholars, Acts 1-2 covers approximately fifty days; Acts 3:1-9:31 covers around four years; Acts 9:32-12:24 covers around ten years; Acts 12:25-16:5 covers about five years; Acts 16:6-19:41 covers about six years; and Acts 20:1-28:31 covers around seven years. David Wenham and Steve Walton, *Exploring the New Testament: A Guide to the Gospels and Acts*, third edition (Downers Grove, IL: InterVarsity Press, 2021), 1:334.

47. Note that when piecing together the timeline found in history (regarding Herod) and Paul's sequence of events in Galatians 1 and 2, Luke's account in Acts 11 and 12 does not appear to be in chronological order. This is why the order of certain events differs slightly from Acts in this section of the book. Witherington confirms, saying, "Acts 12 then records some events which happened before Acts 11." Ben Witherington III, *The Acts of the Apostles*, 368.

and persuades him to come to Antioch.[48] For the next year, Barnabas and Saul enjoy body life in Antioch.[49] They nurture it as well. Barnabas acts as Saul's mentor.[50]

The two men complement one another magnificently. Barnabas is older, more respected, and more experienced. He is noted for his kindness, sensitivity, and empathy. Saul, on the other hand, is brilliant with a razor-sharp intellect, an amazing grasp of the Hebrew Scriptures, and unparalleled passion.[51] With Barnabas in the lead and Paul as his "right-

48. Bruce says this probably took place in A.D. 45. F.F. Bruce, *Paul: Apostle of the Heart Set Free*, 133. For details on Paul's time in Antioch, see Martin Hengel, et al., *Paul Between Damascus and Antioch*, chap. 8; W.J. Conybeare and J.S. Howson, *The Life & Epistles of St. Paul* (Grand Rapids, MI: Eerdmans, 1966), 90-107.

49. "Body life" is a term I use for the experience of the body of Christ; i.e., community life under Christ's headship. Ray Stedman popularized the term and possibly coined it.

50. Many scholars confirm that Barnabas mentored Saul. Orlando Rivera, "Mentoring Stages in the Relationship between Barnabas and Paul," *Journal of Biblical Perspectives in Leadership*, 2007; C.W. Stenschke, "When the Second Man Takes the Lead: Reflections on Joseph Barnabas and Paul of Tarsus and Their Relationship in the New Testament," *Koers - Bulletin for Christian Scholarship/Bulletin vir Christelike Wetenskap*, vol 75, no 3 (July 26, 2010): a94. Wright says Saul was Barnabas' protégé. N.T. Wright, *Paul: A Biography*, 115. According to Bence, "In the Barnabas-Saul partnership, they could accomplish two goals. Of course, Saul could help disciple the Gentiles. But at the same time, Barnabas could mentor Saul, as Saul developed his own rich potential." Philip Bence, *Acts: A Bible Commentary in the Wesleyan Tradition*, Logos edition (Indianapolis, IN: Wesleyan Publishing House, 1998), 121. Luke Timothy Johnson states that Barnabas acted as Saul's patron (sponsor) in *The Acts of the Apostles*, Sacra Pagina (Collegeville, MN: Liturgical Press, 1992), 204. Johnson agrees that Barnabas also served as Saul's mentor. Personal correspondence with Luke Timothy Johnson, 7/28/23. The ordering of their names is a strong clue that points to a mentoring relationship. Luke uses "Barnabas and Saul" (Acts 11:30; 12:25; 13:2, 7). In the first century, authors indicated priority by how they ordered people's names. Later, however, the priority would shift, and it would become "Paul and Barnabas" when Paul took the lead (Acts 13:43, 46, 50). See F.F. Bruce, *The Pauline Circle*, 18-19; Alan Bandy, *An Illustrated Guide to the Apostle Paul*, 41. Barnabas sat under the ministry of the Twelve for around a decade in Jerusalem. Antioch would be the first real experience of body life that Saul received for any significant length of time (at least three years). While Saul received his gospel directly from Jesus, he learned what working with an ekklesia entailed by observing and laboring side-by-side with Barnabas, who observed the Twelve do it in Jerusalem. Therefore, from an experiential standpoint, the idea that Saul learned from Barnabas is obvious. According to Fairchild, "Barnabas certainly influenced Paul." Personal correspondence with Mark Fairchild, 8/4/23.

51. R. Kent Hughes, *Acts*, 161-162.

hand man,"[52] the two men gather with the ekklesia and teach God's word to the thriving community.[53]

While in Antioch, Saul possibly lodges with Simon of Cyrene, also called Simeon (who carried the cross of Jesus), and his family.[54] This includes his wife, who cares for Saul with the consideration of a mother and Simon's two sons, Rufus and Alexander.[55] In Antioch, the disciples of Jesus are designated "Christians." This title means "Christ's people."[56]

When he [Barnabas] had found him [Saul], he brought him to Antioch. For a whole year they were gathered together with the assembly, and taught many people. The disciples were first called Christians in Antioch. (Acts 11:26)

The believers don't call *themselves* Christians, nor is the name given to them by the Jews.[57] (Unconverted Jews don't believe Jesus is the Christ/Messiah.) Instead, their Greek-speaking

---

52. Simon Kistemaker, *Exposition of the Acts of the Apostles*, Logos edition (Grand Rapids, MI: Baker, 1990), 422.

53. Acts 11:26. Saul and Barnabas "assembled with the ekklesia" and taught the believers. Dunn points out that the "whole year" was only part of the time they spent in Antioch. James D.G. Dunn, *The Acts of the Apostles*, 156. See also N.T. Wright, *Paul: A Biography*, 92. For further details on the ekklesia in Antioch, see William Ramsay, *St. Paul the Traveler and Roman Citizen*, chap. 3. Scholars differ on how long Saul spent in Antioch. The estimates range from three years to ten years. See Clinton Arnold, ed., *Zondervan Illustrated Bible Backgrounds Commentary*, 2b:103.

54. Acts 13:1; Mark 15:21; Romans 16:13. J.D. Douglas, et al., eds., *New Bible Dictionary*, 1040. F.F. Bruce makes a plausible case that Saul likely lodged with Simon/Simeon of Cyrene and his family in *Romans: An Introduction and Commentary*, revised edition, TNTC (Grand Rapids, MI: Eerdmans, 1985), 260-261.

55. F.F. Bruce, *Paul: Apostle of the Heart Set Free*, 148-149; *The Book of the Acts*, 238; *The Pauline Circle*, 93-94; Douglas Moo, *Epistle to the Romans*, NICNT (Grand Rapids, MI: Eerdmans, 1996), 925. Simon/Simeon of Cyrene carried the cross of Christ part of the way to Calvary. Mark 15:21. Rufus is mentioned in a letter written by Paul later in the story (Romans 16:13). Clinton Arnold, ed., *Zondervan Illustrated Bible Backgrounds Commentary*, 3:93.

56. Or "Messiah's people."

57. N.T. Wright, *Paul: A Biography*, 93. Witherington doesn't think the believers used the term "Christians" for themselves before the second century. Until this point, those who followed Jesus were called "disciples" (Acts 6:1), "saints" (Acts 9:13), "brothers" or "brethren" (Acts 1:16; 9:30), "believers" (Acts 10:45), those "being saved" (Acts 2:47), and the people "of the Way" (Acts 9:2). They were also called Nazarenes and followers of the Way. Ben Witherington III, *The Acts of the Apostles*, 371; John Stott, *The Message of Acts*, 205. Some scholars believe the term "Christians" was used derisively, wherein the unbelievers mocked them for being "Christ's people," a taunting nickname. Richard Longenecker, *Luke-Acts*, 852-853; Edwin Judge, *The Social Pattern of the Christian Groups in the First Century*, 45. Keener believes it was a mocking political designation, "partisans of the Jewish Messiah." Personal correspondence with Craig Keener, 12/4/23. Antiochians

neighbors label them "Christians" because the disciples constantly talk about Christ. The Christians in Antioch are consumed with Jesus, and out of the abundance of the hearts the mouths speak.[58] The new movement is also called "The Way"—a term the followers of Jesus use for the way of salvation and the way of life, embodied in Christ Himself.[59] In Palestine, the Christians are known as "Nazarenes," because they follow Jesus of Nazareth.[60]

In Antioch, the ministries of Barnabas and Saul bear much fruit. As the ekklesia grows beneath their tutelage,[61] two Gentiles in the Antioch assembly begin to stand out. Their names are Luke[62] and Titus.[63] Both men will play key roles in the unfolding drama. Titus

were known for making fun of people, so "Christian" was probably a mocking term. Years later, it became a legal charge as shown in 1 Peter 4:16. Craig Keener, "Lessons on Acts," Session 20.

58. Stott agrees that they were called Christians "because the word 'Christ' was constantly on their lips." John Stott, *The Message of Acts*, 205. According to N.T. Wright, "The followers of Jesus were thinking and speaking in such a way that they were thought of as 'the king's people,' 'Messianists,' *Christians*." N.T. Wright, *Acts for Everyone: Part One*, 178. The first-century Christians were a people obsessed with Jesus. "Jesus" appears about nine hundred times in the New Testament, His name appearing once every eight verses on average. Nijay Gupta, *Strange Religion: How the First Christians Were Weird, Dangerous, and Compelling* (Grand Rapids, MI: Brazos Press, 2024), 205-206.

59. John 14:6; Acts 9:2; 19:9, 23; 22:4; 24:14; 16:17; 18:25-26. Clinton Arnold, ed., *Zondervan Illustrated Bible Backgrounds Commentary*, 2b:76. By contrast, the only times the term "Christian" (*christianos*) appears in the New Testament is in Acts 11:26; 26:28; 1 Peter 4:16. Even so, throughout this book I will sometimes use the term "Christian" to describe the believers.

60. Acts 24:5. Clinton Arnold, ed., *Zondervan Illustrated Bible Backgrounds Commentary*, 2b:236; Edwin Judge, *The Social Pattern of the Christian Groups in the First Century*, 45. Jesus was also known by this nickname, "Nazarene." Matthew 2:23. Hans Leitzmann, *A History of the Early Church*, 1:131; William Ramsay, *St. Paul the Traveler and Roman Citizen*, 54.

61. While there were certainly others who ministered in the ekklesia in Antioch (Acts 13:1), Barnabas and Saul stood out beyond the rest. Both had an apostolic calling which will become apparent later in the story.

62. According to church tradition, Luke was from Antioch of Syria. Eusebius, *The History of the Church*, 3.4; William Ramsay, *St. Paul the Traveler and Roman Citizen*, 168, 302-304; J.B. Lightfoot, *The Acts of the Apostles*, 187; Robert Gundry, *A Survey of the New Testament*, third edition (Grand Rapids, MI: Zondervan, 1994), 206; Johannes Weiss, *Earliest Christianity: A History of the Period A.D. 30-150*, volume 1 (New York, NY: Harper & Brothers, 1959), 278; Eckhard Schnabel, *Acts,* 24. Aside from being an Antiochian by birth, Luke was probably a God-fearing Gentile before he believed on Christ. F.F. Bruce, *The Pauline Circle*, 40; *Paul: Apostle of the Heart Set Free*, 133. The remarks about Luke in this chapter, and those to come, are expanded in F.F. Bruce, *The Pauline Circle*, 35-43. Some, like Alan Bandy, believe Luke was Macedonian (likely from Philippi). Later in the story, Luke will become an "inseparable" companion to Paul, something echoed in the early patristic writers. Irenaeus, *Against Heresies*, 3.14.1; Clement of Alexandria, *Miscellanies*, 5.12; Jerome, *Lives of Illustrious Men*, 7.

63. That Titus was from Antioch is a natural inference from Galatians 2:1-3. Wilson agrees that "Titus was a Gentile most probably from Antioch." Personal correspondence with Mark Wilson, 9/4/23. Alternatively,

will one day become an apostolic worker,[64] but only after he's had time to develop spiritually in the Antioch assembly.[65] Luke is a Gentile itinerant (traveling) physician who plies his trade in places like Troas and Philippi.[66] (Titus is possibly Luke's brother.[67])

Jerusalem Gets Relief from Antioch
A.D. 46 – 47[68]

Just as Agabus had prophesied, the famine strikes Judea hard, deeply affecting the Jerusalem assembly.[69] When the assembly in Antioch receives word of the famine, the church

---

some scholars believe Titus was among the first converts to Christ in Europe. Rainer Riesner, *Paul's Early Period*, 269. Craig Keener believes Titus was a South Galatian, but it's difficult to be certain since Titus is never mentioned in Acts. Personal correspondence with Craig Keener, 7/14/16.

64. In the New Testament, the term "worker" denotes the apostolic ministry. Matthew 9:37-38; Romans 16:21; 1 Corinthians 3:9; Galatians 2:9; Philippians 2:25; Colossians 1:7; 2 Timothy 2:15 (all in the NLT).

65. For details on how Titus is described throughout Paul's letters, see Eckhard Schnabel, *Paul the Missionary*, 252-253. Later Paul will call him a "fellow worker" (2 Corinthians 8:23, ESV).

66. Ben Witherington III, *New Testament History*, 256. That Luke was a physician, see Colossians 4:14. Even though Luke was likely from Syrian Antioch, he could have traveled back and forth from Troas and Philippi for his work. Philippi was famous for its school of medicine, producing doctors throughout the empire. Ben Witherington III, *The Acts of the Apostles*, 485, 490. Meeks speculates that Luke (who had a Latin name) could have been a manumitted (freed) slave. Doctors were often slaves. Wayne Meeks, *The First Urban Christians*, 57. For further details on Luke, see Craig Keener, *Acts*, 1:402-422. Luke's firsthand account begins in Acts 16:10ff. See also F.F. Bruce, *Paul: Apostle of the Heart Set Free*, 149. When Luke uses the "we" passages in Acts 16, 20, 21, 27, and 28, it is because he was present.

67. For this conclusion, see *Paul: Apostle of the Heart Set Free*, 339, n. 5; William Ramsay, *St. Paul the Traveler and Roman Citizen*, 304; Alexander Souter, "A Suggested Relationship between Titus and Luke," *Expository Times* 18:1906-1907a-b, 285, 335-336. This would explain why Luke never mentions Titus in the book of Acts, which had to do with Luke being objective according to the standards of the time. Luke also doesn't mention himself, which according to Bruce, could be due to his modesty. F.F. Bruce, *The Pauline Circle*, 64.

68. Ben Witherington III, *The New Testament Story*, 274; *The Acts of the Apostles*, 368; N.T. Wright, *Paul: A Biography*, 95. The famine in Judea could have stretched to A.D. 48. While it started in A.D. 45/46, its effects occurred a bit later. Ben Witherington III, *The Acts of the Apostles*, 368.

69. According to Suetonius, droughts and poor harvests (which create famines) occurred in succession during the reign of Claudius (A.D. 41-54). *Life of Claudius*, 18.2. The famine in Judea in A.D. 46-47 is attested by Josephus in *The Antiquities of the Jews*, 3.320-321; 20.51-53, 101. The famine may have started after the death of Herod Agrippa. The effects of the shortage of food were keenly felt in Judea in A.D. 46-48. Alan Bandy, *An Illustrated Guide to the Apostle Paul*, 49. Stott says the famine in Judea didn't end until 57. John

quickly organizes the relief fund and selects Barnabas and Saul to bring it to the elders in Jerusalem.[70] Saul and Barnabas leave Antioch and head toward Jerusalem to deliver the fund.[71] They bring Titus, a Gentile representative of the assembly in Antioch.[72] The journey from Antioch to Jerusalem is more than 300 miles. When they arrive in the holy city, Saul, Barnabas, and Titus graciously hand the collection over to the Jerusalem elders.

While there, the three men have a private meeting with Peter, James (the Lord's half-brother), and John, the "pillars" of the Jerusalem ekklesia.[73] In this meeting, Saul and Barnabas give a report on their ministry to the Gentiles and share their desire to continue

---

Stott, *The Message of 1 & 2 Thessalonians: The Gospel & the End Time* (Downers Grove, IL: InterVarsity Press, 1991), 57.

70. Acts 11:30. This is the first mention of elders in the Jerusalem assembly. Most likely, it took years for some of the "brothers" in Jerusalem to become "elders." Also, when Paul said he "went up" to Jerusalem "by revelation" (Galatians 2:2), he was presumably referring to the revelation given to Agabus about the coming famine (Acts 11:28). John Drane, *Paul: An Illustrated Documentary*, 34.

71. This was Paul's second post-conversion visit to Jerusalem. His first visit is recorded in Acts 9:26-29. Eckhard Schnabel, *Acts*, 455.

72. Galatians 2:1. F.F. Bruce, *Paul: Apostle of the Heart Set Free*, 150-159; Darrell Bock, *Acts*, 31ff., 486-493. I agree with F.F. Bruce, Ben Witherington, N.T. Wright, Michael Bird, Darrell Bock, David deSilva, John Drane, et al. who believe the meeting mentioned in Galatians 2 likely occurred during this time (Acts 11), and it's not the meeting that took place in Acts 15 (the Jerusalem council). Other first-rate scholars like Craig Keener, J.B. Lightfoot, James D.G. Dunn, et al. believe Galatians 2 and Acts 15 describe the same meeting. Craig Keener, *Acts*, 3:2195-2211; James D.G. Dunn, *Beginning from Jerusalem*, 446ff. Dunn admits that the difference in views on this point "is not important theologically" (447). Both positions have strong arguments to support them. Which view a person adopts determines whether Galatians was written before or after the Jerusalem council in Acts 15. Schnabel asserts, "There is sufficient evidence to suggest that the famine-relief visit described in Acts 11:27-30 is identical with Paul's second visit to Jerusalem fourteen years after his conversion, described in Galatians 2:1-10." Eckhard Schnabel, *Early Christian Mission*, 2:988. Drane agrees and sketches out the reasons in *Paul: An Illustrated Documentary*, 36-39. See also Ben Witherington III, *The Acts of the Apostles*, 90-97; Richard Longenecker, *The Ministry and Message of Paul*, 39; Colin Hemer, *The Book of Acts in the Setting of Hellenistic History*, 247-251; F.F. Bruce, *The Book of the Acts*, 231, 282-285; Thomas Schreiner, *Galatians: Zondervan Exegetical Commentary on the New Testament* (Grand Rapids, MI: Zondervan, 2010), 29. Most of the scholars admit we cannot be certain. For discussions on the complications with combining the narrative in Acts with Galatians chapters 1 and 2, see Philip Bence, *Acts*, 122-125; Robert Jewett, *A Chronology of Paul's Life*, chaps. 4 and 5.

73. The men in this triumvirate were regarded as the pillars, or "sustaining structure," of the new community in Jerusalem. N.T. Wright, *Paul: A Biography*, 134. The meeting was held because Saul needed their endorsement for his mission to the Gentiles. Personal correspondence with Ben Witherington III, 7/18/16. In Galatians 1:11-24, Paul tells the story of his conversion up until the time he met Peter, James, and John.

to reach the uncircumcised.[74] Unfortunately, several "false brethren" from the circumcision party show up to the meeting.[75] They are undercover agents who infiltrate the meeting with an agenda to put the Gentiles in Antioch under the Mosaic Law.

Since Titus is not circumcised, they make him an issue.[76] So they pressure Titus to be circumcised and become a "full Jew" and a "legitimate part" of the Jesus family.[77] Titus rejects their demands and dismisses their pressure.[78] Peter, James, and John are also unconvinced by the circumcision party's arguments, and they approve Saul's gospel of grace.[79]

The three apostles give Saul and Barnabas "the right hand of fellowship." They agree that the chief sphere of ministry for Saul and Barnabas will be the Gentile world, while the chief sphere of ministry for Peter, James, and John will be the Jewish world. The three "pillars" only request that Saul and Barnabas continue to remember the impoverished believers in Jerusalem—a request that Saul already had on his heart.[80] (The poverty in Jerusalem is known

74. Strongly implied from Galatians 2:7-9.

75. Paul calls them "false brothers" in Galatians 2:4, ESV. These were the "hardline Jews" of the Jerusalem ekklesia mentioned earlier. I agree with Witherington that Paul didn't consider them to be true followers of Jesus, despite their claim. Personal correspondence with Ben Witherington III, 7/18/16.

76. Galatians 2:1-5.

77. N.T. Wright, *Paul: A Biography*, 98.

78. Galatians 2:3. The "pillars" should also be credited here because they didn't back the circumcision party's demands, and they let Titus "off the hook." Personal correspondence with David deSilva, 1/18/24.

79. This reconstruction is based on mirror-reading what Paul says about the meeting in Galatians 2 (which I along with other scholars believe was private). Paul's gospel of grace has been called "Law-free" by theologians and scholars. (For example, see Ben Witherington III, *Grace in Galatia*, 153.) Paul wasn't against the Law; he believed God's Law was good and holy. However, Paul's gospel was free from obeying the Law of Moses for salvation and sanctification. See 1 Corinthians 9:20-21, Romans 7–8, and Galatians 5 where Paul discusses being under the law of Christ to follow the Holy Spirit, who enables a person to obey God, as opposed to being under the Law of Moses, which is seeking to please God in the energy of the flesh. According to Paul, those who are under grace and led by the Spirit are not under the Law (Galatians 5:18; Romans 6:13-14), and they do not fulfill the desires of the flesh (Galatians 5:16; Romans 8:1-4). Paul's critics were correct when they alleged that he taught that Gentiles weren't obligated to follow the Law of Moses and circumcise their children or follow the Mosaic traditions (Acts 21:21). One of the best expositions of Paul's gospel in print is *Paul: Apostle of the Heart Set Free* by F.F. Bruce. See also "Jesus vs. Moses" at frankviola.org/jesusvsmoses for an extensive treatment of Paul's view of the Law. According to Paul, those who follow the Spirit of Christ fulfill the moral dictates of the Law (Romans 8:1-4). See also Ezekiel 36:25-27; Jeremiah 31:33-34; Hebrews 8:7-13; 10:15-16 for how the Spirit writes God's moral law on the hearts and minds of those who are part of the new covenant.

80. Galatians 2:6-10. The "poor" in verse 10 likely refers to those in Jerusalem who didn't have enough resources to "maintain life even at subsistence level." James D.G. Dunn, *Beginning from Jerusalem*, 458. For

throughout the Jewish world. Possibly up to two-thirds of its inhabitants are supported by public or private charity.[81] Later, Saul will take up a collection from all the Gentile ekklesias he will raise up to relieve the chronic poverty of the Jerusalem church.[82])

Saul, Barnabas, and Titus head back home to Antioch of Syria.[83] On their return, they take with them Barnabas' young cousin, John Mark,[84] who will become their assistant.[85] ("John" is his Jewish name, while "Mark" or "Marcus" is his Roman name. He is the same Mark who authored the Gospel of Mark.[86])

A Prayer Meeting That Changes History
Spring 47

The ekklesia in Antioch is now about six years old. A prayer meeting is called, and five gifted men from the assembly are present. These men are prophets and teachers, and they are culturally and racially diverse.[87] The men come together fasting and ministering unto the Lord.[88] They are:

Paul, helping the poor within the Jesus family was a mark of love. N.T. Wright, *Paul: A Biography*, 218. For a detailed analysis of Greco-Roman poverty and Paul's theology of the poor, see Bruce Longenecker, *Remember the Poor: Paul, Poverty, and the Greco-Roman World* (Grand Rapids, MI: Eerdmans, 2010).

81. Jerome Murphy-O'Connor, *Paul: His Story*, 106.

82. Paul's plan to collect money for the poor believers in Jerusalem was carried out over a span of about ten years. Paul Barnett, *Paul: Missionary of Jesus*, 153.

83. We assume that Titus went back with them. N.T. Wright, *Paul: A Biography*, 100.

84. Colossians 4:10.

85. Acts 13:5; Colossians 4:10. As a "helper," Mark likely assisted the apostles with their daily needs. Clinton Arnold, ed., *Zondervan Illustrated Bible Backgrounds Commentary*, 2b:119.

86. Barry Beitzel, *Lexham Geographic Commentary on Acts through Revelation*, 311. We will call him "Mark" throughout the rest of the story. For details on Mark, see F.F. Bruce, *The Pauline Circle*, 73-80. For a comprehensive treatment of the narrative found in Acts 3 to Acts 12, with a focus on Peter's ministry, see Craig Keener, *Acts*, 2:1042-1979.

87. This fact is notable. Two were from northern Africa, one from Cyprus, another from Cilicia, and one from Palestine. Interestingly, none of the five men were from Syria where Antioch is located. Clinton Arnold, ed., *Zondervan Illustrated Bible Backgrounds Commentary*, 2b:117.

88. Acts 13:1-2.

- Simeon called Niger ("Niger" is his nickname,[89] indicating he is of dark complexion)[90]
- Lucius of Cyrene[91]
- Manaen (an aristocrat from Palestine, probably the foster brother of Herod Antipas—a son and successor of Herod the Great)[92]
- Barnabas (from Cyprus)
- Saul (from Cilicia)

The Spirit Sends Barnabas and Saul

A historic moment is about to take place. Just as the Father called and sent His Son, and just as the Son called and sent the Twelve, the Holy Spirit takes up the role of sending those whom God has called to His work.[93]

> *As they ministered to the Lord and fasted, the Holy Spirit said, "Now separate to Me Barnabas and Saul for the work to which I have called them." ...So, being sent out by the Holy Spirit, they went down to Seleucia.... (Acts 13:2, 4, NKJV)*[94]

89. Mark 15:21.

90. "Simeon called Niger" (Acts 13:1, NIV). "Niger" means black (probably pronounced "nee-gare" or "nair-jr"). Dunn believes Simeon was a black man. James D.G. Dunn, *The Acts of the Apostles*, 172. Bruce agrees that "he was presumably of dark complexion." F.F. Bruce, *The Book of the Acts*, 244. According to Guthrie, Simeon Niger had a Jewish and Latin name. Donald Guthrie, *The Apostles*, 95.

91. While it cannot be proven, the idea that Lucius is the same person as Luke is not outside the realm of possibility. James D.G. Dunn, *Romans 9–16*, WBC, Logos edition (Dallas, TX: Word Books, 1988), 909; Ben Witherington III, *Paul's Letter to the Romans: A Socio-Rhetorical Commentary* (Grand Rapids, MI: Eerdmans, 2004), 399. But along with Bruce, I am unconvinced of this connection. F.F. Bruce, *Paul: Apostle of the Heart Set Free*, 149. To my mind, Luke was a Gentile, while Lucius was Jewish (see Romans 16:21).

92. Manaen was said to be "the foster brother of Herod the tetrarch" (Acts 13:1, WEB). He was a member of the upper class and came from Palestine. Rainer Riesner, *Paul's Early Period*, 111; Ben Witherington III, *The Acts of the Apostles*, 392-393; F.F. Bruce, *Paul: Apostle of the Heart Set Free*, 149. Presumably, he was an elderly teacher in the ekklesia in Antioch. Colin Hemer, *The Book of Acts in the Setting of Hellenistic History*, 166. Since Herod Antipas ruled Galilee from A.D. 4 to 34, some scholars believe Manaen was also from Galilee (in Palestine). If he was, he may have heard Jesus teach. Clinton Arnold, ed., *Zondervan Illustrated Bible Backgrounds Commentary*, 2b:117.

93. John 20:21; Acts 13:2.

94. Luke doesn't tell us exactly *how* the Holy Spirit spoke, but it's possible that the Spirit spoke through one of the prophets in the gathering. W.J. Conybeare and J.S. Howson, *The Life & Epistles of St. Paul*, 110.

Like the Twelve, Barnabas and Saul are now "sent ones"—apostles.[95] But their sending has not been without preparation. Barnabas has lived in the experience of the body of Christ for over fifteen years.[96] He was also mentored by the Twelve, who were mentored by Jesus. Saul has lived in the experience of the body of Christ in Antioch for two or three years, and he was mentored by Barnabas, who was mentored by the Twelve.[97] The other three men (Lucius, Simeon, and Manaen) lay hands on Barnabas and Saul (on behalf of the Antioch assembly) and send them off to the Lord's work[98]—which is to preach the gospel and establish kingdom communities.

95. Paul/Saul and Barnabas are called "apostles" in Acts 14:3-4, 14. (Barnabas is also called an apostle in 1 Corinthians 9:5-6.) James D.G. Dunn, *The Acts of the Apostles*, 190. The two men became apostles when they were sent out by the ekklesia in Antioch. The Greek word *apostolos* means "a sent one." The word is derived from the verb "to send out" (*apostellein*). John Barry, et al., "Apostle," *The Lexham Bible Dictionary*. Planting ekklesias was the function of an apostle in the first century. Richard Plummer, et al., *Paul's Missionary Methods*, 161; Robert Banks, *Paul's Idea of Community*, chap.16; Watchman Nee, *The Normal Christian Church Life*, chaps. 6-7; Frank Viola, *Finding Organic Church*, chaps. 1-4. For a list drawn from the New Testament where Paul speaks of himself as an apostle, as well as other designations indicating his divine calling, see James D.G. Dunn, *Beginning from Jerusalem*, 522-523. For details on Paul's self-identity as a follower of Christ and an apostle, see James D.G. Dunn, *Jesus, Paul, and the Gospels*, chaps. 6-7. Paul saw himself as a royal emissary to declare Jesus as Lord of the world, which meant Caesar was not. N.T. Wright, *Paul: In Fresh Perspective*, 161-163. Apostles were often prophets, teachers, and evangelists also. Paul, for instance, described himself as an apostle, preacher, and teacher (1 Timothy 2:7; 2 Timothy 1:11).

96. We know that Barnabas was part of the church in Jerusalem in A.D. 30 or 31. (He first appears in Acts 4:36.) Around A.D. 41, he went to Antioch of Syria, so he would have had around ten years of body life in Jerusalem and around seven years of body life in Antioch before he was sent out.

97. For a discussion of how God raises up and sends apostolic workers to plant kingdom communities, including biblical support for the arguments, see my book *Finding Organic Church*, chaps. 1-3.

98. Acts 13:2-4. In the New Testament, the term "work" refers to the apostolic ministry of founding kingdom communities, while the word "church" (ekklesia) refers to local kingdom communities. For a discussion on the difference between the "work" and the "church," see my book *Finding Organic Church*, chap. 2; Robert Banks, *Paul's Idea of Community*, chap.16; Watchman Nee, *The Normal Christian Church Life*, chaps. 6-7. For a discussion on the term "worker" as it is used in the New Testament, see Eckhard Schnabel, *Paul the Missionary*, 249. The sending of Paul and Barnabas not only reflected their apostolic calling and work, but it may have included the idea that the church paid their traveling fare. Craig Keener, "Lessons on Acts," Session 21.

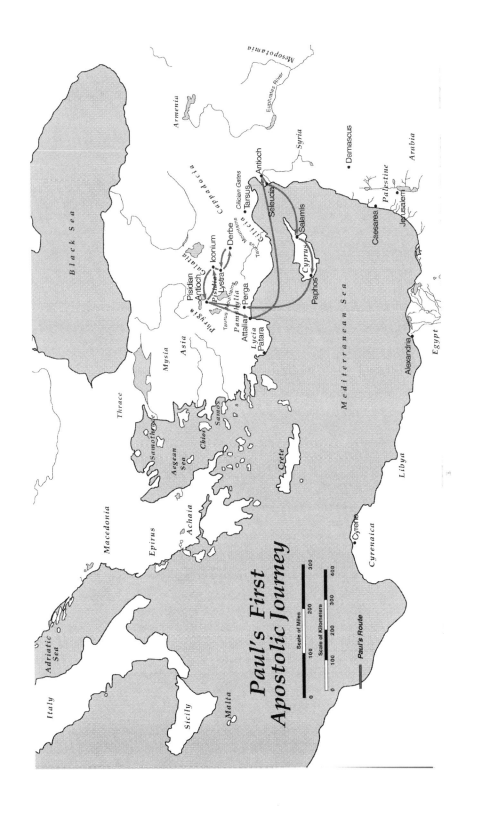

Paul's First Apostolic Journey

CHAPTER 9

THE GALATIAN CHRONICLE

A.D. 47 – A.D. 50

But they, passing on from Perga, came to Antioch of Pisidia. They went into the synagogue on the Sabbath day, and sat down. After the reading of the law and the prophets, the rulers of the synagogue sent to them, saying, "Brothers, if you have any word of exhortation for the people, speak." Paul stood up, and beckoning with his hand said, "Men of Israel, and you who fear God, listen." (Acts 13:14-16)

PREVIEW OF PAUL'S FIRST APOSTOLIC JOURNEY[1]

Duration: Two years

Dates: A.D. 47-49[2]

1. The term "apostolic journey" is preferred over the oft-repeated "missionary journey." The phrase "missionary journey" seems to find its origin in the nineteenth-century German commentaries on Paul, and it was probably influenced by the rise of world missionary work in the eighteenth and nineteenth centuries. The old commentaries by Adolf Schlatter confirm this. Paul was not engaging in "missionary" activity where the goal was leading individual souls to faith and repentance. Rather, Paul was seeking to raise up kingdom communities to fulfill God's eternal purpose. His journeys, then, were church planting trips. Again, apostles were sent out to preach the gospel of the kingdom and raise up ekklesias; hence, "apostolic journey" is more accurate to describe this work. Some scholars estimate that Paul traveled 1,400 miles on this first apostolic trip. Rose Publishing, *Rose Chronological Guide to the Bible* (Peabody, MA: Rose Publishing, 2019), 153.

2. The majority of this journey took place in A.D. 47 and 48. F.F. Bruce, *The Defense of the Gospel in the New Testament*, 70-71; *Paul: Apostle of the Heart Set Free*, 475; John A.T. Robinson, *Redating the New Testament*, 52. Witherington believes much of it took place in A.D. 48. Ben Witherington III, *The Acts of the Apostles*, 83.

Kingdom Communities Planted: (4) Pisidian Antioch, Iconium, Lystra, and Derbe[3]

Time Planting:

Pisidian Antioch = Three to six months

Iconium = Three to six months

Lystra = One to three months

Derbe = One to three months

Barnabas and Saul leave Antioch of Syria and head west. Barnabas takes the lead role,[4] and Mark comes along as their attendant.[5] He carries luggage and other necessary items, but he's more than a "grunt worker." Mark is an eyewitness to the events leading up to the death of Jesus, an experience that proves useful in proclaiming the gospel.[6] The three men head to Antioch's port city, Seleucia, sixteen miles from Antioch.[7] From there, they sail off to the small island of Cyprus (sixty-two miles offshore from Antioch of Syria).[8]

3. For a highly detailed treatment of Paul's first apostolic journey, see Craig Keener, *Acts*, 2:1980-2191; William Ramsay, *St. Paul the Traveler and Roman Citizen*, chap. 4; W.J. Conybeare and J.S. Howson, *The Life & Epistles of St. Paul*, 108-180.

4. Before Acts 13:7, Luke lists the pair as "Barnabas and Saul," which indicates Barnabas was in the lead. F.F. Bruce, *The Pauline Circle*, 18-19; N.T. Wright, *Paul: A Biography*, 115.

5. Acts 13:5. I believe Mark was young. The reference to a "young man" in Mark 14:51-52 is probably John Mark himself. This was a common view held by the church fathers. William Lane, *The Gospel According to Mark*, NICNT (Grand Rapids, MI: Eerdmans, 1974), 528. Weima rightly observes that "there is a parallel in the personnel of the first two journeys: Barnabas and Saul are the two 'senior' members of the team, while John Mark is the 'junior' member. Later Paul and Silas will be the two 'senior' members, while Timothy will be the 'junior' member." Personal correspondence with Jeffrey Weima, 12/28/23.

6. Ben Witherington III, *The New Testament Story*, 77. Bandy observes, "It's likely that as a child Mark would have seen and heard Jesus during his earthly ministry. As an eyewitness, Mark would have been an important addition to the ministry team in providing firsthand accounts about Jesus. Another likely reason Mark joined the team was because he and Barnabas were cousins (Col. 4:10)." Alan Bandy, *An Illustrated Guide to the Apostle Paul*, 50. See also N.T. Wright, *Mark for Everyone* (Louisville, KY: Westminster John Knox Press, 2004), 200; Richard Bauckham, *Jesus and the Eyewitnesses*, 198-199.

7. Acts 13:4. Ben Witherington III, *The Acts of the Apostles*, 394. Seleucia was only five miles from the mouth of the Orontes River. Clinton Arnold, ed., *Zondervan Illustrated Bible Backgrounds Commentary*, 2b:118.

8. Barry Beitzel, *Lexham Geographic Commentary on Acts through Revelation*, 299. Bandy believes this took place in mid-to-late summer of A.D. 46. Alan Bandy, *An Illustrated Guide to the Apostle Paul*, 59. Cyprus was a

Cyprus belongs to the province of Cilicia.[9] The principal export is copper from which it derives its name.[10] Cyprus is the third largest island in the Mediterranean. The island is 138 miles long, sixty miles wide.[11] It is made up mostly of Greeks, but it also contains a large Jewish population. Cyprus is full of beauty,[12] and it is Barnabas' native land. (He probably still has family there.[13])

A Visit to Cyprus
A.D. 47[14]

Barnabas, Saul, and Mark come by ship to a model Roman city in east Cyprus called Salamis, home to a large Jewish community with several synagogues.[15] Salamis is the chief city of Cyprus.[16] Barnabas and Saul quickly begin preaching the jaw-dropping gospel of the kingdom in the synagogues.[17] This pattern will become a common practice for Saul/

Roman province during the first century, and there were Greeks, Romans, and some Jewish colonies living in the cities as well as in small settlements. Personal correspondence with Eckhard Schnabel, 8/25/23.

9. The Roman Empire was divided up into provinces, which were administrative districts. The provinces were either imperial or senatorial. Cyprus was senatorial while Cilicia was imperial. For details, see Gary Burge, et al., *The New Testament in Antiquity*, 97.

10. Barnabas possibly sold a field containing copper when he pooled his money to help the Jerusalem assembly years earlier.

11. It is also 3,571 square miles. Joel Green, et al., *The World of the New Testament*, 498-499.

12. Mark Fairchild, "The Last Apostle," documentary film.

13. N.T. Wright, *Paul: A Biography*, 113. According to Fairchild, John Mark was also a native Cyprian. Mark Fairchild, "The Last Apostle," documentary film. Since Mark was a cousin of Barnabas, Mark may well have come from Cyprus too. Personal correspondence with Jeffrey Weima, 12/28/23.

14. According to Bruce, the trip to Cyprus and much of Galatia occurred between A.D. 47-48. F.F. Bruce, *Paul: Apostle of the Heart Set Free*, 475.

15. Acts 13:5. See also Craig Keener, et al., *Journeys of the Apostle Paul*, 32; Ben Witherington III, *The Acts of the Apostles*, 395; W.J. Conybeare and J.S. Howson, *The Life & Epistles of St. Paul*, 111; Mark Fairchild, "The Last Apostle," documentary film. According to Keener, Salamis had an estimated population of over 100,000. (Its theater seated 15,000.) Craig Keener, *The IVP Bible Background Commentary: New Testament*, 358.

16. It was also a port city, perhaps sixty miles from Seleucia. Craig Keener, *The IVP Bible Background Commentary: New Testament*, 358.

17. Synagogue members customarily invited visiting rabbis to read Scripture and provide instruction. Alan Bandy, *An Illustrated Guide to the Apostle Paul*, 55. The earliest look at synagogue worship comes from Philo of Alexandria. Some synagogues met in homes, while others gathered in buildings designed for worship.

Paul. He will proclaim the gospel to the Jews first and afterward bring his message to the Gentiles. (Saul/Paul will also be persecuted by the Jews in virtually every city he enters.[18])

For I am not ashamed of the gospel, because it is the power of God that brings salvation to everyone who believes: first to the Jew, then to the Gentile. (Romans 1:16, NIV)[19]

The men traverse the island from east to west, preaching in the synagogues. When they come to the west side of the island, they stop in a town called Paphos, the administrative capital of Cyprus.[20] There, Barnabas and Saul preach the gospel, but the synagogue leaders reject and punish them. The two apostles are tied to a pillar and whipped.[21] They receive the "forty less one" beating, which is horrific. The brutal beating they endure is one of five that Saul/Paul will receive from the Jews in the years to come.[22]

Synagogue worship included prayer, religious study, Scripture reading, and exposition. Ben Witherington III, *Letters and Homilies for Hellenized Christians*, 1:40.

18. This pattern will emerge as the story goes on. Schnabel argues that the motivational factors for the unbelieving Jews to oppose Paul were jealousy, fear of losing political influence, unbelief in his message, and pressure from Jews in other cities. See Eckhard Schnabel, *Early Christian Mission*, 2:1020-1023.

19. See also Romans 2:9-10.

20. Paphos is the political center of the island. Craig Keener, et al., *Journeys of the Apostle Paul*, 35. The distance between Salamis and Paphos was about 112 miles, which took seven days or more on foot. Barry Beitzel, *Lexham Geographic Commentary on Acts through Revelation*, 299-300. For details on Paphos, see Eckhard Schnabel, *Early Christian Mission*, 2:1082.

21. The "column of the flagellation of St. Paul" remains in the city as a testimony to the beating of the two men. A photo of the column appears in Craig Keener, et al., *Journeys of the Apostle Paul*, 37 (with a description on page 36). See also Otto F.A. Meinardus, *St. Paul in Ephesus*, 16-18. While this tradition cannot be proven, a number of scholars believe it is true, as do I.

22. The "forty stripes minus one" was the official punishment administered by Jews on fellow Jews in the synagogues. Rainer Riesner, *Paul's Early Period*, 149. There is no record of a synagogue lashing in the book of Acts, so the other four floggings probably took place during the "Levantine span of years" (Damascus, Arabia, Syria-Cilicia) from A.D. 34 to 47. Paul Barnett, *Paul: Missionary of Jesus*, 78ff., 198. Alan Bandy agrees. Personal correspondence with Bandy, 6/27/23. According to Mark Fairchild, "The whippings by the Jews could have been a result of Paul's ministry in the synagogues of Cilicia. There are a large number of Jewish tombs and evidence of as many as seven synagogues in Rough Cilicia. Some are located on the coast, but others are deeper into the interior, as far as Diocaesarea." Personal correspondence with Fairchild, 2/23/23. Craig Keener agrees, guessing that many of Paul's synagogue beatings took place in Tarsus. "Lessons on Acts," Session 18. See also John Stott, *The Message of Acts*, 204.

Five times I received forty stripes minus one from the Jews. (2 Corinthians 11:24)

As the men begin to recover, they run into a Jewish magician and false prophet named Bar-Jesus (also called Elymas, which is Semitic for "sorcerer"). Bar-Jesus is an attendant to the governor (proconsul) of Cyprus—Sergius Paulus. Sergius Paulus is an intelligent man, and he hears that Paul and Barnabas have been preaching a message they claim to be God's word. The governor is intrigued and invites the men to speak to him about their "religion."

As Barnabas and Saul share Christ with the governor, Bar-Jesus, who enjoys influence as Sergius' personal sorcerer, rudely interrupts them. In response, Saul gives Bar-Jesus a withering stare and rebukes him. Immediately, the hand of the living God falls upon the sorcerer, and Bar-Jesus is struck blind.[23] Sergius Paulus is mesmerized by Paul's message and impressed by the miraculous event. As a result, he becomes a believer.[24]

Then the proconsul, when he saw what was done, believed, being astonished at the teaching of the Lord. (Acts 13:12)

The proconsul becomes Barnabas and Saul's first recorded Gentile convert to Jesus. Saul falls ill.[25] Sergius Paulus has relatives in a land called Pisidia in the province of Galatia,[26] so he encourages Saul and Barnabas to visit Pisidia to receive medical help (from the proconsul's relatives). But he also wants him to share the gospel with his family.[27] Saul agrees, and the three men head due north toward Pisidia.

23. In his rebuke, Saul calls Bar-Jesus "Bar-Satan" (or "son of the devil"). Acts 13:10. Ben Witherington III, *The Acts of the Apostles*, 402.

24. Sergius Paulus was "astonished" at the teaching of the Lord because the power of God he witnessed confirmed that Jesus truly was the world's rightful Lord. N.T. Wright, *Paul: A Biography*, 115.

25. We can only speculate about what the illness was, but it wasn't debilitating since Paul continued to travel. At the same time, Paul's sickness was detectable by observers. Inferred from Galatians 4:13-14, NIV.

26. Acts 13:6-12. See Douglas Campbell, *Paul: An Apostle's Journey*, 43; Alan Bandy, *An Illustrated Guide to the Apostle Paul*, 59.

27. I credit David deSilva for this reconstruction which he shared with me over lunch on 8/22/22. The reconstruction is based on two facts: (1) In Galatians 4:13, Paul wrote that it was his illness that brought him to the region to preach, and (2) Sergius Paulus had relatives in Pisidia, the region where the two apostles went next. Witherington suggests that Sergius Paulus may have written a letter of recommendation to his family connections for Saul and Barnabas to receive aid. Ben Witherington III, *The Acts of the Apostles*, 403.

Sailing to Galatia

Saul, Barnabas, and Mark set sail on the Mediterranean Sea from Paphos (in Cyprus) to Perga (in Pamphylia),[28] a journey of about 186 miles.[29] The voyage from Paphos to Perga is treacherous. The seas are rough. Consequently, this journey might have been the occasion of one of Paul's shipwrecks.[30]

...Three times I suffered shipwreck.... (2 Corinthians 11:25)

Perga is a nearby port for travel to Pisidian Antioch.[31] It's a leading city in Asia Minor with a sizeable population[32] and the capital of the Roman province of Pamphylia.[33] The massive city contains a large stadium that seats up to 14,000, along with Roman baths, a large gymnasium, an agora (forum), water fountains, and three aqueducts.[34]

Keener agrees that this reconstruction is plausible. Craig Keener, "Lessons on Acts," Session 22. See also Alan Bandy, *An Illustrated Guide to the Apostle Paul*, 57; Eckhard Schnabel, *Early Christian Mission*, 2:1088.

28. Perga was located on the coastal road from Ephesus to Tarsus. It was the primary city of Pamphylia. F.F. Bruce, *Paul: Apostle of the Heart Set Free*, 162.

29. Barry Beitzel, *Lexham Geographic Commentary on Acts through Revelation*, 300. According to the same source, the distance the apostolic workers traveled by ship from Antioch of Syria to Perga was over 300 miles, which likely took four to ten days.

30. While the exact sea route and distance is not specified, they traveled north across the Mediterranean Sea to the city of Perga. It was probably somewhat longer than the 186 mile straight-line distance, perhaps around 200-250 sea miles, accounting for the need to follow coastlines and currents between the two regions. About ten years later, Paul will mention being involved in three shipwrecks (2 Corinthians 11:25). This doesn't count the shipwreck he experienced on his way to Rome, which occurred after 2 Corinthians was written. Luke mentions at least nine sea voyages and only one shipwreck, which occurred after Paul penned 2 Corinthians. So it's probable to assume that this was the location of one of the apostle's shipwrecks.

31. Like many cities in the ancient world, Perga was located not right on the coast, where it would have been vulnerable to attack by sea (especially from pirates), but inland a few miles, along a river on which goods could be transported from larger ships that docked on the coast. Personal correspondence with Jeffrey Weima, 12/28/23.

32. Clinton Arnold, ed., *Zondervan Illustrated Bible Backgrounds Commentary*, 2b:124.

33. Alan Bandy, *An Illustrated Guide to the Apostle Paul*, 59. According to Mark Wilson, Perga's status as Pamphylia's capital is now disputed due to its location in Galatia during Paul's era.

34. Clinton Arnold, ed., *Zondervan Illustrated Bible Backgrounds Commentary*, 2b:124. Perga was a beautiful city that trained artists and sculptors. Mark Fairchild, "The Last Apostle," documentary film. We aren't sure if the apostles preached the gospel in Perga at this time (Acts 13:13), but they would do so on their return

At this point, there is a shift in ministry priority. Saul takes the lead ahead of Barnabas.[35] He also begins using his Greco-Roman name "Paul" (*Paulus*) instead of his Jewish name "Saul."[36]

Sharpening the Focus: In the first century, passenger ships do not exist. A traveler must find a merchant sailing ship or cargo ship with space. The bigger the ship, the safer the travel. (The biggest ships are grain ships.) Sailing is dangerous but inexpensive.[37] Except for emergencies, no sailing is done during the winter months, due to the inclement weather.[38] From November 11 to March 10, the seas often become treacherous. March 11 to May 26 and September 15 to November 10 are hazardous, but still sailable. The prime time for sailing is May 27 to September 14.[39]

No matter what time of year, pagan sailors always wait for an omen from the gods before they set out to sea. A sacrifice is typically made beforehand, and the entrails of the animal are read to determine if sailing is favorable.[40] (The Alexandrian ship that Paul will later take to get to Rome will have the figureheads of the twin gods, Castor and Pollux, attached to it. The pagans believe these gods provide protection from storms, as in Acts 28:11.)

In the region Paul and Barnabas now travel, the Etesian winds can cause problems. The Etesian winds are prevailing northerly, monsoonal winds that appear sporadically in the summer and early fall. The winds flow into the Aegean Sea and into the eastern Mediterranean, from north to south, potentially creating a difficult headwind

---

(Acts 14:25). According to Bandy, when the men arrived in Perga, the Taurus Mountains were "shimmering in a haze from the oppressive summer heat." Alan Bandy, *An Illustrated Guide to the Apostle Paul*, 59.

35. From this point (Acts 13:13), Luke switches from writing "Barnabas and Saul" (Acts 11:26, 30; 12:25; 13:2, 7) to "Paul and Barnabas," indicating that Paul took the lead. F.F. Bruce, *The Pauline Circle*, 18-19. Before this point, Saul/Paul was Barnabas' junior partner. N.T. Wright, *Paul: A Biography*, 115.

36. F.F. Bruce explains Paul's three Roman names in *The Book of the Acts*, 249, n. 25.

37. Mark Fairchild, "The Last Apostle," documentary film.

38. Travel was difficult during the winter, not only by sea, but also by land. Craig Keener, *Acts*, 3:2310.

39. Craig Keener, et al., *NIV Cultural Backgrounds Study Bible*, 2095; Ben Witherington III, *A Week in the Fall of Jerusalem*, 65-66; F.F. Bruce, *The Book of the Acts*, 481; Rainer Riesner, *Paul's Early Period*, 308.

40. Sacrifices were ubiquitous in pagan temples throughout the Roman Empire. Bruce Longenecker, *In Stone and Story*, 65.

for a ship sailing due north. They are unpredictable and can become quite strong, creating an additional challenge.

After their sea travel to Perga, the men must cross over the massive Taurus Mountains to get to Pisidia, a journey of between 125 and 156 miles.[41] The ordinary rate of travel by foot in the first century is eighteen to twenty miles a day, shrinking to twelve to fifteen a day in mountains.[42] The journey from Perga to Pisidia takes about three weeks.[43] It's a dangerous trip, uphill all the way, over rough terrain.[44] The roads abound with robbers.[45] The rivers in this area are also known to overflow easily, causing many to drown.[46]

Travelers carry their possessions in knapsacks.[47] They risk kidnapping, robbery, health problems, and other dangers. Paul and Barnabas undoubtedly have to stop at the local inns on their journey. Inns are noted for their filthy sleeping quarters, adulterated wine, extortionate innkeepers, gamblers, thieves, and prostitutes. Not to mention their bug-infested beds.[48]

41. Craig Keener, *Acts*, 2:2035. Paul had to be in great shape to hike all the mountains he climbed on his travels, including the Taurus Mountains. Mark Fairchild, "The Last Apostle," documentary film.

42. Craig Keener, et al., *Journeys of the Apostle Paul*, 61. This was known as a "day's journey." Personal correspondence with Alan Bandy, 6/27/23. Other historians estimate twenty-five miles per day may be more likely. Clinton Arnold, ed., *Zondervan Illustrated Bible Backgrounds Commentary*, 2b:69. Roman soldiers could cover thirty-five miles in a day. Gary Burge, *A Week in the Life of a Roman Centurion*, 33. The optimum speed of a ship was one hundred miles per day. For more details on travel in the first century, see Craig Keener, *Acts*, 3:2376-2377.

43. Mark Fairchild, "The Last Apostle," documentary film. Bandy believes they traveled the Via Sebaste, so they were climbing in elevation, but they were not in the mountains the entire time. Personal correspondence with Alan Bandy, 12/6/23.

44. Craig Keener, "Lessons on Acts," Session 22.

45. Travel was among the most dangerous activities in the ancient world. For this reason, Jewish priests would pray and fast two days a week for a traveler's safety. Craig Keener, *The IVP Bible Background Commentary: New Testament*, 519. For dangers on the road during the first century, including inns, see Jerome Murphy-O'Connor, *Paul: His Story*, 49-52; W.J. Conybeare and J.S. Howson, *The Life & Epistles of St. Paul*, 129.

46. Otto F.A. Meinardus, *St. Paul in Ephesus*, 22.

47. Craig Keener, et al., *Journeys of the Apostle Paul*, 60-61; Ben Witherington III, *The Acts of the Apostles*, 636-641.

48. Craig Keener, "Lessons on Acts," Session 25. Inns and taverns often doubled as low-class brothels. Craig Keener, *The Gospel of Matthew*, 509. Inns were often spaced out, with a day's journey between each.

Well-to-do Romans avoid these inns at all costs. So do Jews (and Christians, later on) due to their bad reputations.[49] Jews who travel rely on the hospitality of friends who live in private homes.[50] Paul and Barnabas, most likely, do not have this luxury.[51] Their destination is Antioch of Pisidia, the "new Rome."[52] The city sits on the southern foothills of the Sultan Mountains,[53] 3,600 feet above sea level.[54] Like Rome, the city is spread over seven little hills and divided up into seven districts, each on one of the seven hills.[55] As a typical Roman colony, its architecture and governmental structure resemble Rome.[56] The temple to Augustus sits on the east end of the town square. The city also contains a bath house and a theater.[57] The city is relatively prosperous and is home to many senators and high-ranking Romans.[58]

The recent shipwreck, coupled with the threat of bandits who haunt the hazardous Taurus Mountains, greatly discourages Mark from continuing the journey.[59] In addition, Mark never

---

James D.G. Dunn, *Beginning from Jerusalem*, 517. For further details on inns in the first century, see Craig Keener, *Acts*, 3:2414-2416.

49. Roger Gehring, *House Church and Mission*, 183.

50. This will also be true for the Christians later on. Roger Gehring, *House Church and Mission*, 183.

51. They were forced to sleep in the open air at times. Personal correspondence with David deSilva, 1/18/24.

52. Pisidian Antioch has been called "the metropolis of Gentile Christianity, the new Rome, as it were, of the Christian world." H.D.M., Spence-Jones, ed., *Acts of the Apostles: Exposition and Homiletics* (New York, NY: Funk & Wagnalls Company, 1909), vol. 2, 96. See also Elaine Gazda and Diana Ng, eds., *Building a New Rome: The Imperial Colony of Pisidian Antioch, 25 BC - AD 700* (Ann Arbor, MI: Kelsey Museum of Archaeology, 2011).

53. For a visual sketch of ancient Pisidian Antioch, see Peter Walker, *In the Steps of Paul: An Illustrated Guide to the Apostle's Life and Journeys* (Grand Rapids, MI: Zondervan, 2008), 87-90.

54. Craig Keener, *Acts*, 2:2035; William Ramsay, *St. Paul the Traveler and Roman Citizen*, 89; Ben Witherington III, *The Acts of the Apostles*, 405.

55. Clyde Fant and Mitchell Reddish, *A Guide to Biblical Sites in Greece and Turkey*, 152.

56. N.T. Wright, *Paul: A Biography*, 117.

57. Craig Keener, *Acts*, 2:2039-2040.

58. Craig Keener, *Acts*, 2:2038.

59. Fairchild believes Paul originally intended to go to Rome on this first journey. But when the governor (Sergius Paulus) asked him to go to Pisidian Antioch, he changed his plans. This change of plans may be one of the reasons John Mark went back home. The Taurus Mountains were intimidating and very dangerous. The roads were loaded with former pirates who became thieves and robbers. Dangerous animals were also

anticipated the more extended trip into the high parts of Galatia where Paul and Barnabas are headed.[60] Years later, Paul will think back on this journey and pen these words:

I have been in travels often, perils of rivers, perils of robbers.... (2 Corinthians 11:26)

Mark may also be troubled that Paul is now the leader of the apostolic mission with his cousin taking second place.[61] All of this causes Mark to become homesick, so he heads back to Jerusalem. Paul, however, views Mark's departure as unfaithful abandonment.[62] In addition to all these setbacks, Paul is still sick.[63]

A Kingdom Community Is Planted in Antioch of Pisidia A.D. 47 – 48[64]

When Paul and Barnabas arrive in the region of Pisidia,[65] they stop at a Roman colony called Antioch of Pisidia.[66]

present. John Mark may have felt this was far beyond what he signed up for. Mark Fairchild, "The Last Apostle," documentary film. Scholars have offered other reasons as well, such as the concern that Mark may have heard about the effect that a ministry to the Gentiles would have on the Jerusalem church. Richard Longenecker, *The Ministry and Message of Paul*, 43; Mark Wilson, *Biblical Turkey*, 96.

60. F.F. Bruce, *Paul: Apostle of the Heart Set Free*, 163. The large Roman province of Galatia included Pisidian Antioch, Derbe, Lystra, and Iconium. Clinton Arnold, ed., *Zondervan Illustrated Bible Backgrounds Commentary*, 2b:126.

61. See F.F. Bruce, *The Pauline Circle*, 18-19; J.D. Douglas, et al., eds., *New Bible Dictionary*, 125; Roland Allen, *Missionary Methods: St. Paul's or Ours?* (Grand Rapids, MI: Eerdmans, 1962), 10. In previous notes, I explained that the ordering of their names in Luke's account is significant and implies priority. "That Barnabas was Paul's senior partner in the relationship is evident from the fact that Barnabas' name is mentioned before Paul's name in all Acts accounts thus far [before Acts 13]...." Jon Daniels, "Barnabas" (Person) in D.N. Freedman, ed., *The Anchor Yale Bible Dictionary*.

62. Acts 13:13; 15:37-38.

63. Ramsay suggests that Paul contracted malaria in Pamphylia and sought relief in the highland region, bringing him to Galatia. William Ramsay, *St. Paul the Traveler and Roman Citizen*, 88-90. I disagree with Ramsay that malaria was Paul's thorn in the flesh, but it's possible he did contract the illness at this time.

64. F.F. Bruce, *Paul: Apostle of the Heart Set Free*, 475.

65. Pisidia is known for its rugged and independent warrior traditions. The warrior gods were prominent there. Craig Keener, *Acts*, 2:2033.

66. Antioch of Pisidia is not to be confused with Antioch of Syria. It literally means "Antioch near Pisidia," and it's actually in Phrgyia. Alan Bandy, *An Illustrated Guide to the Apostle Paul*, 62.

Sharpening the Focus: The Romans divided the political province of South Galatia into the following regions: Pisidia, Lycaonia, and Phrygia.[67] Antioch of Pisidia is located in what is today west central Turkey.[68] It's a Roman colony belonging to Phrygia, rather than to Pisidia. (Its technical name is "Antioch-near-Pisidia."[69])

The population is around 10,000,[70] and the city is adorned with buildings. The most prominent feature in the city is a great temple dedicated to Augustus and Roma, with a large courtyard surrounded by porticoes and a monumental entryway. A long list of Augustus's achievements, known as the "Deeds of the Divine Augustus," is engraved on the walls of the propylon (monumental gateway) of the temple of Augustus and Roma.[71]

Pisidian Antioch is the civil and administrative center of the Galatian province. The intellectual section of the city is Greek, while most of the population is Phrygian.[72] The Phrygians are a nonviolent (and unwarlike) people who have been subject to other races for centuries. Greek, as well as Phrygian, is spoken in Pisidian Antioch. A well-established minority of Jews live there, but it is not large, since it appears there is only one synagogue in the city.[73]

67. Although scholars often refer to "South Galatia" (versus "North Galatia"), these are not the official names of the Roman province. It was simply called "Galatia" in the first century. Therefore, I will use "Galatia" from here onward in the main text to describe this region.

68. For details on Galatia and the Galatians, see Colin Hemer, *The Book of Acts in the Setting of Hellenistic History*, chap. 7.

69. Craig Keener, "Lessons on Acts," Session 22.

70. Based on the demographic studies of Andrew Wilson and J.W. Hansen, Mark Wilson estimates the urban population (excluding the chora) of Pisidian Antioch to be 10,000. Personal correspondence with Mark Wilson, 4/11/23. Keener says there were at least 5,000 Roman colonists in the city. Craig Keener, "Lessons on Acts," Session 22.

71. Personal correspondence with Jeffrey Weima, 12/28/23; personal correspondence with David deSilva, 1/18/24. The imperial cult had long existed in all major cities throughout the provinces of the Eastern Roman empire. Bruce Winter, *Seek the Welfare of the City*, 125; James D.G. Dunn, *Beginning from Jerusalem*, 550. For details on the emperor and the gods, see John Barclay, *Pauline Churches and Diaspora Jews*, 351-355.

72. For this reason, the region is called Phrygia and Galatia, or "Phrygian Galatia." Acts 16:6. Ben Witherington III, *The Acts of the Apostles*, 405. For details, see Craig Keener, *Acts*, 3:2324-2326.

73. Otto F.A. Meinardus, *St. Paul in Ephesus*, 23. Weima observes, "It only took ten males to form a synagogue, so there may well have been a number of synagogues in the city. Acts describes Paul and Barnabas

Antioch of Pisidia is nestled in a wide-open plain located in the foothills of a dangerously high mountain range. The two apostolic workers can see the mountains from a distance.[74] When they arrive in the city, they seek out the synagogue community. They are probably housed by a fellow Jew, instead of at an inn.[75] On the Sabbath, Paul and Barnabas visit the local synagogue and sit down on one of the stone benches along the walls.[76]

The synagogue audience is made up of Jews, proselytes, and God-fearers.[77] After the Law and the Prophets are read (which is customary in the synagogue service), there is a time for guests to give a word of exhortation.[78] Spotting that one of his visitors is a Pharisee,[79]

going to the main synagogue building where they are invited to speak and teach." Personal correspondence with Jeffrey Weima, 12/28/23.

74. Alan Bandy, *An Illustrated Guide to the Apostle Paul*, 62.

75. Craig Keener, *Acts*, 2:2045.

76. Acts 13:14. Synagogues generally had stone benches along two or three walls with rows of wooden benches in the middle. Clinton Arnold, ed., *Zondervan Illustrated Bible Backgrounds Commentary*, 2b:126. People of status and the elders sat on the benches around the synagogue walls. In less prosperous synagogues, people of lower status sat on the floors. Those invited to speak would sit in a seat of special honor, known as "Moses' seat" (Matthew 23:2). Craig Keener, *Acts*, 2:2044.

77. Jews were Israelites by birth. The males were circumcised on the eighth day after birth, which showed they had a covenant with God. Proselytes were Gentiles who converted to Judaism. The males were circumcised and ceremonially bathed. They offered a sacrifice and vowed to keep the Law of Moses. Proselytes had become complete Jews. As such, they were full members of the synagogue. God-fearers were Gentiles who followed the God of Israel, but they were not circumcised. Therefore, they were not full members of the synagogue. According to Schnabel, "Gentile proselytes would have kept the entire Law, while God-fearers would have believed in Yahweh and some perhaps kept a few laws allowing them to regularly attend the synagogue." Eckhard Schnabel, *Early Christian Mission*, 1:122; personal correspondence with Schnabel, 8/25/23; Bruce Winter, *Seek the Welfare of the City*, 136-137. Even though Judaism was tolerated in the Roman Empire, Roman officials often acted against Jews who openly proselytized Gentiles. David deSilva, *Paul and the Macedonians: The Life and Letters of Paul* (Nashville, TN: Abingdon Press, 2001), 19. For more on this topic, see Mark Fairchild's discussion on Paul, God-fearers, and Judaizers in *Christian Origins in Ephesus & Asia Minor*, second edition (Peabody, MA: Hendrickson, 2017), 50-52.

78. For details on the synagogue service (liturgy), see Ernest De Witt Burton, "The Ancient Synagogue Service," *The Biblical World* 8, no. 2 (1896): 143-148; Fr. Silouan Thompson, "First-Century Christian Synagogue Liturgy," published in SILOUAN, September 15, 2007.

79. The prayer shawl was an identifiable mark that Paul was a Pharisee. Ben Witherington III, *Invitation to the New Testament*, 24. Pharisees also wore long robes with lengthy tassels and sported wide leather boxes (*tefillin*) that had some of the commandments inside, as Moses commanded for male Jews (Matthew 23:5, NLT). N.T. Wright, *Paul: A Biography*, 27. The *tefillin* (or phylacteries) were worn on the forehead and arm (literally, "hand"). Exodus 13:9, 16; Deuteronomy 6:8 (NIV). I believe Paul wore his Pharisaical "garb" when

the synagogue ruler[80] asks Paul if he would like to address the congregation. The apostle stands up and introduces himself as a student of the great teacher Gamaliel. With this remark, Paul gains his audience's full attention.[81]

Paul launches into the story of Israel.[82] Following his narrative, he quotes the Psalms and Isaiah and then drops a bombshell. He announces that the long-awaited Messiah, the new David, has arrived! His name is Jesus, and the Jerusalem leaders had Him executed. But God raised Him from the dead. Paul ends his stirring message by quoting a warning from the prophet Habakkuk.

Paul's shocking announcement that the promised Messiah has come holds everyone spellbound. His message also contains similarities with the message Stephen delivered the day he was stoned.[83] (Paul likely heard Stephen's message firsthand and remembered it,[84] so perhaps this was his way of honoring him.) When the apostle finishes, the audience is

---

he visited the synagogues because it gave him instant clout with his audience. According to Witherington, there were few (if any) Pharisees in the Diaspora, since they existed in Israel and were connected to the temple. Personal correspondence with Ben Witherington III, 6/24/22. Since this was likely the case, the Jews in the synagogue would immediately recognize that Paul was from Judea (and thus, he knew the Scriptures well). The Jews in the Diaspora visited Jerusalem every year, so they could recognize a Pharisee. For Paul, wearing the Pharisaical "garb" was for witness (1 Corinthians 9:20). We see how Paul referenced his training under Gamaliel in Acts 22:3 as he spoke to a Jewish audience. Meinardus says Paul entered the synagogue wearing the tallit, the garment worn by Jews at prayer. Perhaps Barnabas did also. Otto F.A. Meinardus, *St. Paul in Ephesus*, 26. Paul likely wore a basic tunic, and in the winter, probably a robe on top of it. He likely traveled with a prayer shawl, much like Jesus did in the story of the woman with the flow of blood. He would need it when offering prayer, covering his head in the process. Personal correspondence with Ben Witherington III, 8/19/21. Keener speculates that Pharisees may have worn the *tzitzit*, since it was commanded in Numbers 15:38. Personal correspondence with Craig Keener, 1/8/19.

80. The synagogue ruler was called the *archisynagogos*.

81. Once Paul mentioned that he was from Judea and was trained by the renowned teacher Gamaliel, he would have had instant respect in the synagogue. It would be like having an Ivy League graduate speak at a rural school. Jeffrey Weima, *1-2 Thessalonians*, 27.

82. The message found in Acts 13:16-41 is the longest recording of the kind of message Paul typically preached to a predominantly Jewish audience. The key ideas in it were undoubtedly repeated many times throughout the rest of Paul's apostolic activity when he preached in the synagogues, even though Luke doesn't repeat Paul's full messages elsewhere. Personal correspondence with Jeffrey Weima, 12/28/23.

83. Compare Acts 7:2-53 with Acts 13:16-41. The main points in the narrative are repeated in both messages. The main difference is that Stephen didn't get to the arrival of Jesus in his talk, while Paul did.

84. Ben Witherington III, *The Acts of the Apostles*, 265.

electrified, and they beg Paul to continue preaching the next Sabbath. Many of the Jews and proselytes follow Paul and Barnabas out of the synagogue, pelting them with questions. The two apostolic workers urge those who've trusted in Jesus to persevere in God's grace.[85]

News about Paul's earthshaking message spreads throughout the city. When the next Sabbath arrives, a large percentage of the city pours into the synagogue to hear Paul preach.[86] The favorable response and large crowd incite the Jewish leaders to jealousy. In their envy, they begin to contradict Paul while he speaks. They even revile and slander him.[87] They also attempt to discount his message by pointing out that he is sick.[88] (In the mind of an ancient Jew, illness is a visible sign that God's hand is against a person.[89])

but you know that because of weakness in the flesh I preached the Good News to you the first time. That which was a temptation to you in my flesh, you didn't despise nor reject; but you received me as an angel of God, even as Christ Jesus. (Galatians 4:13-14)

Paul and Barnabas leave the synagogue and begin preaching the gospel to the Gentiles. The Gentiles receive Paul as a messenger of God, despite his sickness.[90] Many of them believe his message and put their faith in Jesus.[91] The high-voltage gospel the two

85. The narrative you just read is based on Acts 13:13-43. See also N.T. Wright, *Paul: A Biography*, 118. Respected rabbis in the Diaspora *stood* when they spoke in the synagogue, while rabbis in Judea *sat* while they spoke. Craig Keener, "Lessons on Acts," Session 23. According to Keener, in Luke 4:16ff., Jesus stood to read, but then sat to teach. Personal correspondence with Craig Keener, 3/18/24. Most synagogues could afford a few scrolls. Some could even afford one from each section of the Hebrew canon, but it's likely there were entire books of the Hebrew Scriptures in the Judean temple. The common experience of having a complete Bible is a modern invention. Joel Green, et al., *The World of the New Testament*, 355.

86. Luke's wording conveys a large number. "The next Sabbath almost the whole city gathered to hear the word of the Lord" (Acts 13:44, ESV). The synagogue must have been packed solid.

87. Acts 13:45, NLT and ESV.

88. From Galatians 4:13, we know that Paul was ill. It's likely his audience knew and some held it against him.

89. Sickness, as well as loss of wealth and misery, were regarded as signs of divine wrath. Max Weber, *Ancient Judaism* (London: George Allen and Unwin, 1952), 370. The belief that sickness was a sign of God's judgment was held among both Jews and Gentiles. Craig Keener, *The IVP Bible Background Commentary: New Testament*, 534.

90. Galatians 4:13-14.

91. Faith is trusting allegiance to the new ruler, King Jesus. The faith that justifies a person is a "believing loyalty which upstages that demanded by Caesar." N.T. Wright, *Pauline Perspectives*, 247. Paul didn't see his

apostles proclaim quickly spreads throughout the region. In a few months' time, the local Jewish leaders go to the Gentile civic authorities and stir up the God-fearing women of high standing and the leading men against the two apostolic workers.[92] As a result, Paul and Barnabas are legally banished from the district.[93] And as part of the formal banishing process, they are beaten with birch rods.[94]

Three times I was beaten with rods…. (2 Corinthians 11:25)

Following the instructions Jesus gave to the Twelve, the two men shake the dust off their feet and leave the city.[95] Yet when Paul and Barnabas depart, they leave behind a kingdom community—an assembly of God's people in Pisidian Antioch, called to bear God's image and exercise His authority. This kingdom community is mostly Gentile. It's an alternative family made up of spiritual brothers, sisters, fathers, mothers, and children, both Gentile and Jew.[96] The new converts are filled with joy and with the Holy Spirit.[97]

---

gospel as a set of ideas or the promise of an emotional experience. Instead, he saw it as the vehicle by which the living God would capture hearts to give their total allegiance to Jesus. When people exercised faith in Paul's gospel, they would become part of a shared-life community of love where members laid their lives down for one another and were willing to sacrifice themselves for their Lord, Jesus Christ. N.T. Wright, *Paul for Everyone: Galatians and Thessalonians,* 140.

92. Acts 13:50, NIV. For details on this text, see Craig Keener, *The IVP Bible Background Commentary: New Testament,* 361. The leading men of the city may have been Roman magistrates. Ben Witherington III, *The Acts of the Apostles,* 417.

93. They were forced to leave the district, expelled from Pisidian Antioch. Eckhard Schnabel, *Acts,* 590.

94. This scenario is plausible. A beating with rods was sometimes part of the process in expelling a person from a Roman city. Given the timeline, the options for Paul's three beatings (2 Corinthians 11:25; 6:5) could have taken place in Pisidian Antioch, Lystra, or Troas, beyond the beating in Philippi (which comes later in our story). Since they were all Roman colonies, those options are likely. For this reason, following Ramsay, I've concluded that one of these beatings occurred in Antioch of Pisidia. William Ramsay, *St. Paul the Traveler and Roman Citizen,* 97. Corinth was an unlikely option. See Craig Keener, *Acts,* 3:2482. More on this later.

95. Acts 13:51.

96. Family is the dominating metaphor throughout the New Testament. Frank Viola, *Reimagining Church,* chap. 5. In Paul's letters, "brothers/sisters" is used 139 times, "father" is used sixty-three times, "sons" is used seventeen times, and "child" is used thirty-nine times. Joseph Hellerman, *When the Church Was a Family,* 77. For details on how the ekklesias Paul raised up operated as alternative families, see Joseph Hellerman, *The Ancient Church as Family,* chap. 4.

97. Acts 13:52.

A Kingdom Community Established in Iconium

As the blood dries on their backs, Paul and Barnabas journey ninety-three miles southeast[98] to the frontier town of Iconium. The two men take the Roman military road called the Via Sebaste, a road that will later lead them to the towns of Lystra and Derbe.[99] Iconium is a Greek city[100] where Phrygian and Greek are spoken.[101] It's located on the northwest edge of a fertile and high platcau, 3,770 feet above sea level.[102]

As is their custom, Paul and Barnabas visit the synagogue and preach Christ boldly with utter dependence on the Holy Spirit.[103] Their message is so effective that many believe in Jesus, both Jews and God-fearers. The gospel of grace[104] they boldly preach is confirmed by signs and wonders.[105] The apostolic workers spend considerable time in the city, raising up a new kingdom community.[106]

98. F.F. Bruce, *The Book of the Acts*, 268. Keener says this was probably a four-day walk. Craig Keener, "Lessons on Acts," Session 23.

99. The Via Sebaste was built under Augustus in 6 B.C. It connected six military colonies, including Antioch of Pisidia. Douglas Campbell, *Paul: An Apostle's Journey*, 42.

100. The city became part of the empire in 25 B.C., and it received the name "Claudiconium" from Claudius. F.F. Bruce, *The Book of the Acts*, 268-269.

101. According to Keener, the people of Iconium didn't understand Greek very well, so the two apostles may have used an interpreter. Craig Keener, "Lessons on Acts," Session 23.

102. Alan Bandy, *An Illustrated Guide to the Apostle Paul*, 65. There is very little that can be seen of the ancient city of Iconium today, so nobody can give an educated guess on the population. Fairchild estimates (wildly) that the population of Iconium was between 5,000 to 10,000. Personal correspondence with Mark Fairchild, 8/23/23. Wilson estimates perhaps 20,000 to 25,000. Personal correspondence with Mark Wilson, 8/4/23. "Iconium was the most important assize center in western Lycaonia." Personal correspondence with Eckhard Schnabel, 8/25/23. (An "assize" was the regular tour of a Roman magistrate/proconsul who visited the most important cities/towns in his province to hold court and administer justice.)

103. The message of the gospel of the kingdom is the same as preaching Christ, the King. Compare Acts 8:4-5 with 8:12; Acts 17:2-3 with 17:7. In Acts 28:31 (NIV), proclaiming the kingdom and the Lord Jesus Christ are mentioned together.

104. The message of the kingdom is also called "the gospel of grace." For an explanation, see Frank Viola, *Insurgence*, 37-40.

105. Acts 14:3. Throughout Acts, miracles in Paul's ministry are only recorded in five towns in four provinces. Roland Allen, *Missionary Methods*, 41-48. However, we know Paul did miracles in Corinth according to 2 Corinthians 12:12, even though they aren't mentioned in Acts. See also Romans 15:18-19.

106. Acts 14:3.

Unfortunately, the unbelieving Jewish leaders in Iconium replay the reaction of those in Pisidian Antioch. Jealous and agitated, they begin poisoning the minds of the people and dissuade them from heeding the two apostles. As a result, the city is bitterly divided. Some side with the Jewish leaders while others side with Paul and Barnabas. Some of the Jewish leaders, Gentiles, and city rulers hatch a plot to stone the two men.

When Paul and Barnabas get wind of the news, they leave the city, barely escaping the mob violence.[107] But as they depart Iconium, they leave behind a kingdom community—the body of Jesus Christ that expresses God's image and authority.[108] The two men head toward the Lycaonian cities of Lystra and Derbe, as well as the surrounding countryside.[109] There they continue preaching the heart-transforming gospel of the kingdom.

A Kingdom Community Established in Lystra

Paul and Barnabas take the Via Sebaste twenty-one miles southwest to a Roman colony called Lystra.[110] It's a primitive town built on a small hill. The population is estimated at around 3,000.[111] The old Lycaonian language is still spoken here as well as Greek. Since Lystra is a Roman colony, the language of the courts and the Roman soldiers is Latin.[112] There is no synagogue, indicating there are hardly any Jews present. So Paul

107. Jesus taught His disciples that when your detractors persecute you in one town, flee to another (Matthew 10:23; Luke 9:5; 10:11). Paul would do this often.

108. Acts 14:1-7.

109. Paul's travels through Lycaonia may have also been fraught with "dangers from bandits" (2 Corinthians 11:26, NIV), including when they revisited the new assemblies and returned back to Syrian Antioch. James D.G. Dunn, *Beginning from Jerusalem*, 433, n. 90, and 516.

110. Barry Beitzel, *Lexham Geographic Commentary on Acts through Revelation*, 306. Lystra was made a Roman colony by Augustus in 25 B.C. According to Dunn, the journey from Iconium to Lystra took about six hours on foot. James D.G. Dunn, *The Acts of the Apostles*, 192. Lystra was an older town, a prosperous city and "sister" to Pisidian Antioch. Eckhard Schnabel, *Acts*, 605.

111. This estimate includes women and children. Mark Wilson, *Biblical Turkey*, 167. Witherington speculates that the population was larger, around 20,000. Personal correspondence with Ben Witherington III, 6/23/05.

112. Personal correspondence with Ben Witherington III, 2/12/04.

and Barnabas preach the gospel to the pagans in the city and begin raising up a kingdom community.[113]

Residents of Lystra are familiar with an old legend that the Greek gods Zeus and Hermes once visited the city.[114] As the story goes, the two gods appeared as homeless humans looking for a place to stay. After they were rejected by the town, an elderly couple took the gods into their home. The gods turned their modest house into a palace, and the palace became the temple of Zeus.[115]

At some point during his stay in Lystra, Paul heals a lame man who has been disabled from birth. After witnessing the miracle, the Lycaonians think Paul is Hermes (because he is the lead speaker) and Barnabas is Zeus.[116] They conclude the two gods have returned to Lystra! The priest of Zeus brings oxen and wreaths to the city gates. He intends to offer a sacrifice to the two apostles because he believes they are divine. When Paul and Barnabas figure out what's happening, they tear their clothes and run out among the crowd.[117] They tell the people they are mere mortals and command them to stop sacrificing to them. They also add this question:

Men, why are you doing these things? We also are men with the same nature as you, and preach to you that you should turn from these useless things to the living God, who made the

113. Luke greatly abridges his narrative, so we can only guess how long the apostles were in Lystra. But they were there long enough to make enough disciples to lay the foundation for an assembly (as the story will later reveal). See Craig Keener, *Acts*, 2:2176.

114. Hermes, whose Roman name was Mercury, was the clever messenger of the Greek gods. Zeus, whose Roman name was Jupiter, was the father of all the Greek gods as well as humans. For details, see Clinton Arnold, ed., *Zondervan Illustrated Bible Backgrounds Commentary*, 2b:134.

115. This is the story of Baucis and Philemon. The legend is found in Ovid, *Metamorphoses*, 8.616-724. According to Ovid, the names of the gods who visited the city were Jupiter and Mercury (the Roman equivalents of Zeus and Hermes). I. Howard Marshall, *Acts*, 237; F.F. Bruce, *The Book of the Acts*, 274; Craig Keener, et al., *Journeys of the Apostle Paul*, 44-45; James D.G. Dunn, *The Acts of the Apostles*, 190; John Byron, *A Week in the Life of a Slave*, 60.

116. It's also possible that they called Barnabas "Zeus" because he may have had a more impressive appearance than Paul or because he was the older of the two. James D.G. Dunn, *The Acts of the Apostles*, 190; Eckhard Schnabel, *Acts*, 607-608.

117. At first, Paul and Barnabas didn't understand what was happening because they didn't understand the Lycaonian language. F.F. Bruce, *Paul: Apostle of the Heart Set Free*, 169; Ben Witherington III, *The Acts of the Apostles*, 424. "It wasn't until they saw the bulls going to be offered in sacrifice to them that they responded." Personal correspondence with Alan Bandy, 12/6/23.

heaven, the earth, the sea, and all things that are in them, who in bygone generations allowed all nations to walk in their own ways. (Acts 14:15-16, NKJV)

Despite their attempts, Paul and Barnabas fail to persuade the Lycaonians to stop sacrificing to them. Not long after, the Jewish leaders from Pisidian Antioch and Iconium descend on the city and incite the crowds against Paul and Barnabas. In a head-snapping turn of events, the Lycaonians suddenly turn on the two men. They stone Paul and drag him out of the city, leaving him for dead.[118]

...Once I was stoned.... (2 Corinthians 11:25)

A young man named Timothy (also called Timotheus) watches the drama unfold.[119] He, along with his mother Eunice and his grandmother Lois, have been converted under Paul's preaching.[120] They all live in Lystra.[121] Timothy is probably in his late teens.[122] Lois and Eunice are Jews, but Timothy's father is Greek.[123] From his childhood, Timothy has learned the Hebrew Scriptures.[124]

The believers in Lystra gather around Paul, and he miraculously rises up healed. The stoning, however, leaves wounds on his body that will turn into permanent scars. Paul will

118. For details, see Alan Bandy, *An Illustrated Guide to the Apostle Paul*, 68.

119. In 2 Timothy, Paul confirms that Timothy was likely present during this dramatic event. "You, however, have observed...my persecutions, and the sufferings that came upon me in Antioch, Iconium, and Lystra." 2 Timothy 3:10-11, BSB.

120. 2 Timothy 1:5. It appears that Paul converted all of them to Christ. Ben Witherington III, *The Acts of the Apostles*, 474, n. 15. It's likely that Timothy's mother married a Roman citizen in the colony. Mark Wilson, *Biblical Turkey*, 168.

121. Timothy was a native of Lystra in South Galatia. Douglas Moo, *Epistle to the Romans*, 934. The remarks about Timothy in this chapter and those to come are expanded in more detail in F.F. Bruce's *The Pauline Circle*, 29-34; Ben Witherington III, *Paul's Letter to the Philippians: A Socio-Rhetorical Commentary* (Grand Rapids, MI: Eerdmans, 2011), 43-45.

122. This is the opinion of several scholars. David deSilva thinks Timothy was close to twenty during this time. Personal correspondence with deSilva, 10/15/22. Witherington agrees, suggesting that Timothy was probably in his teens when he first met Paul and around twenty when Paul came through Lystra the second time. Personal correspondence with Ben Witherington III, 10/18/22.

123. Acts 16:1-3. Judeans treated intermarriage with Gentiles as an invitation for God's wrath. Craig Keener, "Lessons on Acts," Session 24.

124. 2 Timothy 3:15. Timothy's parents were wealthy enough to secure some scrolls of the Scriptures that his mother utilized to teach him. James D.G. Dunn, *Beginning from Jerusalem*, 663-664, n. 22.

regard these scars, together with the many lesions on his back, as trophies signifying that he was privileged to suffer for His Master Jesus in his physical body.[125]

...for I bear the marks of the Lord Jesus branded on my body. (Galatians 6:17)[126]

Paul and Barnabas walk back into the city to retrieve their belongings. The next day they make their exit, but they leave behind a community of Jesus-followers who are part of the kingdom of God.[127] The body of Jesus Christ is alive in the city of Lystra!

A Kingdom Community Raised Up in Derbe

Making their exit from Lystra, the two apostles head eighty-six miles southeast to a tiny frontier town called Derbe.[128] In Derbe, they begin preaching the gospel of Christ, and many disciples are made.[129] One of them is a man named Gaius.[130]

125. The marks on Paul's body were similar to the branding marks that masters put on their slaves. This is probably how Paul viewed them. F.F. Bruce, *Paul: Apostle of the Heart Set Free*, 171. The marks were incurred from his sufferings. N.T. Wright, *Paul: A Biography*, 124; John Stott, *The Message of Galatians: Only One Way* (Downers Grove, IL: InterVarsity Press, 1968), 182.

126. The Greek word for "bear" in this text is the same term used when Jesus carried His cross (John 19:17) and also in His exhortation for His followers to bear their crosses daily (Luke 14:27). Thomas Schreiner, *Paul, Apostle of God's Glory in Christ*, 97.

127. Acts 14:8-20.

128. Barry Beitzel, *Lexham Geographic Commentary on Acts through Revelation*, 306. Accounting for rest stops, terrain, and less than ideal road conditions, a realistic estimate for the travel time from Lystra to Derbe would have been four to six days of walking. The population of Derbe was less than 30,000. Personal correspondence with Ben Witherington III, 6/23/05; Craig Keener, *The IVP Bible Background Commentary: New Testament*, 364.

129. We don't know how long Paul was in Derbe as Luke abridges the story in one verse (Acts 14:21). But in order to have "made many disciples" and lay the foundation for a new assembly, he must have been in the town for at least a month. Also, Derbe wouldn't have been a natural place to preach the gospel and raise up a church. Wilson thinks someone heard Paul's preaching and invited him to Derbe. It would have also been a safe place to recover from the stoning he endured in Lystra. Personal correspondence with Mark Wilson, 9/4/23. For further details on Paul's time in Derbe, see Alan Bandy, *An Illustrated Guide to the Apostle Paul*, 69. If a synagogue was in Derbe, Paul undoubtedly preached there. But little is known about Derbe; it is only now being excavated. Personal correspondence with Mark Fairchild, 8/4/23.

130. Acts 20:4.

There is now an assembly—a kingdom community—in Derbe, bearing witness to God's kingdom.[131]

When Paul and Barnabas raised up the four churches in Galatia, they taught the new believers a number of things beyond the call to repent and believe the gospel. The two apostles demonstrated dramatically the crucifixion of Jesus.[132] They also warned the churches that those who practice the defiling deeds of the flesh will not inherit the kingdom of God.[133] After preaching in Derbe, Paul and Barnabas retrace their steps.[134] Despite the fact that they have been driven out of Lystra, Iconium, and Pisidian Antioch, they revisit each city.[135] They briefly meet with each of the four kingdom communities to strengthen, encourage, and warn the new disciples about the trials that lie ahead.

...through many afflictions we must enter into God's Kingdom. (Acts 14:22)[136]

After prayer and fasting, the apostles identify the older men in each assembly, those who have matured the most. They publicly acknowledge these men as "elders."[137]

131. For details on Paul's trip to Iconium, Lystra, and Derbe, see James D.G. Dunn, *Beginning from Jerusalem,* 429ff.

132. Galatians 3:1. Barnett points out that the two apostles "publicly portrayed" Jesus Christ as crucified among the Galatians. This verbal demonstration suggests that "perhaps one or both had witnessed the crucifixion of Jesus." Paul Barnett, *From Jerusalem to Illyricum*, 53. Even if they hadn't, they described it vividly.

133. Galatians 5:19-21. Paul writes "I warn you, as I did before" in verse 21 (NIV) referring to the time when he was among them. Some translations use "works" or "acts" of the flesh in verse 19.

134. From Derbe, they could have crossed the Taurus Mountains. Craig Keener, *The IVP Bible Background Commentary: New Testament*, 364. For further details on the ekklesias planted in south Galatia, see William Ramsay, *St. Paul the Traveler and Roman Citizen*, chaps. 5, 6, 8.

135. Dunn explains the problems on this part of the trip and their return to Syrian Antioch, also pointing out that the road beyond Lystra may not have been paved. James D.G. Dunn, *Beginning from Jerusalem*, 433. While Luke only mentions Derbe and Lystra (Acts 16:1), I agree with Bandy that they also visited Iconium and Pisidian Antioch. Alan Bandy, *An Illustrated Guide to the Apostle Paul*, 81. Acts 16:4 says they traveled "from town to town," delivering the decisions made by the apostles and elders in Jerusalem.

136. Regarding this text, I agree with Keener that one of the main messages of discipleship is suffering for the kingdom of God. Craig Keener, "Lessons on Acts," Session 23.

137. Paul was not installing people into an "office" called "elder." He was publicly recognizing a function that was already taking place. The word often translated "appoint" in Acts 14:23 is better translated "chosen" (Berean Literal Bible). The word carries the idea of public acknowledgment, rather than an installation into an office. According to Robert Banks, "the sense of the word 'appoint' is captured in Paul's declaration in 1 Corinthians 16:15-16 about Stephanas and those like him, as well as in his and Titus' decision in Acts

Paul and Barnabas commend each assembly to the Lord Jesus Christ, and they depart.[138]

Sharpening the Focus: If we consider their travel time, Paul and Barnabas spend only one to five months planting each kingdom community in Galatia.[139] This pattern will continue throughout Paul's entire ministry, with the exceptions of Corinth and Ephesus. He will spend a short time laying a solid foundation for an infant community of Jesus' disciples in Galatia. He will then abandon the community for a long time without human headship.[140]

Two years will pass before Paul returns to see the Galatian believers. Most of the converts in Galatia are heathen Gentiles. Some among them are God-fearers and

---

16:1-3 to add Timothy to their apostolic team. It means to *publicly announce* or *acknowledge* someone based on others' appreciation or endorsement." Personal correspondence with Banks, 7/1/22. Translations that use the term "office" for elders and overseers do not reflect the original Greek. For a detailed discussion on the functional nature of elders and all leadership in the first century (as opposed to offices and positions), see Robert Banks, *Paul's Idea of Community*, chap. 14; Wayne Meeks, *The First Urban Christians*, 134-136; Frank Viola, *Reimagining Church*, chaps. 8-10. Elders, shepherds (pastors), and overseers were different names for the same function (Acts 20:17, 28; 1 Peter 5:1-4; 1 Timothy 3:1; Philippians 1:1, etc.). "…From Jerusalem to Corinth, the churches were nurtured in homes, received oversight from their familial *episkopoi* (overseers), who were naturally known by the collective title of *presbuteroi* (elders)." Roger Gehring, *House Church and Mission*, 273. See also Alastair Campbell, *The Elders: Seniority within Earliest Christianity* (Edinburgh: T&T Clark, 1994). According to Ben Witherington III, "the term 'elder' means normally just what it says. In antiquity, older persons had more respect and were thought to have more wisdom. This is precisely why Timothy or Titus would have trouble with some despising their youth." Personal correspondence with Witherington 9/28/00. Interestingly, there is no mention of elders in the sending church—the assembly in Syrian Antioch. James D.G. Dunn, *The Acts of the Apostles*, 193.

138. Acts 14:20-23. On this first apostolic journey, the team preached the gospel to a wide range of people: God-fearers, women of high standing, leading men of the city, etc. Acts 13:16, 26, 50. They also preached in large cities and in small towns and villages. Craig Keener, et al., *Journeys of the Apostle Paul*, 49.

139. This is based on the timeline I've documented. Remember, Luke compresses his narrative.

140. Some of the churches in Galatia (Pisidian Antioch, for example) hadn't seen Paul for almost a year to fifteen months after he and Barnabas left them. Also, elders (overseers/shepherds) are never referred to as "heads" of a church in the New Testament. The phrase "head of the church" is only reserved for Christ (Ephesians 5:23; Colossians 1:18).

Jews.[141] The Gentiles were once "unwashed" pagans. They come from a background racked with superstition, worshipping false gods, and immorality. The Gentile, God-fearing believers had regularly attended the synagogue to hear about the God of Israel. The believing Jews are the clean-cut, cultured, morally conscious members of the assembly. The new converts in Galatia do not have Bibles. The New Testament hasn't been written yet, and the Old Testament is difficult to access.

It's possible that a Jew in one of the four ekklesias could have one or two Old Testament scrolls. But it is highly doubtful that any synagogue had an entire Old Testament, much less the ekklesias of God.[142] Yet even if every convert had an entire Bible, it would profit them little, because an estimated 90 percent of the Roman Empire is functionally illiterate.[143] In a few Hellenistic cities, the literacy rate may be as high as 20 to 30 percent.[144] But in the Western provinces of the empire, it is unlikely that the literacy rate is as high as 5 to 10 percent.

Letter writers, stenographers, occasional poets, and legal scribes make up only 4 percent of the population, at best. One or two people out of every ten could write.[145] Those who can write often become farsighted by the age of forty. Thus, they will need an amanuensis (a secretary who serves as a professional scribe) to pen their letters.[146]

141. For a detailed analysis of Paul and Barnabas' apostolic work in Galatia, see Eckhard Schnabel, *Early Christian Mission*, 2:1089-1124.

142. Synagogues possessed some scrolls of the Old Testament. Scrolls were expensive and rarely, if ever, loaned out. Memorization in the oral culture of the first century was primary. Elite persons could copy scrolls for personal use or study. Personal correspondence with Ben Witherington III, 8/19/21.

143. An estimated 5 to 10 percent of the entire Mediterranean world could read with any proficiency. Joel Green, et al., *The World of the New Testament*, 348; David Capes, et al., *Rediscovering Paul*, 99-101; Craig Evans, et al., eds., *Dictionary of New Testament Background*, 645. For a detailed argument that literacy was between 5 and 10 percent in the ancient world, see William Harris, *Ancient Literacy* (Cambridge, MA: Harvard University Press, 1989). The ancient world was an oral culture. While most of the early believers could not read, they were accustomed to hearing documents read. So they were attuned to careful listening and even memorization as their primary way of encountering Scripture. Personal correspondence with Alan Bandy, 12/6/23. Literacy was higher among males. It was also higher in cities than in the countryside. Personal correspondence with Craig Keener, 7/18/16.

144. Eckhard Schnabel, *Early Christian Mission*, 1:631.

145. Ben Witherington III, *Invitation to the New Testament*, 176.

146. Jerome Murphy-O'Connor, *Paul the Letter-Writer*, 6ff.; Benjamin Laird, *Creating the Canon*, 15-19.

This may be one of the reasons that Paul used an amanuensis to write some of his epistles (e.g., Romans 16:22).[147] Another reason is to save time.

With his own hand, Paul would often sign the last part of the letter to confirm its authenticity.[148] In some cases, trusted amanuenses had great freedom to shape the form, style, and even the content of an author's letter. Sometimes Paul would add a marginal note with his own hand (e.g., Philemon 19).[149]

The poverty among the Galatians is daunting. Many of the freedmen in the community live on the borders of human survival. They attempt to find work every day in the marketplace. When they work, they are paid a day's wage (one Roman denarius). This amount buys barely enough food to feed their families.[150] Keep in mind that these new Galatian ekklesias are surrounded by Gentile immorality and idolatry. And there are Jews in their towns who hate the new faith. As is the case with much of the empire, for most of its population, first-century Galatia is a thankless, loveless, horrible place to live. Yet this is the world into which two apostolic workers from Antioch of Syria arrive to establish an assembly of Jesus Christ, that is, a colony from heaven.[151]

In the face of these insurmountable problems, Paul and Barnabas only spend three to five months with the new disciples. The apostles teach them all they can about Christ, and then they leave them on their own. After their brief revisit, the new Christians in Galatia will not see the hair of a genuine apostle for almost two years.

---

147. Even when Paul used an amanuensis, the style of his letters was largely his own. F.F. Bruce, *Paul: Apostle of the Heart Set Free*, 16. Paul mentions making use of an amanuensis five times in his letters, where he ends the letter with his own hand to verify its authenticity. William Ramsay, *St. Paul the Traveler and Roman Citizen*, 141. Some scholars assume that all the New Testament letters were penned with the assistance of a secretary. Joel Green, et al., *The World of the New Testament*, 359, 364.

148. Galatians 6:11; 2 Thessalonians 3:17; 1 Corinthians 16:21; Colossians 4:18.

149. According to Weima, "In typical fashion of that day, Paul would take over from his secretary and write the final words of the letter 'in my own hand.' In some cases, like the ending of Galatians (6:11-18), Paul was so upset with his readers that he used his 'autograph' (writing in his own hand) to make some important final points." Personal correspondence with Jeffrey Weima, 12/28/23.

150. The poorest people ate very little besides wheat and barley. Reta Halteman Finger, *Of Widows and Meals*, 121-122.

151. This wasn't just the case with the region of Galatia. Life throughout the Roman Empire was brutish, nasty, harsh, short, and often filled with unrelenting cruelty. Lewis Lord, "The Year One," 38-45; Michael Green, *Evangelism*, 15.

However, the gospel that Paul and Barnabas preached was rich and high enough to equip the Galatian communities to survive without outside help. The message they proclaimed radically transformed these formerly pagan, superstitious, self-centered, and unhappy Gentiles. It inspired them to love one another deeply, filling them with the radiant joy of Christ which became evident in their songs and smiles.

How did these two men from Antioch of Syria pull off such an impossible feat? The answer: They stand in the lineage that stretches back to God Himself, when He called, prepared, and sent the eternal Son to the apostolic ministry.[152] Like Jesus and the Twelve before them, Paul and Barnabas were called, trained, and sent. They preached an indwelling Christ to the Galatians out of their own experience, a Christ who would sustain them through the pressures of life.

The kingdom communities in Galatia are classless societies. All social distinctions are erased. Jew and Gentile, slave and free, rich and poor no longer exist in Christ (Galatians 3:28; Colossians 3:10-11).[153] The believers see themselves as part of the same family, a new race, part of a new colony from the heavenly realm. Because the ex-pagan Jesus-followers no longer participate in the festivals and feasts of Greek religion and the Roman imperial cult, they experience "profound alienation" from their blood relatives, some of whom disown them.[154]

While they feel the sting of abandonment by their blood families, Paul will remind them that they are part of the "household of faith."[155] They have been adopted into the family of God, where the Creator of all things is now their *Abba* (Father). They

152. For the unbroken pattern of how God calls, prepares, and sends apostolic workers, see Frank Viola, "When Giants Walked the Earth (The Real Apostolic Succession)" at frankviola.org/giants.

153. The "status-leveling equality" that marked the early Christians was remarkable. Nijay Gupta, *Strange Religion,* 190. One scholar points out there are about thirty extant letters written by Christians before Constantine. According to these letters, the Christians typically dropped their general family name, which indicated their social status. They also called one another "brother" and "sister." Graydon Snyder, *Ante Pacem: Archaeological Evidence of Church Life Before Constantine* (Macon, GA: Mercer University Press, 1985), chap. 7.

154. Calvin Roetzel, *The World That Shaped the New Testament,* 102. This was also due to the fact that the early believers were overturning Greco-Roman customs and traditions. For details, see D. Clint Burnett, *Paul and Imperial Divine Honors,* 1-57.

155. Galatians 6:10. The Jewish believers also experienced ostracization from their blood kin. This practice continues today in some Orthodox Jewish communities, where families observe a week-long mourning period upon learning that a child has converted to Jesus.

have become children of the living God, children of the promise, and children of free-dom.[156] As such, they eat together, work together, greet each other with a holy kiss,[157] raise their children together, take care of one another, marry one another, and eventually, bury each other. The joy and love the Galatian believers have for one another begins to shake the Roman Empire to its foundations.

Paul and Barnabas draw fresh lines across the Mediterranean world. From Pisidian Antioch, they return to Pamphylia, the narrow coastal plain nestled between the Mediterranean Sea and the Taurus Mountains.[158] They revisit Perga and enter through the enormous Hellenistic gate with its two tall towers on each side.[159] And they begin preaching the gospel in the city.[160]

After leaving Perga, they travel the short distance to the city of Attalia on the coast of the Pamphylian Gulf. From Attalia, they sail back to Antioch of Syria, the city from which they were sent. (It is on this trip to Antioch that Paul's second shipwreck may have occurred.[161]) When they arrive in Antioch, the two men gather everyone in the kingdom

---

156. Galatians 1:4; 4:6-7; 3:26; 4:28, 31.

157. Kissing was widely practiced among relatives and close friends in the ancient world as a greeting. A "holy kiss" emphasized the non-erotic nature of the kiss, which was usually a light kiss on the mouth. Craig Keener, *Romans*, 188. Paul's exhortation to greet one another with a holy kiss was a standard item in his epistles to the churches (Romans 16:16; 1 Corinthians 16:20; 2 Corinthians 13:12; 1 Thessalonians 5:26). Peter also encouraged the kiss of love (1 Peter 5:14). The kiss represented friendship as well as unity and reconciliation. Later in church history, it was called the "kiss of peace." For details, see Ben Witherington III, *1 and 2 Thessalonians: A Socio-Rhetorical Commentary* (Grand Rapids, MI: Eerdmans, 2006), 175-176; F.F. Bruce, *1 & 2 Thessalonians*, 134.

158. Alan Bandy, *An Illustrated Guide to the Apostle Paul*, 59.

159. Mark Fairchild, "The Last Apostle," documentary film.

160. Acts 14:24-25. Luke doesn't mention a synagogue in Perga, but there were Jews in Pamphylia at the time. Mark Wilson, *Biblical Turkey*, 94.

161. 2 Corinthians 11:25. The trip from Attalia to Syrian Antioch was approximately 300-350 sea miles, a plausible stretch for a shipwreck. (The straight-line distance between their modern locations is around 220 miles.) See my earlier note on a likely place for Paul's first shipwreck (from Paphos to Perga). Since Luke doesn't mention Paul's first three shipwrecks, inductive reasoning is required to form an educated guess.

community and share a report on all that God has done.[162] Paul and Barnabas will rest in Syrian Antioch for about a year.[163]

Meanwhile, in Rome, Emperor Claudius issues a decree[164] expelling the Jews from the "Eternal City" (Rome).[165] The Jews are rioting over their views about Christ.[166] Many Jewish Christ-followers are forced to leave the city. They caused a ruckus in the city, disturbing the much promoted "Pax Romana" (Roman peace) by proclaiming in the synagogues that Jesus is the Messiah.

Some of the banished Jews flee to the city of Corinth located in the province of Achaia (Southern Greece).[167] A Roman Jew named Aquila, and his wife (Priscilla) are among

162. Acts 14:27.

163. Luke says, "they stayed there [Syrian Antioch] a long time with the disciples" (Acts 14:28, NIV). Some scholars believe it could have been months up to a year. Clinton Arnold, ed., *Zondervan Illustrated Bible Backgrounds Commentary*, 2b:138. Given my timeline, approximately a year fits well.

164. Most scholars date the edict at A.D. 49. Darrell Bock, *Acts*, 578; Ben Witherington III, *Invitation to the New Testament*, 336; *The Acts of the Apostles*, 545; Craig Keener, *Acts*, 3:2684; F.F. Bruce, *The Defense of the Gospel in the New Testament*, 55; James D.G. Dunn, *The Acts of the Apostles*, 240. It's unlikely that all 40,000 Jews were actually expelled. James D.G. Dunn, *The Acts of the Apostles*, 241. The "ringleaders," whose actions caused the riots, may have been the main targets. Rainer Riesner, *Paul's Early Period*, 192. Some historians estimate that the number of Jews who were living in Rome before Claudius expelled them in A.D. 49 was between 40,000 to 50,000. Eckhard Schnabel, *Acts*, 756. According to Jewett, "It was all the agitators rather than all 50,000 Jews in Rome who were banned…." Robert Jewett, *A Chronology of Paul's Life*, 37. From the first year of Claudius' reign (A.D. 41), he looked on the Jews with suspicion and forbade them to gather according to their ancestral customs. Then in A.D. 49, his tolerance ran out, and he expelled them. Clinton Arnold, ed., *Zondervan Illustrated Bible Backgrounds Commentary*, 2b:181-182.

165. While the term "Eternal City" probably wasn't in use for Rome prior to Hadrian's reign (second century), I'm using it in this book as an alternative for "Rome" at times.

166. "The Jews, who by the instigation of one Chrestus were evermore tumultuous, he banished from Rome." Suetonius, *Life of Claudius*, 25.4; Orasius, *History Against the Pagans*, 7.6.15ff. "Chrestus" was a common slave name and might have been Suetonius's mistake for *Christus*. By contrast, the Roman historian Tacitus (*Annals*, 15.44) gets the name right in his account of the persecution under Nero. See also Peter Lampe, *From Paul to Valentinus: Christians at Rome in the First Two Centuries* (Minneapolis, MN: Fortress Press, 2003), 12-13; Richard Longenecker, *The Ministry and Message of Paul*, 66-67; Ben Witherington III, *The Acts of the Apostles*, 540-541; F.F. Bruce, "The Early Church in the Roman Empire," *The Bible Student* 56 (Bangalore, India: March-April 1933): 30-32; *Jesus and the Christian Origins of the New Testament* (Grand Rapids, MI: Eerdmans, 1974), 20-21.

167. In 44 B.C., Corinth was rebuilt by Julius Caesar as a Roman city, and it wasn't terribly far from the lower eastern boot of Italy.

them.[168] The couple was likely present in Jerusalem during the feast of Pentecost when Peter preached the gospel. After their conversion, they went back to their hometown in Rome with Peter's words ringing in their ears.[169] Because Rome has expelled so many Jews, Gentiles in all the Roman colonies regard Jews with even greater suspicion than before.

Peter Visits Antioch of Syria[170]

Peter pays a visit to the assembly in Syrian Antioch.[171] While there, he enjoys table fellowship (shared meals) with the Gentile believers. When the kingdom community in Jerusalem hears that Peter is eating with Gentiles,[172] James (the Lord's half-brother) sends a delegation of Jewish Christ-followers to investigate and send a message to Peter.[173] Peter's free fellowship with Gentiles is creating a scandal in Jerusalem (since devout Jews are offended by Peter for eating with Gentiles). Peter's action is also hurting the Jerusalem church's efforts at reaching unbelieving Jews with the gospel message.[174] The men who send the message are part of the circumcision party.[175]

---

168. Acts 18:2. We will see more of them later in our story.

169. Personal correspondence with Ben Witherington III, 1/28/22. This is a plausible guess based on Acts 2:10. Jews from Rome were in the city when Peter began to preach (Acts 2:14ff.). Bruce also believed the couple were Christians before Paul met them in Corinth. F.F. Bruce, *Paul: Apostle of the Heart Set Free*, 382. Schnabel says, "Luke's account gives the impression that Priscilla and Aquila were believers when Paul met them in Corinth." Eckhard Schnabel, *Acts*, 756.

170. From A.D. 34-47, Peter was involved in frequent travel within Judea (Samaria, Lydda, Joppa, Caesarea). After A.D. 47, we see him traveling outside of Judea increasingly. He appears to have worked mainly among non-Palestinian, Greek-speaking Jews outside Judea. Paul Barnett, *Bethlehem to Patmos*, 210-211.

171. I believe (as do other scholars) that this visit took place after Paul and Barnabas completed their first apostolic journey. Clinton Arnold, ed., *Zondervan Illustrated Bible Backgrounds Commentary*, 3:277.

172. Pious Jews weren't supposed to eat with Gentiles. Craig Keener, *The IVP Bible Background Commentary: New Testament*, 528.

173. Galatians 2:12. Schreiner agrees that James instructed these men to go to Antioch to talk to Peter. Thomas Schreiner, *Galatians*, 140. However, what they ended up telling Peter went far beyond what James had in mind.

174. For evidence supporting this interpretation, see F.F. Bruce, *Paul: Apostle of the Heart Set Free*, 176-177.

175. I agree with those scholars who believe these are the same men mentioned in Acts 15:1. N.T. Wright, *Paul: A Biography*, 144; F.F. Bruce, *The Epistle to the Galatians: A Commentary on the Greek*, NIGTC (Grand Rapids, MI: Eerdmans, 1982), 130; Ben Witherington III, *The Acts of the Apostles*, 95-96, 450; Eckhard Schnabel,

The circumcision party plans to do more than James requested. They scheme to confront the apostle face-to-face[176] and push circumcision on the Gentile believers. In the minds of the circumcision party, loyal Jews must be circumcised. If a man professes to be converted to the God of Israel, he must believe in Jesus *and* be circumcised, as well as keep the entire Law. For the circumcision party, table fellowship with uncircumcised Gentiles is immoral, and loyal Jesus-followers should never participate in it.[177]

The members of the circumcision party seek to ensure that all Jesus-followers continue to conform to the laws of Moses.[178] So with great zeal, they aim to persuade the Gentile converts to do the same.[179] The circumcision party arrives in Antioch and meets with Peter. They persuade him to no longer enjoy table fellowship with his Gentile brethren. We can imagine their conversation to have been something like this:

In Jerusalem, we've heard that you are habitually having table fellowship with Gentiles. Your actions are causing a huge scandal among our more conservative brethren in the assembly.

Acts, 628. Bock agrees this is a plausible view. Darrell Bock, *Acts,* 495. James didn't tell the delegation to push circumcision on the Gentiles; they did that on their own. If this is true, in Acts 15:24, James was saying he didn't authorize them to push circumcision on the believers. Instead, "they exceeded the terms of their commission." F.F. Bruce, *The Book of the Acts,* 286. "They clearly went beyond what James wanted them to do." Personal correspondence with Ben Witherington III, 7/18/16. See also John Stott, *The Message of Galatians,* 50-52; Alan Cole, *Galatians: An Introduction and Commentary,* revised edition, TNTC (Grand Rapids, MI: Eerdmans, 1989), 116. Note that the "circumcision party" was a label Paul and Luke gave these men years later as they looked back.

176. In Galatians 2:14, Paul tells Peter he was living like a Gentile and not like a Jew. I agree with Schreiner and Barnett who point out that a natural reading of this text suggests Peter was eating foods that were ceremonially unclean and unlawful for Jews to consume. Thomas Schreiner, *Galatians,* 139-142; Paul Barnett, *Jesus & the Rise of Early Christianity,* 285; *From Jerusalem to Illyricum,* 63.

177. N.T. Wright sketches out the problem well in *Paul: A Biography,* 142ff. For a discussion on how the Pharisaic Jews perceived circumcision versus how the Gentiles viewed it, see Clinton Arnold, ed., *Zondervan Illustrated Bible Backgrounds Commentary,* 2b:139.

178. The circumcision party isn't as happy with the assembly in Antioch as Barnabas is because it's not "Jewish enough" for them. Craig Keener, "Lessons on Acts," Session 24.

179. The term "Judaizer" refers to someone whose mission is turning people into Judeans by demanding they accept Judean practices. The men who visited Antioch came from Judea, specifically, Jerusalem (Acts 15:1). They were part of the believing Pharisees mentioned in Acts 15:5. Paul viewed them as false brethren. James D.G. Dunn, *The Acts of the Apostles,* 199; F.F. Bruce, *Paul: Apostle of the Heart Set Free,* 175; Ben Witherington III, *The Acts of the Apostles,* 95-96.

It's also becoming common knowledge outside the assembly, and it's seriously hindering our attempts to evangelize our fellow Jews. More seriously, your actions are putting the other apostles in Jerusalem in danger, since the militant Jews in Jerusalem view any fraternization with Gentiles to be the conduct of traitors.[180]

Fearful of offending his brethren in Jerusalem, Peter begins eating exclusively with the Jewish believers in the Antioch assembly.[181] The rest of the Jews in the church follow suit, creating a division in the ekklesia between Jewish and Gentile believers. Even Barnabas, the man who preached the gospel of grace with Paul to numerous Gentiles in Syrian Antioch and Galatia, sides with the Jews and stops eating with the Gentile believers.[182] When Paul discovers what is happening,[183] he is so angered that he publicly rebukes Peter for his hypocrisy.[184]

180. I created this conversation based on the sources I've cited in the notes in this section, especially F.F. Bruce's work. Note also that the mid-forties witnessed a revival of militancy among Judean freedom-fighters. Tiberius Julius Alexander, procurator of Judea, crucified two of their leaders—Jacob and Simon—sons of Judas, the man who led the revolt against the census in A.D. 6. These militants regarded any Jews who fraternized with the uncircumcised as traitors. F.F. Bruce, *The Epistle to the Galatians*, 130.

181. On occasion, the Jerusalem apostles "crumbled before the pressure of the counter-mission wing of the Jerusalem church." Paul Barnett, *Paul: Missionary of Jesus*, 203. Scholars debate who "the circumcision" is in Galatians 2:12, but I believe (along with Barnett) that it's reasonable to conclude it was "the circumcision party" (ESV). See also Alan Cole, *Galatians*, 116; John Stott, *The Message of Galatians*, 52. For alternative interpretations, see Thomas Schreiner, *Galatians*, 143-144; Richard Longenecker, *Galatians*, 74-75; Ben Witherington III, *Grace in Galatia*, 156.

182. "And the rest of the Jews joined him in his hypocrisy, so that even Barnabas was carried away with their hypocrisy" (Galatians 2:13). There is no evidence that Peter or Barnabas shared the view of the Judaizers. They both lived and ate like Gentiles, only withdrawing after the pressure exerted by the agitators. Ben Witherington III, *The Acts of the Apostles*, 455.

183. Note that the church in Antioch was very large, so the assembly doubtlessly gathered in different homes throughout the entire city. This explains why Paul eventually discovered what was taking place. It's also possible that he was visiting a nearby town when Peter met with the Judaizers.

184. Paul's rebuke to Peter is recorded in Galatians 2:14-21. Bruce observes that the rebuke was public as well as personal ("to his face"). Paul appears to have been following what he'd later write in 1 Timothy 5:20. Namely, those who sin in public should be rebuked in public. Otherwise, Matthew 18:15ff. would have probably been followed. F.F. Bruce, *The Epistle to the Galatians*, 132. "Paul's rebuke of Cephas occurred before all the members of the Antioch church in open session…not just before the Jewish believers…." Richard Longenecker, *Galatians*, WBC (Grand Rapids, MI: Zondervan, 1990), 77. Some scholars believe Paul's rebuke to Peter caused the church in Antioch to withdraw their support for Paul, so Paul began his apostolic trips

But when Peter came to Antioch, I had to oppose him to his face, for what he did was very wrong. ...other Jewish believers followed Peter's hypocrisy, and even Barnabas was led astray by their hypocrisy. (Galatians 2:11, 13, NLT)

The circumcision party defends Peter, and Paul has it out with them. For Paul, nothing less than the gospel is at stake. Barnabas realizes that Paul is right and sides with him. A full-scale debate ensues between the Jerusalem circumcision party and Paul and Barnabas over the matter of circumcision.[185] The circumcision party insists that the Gentile believers must be circumcised and keep the Law of Moses to be saved and included in God's covenant people.[186] Paul and Barnabas vehemently disagree, and they sharply debate them.[187]

The two apostles argue that all who believe in Jesus as the Messiah are part of the same family—God's family—made up of both Jew and Gentile. It's Christ's risen life that binds them together, not the Law of Moses. Gentile believers, therefore, can enjoy table fellowship with Jewish believers because they are all part of the same family.[188]

Fire Falls on the Galatian Churches
Early 49[189]

Peter returns to Jerusalem,[190] but the circumcision party leaves Syrian Antioch and makes the long, perilous trip to Galatia to visit all four kingdom communities that Paul and

---

without their help. I agree with Wright, however, that this is a mistaken conclusion. Paul returned to Antioch after his initial journeys without any issues. N.T. Wright, *Paul: A Biography*, 152.

185. Bruce gives a helpful overview of the Gentile problem in *Paul: Apostle of the Heart Set Free*, 173-187. For a discussion on how critical circumcision was to Jewish identity, see James D.G. Dunn, *The Acts of the Apostles*, 198.

186. They essentially demanded that the Gentiles become Torah-observant Jews. Jerome Murphy-O'Connor, *Paul: His Story*, 99.

187. Acts 15:2, NIV.

188. See Paul's argument in Galatians chapters 3 through 4.

189. Ben Witherington III, *The Acts of the Apostles*, 83.

190. Neither Acts nor Galatians tell us how Peter reacted to Paul's argument, but we can safely assume from what unfolds later in the story (Acts 15) that he was persuaded by what Paul had to say regarding eating with the Gentiles.

Barnabas raised up.[191] (The circumcision party is aware of the mission in Galatia. On their way to Galatia, they make a stop at the ekklesias in Cilicia and share their Law-based gospel with them.[192])

Their objective is clear: to overturn Paul's work and persuade the Gentile believers to accept the knife (circumcision) and follow the entire Law of Moses, just as they recently attempted in Antioch of Syria.[193] Months later, James will rebuke these men in his letter to the Gentile believers in Syrian Antioch and Cilicia saying:

191. Witherington notes that "the Judaizers seem to have left Jerusalem, gone to Antioch, and then continued following Paul and Barnabas's footsteps to the newly founded churches in Galatians sometime in A.D. 49…they appear again at Acts 15:2, 5." Ben Witherington III, *The Acts of the Apostles*, 444. Witherington confirms that the agitators in Acts 15:1 were the Judaizers who visited the churches in Galatia. They had plenty of time to make a trip to Galatia and then get back to Jerusalem for the Jerusalem council. Personal correspondence with Ben Witherington III, 7/18/16.

192. If you look at a map of the first century, Cilicia is on the way from Syrian Antioch to the region of Galatia. So the Judaizers left Antioch, visited the fellowships in Cilicia and spread their legalistic gospel there. After this, they traveled to Galatia where they did the same thing. Acts 15:23ff. and the letter to the Galatians confirm this scenario.

193. Ben Witherington III, *The Acts of the Apostles*, 450. Not only is the controversial issue the same in Acts 15:1 and Galatians 2:14-21; 6:15-16, but notice that the wording is the same in Galatians 5:10 ("he who *troubles* you") and Acts 15:24 ("some who went out from us have *troubled* you with words, unsettling your souls" [emphasis added]). The Greek word in both passages, *tarassō*, is identical. Because this word means to "trouble" or "agitate," some scholars call this group the "agitators." Alan Bandy, *An Illustrated Guide to the Apostle Paul*, 66. These people were not Jews outside the Jesus movement. ("Jesus movement" is a term historians use for the Christian faith.) Instead, they were professing believers in Jesus who were Jewish. They weren't the Jerusalem apostles nor their emissaries. Richard Horsley, ed., *Paul and Politics*, 152, 154. This is the same group that went to Antioch and Galatia, the "false brothers" mentioned in Galatians 2:4. Ben Witherington III, *New Testament History*, 244; David Capes, et al., *Rediscovering Paul*, 127-129; Paul Barnett, *Paul: Missionary of Jesus*, 142-143; Eckhard Schnabel, *Early Christian Mission*, 2:1004; Mark Fairchild, *Christian Origins in Ephesus & Asia Minor*, 51. A point made by those who hold that Galatians was written *after* Acts 15 is that "James's/Jerusalem's decree against the circumcisionists addressed Syria and Cilicia *only* which suggests that before the Jerusalem council (Acts 15), the circumcisionists had not yet reached Galatia." Personal correspondence with Craig Keener, 12/4/23. This is an astute observation. However, scholars like David deSilva hold that Galatians was written *before* Acts 15, since the circumcision party couldn't very well make a persuasive case in Galatia after the events of Acts 15 and the decision of the apostolic council, and Paul would have had the trump card that he would not have failed to play in his letter, had the official ruling of the apostolic council been available to him in Galatia. For a detailed discussion, see deSilva, *Letter to the Galatians*, 50-53. According to Blomberg, "Maybe the answer is as simple as the most immediately precipitating incident occurred in

> *Because we have heard that some who went out from us have troubled you with words, unset-tling your souls, saying, 'You must be circumcised and keep the law,' to whom we gave no commandment... (Acts 15:24)*[194]

Clearly, James does not authorize the circumcision party with their gospel of legalism.[195] Paul will later call the members of the circumcision party "agitators," and they are led by one unnamed man.[196]

A Thorn in the Flesh

> *...But he who troubles you will bear his judgment, whoever he is. (Galatians 5:10)*

Paul will refer to this unnamed man as his "thorn in the flesh."[197] On three separate occasions, the apostle will ask the Lord to remove the thorn from his life. But Jesus will respond, "My grace is sufficient for you, for my power is made perfect in weakness."[198] The Lord chooses not to remove the thorn from Paul's life, yet He will rescue Paul *through* the sufferings that the thorn inflicts upon him. For years to come, the "thorn"—this unnamed Judaizer who is part of the circumcision party—will obsessively seek to destroy Paul's work.

Syrian Antioch—the administrative center of the combined provinces of Syria and Cilicia." Personal correspondence with Craig Blomberg, 12/14/23. The issue is complicated and both views have their strengths and weaknesses. In a future note, I offer another possible reason why Galatia isn't mentioned in Acts 15:23 in the letter written by the apostles and elders in Jerusalem.

194. The letter was penned by the apostles and the elders (with the approval of the whole church). James, of course, was one of the authors (Acts 15:22ff.).

195. N.T. Wright, *Paul: A Biography*, 167.

196. Galatians 3:1; 5:10. Barnett agrees that the agitators (Galatians 5:12) were headed up by one man. Paul Barnett, *Paul: Missionary of Jesus*, 144.

197. Keener agrees that "Paul's opponents were his thorn," and says the idea that they were headed up by one man is possible. Personal correspondence with Craig Keener, 12/4/23. Bandy holds that my view on the thorn "has much merit" and "is the most likely" perspective. Personal correspondence with Alan Bandy, 12/6/23.

198. 2 Corinthians 12:9.

Under God's sovereign hand, he (the thorn) is given to Paul to keep him humble amid the glorious revelations of Christ that the apostle has received from God.[199] During His earthly ministry, Jesus predicted this kind of suffering when he upbraided the Pharisees.

Therefore, behold, I send to you prophets, wise men, and scribes. Some of them you will kill and crucify; and some of them you will scourge in your synagogues and persecute from city to city.... (Matthew 23:34)

Just as Paul (who was once a Pharisee) had persecuted the followers of Jesus "from city to city," Paul's thorn and the accompanying group of "agitators" will pursue the believers in Paul's assemblies "from city to city." In addition, the unbelieving Jews will persecute Paul in every town he steps into.

Sharpening the Focus: For generations, Bible commentators have offered multiple theories about the identity of Paul's thorn in the flesh. The most popular theories range from various and sundry illnesses (malaria, epilepsy, ophthalmia, etc.), to haunting guilt for persecuting the church, to a sexual addiction Paul never overcame.

I've never found any of these common theories persuasive or satisfactory. To my mind, if we take the text, just as it is written, and compare it with other texts using similar language, then step back to take a fresh look at the New Testament narrative in its chronological sequence, an entirely different picture emerges—one I personally find compelling.

Let's first look carefully at the text:

By reason of the exceeding greatness of the revelations, that I should not be exalted excessively, a thorn in the flesh was given to me: a messenger of Satan to torment me, that I should not be exalted excessively. Concerning this thing, I begged the Lord three times that it might depart from me. He has said to me, "My grace is sufficient for you, for my power is made perfect in weakness." Most gladly therefore I will rather glory in my weaknesses, that the power of Christ may rest on me. Therefore I take pleasure in weaknesses, in injuries, in

199. 2 Corinthians 12:1-10.

necessities, in persecutions, and in distresses, for Christ's sake. For when I am weak, then am I strong. (2 Corinthians 12:7-10)

Paul plainly identifies the thorn.[200] It was a "messenger of satan" with the malicious purpose to torment Paul. The word "torment" means "to strike with the fist, to rain blows upon, to treat with violence." It's often translated as "harass." When Paul asks the Lord to remove the thorn, the Savior responds, "My power is perfected in weakness" (v. 9, NASB). Paul immediately says that he would rather "boast in my weaknesses" so Christ's power may dwell in him (v. 9, NASB).

What's telling here is that Paul's entire discussion in chapter 11 (just before he mentions the thorn in the flesh) is about his "weaknesses." The context of 2 Corinthians 11:16ff. are the false apostles who caused him great trouble. He then gives a robust list of hardships that he endured for the gospel:

- imprisonment
- flogging
- being exposed to death
- forty lashes (five times)
- beaten with rods (three times)
- being stoned
- being shipwrecked (three times)
- spending a night and day in the open sea
- being in danger of rivers
- being in danger of bandits
- being in danger from his fellow Jews
- being in danger from Gentiles
- being in danger in the city and country

200. Barnett argues that the Greek word *skolops* translated "thorn" is used for a stake, thorn, or spike. It, therefore, seems to connote violence. However, when used in the LXX (Septuagint), it means only "splinter" or "thorn." Paul Barnett, *The Second Epistle to the Corinthians*, NICNT (Grand Rapids, MI: Eerdmans, 1997), 569. See also F.F. Bruce, *1 and 2 Corinthians*, 248.

- being in danger at sea
- being in danger from false believers
- going without sleep
- going without food
- being cold and naked
- the daily pressure of his concern for the ekklesias he raised up[201]

Interestingly, he describes all his sufferings as "weaknesses," never once mentioning being sick or ill (see 11:30). The word "weakness" in 11:30 is the same Greek word that's used for "weaknesses" in 12:5 and 12:9-10. In 12:10, in addition to "weaknesses," he mentions "insults, hardships, persecutions, and difficulties."[202] He never mentions sickness or illness, which is odd if the thorn were a physical sickness of some kind. (The Greek word *angelos*—translated "messenger" in 12:7—tends to be used for personal beings, not impersonal instruments like sickness, psychological problems, eye trouble, etc.[203])

Paul begins his argument in chapter 11 by talking about the "false apostles" and "deceitful workers" who transform themselves as angels of light. He goes on to say that even satan disguises himself as an angel of light (11:14). Interestingly, the Greek word for "angel" in 11:14 is the same word for "messenger" in 12:7 (which Paul refers to as a "thorn").

201. Paul's list in 2 Corinthians 11:24-28 reads like a parody of the famous inscription of Augustus in which the emperor cataloged the glories of his reign (*Acts of Augustus*, 1.4). In 2 Corinthians 11, however, Paul lists his sufferings and losses rather than his achievements. Clinton Arnold, ed., *Zondervan Illustrated Bible Backgrounds Commentary*, 3:250.

202. Barnett observes that in 2 Corinthians 11 through 12, Paul presents himself as a man of weakness, meaning, he is a "man of suffering," just like his Lord (Isaiah 53:3, NIV). Paul Barnett, *The Second Epistle to the Corinthians*, 566.

203. Some have tried to argue that Paul had an eye disease based on the phrase "pluck your eyes out" in Galatians 4:15. But this is not a reference to Paul having eye trouble. Rather, it was a familiar figure of speech similar to someone saying, "You'd give your left arm for someone." N.T. Wright, *Paul: A Biography*, 123. It was a graphic idiom for going to the extreme to benefit another person. Richard Longenecker, *Galatians*, 193; Craig Keener, *1–2 Corinthians*, NCBC (New York, NY: Cambridge University Press, 2005), 240, n. 273. It was also a familiar expression for affection in antiquity. Personal correspondence with Craig Keener, 5/1/16.

For such men are false apostles, deceitful workers, masquerading as Christ's apostles. And no wonder, for even Satan masquerades as an angel of light. It is no great thing therefore if his servants also masquerade as servants of righteousness, whose end will be according to their works. (2 Corinthians 11:13-15)

Paul tells us that these "false apostles" are "servants" of satan. That is, they are messengers of the devil, doing his bidding. They masquerade themselves as messengers of light just as satan does. They traffic in slander, innuendo, misrepresentation, and defamation (see Acts 13:45; 2 Corinthians 6:8; 1 Timothy 6:4, NLT). They also bring persecution by stirring up the people, whether fellow Jews or Gentiles (as in Acts 17; 2 Corinthians 12:10). Right after Paul mentions his thorn in the flesh (12:7), he says that he is not inferior to the best apostles and he worked the signs of a real apostle in their midst.

...for I am in no way inferior to the very best apostles, though I am nothing. Truly the signs of an apostle were worked among you in all perseverance, in signs and wonders and mighty works. (2 Corinthians 12:11-12)

Consequently, if we view 2 Corinthians 11 and 12 as a discussion about the weaknesses in which Paul boasts, we begin to make better sense of what his thorn was all about. In the Old Testament, the term "thorn" is used as a metaphor for a person or group that persecutes God's people:

But if you do not drive out the inhabitants of the land from before you, then those you let remain of them will be like pricks in your eyes and thorns in your sides. They will harass you in the land in which you dwell. (Numbers 33:55)[204]

In this context, God's enemies are called "thorns" in Israel's sides (flesh) that "vex" and torment them. These "thorns" were human beings motivated by God's enemy. When we read the New Testament as a narrative, taking it in its chronological sequence, we discover something interesting. Everywhere Paul planted a church, a group of detractors opposed

204. See also Joshua 23:13 and Judges 2:3.

his ministry and made a calculated effort to discredit his apostolic authority and assail his character in the eyes of the Christians for whom he cared.

In Galatians, Paul indicates this group of detractors was headed up by one man in particular. Paul refers to the detractors saying: "Only there are *some* who trouble you and want to pervert the Good News of Christ" (Galatians 1:7); "I wish that *those* who disturb you would cut *themselves* off" (Galatians 5:12).

He refers to the one man heading them up saying: "But *he* who troubles you will bear his judgment, whoever *he* is" (Galatians 5:10).[205] At the end of the letter, Paul says something else worth noting:

> *From now on, let no one cause me any trouble, for I bear the marks of the Lord Jesus branded on my body. (Galatians 6:17)*

You can almost hear a prayer behind this statement in which Paul is asking the Lord to remove this person who is troubling him and the churches.

Putting all this together, an important picture emerges. Paul's thorn was likely a man (inspired by satan) obsessed with discrediting Paul and his ministry, just as the religious leaders in Jerusalem were obsessed with destroying Jesus and His ministry. This man followed Paul wherever he traveled, beginning in Galatia (Acts 14ff.). He was from the church in Jerusalem, most likely a Pharisee who converted (Acts 15:5).[206] And he made it his mission to subvert Paul's gospel and undermine Paul's work.

This "messenger" or "servant" of satan was in league with a group of others who followed him (Galatians 1:7; 5:12). They followed in Paul's footsteps to the churches in Galatia, Thessalonica, and then to Corinth. (I will later argue that he is the ringleader of the "super-apostles" whom Paul mentions in 2 Corinthians chapters 11 through 12.)[207] Paul responds to their accusations in Galatians 1:10-24; 2:1-18; 1 Thessalonians

---

205. Also compare what Paul says about the "one" person in 2 Corinthians 11:4, NASB with Galatians 1:9, NASB. The wording is almost identical.

206. I believe this man was Paul's peer in gifting, intelligence, zeal, and uncommon devotion to his cause.

207. Witherington agrees that the opponents in Corinth were headed up by a "ringleader" and argues the point from the Greek. Ben Witherington III, *Conflict and Community in Corinth*, 447.

2:3-6; 2 Corinthians 10 through 12. On three occasions, Paul asked the Lord to remove this person from his life. He was a torment, frustration, and harassment to Paul and his work. But the Lord answered and said that His grace was sufficient.

The Lord didn't remove the thorn. He instead enabled Paul to bear with it. Near the end of his life, Paul would reflect on the persecutions he endured in Galatia saying,

You, however, know all about my teaching, my way of life, my purpose, faith, patience, love, endurance, persecutions, sufferings–what kinds of things happened to me in Antioch, Iconium and Lystra, the persecutions I endured. Yet the Lord rescued me from all of them. (2 Timothy 3:10-11, NIV)

The persecutions and afflictions still came, but they didn't stop Paul from moving forward. By God's grace, Paul *endured* them all, for God's grace was sufficient. While this text probably isn't referring specifically to Paul's "thorn," the principle involved is the same. The men who visited Galatia and Corinth with their "gospel" seemed to have been fellow Hebrews from the Jerusalem church (although operating without its approval and misrepresenting the assembly—see 2 Corinthians 11:22 and Galatians chapter 1 through chapter 2). That is, these men were recognized Christians—in name at least.

To my mind, this interpretation fits the evidence better than the alternatives. And it's one that is confirmed by the experience of many servants of God. Jerome Murphy-O'Connor writes,

The nature of the thorn in the flesh has intrigued commentators from the early patristic period to the present day. But a common-sense look at what Paul actually did in the course of his lifetime excludes any bodily or psychiatric disease.... The only hypothesis for which a serious case can be made is that by the thorn in the flesh Paul meant opposition to his ministry from within the Jesus movement. His mention of "a messenger of Satan" implies an external, personal source of affliction, and previously he had identified as 'servants of Satan' (2 Cor. 11:14-15) his Antiochean adversaries in Corinth....[208]

208. Jerome Murphy-O'Connor, *Paul: His Story*, 191. Murphy-O'Connor identifies the "Antiochean adversaries" as the Judaizers who visited Antioch, Galatia, and Corinth. Likewise, Paul Barnett argues that

Barnett is in agreement saying, "More plausibly, Paul's *skolops* [thorn] is the rise of the Judaizing, anti-Paul movement, such as was then all too obvious in Corinth."[209]

The agitators[210] arrive in Galatia and begin visiting the four assemblies.[211] Introducing themselves as brothers from the Jerusalem assembly—the one the original apostles of Jesus founded[212]—they tell the new converts in Galatia the following:

- Jerusalem is the center of God's work on earth. The twelve apostles are the only authorities who can define the true gospel because they were commissioned by Jesus Himself. Paul did not come from Jerusalem, he was not commissioned by Jesus, and he was never part of the Twelve. We, however, live with the Twelve!

- Paul visited Jerusalem shortly after his conversion and spent some time with the apostles there. The apostles instructed him in the basic principles of the gospel

the Jerusalem-based countermission (a term he uses for the circumcision party) followed Paul to most of the assemblies he raised up. Paul Barnett, *Paul: Missionary of Jesus*, chap. 9. Barnett writes, "A significant source of Paul's missionary sufferings was the countermission of the Jerusalem-based Jewish Christians who sought to impose circumcision on the Gentile believers" (191).

209. Paul Barnett, *The Second Epistle to the Corinthians*, 570. In addition, after reading my thesis on Paul's thorn, Barnett remarked, "There is the reasonable possibility Paul was referring to the Jewish counter-missionaries. Your case is well worth arguing." Personal correspondence with Barnett, 1/14/24.

210. These are the Judaizers. For details on the debate over their identity, see Thomas Schreiner, *Galatians*, 39-46. Schreiner argues that the opponents (rival teachers, agitators) are Judaizers.

211. After the agitators visit Galatia, they will visit the churches that Paul will plant in Greece, leveling the same accusations against him as they did in Galatia. In his magnificent book, Barnett confirms my theory of a unified attempt to thwart Paul's work. Paul Barnett, *Paul: Missionary of Jesus*, 144-153, 157. Barnett also discusses the influence of the countermission in Rome (152). Alan Bandy supports this reconstruction saying, "We do see clear instances where Paul's opponents would travel great distances to cities where Paul was ministering to oppose the gospel work being done. As such, it actually is very likely that a highly organized attempt at deconstructing Paul's ministry indeed was the case. Your case is very plausible." Personal correspondence with Alan Bandy, 12/6/23.

212. Longenecker agrees that the agitators were most likely Jewish "Christians" claiming the authority of the home church in Jerusalem. They saw James as the official leader of the strict Law-abiding group in the church, even though James wasn't in line with what they were doing. Richard Longenecker, *Paul, Apostle of Liberty*, 196.

and authorized him to preach the message he learned from them. But when he left Jerusalem and returned to Cilicia, Paul modified his gospel to make it more acceptable to the Gentiles. He removed "the hard parts," especially circumcision, Sabbath-keeping, and observing the Jewish dietary laws.

- Paul's gospel is deficient. Because Paul is a people pleaser, he preaches an easy gospel and omits the difficult parts.

- The gospel that Paul proclaims is not supported by the apostles or the Jerusalem assembly. Believing in Jesus coupled with obeying the Law of Moses justifies as well as sanctifies a person before God.

- In order to be part of "the Israel of God" and demonstrate that a person is part of God's covenant family, you (all the males) must be circumcised.[213]

- Peter is the chief apostle.[214] Yet Paul had the arrogance and audacity to rebuke him to his face! (We saw this happen in Syrian Antioch with our own eyes.) This horrible act proves that Paul is a freelancer, a rogue doing independent work in conflict with the ministry of the Twelve.

- Paul is inconsistent in his views. While he doesn't preach circumcision to the Gentiles, he secretly preaches it to the Jews.[215]

- Paul is insincere. He adapts his gospel to his environment, a classic trait of a people pleaser.[216]

---

213. This explains why Paul uses the phrase "Israel of God" in Galatians 6:16, NIV.

214. Evangelical scholars are in agreement on this point. See Paul Barnett, *From Jerusalem to Illyricum,* 161; Herbert Lockyer, ed., *Nelson's Illustrated Bible Dictionary,* 824; J.D. Douglas, et al., eds., *New Bible Dictionary,* 917.

215. Paul *formerly* preached circumcision before his conversion. In this regard, he advanced in Judaism beyond his peers (Galatians 1:14). To further their arguments, most detractors will typically point to what a person once believed and practiced, even if those beliefs and practices were abandoned long ago.

216. Galatians 5:11. I give more detail on what provoked Paul to write Galatians as well as provide a deep dive into the letter in my master class *Spiritual Graffiti: Galatians in 3D* at thedeeperchristianlife.com/classes. This master class (along with all my other master classes) presents the epistle to the right brain and the left brain as well as to the heart.

Approximately six years later, Paul will write that fire will fall on every worker's labor. Fire now falls on Galatia by the hand of the circumcision party. This crisis will be the first test on Paul's work, and it will reveal whether or not he built with imperishables.

According to the grace of God which was given to me, as a wise master builder I laid a foundation, and another builds on it. But let each man be careful how he builds on it. For no one can lay any other foundation than that which has been laid, which is Jesus Christ. But if anyone builds on the foundation with gold, silver, costly stones, wood, hay, or stubble, each man's work will be revealed. For the Day will declare it, because it is revealed in fire; and the fire itself will test what sort of work each man's work is. (1 Corinthians 3:10-13)[217]

The circumcision party is still in Galatia, and the Galatian converts are troubled and confused. Some of them depart from the gospel that Paul and Barnabas preached, seeking to be justified by the Law. Others in the assembly write a letter to Paul asking him why he failed to tell them "the whole gospel."[218] Timothy also writes a letter to Paul. In it, he explains what is happening in Lystra and Iconium.[219] Timothy is not moved by the circumcision party and stands against it.[220]

Due to the circumcision party's influence, some of the Gentile men are considering circumcision.[221] The believers are also exhibiting the works of the carnal nature,[222]

217. While 1 Corinthians 3:10-13 has the day of judgment in view, it has present application as well. Fire will fall on every true work of God in *this life* and will reveal the quality of material with which it was built. Concerning spiritual work, there is a connection between what happens in this life and what is brought into the next. In God's work, *quality* is more important than *quantity*, and the difference is often manifested in this lifetime when fire falls on a servant of God's work through opposition, persecution, defamation, targeted harassment, etc.

218. It's also possible that some in the Galatian churches traveled to where Paul was located and rehearsed what was happening. Or they carried letters to him (as was the case with the Corinthian church later in the story). Either way, the news got to Paul, and he responded by letter (Galatians).

219. There is division in the four ekklesias in Galatia because of the Judaizers and their influence, so it's plausible that Paul heard from more than one person in these communities.

220. While this scenario cannot be proven, it's reasonably derived from how Timothy is portrayed in the book of Acts and the epistles (Acts 16:2, etc.).

221. Inferred from Galatians 5:2-3. See also Thomas Schreiner, *Galatians*, 34; Ben Witherington III, *Grace in Galatia*, 380.

222. Inferred from Galatians 5:13-18. I side with those scholars who believe Paul was tackling specific issues in the Galatian churches. David deSilva observes that Galatians 5:13 through 6:10 are not an afterthought,

particularly pride, envy, and strife.[223] One person has fallen into an egregious sin and is in need of restoration, but the believers are not sure how to handle it.[224]

Paul, who is still in Syrian Antioch, receives both letters from the Galatian ekklesias. The news from Galatia perplexes and angers him.[225] He is astonished, amazed, and shocked that the new converts have so quickly deserted the Lord by turning to a different gospel.[226]

---

but "an integral, essential part of his counterargument against the position of the rival teachers, who would have been readily able to present the Torah as the reliable guide to virtue and the Torah-observant life as the discipline that would develop virtue and inhibit vice that the Galatians knew they sorely needed." David deSilva, *Letter to the Galatians,* 22. For the debate, including scholars who agree with my position, see Richard Longenecker, *Galatians,* 235-271; F.F. Bruce, *The Epistle to the Galatians,* 240, 260.

223. Clearly, the agitators created communal strife in the assemblies. "But if you bite and devour one another, be careful that you don't consume one another" (Galatians 5:15). "Let's not become conceited, provoking one another, and envying one another" (Galatians 5:26). These statements cohere with the claims that the rival teachers had "agitated" or "troubled" the ekklesias (5:12). "The introduction of the new teaching into the Galatian churches appears to have provoked controversy and quarrels." F.F. Bruce, *The Epistle to the Galatians,* 242.

224. Inferred from Galatians 6:1-8. According to Fung, the man referred to in this text "obviously refers to a member of the Christian community." Ronald Fung, *The Epistle to the Galatians* (Grand Rapids, MI: Eerdmans, 1988), 284. Bruce agrees saying, "The general teaching of 5:13–26 is now applied to some more specific situations…. Whatever form it takes, the offender must be rehabilitated, and not made to feel like a pariah." F.F. Bruce, *The Epistle to the Galatians,* 260. According to George, "Clearly Paul was responding to a real life situation in which concrete acts of wrongdoing such as those he had just listed among the works of the flesh were disrupting both the Galatians' relationship to God and their fellowship with one another. What were the believers to do in such a situation?" Timothy George, *Galatians,* TNAC, Logos edition (Nashville, TN: Broadman & Holman, 1994), 409. Schreiner is right when he observes that "social sins that disrupt the community predominate the vice list. Eight different words describe the sins that foment discord in the church." Thomas Schreiner, *Galatians,* 347. In short, I agree with the sentiment that "these verses obviously had some relationship to the Galatians or they would not have been included." Philip Comfort, ed., *Cornerstone Biblical Commentary* (Carol Stream, IL: Tyndale, 2008), vol. 14:327.

225. The entire scenario I've described is derived from mirror-reading Paul's words in Galatians. The rest of the New Testament epistles will employ this same method.

226. Galatians 1:6 says, "I am astonished that you are so quickly deserting him who called you in the grace of Christ and are turning to a different gospel…" (ESV). The NASB uses the word "amazed," and the NLT uses "shocked." See also Galatians 4:20, "perplexed" (ESV, NIV).

PAUL WRITES GALATIANS

Year: A.D. 49[227]

From: Antioch of Syria[228]

To: The four assemblies in Galatia: Pisidian Antioch, Iconium, Lystra, and Derbe (each are between one and two years old)[229]

Author: Paul[230]

227. The early part of A.D. 49. Ben Witherington III, *The New Testament Story*, 276; David and Pat Alexander, eds., *Handbook to the Bible*, 711; John Drane, *Paul: Libertine or Legalist?* (London: SPCK, 1975), 140ff. Drane, along with countless other scholars including William Ramsay later in his life, set the date to A.D. 49. William Ramsay, *St. Paul the Traveler and Roman Citizen*, 153. See also Ben Witherington III, *The New Testament Story*, 52-54, 276. David deSilva dates the composition of the book at A.D. 48 or 49. *The Letter to the Galatians*, 60-61. For details on the early date of Galatians, see Ben Witherington III, *The Acts of the Apostles*, appx. 1. The bulk of Paul's letters were written between A.D. 47 and 57, during his first three apostolic journeys. They also give us the earliest written references to Jesus (even before the Gospels were written). For more information on when Galatians was composed, see Richard Longenecker, *Galatians*, lxxiii-lxxxviii; Donald Guthrie, *New Testament Introduction*, revised edition (Downers Grove, IL: InterVarsity Press, 1990), 465-488.

228. Ben Witherington III, *Invitation to the New Testament*, 195. Other alternatives have been offered, including Corinth and Rome. Craig Keener, *Galatians: A Commentary* (Grand Rapids, MI: Baker Academic, 2019), 6-7. However, I agree with Witherington and others that Paul was in Syrian Antioch when he wrote the letter.

229. William Ramsay is noted for the "South Galatian theory," which states that Paul wrote Galatians to the churches in the political province of Galatia, i.e., an area that the Roman government designated "Galatia"—a province including Lystra, Derbe, Iconium, etc. Most New Testament scholars, as well as archaeologists, hold to this theory. Personal correspondence with Craig Keener, 5/1/16; Mark Fairchild, "The Last Apostle," documentary film. Most of Phrygia was in the southern part of the Roman province called "Galatia." North Galatia was less populated, and it's not mentioned in Acts or Galatians. The "North Galatian theory" was held by many of the church fathers through the Reformation. But the evidence strongly favors the "South Galatian theory." Craig Keener, "Lessons on Acts," Session 24; Darrell Bock, *Acts*, 526-527; John Drane, *Paul: An Illustrated Documentary*, 50-54; N.T. Wright and Michael Bird, *The New Testament in Its World*, 399-400. For detailed discussions of the North vs. South Galatian hypothesis, see Richard Longenecker, *Galatians*, lxiii-lxxii; David deSilva, *The Letter to the Galatians*, 39-48.

230. "No significant scholarly debate exists on whether Paul wrote Galatians. Indeed, Galatians is often identified as quintessentially Pauline." Thomas Schreiner, *Galatians*, 22; Richard Longenecker, *Galatians*, lvii-lix. Paul adds that he wrote the letter with "all the brothers who are with me" (Galatians 1:2), referring to some of the believers who were in the church in Syrian Antioch where Paul was located at the time.

Contextual Summary: Galatians is the first piece of Christian literature that has survived.[231] The letter is a monumental statement against legalism in every form. It is a polemical piece written in a frantic tone, Paul's first salvo.[232] The apostle writes this blistering epistle in white heat.[233] He answers every argument the circumcision party (the Judaizers) employed to persuade the Galatians into following the Law of Moses.[234]

Galatians is the Magna Carta of the Christian faith. It's an explosive missive arguing that justification and sanctification are by grace through faith in Jesus Christ and the work of the Holy Spirit, not by the works of the Law.[235] The age to come has already launched in Jesus and has burst into the present evil age. Circumcision, then,

231. Alan Bandy, *An Illustrated Guide to the Apostle Paul*, 70. If Galatians is Paul's first letter as F.F. Bruce, Ben Witherington, N.T. Wright, Michael Bird, David deSilva, and many others have argued, and Galatians is the first surviving epistle in the New Testament, this makes it the first extant Christian document. Paul Barnett, *Paul: Missionary of Jesus*, 9; Bruce Longenecker, ed., *The New Cambridge Companion to St. Paul* (New York, NY: Cambridge University Press, 2020), 4. According to Craig Keener and Darrell Bock, most evangelical scholars believe Galatians was Paul's first surviving letter. Personal correspondence with Craig Keener, 12/18/14 and Darrell Bock, 7/14/23. See also Paul Barnett, *From Jerusalem to Illyricum*, 151.

232. Ben Witherington III, *Invitation to the New Testament*, 193-198.

233. Paul's anger toward the Judaizers shows through in his vitriolic remarks, like in Galatians 1:9; 3:1; 5:4, 12. See David Capes, et al., *Rediscovering Paul*, 126-127; E.P. Sanders, *Paul: The Apostle's Life, Letters, and Thought*, 475ff. The churches were in danger of contamination by the false teachers, so Paul uses language that sounds coarse and malicious, though his motivation is out of love for God's people. John Stott, *The Message of Galatians*, 136.

234. While many theories abound as to who Paul's opponents were in Galatia, "the traditional view that the opponents were Judaizers is still the most satisfying." Thomas Schreiner, *Galatians*, 39. (Schreiner presents contrary theories and responds to each one in 39-52.)

235. The phrase "works of the Law" refers to the human attempt to keep God's Law in one's energy, including circumcision, Sabbath-keeping, festival observance, purity washings, and dietary rules. The term "works" implies human effort (Romans 4:4). Paul Barnett, *From Jerusalem to Illyricum*, 66-67. Even though Paul wrote his many epistles mainly to Gentiles, he cites and quotes many Old Testament passages. Altogether, there are over one hundred explicit quotes from the Hebrew Scriptures in the Pauline corpus. More than 90 percent of them appear in Galatians, 1 and 2 Corinthians, and Romans. James D.G. Dunn, *The Theology of Paul the Apostle*, 170. Some of the most helpful works on Galatians are written by F.F. Bruce (*The Epistle to the Galatians*, NIGTC); Ben Witherington III (*Grace in Galatia: A Commentary on Paul's Letter to the Galatians*); Richard Longenecker, *Galatians*, WBC); John Stott (*The Message of Galatians: Only One Way*); David deSilva (*Letter to the Galatians*).

is nothing, and neither is uncircumcision. What matters is the new creation, the kingdom of God come to earth.

God's people, therefore, are no longer obligated to keep the 613 laws of Moses, including circumcision, the Sabbath, and the dietary laws, all of which Jews viewed as the badges of participating in God's family.[236] Paul's burden in the letter is the reconciliation of Jew and Gentile into the Messiah's one family.[237]

Throughout the letter, Paul will connect with the slaves who populate the Galatian ekklesias. He will use the word "slave" (or its derivative) some sixteen times. Many of his metaphors contrast with freedom (examples: "bondage," "confinement," "custodianship," "minor child," and "slavery"). The gospel of the kingdom is also called the gospel of liberty. It sets people free from the bondage of the flesh as well as the bondage of the Law.[238] Paul reminds the Galatians they are free from the Law and

236. Ben Witherington III, *Invitation to the New Testament*, 199. For a summary of the "new perspective on Paul," which some scholars affirm with respect to Paul's view of the Law, see I. Howard Marshall, Stephen Travis, and Ian Paul, *Exploring the New Testament: A Guide to the Letters and Revelation*, third edition (Downers Grove, IL: InterVarsity Press, 2021), 2:58-59. For arguments for and against "the new perspective," see E.P. Sanders, *Paul: The Apostle's Life, Letters, and Thought*, 631ff.; Ben Witherington III, *Paul's Letter to the Romans*, 102-107; Richard Longenecker, *The Epistle to the Romans*, NIGTC (Grand Rapids, MI: Eerdmans, 2016), 362-370; David deSilva, *An Introduction to the New Testament*, 453-454; Mark Nanos and Magnus Zetterholm, eds., *Paul within Judaism: Restoring the First-Century Context to the Apostle* (Minneapolis, MN: Fortress Press, 2015); Paul Barnett, *A Short Book about Paul,* chap. 17; Michael Bird, Ruben Bühner, Jörg Frey, and Brian Rosner, eds., *Paul within Judaism: Perspectives on Paul and Jewish Identity* (Tübingen: Germany, Mohr Siebeck, 2023). The idea that the "works of the Law" only refers to circumcision, Sabbath-keeping, and the Jewish dietary laws appears to conflict with Paul's remarks in Galatians 5:2-3. Bruce Longenecker argues convincingly that Paul's opponents wanted the Galatians to keep the *whole* Law and didn't restrict themselves to pushing circumcision only. Bruce Longenecker, *The Triumph of Abraham's God: The Transformation of Identity in Galatians* (Nashville, NT: Abingdon, 1998), 30-33. See also Thomas Schreiner, *Galatians*, 44-45.

237. N.T. Wright, *Paul: A Biography*, 172. As a whole, the Jewish people believed they were destined for greatness while the Gentiles were destined for judgment. Paul was far ahead of his time, for he believed in a salvation that extended to the Gentiles. A big part of Paul's message was reconciliation: reconciliation with God and reconciliation between people. Mark Fairchild, "The Last Apostle," documentary film.

238. To see the majority of my work on the Christian's relationship to the Law of Moses, see my article "Jesus vs. Moses" at frankviola.org/jesusvsmoses. The article includes quotes from numerous scholars on the meaning of Galatians 4:8-11. For a superb analysis of the theme of freedom in the letter, see John Stott, *The*

holy in Christ. The impartation of God's life and His righteousness does not come by obeying the Law. It comes by faith in Christ. The Law was designed to lead people to the Savior.[239]

The Galatian believers, both Gentile and Jew, are Abraham's seed, children of God, and heirs of His kingdom.[240] Jerusalem is not the center of all things, as the Judaizers believe. What counts is the new Jerusalem, which is from above. Those who allege the Law must be observed in order to become part of God's family proclaim "another gospel." The Judaizers want to win the Galatian believers over and alienate them from Paul and Barnabas for their own selfish ends.[241] Ironically, the Judaizers don't keep the Law themselves, despite what they preach.[242]

Later in the letter, the apostle deals with the current problems of pride, envy, and strife in the assembly.[243] He explains that they don't need the Law to live above the flesh. Instead, if they walk in the Spirit, they will automatically fulfill God's moral will.[244] Paul is also concerned that some of the Galatians who rejected the legalistic teachings of the circumcision party may wrongly equate freedom in Christ with license to fulfill the lusts of the flesh.[245] When he was among them, Paul told the Galatians

---

Message of Galatians, 139-144. Richard Longenecker sums up Paul's view of Christ and the Law beautifully in his book *Paul, Apostle of Liberty*, 243-246.

239. Galatians 3:21-25.

240. Galatians 3:29 through 4:7.

241. Galatians 4:17-20.

242. Galatians 6:13.

243. Galatians 5:26. Pride is always at the root of strife and contention. Proverbs 13:10, NKJV.

244. For Paul, the Galatians didn't need the Torah to live a self-controlled life. They were given the Holy Spirit to accomplish this. If a person walks in love (that is, by the Spirit), they will fulfill the entire Law (Galatians 5:14, 16). To Paul's mind, the Law (Torah) isn't something to be "done" by Christians. It's "fulfilled" by Christians when they walk in the Spirit. The rival teachers were probably saying, "If you do not live according to the Mosaic law, then you have no way to check sinful living." Richard Longenecker, *Galatians*, 89. They were also likely alleging that the Jewish law was the divinely appointed way to curb libertinism and the sins of the flesh (xcviii). See also Alan Cole, *Galatians*, 211. Paul refutes this idea in Galatians 5:13-26 stating that only the Holy Spirit is needed to live above the flesh. For these ideas, see David deSilva, *Letter to the Galatians*, 450-451, 445-446; Thomas Schreiner, *Galatians*, 47; Ben Witherington III, *Grace in Galatia*, 385.

245. Inferred from Galatians 5:13. See also Timothy Keller, *Galatians for You* (Epsom: The Good Book Company, 2013), 142. To my mind, Galatians 5:15 and 5:26 along with Galatians 6:1-8 make plain that

that certain fleshly practices would bar people from entering God's kingdom. Given the problems the Galatian churches are facing now, he reminds them again.[246]

In Paul's zeal to preserve the liberating gospel of Christ, he writes this letter using bitter metaphors and scathing indictments against the Judaizers. (Paul describes circumcision as being "severed" from Christ and adds his wish that those who insist on circumcision "mutilate" themselves![247]) Paul is so angry and worried about his Galatian converts that he cannot bring himself to give thanks to God for them in a thanksgiving section that marks the beginning of his later letters. Instead of opening with thanksgiving or blessing, as Paul will typically do in his other epistles, he opens with a stern rebuke.[248]

His fury is directed toward the circumcision party, and his surprise is aimed at the Galatian believers.[249] Nevertheless, Paul is confident that the Galatians will receive

some fleshly living was going on in the churches. Paul tells the Galatians not to allow their liberty in Christ to become a license to live in the flesh (Galatians 5:13). Longenecker says, "The danger of libertinism, however, was also present within the Galatian churches, being there in an indigenous fashion from the very first. And Paul must also deal with that as a threat to the freedom that believers have in Christ, which he does in the remainder of the body of Galatians in 5:13–6:10." Richard Longenecker, *Galatians*, 235.

246. Inferred from Galatians 5:19-20. I agree with Longenecker who states, Galatians 5:13-21 "implies quite clearly that the Galatian churches were having ethical problems or at least were acutely conscious of ethical failures…. In addition to this judaizing threat brought in from the outside, there was in the Galatian churches the threat of libertinism, which appears to have been present from the very beginning." Richard Longenecker, *Galatians*, xcviii-xcix. Paul argues against (1) any charge that Christian freedom encourages libertinism, and (2) any attempt to put Christian living on a legal basis (82). Witherington agrees that in Galatians 5 through 6, Paul is dealing with specific problems the Galatians were experiencing. Ben Witherington III, *Grace in Galatia*, 379.

247. Different translations use "mutilate," "castrate," and "emasculate." Galatians 5:12, NLT, NRSV, ESV. See also E.P. Sanders, *Paul: The Apostle's Life, Letters, and Thought*, 493.

248. See Galatians 1:1-10 and compare with 1 Thessalonians 1:2; 2 Thessalonians 1:3; 1 Corinthians 1:4; Romans 1:8; Philippians 1:3. I give credit to Jeffrey Weima for this observation.

249. In Galatians 6:13, Paul says the Judaizers only wanted the believers to be circumcised "so they can boast about it and claim you as their disciples" (NLT). The Judaizers could also tell non-believing Jews that the gospel makes Gentiles Jewish proselytes. This would make the gospel of Jesus more appealing to Jews. Richard Longenecker, *The Ministry and Message of Paul*, 52.

his letter and "adopt no other view."[250] He urges them to throw the agitators out of the churches.[251] He begins the letter with greetings of grace and peace, and he ends it the same way.[252] But again, there is no thanksgiving for the churches. The letter is brought to Galatia by someone Paul knows in the ekklesia in Antioch of Syria, possibly Titus.[253]

Galatians

Paul, an apostle—not from men, nor through man, but through Jesus Christ, and God the Father, who raised him from the dead—and all the brothers[a] who are with me, to the assemblies of Galatia: Grace to you and peace from God the Father and our Lord Jesus Christ, who gave himself for our sins, that he might deliver us out of this present evil age, according to the will of our God and Father—to whom be the glory forever and ever. Amen.

I marvel that you are so quickly deserting him who called you in the grace of Christ to a different "good news," but there isn't another "good news." Only there are some who trouble

---

250. I agree with Longenecker that "in all probability, the Galatian Christians were won back to the Pauline gospel" by this letter. Richard Longenecker, *Paul, Apostle of Liberty*, 198.

251. See Galatians 4:30. "The language of casting out and expulsion makes perfectly good sense and is apt if Paul is talking about the agitators who have made themselves a part of the Galatian Christian communities...." Ben Witherington III, *Grace in Galatia*, 338. "Paul implies that his audience should send away the spiritual Ishmaelites—those trying to tie them to the Sinai covenant rather than the superior promise." Craig Keener, et al., *NIV Cultural Backgrounds Study Bible*, 2052. Richard Longenecker agrees saying, "the Galatian believers should 'cast out' the Judaizers and their influence from the Christian congregations of Galatia." Richard Longenecker, *Galatians*, 271.

252. Galatians 1:3 and 6:16-18.

253. While we cannot be sure who brought the letter, Titus is a plausible candidate and confirmed by Witherington. Personal correspondence with Ben Witherington III, 7/18/16 and 4/4/22. For an overview of Galatians, see David deSilva, *An Introduction to the New Testament*, chap. 12; N.T. Wright and Michael Bird, *The New Testament in Its World*, chap. 17; Clinton Arnold, ed., *Zondervan Illustrated Bible Backgrounds Commentary*, 3:265-298.

you and want to pervert the Good News of Christ. But even though we, or an angel from heaven, should preach to you any "good news" other than that which we preached to you, let him be cursed.

As we have said before, so I now say again: if any man preaches to you any "good news" other than that which you received, let him be cursed. For am I now seeking the favor of men, or of God? Or am I striving to please men? For if I were still pleasing men, I wouldn't be a servant of Christ.

But I make known to you, brothers, concerning the Good News which was preached by me, that it is not according to man.

For I didn't receive it from man, nor was I taught it, but it came to me through revelation of Jesus Christ. For you have heard of my way of living in time past in the Jews' religion, how that beyond measure I persecuted the assembly of God and ravaged it.

I advanced in the Jews' religion beyond many of my own age among my countrymen, being more exceedingly zealous for the traditions of my fathers. But when it was the good pleasure of God, who separated me from my mother's womb and called me through his grace to reveal his Son in me, that I might preach him among the Gentiles, I didn't immediately confer with flesh and blood, nor did I go up to Jerusalem to those who were apostles before me, but I went away into Arabia. Then I returned to Damascus.

Then after three years I went up to Jerusalem to visit Peter, and stayed with him fifteen days. But of the other apostles I saw no one except James, the Lord's brother. Now about the things which I write to you, behold,[b] before God, I'm not lying. Then I came to the regions of Syria and Cilicia. I was still unknown by face to the assemblies of Judea which were in Christ, but they only heard: "He who once persecuted us now preaches the faith that he once tried to destroy." So they glorified God in me.

Then after a period of fourteen years I went up again to Jerusalem with Barnabas, taking Titus also with me. I went up by revelation, and I laid before them the Good News which I preach among the Gentiles, but privately before those who were respected, for fear that I might be running, or had run, in vain. But not even Titus, who was with me, being a Greek, was compelled to be circumcised.

This was because of the false brothers secretly brought in, who stole in to spy out our liberty which we have in Christ Jesus, that they might bring us into bondage, to whom we gave no place in the way of subjection, not for an hour, that the truth of the Good News might continue with you.

But from those who were reputed to be important—whatever they were, it makes no difference to me; God doesn't show partiality to man—they, I say, who were respected imparted nothing to me, but to the contrary, when they saw that I had been entrusted with the Good News for the uncircumcised, even as Peter with the Good News for the circumcised—for he who worked through Peter in the apostleship with the circumcised also worked through me with the Gentiles—and when they perceived the grace that was given to me, James and Cephas and John, those who were reputed to be pillars, gave to Barnabas and me the right hand of fellowship, that we should go to the Gentiles, and they to the circumcision. They only asked us to remember the poor—which very thing I was also zealous to do.

But when Peter came to Antioch, I resisted him to his face, because he stood condemned. For before some people came from James, he ate with the Gentiles. But when they came, he drew back and separated himself, fearing those who were of the circumcision. And the rest of the Jews joined him in his hypocrisy, so that even Barnabas was carried away with their hypocrisy.

But when I saw that they didn't walk uprightly according to the truth of the Good News, I said to Peter before them all, "If you, being a Jew, live as the Gentiles do, and not as the Jews do, why do you compel the Gentiles to live as the Jews do? We, being Jews by nature, and not Gentile sinners, yet knowing that a man is not justified by the works of the law but through faith in Jesus Christ, even we believed in Christ Jesus, that we might be justified by faith in Christ, and not by the works of the law, because no flesh will be justified by the works of the law. But if while we sought to be justified in Christ, we ourselves also were found sinners, is Christ a servant of sin? Certainly not! For if I build up again those things which I destroyed, I prove myself a law-breaker. For I, through the law, died to the law, that I might live to God. I have been crucified with Christ, and it is no longer I who live, but Christ lives in me. That life which I now live in the flesh, I live by faith in the Son of God, who loved me, and gave himself up for me. I don't reject the grace of God. For if righteousness is through the law, then Christ died for nothing!"

Foolish Galatians, who has bewitched you not to obey the truth, before whose eyes Jesus Christ was openly portrayed among you as crucified? I just want to learn this from you: Did you receive the Spirit by the works of the law, or by hearing of faith? Are you so foolish? Having begun in the Spirit, are you now completed in the flesh? Did you suffer so many things in vain, if it is indeed in vain?

He therefore who supplies the Spirit to you and does miracles among you, does he do it by the works of the law, or by hearing of faith? Even so, Abraham "believed God, and it was counted to him for righteousness." Genesis 15:6 Know therefore that those who are of faith are children of Abraham.

The Scripture, foreseeing that God would justify the Gentiles by faith, preached the Good News beforehand to Abraham, saying, "In you all the nations will be blessed." Genesis 12:3; 18:18; 22:18 So then, those who are of faith are blessed with the faithful Abraham. For as many as are of the works of the law are under a curse. For it is written, "Cursed is everyone who doesn't continue in all things that are written in the book of the law, to do them." Deuteronomy 27:26 Now that no man is justified by the law before God is evident, for, "The righteous will live by faith." Habakkuk 2:4 The law is not of faith, but, "The man who does them will live by them." Leviticus 18:5

Christ redeemed us from the curse of the law, having become a curse for us. For it is written, "Cursed is everyone who hangs on a tree," Deuteronomy 21:23 that the blessing of Abraham might come on the Gentiles through Christ Jesus, that we might receive the promise of the Spirit through faith. Brothers, speaking of human terms, though it is only a man's covenant, yet when it has been confirmed, no one makes it void or adds to it.

Now the promises were spoken to Abraham and to his offspring.[c] He doesn't say, "To descendants[d]," as of many, but as of one, "To your offspring," Genesis 12:7; 13:15; 24:7 which is Christ. Now I say this: A covenant confirmed beforehand by God in Christ, the law, which came four hundred thirty years after, does not annul, so as to make the promise of no effect. For if the inheritance is of the law, it is no more of promise; but God has granted it to Abraham by promise.

Then why is there the law? It was added because of transgressions, until the offspring should come to whom the promise has been made. It was ordained through angels by the hand of a mediator.

Now a mediator is not between one, but God is one. Is the law then against the promises of God? Certainly not! For if there had been a law given which could make alive, most certainly righteousness would have been of the law. But the Scripture imprisoned all things under sin, that the promise by faith in Jesus Christ might be given to those who believe.

But before faith came, we were kept in custody under the law, confined for the faith which should afterwards be revealed. So that the law has become our tutor to bring us to Christ, that we might be justified by faith. But now that faith has come, we are no longer under a tutor.

For you are all children of God, through faith in Christ Jesus. For as many of you as were baptized into Christ have put on Christ. There is neither Jew nor Greek, there is neither slave nor free man, there is neither male nor female; for you are all one in Christ Jesus. If you are Christ's, then you are Abraham's offspring and heirs according to promise.

But I say that so long as the heir is a child, he is no different from a bondservant, though he is lord of all, but is under guardians and stewards until the day appointed by the father. So we also, when we were children, were held in bondage under the elemental principles of the world.

But when the fullness of the time came, God sent out his Son, born to a woman, born under the law, that he might redeem those who were under the law, that we might receive the adoption as children. And because you are children, God sent out the Spirit of his Son into your hearts, crying, "Abba,[e] Father!" So you are no longer a bondservant, but a son; and if a son, then an heir of God through Christ.

However at that time, not knowing God, you were in bondage to those who by nature are not gods. But now that you have come to know God, or rather to be known by God, why do you turn back again to the weak and miserable elemental principles, to which you desire to be in bondage all over again? You observe days, months, seasons, and years. I am afraid for you, that I might have wasted my labor for you.

I beg you, brothers, become as I am, for I also have become as you are. You did me no wrong, but you know that because of weakness in the flesh I preached the Good News to you the first time. That which was a temptation to you in my flesh, you didn't despise nor reject; but you received me as an angel of God, even as Christ Jesus.

What was the blessing you enjoyed? For I testify to you that, if possible, you would have plucked out your eyes and given them to me. So then, have I become your enemy by telling you the truth? They zealously seek you in no good way. No, they desire to alienate you, that you may seek them. But it is always good to be zealous in a good cause, and not only when I am present with you.

My little children, of whom I am again in travail until Christ is formed in you—but I could wish to be present with you now, and to change my tone, for I am perplexed about you. Tell me, you that desire to be under the law, don't you listen to the law? For it is written that Abraham had two sons, one by the servant, and one by the free woman. However, the son by the servant was born according to the flesh, but the son by the free woman was born through promise.

These things contain an allegory, for these are two covenants. One is from Mount Sinai, bearing children to bondage, which is Hagar. For this Hagar is Mount Sinai in Arabia, and answers to the Jerusalem that exists now, for she is in bondage with her children. But the Jerusalem that is above is free, which is the mother of us all. For it is written, "Rejoice, you barren who don't bear. Break out and shout, you who don't travail. For the desolate have more children than her who has a husband." Isaiah 54:1

Now we, brothers, as Isaac was, are children of promise. But as then, he who was born according to the flesh persecuted him who was born according to the Spirit, so also it is now. However what does the Scripture say? "Throw out the servant and her son, for the son of the servant will not inherit with the son of the free woman." Genesis 21:10 So then, brothers, we are not children of a servant, but of the free woman.

Stand firm therefore in the liberty by which Christ has made us free, and don't be entangled again with a yoke of bondage. Behold, I, Paul, tell you that if you receive circumcision, Christ will profit you nothing. Yes, I testify again to every man who receives circumcision that he is a debtor to do the whole law. You are alienated from Christ, you who desire to be justified by the law. You have fallen away from grace. For we, through the Spirit, by faith wait for the hope of righteousness.

For in Christ Jesus neither circumcision amounts to anything, nor uncircumcision, but faith working through love. You were running well! Who interfered with you that you should not obey the truth? This persuasion is not from him who calls you. A little yeast grows through the whole lump. I have confidence toward you in the Lord that you will think no other way. But he who troubles you will bear his judgment, whoever he is.

But I, brothers, if I still preach circumcision, why am I still persecuted? Then the stumbling block of the cross has been removed. I wish that those who disturb you would cut themselves off. For you, brothers, were called for freedom. Only don't use your freedom for gain to the flesh, but through love be servants to one another. For the whole law is fulfilled in one word, in this: "You shall love your neighbor as yourself." Leviticus 19:18 But if you bite and devour one another, be careful that you don't consume one another.

But I say, walk by the Spirit, and you won't fulfill the lust of the flesh. For the flesh lusts against the Spirit, and the Spirit against the flesh; and these are contrary to one another, that you may not do the things that you desire.

But if you are led by the Spirit, you are not under the law.

Now the deeds of the flesh are obvious, which are: adultery, sexual immorality, uncleanness, lustfulness, idolatry, sorcery, hatred, strife, jealousies, outbursts of anger, rivalries, divisions, heresies, envy, murders, drunkenness, orgies, and things like these; of which I forewarn you, even as I also forewarned you, that those who practice such things will not inherit God's Kingdom.

But the fruit of the Spirit is love, joy, peace, patience, kindness, goodness, faith,[f] gentleness, and self-control. Against such things there is no law. Those who belong to Christ have crucified the flesh with its passions and lusts.

If we live by the Spirit, let's also walk by the Spirit. Let's not become conceited, provoking one another, and envying one another.

Brothers, even if a man is caught in some fault, you who are spiritual must restore such a one in a spirit of gentleness; looking to yourself so that you also aren't tempted. Bear one another's burdens, and so fulfill the law of Christ. For if a man thinks himself to be something when he is nothing, he deceives himself. But let each man examine his own work, and then he will have reason to boast in himself, and not in someone else. For each man will bear his own burden.

But let him who is taught in the word share all good things with him who teaches. Don't be deceived. God is not mocked, for whatever a man sows, that he will also reap. For he who sows to his own flesh will from the flesh reap corruption. But he who sows to the Spirit will from the Spirit reap eternal life. Let's not be weary in doing good, for we will reap in due season, if we don't give up. So then, as we have opportunity, let's do what is good toward all men, and especially toward those who are of the household of the faith.

See with what large letters I write to you with my own hand. As many as desire to make a good impression in the flesh compel you to be circumcised; just so they may not be persecuted for the cross of Christ. For even they who receive circumcision don't keep the law themselves, but they desire to have you circumcised, that they may boast in your flesh.

But far be it from me to boast, except in the cross of our Lord Jesus Christ, through which the world has been crucified to me, and I to the world. For in Christ Jesus neither is circumcision anything, nor uncircumcision, but a new creation. As many as walk by this rule, peace and mercy be on them, and on God's Israel.

From now on, let no one cause me any trouble, for I bear the marks of the Lord Jesus branded on my body.

The grace of our Lord Jesus Christ be with your spirit, brothers. Amen.

a. 1:2 The word for "brothers" here and where context allows may also be correctly translated "brothers and sisters" or "siblings."

b. 1:20 "Behold," from "ἰδού," means look at, take notice, observe, see, or gaze at. It is often used as an interjection.

c. 3:16 or, seed.

d. 3:16 or, seeds.

e. 4:6 Abba is a Greek spelling for the Aramaic word for "Father" or "Daddy" used in a familiar, respectful, and loving way.

f. 5:22 or, faithfulness.

> **Sharpening the Focus:** Most people write letters on sheets of papyrus. (Those too poor to afford papyrus write on broken pieces of pottery called *ostraca*.) Papyrus is a light and tough material made from the stalks of the papyrus plant, woven and pressed together. A normal sheet is about the same size as a standard sheet of American paper, around eleven inches high by eight inches wide.[254]

254. Ben Witherington III, *Invitation to the New Testament*, 5; Wayne Meeks, ed., *Library of Early Christianity*, 8:117-118.

For longer documents, the papyrus sheets are glued side-by-side on a stick to form a roll (also called a "scroll"). Once the scroll has been written upon, it's rolled up and tied with pieces of thread. One roll is called a "volume" (from the Latin *volumen*, "something rolled up"). A volume is twenty to thirty-five feet long and eight to ten inches high.[255] (Authors write to fit volumes. Luke's two-volume work, Luke-Acts, is an example.[256]) The Gospel of Luke (the longest Gospel) contains the maximum number of letters and words that could fit onto twenty papyrus sheets glued together. Important documents are normally sealed with hot wax on top of the threads. A seal is then placed on the scroll to reserve its contents for its recipient.

Since papyrus reeds are not available everywhere, another important material for letter writing is parchment.[257] Parchment is made from animal skins and twice as expensive as papyrus.[258] While most of the New Testament authors will use scrolls, a few of them may use codices (plural for "codex," a book with pages bound together in modern style).[259] Writers use a reed pen and black ink made of soot, gum, and water.

Words are usually written in all capital (*uncial*) letters and written without any word breaks, indentation, or punctuation.[260] Chapters and verses are also lacking in first-century writing.[261] (They were later added to the New Testament by editors.) This is for economic reasons, because the less papyrus used, the less expensive to produce.[262] For note-taking and the like, people often write on a wooden tablet using

255. Ben Witherington III, *The New Testament Story*, 9.

256. Ben Witherington III, *The Acts of the Apostles*, 172.

257. See 2 Timothy 4:13.

258. Joel Green, et al., *The World of the New Testament*, 354. For the number of lines and estimated expense of each of Paul's letters, see David Capes, et al., *Rediscovering Paul*, 113, 116. Most of Paul's letters were expensive to write because they were unusually long. See also Mark Wilson, *Biblical Turkey*, 279.

259. Paper wasn't invented until about A.D. 100 (by the Chinese), but it took over 1,000 years to reach the Mediterranean population. For a detailed discussion on the differences between parchment and papyrus, along with the use of the codex, see Joel Green, et al., *The World of the New Testament*, 351-356. Christians played a significant role in popularizing the codex, being among the earliest groups to widely adopt and spread its use.

260. The technical term for this is *scriptio continua*. Personal correspondence with Jeffrey Weima, 12/28/23.

261. Ben Witherington III, *The New Testament Story*, 9.

262. Ben Witherington III, *Invitation to the New Testament*, 5.

a thick wax coating on one side. They use a wooden stylus to etch the wax surface for temporary writing which can be smoothed out and removed later.[263]

Regarding the delivery of letters, ordinary people cannot use the imperial postal system. They must rely on messengers who can hand-deliver the letters to their recipients.[264] In other words, Paul's letters are normally carried by private carriers, people he knows and trusts.[265] His letters (as well as the rest of the New Testament) are written in *koiné* Greek—the common trade language of the Roman world, used by the masses, the merchants, and the marketplace.[266]

The culture of the ancient world was preliterate and preprint.[267] Consequently, the ancients have a remarkable capacity for memory and recall.[268] This is why the words of Jesus can be passed on by spoken tradition over a period of years and still be reliable.[269] With respect to the Old Testament, in the first century, both Greek-speaking Jews and Christians use the Septuagint (or the LXX, which means "seventy"). This is a translation of the Hebrew Bible, created before the third century B.C. in

263. Gary Burge, *A Week in the Life of a Roman Centurion*, 91.

264. Craig Keener, *Acts*, 3:2283; Joel Green, et al., *The World of the New Testament*, 362-364; Benjamin Laird, *Creating the Canon*, 19-22.

265. David Capes, et al., *Rediscovering Paul*, 117. For example, Paul sent some of his letters with Phoebe and Tychicus.

266. *Koiné* means "common." Scott Korb, *Life in Year One*, 19. The writings of the New Testament were penned between A.D. 45 and A.D. 100. Robert Hutchinson, *The Dawn of Christianity*, xviii.

267. As previously noted, the ancient world was an oral culture. Second Temple Judaism was also an oral society. Jewish literacy in the first century ran less than 10 percent. Literate Jews were almost always royal officials, priests, Pharisees, and scribes. Most who followed Jesus were "technically illiterate." James D.G. Dunn, *Jesus, Paul, and the Gospels*, 8-9.

268. The absolute staple of ancient education was repetition and memorization in short redundancy. Personal correspondence with Ben Witherington III, 1/2/06.

269. Ben Witherington III, *Invitation to the New Testament*, 7; *The New Testament Story*, 3ff.; *A Week in the Fall of Jerusalem*, 56-57; Gary Burge, et al., *The New Testament in Antiquity*, 119; N.T. Wright, *The Challenge of Jesus*, 26. Regarding the reliability of the New Testament as a whole, "roughly ninety-four percent of its content is identical in the extant manuscripts." Michael Shepherd, *An Introduction to the Making and Meaning of the Bible*, 58. The remaining variations are minor and do not change any theological or doctrinal point of the historical Christian faith.

Alexandria, Egypt, to the second century A.D. in Palestine. The majority of New Testament citations of the Old Testament are derived from the Septuagint.

In the Greco-Roman world, private letters average around ninety words, while literary letters from orators and statesmen average around 200 words. By contrast, the average length of Paul's letters is about 1,300 words. Paul, therefore, creates a new literary form that we call the "epistle," which is far longer than most letters, theological in its character, and communal in its nature.[270] Paul of Tarsus is a brilliant and deliberate letter writer. The ingenious way he crafts his epistles makes this plain.[271]

The Jerusalem Council
Late 49[272]

The agitators have left their imprint on the church in Syrian Antioch. Some of the Gentile believers wonder if they really must be circumcised as the circumcision party alleges. To resolve this matter, the Antioch assembly sends Paul, Barnabas, and some other believers

270. Robert Gundry, *A Survey of the New Testament*, 341.

271. For details on this point and an analysis of how Paul crafted his letters, including the opening, thanksgiving, body, and closing, see Jeffrey Weima, *Paul the Ancient Letter Writer: An Introduction to Epistolary Analysis* (Grand Rapids, MI: Baker Academic, 2016); Jerome Murphy-O'Connor, *Paul the Letter-Writer*. Historical context is not the only consideration in understanding Paul's letters. "Epistolary analysis" is also necessary. David Capes, et al., *Rediscovering Paul*, chap. 3; Wayne Meeks, ed., *Library of Early Christianity*, 8:158-182; David deSilva, *Paul and the Macedonians*, 23-26. For a discussion on how the entire New Testament was composed, including details about its original readers, see Benjamin Laird, *Creating the Canon*, chaps. 1 and 3.

272. The latter part of A.D. 49. Ben Witherington III, *The New Testament Story*, 276; F.F. Bruce, *Paul: Apostle of the Heart Set Free*, 475. Longenecker, along with many other scholars, agree with the A.D. 49 date. Richard Longenecker, *The Ministry and Message of Paul*, 53. This same year "the Passover disturbances" took place in Jerusalem, and 20,000 to 30,000 Jews were killed as a result. Rainer Riesner, *Paul's Early Period*, 354. For more information on the brutal massacre of Jews in the temple precincts in Jerusalem on Passover A.D. 49, see John Stott, *The Message of 1 & 2 Thessalonians*, 57; Jeffrey Weima, *1-2 Thessalonians*, 177. This tragedy, as well as Claudius' decree expelling the Jews from Rome, could be what Paul had in mind when he later penned 1 Thessalonians 2:16, which says, "But wrath has come on them [the Jews] to the uttermost."

to Jerusalem[273] to find out if the circumcision party represents the voice of the twelve apostles, the elders, and the entire Jerusalem church.[274]

As the men journey south toward Jerusalem (about a twenty-five-day walk), Paul and Barnabas report to the saints in Phoenicia and Samaria about God's work among the Gentiles. The believers in those regions rejoice at the news.[275] When Paul and Barnabas arrive in Jerusalem, the assembly, apostles, and elders welcome them. But some in the circumcision party stand up to protest, asserting that the Gentiles must be circumcised and keep the Law of Moses.[276]

A debate ensues among the apostles and elders, and Paul and Barnabas are drawn into the simmering conflict. The tension is palpable. After much discussion, Peter reminds everyone that God decided the issue when He poured His Holy Spirit upon Cornelius and his household. They received the Spirit, not by observing the Law, but by trusting in Jesus without circumcision. His thundering statement is:

He [God] did not discriminate between us and them [the Gentiles], for he purified their hearts by faith. Now then, why do you try to test God by putting on the necks of Gentiles a yoke that neither we nor our ancestors have been able to bear? No! We believe it is through the grace of our Lord Jesus that we are saved, just as they are. (Acts 15:9-11, NIV)

Paul and Barnabas follow Peter's speech. They report on the signs and wonders God accomplished through them among the Gentiles, confirming their gospel of grace.[277] The assembly witnesses the conversation and everyone falls silent.[278] James (the Lord's

---

273. Acts 15:2-3.

274. According to Acts, this was Paul's third visit to Jerusalem as a disciple of Jesus. For a detailed sketch and timeline, see Ben Witherington III, *The Acts of the Apostles*, 440-452. For a fuller discussion on the council, see Martin Hengel, *Acts and the History of Earliest Christianity*, chap. 10.

275. Acts 15:3.

276. Again, it was not only that they pushed circumcision; they demanded that the Gentiles keep the entire Law of Moses (Acts 15:5). This is significant since they continued to make this demand throughout the narrative. Clinton Arnold, ed., *Zondervan Illustrated Bible Backgrounds Commentary*, 2b:140.

277. This was strategic, as the Jews put a lot of stock in signs and wonders. Acts 15:12; 1 Corinthians 1:22.

278. According to Acts 15:6, the apostles and elders discussed the issue, but in Acts 15:12, the assembly is present also. According to Weima, "The Greek text of Acts 15:12 does not use a word that requires a reference to the broader assembly of Christians. It is just as likely (perhaps even more likely) that the 'assembly' is the collective term used to refer to those that are identified in 15:6 as attending this gathering: 'the apostles

half-brother) speaks next, and he summarizes Peter's argument. James references the prophecy from Amos, that the tabernacle of David would be restored and the Gentiles would receive salvation.[279]

In his speech, James offers a compromise to please both the Jews and Gentiles in the ekklesias. Agreeing with Peter's words about salvation by grace, he concludes that to help the Gentiles and Jews get along in the kingdom communities, the Gentiles should observe four stipulations: They should abstain from food polluted by idols, fornication (sexual immorality),[280] strangled animals (animals with undrained blood), and consuming blood.[281] No other burden should be laid upon the Gentiles.[282]

---

and the elders.' Personal correspondence with Jeffrey Weima, 1/4/24. This may be true, but the NKJV and the NASB use the term "multitude" while the NIV uses "whole assembly." Since Acts 15:22 mentions the "whole church" (NIV) as being separate from the apostles and elders, I believe the whole assembly was observing the discussion. On the other hand, the apostles and elders probably made up a sizeable group, so the term could refer to just the apostles and elders or to the entire assembly. Craig Keener, *Acts*, 3:2240-2241.

279. Amos 9:11-12; Acts 15:13-21. For an analysis of James' speech in Acts 15, see Ben Witherington III, ed., *History, Literature and Society in the Book of Acts*, chap. 7.

280. Jews "detested as horrible premarital sex, adultery, prostitution, and frequently even lust, which some viewed as visual adultery." Craig Keener, *Acts*, 3:2273.

281. Food polluted or offered to idols (Acts 15:20, 29) refers to the fact that most cities in the Roman world sold meat in the meat markets supplied by local temples and offered to pagan gods. In most pagan homes, before wine was consumed, a libation was made to some god and poured out. For a Jew to consume either food or drink offered to idols would render them unclean. James D.G. Dunn, *The Acts of the Apostles*, 205.

282. Witherington argues that these prohibitions are all related to attending temple feasts. Ben Witherington III, *The Acts of the Apostles*, 462-467. Others believe they are related to the Noachide laws. Craig Keener, *Acts*, 3:2260ff. According to David deSilva, "In the case of Acts 15, we see a compromise solution to the presenting problem: how can Jews (whom God set apart from the nations for himself) mingle freely with Gentiles in this new social entity that we call 'the Church' without polluting themselves? The answer was to impose a few token purity regulations upon Gentile believers (often associated with the so-called Noachide laws—but strangely not entirely overlapping with them) as a means of ensuring non-contaminating contact." Personal correspondence with deSilva, 3/23/22. Other scholars believe these prohibitions closed the door to demonic activity (e.g., 1 Corinthians 10:20). Clinton Arnold, ed., *Zondervan Illustrated Bible Backgrounds Commentary*, 2b:145-146. Bruce gives an insightful look at these prohibitions, arguing that Paul later rescinded the food laws. Therefore, they had temporary application (see 1 Timothy 4:4-5; 1 Corinthians 8). Fornication, deplorable according to Jewish standards, is upheld throughout the entire New Testament. F.F. Bruce, *Answers to Questions*, 80-81.

The assembly accepts James' suggestion.[283] The decision is reached by consensus, and the Holy Spirit stands with it. The four prohibitions represent practices that are highly offensive to Jewish sensibilities. They are known as the "heinous vices of heathenism."[284] The apostles, elders, and assembly in Jerusalem decide to write a letter outlining these prohibitions for the Gentile believers to read.[285] They write it not only to the ekklesia in Syrian Antioch, but also to the assemblies in Cilicia and throughout Syria.[286] The letter opens with the apostles and elders calling the Gentile believers in Antioch, Syria, and Cilicia their "brothers"—a significant statement in light of the debate.[287]

283. No doubt the strict Jewish believers consented with a heavy heart. But as the story unfolds, some of them didn't abide by this stipulation and continued their mission to persuade the Gentile believers to be circumcised and keep the Mosaic Law.

284. Richard Longenecker, *The Ministry and Message of Paul*, 56.

285. The letter is written in the style of an official encyclical document. Darrell Bock, *Acts*, 511; Eckhard Schnabel, *Acts*, 647. The Jerusalem council "stands as the watershed in the design and construction of the narrative in Acts." Richard Longenecker, *Paul, Apostle of Liberty*, 233. The typical papyrus letter averaged eighty-seven words. The apostolic letter that appears in Acts 15 is just under one hundred words. Craig Keener, *The IVP Bible Background Commentary: New Testament*, 272.

286. Acts 15:23. These ekklesias in Cilicia and Syria were probably founded through the witness of the ekklesia in Syrian Antioch. Richard Longenecker, *The Ministry and Message of Paul*, 61. "We need not wonder that there were congregations in Syria and in Cilicia; the first dispersion had carried the gospel as far as Antioch, and that means also to other places, and since that time Christians had spread out from these new centers." R.C.H. Lenski, *The Interpretation of the Acts of the Apostles*, 621. The Judaizing "agitators" not only created anxiety and perplexity in Syria (i.e., Antioch), but they also did the same in Cilicia. W.J. Conybeare and J.S. Howson, *The Life & Epistles of St. Paul*, 195. The circuit letter first went to the Gentile believers in Syrian Antioch and Cilicia (Acts 15:41). But Paul and Silas later delivered it to the ekklesias in southern Galatia (Acts 16:4). Simon Kistemaker, *Exposition of the Acts of the Apostles*, 561. "It is plausible that Silas, one of the two envoys that the apostles and elders had sent to Syria and Cilicia, had made copies of the letter… one of which he carried to the churches in South Galatia." Eckhard Schnabel, *Acts*, 666.

287. Acts 15:23, ESV. According to Bruce, "The letter is addressed to the Gentile Christians of Antioch and of the united province of Syria-Cilicia, of which Antioch was the capital. The recently founded churches in South Galatia may have been envisaged as coming within the scope of the letter, but they are not mentioned." F.F. Bruce, *The Book of the Acts*, 298. It appears that there were churches in Syria other than Antioch. Tyre and Sidon were among them. Eckhard Schnabel, *Acts*, 648. The reason why the letter wasn't addressed to Galatia along with Antioch, Syria, and Cilicia was perhaps because the issue originated from Antioch, Syria (whose neighbor was Cilicia), and Paul (who was present at the council) may have said, "I've recently sent a letter to the ekklesias in Galatia, so there's no need to pile on with this decree. I will just bring it with me as a confirmation to my letter when I visit them again." (I owe this scenario to Tim Oslovich.) Note that Antioch was the hub for the double province of Syria and eastern Cilicia. Darrell Bock, *Acts*, 511. According

Because we have heard that some who went out from us have troubled you with words, unsettling your souls, saying, "You must be circumcised and keep the law," to whom we gave no commandment.[288]

The whole ekklesia, the Twelve, and the Jerusalem elders select two of their prophets[289] to journey back to Syrian Antioch with Paul and Barnabas. The prophets, Judas Barsabbas[290] and Silas (also called Silvanus),[291] play a specific role. It is to authenticate the letter.[292] Silas is a Roman citizen and a kindred spirit with Paul.[293] He is literate and has training in Greek and rhetoric.[294] As prominent members of the Jerusalem assembly, Judas and Silas have earned the esteem of their fellow believers. The two men "risked their lives for the name of our Lord Jesus Christ."[295]

Paul, Barnabas, Judas, and Silas make their way back to Antioch of Syria to deliver the letter to the assembly there. When they arrive, they gather the church and read the letter. The letter greatly encourages the Antioch believers, and they rejoice. Judas and Silas stay in Syrian Antioch for a time, encouraging and strengthening the believing community

---

to Schnabel, "Acts 15:23 attests other churches in Syria and also in Cilicia, who would have heard of the problems in Antioch, which seems to be the reason why these two regions are mentioned." Personal correspondence with Eckhard Schnabel, 1/9/24.

288. Acts 15:24. Compare with Galatians 1:7; 5:10, 12, ESV.

289. Judas and Silas are described as "prophets" in Acts 15:32.

290. This person is not to be confused with Joseph/Justus Barsabbas mentioned in Acts 1:23.

291. Silvanus was his Latin (Roman) name, while Silas was his Jewish name. F.F. Bruce, *The Pauline Circle*, 24. Silas and Judas were called "chief men among the brethren," denoting the spiritual clout they held in the eyes of the ekklesia in Jerusalem (Acts 15:22, KJV and ASV).

292. Acts 15:22. The wording in the Greek, "sent forth," implies that the church in Jerusalem provided financially for their trip. Craig Keener, *Acts*, 3:2224. The controversy provoking this letter was temporary. By A.D. 70, the matter was no longer significant. F.F. Bruce, *The Spreading Flame: The Rise and Progress of Christianity from Its First Beginnings to the Conversion of the English* (Grand Rapids, MI: Eerdmans, 1958), 110-111. For further details on the Jerusalem council, see William Ramsay, *St. Paul the Traveler and Roman Citizen*, chap. 7; Craig Keener, *Acts*, 3:2215-2296.

293. F.F. Bruce, *The Pauline Circle*, 26; *The Spreading Flame*, 111.

294. Ben Witherington III, *Letters and Homilies for Hellenized Christians*, 2:50.

295. Acts 15:26. Some scholars prefer the translation "devoted" or "dedicated" rather than "risked." However, true devotion to Christ and the willingness to risk one's life for Him go together. Craig Keener, *Acts*, 3:2290.

there. When their time expires, the Antioch church sends them back to Jerusalem with salutations of peace. Paul and Barnabas stay in Antioch, teaching and preaching the word of God along with many others in the church.[296]

Crisis in the Jewish Kingdom Communities

The Twelve leave Jerusalem again and begin traveling.[297] Peter retraces the steps of Paul and ministers to the churches Paul raised up, just as he retraced the steps of Philip. The dispersed Jewish believers in Palestine and beyond suffer oppression from unconverted Jews and Gentiles in their cities. The limited agricultural land cannot support a growing population in Palestine and in other regions. Those deprived of land are forced to become hired laborers. For this reason, rich landowners rob some Christians of their land. A number of Jesus-followers are hauled into court by wealthy men who scorn their faith.

In addition, rich farmers are oppressing their poor laborers, and tension between landlords and tenants grows, even breaking out into violence. In Rome, grain shortages lead to rioting. This also happens in Palestine. At the same time, the influx of Hellenistic goods causes a class of wealthy merchants to emerge. Some Christians seek opportunities to become prosperous traders. And the wealthy members of the assemblies receive undue favoritism while the poor believers fear offending them.[298]

Additionally, as the Jewish Christians hear vague rumors about the council in Jerusalem, they conclude that the Gentile and Jewish believers in Syrian Antioch and elsewhere have positioned themselves against the Law of Moses under Paul's influence. They hear a

296. "Paul and Barnabas also remained in Antioch, teaching and preaching the word of the Lord, with many others also." Acts 15:35, NKJV.

297. We don't see the Twelve in Jerusalem after Acts 15. Only James and the elders are mentioned in Acts 21:18. See Paul Barnett, *Bethlehem to Patmos,* 198. Since James (the Lord's brother) is called an "apostle" (Galatians 1:19), it's reasonable to believe that he traveled also, since all apostolic workers are itinerant and travel.

298. The scenario presented in this section is based on information in Clinton Arnold, ed., *Zondervan Illustrated Bible Backgrounds Commentary,* 4:89; Ben Witherington III, *Letters and Homilies for Hellenized Christians,* 3:385-555; David deSilva, *An Introduction to the New Testament,* 724, including n. 14; Craig Keener, *The IVP Bible Background Commentary: New Testament,* 669-670; Douglas Moo, *James,* 92; Scot McKnight, *The Letter of James,* NICNT, Logos edition (Grand Rapids, MI: Eerdmans 2011), 196-198, 383-410.

corrupted version of grace that is wrongly ascribed to Paul. The version alleges that good works have nothing to do with salvation.[299]

Believing that the Twelve also hold this position, some of the Jewish Christians are falling in love with the world. They are injuring one another with uncontrolled critical speech that springs from envy. The well-to-do believers are discriminating against the poor, giving preferential treatment to the rich. A number of the worldly believers have ambitions to become teachers within the church. Some in the assemblies are also sick.

The crisis reaches the ears of James (the Lord's half-brother), and he becomes burdened to address it. So he writes a letter to the kingdom communities dispersed among the nations.[300]

JAMES WRITES HIS LETTER (JAMES)

Year: A.D. 49[301]

299. Witherington argues that the letter of James was written to correct a misunderstanding of Paul's doctrine. Ben Witherington III, *Invitation to the New Testament,* 281. According to Douglas Moo, "the scenario that makes best sense is to think that he [James] is writing to oppose a misunderstood form of Paul's teaching. The readers of the letter, scattered by persecution into areas near Antioch, have become acquainted with a perverted form of the Pauline viewpoint, with the slogan 'faith alone justifies' as its hallmark. James writes, then, to counter this false view of the relationship between faith, works, and salvation. James and Paul, when properly interpreted in their own contexts, are not opposed to one another on this point." Douglas Moo, *The Letter of James*, PNTC, Logos edition (Grand Rapids, MI: Eerdmans, 2000), 121.

300. "The phrase 'scattered among the nations' translates a Greek phrase meaning, literally, 'in the diaspora.' 'Diaspora,' or 'Dispersion' (NRSV), became a technical name for all the nations outside of Palestine where Jewish people had come to live." Douglas Moo, *The Letter of James*, 50.

301. Rose Publishing, *Rose Chronological Guide to the Bible*, 157. If James responded to Paul's message, the letter was probably written in A.D. 49 or after. Craig Blomberg, et al., *From Pentecost to Patmos*, 571. Siding with Guthrie and others, I believe the letter was written before A.D. 50. Donald Guthrie, *New Testament Introduction*, 749ff. Witherington says "the document was written at least by the A.D. 50s." Ben Witherington III, *Invitation to the New Testament*, 283. One popular chronological Bible confirms, placing James immediately after Galatians. *The Chronological Study Bible* (Nashville, TN: Thomas Nelson, 2008), 1284. See also Donald Guthrie, *The Apostles*, chaps. 8-9. Other scholars estimate the letter was written between A.D. 44 and 48. Clinton Arnold, ed., *Zondervan Illustrated Bible Backgrounds Commentary*, 3:87. Since Paul's liberating gospel was proclaimed and embraced in Antioch of Syria as early as the 40s, it's possible that James was responding to a corrupt version of it. According to Longenecker, "Paul's letters are the earliest Christian documents in

From: Jerusalem[302]

To: The dispersed Jewish believers in the empire[303]

Author: James, the half-brother of Jesus. He is often called "James the Righteous" or "James the Just." Both names signify his faithful observance of the Law.[304]

---

existence." Bruce Longenecker, ed., *The New Cambridge Companion to St. Paul*, 4. If true, it means Galatians was written before James. Wright and Bird state, "the polemic about faith and works fits with a date during Paul's lifetime…." N.T. Wright and Michael Bird, *The New Testament in Its World*, 736. According to Robinson "it is likely to have been written not long before the incident of Acts 15:1." John A.T. Robinson, *Redating the New Testament*, 126, online version. Moo believes the date of the letter is likely the late 40s. Douglas Moo, *James*, TNTC (Grand Rapids, MI: Eerdmans, 1985), 34. Even though James was responding to misrepresentations of Paul's teaching, the two men actually agreed. Their audiences and emphases were merely different. See Clinton Arnold, ed., *Zondervan Illustrated Bible Backgrounds Commentary*, 3:101. Arguments that the letter was written after A.D. 100 and is pseudepigraphical have been successfully debunked. Eckhard Schnabel, *New Testament Theology*, 35. Most evangelical scholars believe that the epistle of James was written between A.D. 45 and 65, with the majority favoring the narrower range of A.D. 48 to 50 as the most likely time of composition.

302. Douglas Moo, *James*, 35.

303. James 1:1. The "dispersion" included Jews throughout the Roman Empire. James no doubt met Jews from many different nations at the regular feasts in Jerusalem. Craig Keener, *The IVP Bible Background Commentary: New Testament*, 672. The audience was Jewish-Christian, some of whom were poor. They were hauled into court by the wealthy and oppressed by big landowners (James 2:4-6; 5:1-11). Clinton Arnold, ed., *Zondervan Illustrated Bible Backgrounds Commentary*, 4:89. One scholar believes the letter was written to "believers living in Jewish ghettos throughout the Roman world." This would include Antioch of Syria, which had ties to the Jerusalem church. James was an "encyclical letter" to Jews in the Diaspora. Patrick Hartin, *James*, Sacra Pagina (Collegeville, MN: Liturgical Press, 2003), 27.

304. Patrick Hartin, *James*, 16-27; Jonathan Bernier, *Rethinking the Dates of the New Testament*, 196-210; Craig Keener, *The IVP Bible Background Commentary: New Testament*, 668-669; N.T. Wright and Michael Bird, *The New Testament in Its World*, 734-735; Scot McKnight, *The Letter of James*, 37. James was the younger brother of Jesus. Douglas Moo, *James*, 21-22. Some scholars believe a different James wrote the letter. Guthrie delves deep into the debate, but argues for the traditional view that James, brother of Jesus, was the author. Donald Guthrie, *New Testament Introduction*, 723-746. "But if James the Lord's brother wrote this letter, why does he not mention his special relationship to Jesus? Probably because being a brother of Jesus gave James no authority to admonish other Christians as he does in this letter." Douglas Moo, *The Letter of James*, 48.

Contextual Summary: James encourages the Jewish believers in a time of trial. His primary focus is on faithfulness during temptation, especially as it relates to one's inward desires. He emphasizes consistency of faith with action, which includes a person's speech.[305]

The letter opens with an encouragement regarding trials and a promise that God will grant wisdom to those who ask for insight when they are undergoing affliction. In reply to false rumors that some have heard about the Jerusalem council, James distinguishes between the works of the Law and the works of faith. He also issues a rebuke to the false doctrine of faith without works.[306] He argues that true faith produces good works. (Paul made the same point in Galatians 5:6.)

James reproves worldliness among the believers. He admonishes those who are showing favoritism to the wealthy and rebukes the rich for discriminating against the poor. He chastises the rich merchants and wealthy farmers. He exhorts his readers to be doers of God's word rather than passive hearers. He reproves critical speaking, slander, and exhorts the sick to ask the elders to pray for their healing.

The letter alludes to Jesus' "Sermon on the Mount" at least twenty times.[307] It also draws a great deal from the Wisdom literature of the Old Testament (namely, Proverbs).[308]

---

305. David deSilva, *An Introduction to the New Testament*, 730-735.

306. I agree with Dunn that James was responding to those who seized on Paul's slogan of justification by faith but misinterpreted it. James D.G. Dunn, *Unity and Diversity in the New Testament*, 251. Paul's polemic against the "works of the law" in Galatians and Romans is not a polemic against "good works." They aren't the same. David deSilva, *An Introduction to the New Testament*, 453.

307. Paul Barnett, *The Birth of Christianity*, 128-132.

308. Ben Witherington III, *The New Testament Story*, 56. For an overview of James, see David deSilva, *An Introduction to the New Testament*, chap. 21; N.T. Wright and Michael Bird, *The New Testament in Its World*, chap. 31; Clinton Arnold, ed., *Zondervan Illustrated Bible Backgrounds Commentary*, 3:87-119.

James

James, a servant of God and of the Lord Jesus Christ, to the twelve tribes which are in the Dispersion: Greetings.

Count it all joy, my brothers,[a] when you fall into various temptations, knowing that the testing of your faith produces endurance. Let endurance have its perfect work, that you may be perfect and complete, lacking in nothing.

But if any of you lacks wisdom, let him ask of God, who gives to all liberally and without reproach, and it will be given to him. But let him ask in faith, without any doubting, for he who doubts is like a wave of the sea, driven by the wind and tossed. For that man shouldn't think that he will receive anything from the Lord. He is a double-minded man, unstable in all his ways.

But let the brother in humble circumstances glory in his high position; and the rich, in that he is made humble, because like the flower in the grass, he will pass away. For the sun arises with the scorching wind and withers the grass, and the flower in it falls, and the beauty of its appearance perishes. So the rich man will also fade away in his pursuits.

Blessed is a person who endures temptation, for when he has been approved, he will receive the crown of life, which the Lord promised to those who love him. Let no man say when he is tempted, "I am tempted by God," for God can't be tempted by evil, and he himself tempts no one. But each one is tempted when he is drawn away by his own lust and enticed. Then the lust, when it has conceived, bears sin.

The sin, when it is full grown, produces death. Don't be deceived, my beloved brothers. Every good gift and every perfect gift is from above, coming down from the Father of lights, with whom can be no variation, nor turning shadow. Of his own will he gave birth to us by the word of truth, that we should be a kind of first fruits of his creatures.

So, then, my beloved brothers, let every man be swift to hear, slow to speak, and slow to anger; for the anger of man doesn't produce the righteousness of God. Therefore, putting away all filthiness and overflowing of wickedness, receive with humility the implanted word, which is able to save your souls.[b]

But be doers of the word, and not only hearers, deluding your own selves. For if anyone is a hearer of the word and not a doer, he is like a man looking at his natural face in a mirror;

for he sees himself, and goes away, and immediately forgets what kind of man he was. But he who looks into the perfect law of freedom and continues, not being a hearer who forgets, but a doer of the work, this man will be blessed in what he does.

If anyone among you thinks himself to be religious while he doesn't bridle his tongue, but deceives his heart, this man's religion is worthless. Pure religion and undefiled before our God and Father is this: to visit the fatherless and widows in their affliction, and to keep oneself unstained by the world.

My brothers, don't hold the faith of our Lord Jesus Christ of glory with partiality. For if a man with a gold ring, in fine clothing, comes into your synagogue,[c] and a poor man in filthy clothing also comes in, and you pay special attention to him who wears the fine clothing and say, "Sit here in a good place;" and you tell the poor man, "Stand there," or "Sit by my footstool" haven't you shown partiality among yourselves, and become judges with evil thoughts?

Listen, my beloved brothers. Didn't God choose those who are poor in this world to be rich in faith, and heirs of the Kingdom which he promised to those who love him? But you have dishonored the poor man. Don't the rich oppress you, and personally drag you before the courts? Don't they blaspheme the honorable name by which you are called? However, if you fulfill the royal law according to the Scripture, "You shall love your neighbor as yourself," Leviticus 19:18 you do well.

But if you show partiality, you commit sin, being convicted by the law as transgressors. For whoever keeps the whole law, and yet stumbles in one point, he has become guilty of all. For he who said, "Do not commit adultery," Exodus 20:14; Deuteronomy 5:18 also said, "Do not commit murder." Exodus 20:13; Deuteronomy 5:17 Now if you do not commit adultery, but murder, you have become a transgressor of the law. So speak and so do, as men who are to be judged by a law of freedom. For judgment is without mercy to him who has shown no mercy. Mercy triumphs over judgment.

What good is it, my brothers, if a man says he has faith, but has no works? Can faith save him? And if a brother or sister is naked and in lack of daily food, and one of you tells them, "Go in peace. Be warmed and filled;" yet you didn't give them the things the body needs, what good is it? Even so faith, if it has no works, is dead in itself. Yes, a man will say, "You have faith, and I have works." Show me your faith without works, and I will show you my faith by my works.

You believe that God is one. You do well. The demons also believe, and shudder. But do you want to know, vain man, that faith apart from works is dead? Wasn't Abraham our father justified by works, in that he offered up Isaac his son on the altar? You see that faith worked with his works, and by works faith was perfected. So the Scripture was fulfilled which says, "Abraham believed God, and it was accounted to him as righteousness," <u>Genesis 15:6</u> and he was called the friend of God.

You see then that by works, a man is justified, and not only by faith. In the same way, wasn't Rahab the prostitute also justified by works, in that she received the messengers and sent them out another way? For as the body apart from the spirit is dead, even so faith apart from works is dead.

Let not many of you be teachers, my brothers, knowing that we will receive heavier judgment. For we all stumble in many things. Anyone who doesn't stumble in word is a perfect person, able to bridle the whole body also. Indeed, we put bits into the horses' mouths so that they may obey us, and we guide their whole body. Behold,[d] the ships also, though they are so big and are driven by fierce winds, are yet guided by a very small rudder, wherever the pilot desires.

So the tongue is also a little member, and boasts great things. See how a small fire can spread to a large forest! And the tongue is a fire. The world of iniquity among our members is the tongue, which defiles the whole body, and sets on fire the course of nature, and is set on fire by Gehenna.[e] For every kind of animal, bird, creeping thing, and sea creature, is tamed, and has been tamed by mankind; but nobody can tame the tongue. It is a restless evil, full of deadly poison.

With it we bless our God and Father, and with it we curse men who are made in the image of God. Out of the same mouth comes blessing and cursing. My brothers, these things ought not to be so. Does a spring send out from the same opening fresh and bitter water? Can a fig tree, my brothers, yield olives, or a vine figs? Thus no spring yields both salt water and fresh water.

Who is wise and understanding among you? Let him show by his good conduct that his deeds are done in gentleness of wisdom. But if you have bitter jealousy and selfish ambition in your heart, don't boast and don't lie against the truth. This wisdom is not that which comes down from above, but is earthly, sensual, and demonic.

For where jealousy and selfish ambition are, there is confusion and every evil deed. But the wisdom that is from above is first pure, then peaceful, gentle, reasonable, full of mercy and good fruits, without partiality, and without hypocrisy. Now the fruit of righteousness is sown in peace by those who make peace.

Where do wars and fightings among you come from? Don't they come from your pleasures that war in your members? You lust, and don't have. You murder and covet, and can't obtain. You fight and make war. You don't have, because you don't ask. You ask, and don't receive, because you ask with wrong motives, so that you may spend it on your pleasures. You adulterers and adulteresses, don't you know that friendship with the world is hostility toward God?

Whoever therefore wants to be a friend of the world makes himself an enemy of God. Or do you think that the Scripture says in vain, "The Spirit who lives in us yearns jealously"? But he gives more grace. Therefore it says, "God resists the proud, but gives grace to the humble." Proverbs 3:34

Be subject therefore to God. Resist the devil, and he will flee from you. Draw near to God, and he will draw near to you. Cleanse your hands, you sinners. Purify your hearts, you double-minded. Lament, mourn, and weep. Let your laughter be turned to mourning, and your joy to gloom. Humble yourselves in the sight of the Lord, and he will exalt you.

Don't speak against one another, brothers. He who speaks against a brother and judges his brother, speaks against the law and judges the law. But if you judge the law, you are not a doer of the law, but a judge. Only one is the lawgiver, who is able to save and to destroy. But who are you to judge another?

Come now, you who say, "Today or tomorrow let's go into this city, and spend a year there, trade, and make a profit." Whereas you don't know what your life will be like tomorrow. For what is your life? For you are a vapor that appears for a little time, and then vanishes away. For you ought to say, "If the Lord wills, we will both live, and do this or that." But now you glory in your boasting. All such boasting is evil. To him therefore who knows to do good, and doesn't do it, to him it is sin.

Come now, you rich, weep and howl for your miseries that are coming on you. Your riches are corrupted and your garments are moth-eaten. Your gold and your silver are corroded, and their corrosion will be for a testimony against you and will eat your flesh like fire. You have laid up your treasure in the last days.

Behold, the wages of the laborers who mowed your fields, which you have kept back by fraud, cry out, and the cries of those who reaped have entered into the ears of the Lord of Armies.[f] You have lived in luxury on the earth, and taken your pleasure. You have nourished your hearts as in a day of slaughter. You have condemned and you have murdered the righteous one. He doesn't resist you.

Be patient therefore, brothers, until the coming of the Lord. Behold, the farmer waits for the precious fruit of the earth, being patient over it, until it receives the early and late rain. You also be patient. Establish your hearts, for the coming of the Lord is at hand.

Don't grumble, brothers, against one another, so that you won't be judged. Behold, the judge stands at the door. Take, brothers, for an example of suffering and of perseverance, the prophets who spoke in the name of the Lord. Behold, we call them blessed who endured. You have heard of the perseverance of Job, and have seen the Lord in the outcome, and how the Lord is full of compassion and mercy.

But above all things, my brothers, don't swear—not by heaven, or by the earth, or by any other oath; but let your "yes" be "yes," and your "no," "no," so that you don't fall into hypocrisy.[g]

Is any among you suffering? Let him pray. Is any cheerful? Let him sing praises. Is any among you sick? Let him call for the elders of the assembly, and let them pray over him, anointing him with oil in the name of the Lord, and the prayer of faith will heal him who is sick, and the Lord will raise him up.

If he has committed sins, he will be forgiven. Confess your offenses to one another, and pray for one another, that you may be healed. The insistent prayer of a righteous person is powerfully effective. Elijah was a man with a nature like ours, and he prayed earnestly that it might not rain, and it didn't rain on the earth for three years and six months. He prayed again, and the sky gave rain, and the earth produced its fruit.

Brothers, if any among you wanders from the truth and someone turns him back, let him know that he who turns a sinner from the error of his way will save a soul from death and will cover a multitude of sins.

a. 1:2 The word for "brothers" here and where context allows may also be correctly translated "brothers and sisters" or "siblings."

b. <u>1:21</u> or, preserve your life.

c. <u>2:2</u> or, meeting.

d. <u>3:4</u> "Behold," from "ἰδοὺ," means look at, take notice, observe, see, or gaze at. It is often used as an interjection.

e. <u>3:6</u> or, Hell.

f. <u>5:4</u> Greek: Sabaoth (for Hebrew: Tze'va'ot).

g. <u>5:12</u> TR reads "under judgment" instead of "into hypocrisy."

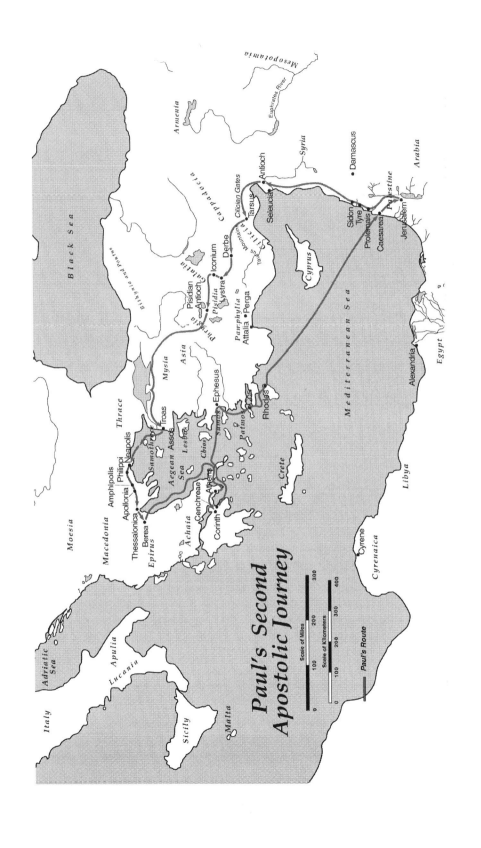

Paul's Second Apostolic Journey

Scale of Miles
0   100   200   300

Scale of Kilometers
0   100   200   300   400

Paul's Route

CHAPTER 10

THE GRECIAN CHRONICLE

A.D. 50 – A.D. 52

...Barnabas took Mark with him and sailed away to Cyprus, but Paul chose Silas and went out, being commended by the brothers to the grace of God. He went through Syria and Cilicia, strengthening the assemblies. (Acts 15:39-41)

PREVIEW OF PAUL'S SECOND APOSTOLIC JOURNEY[1]

Duration: Two years[2]

Dates: A.D. 50-52[3]

Kingdom Communities Planted: (4) Philippi, Thessalonica, Berea,[4] Corinth[5]

1. Some scholars estimate that Paul traveled 2,800 miles on this apostolic trip. Rose Publishing, *Rose Chronological Guide to the Bible*, 154.

2. James D.G. Dunn, *Beginning from Jerusalem*, 515.

3. Ben Witherington III, *The New Testament Story*, 274. F.F. Bruce, *1 & 2 Thessalonians*, xxxiv-xxxv. Some scholars believe this journey spanned three to four years. Craig Keener, *Acts*, 3:2298-2299.

4. Also spelled "Beroea."

5. Dunn calls this trip, along with Paul's later journey to Ephesus, "the Aegean mission." He regards it as one mission instead of two separate missions. James D.G. Dunn, *The Acts of the Apostles*, 212; *Beginning from Jerusalem*, 660. The Aegean mission was the heart of Paul's apostolic work. His aim for the second journey was to revisit the ekklesias he and Barnabas planted, share the Jerusalem council's letter, and raise up new ekklesias in other regions. Alan Bandy, *An Illustrated Guide to the Apostle Paul*, 83. For a highly detailed treatment of Paul's second apostolic journey, see Craig Keener, *Acts*, 3:2297-2779; W.J. Conybeare and J.S. Howson, *The Life & Epistles of St. Paul*, 181-330.

Time Planting:

Philippi = Two to three months

Thessalonica = Three to four months[6]

Berea = Two months[7]

Athens = Between two and four weeks[8]

Corinth = Eighteen months[9]

6. James D.G. Dunn, *Beginning from Jerusalem*, 515; Leon Morris, *1 and 2 Thessalonians*, revised edition, TNTC (Grand Rapids, MI: Eerdmans, 1984), 23, n. 3. While Acts 17:2 states that Paul went to the synagogue in Thessalonica for "three Sabbath days" (NIV), we can be sure Paul was in Thessalonica for more than three weeks. He needed time to set up his leatherworking business as well as receive two gifts from the assembly in Philippi. Luke compresses his narrative in Acts 17 (just as he does elsewhere). The first three weeks of Paul's ministry in the city was to the Jews in the synagogue, but he quickly changed his focus to the pagans. We know this because most of the ekklesia in Thessalonica was made up of pagans. This is clear from 1 Thessalonians 1:9. F.F. Bruce, *1 & 2 Thessalonians*, xxii. For details on Paul's time in Thessalonica, see Jeffrey Weima, *1-2 Thessalonians*, 26-27, 38. According to Weima, "Paul was clearly in Thessalonica longer than 'three sabbaths' on at least three specific grounds and thus we typically refer to Paul being in the city for 'three plus' weeks; i.e., more than three weeks and for an undefined longer period. A time period of three to four months is certainly possible." Personal correspondence with Jeffrey Weima, 1/27/23. Riesner believes Paul founded the church in three months, after which he was run out of town. Rainer Riesner, *Paul's Early Period*, 414. Others speculate Paul was in the city for four months. Nijay Gupta, *1 & 2 Thessalonians*, CINT (Grand Rapids, MI: Zondervan, 2019), 28. Ramsay estimates Paul was in Thessalonica from December 50 to May 51 (six months). William Ramsay, *St. Paul the Traveler and Roman Citizen*, 180. Longenecker believes Paul was in the city founding the ekklesia three to six months. Bruce Longenecker, et al., *Thinking Through Paul*, 61.

7. James D.G. Dunn, *Beginning from Jerusalem*, 514-515.

8. Robert Jewett, *A Chronology of Paul's Life*, 60. Fairchild agrees that Paul was probably in Athens two to four weeks. Personal correspondence with Mark Fairchild, 8/23/23. Paul's time in Athens was very short. He left the city "almost straightaway." James D.G. Dunn, *The Acts of the Apostles*, 238.

9. Acts 18:11. For travel details on Paul's second apostolic trip, see Robert Jewett, "Mapping the Route of Paul's 'Second Missionary Journey' from Dorylaeum to Troas," *Tyndale Bulletin* vol. 48, no. 1 (1997): 1-22; James D.G. Dunn, *Beginning from Jerusalem*, chap. 31.

A.D. 50

Paul and Barnabas decide to revisit the kingdom communities they established in Galatia to check on their progress. Before they depart, however, the two men have a falling out over Mark. Barnabas wants to take Mark on the trip, giving him a second chance. (They are cousins, after all.) Paul refuses, feeling that Mark deserted them on the first apostolic journey and isn't reliable.[10] The disagreement is so severe that Paul and Barnabas part ways.[11]

Barnabas and Mark head to the island of Cyprus (Barnabas' native land),[12] and they continue their ministry there.[13] Paul takes Silas with him to Galatia.[14] Silas has been part of the Jerusalem assembly for about twenty years, and he was trained under the Twelve.[15] Paul and Silas are approved by the assembly in Antioch of Syria, and the church sends[16]

10. According to Conybeare and Howson, the fault of the disagreement lay with both parties. Human weakness and partiality led to misunderstanding. W.J. Conybeare and J.S. Howson, *The Life & Epistles of St. Paul*, 193.

11. Mark Fairchild, "The Last Apostle," documentary film. It is likely that Barnabas lived with his cousin, John Mark, while he was in Jerusalem, thus strengthening the familial bond they shared. Barry Beitzel, *Lexham Geographic Commentary on Acts through Revelation*, 311. The schism didn't permanently damage either relationship. Paul highly regards Barnabas in 1 Corinthians 9:6, and he commends John Mark in Colossians 4:10 and 2 Timothy 4:11. Richard Longenecker, *The Ministry and Message of Paul*, 60.

12. Barnabas appears to have departed on his trip before Paul did on his. W.J. Conybeare and J.S. Howson, *The Life & Epistles of St. Paul*, 194-195. At this point, Barnabas and Mark fade from the Acts narrative. N.T. Wright, *Paul: A Biography*, 173.

13. Otto F.A. Meinardus, *St. Paul in Ephesus*, 11. According to tradition, Barnabas remained in Cyprus until his passing. William Ramsay, *St. Paul the Traveler and Roman Citizen*, 143.

14. Acts 15:36-40. For details on Silas, see F.F. Bruce, *The Pauline Circle*, 23-28. Regarding Acts 15:34, some later Greek manuscripts (reflected by the KJV) add that Silas remained in Antioch while Judas returned to Jerusalem. This detail, however, is not present in the early manuscripts on which most modern translations are based. Ben Witherington III, *The Acts of the Apostles*, 470, n. 456. Therefore, Silas may have returned to Jerusalem, and when Paul sent word to him, he made the twenty-five-day trip back to Antioch to meet Paul.

15. This calculation assumes that Silas was part of the Jerusalem church from the beginning, which is a reasonable conjecture. Given his stature in the Jerusalem church (he was one of the "chief men among the brethren" according to Acts 15:22), the thesis is plausible. "Certainly he must have been a believer for a long time." Personal correspondence with Craig Keener, 12/4/23.

16. Acts 15:40, NLT and ESV. The Greek word translated "left" and "departed" in these versions is *exerchomai*, and it's also translated "go forth" and "go away" multiple times in the KJV. Thus, the word carries the idea of sending.

the two apostles[17] to God's gracious care. Silas is not only gifted prophetically, but he is authorized to interpret the Jerusalem decree and validate its authenticity.[18]

The two men set off on foot, first visiting and strengthening the assemblies in Syria and Cilicia.[19] Afterward, the men head up through Tarsus, trekking across the craggy Taurus Mountains. They walk through the Cilician gates into Cappadocia[20] and set out by land to visit the four assemblies in the hill countries of Galatia, beginning with Derbe and Lystra.[21]

Timothy of Lystra

When Paul and Silas come to Lystra, they take note of Timothy, a young man who shows strong signs of being called to the Lord's work. Timothy is around twenty years old now,[22] and he is highly regarded by the believers in Lystra and Iconium.[23] (In time, Timothy will become a spiritual giant.[24])

17. Silas and Timothy are called "apostles" in 1 Thessalonians 2:6 (with 1:1), just as Barnabas is called an apostle in Acts 14:3-4, 14; 1 Corinthians 9:5-6. The New Testament makes clear that all three men (Paul, Barnabas, and Silas) were involved in planting kingdom communities, which is the work of an apostle.

18. Ben Witherington III, *New Testament History*, 252. It's also possible that Silas was an eyewitness to the resurrection of Jesus. Charles Wanamaker, *The Epistle to the Thessalonians*, NIGTC (Grand Rapids, MI: Eerdmans, 1990), 69. Even though the limits of the decree are Syria and Cilicia, the two men would bring the decree to the Galatians (Acts 16:4). Craig Keener, "Lessons on Acts," Session 25.

19. Acts 15:40-41. Instead of taking a boat from Seleucia to Attalia, they took an overland route which enabled them to visit the ekklesias in the regions Paul had previously been. Clinton Arnold, ed., *Zondervan Illustrated Bible Backgrounds Commentary*, 2b:148. Ben Witherington explores why the men chose the overland route when returning to Galatia in *The Acts of the Apostles*, 473.

20. The distance from Tarsus to Derbe was about 150 miles. Alan Bandy, *An Illustrated Guide to the Apostle Paul*, 81. It is unlikely they attempted the climb through the Cilician Gates during the winter. James D.G. Dunn, *Beginning from Jerusalem*, 515. Bandy believes they went in the spring when the winter snows melted. Personal correspondence with Alan Bandy, 12/6/23.

21. Richard Longenecker, *The Ministry and Message of Paul*, 61; Colin Hemer, *The Book of Acts in the Setting of Hellenistic History*, 111. According to Acts 18:23, the two apostles strengthened the assemblies in Galatia and Phrygia.

22. "This is a reasonable conjecture." Personal correspondence with Ben Witherington III, 10/18/22. Stott agrees. John Stott, *The Message of 2 Timothy: Guard the Gospel* (Downers Grove, IL: InterVarsity Press, 1973), 19.

23. Acts 16:2. Lystra was closer to Iconium than to Derbe, hence why Luke grouped them together when referring to Timothy (Acts 16:2). William Ramsay, *St. Paul the Traveler and Roman Citizen*, 145.

24. For a marvelous discussion on Timothy's role in the New Testament narrative and his relationship to Paul, see F.F. Bruce, *The Pauline Circle*, chap. 4; James D.G. Dunn, *The Acts of the Apostles*, 216.

Paul and Silas decide to take Timothy with them for the rest of the trip.[25] The assembly in Lystra approves this decision. Paul and the elders of the assembly lay hands on Timothy. Spiritual gifts are imparted to him, and prophetic utterances are spoken over him.[26] Paul and his companions leave Lystra and travel to the other regions of Phrygia and Galatia (or more accurately, Phrygian Galatia).[27] Although Timothy's mother is Jewish, he's never been circumcised.[28] Consequently, Paul circumcises Timothy so his uncircumcised state will not hinder the work.[29] Because the Jews regard Timothy as a Jew (through his mother), for him to remain uncircumcised would make it appear that he is an apostate.[30] This, in turn, would jeopardize Paul's link to the synagogue.

25. Timothy replaced the role of John Mark just as Silas replaced the role of Barnabas. David Bauer, *The Book of Acts as Story*, 195. Note that the journeys of Paul took months. While he traveled, he trained his disciples and apprentices. This became a pattern on this second trip as well as on subsequent apostolic/church planting trips. Mark Fairchild, "The Last Apostle," documentary film.

26. 1 Timothy 1:18; 4:14; 2 Timothy 1:6. Craig Keener, *Acts*, 3:2322.

27. Acts 16:6. The expression is better translated "the region of Phrygian Galatia." Clinton Arnold, ed., *Zondervan Illustrated Bible Backgrounds Commentary*, 2b:150.

28. Mixed marriages were forbidden in Judaism. However, whenever they took place, the children were to be reared as Jews. Darrell Bock, *Acts*, 522. For details on the scholarly debate about Timothy's ethnicity and Paul's decision to circumcise him, see James D.G. Dunn, *The Acts of the Apostles*, 475-476. Circumcision would have been painful since surgeries were performed on just about every part of the human body without conventional sedatives. Gary Burge, *A Week in the Life of a Roman Centurion*, 47. There were no pain killers during this time, but orally ingested alcohol was available. Personal correspondence with Craig Keener, 5/1/16. According to Gary Burge, the two chief anesthetics were opium (mixed with wine) and powdered mandrake. At best, these would give a person a little more than drowsiness. Surgeries, then, were fast because they were so traumatic. Personal correspondence with Gary Burge, 7/12/22. Bandy believes Timothy's pedigree is one of the reasons why Paul wanted to take him on the trip. He would be ideal for the Jew/Gentile nature of the mission because he could navigate both worlds. Personal correspondence with Alan Bandy, 12/6/23.

29. Paul didn't circumcise Timothy for salvation, but for witness. Ben Witherington III, *New Testament History*, 252-253. Had Timothy not been circumcised, and had it become known, he would have been violently denounced in every synagogue, preventing the open presentation of the gospel. Paul probably circumcised Timothy in Iconium. W.J. Conybeare and J.S. Howson, *The Life & Epistles of St. Paul*, 204-206. We don't know how the Jews verified that Timothy was circumcised, but it would have been obvious in the baths. Personal correspondence with Craig Keener, 5/1/16.

30. James D.G. Dunn, *The Acts of the Apostles*, 216.

During this season of travel throughout Syria, Cilicia, and Galatia,[31] they read the letter from the Jerusalem council to all the kingdom communities in the area.[32] As a result, the churches are strengthened in the faith, and they increase in number.[33] Note that the Galatian assemblies have not seen the face of an apostle for over a year. Yet Paul and Silas make a wonderful discovery. *Although the Galatian communities were thrown into the crucible of crisis, they survived!* They received and embraced Paul's letter.[34] Paul's gospel held, and his work proved to be made of "gold, silver, and precious stone."[35]

Paul wants to travel westward into the Roman province of Asia to preach the gospel, but the Holy Spirit forbids him from doing so. When he and his companions come to the border of Mysia, they try to head north to Bithynia, but the Spirit prevents them again.[36] They also have more run-ins with bandits.[37]

A Visit to Troas

Paul, Silas, and Timothy head northwest to a Roman colony called Troas. Troas is about 600 miles northwest of Antioch of Syria.[38] Its population is about 100,000, a large city by ancient

31. Luke uses the term "Phrygia and Galatia" in Acts 16:6, referring to Phrygian Galatia (Phrygia Galatica) as opposed to Asian Galatia. In general, Luke mostly uses ethnic and regional designations while Paul uses provincial designations in his epistles. Ben Witherington III, *New Testament History*, 253; *The Acts of the Apostles*, 478. The men likely passed through the Cilician Gates on this leg of the trip. Rainer Riesner, *Paul's Early Period*, 281.

32. Acts 15:41; 16:4. Witherington believes the decrees from the council were also read to the Thessalonian and Corinthian believers, later. Ben Witherington III, *The Acts of the Apostles*, 477.

33. Acts 16:1-5, NET.

34. The epistle we know as "Galatians." For evidence supporting this conclusion, see David Capes, et al., *Rediscovering Paul*, 148-149.

35. Paul used this metaphor in 1 Corinthians 3:10-12 for a work built from reliance on God's life rather than human strength and ingenuity. For details on serving God in the Spirit rather than in the energy of the flesh, see Frank Viola, "The Two Anointings" and "Serving in the Newness of the Spirit" on the Christ is All podcast, episodes #200 and #201 at frankviola.org/thechristisallpodcast.

36. Acts 16:6-8. For details on this part of the story, see Alan Bandy, *An Illustrated Guide to the Apostle Paul*, 84-85. For information on ancient Bithynia, see Mark Wilson, *Biblical Turkey*, 347-348.

37. 2 Corinthians 11:26. Bandits traveled on the desolate borders of Bithynia and Mysia. Barry Beitzel, *Lexham Geographic Commentary on Acts through Revelation*, 191. They would have also likely encountered bandits along many of the remote regions they traveled. Personal correspondence with Alan Bandy, 12/6/23.

38. The route from Pisidian Antioch to Troas was about 590 miles, which required about thirty-eight days of walking. Barry Beitzel, *Lexham Geographic Commentary on Acts through Revelation*, 336. Troas was the chief

standards.[39] They arrive in Troas weary, puzzled, and disheartened because they have received no clear guidance on their next step.[40] Paul, however, receives a vision in the night.[41] He sees a Macedonian man beseeching him to come to Macedonia and offer help. The workers interpret the vision to mean that God is calling them to preach the gospel in Macedonia.[42] So in the morning, they step boldly into the glorious unknown and head to the Greek-speaking region of Macedonia, a Roman province in what is now Northern Greece.[43] Luke, having traveled to Troas to join Paul, Silas, and Timothy, accompanies them to Macedonia.[44]

A Kingdom Community Is Planted in Philippi

From Troas, the men sail across the Aegean Sea and come to a mountainous island called Samothrace, which rises to almost 6,000 feet.[45] The next day, they arrive at Neapolis, the port city of Philippi.[46] The trip from Troas to Neapolis takes only two days due to favorable

---

port for traveling to Macedonia from Asia Minor. Mark Fairchild, *Christian Origins in Ephesus & Asia Minor*, 103; Darrell Bock, *Acts*, 528. For further details on ancient Troas, see Mark Wilson, *Biblical Turkey*, 376-379.

39. Craig Keener, "Lessons on Acts," Session 25.

40. N.T. Wright, *Paul: A Biography*, 177.

41. Acts 16:9. It's possible that Paul's vision in the night was a dream. Ben Witherington III, *The Acts of the Apostles*, 479.

42. The "we" passages, which begin in Acts 16:10, are initially set in Troas, not Macedonia. Therefore, the man in the vision couldn't have been Luke (as some have suggested). See Ben Witherington III, *The Acts of the Apostles*, 479-480. God must have a sense of humor, since after seeing a "*man* of Macedonia" the first significant person Paul meets in Macedonia is Lydia, a woman! Alan Bandy agrees that this may be a case of the irony of God. Personal correspondence with Bandy, 12/24/23.

43. For a detailed analysis of Paul and Silas' apostolic work in Macedonia and later in Achaia, see Eckhard Schnabel, *Early Christian Mission*, 2:1125-1197. For information on the Jewish community in both regions, see Bruce Winter, et al., eds., *The Book of Acts in Its First Century Setting*, vol. 5, chap. 10.

44. Acts 16:8-11.

45. Bock says the island had a mountain peak of 5,777 feet. Darrell Bock, *Acts*, 532. According to Bandy, "They seem to have stayed overnight in Samothrace instead of merely passing it by." Personal correspondence with Alan Bandy, 12/6/23. According to Weima, "The boat on which they were traveling likely spent the evening moored on the north side of the island, protected from the prevailing winds." Personal correspondence with Jeffrey Weima, 12/28/23.

46. F.F. Bruce, *Philippians*, NIBC (Peabody, MA: Hendrickson, 1989), 7. Neapolis was the harbor city of Philippi. It lay to the northwest along the Via Egnatia, the main east-west highway through Macedonia. Alan Bandy, *An Illustrated Guide to the Apostle Paul*, 89.

weather. (On the return leg of his third apostolic journey, it will take Paul five days to sail the other direction, from Neapolis to Troas.[47])

The men take the great Roman road called the Via Egnatia (the "Egnatian Way") to travel the ten miles from Neapolis to Philippi.[48] This is a large, marble-covered military road that runs across the Balkan Peninsula from the Aegean Sea to the Adriatic.[49] Finally, Paul, Silas, Timothy, and Luke arrive in the Roman colony of Philippi.

Sharpening the Focus: Philippi is a Roman city where retired Roman soldiers had been given appropriated land upon their retirement after the decisive battle between Octavian (Augustus) and Marc Antony in 31 B.C.[50] It's one of the chief cities in the province of Macedonia, and it is thoroughly Romanized.[51] The population is between 5,000 and 10,000, and the wall circumference is two miles.[52] Philippi is a wealthy

47. Acts 20:6. The sea journey from Troas to Neapolis was 137 miles. Samothrace lay halfway between Troas and Neapolis. Barry Beitzel, *Lexham Geographic Commentary on Acts through Revelation*, 337.

48. Barry Beitzel, *Lexham Geographic Commentary on Acts through Revelation*, 339; Jeffrey Weima, *1-2 Thessalonians*, 25. The Via Egnatia extended about 530 miles. Paul Davies, "The Macedonian Scene of Paul's Journeys," *The Biblical Archaeologist* 26, no. 3 (1963): 91. See also 91-106 for details on Paul's second apostolic journey. Roman roads were no more than twenty feet wide, but they were better and safer than most European roads before the year 1850. Craig Keener, "Lessons on Acts," Session 27. The Romans knew how to build durable roads. After 2,000 years, many of them have survived. They often had milestones to mark distances. Mark Fairchild, "The Last Apostle," documentary film. The Via Egnatia was a well-paved, well-traveled road. Personal correspondence with Alan Bandy, 6/27/23.

49. Philippi, Amphipolis, Apollonia, and Thessalonica all stood on the Egnatian Way. The Egnatian Way was the most direct route between Rome and the East.

50. Personal correspondence with Jeffrey Weima, 12/28/23.

51. For details on the city, see F.F. Bruce, *In the Steps of the Apostle Paul* (Grand Rapids, MI: Kregel, 1995), 32-33.

52. Barry Beitzel, *Lexham Geographic Commentary on Acts through Revelation*, 338. Some scholars believe the city more likely had a population between 5,000 and 15,000. Alan Bandy, *An Illustrated Guide to the Apostle Paul*, 90. According to Ben Witherington, it may have been as large as 20,000. Personal correspondence with Witherington, 4/4/22. "The city was on a hill, with woods to the north, marsh on the south as far as the sea, gorges on the east, and fertile plain on the west." Craig Keener, *Acts*, 3:2380.

city.[53] The chief language is Latin, though many speak Greek.[54] Philippi is naturally beautiful, displaying a plethora of hundred-petaled roses. (The other parts of the empire have few.[55])

Two temples stand in the forum, dedicated to the emperor.[56] The city is governed by a proconsul (governor), whose headquarters are in Thessalonica. Consequently, the supreme authority to which a Philippian can appeal is in another city. The city was given the highest honor of all—the *ius italicum*—making it an Italian city in every legal respect. In short, Philippi is a microcosm of Rome.[57] Later historians will call it "little Rome."[58] The city is proud of its association with Rome. It is governed according to Roman law, and like all colonies, it is an extension of the Eternal City.[59]

Philippian citizens are also granted Roman citizenship.[60] Paul will draw on this imagery when he writes Philippians.[61] There is a strong presence of the imperial cult, deifying Julius, Augustus, and Claudius.[62] There is no synagogue in Philippi—the Jewish population is too sparse in the city. A synagogue requires a *minyan*, a quorum of ten male Jews.[63] The Jews in the city maintain a *proseuchē*—in this case, it's a

53. Darrell Bock, *Acts*, 533. Philippi's gold mines, which also produced gems, were an important source of the city's wealth. Craig Keener, *Acts*, 3:2381.

54. Eighty percent of the inscriptions in Philippi are in Latin, compared to 40 percent in Pisidian Antioch. Both were Roman colonies. Ben Witherington III, *The Acts of the Apostles*, 488.

55. Craig Keener, *Acts*, 3:2388. For a visual sketch of ancient Philippi, see Peter Walker, *In the Steps of Paul*, 104-106.

56. Barry Beitzel, *Lexham Geographic Commentary on Acts through Revelation*, 338. "The imperial cult venerated not just individual Roman emperors (after their death), but more broadly the Roman state personified as a goddess, Roma." Personal correspondence with Jeffrey Weima, 12/28/23.

57. Ben Witherington III, *The Acts of the Apostles*, 488.

58. Darrell Bock, *Acts*, 533; Douglas Campbell, *Paul: An Apostle's Journey*, 46.

59. David deSilva, *Paul and the Macedonians*, 14.

60. Craig Keener, "Lessons on Acts," Session 25.

61. Philippians 3:20.

62. David deSilva, *Paul and the Macedonians*, 15.

63. F.F. Bruce, *Paul: Apostle of the Heart Set Free*, 219.

temporary place of prayer in the open air, near a river where people can wash their hands. This is keeping in line with Jewish purity rites.[64]

A great deal of anti-Jewish sentiment exists in Rome. Philippi is aligned with the empire's anti-Judaic sensibilities, supporting the Jewish expulsion from Rome in A.D. 49.[65] For this reason, prejudice against the Jews is running high in the city when Paul and Silas come there. (The Romans complained that the Jews were converting people, which meant that more people no longer worshipped Caesar or the gods.[66])

When Paul, Silas, Timothy, and Luke arrive in Philippi, they search for a synagogue (also called a "place of prayer").[67] But they find none.[68] So they head toward the nearest river and meet a group of God-fearing women gathering at a *proseuchē* along the banks of the Gangites River.[69] A lucrative merchant from Thyatira named Lydia is one of them.[70] Lydia

64. Leon Morris, *The First and Second Epistles to the Thessalonians*, 2; James D.G. Dunn, *Beginning from Jerusalem*, 670.

65. Craig Keener, "Lessons on Acts," Session 26.

66. Craig Keener, "Lessons on Acts," Session 26.

67. Craig Keener, et al., *Journeys of the Apostle Paul*, 67.

68. A place of prayer (or "prayer house") was another name for a synagogue. Craig Keener, "Lessons on Acts," Session 25. They were especially called "prayer houses" in the Diaspora. Robert Banks, *Paul's Idea of Community*, 9.

69. They met on Sabbaths and holy days to recite prayers and give thanks. Craig Keener, "Lessons on Acts," Session 25. An arch stood between the city and the river Gangites, crossing the Egnatian way. The place of prayer may have lain west of the arch. F.F. Bruce, *In the Steps of the Apostle Paul*, 33-34; James D.G. Dunn, *The Acts of the Apostles*, 219. For details on the Gangites River as the likely location, see Craig Keener, *Acts*, 3:2386-2387.

70. The fact that Lydia had a house and a "household" (nuclear family, kinsfolk, servants, and other dependents) made her a woman of means and social significance. Her trade also confirms this. Royal purple (the murex dye) was a luxury item in the first century. Those who traded it were typically members of Caesar's household. Craig Keener, "Lessons on Acts," Session 25; *Acts*, 3:2396-2403. Roman citizens usually wore an expensive white toga, often marked with purple to denote their status. Magistrates and senators often wore togas with purple bands. Purple dye was incredibly expensive. Douglas Campbell, *Paul: An Apostle's Journey*, 46.

is a God-fearing Gentile and a woman of high standing.[71] She is also pious and single.[72] Paul preaches Christ to the women who gather for prayer in the morning, and God opens Lydia's heart to receive the message.

As a result, Lydia becomes the first convert in Europe. She and her household are immediately baptized, and she opens her home, insisting that the men stay with her.[73] Lydia has a large enough house to accommodate all four men, along with her household.[74] Undoubtedly, the men find Lydia's hospitality a blessing, since they don't have to suffer the perils of staying in an inn. Later, Paul will honor Lydia as a partner in God's work.[75]

71. Some scholars believe Lydia was a freed slave who ran her own business. Douglas Campbell, *Paul: An Apostle's Journey*, 47. For further details on Lydia and her social standing, see Craig Keener, *Acts*, 3:2393-2408. In Acts 17, Luke mentions Greek women of high standing who were converted to Christ. Luke wanted readers to know that women were attracted to the gospel, that Paul persuaded those of social prominence to the truth (affirming its power), and that Paul's arguments from the Hebrew Scriptures persuaded not just Jews, but God-fearers also. This was the primary reason the Jews in the synagogue were ignited with jealousy, a repeated pattern in Acts. David Bauer, *The Book of Acts as Story*, 201-202.

72. Lydia may have been widowed or divorced. Craig Keener, "Lessons on Acts," Session 25; Darrell Bock, *Acts*, 535; William Ramsay, *St. Paul the Traveler and Roman Citizen*, 170. Some scholars believe she was divorced, since most women who exclusively owned homes in the first century were divorced rather than widowed. Craig Keener, *Acts*, 3:2406.

73. Acts 16:40. It was considered a great honor to host a prophet. Also, Judaism respected women. For this reason, many Gentile women were attracted to it. Far more women than men followed Judaism. Craig Keener, "Lessons on Acts," Session 25.

74. Most people in Paul's day were not wealthy enough to own a house. Those who did, like Lydia, were well-to-do, so her business was substantial. Jeffrey Weima, *1-2 Thessalonians*, 27-28; James D.G. Dunn, *Beginning from Jerusalem*, 671. For a discussion on Paul's hosts and hostesses throughout the New Testament story, see F.F. Bruce, *The Pauline Circle*, 91-100. Only the wealthy could afford clothes treated with purple dye, which was Lydia's business. Lydia was the first woman of high social standing to be one of Paul's associates. Others like Phoebe, Priscilla, and Nympha would follow. James D.G. Dunn, *The Acts of the Apostles*, 219.

75. According to Philippians 1:4-5, Paul regarded the ekklesia in Philippi to be a partner in the gospel "from the first day until now" (NIV). Since Lydia was a woman of means who housed the apostle and his co-workers in Philippi, as well as helped Paul financially on more than one occasion, it's logical to conclude that Paul primarily had her in mind when he penned these words. See also F.F. Bruce, *The Pauline Circle*, 94-95. Some believe Lydia was the "yokefellow" Paul mentioned in Philippians 4:3, KJV. Bruce doubts this, on the grounds of the Greek form of the word. *The Pauline Circle*, 95. Even so, like Jesus, Paul elevated women throughout his ministry—so much so that they were his partners in the work. David Balch, et al., *Early Christian Families in Context*, 159-184; Robert Banks, *Paul's Idea of Community*, chap. 12; Craig Keener, *Paul, Women, and Wives: Marriage and Women's Ministry in the Letters of Paul* (Grand Rapids, MI: Baker Academic, 1992). The role of women in Paul's ministry was far greater than it was in Judaism. Wayne Meeks,

Day after day, the men gather with the women by the river.[76] On one particular day, a slave girl possessed with a high-powered demon shows up. She has been taken over by a python spirit associated with Apollo.[77] The spirit gives her the ability to predict the future. The slave girl follows the apostolic workers, mocking them out loud. After many days, Paul's tolerance runs out.[78] He casts the python spirit out of her in the name of Jesus Christ. The girl is instantly delivered and loses her power of clairvoyance. When her owners find this out, they're infuriated because they cannot continue making money from her powers.

The girl's owners seek out Paul and Silas and aggressively drag them through the marketplace (known as the agora in Greek, the forum in Latin). It is located at the base of the acropolis.[79] The apostles are hauled before the city magistrates (also called *praetors*).[80] The slave girl's owners accuse the men of disturbing the peace and introducing illegal customs.[81]

The First Urban Christians, 81. For a discussion on the place of women throughout the New Testament, see Ben Witherington III, *Women in the Earliest Churches* (New York, NY: Cambridge University Press, 1988); Roger Gehring, *House Church and Mission*, 210-225. It's been estimated that 18 percent of Paul's co-workers were women. Eckhard Schnabel, *Paul the Missionary*, 251; *Early Christian Mission*, 1:284-287. Throughout Acts, Luke chronicles how the gospel influenced the progress of women. Ben Witherington III, *The Acts of the Apostles*, 339. Helpful surveys of women in the church can be found in F.F. Bruce, *A Mind for What Matters*, chap. 17; Nijay Gupta, *Tell Her Story*, chap. 6.

76. For more on Lydia and the gathering place in Philippi, see James D.G. Dunn, *Beginning from Jerusalem*, 670-671.

77. A python spirit is a demon inspired by Apollo, the python deity that was often consulted through the oracle at Delphi. F.F. Bruce, *The Book of the Acts*, 312; James D.G. Dunn, *Beginning from Jerusalem*, 671-672; Craig Keener, "Lessons on Acts," Session 25; William Ramsay, *St. Paul the Traveler and Roman Citizen*, 172. The god is called "Pythian Apollo" because he defeated Python. Hence, both he and the spirit are named after Python. Personal correspondence with David deSilva, 1/18/24.

78. According to some translations, Acts 16:18 says Paul was "annoyed." Others say he was "distressed." Undoubtedly, Paul was disturbed that the female slave was hampering his gospel message, but I don't doubt that he was also annoyed by her behavior.

79. Otto F.A. Meinardus, *St. Paul in Greece*, 25. The traditional Greek agora was square, while the Roman forum was rectangular. Like Corinth, Philippi's forum followed the Roman model. Craig Keener, *Acts*, 3:2467.

80. The marketplace in Philippi was 230 feet by 485 feet. Craig Keener, "Lessons on Acts," Session 26. Magistrates typically followed a mob's desires. Magistrates sat on a raised judgment seat in the marketplace to render their verdicts. Darrell Bock, *Acts*, 537. For details, see Ben Witherington III, *The Acts of the Apostles*, 496.

81. For details on the charges and the punishment, see Darrell Bock, *Acts*, 538-539.

They emphasize that Paul and Silas are Jews, an important detail given the antisemitism in the Roman colony.[82]

It is a moment of high drama. Hearing the charges, the surrounding crowd is incited against Paul and Silas, and they join the attack. The magistrates order the two men to be stripped and beaten[83] by the *lictors* (police attendants). With no trial, Paul and Silas are completely unclothed and severely battered with birch rods.[84] The men are shamed, humiliated, and left with open wounds.[85] They are thrown in jail, and a jailer is ordered to guard them securely. The two apostles are placed in the most secure cell. Their feet are placed in wooden stocks, causing extreme discomfort.[86]

...having suffered before and been shamefully treated, as you know, at Philippi.... (1 Thessalonians 2:2)

The sanitary conditions of the jail are horrific. Rodents abound. Like all prisoners, the men aren't cared for, so they must rely on their friends to bring them food.[87] Because

---

82. The accusers played the "Jew card" because antisemitism was running at high tide in Philippi due to the recent expulsion of Jews from the mother city (Rome). Personal correspondence with Jeffrey Weima, 2/10/22.

83. Acts 16:22. The Greek verb indicates the special Roman form of punishment, that of being beaten with the rods of the *lictors*. The *lictors* ("rod bearers") carried bundles of rods (called *fasces*) as a sign of their office. Craig Keener, "Lessons on Acts," Session 25; Alan Bandy, *An Illustrated Guide to the Apostle Paul*, 94. Being stripped was the normal procedure before a beating, and it was especially humiliating for a Jew. Craig Keener, *Acts*, 3:2477-2478.

84. This was likely the second time Paul was beaten with rods. He would be beaten one more time over the next six years (2 Corinthians 11:25). Regarding the third beating (and perhaps others later), Mark Fairchild says, "The beatings with rods were probably Roman punitive actions against Paul. These beatings were at the coastal cities where there were Roman administrators. I would suggest Elaiussa Sebaste (Ayaş today) as the most likely place, but Korykos and Seleucia ad Calycadnum are other possibilities." Personal correspondence with Fairchild, 2/23/22.

85. It's highly likely that the guidance Paul received in Acts 16:9 helped him endure the suffering, because he knew he was in the sweet spot of God's will.

86. The inner prison and wooden stocks were reserved for the worst criminals. Alan Bandy, *An Illustrated Guide to the Apostle Paul*, 94.

87. Jails were known for their filth. They had no toilet facilities. The unclean conditions could infect their wounds. Floors were cold and damp, and there was no rug. Wood stocks were fastened to the floor and often used for torture. The prisoner in stocks had to sleep on his side or in a sitting position. Changing positions to

Paul and Silas are Roman citizens, the beatings were illegal.[88] (Roman citizens are exempt from degrading treatment like scourging and exempt from arrest except in extreme cases. They also have the right to appeal to the emperor.[89]) Years before, Paul received opposition instigated by furious Jews who alleged that he was disloyal to Moses and the traditions. In Philippi, Gentiles instigate the opposition, alleging that he is disloyal to Rome.[90]

At midnight, Paul and Silas sit bruised, bleeding, and sore in the complete darkness of a jail cell. Their backs are covered with tender welts and they suffer pain in their legs.[91] Yet the two men pray and sing hymns to the Lord.[92] The other prisoners listen with wonder and surprise. Suddenly, an earthquake shakes the foundations of the jail, the doors fling open, and every prisoner's stocks come loose.[93]

The jailer awakens and realizes the jail doors are open. Thinking the prisoners have escaped, he is overwhelmed with dread and draws his sword to kill himself.[94] Shouting, Paul pleads for the jailer not to harm himself because none of the inmates have left. The jailer asks for torches to see the prisoners. After he verifies they haven't escaped, he falls down trembling before Paul and asks what he must do to be saved.[95] He then brings Paul and Silas near his home to hear the word of salvation.

---

avoid cramping was nearly impossible. The discomfort of a prisoner could turn to excruciating pain simply by increasing the distance between the left and right foot. Craig Keener, "Lessons on Acts," Session 26; *Acts*, 3:2477; N.T. Wright, *Paul: A Biography*, 182. Brian Rapske's volume, *Paul in Roman Custody*, vol. 3 in *The Book of Acts in Its First Century Setting* is the most thorough treatment on this subject.

88. For details on the charges, see Darrell Bock, *Acts*, 544.

89. It's possible that Paul and Silas cried out, "*Civis Romanus Sum,*" which means, "I am a Roman citizen." But their plea wasn't heard amid the commotion preceding their unjust beating. Non-citizens could be beaten without a trial to secure evidence.

90. N.T. Wright, *Paul: A Biography*, 181. This will become a pattern in the apostle's life as well as in the life of the assemblies: opposition from both Jews and Gentiles due to disloyalty.

91. Craig Keener, "Lessons on Acts," Session 26.

92. Paul and Silas undoubtedly knew the words of Jesus in Matthew 5:10-12, which were repeated to them by some of the Twelve. See Matthew 28:20.

93. Philippi was an earthquake-prone area. Craig Keener, "Lessons on Acts," Session 26; N.T. Wright, *Paul: A Biography*, 182; Ben Witherington III, *The Acts of the Apostles*, 497.

94. Allowing prisoners to escape was a capital offense.

95. The jailer was not asking to be saved from the consequences of letting the prisoners escape (execution), which he wrongly thought occurred. Word got out in the city that Paul and Silas were preaching a spiritual salvation. This is what the jailer was inquiring about. Craig Keener, "Lessons on Acts," Session 27.

The two apostles proclaim Christ to him and his household, and they receive the message.[96] The jailer bathes the wounds of the two men at a well in the prison courtyard. He and his household are all baptized in the middle of the night (perhaps at the same well).[97] The jailer then brings Paul and Silas into his house and feeds them.[98] As he talks with the two apostles over a meal, he is filled with the joy of salvation. Paul and Silas willingly return to the jail.[99] At daybreak, the magistrates send word to the officers to release Paul and Silas. When the jailer lets Paul know the seemingly good news, Paul protests. He argues that he and Silas are Roman citizens, and it was illegal for them to have been publicly beaten without a trial.[100]

Since they were unlawfully shamed in public as criminals, Paul demands they be officially exonerated of the charges and escorted out of jail in public view rather than in secret.[101] Paul's appeal turns the tables on the magistrates. They charged him with being disloyal to Rome, but they were the ones who had broken Roman law.[102]

96. In the first century, when the head of a household converted to a new religion or faith, the whole household followed his or her lead. This is what took place with the jailer's household, as well as with Lydia's. E. Randolph Richards and Brandon O'Brien, *Misreading Scripture with Western Eyes* (Downers Grove, IL: InterVarsity Press, 2012), 104ff.; Craig Keener, "Lessons on Acts," Session 27.

97. Given the circumstances and the time (the middle of the night), a well would be the most likely location for the baptism. A nearby fountain would be an equally probable option. James D.G. Dunn, *Beginning from Jerusalem*, 674; *The Acts of the Apostles*, 223; John Byron, *A Week in the Life of a Slave*, 24. For all the options on where the baptisms could have taken place, see Craig Keener, *Acts*, 3:2513.

98. The jailer risked getting into hot water by dining with the prisoners. Craig Keener, "Lessons on Acts," Session 27.

99. The narrative you just read is a reconstruction of Acts 16:12-34. The fact that Paul and Silas returned to the jail is inferred from Acts 16:36-37.

100. To prove their Roman citizenship, Paul and Silas may have been carrying a *testatio*—a certified private copy of evidence of their birth and citizenship inscribed on the wax surface of a small wooden *diptych*, which was a pair of folding tablets. The document was called *diploma civitas Romanae,* and it recorded a person's citizenship. Either way, Paul's citizenship would have been on record in Tarsus. It was a capital offense to falsely claim Roman citizenship, so people rarely dared it. Craig Keener, "Lessons on Acts," Session 27; F.F. Bruce, *Paul: Apostle of the Heart Set Free*, 39; Darrell Bock, *Acts*, 544-545; Clinton Arnold, ed., *Zondervan Illustrated Bible Backgrounds Commentary*, 2b:225-226. For details on Paul's citizenship, see Ben Witherington III, *The Acts of the Apostles*, 679-683.

101. Acts 16:37.

102. N.T. Wright, *Paul: A Biography*, 184.

Hearing that Paul and Silas are Roman citizens mortifies the magistrates, so they comply with Paul's request.[103] They publicly escort the two apostles out of jail and urge them to leave the city. But Paul and Silas are in no hurry to depart. They visit Lydia and encourage the new believers.[104] The ekklesia in Philippi is not only made up of women now, but "brothers" are present also.[105] As they stride out of the city, they take Timothy with them, but they leave Luke behind.[106]

Philippi now has a kingdom community, an assembly of God's people. And it's mostly populated by God-fearing women. Lydia, Euodia, and Syntyche (all women) are part of the assembly.[107] So is a man named Clement.[108] The church meets in Lydia's home.[109] The body of Jesus Christ—a face-to-face community and colony of heaven[110] bearing God's image and authority—is now present in the Roman colony.

A Kingdom Community Is Planted in Thessalonica[111]

Paul, Silas, and Timothy head west on the Egnatian Way. Because their beating was so brutal, the clothes on Paul and Silas' backs cause pain and discomfort on their still fresh wounds.[112] After passing through the towns of Amphipolis (about thirty miles southwest of

103. They were fearful because they didn't want to jeopardize their good relationship with Rome and threaten Philippi's standing as a proud colony. As a penalty for their mistake, the magistrates could be removed from public office and disqualified from holding office again, and the city could have had its privileges revoked. Craig Keener, *Acts*, 3:2528.

104. N.T. Wright, *Paul: A Biography*, 184.

105. Acts 16:40, NIV. Craig Keener, *Acts*, 3:2531.

106. Luke appears to have remained in Philippi for about seven years until he joined Paul again on the return leg of the apostle's third apostolic journey. This is suggested by the fact that the "we" sections of Acts (use of first-person plural) stop in Philippi, and don't start up again until later in Acts. Personal correspondence with Jeffrey Weima, 12/28/23.

107. Philippians 4:2; Acts 16:14ff.

108. Philippians 4:3.

109. Given Lydia's social status and the fact that she housed the apostles in the beginning of the church plant makes this a reasonable conclusion. Bandy agrees. Personal correspondence with Alan Bandy, 12/6/23.

110. Philippians 3:20, Moffatt, New Translation (MNT). "But we are a colony of heaven…."

111. Paul founded the church in Thessalonica in A.D. 50. Personal correspondence with Jeffrey Weima, 4/23/23. David deSilva agrees that "A.D. 50 is reasonable." Personal correspondence with deSilva, 4/24/23.

112. Craig Keener, "Lessons on Acts," Session 27.

Philippi) and Apollonia (twenty-seven miles farther), they travel an additional thirty-five miles and arrive in the thriving port city of Thessalonica.[113] Totaling all three legs of the trip, Thessalonica is almost one hundred miles southwest of Philippi.[114]

Sharpening the Focus: Thessalonica is the capital of Macedonia and the largest city in Northern Greece.[115] The population is between 65,000 and 100,000.[116] The city is ninety-two miles away from Philippi.[117] Its circuit is around four-and-a-half miles.[118] Though the city is predominantly Greek, it contains a considerable number of Italians and Thracians.[119] Jews make up a small minority,[120] but there is a large enough population to support a synagogue.[121]

Thessalonica is the first major city east of Rome on the Via Egnatia. Consequently, it's a likely place Jewish refugees settled after they were expelled from Rome in A.D.

---

113. Jeffrey Weima, *1-2 Thessalonians*, 25. The entire trip took four or five days, possibly six. Barry Beitzel, *Lexham Geographic Commentary on Acts through Revelation*, 339. According to Witherington, they may have traveled by horse or mule. Ben Witherington III, *The Acts of the Apostles*, 502.

114. Weima believes Paul and his team didn't preach in Amphipolis or Apollonia because both cities lacked the presence of Jews.

115. Barry Beitzel, *Lexham Geographic Commentary on Acts through Revelation*, 337.

116. Jeffrey Weima, *1-2 Thessalonians*, 2-3. Other scholars estimate higher numbers (as high as 200,000). Bruce Longenecker, *In Stone and Story*, 22. Keener believes the real population was lower than 200,000. Craig Keener, *The IVP Bible Background Commentary: New Testament*, 374. Others estimate far lower numbers (40,000). Even so, along with Rome, Alexandria, Ephesus, and Antioch, Thessalonica was a "giant city" during the first century. Most cities in the first century only had 20,000 residents. Thessalonica had a much larger population. Craig Keener, *Acts*, 3:2537. Witherington estimates 60,000 to 80,000, with 100,000 living just outside the walls. Ben Witherington III, *1 and 2 Thessalonians*, 4. This is about the same as Weima's estimate, which I deem accurate.

117. Jeffrey Weima, *1-2 Thessalonians*, 25.

118. H.L. Hendrix, "Thessalonica" (Place) in D.N. Freedman, ed., *The Anchor Yale Bible Dictionary*. The height of the walls extended from eight meters to over ten (which is around twenty-six to thirty-two feet). The circuit of the city was confirmed by personal correspondences with Jeffrey Weima, 6/14/22, and David Bauer, 3/20/22. For a visual sketch of ancient Thessalonica, see Peter Walker, *In the Steps of Paul*, 106-107.

119. N.T. Wright and Michael Bird, *The New Testament in Its World*, 417.

120. Craig Keener, *The IVP Bible Background Commentary: New Testament*, 374.

121. Dunn speculates that the Jewish population was significant, but admits the supporting epigraphical data is slim. James D.G. Dunn, *Beginning from Jerusalem*, 676-677.

49. It's a free Greek city, not a Roman colony.[122] It mints its own coins and has its own form of government. Nevertheless, the city has close ties with Rome and the emperor; thus, it's sensitive to anything that might cause it to lose its "favored city" status. The *politarchs* are particularly sensitive to any problems coming from the Jews.[123]

Thessalonica is also a center for communication and trade. It's an urban metropolitan city, with a diverse population and many religions, combining Greek, Roman, and Eastern ways of life. Yet it's not a philosophical or educational center (like Athens).[124] The imperial cult is important in Thessalonica.[125] Beyond the emperor (who is worshiped), the major gods recognized in the city are Dionysus, Serapis, Isis, and Cabirus.[126] The city also worships the traditional Greek pantheon, including Zeus, Apollo, Hades, Poseidon, etc.[127]

Like most Greco-Roman cities, Thessalonica is marked by sexual laxity and promiscuity. The immorality is not restricted to pagan temples. It also takes place at inns and taverns where prostitutes are kept for sexual entertainment.[128] The general attitude in the city, as well as throughout the empire among the Gentiles, is that "mistresses we keep for the sake of pleasure, concubines for the daily care of our persons, but wives to bear us legitimate children and to be faithful guardians of our households."[129] By

122. The city was given free status, governed by its own patriarchs, in 42 B.C. F.F. Bruce, *Paul: Apostle of the Heart Set Free*, 223.

123. Ben Witherington III, *New Testament History*, 263.

124. Ben Witherington III, *1 and 2 Thessalonians*, 5.

125. Craig Blomberg, et al., *From Pentecost to Patmos*, 203. This is one of the reasons why Paul used imperial language throughout 1 and 2 Thessalonians. "Caesar's grip was on the hearts and minds of the humble tradespeople, craftspeople, slaves, servants, and day laborers." Richard Horsley, et al., *The Message and the Kingdom*, 154. For a detailed treatment of the imperial divine honors and the influence they had on Paul and the Thessalonian church, see D. Clint Burnett, *Paul and Imperial Divine Honors*, chap. 3.

126. Egyptian gods were extremely popular in Thessalonica. Personal correspondence with Jeffrey Weima, 2/10/22. For details on the favored religions in the city, see Jeffrey Weima, *1-2 Thessalonians*, 9-23.

127. Gene Green, *The Letters to the Thessalonians* (Grand Rapids, MI: Eerdmans, 2002), 43.

128. For a discussion on women and dining in the ancient world, see Reta Halteman Finger, *Of Widows and Meals*, chap. 11.

129. Demosthenes, *Orations*, 59.22.

stark contrast, the high standard of sexuality among the Jews is respected in the Diaspora.[130] The women of Macedonia are noted for their independence.[131]

Many Jews live in Thessalonica and share in the city's wealth. At the same time, unemployment is high, and a large part of the population probably lives on the public distribution of grain.[132] A famine will hit Greece in A.D. 51, and there will be earthquakes and widespread panic throughout the region. These catastrophes will be viewed as divine judgment from the gods because of the Christians.[133] The converts in the ekklesias that Paul will raise up are a mixture of slaves, freedmen, and well-to-do people. Most of the assemblies also include merchants, scribes, and city officials. This is also true of the assembly in Thessalonica.[134]

The three men come to the triumphal gate—a triple Roman arch gate that stands at the entrance of the city.[135] As they walk through the city, they spot the statue of Augustus (with his raised upright hand). They also see the temple dedicated to Augustus in the

130. F.F. Bruce, *1 & 2 Thessalonians,* 87. The Jews believed that fornication (sexual intercourse outside of marriage) was a serious sin before God, so they were known for their monogamous marriages.

131. F.F. Bruce, *The Book of the Acts,* 323. For further details on the city of Thessalonica during Paul's day, see Jeffrey Weima, *1-2 Thessalonians,* 1-40. Similarly, Roman wives generally remained under the legal guardianship of their fathers rather than their husbands. Thus, within marriage, they had more independence than any other women in the Greco-Roman world, including the ability to divorce their husbands. David Capes, et al., *Rediscovering Paul,* 42.

132. According to Riesner, this was also true in other large cities in the empire, not just Thessalonica. Rainer Riesner, *Paul's Early Period,* 376.

133. Bruce Winter, *Seek the Welfare of the City,* 52-53. Pagans believed the Christians caused economic distress because they didn't participate in the pagan cults. Personal correspondence with Christoph Heilig, 1/30/23. This will become a significant factor in anti-Christian sentiment in the second and third centuries. Personal correspondence with David deSilva, 1/18/24.

134. Wayne Meeks, *The First Urban Christians,* chap. 2. Meeks points out that in Paul's letters (not counting the Pastorals), sixty-five individuals are named. In Acts, thirteen are named who are in association with Paul. While none of them were part of the uber rich, many were well-to-do (55-73).

135. Personal correspondence with Jeffrey Weima, 3/9/22.

distance.[136] They behold Mount Olympus—the supposed location of the gods—a mere fifty miles away.[137]

For three consecutive Sabbaths, Paul, Silas, and Timothy visit the Jewish synagogue in Thessalonica.[138] With fiery passion[139] and great power,[140] Paul preaches that Jesus of Nazareth is the promised Christ, proving his case by skillfully wielding the Hebrew Scriptures. This is incredible news to the Jews in Northern Greece, and it provokes either belief or hostility. Some of the Jews receive the message, along with a relatively large number of God-fearing Greeks and quite a few prominent women.[141]

A Hellenistic Jew named Jason, a man of wealth, is converted. He opens his home to the apostolic workers, a home that's large enough to host them all.[142] Those who believe the

136. Ben Witherington III, *1 and 2 Thessalonians*, 5.

137. John Stott, *The Message of 1 & 2 Thessalonians*, 39. According to Weima, a person can see Mount Olympus on a clear day from Thessalonica. Personal correspondence with Jeffrey Weima, 3/9/22.

138. Synagogues were known for more than worship. They were centers for education and also operated like modern hotels, showing hospitality to visitors from out of town. Since Paul was seen as a "Harvard grad" (a student of the great Gamaliel), the synagogue probably extended hospitality to him and his companions in the very beginning. Personal correspondence with Jeffrey Weima, 2/10/22.

139. Ramsay argues that Paul was an impassioned orator and regularly made many gestures with his hands while he spoke. William Ramsay, *St. Paul the Traveler and Roman Citizen*, 40.

140. When Paul preached the gospel, God's power came through his words (1 Thessalonians 1:5; 1 Corinthians 1:18; 2:4-5; 4:20; Romans 1:4, 16).

141. The prominent women mentioned in Acts 17:4 could also mean the wives of prominent men. Darrell Bock, *Acts*, 551; Gene Green, *The Letters to the Thessalonians*, 49. Witherington suggests that one of them could have been the wife of Aristarchus. Ben Witherington III, *1 and 2 Thessalonians*, 41. Macedonia permitted women to have significant social, religious, and political roles since the Hellenistic era. Ben Witherington III, *The Acts of the Apostles*, 492. According to some scholars, women could be counted as part of the ten (quorum) required to build a synagogue. Women were active in the synagogues and participated fully in the life of the community (except for reading Scripture publicly). There was no special women's section in the synagogues or divider that separated the sexes. Shmuel Safrai, "The Place of Women in First-Century Synagogues: They Were Much More Active in Religious Life Than They Are Today," published in CBE International, January 31, 2002. Even though the ekklesia in Thessalonica was about fifty people tops, when a quorum or *minyan* is only ten or twelve in a synagogue, anything over twenty can be considered a "large number." Personal correspondence with Ben Witherington III, 3/28/22. This is significant in understanding Luke's wording in Acts 17:4, 12.

142. Otto F.A. Meinardus, *St. Paul in Greece*, 31. Jason was a man of financial means, since he owned a house large enough to accommodate the Thessalonian ekklesia. He was also well-off enough to be able to post bond. Rainer Riesner, *Paul's Early Period*, 350; F.F. Bruce, *The Pauline Circle*, 96; James D.G. Dunn, *The*

earth-shattering gospel of the kingdom Paul preaches begin gathering in Jason's home.[143] The apostle presents a crucified and resurrected Messiah who has been made Lord of the world and requires everyone's believing obedience.[144] A crucified Messiah is non-sensical—an absurd contradiction to the Jewish mind and complete foolishness to the Greek mind.[145]

Paul, well aware of this, readily depends on the Holy Spirit to create faith in the hearts of those who hear his controversial gospel.[146] And the Spirit does just that. Consequently, converts to Jesus Christ are made in Thessalonica. Most of them are Greeks, and their first impulse is to abandon their idols and repent of their fornication.[147] (Idolatry and fornication are a way of life in Greece. Prayer and sacrifices to the gods are a normal part of the day. Idolatry is practiced everywhere; it's part of the fabric of society. If a person plants a tree, or goes on a trip, or if a family member gets married, they pray to the relevant god.[148]

Acts of the Apostles, 228; *Beginning from Jerusalem*, 679. Green says Jason was "sufficiently rich." Gene Green, *The Letters to the Thessalonians*, 29. The Jason mentioned in Acts 17:6 is likely the Jason listed in Romans 16:21, who Paul says was a Jew. Craig Keener, et al., *NIV Cultural Backgrounds Study Bible*, 1911. Jason may have also provided work (and a workshop) for Paul and Silas. Craig Keener, *Acts*, 3:2549-2550. Luke, the author of Acts, wrote as though his audience knew who Jason was. See also W.J. Conybeare and J.S. How-son, *The Life & Epistles of St. Paul*, 256.

143. Witherington believes Jason was the first convert in Thessalonica. Ben Witherington III, *1 and 2 Thessalonians*, 36-37.

144. Paul reframed the central terms used by and about Caesar (e.g., "good news," "Lord," "Savior," "justice," "salvation," "peace," "power," "faith/loyalty," etc.) and applied them to Jesus and God's kingdom. N.T. Wright, *Paul: A Biography*, 324-325.

145. 1 Corinthians 1:22-25. N.T. Wright, *Paul: A Biography*, 213-214; *The Challenge of Jesus*, chap. 4.

146. 1 Thessalonians 1:5.

147. 1 Thessalonians 1:9; 4:2ff.

148. N.T. Wright, *Paul for Everyone: Galatians and Thessalonians*, 91-92. Giving up idols in Paul's day would be like giving up smart phones and computers in our day. It was a huge risk for the Thessalonians to turn away from idols to serve the living God, given how highly their pagan neighbors regarded idol worship. In the ancient world of Paul's day, there was no separation between secular and spiritual. All of life was sacred, and the gods and goddesses were everywhere. Personal correspondence with Jeffrey Weima, 2/10/22. For a detailed analysis of the Greco-Roman gods during the first century and their relationship to the early Christians, see Bruce Longenecker, ed., *Greco-Roman Associations, Deities, and Early Christianity* (Waco, TX: Baylor University Press, 2022). For an analysis of Greco-Roman philosophy, religion, and voluntary associations, see Richard Longenecker, ed., *Community Formation in the Early Church and in the Church Today*, chap. 1.

When ships arrive at a harbor, an offering is made to a god or goddess.[149] Military action starts and concludes with sacrifice and prayer.[150])

Forsaking idols means no longer dining in the pagan temples as well as no longer engaging in the regular pagan religious festivals.[151] If a person refuses to worship the gods, they can be stoned in the streets.[152] All of this puts the members of the new ekklesia out of favor with friends, relatives, and business associates.[153] It also puts their lives at risk.[154]

The gospel of Jesus Christ is a threat to the normative way of life in Thessalonica. Rejecting idolatry and fornication incurs the social harassment of the Greek community.[155] Even more striking, the Christians' refusal to worship the emperor constitutes treason.[156] Their hope in a returning agent of God (Jesus) who will completely upset the Roman order is nothing less than seditious.[157]

As Paul spends time laying the foundation for the new ekklesia, he speaks about the kingdom of God, both its present and future dimensions. He tells the new believers about their hope, which will be fully realized at the second coming of Christ. He speaks to them

149. David Capes, et al., *Rediscovering Paul*, 46.

150. Craig Keener, et al., *Journeys of the Apostle Paul*, 72-73.

151. Meat was sold at the markets as well as in the pagan temples. And it was often offered to idols. Otto F.A. Meinardus, *St. Paul in Greece*, 90.

152. Ramsay MacMullen, *Paganism in the Roman Empire* (New Haven, CT: Yale University Press, 1981), 62; Nijay Gupta, *1 & 2 Thessalonians*, 61.

153. Ben Witherington III, *1 and 2 Thessalonians*, 43. The citizens of the city were irritated by the Thessalonian believers, viewing them as useless rabble, responsible for disorder. They saw them as instigators of confusion and insurrection because they denied the gods and wouldn't pay homage to Caesar. Thessalonica was so enamored with Rome they dedicated four temples to the emperor. In 1 Thessalonians 2:14, Paul refers to the pagans in the city as "fellow-citizens" or "your own countrymen."

154. For details on how the first-century Christians were viewed as weird, dangerous, subversive, and a threat to the Roman order, see Nijay Gupta, *Strange Religion*. Similarly, for a thorough overview of the historical, social, and religious context of the Jesus movement in the Greco-Roman world along with how the Christians differed from the pagans, see Markus Öhler, *History of Early Christianity: Religion, Culture, Identity* (Waco, TX: Baylor University Press, 2024).

155. The rejection of idol worship and participation in the pagan festivals brought the anger and resentment of the city on the Christians. The city saw them as antisocial atheists (because they denied the gods). Bruce Longenecker, *In Stone and Story*, 47. They also feared the Christians would anger the gods, who would then bring plagues, famine, disease, etc. upon the entire city. Jeffrey Weima, *1-2 Thessalonians*, 108-109.

156. Craig Keener, et al., *Journeys of the Apostle Paul*, 73.

157. 1 Thessalonians 1:9-10; 2:19; 3:13; 4:15; 5:23.

about the day of the Lord and all it means for them and the world.[158] Paul labors with the new assembly as a nursing mother who cares for her children. He compares himself and his companions to gentle, innocent infants[159] among them, yet he's also like a father who confidently educates and implores his children.[160] As is his custom, Paul begins mending tents to pay for his expenses. He and Silas work early in the mornings and late in the evenings.[161]

Remarkably, the apostle pays his own way in everything, including food and rent.[162] He refuses to be a burden to the Thessalonian believers while he serves them with the gospel.[163] By his example of hard work, Paul teaches the assembly to labor with their own hands, even though manual labor is abhorrent to most Greeks. The apostle evangelizes as well as disciples his new converts from his workshop.[164] He talks to them about the importance of

158. 1 Thessalonians 5:1-2; 2 Thessalonians 2:5.

159. According to Weima, the manuscript support for "infants" is stronger than "gentle" in 1 Thessalonians 2:7, the former conveying the idea of innocence, the opposite of what Paul's detractors accused him of. Jeffrey Weima, *1-2 Thessalonians*, 144-145, 187, 285.

160. 1 Thessalonians 2:7-11.

161. 1 Thessalonians 2:9. Ben Witherington III, *New Testament History*, 262. In 1 Thessalonians 2:9, Paul uses the plurals "we" and "our" in describing his labor, possibly indicating that Silas was also involved in the leatherworking practice.

162. 2 Thessalonians 3:8. If Paul and Silas were staying with Jason, which is highly plausible from Acts 17:7, the apostle insisted on paying Jason room and board. John Stott, *The Message of 1 & 2 Thessalonians*, 53. This doesn't discount the fact that the church in Philippi helped Paul financially while he was in another city. The point is that the apostle refused to take money from the church in Thessalonica *while* he was present planting it.

163. Paul's pattern was to labor with "his hands" while he worked with a church (1 Corinthians 4:12; 9:15-18; Acts 20:34; 1 Thessalonians 2:9; 2 Thessalonians 3:8). He only accepted contributions from an assembly *after* it was established and he was on the road, ministering in other locations. Jeffrey Weima, *1-2 Thessalonians*, 150-151.

164. It's more plausible that Paul had a workshop rather than a spot in the marketplace. Workshops in the ancient world were similar to the old-time barbershops in America, where people talked and caught up on current news. Paul conducted evangelism and discipleship in the semiprivate workshop as well as in the marketplace. Jeffrey Weima, *1-2 Thessalonians*, 28-29, 151; personal correspondence with Weima, 2/10/22; Rainer Riesner, *Paul's Early Period*, 377; Bruce Longenecker, *In Stone and Story*, 48; Jerome Murphy-O'Connor, *Paul: His Story*, 73. Business was usually undertaken in a person's house. Ben Witherington III, *The Acts of the Apostles*, 338. Consequently, Paul's workshop may have been in a room in Jason's house, or an *insula,* an apartment building with living spaces on the upper floor. The artisan shops in the *insula* would have opened onto the street. David deSilva, *Paul and the Macedonians*, 21-22. Paul's business would have put him in regular contact with Jews and Gentiles. Ben Witherington III, *1 and 2 Thessalonians*, 37-38. Some in the ekklesia in

manual labor and not being a burden on others as financial dependents. He gives them the following standard: "If someone is not willing to work, let him not eat."[165]

While Paul labors in Thessalonica, the assembly in Philippi graciously sends at least two financial gifts to help him and his companions.[166]

You yourselves also know, you Philippians, that in the beginning of the Good News, when I departed from Macedonia, no assembly shared with me in the matter of giving and receiving but you only. For even in Thessalonica you sent once and again to my need. (Philippians 4:15-16)

The ekklesia in Thessalonica is made up mostly of ex-pagans, along with some God-fearers and some Jews.[167] It contains some wealthy members, but the majority are manual workers, part of the lower class of society.[168] As Paul is laying the foundation for the new church, he explains that sexual purity is the will of God, and it pleases Him.[169] He warns the believers about the divine consequences of using their bodies immorally and taking advantage of one another[170] (a common practice among the Gentiles). The apostle also passes on the apostolic tradition to the young church.[171]

Thessalonica were probably artisans like Paul, and most of the congregation belonged to the working class. Rainer Riesner, *Paul's Early Period*, 377. Artisans and laborers who didn't work daily needed the financial help of the others in the congregation, but such help given out of love wasn't to be exploited. Charles Wanamaker, *The Epistle to the Thessalonians*, 163.

165. 2 Thessalonians 3:10. See also 1 Thessalonians 4:11. Paul was not referring to those who were unable to work due to disability, illness, or unavoidable unemployment. Paul was addressing those members of the Thessalonian church who, despite being able-bodied, refused to work and instead exploited the generosity of their fellow believers. Personal correspondence with Jeffrey Weima, 12/28/23.

166. Rainer Riesner, *Paul's Early Period*, 363. We aren't told who brought the gifts to Paul from Philippi. An educated guess would be that the gifts were brought to Paul from Clement, a man in the Philippian assembly whom Paul held in high regard (Philippians 4:3). Titus may have also brought one or more gifts. If so, he would have been visiting Philippi at the time. Personal correspondence with Ben Witherington III, 1/27/22; J.B. Lightfoot, *The Acts of the Apostles*, 227.

167. Jeffrey Weima, *1-2 Thessalonians*, 28. 1 Thessalonians 1:9 and 4:3-8 support this inference.

168. James D.G. Dunn, *Beginning from Jerusalem*, 633.

169. Inferred from 1 Thessalonians 4:1-5.

170. Inferred from 1 Thessalonians 4:6-8.

171. 2 Thessalonians 2:15; 3:6, ESV. The apostolic tradition refers to the teachings, practices, and way of life that the apostles, particularly Paul, passed on to the early Christian churches both in person and by letter.

Paul and Silas preach the politically and religiously subversive gospel of the kingdom throughout the city. They discuss the return of Jesus, the worship of the one true God, and they implore the Gentiles to forsake their idols. All of this makes Paul an enemy of the state.[172] Despite the backlash, Paul continues to proclaim the gospel and build the young assembly.

You became imitators of us and of the Lord, having received the word in much affliction, with joy of the Holy Spirit...we grew bold in our God to tell you the Good News of God in much conflict. (1 Thessalonians 1:6; 2:2)

The apostle informs the new converts that they are destined to suffer and thus they will face afflictions.[173] He encourages them with stories of how the kingdom communities in Judea endured their persecutions, holding them up as a model for imitation.[174] The opposition in Thessalonica increases, and the Jewish leaders spread a rumor that Paul and Silas are criminals. (They heard about their imprisonment in Philippi.)

The Jewish leaders boil over with jealousy and view Paul as a synagogue splitter. So they stir up some local ruffians[175] to instigate a tumult in the agora of the city.[176] A day at

---

This tradition was based on the teachings of Jesus and considered authoritative for all believers. It includes many elements, including the importance of earning one's livelihood through honest work. For details, see Jeffrey Weima, *1-2 Thessalonians*, 557-559.

172. The opposition came from both Jews and pagans in the city. The resistance wasn't only because Paul preached another king. It was also because there was a community of people forming around that message and acting on it (Acts 17:4ff.) Those who believed and proclaimed the revolutionary kingdom message were considered seditious. Andy Johnson, *1 & 2 Thessalonians* (Grand Rapids, MI: Eerdmans, 2016), 11.

173. 1 Thessalonians 3:3-4.

174. 1 Thessalonians 2:14.

175. The ruffians were also called "agora men." They frequented the marketplace, probably as unemployed day laborers who were malcontented and given to agitation. Ben Witherington III, *The Acts of the Apostles*, 506.

176. Acts 17:4-5 makes plain that the Jewish leaders were jealous because they were losing synagogue members (and undoubtedly donors) to the new faith from among the God-fearers. The Jewish community saw Paul as a sheep-stealer, taking rich and powerful members away from the synagogue to follow his new faith. Personal correspondence with Jeffrey Weima, 2/10/22. This is why they plotted against him. Jews were already on shaky ground, since Claudius had been marginalizing them throughout the empire from A.D. 41 to 49. Ben Witherington III, *1 and 2 Thessalonians*, 39. The use of a mob was a normal tactic within the

the marketplace quickly descends into mayhem. The mob forms and begins a riot. The malcontents thunder through the streets and storm Jason's residence to search for Paul and Silas. Their intention is to bring them before the citizen assembly for trial.[177] Paul and Silas are not present, so the mob changes its plan and drags Jason and some of the new converts before the *politarchs* (city officials).[178]

They accuse Jason of harboring enemies of Rome. They charge Paul and Silas in absentia with two very dangerous accusations: disturbing the peace and violating the decrees of Caesar[179] by proclaiming a rival king.[180]

When they didn't find them, they dragged Jason and certain brothers before the rulers of the city, crying, "These who have turned the world upside down have come here also, whom Jason

history of Greek democracy. James D.G. Dunn, *The Acts of the Apostles*, 229. The ruffians were likely paid by the Jewish opposition to cause the riot. Personal correspondence with Alan Bandy, 12/6/23.

177. Gene Green, *The Letters to the Thessalonians*, 50-51. The citizen assembly (or town council), *dēmos* in the Greek, collaborated with the *politarchs*. Ben Witherington III, *1 and 2 Thessalonians*, 4. Most translations render this governmental body "the people" or "the crowd." The CSB does better by translating it "the public assembly." The *politarchs* were the power brokers between Rome and the city. Jeffrey Weima, *1-2 Thessalonians*, 32; Ben Witherington III, *The Acts of the Apostles*, 507.

178. The distinction between the citizen assembly and the *politarchs* (city officials) is revealed in the Greek in Acts 17:5 (the public assembly) and Acts 17:6 (the *politarchs*). For details on the governmental structure of Thessalonica and the differences between the citizen assembly and the *politarchs*, see Weima, *1-2 Thessalonians*, 7-9.

179. The decrees of Caesar likely included the loyalty oath paid to the emperor by all the citizens of Thessalonica. Paul Barnett, *From Jerusalem to Illyricum*, 75.

180. In A.D. 16, Emperor Tiberius issued an imperial decree banning the prediction of a new king throughout the empire. For details on the two charges against Paul and Silas, see Jeffrey Weima, *1-2 Thessalonians*, 32-35. Interestingly, some scholars believe the accusation was a misrepresentation. In contrast, I believe N.T. Wright gets it right in saying that they fully understood what Paul was preaching and their accusation was true. The apostles were preaching that Jesus of Nazareth was Lord and Caesar was not. N.T. Wright, *Acts for Everyone: Part Two*, 78. That message caused riots to break out wherever Paul preached. The apostle was fomenting a spiritual insurgence, boldly proclaiming the gospel of the kingdom of God in the major cities. The charge against Paul and Silas is similar to the charge laid at the feet of Jesus (Luke 23:2, 38). Andy Johnson, *1 & 2 Thessalonians*, 12. Ironically, in Philippi, Paul was accused by pagans of promoting Jewish customs that were illegal for Romans. But in Thessalonica, he was accused by Jews of teaching against the decrees of Rome. N.T. Wright, *Paul: A Biography*, 227.

has received. These all act contrary to the decrees of Caesar, saying that there is another king, Jesus!" (Acts 17:6-7)[181]

Thessalonica already has a "savior" and "lord" who provides "peace and security." It is Caesar. So any competitor will suffer the consequences.[182] The apostolic workers and their followers are viewed as social deviants, at odds with beloved Rome.[183] Jason and all others who follow Paul's gospel have broken Roman law and must be held accountable.

Paul has been telling the people to forsake their idols (which likely included the statue of the emperor). This is another crime against the state.[184] Consequently, the *politarchs* (numbering five or six) interrogate Jason.[185] After the interrogation, they make him post a financial bond to ensure there is no more trouble. They warn Jason that if Paul and Silas don't leave the city, they will confiscate his property. The same thing will happen if Paul and Silas return. Therefore, the two apostles are legally banned from Thessalonica.

Upon hearing this news, some of the believers in Thessalonica find Paul and Silas and secretly send them off under the cloak of darkness.[186] But Paul, in concern for the new believers, leaves Timothy behind to encourage the Thessalonians in their faith in the wake of Paul and Silas' hasty departure.[187]

Paul has developed a deep affection for the Thessalonians. He feels torn apart from them like a father bereaved of his children.[188] But even though the two apostles are run out of town, a multiethnic kingdom community—an assembly that expresses Jesus Christ—now

181. The word translated "king" in Acts 17:7 was the same title used of the emperor in the east. The theme of the kingship of Jesus runs all throughout Luke-Acts. Calling Jesus King and Messiah was subversive to the existing empire. Luke Timothy Johnson, *The Acts of the Apostles*, 307.

182. Richard Horsley, *Jesus and Empire*, 12.

183. N.T. Wright and Michael Bird, *The New Testament in Its World*, 418.

184. Ben Witherington III, *1 and 2 Thessalonians*, 40. The exhortation to stop worshipping idols and turn to the living God was viewed by Gentiles as a "Jewish" message to be disloyal to the imperial cult and the cults of the gods on whose favor the well-being of the city depended. N.T. Wright, *Paul: A Biography*, 181.

185. Ben Witherington III, *New Testament History*, 263; *The Acts of the Apostles*, 507; Darrell Bock, *Acts*, 552; F.F. Bruce, *New Testament History*, 308, n. 12; Jeffrey Weima, *1-2 Thessalonians*, 32.

186. Night travel was especially dangerous due to robbers. Craig Keener, *Acts*, 3:2559-2560.

187. Paul will later relate that he deliberately left Timothy in Thessalonica after the apostle was run out of town to make sure these troubling events did not weaken the faith of the believers (1 Thessalonians 3:1ff.). For deSilva's reconstruction, see David deSilva, *An Introduction to the New Testament*, 461-472.

188. 1 Thessalonians 2:17. Charles Wanamaker, *The Epistle to the Thessalonians*, 120.

exists in Thessalonica. The church has four distinguished converts: Jason, Aristarchus, Secundus, and Demas. Jason and Aristarchus are well-to-do Jews; Secundus and Demas are Gentiles.[189] All of them will reappear later in the story.[190]

A Kingdom Community Is Planted in Berea

Paul and Silas walk forty-five miles due west on the Via Egnatia. A short distance off the Via Egnatia,[191] they come to a resort-like town called Berea.[192] The trip takes two to three days, and they travel by land.[193] Berea is a small town off the beaten path.[194] It sits on a

189. See Colossians 4:14; Romans 16:21; Philemon 24. For details, see F.F. Bruce, *The Pauline Circle*, 86, 96, 98; Rainer Riesner, *Paul's Early Period*, 348; Craig Keener, *Acts*, 3:2550-2551. Secundus was "a gentile Christian from Thessalonica who accompanied Paul on his final journey from Greece to Jerusalem (Acts 20:4)." Geoffrey Bromiley, "Secundus," in *The International Standard Bible Encyclopedia*, revised edition (Grand Rapids, MI: Eerdmans, 1979-1988). Keener believes Secundus was likely a person of status. Craig Keener, *Acts*, 3:2955. And he was probably a Roman citizen. Jeffrey Weima, *1-2 Thessalonians*, 30; Rainer Riesner, *Paul's Early Period*, 351. Slaves who were freed by Roman citizens typically gained Roman citizenship themselves. Bruce Longenecker, *In Stone and Story*, 19. For the social status of Aristarchus, see Gene Green, *The Letters to the Thessalonians*, 29; Ben Witherington III, *1 and 2 Thessalonians*, 41.

190. Acts 17:5; 20:4; 2 Timothy 4:10 (the latter text presumes Demas was from Thessalonica). Jason, Aristarchus, and Secundus were probably converted to Christ during this period. F.F. Bruce, *The Book of the Acts*, 323. It's plausible that Demas was also.

191. They likely walked. Personal correspondence with Mark Fairchild, 8/4/23.

192. Barry Beitzel, *Lexham Geographic Commentary on Acts through Revelation*, 339; Herbert Lockyer, ed., *Nelson's Illustrated Bible Dictionary*, 146. It is probable that the Greeks went to Berea in the summer to cool off. Personal correspondence with Mark Wilson, 9/4/23. According to Darrell Bock, Berea was hilly around the city, but relatively flat within. It had a major marketplace (agora) and a stadium. Personal correspondence with Bock, 7/14/23. Berea was described as an "out-of-the-way-town," which means it was located off the Via Egnatia. F.F. Bruce, *The Book of the Acts*, 327. Some scholars believe Paul arrived in Berea during the summer. Personal correspondence with Alan Bandy, 6/27/23 and Mark Fairchild, 8/4/23. For details on Berea, see Eckhard Schnabel, *Early Christian Mission*, 2:1195. The remains of the agora, public baths, streets, and city wall still survive. Personal correspondence with Eckhard Schnabel, 8/25/23.

193. Barry Beitzel, *Lexham Geographic Commentary on Acts through Revelation*, 339-340. If one believes the average person could walk eighteen to twenty-five miles a day, it's possible the trip took two days. Personal correspondence with Alan Bandy, 6/27/23.

194. Ben Witherington III, *The Acts of the Apostles*, 509; personal correspondence with Mark Fairchild, 8/4/23. Bandy estimates the population may have been between 10,000 and 20,000. Personal correspondence

slope overlooking a stream.[195] Located in the foothills of Mount Bermium, Berea is rich and fertile, so farms are in abundance.[196] (Likely, the believers in Thessalonica felt Berea would be a safe location for the two workers after they got run out of their city.[197])

Berea is made up of older, high-class folk. Many Jewish merchants live there. It's a Roman trading town, and it sports a high degree of literacy (which is unusual in the empire).[198] Like Thessalonica, Berea is also ruled by *politarchs*.[199] But they are completely independent from the *politarchs* in Thessalonica.[200] As is their custom, the apostles visit the synagogue to preach Christ. Paul ministers, but he isn't preaching to a passive audience. He dialogues with the Jews, exchanging ideas and opinions with them.[201]

The Bereans are open-minded students of the Hebrew Scriptures. They are gracious, cordial, and fair-minded, eagerly evaluating Paul's message against the Hebrew Bible to see if what he is preaching is accurate.[202] Paul finds this an exceptional experience, since

with Alan Bandy, 6/27/23. Wilson estimates 20,000 to 25,000. Personal correspondence with Mark Wilson, 9/4/23.

195. In the city, there were waterfalls tied to a river, the Tripotamos. Personal correspondence with Darrell Bock, 7/14/23. In addition, the Haliacmon River coursed just southeast of the city before flowing into the Aegean Sea. Personal correspondence with Mark Wilson, 9/4/23. A traveler headed to Athens would pass through Berea. Darrell Bock, *Acts*, 555.

196. Craig Keener, *Acts*, 3:2561. According to Darrell Bock, Berea sat at the base of the Bermio (or Vermio) range, north of Mount Olympus. Personal correspondence with Bock, 7/14/23.

197. Since it was an "out-of-the-way" town, Berea didn't fit Paul's typical strategy of bringing the gospel to urban centers. He and the Thessalonian believers probably chose Berea because it sat outside of Thessalonica's jurisdiction. James D.G. Dunn, *Beginning from Jerusalem*, 681. Given this fact, entering Berea probably wasn't part of Paul's original travel plan. He simply fled there to avoid the political charges from Thessalonica. Jeffrey Weima, *1-2 Thessalonians*, 35.

198. The city is not insignificant, due to its trading and Jewish synagogue. Rainer Riesner, *Paul's Early Period*, 360.

199. Ben Witherington III, *New Testament History*, 264.

200. The decision made by the Thessalonian officials against Paul and Silas held no authority in Berea. Ben Witherington III, *The Acts of the Apostles*, 509.

201. Paul's method of "dialogue" continued in other cities where he presented the gospel. James D.G. Dunn, *Beginning from Jerusalem*, 678.

202. Luke's description implies that the synagogue in Berea functioned as a study center, where scrolls of the Scriptures were kept and people from the Jewish community could visit and study them daily (not just on the Sabbath). James D.G. Dunn, *Beginning from Jerusalem*, 681. They probably had a Torah scroll and scrolls of other Scriptures, most likely in a Greek translation. Craig Keener, *Acts*, 3:2562. Synagogues typically contained a niche for the chest used to hold Scripture scrolls. Personal correspondence with James Ware,

he's been rejected and thrown out of most of the cities where he has preached.[203] The Jewish synagogue leaders in Berea express no hostility. In fact, many of the Berean Jews believe in Christ as a result of Paul's message, including some upper-class Greek women. In addition, a Jew named Sopater (also called Sosipater) is one of the distinguished converts in the new ekklesia in Berea.[204]

Timothy leaves Thessalonica and rejoins Paul and Silas in Berea. What happens next mirrors what took place during the first apostolic journey in Lystra. Some of the Jewish leaders from Thessalonica hear that Paul and Silas are preaching in Berea. So they descend on the town and stir up the crowds against the two workers. Several of the Berean believers try to spare Paul, so they take him to the coast and escort him by sea to Athens.[205] The route from Berea to Athens is 320 miles, nearly a four-week journey.[206] Silas and Timothy stay behind to encourage the newly founded Berean assembly. There is now an assembly of God's people in the little town of Berea. The kingdom has come to Berea and gained a

---

10/4/02, and Craig Keener, 7/8/21. The scrolls may have been read on a table in the center of the synagogue. Since they were hand copies, smaller synagogues might not have had many. They would likely have had the Torah (Pentateuch), Isaiah, and the Psalms. That's why these are overwhelmingly the most quoted or alluded to books in the New Testament. Personal correspondence with Craig Keener, 7/8/21 and Ben Witherington III, 8/19/21.

203. F.F. Bruce, *Paul: Apostle of the Heart Set Free*, 167; Jeffrey Weima, *1-2 Thessalonians*, 36.

204. Paul calls Jason and Sopater "my fellow Jews" in Romans 16:21, NIV. Bruce believes Sopater and Sosipater are identical, and he was "evidently a Jew by birth." F.F. Bruce, *In the Steps of the Apostle Paul*, 35. In his letters, Paul refers to people by their formal names, while Luke refers to them by their familiar names. Paul uses the name "Sosipater" while Luke calls him "Sopater." In the same way, Paul speaks of "Prisca" (in the epistles) while Luke (in Acts) calls her "Priscilla." Paul also speaks of "Silvanus" while Luke calls him "Silas." F.F. Bruce, *The Pauline Circle*, 45; *Romans*, revised edition, TNTC (Grand Rapids, MI: Eerdmans, 1985), 257; James D.G. Dunn, *Romans 9–16*, 909.

205. According to Acts 17:15, some of the Berean Christians "escorted" Paul to Athens. F.F. Bruce, *New Testament History*, 311; James D.G. Dunn, *The Acts of the Apostles*, 229; N.T. Wright, *Paul: A Biography*, 189. A strong tradition supports the sea-travel opinion. H.V. Morton, *In the Steps of St. Paul* (Cambridge, MA: Da Capo Press, 2002), 293-294. "Sea travel was the most convenient way to reach Athens." Craig Keener, *Acts*, 3:2564. Bandy agrees that the men sailed to Athens. Personal correspondence with Alan Bandy, 6/27/23. Other scholars believe Paul traveled to Athens by land. Darrell Bock, *Acts*, 557.

206. Barry Beitzel, *Lexham Geographic Commentary on Acts through Revelation*, 341. The implication from Acts 17:14 is that this was a journey by boat. It was also difficult to journey south by land through the Olympian Mountains. Jeffrey Weima, *1-2 Thessalonians*, 37. Some scholars calculate 195 miles from Berea to Athens. Darrell Bock, *Acts*, 557.

foothold there.[207] After arriving in Athens, Paul asks the brethren escorting him to instruct Silas and Timothy to come to Athens as soon as possible.[208]

Rejection in Athens

The Berean disciples leave Paul in Athens alone. Located in Achaia (Southern Greece), Athens is the cradle of Greek philosophy and democracy. It's a free Greek city, a small university town described as a "provincial backwater"[209] with a population of about 25,000.[210] Upon arriving at Piraeus, the city's main harbor, Paul enters the city through the Double Gate (Dipylon) on the west side.[211] He beholds the Temple of Demeter with the statue of the goddess and her daughter. As he moves farther, he sees the statue of Poseidon.[212]

The city is running over with idols and pagan temples. Wherever Paul turns, statues, temples, and shrines fill his horizon.[213] The square pillars each mounted by a head of Hermes surround him.[214] Athens features a temple, an altar, and a cult for every pagan taste. Athena is worshipped on the acropolis, the high point of the city.[215] She is the goddess of wisdom and the patron goddess of the city. Three temples dedicated to her rest on the acropolis, as well as a small temple in the agora. She is also worshipped in the council chamber.

207. For further details on the three ekklesias planted in Macedonia (Philippi, Thessalonica, and Berea), see William Ramsay, *St. Paul the Traveler and Roman Citizen*, chaps. 9-10.

208. The narrative you just read is based on Acts 17:10-15.

209. Weima adds nuance saying, "The glory days of Athens were in the past. Nevertheless, it still had a glorious reputation which caused many wealthy and powerful figures from the ancient world to donate and sponsor public buildings in Athens. Luke's description of Paul's ministry in Athens certainly presumes this renowned reputation of the city." Personal correspondence with Jeffrey Weima, 12/28/23.

210. Craig Evans, et al., eds., *Dictionary of New Testament Background*, 139.

211. Personal correspondence with Alan Bandy, 12/6/23.

212. Otto F.A. Meinardus, *St. Paul in Greece*, 41-42.

213. Some of these pillar-statues sported phalluses. Idolatry and sexual immorality were joined together in the ancient world, as the apostolic decree indicates (Acts 15:20, 29). Ben Witherington III, *The Acts of the Apostles*, 512-513.

214. F.F. Bruce, *The Book of the Acts*, 330.

215. Personal correspondence with Jeffrey Weima, 12/28/23.

Zeus is worshipped in the stoa, the major commercial building for shopping located on the west side of the agora (marketplace).[216] Athenians worship other gods like Demeter, Apollo, Artemis, Aphrodite, Ares, Hermes, Isis, and Serapis as well as the emperor.[217] According to one ancient proverb, there are more gods than men in Athens.[218] Early into Paul's stay in Athens, Timothy and Silas rejoin him.[219]

As the forest of idols in Athens fills Paul's eyes, his spirit is grieved. And he is both angered and distressed.[220] He then takes note of one curious altar with the inscription: "TO THE UNKNOWN GOD."[221]

Meanwhile, the assembly in Thessalonica weighs heavy on Paul's heart. He was prevented from completing the foundation he began to lay there and the church is under severe persecution. As a result, the apostle experiences a form of separation anxiety.[222] He desperately longs to see the young assembly, so he lifts up the believers to the Lord day and night,[223] asking God to make a way for him to revisit them. Paul makes several attempts to

216. The agora in Athens was "more than a typical marketplace; it was the civic, economic, cultural, and intellectual heart of the city." Alan Bandy, *An Illustrated Guide to the Apostle Paul*, 105. In the agora, slaves were ransomed and redeemed for a fee. In his letters, Paul uses the language of redemption that was commonly spoken in the agora to make theological points. Mark Wilson, *Biblical Turkey*, 118.

217. Eckhard Schnabel, *Paul the Missionary*, 179ff. Weima observes, "A modest shrine/temple dedicated to Augustus was placed immediately in front of the Parthenon. Thus, the imperial cult was present during the period when Paul visited the city." Personal correspondence with Jeffrey Weima, 12/28/23.

218. Otto F.A. Meinardus, *St. Paul in Greece*, 44.

219. This is a plausible deduction. According to Keener, "Paul is alone in Athens (Acts 17:15-16) until Timothy joins him (Acts 17:15). We could then suppose that after Silas and Timothy join him in Athens, Paul can send Timothy back to Thessalonica; the 'we' left at Athens would thus be Paul and Silas (1 Thess. 3:1)." Craig Keener, *Acts*, 3:2570-2571. Paul sent Silas somewhere in Macedonia, and both men rejoined Paul in Corinth (Acts 18:5). Weima is in agreement with this reconstruction. Jeffrey Weima, *1-2 Thessalonians*, 208. Keener gives a detailed analysis on Paul, Silas, and Timothy in Athens based on a reconstruction of the material in Acts and the epistles in *Acts*, 3: 2570-2578. (Acts 18:5 doesn't contradict this reconstruction.)

220. The words "greatly distressed" in Acts 17:16 (NIV) also mean to anger, provoke, or irritate. David Bauer, *The Book of Acts as Story*, 205.

221. Acts 17:23, ESV, KJV, NKJV. Some translations render it "TO AN UNKNOWN GOD" (NIV, NASB, WEB).

222. 1 Thessalonians 2:17; 3:1, 5.

223. 1 Thessalonians 3:9-10.

get back into the city,[224] but because the principalities and powers in the city have banned him and Silas, satan (who controls these powers) thwarts his efforts. The ban is still in force.

> *For we wanted to come to you—certainly I, Paul, did, again and again—but Satan blocked our way. (1 Thessalonians 2:18, NIV)*

The apostle is frustrated and anxious about the spiritual state of the believers since he knows they are under great pressure. He is gravely concerned they will crack under the weight.[225] Knowing that the ban doesn't apply to Timothy, he sends his apprentice back to Thessalonica to encourage the assembly and find out how it's holding up under the persecution.[226] He sends Silas to Philippi.[227]

Paul visits the synagogue in Athens and presents Christ to the Jews and God-fearers. But he does so in dialogue form.[228] He also proclaims Jesus in the agora—the Athenian marketplace adorned with public buildings and colonnades. While he's preaching, some of the Stoic and Epicurean philosophers engage Paul in a debate.[229] Stoics believe humans should be free from all passion, thus they suppress their affections and accept all things as the will of the gods. Epicureans believe the chief aim of life is the pursuit of mental pleasure.[230] They also teach that pain, suffering, and superstitions should be avoided.[231]

224. The Greek in 1 Thessalonians 2:17-18 supports this conclusion. See Jeffrey Weima, *1-2 Thessalonians*, 198-199; Rainer Riesner, *Paul's Early Period*, 360.

225. 1 Thessalonians 3:5. See also 2 Corinthians 11:28.

226. 1 Thessalonians 3:1-5.

227. While we cannot be certain if Silas went to Philippi, he did go to Macedonia (Acts 18:5), and Philippi seems the most plausible option in the region. I presume he went there to encourage the church and receive a report on its progress. Upon leaving, he brought back another financial gift for Paul (2 Corinthians 11:8-9; Philippians 4:15). Bock agrees that Silas probably went to Philippi. Darrell Bock, *Acts*, 557. The scenario I've painted is derived from piecing together Acts 17:15, 18:5, and 1 Thessalonians 3:2.

228. James D.G. Dunn, *Beginning from Jerusalem*, 682.

229. Interestingly, many educated Jews believed the Greek philosophers plagiarized Moses. Craig Keener, *Acts*, 3:2607.

230. Craig Keener, *Acts*, 3:2584-2591.

231. For more information on the differences between the Stoics and Epicureans, see James D.G. Dunn, *The Acts of the Apostles*, 233; Clinton Arnold, ed., *Zondervan Illustrated Bible Backgrounds Commentary*, 2b:172-173.

Some of the philosophers assert that Paul is a babbler—a *spermologos* (seed-picker or scavenger).[232] Others say he declares foreign gods. He preaches the resurrection of the dead, which is a laughable concept to the Greek mind.[233] But the Athenians wrongly assume that when Paul mentions the resurrection, he is referring to foreign gods.[234] Fascinated by his message, the philosophers bring Paul to the Areopagus (also known as Mars Hill) to share his beliefs.[235] The Areopagus is the city council—or court—that decides moral and religious matters.[236] The council meets in the Royal Colonnade in the agora,[237] located to the northwest of the acropolis.[238]

Paul is not brought there to stand trial. Instead, they ask the apostle to share his "new" teaching so they can determine its validity as a religion. (The Athenians have a passion for anything "new," making it the talk of the town. Consequently, they are eager to hear Paul's message.[239]) The apostle begins his talk by mentioning the altar dedicated "TO THE UNKNOWN GOD."

232. Darrell Bock, *Acts*, 561-562; James D.G. Dunn, *Beginning from Jerusalem*, 685. The Greek word *spermologos* refers to those who loafed about in the agora, serving up sound bites of philosophy they picked up from various sources.

233. The Greeks believed in the immortality of the soul, but not the resurrection of the body. They firmly believed a dead person remained dead. Darrell Bock, *Acts*, 570.

234. James D.G. Dunn, *The Acts of the Apostles*, 234. The Greek word for resurrection is *anastasis*. Therefore, the Athenians probably assumed Paul was proclaiming a male deity (Jesus) and a female deity (Anastasia). Ben Witherington III, *New Testament History*, 267; N.T. Wright, *Acts for Everyone: Part Two*, 84.

235. During this period, the Areopagus was an aristocratic body composed of the local elite. It was the "Supreme Court" of Athens. Areopagus means "the hill of Ares." The Areopagus in Athens took its name from the Greek god of war (Ares). His Roman name was Mars. The hill of Ares/Mars was the original meeting place for the Areopagus. During Paul's day, however, the council met in the Royal Porch in the Athenian marketplace (except when investigating cases of homicide). Craig Keener, *Acts*, 3:2600ff.; N.T. Wright, Lecture 2, The Soularize Conference.

236. The Areopagus was not primarily a location, but an assembly—a governing body in judicial, religious, and financial matters. Ben Witherington III, *New Testament History*, 267. The Areopagites were probably people of wealth and status. Craig Keener, *Acts*, 3:2601.

237. F.F. Bruce, *Jesus and Paul: Places They Knew* (Nashville, TN: Thomas Nelson, 1983), 99. When Luke says Paul stood in the middle of the Areopagus (Acts 17:22), it means he stood in the midst of the court. F.F. Bruce, *In the Steps of the Apostle Paul*, 40.

238. James D.G. Dunn, *The Acts of the Apostles*, 234. The acropolis was the highest point of the city.

239. In Acts 17, Luke alludes to the story of Socrates who was tried in Athens for introducing new gods. Paul was examined for introducing foreign gods, and he began his speech with the same words Socrates used

There is an incredible story behind this altar. Hundreds of years before, a plague fell on Athens. The Athenians believed that a certain god had cursed them. In response, they sacrificed to all the gods, but nothing worked. They concluded, therefore, that the gods refused to be appeased. So they fetched a wise man named Epimenides, a philosopher from Crete. When Epimenides came to Athens, the Athenians thought, "He will know how to appease the god we offended and deliver our city from the plague."

Epimenides said to them, "Tomorrow at sunrise bring a flock of sheep. Bring some stonemasons and a large supply of stones. The sheep must all be healthy and have different colors, some white and some black. You must prevent them from grazing after their night's rest. They must be hungry sheep. The next morning, release all the sheep upon this sacred slope and permit each animal to graze where it wants. Watch them closely." The philosopher prayed, "Dear unknown god, behold the plague. If you would have compassion and help us, behold this flock of sheep, and cause any sheep that pleases you to lie down upon the grass instead of grazing." Within minutes, several sheep were resting on the grass.

The philosopher said, "Separate the sheep and mark the place where each sheep laid down. Let the stonemasons build altars. One altar on each animal's resting place."[240] The stonemasons carved "TO THE UNKNOWN GOD" on the altars, and they sacrificed each dedicated sheep upon them. By dawn the next day, the plague began to dissipate. And within a week, it was gone. The Athenians and Epimenides quickly praised the unknown God.[241]

With this story in mind, Paul tells the people of Athens, "You worship something unknown to you, and I am here to reveal who this unknown God is!"[242] Tailoring his

---

in his defense: "Men, Athenians." Craig Keener, et al., *Journeys of the Apostle Paul*, 44. The charge of introducing foreign gods is what led to Socrates' death. Plato, *Apology of Socrates*, 23B-C; Craig Keener, *Acts*, 3:2604.

240. This is a paraphrase of what the philosopher (Epimenides) told them. William Larkin Jr., *Acts: The IVP New Testament Commentary Series*, Logos edition (Downers Grove, IL: InterVarsity Press, 1995), Acts 17:22-23. For further details on the story, see Don Richardson, *Eternity in Their Hearts* (Minneapolis, MN: Bethany House, 1981), chap. 1; Craig Keener, *Acts*, 3:2631-2632; F.F. Bruce, *The Spreading Flame*, 115-116.

241. "They thought in terms of unknown gods, but naturally Paul appeals to the one God unknown to them who is real." Personal correspondence with Craig Keener, 12/4/23.

242. This is my paraphrase of Acts 17:23.

message to the Greek mind, Paul quotes a few Greek poets.[243] He does this to show that some of the truths he proclaims already exist within Athenian culture.[244]

He then shares about Jesus, the man whom the one true God raised from the dead and appointed to be judge of the world.[245] When he starts speaking about the resurrection, however, some of the Athenians scoff and sneer at him.[246] The concept of a bodily resurrection is utter foolishness to their ears.[247] Others, however, seek to hear Paul again on the matter.

Paul will later reflect on his Athens experience when he writes these words:

Where is the wise? Where is the scribe? Where is the lawyer of this world? Hasn't God made foolish the wisdom of this world? For seeing that in the wisdom of God, the world through its wisdom didn't know God, it was God's good pleasure through the foolishness of the preaching to save those who believe. For Jews ask for signs, Greeks seek after wisdom, but we preach Christ crucified: a stumbling block to Jews, and foolishness to Greeks...God chose the foolish things of the world that he might put to shame those who are wise. God chose the weak things of the world that he might put to shame the things that are strong. God chose the lowly things of the world, and the things that are despised, and the things that don't exist, that he might bring to nothing the things that exist, that no flesh should boast before God. (1 Corinthians 1:20-23, 27-29)

243. In Acts 17:28, Paul quotes Epimenides the Cretan and Aratus the Stoic poet, respectively. James D.G. Dunn, *The Acts of the Apostles*, 236. Paul was conversant with Greco-Roman philosophy and poetry. In 1 Corinthians 15:33, he quotes Menander, the author of the Greek comedy, *Thais*. Darrell Bock, *Acts*, 568. Paul's speech, recorded in Acts 17, takes about two-and-a-half minutes to read. Wright believes the actual message was closer to two-and-a-half hours. N.T. Wright, Lecture 2, The Soularize Conference. Luke clearly compresses Paul's speech (as he often does with spoken messages). I agree with Wright that it probably went on for at least an hour instead of two minutes. Luke just rehearses the highlights. N.T. Wright, *Paul: A Biography*, 195.

244. N.T. Wright, *Paul: A Biography*, 202.

245. Acts 17:24-31. The idea of "judging the world" in the full biblical sense means to set it right as well as call it to account. N.T. Wright, *Acts for Everyone: Part Two*, 92.

246. The Greek term Luke uses means to mock or sneer. Darrell Bock, *Acts*, 570.

247. Acts 17:32; 1 Corinthians 1:17-23.

There is little fruit in Athens.[248] By the time Paul leaves the city, only a handful of converts are made, and no assembly is planted.[249] Among the converts are Dionysius, a man of high social standing and a member of the Areopagus,[250] and a woman of status named Damaris.[251]

A Kingdom Community Is Planted in Corinth
Fall 50[252]

From Athens, Paul heads fifty-three miles west to the Roman colony of Corinth.[253] It's basically a three-day trip.[254] Because of his negative experiences in Greece thus far, Paul arrives in Corinth discouraged, dejected, and full of misgivings. He was beaten and imprisoned in Philippi, banned from Thessalonica, driven out of Berea, and rejected in Athens.[255]

---

248. This is the impression that Luke gives us. F.F. Bruce, *The Book of the Acts*, 344; James D.G. Dunn, *Beginning from Jerusalem*, 692. Craig Keener points out that "having an Areopagite—a member of the city council—as a named convert, means they have a great place for a house church." Personal correspondence with Craig Keener, 12/4/23. While this is true, it doesn't mean a church was actually formed.

249. James D.G. Dunn, *The Acts of the Apostles*, 238; Ben Witherington III, *The Acts of the Apostles*, 533. Again, Paul's mission was to raise up kingdom communities, not simply make individual converts. James D.G. Dunn, *Beginning from Jerusalem*, 682-692; Otto F.A. Meinardus, *St. Paul in Greece*, 56. See also the chapter entitled "Kingdom Strategy" at the end of this book. Since Paul's pattern was always to baptize those who came to Christ, the converts in Athens were probably baptized in a fountain house, spring, or river. Craig Keener, *Acts*, 3:2680.

250. James D.G. Dunn, *The Acts of the Apostles*, 238.

251. According to Keener, Damaris was likely a person of status. Craig Keener, *Acts*, 3:2678-2679. She could have been a philosopher or the wife of Dionysius. F.F. Bruce, *The Book of the Acts*, 341-342.

252. According to Bruce, Paul arrived in Corinth in the autumn of A.D. 50. F.F. Bruce, *Jesus and Paul*, 104. Other scholars estimate Paul arrived earlier in A.D. 50.

253. This distance is based on the notion that Paul traveled along the Saronic Gulf via Eleusis, Megara, and Isthmia to Corinth. Barry Beitzel, *Lexham Geographic Commentary on Acts through Revelation*, 341. Paul may have sailed from Piraeus, between the islands of Salamis and Aegina, to the harbor of Cenchreae on the eastern shore of the Isthmus of Corinth. It probably took Paul two or three hours to walk from Cenchreae to Corinth.

254. For a plausible timeline of the movements of Paul and Timothy from Athens to Corinth, see Jeffrey Weima, *1-2 Thessalonians*, 208.

255. Ramsay believes Paul was disillusioned and discouraged from his experience in Athens. William Ramsay, *St. Paul the Traveler and Roman Citizen*, 194.

I was with you in weakness, in fear, and in much trembling. (1 Corinthians 2:3)

Sharpening the Focus: Corinth is the capital of Achaia (Southern Greece).[256] The city is named after the currant, a type of grape that grows in the region.[257] It's a large and prosperous metropolis that's fast becoming the largest and most prosperous city in Greece.[258] Its population is about 80,000.[259] If the towns and villages that Corinth controlled are added, the population rises to 100,000.[260] The circuit of the city is between four and six miles.[261]

One-third of the city is made up of slaves. Corinth is the major clearinghouse and slave market town for slaves shipped from the East westward. As a Roman colony, the architecture in Corinth is Roman, and Latin is the official language. Corinth is essentially a Roman city in a Greek setting. Many of the city's residents (Jew and Gentile) aren't Roman citizens.[262]

The very wealthy live in villas on the slope of the Acrocorinth (a large mountain behind the city).[263] Religiously, the city is pluralistic and includes faith in the Greek gods, especially Aphrodite, Poseidon, and Apollos, as well as the imperial cult.[264] Given that it's a commercial city, Corinth includes a significant and longstanding Jewish community.[265] Some of the Jews in the city have come from Rome because of

256. The city was the seat of government of the Roman province of Achaia from 27 B.C. onward. F.F. Bruce, *Paul: Apostle of the Heart Set Free*, 250.

257. For details on Corinth and Paul's ministry there, see Ben Witherington III, *The Acts of the Apostles*, 535-561.

258. For details, see Alan Bandy, *An Illustrated Guide to the Apostle Paul*, 109-111.

259. James D.G. Dunn, *Beginning from Jerusalem*, 694.

260. Barry Beitzel, *Lexham Geographic Commentary on Acts through Revelation*, 341; Lars Kierspel, *Charts on the Life, Letters, and Theology of Paul*, 48.

261. Strabo, *Geography*, 8.6.21a. By some calculations, forty stadia was almost four miles. According to Jeffrey Weima, the remaining/existing walls of the city are six miles and Strabo's reference could be off. Personal correspondence with Weima 6/14/22.

262. F.F. Bruce, *In the Steps of the Apostle Paul*, 42.

263. Personal correspondence with Bruce Winter, 5/24/02.

264. N.T. Wright, *Paul: A Biography*, 210-211.

265. F.F. Bruce, *The Book of the Acts*, 348.

Emperor Claudius' decree to expel them from the Eternal City. Luke specifically identifies this as the cause of Priscilla and Aquila's relocation to Corinth from Rome.[266]

Corinth sits on a narrow isthmus.[267] And it's a true melting pot. It caters to its many transient merchants and sailors in both food and entertainment.[268] Therefore, you can hear half a dozen languages in addition to the dominant Greek and Latin. Latin is almost as common as Greek. Roman law controls everyday living.[269] The city's municipal government mirrors Rome's.[270] As a "boomtown," its location is strategic for the spread of the gospel.

The city is a major stop on the Roman road system.[271] Consequently, its taverns are numerous and its prostitutes rampant. The city has a reputation for sexual immorality, luxury, self-promotion, and boasting.[272] (In fact, "Corinth" has long been a byword for immorality.[273] In the fourth century B.C., to act "Corinthian" or to "Corinthianize" meant to engage in fornication. In the same vein, a prostitute was called a "Corinthian girl."[274])

Temples devoted to Apollo, Demeter, Isis, Ephesian Artemis, Aphrodite, and other gods populate the city. The satellite ports of Lechaion and Cenchreae have shrines to Poseidon, Aphrodite, and Isis, among others. In one of his letters to the Corinthian

266. Acts 18:2-3.

267. The ismthus is important for connecting mainland Greece with other parts near the region. The dozens of languages in the city stem from the fact that it's a large city with an active trade record of goods traveling from west to east and east to west through its two harbors. Personal correspondence with Jeffrey Weima, 12/28/23.

268. For further details on what life was like in first-century Corinth, see Ben Witherington III, *A Week in the Life of Corinth* (Downers Grove, IL: InterVarsity Press, 2012); F.F. Bruce, *In the Steps of the Apostle Paul*, 41-44. For how ancient Corinth was laid out, see Jerome Murphy-O'Connor, *St. Paul's Corinth* (Collegeville, MN: The Liturgical Press, 2002), 192ff.; Otto F.A. Meinardus, *St. Paul in Greece*, 62-64.

269. David Capes, et al., *Rediscovering Paul*, 178.

270. James D.G. Dunn, *Beginning from Jerusalem*, 694.

271. Craig Keener, et al., *Journeys of the Apostle Paul*, 79ff.

272. F.F. Bruce, *The Book of the Acts*, 346.

273. F.F. Bruce, *Paul: Apostle of the Heart Set Free*, 249. For more on the sexual climate in Corinth, see David Capes, et al., *Rediscovering Paul*, 177.

274. Jerome Murphy-O'Connor, *St. Paul's Corinth*, 56-57.

Christians, Paul will mention "gods" and "lords," referring to the honor Corinthian society pays to the many deities it reveres.[275]

Corinth is socially imbalanced, with few rich and many poor or enslaved.[276] At the same time, it's a magnet for the socially ambitious. There are many opportunities for prosperity. Consequently, social climbing is a major occupation.[277] The city's wealth is augmented by the manufacturing of Corinthian bronze and the Isthmian games.[278] The games are the second largest sports event in the world, next to the Olympics in Olympia. They are held every other year in honor of Poseidon, the god of the sea, and they are underway during Paul's first visit to the city.

The Isthmian victory wreath,[279] a crown of dry, wild celery that Paul refers to as "a perishable crown" (1 Corinthians 9:25, NKJV), is the principal reward presented at the games.[280] Corinth is a highly competitive city, being the first Greek city to have Roman gladiatorial contests. As in other areas of Roman society, Roman wives don't cover their heads in public. This shows their freedom and high status. Prostitutes and fertility priestesses also display their heads uncovered, and no woman covers her head in private at home.[281]

Jewish women and God-fearing women typically cover their heads during synagogue services. Roman and Greek women cover their heads during some pagan religious ceremonies.[282] Men typically cover their heads.[283] And male Roman citizens wear togas and cover their heads during religious rituals.[284] In addition, men in the

275. 1 Corinthians 8:5. F.F. Bruce, *In the Steps of the Apostle Paul*, 41.

276. N.T. Wright, *Paul: A Biography*, 211.

277. Murphy-O'Connor breaks down the different classes in the church, as well as the practice of temples and banquets in *St. Paul's Corinth*, 178-191.

278. Jerome Murphy-O'Connor, *St. Paul's Corinth*, 201ff.

279. Personal correspondence with Craig Keener, 12/4/23. The Isthmian crown was a wreath, not a gold crown.

280. Otto F.A. Meinardus, *St. Paul in Greece*, 85.

281. David Capes, et al., *Rediscovering Paul*, 179-180.

282. Personal correspondence with Jeffrey Weima, 1/13/24.

283. Personal correspondence with Jeffrey Weima, 1/13/24.

284. David Capes, et al., *Rediscovering Paul*, 179-180.

Greco-Roman world normally wear short hair. This includes Jews in both the Diaspora and Palestine.[285]

Prevalent in Corinth is one of the basic building blocks of Greco-Roman society—the patron-client relationship. Patrons are uber-rich individuals who serve as benefactors to less well-to-do people (called "clients").[286] The patron offers advice and protection to the client. In return, the client offers the patron various services, such as campaigning at elections, tending to their needs, and boosting the crowd at family funerals.

Stephanas, Phoebe, and Philemon are some of the patrons Paul will mention in his letters.[287] (Lydia in Philippi is also a patron.) While most of the converts in the kingdom communities Paul founds are poor,[288] a fair number are part of the urban elite.[289] This is partly because Paul's strategy is to plant kingdom communities in the most influential cities on the major trade routes of the empire.[290] First-century Christianity, therefore, is largely an urban movement.[291]

285. E.P. Sanders, *Paul: The Apostle's Life, Letters, and Thought*, 282 (with n. 5).

286. Personal correspondence with Jeffrey Weima, 12/28/23. For a succinct explanation of the patron-client system, see James Papandrea, *A Week in the Life of Rome*, 19. For a more detailed exposition, including the relevance of this background for reading across the New Testament, see David deSilva, *Honor, Patronage, Kinship & Purity*, chaps. 3-4; Amy-Jill Levine and Ben Witherington III, *The Gospel of Luke*, 593-594. In the New Testament, Phoebe (in Cenchreae) and Gaius (in Corinth) were patrons. Both were probably elites in society. Peter Oakes, *Empire, Economics, and the New Testament* (Grand Rapids, MI: Eerdmans, 2020), 118.

287. Like Jesus, Paul treated women as persons worthy of dignity. And he regarded many of them as his co-workers in the gospel, a radical concept in his time. F.F. Bruce, *Paul: Apostle of the Heart Set Free*, 456-463. That Stephanas, Phoebe, and Philemon were persons of wealth, see Wayne Meeks, *The First Urban Christians*, 57-58. Philemon was a benefactor of the Colossian believers. David deSilva, *Honor, Patronage, Kinship & Purity*, 124.

288. 1 Corinthians 1:26. See also James 2:5.

289. For details on the social mobility of the Corinthian believers, see Bruce Winter, *Seek the Welfare of the City*, 146ff. For a conversation on the mobility that marked the first-century Jesus movement, see Wayne Meeks, *The First Urban Christians*, 16-23.

290. For details on Paul's apostolic methods, see the chapter entitled "Kingdom Strategy" at the end of this book.

291. Meeks makes a strong case for this point in his book *The First Urban Christians*. For details on first-century Corinth, the social level of the Corinthian Christians, and the socio-rhetorical natures of Paul's two surviving Corinthian letters, see Ben Witherington III, *Conflict and Community in Corinth*, 5-67. The Jesus

Soon after his arrival in Corinth, Paul meets a man named Aquila, a native of Pontus near the Black Sea.[292] Aquila has a wife named Priscilla (also called Prisca).[293] She is the more impressive personality of the couple.[294] Both are Jews who have been expelled from Rome by Emperor Claudius.[295] Like Paul, they are independent craftsmen—specifically, leatherworkers (tentmakers).[296] The well-to-do couple runs a substantial business,[297] and they are also Jesus-followers.[298]

---

movement began in rural Galilee, but it quickly became an urban movement with the mission of Paul of Tarsus. Gary Burge, et al., *The New Testament in Antiquity*, 95.

292. According to Bandy, Priscilla and Aquila would have arrived in Corinth just a few months before Paul did. Alan Bandy, *An Illustrated Guide to the Apostle Paul*, 112. Ramsay believes Aquila arrived in Corinth six or seven months before Paul did. William Ramsay, *St. Paul the Traveler and Roman Citizen*, 196.

293. Prisca is the diminutive form of Priscilla. Clinton Arnold, ed., *Zondervan Illustrated Bible Backgrounds Commentary*, 3:92. Priscilla was probably freeborn, not a slave. Peter Lampe, "Prisca" (Person) in D.N. Freedman, ed., *The Anchor Yale Bible Dictionary*.

294. According to Bruce, this may explain why both Luke and Paul put her name before her husband's name. F.F. Bruce, *Romans*, 257. Dunn says she "was presumably the more dominant personality." James D.G. Dunn, *The Acts of the Apostles*, 247. Some scholars believe Priscilla was Roman and belonged to the Roman family called *gens Prisca*. If this is true, her name appears first because of her higher social class. For a discussion on how the couple served the kingdom of God, see Nijay Gupta, *Tell Her Story*, chap. 8. For details on this couple, see Eckhard Schnabel, *Acts*, 756-757; F.F. Bruce, *The Pauline Circle*, 44-50.

295. Matthew Novenson, *Paul Then and Now*, 73; Peter Lampe, *From Paul to Valentinus*, 11ff. Priscilla was probably a Jew along with her husband. "Jews married Jews, with probably few exceptions." Personal correspondence with Eckhard Schnabel, 8/25/23.

296. Many translations use "tentmakers" in Acts 18:3. Leatherworkers may be more accurate. The couple "probably lived in a shop front (*taberna*) with small living quarters behind or above. However, since they were able to offer extended hospitality to Paul (Acts 18:3), they seem to have occupied a larger dwelling. But a large dwelling does not necessitate a freestanding house. Some ground-floor apartments had workplaces on each side of the entrance with living quarters, sometimes even a larger upper room, at the back or upstairs." Robert Banks, *Paul's Idea of Community*, 29.

297. James D.G. Dunn, *Beginning from Jerusalem*, 696; W.J. Conybeare and J.S. Howson, *The Life & Epistles of St. Paul*, 300. They hosted more than one assembly in their homes (or apartments) over their lifespans (Romans 16:5; 1 Corinthians 16:19). Because those dwellings were large enough to accommodate the believers, the couple had significant financial status.

298. F.F. Bruce, *The Book of the Acts*, 347; James D.G. Dunn, *Beginning from Jerusalem*, 696; *The Acts of the Apostles*, 241.

Aquila and Priscilla employ Paul to labor in their workshop.[299] Because the Isthmian games are held in Corinth at this time, a great need exists for temporary shelter. Therefore, the three leatherworkers receive plenty of business. Except for the Sabbath, each day they sew durable leather into tents and create (or repair) other leather products which they sell to tourists and sailors in Corinth.[300]

Crisis in Thessalonica
A.D. 50 – 51

Silas and Timothy leave Macedonia and join Paul in Corinth.[301] The assembly in Philippi has sent another financial gift to Paul, and Silas brings it to him.[302] The money enables the apostle to devote himself exclusively to the work of building the ekklesia in Corinth.[303] Timothy brings good news and gives Paul a report:[304]

- The church in Thessalonica is now around fifty people.[305] It is still undergoing harsh

299. Acts 18:3. Peter Lampe, *From Paul to Valentinus*, 187. Craftsmen in the first century often rented workshop spaces (192). Archaeologists in Corinth have excavated a row of workshops approximately nine to twelve feet wide, twelve feet deep, and thirteen feet high, with a doorway about seven-and-a-half feet wide to provide light during working hours. This is suggestive of the conditions under which Paul, Priscilla, and Aquila lived and worked. The couple would have slept in a loft, positioned directly above the workshop, while Paul would have made his bed in the main workroom. Clyde Fant, et al., *A Guide to Biblical Sites in Greece and Turkey*, 51. For further details on Priscilla and Aquila and their workshop, see Craig Keener, *Acts*, 3:2711-2719.

300. Alan Bandy, *An Illustrated Guide to the Apostle Paul*, 112-113.

301. Acts 18:5.

302. 2 Corinthians 11:9; Philippians 4:14-16. As far we know, Philippi is the only church that funded Paul's ministry while he was on the road. See also Darrell Bock, *Acts*, 578. For further details on Paul's ministry in Athens and Corinth, see William Ramsay, *St. Paul the Traveler and Roman Citizen*, chap. 11.

303. "And after Silas and Timothy came down from Macedonia, Paul spent all his time preaching the word...." (Acts 18:5, NLT).

304. 1 Thessalonians 3:6-8.

305. Scholars estimate that the ekklesia in Thessalonica ran around fifty people. Personal correspondence with Jeffrey Weima, 4/21/22. Ben Witherington agrees saying, "I would not think there were over fifty people in the church in Thessalonica." Personal correspondence with Witherington, 1/27/22. This was also the case with most of the churches in the first century. Dunn estimates about forty-five people in the church in Thessalonica. James D.G. Dunn, *Beginning from Jerusalem*, 709. In the same book, Dunn argues that a large house could accommodate fifty people (606-608).

persecution. However, the believers are standing steadfast in the Lord. They are even sounding forth the gospel amid their opposition.

- The believers have pleasant memories of Paul and miss him dearly. But they wonder why the apostle hasn't visited them, especially since his detractors have been spreading awful rumors about his selfish motives in ministering to them.

- Some of the believers from the kingdom communities in Macedonia (Philippi) and Achaia (Corinth) have visited the Thessalonian believers, and they were encouraged by the faith, love, and steadfastness of the Thessalonians in the midst of their local oppression.[306]

- Some well-to-do believers in the church (like Jason and Aristarchus) visit other parts of Macedonia and Achaia on business. While there, they share the gospel in the marketplaces.[307]

- While visiting the ekklesias in Berea and Philippi, the well-to-do believers in Thessalonica financially bless the poor saints in those assemblies.[308]

- Some of the Jews from Jerusalem, the "agitators" who visited Syrian Antioch and Galatia, visit the church in Thessalonica and tell the believers that Paul is a people pleaser, a greedy flatterer driven by impure motives. He is just like the wandering

306. Wayne Meeks, *The First Urban Christians*, 27. We know that the church in Philippi sent Paul a gift on at least two occasions when he was in Thessalonica, so there was contact between the two assemblies in Macedonia (2 Corinthians 11:9; Philippians 4:15ff.). In addition, the church in Corinth (in Achaia) knew about the Thessalonians and their faith (1 Thessalonians 1:8-10).

307. These scenarios are inferred from 1 Thessalonians 1:7-10. The Thessalonians were an encouragement to the believers in other cities and the gospel "rang out" (or "echoed") from them to northern and southern Greece. See also Gene Green, *The Letters to the Thessalonians*, 8; Ben Witherington III, *1 and 2 Thessalonians*, 120; N.T. Wright, *Paul for Everyone: Galatians and Thessalonians*, 91. Because news spread about the ekklesia, Paul didn't have to boast about the Thessalonians in Corinth or elsewhere. Word about them had already gotten out (1 Thessalonians 1:8). F.F. Bruce, *1 & 2 Thessalonians*, 17. Priscilla and Aquila possibly brought Paul news about the Thessalonian believers from reports they heard. Leon Morris, *The First and Second Epistles to the Thessalonians*, 51. When Paul heard the reports that the testimony of the Thessalonians was spreading everywhere, he was like a proud parent whose children just won a game. Personal correspondence with Jeffrey Weima, 2/10/22.

308. This scenario is based on 1 Thessalonians 4:10. (Berea and Philippi are in Macedonia.) In the New Testament, "love" is often translated into financial help. N.T. Wright, *Paul for Everyone: Galatians and Thessalonians*, 121-122.

philosophers who seek the praises of men. (They probably point to the fact that he took money from the Philippians as "evidence" of his greed.) Paul, they claim, also abandoned the Thessalonians when things got rough, proving he's a man of poor character.[309]

- Due to the pressures on the assembly, some of the Gentile believers are struggling with the temptation to revert back to their pagan lifestyle—namely, fornication.[310]

309. Here is my reasoning that the agitators visited Thessalonica. They had already been to Syrian Antioch with their version of the gospel. Then they went to Galatia and trashed Paul's reputation. Later they will show up in Corinth (Southern Greece) to do the same. I imagine these same men visited the assembly in Thessalonica (Northern Greece) blasting Paul's character. They probably left the city before they could unleash their gospel of legalism. In 1 Thessalonians 2:3-6, I see Paul responding to that particular group. Consider that the same language is used in Galatians chapter 1. Namely, (1) The accusation of "people pleasing" (1 Thessalonians 2:4) is found in Galatians 1:10. (2) The accusation that Paul wasn't approved by God and entrusted with the gospel (1 Thessalonians 2:4) is found in Galatians 1:11-12 and 2:7. To me, these details fit my theory. In 1 Thessalonians 2:14-16, Paul switches to the pagan enemies in the city who are oppressing the church along with the unbelieving Jews, though I don't doubt he lumps the Jewish "Christian" agitators with the Jewish enemies of the gospel in his mind. (Paul doesn't see the agitators as genuine brethren as he makes plain in Galatians 2:4.) The whole goal of the agitators is underscored in Galatians 4:17 (NIV): "Those people are zealous to win you over, but for no good. What they want is to alienate you from us, so that you may have zeal for them." According to Keener, "This reconstruction is possible, though since Malherbe's famous article many commentators have argued that Paul simply offers a conventional defense against conventional charges, without having heard these specific charges offered." Personal correspondence with Craig Keener, 12/4/23. Although this is the conventional wisdom currently, the scenario I've presented makes better sense of the material.

310. This a plausible conclusion based on Paul's words in 1 Thessalonians 4:1-8. Clearly, something provoked him to write those words. Paul acknowledges that the believers were walking in purity, yet he *urges* them to do so "more and more" (1 Thessalonians 4:1, NIV). Paul's "urge" implies they all weren't walking perfectly in the area of sexuality. Gordon Fee confirms that a small number in the church were struggling with sexual temptation. According to Fee, Paul's exhortation in 1 Thessalonians 4:1-8 is an "exhortation aimed at so few of them that he feels the need to ease his way into speaking to a decided minority in the context of the gathered people of God." The apostle writes the exhortation in such a way that he wants the believers to "understand that he is aware that not all of them are involved in the errors that need correction." Gordon Fee, *The First and Second Epistles to the Thessalonians*, NICNT (Grand Rapids, MI: Eerdmans, 2009), 139. According to Stott, in 1 Thessalonians 4:1ff., Paul addresses "certain practical problems of Christian conduct which were evidently troubling them" from Timothy's report. That report included "the deficiencies in the Thessalonians' discipleship (3:10) which he proceeds to remedy in chapters 4 to 5." John Stott, *The Message of 1 & 2 Thessalonians*, 75. Bruce agrees saying, "It may be that Timothy, on his return from

- Some in the church have recently died. The believers grieve their loss, and they have questions about what happens to a follower of Jesus when they die. Will they miss the day of the Lord?[311]

- The believers in Thessalonica also want Paul to answer these questions: "How and when will the day of the Lord you told us about arrive? If Jesus really is the world's King, why is there suffering and death? Why isn't He exercising His royal rule and saving us from persecution?"[312]

- Several of the men in the church are acting in disorderly ways with their idle time.[313] Some engage in aggressive evangelism, where they ridicule idols and return evil for evil (perhaps toward those persecuting them).[314]

- Since the church is already in a precarious situation, the failure of some of the believers to live quietly and mind their own business is putting the ekklesia in more jeopardy.[315]

- The disorderly conduct of some in the church has hurt the testimony of the ekklesia in the eyes of outsiders.[316] Those who aren't working are taking advantage of the generosity of the financially better-off believers.[317] (Paul will call these individuals rebelliously idle, disruptive, and disorderly.[318] When he was in the city planting the

---

Thessalonica, reported an undesirable laxity in sexual relations in the church there." F.F. Bruce, *1 & 2 Thessalonians*, 87. See also Craig Keener, *The IVP Bible Background Commentary: New Testament*, 587; Clinton Arnold, ed., *Zondervan Illustrated Bible Backgrounds Commentary*, 3:427.

311. Inferred from 1 Thessalonians 4:13 through 5:4. For details, see Weima's reconstruction and exegesis of 1 Thessalonians 4:13-18. Jeffrey Weima, *1-2 Thessalonians*, 306-337.

312. Gene Green, *The Letters to the Thessalonians*, 47.

313. 1 Thessalonians 5:14.

314. 1 Thessalonians 4:11-12; 5:15. Nijay Gupta, *1 & 2 Thessalonians*, 67. Hence, Paul's instruction to keep a low profile by living a quiet life and acting properly toward those outside the fellowship. Charles Wanamaker, *The Epistle to the Thessalonians*, 163-164.

315. For details, see Ben Witherington III, *1 and 2 Thessalonians*, 40, 121; James D.G. Dunn, *Beginning from Jerusalem*, 710-711.

316. Inferred from 1 Thessalonians 5:15; 4:11-12. See also John Barclay, *Pauline Churches and Diaspora Jews*, 185; F.F. Bruce, *1 & 2 Thessalonians*, 92.

317. Leon Morris, *1 and 2 Thessalonians*, 87.

318. Inferred from 1 Thessalonians 5:14.

ekklesia, he spoke to the believers about the importance of work.[319])

- Some of the believers have grown faint-hearted; their faith and resolve are shaken by the persecution.[320]

- Several of the brethren don't respect those who are selflessly serving the assembly.[321]

- Some are extinguishing the Spirit, despising prophetic utterances.[322]

Upon hearing the news of how the ekklesia has survived under persecution, Paul is overjoyed. He thanks God profusely, but he also knows he must quickly address the church's problems. So he immediately writes a letter to the assembly.[323]

PAUL WRITES 1 THESSALONIANS[324]

Year: A.D. 51[325]

319. You can find these problems in 1 Thessalonians 4 and 5. Jeffrey Weima writes at length about them in *1-2 Thessalonians*, 296-300; 391-393. Meeks believes the majority of the Thessalonian believers were skilled or unskilled manual workers. Wayne Meeks, *The First Urban Christians*, 64-65. Green argues that Paul gave the church a different solution from the norm of taking advantage of the patronage system. Earning money through manual labor was the solution. Gene Green, *The Letters to the Thessalonians*, 211-212. Manual labor was despised among the Greeks. They saw it as the occupation of slaves. For this reason, idleness was epidemic in the city. Gerald Hawthorne, et al., eds., *Dictionary of Paul and His Letters*, 927; Leon Morris, *1 and 2 Thessalonians*, 87.

320. Inferred from 1 Thessalonians 5:14.

321. Those serving would probably include Jason, Aristarchus, Secundus, and possibly Timothy himself (when he visited). Inferred from 1 Thessalonians 5:12-13.

322. Inferred from 1 Thessalonians 5:19-20. This problem might have been due to jealousy by some in the assembly toward those whom God used to prophesy. It also could have been the result of some ex-pagans who were concerned that prophetic ministry is the same as the so-called "prophecy" in the pagan mystery cults.

323. 1 Thessalonians 3:6-9. Verse 6 says, "But Timothy has just now come to us from you...." (NIV). This verse "makes it clear that the letter was written almost immediately upon Timothy's return." Charles Wanamaker, *The Epistle to the Thessalonians*, 60.

324. I give more detail on what provoked Paul to write 1 Thessalonians as well as provide a deep dive into the letter in my master class *Day Moves: 1 Thessalonians in 3D* at thedeeperchristianlife.com/classes.

325. A strong consensus exists among scholars that Paul wrote the letter in late A.D. 50 or early 51. James D.G. Dunn, *Beginning from Jerusalem*, 705, n. 228; Jeffrey Weima, *1-2 Thessalonians*, 39, 170; John A.T.

From: Corinth[326]

To: The assembly in Thessalonica (which is nine to ten months old)[327]

Author: Paul[328]

Contextual Summary: Paul encourages the ekklesia in the face of local persecution and social harassment.[329] He reminds the believers of what he was like when he was among them, along with some of the things he taught. He offers this explanation as a means of reassuring the Thessalonians that his motives were genuine when he ministered to them.

   The apostle opens the letter with undying gratitude for their faithfulness. He then addresses his detractors and responds to their avalanche of accusations and blistering insults. He then takes dead aim at those Jews who colluded with the Roman civic authorities to drive him out of the city and prevent him from returning.[330] The apostle

---

Robinson, *Redating the New Testament*, 84; F.F. Bruce, *1 & 2 Thessalonians*, xxi. Witherington estimates late A.D. 51 or early 52. Ben Witherington III, *1 and 2 Thessalonians*, 39.

   326. Paul Barnett, *A Short Book about Paul*, 12; Leon Morris, *1 and 2 Thessalonians*, 20-21.

   327. Riesner believes Paul wrote the letter six months after he left the city, which would make the church around nine to ten months old. Rainer Riesner, *Paul's Early Period*, 366. Jeffrey Weima agrees that "a time length of six months after Paul left Thessalonica is possible and even probable." Personal correspondence with Weima, 1/27/23.

   328. D. Michael Martin, *1 & 2 Thessalonians*, TNAC (Nashville, TN: Broadman & Holman, 1995), 25. While Timothy and Silvanus (Silas) are mentioned as co-authors, the epistle makes clear that Paul was the primary voice. Charles Wanamaker, *The Epistle to the Thessalonians*, 121. See also 1 Thessalonians 3:5 and 5:27. First Thessalonians is one of Paul's undisputed letters. For a listing of Paul's eight letters co-authored with others (e.g., Sosthenes, Timothy, Silvanus, and "all the members of God's family who are with me"), see Bruce Longenecker, ed., *The New Cambridge Companion to St. Paul*, 9. In those epistles where there were co-senders, Paul was still the main author. Markus Bockmuehl, *The Epistle to the Philippians* (London: A & C Black, 1998), 86.

   329. John Barclay, *Pauline Churches and Diaspora Jews*, 184. The harassment and pressure coming from the assembly's surrounding neighbors came in the form of shame. The Christians, however, had a completely different evaluation of honor and shame. What was shameful in the eyes of the world was an honor for them. See David deSilva, *Honor, Patronage, Kinship & Purity*, 66-93.

   330. The language Paul employs in 1 Thessalonians 2:14-16 is similar to what we read in Acts 5:39 and Matthew 23:13, 32, 34. Bruce Longenecker, et al., *Thinking Through Paul*, 68. The Christians were heretics in the eyes of the Jews, whose leader (Jesus) died under a curse (crucifixion). In addition, the Christians had no

encourages the church in its suffering and reminds the believers they are destined to suffer as followers of Christ.[331] He comforts the assembly concerning the people who have passed away.[332]

Throughout the letter, Paul mentions the second coming of Christ numerous times, which is the church's hope.[333] (He ends every chapter with a reference to it.[334]) In addition, he explains that the day of the Lord will surely come, but it will not be a day of wrath for the believers. Instead, it will be sudden destruction for those who reject Jesus, despite the Roman slogan of the imperial machine, "peace and safety."[335] The apostle also addresses, quite directly, the disorderly brethren who are burdening the church by refusing to work.[336]

---

respect for circumcision, the Law, or the temple, elements esteemed by the Jewish people. Michael Green, *Evangelism*, 13.

331. The Thessalonians faced relentless hostile circumstances and immense pressure. See David deSilva, "Worthy of His Kingdom: Honor, Discourse and Social Engineering in 1 Thessalonians," *JSNT* 64 (1996): 49-79.

332. I agree with Weima who says, "Timothy likely reported the uncertainty many in the church had over a number of members—not just one—who died before the return of Christ." Personal correspondence with Jeffrey Weima, 12/28/23.

333. Hopelessness characterized the vast majority of the ancient world (Ephesians 2:12). Jeffrey Weima, *1-2 Thessalonians*, 316. But according to Paul, God's people "do not grieve like the rest of mankind, who have no hope" (1 Thessalonians 4:13, NIV).

334. Since chapters didn't exist in the original letter, we can say he ended many of his key thoughts with a reference to Christ's return.

335. See 1 Thessalonians 5:1-11. For details on the meaning of the day of the Lord and the Roman slogan "peace and safety," see Jeffrey Weima, *1-2 Thessalonians*, 348-353.

336. Paul deals with this problem in 1 Thessalonians 4:9-12 and makes mention of the same people in 5:14 ("those who are idle and disruptive," NIV). In the ancient world, "to work with your hands" as Paul exhorts means manual labor. Jeffrey Weima, *1-2 Thessalonians*, 296-298.

He closes the epistle by exhorting the young ekklesia to honor those who excel at caring for the believing community[337] and to take care of one another.[338] Throughout the letter, Paul uses Roman imperial language to describe Jesus and the kingdom of God in contrast to Caesar's empire.[339] Shockingly, Paul compares his love for the believers to that of a breast-feeding mother's affection for her child. In the male-dominated, patriarchal world of the first century, a man would rarely compare himself to a woman, let alone a breast-feeding one.[340]

337. "Now we ask you, brothers and sisters, to acknowledge those who work hard among you, who care for you in the Lord and who admonish you. Hold them in the highest regard in love because of their work…." (1 Thessalonians 5:12-13, NIV). Bruce explains that these people are not clergy or those who have titles or authoritative positions. Instead, they are those who care for, protect, and give direction to the assembly. F.F. Bruce, *1 & 2 Thessalonians*, 118-120. Paul probably has in mind Jason, Aristarchus, Secundus, and even Timothy and himself.

338. Paul's exhortation to care for the members of the body (and minister to them) is addressed to the entire church, not to any specific leaders (1 Thessalonians 5:14-15). For an overview of Paul's Thessalonian correspondence, see David deSilva, *An Introduction to the New Testament*, chap. 13; N.T. Wright and Michael Bird, *The New Testament in Its World*, chap. 18; Clinton Arnold, ed., *Zondervan Illustrated Bible Backgrounds Commentary*, 3:405-443.

339. Andy Johnson, *1 & 2 Thessalonians*, 13ff.; Peter Oakes, *Empire, Economics, and the New Testament*, chap. 7; D. Clint Burnett, "Imperial Divine Honors in Julio-Claudian Thessalonica and the Thessalonian Correspondence," *JBL* 139, no. 3 (2020): 567-589. Some examples of imperial language are: Jesus is the true "Lord" and emperor; the true "gospel" is the one proclaimed by the apostles, not the heralds of Rome; "salvation" is found in Christ, not Rome; Jesus is the "Savior," not Caesar; He is also the "Son of God" who brings true "peace and security," etc. These terms were applied to Caesar and Rome, but Paul transferred them to Christ. See Richard Horsley, ed., *Paul and Politics*, chaps. 1, 10; Seyoon Kim, *Christ and Caesar: The Gospel and the Roman Empire in the Writings of Paul and Luke* (Grand Rapids, MI: Eerdmans, 2008). When Paul uses the phrase "peace and security" in 1 Thessalonians 5:3, he is employing Roman imperial language. Jeffrey Weima, "'Peace and Security' (1 Thess. 5:3): Prophetic Warning or Political Propaganda?," *NTS* 58 (2012): 331-359. For further details on how Paul used coded imperial language in this epistle (and others), see N.T. Wright, *Paul: In Fresh Perspective*, chap. 4; *Pauline Perspectives*, chaps. 12, 16, 20, 27; Richard Horsley, ed., *Paul and Empire: Religion and Power in Roman Imperial Society* (Harrisburg, PA: Trinity Press International, 1997); *Paul and Politics*; *Paul and the Roman Imperial Order* (Harrisburg, PA: Trinity Press International, 2004). James D.G. Dunn, *Jesus, Paul, and the Gospels*, 45-46; Christoph Heilig, *The Apostle and the Empire: Paul's Implicit and Explicit Criticism of Rome* (Grand Rapids, MI: Eerdmans, 2022).

340. 1 Thessalonians 2:7, ESV. Personal correspondence with Weima, 4/21/22.

In very strong terms, Paul charges all the believers in the ekklesia to listen to the letter as it is read aloud.[341] Silas probably pens the letter at Paul's dictation,[342] and Timothy likely brings it to the assembly in Thessalonica.[343]

1 Thessalonians

Paul, Silvanus, and Timothy, to the assembly of the Thessalonians in God the Father and the Lord Jesus Christ: Grace to you and peace from God our Father and the Lord Jesus Christ.

We always give thanks to God for all of you, mentioning you in our prayers, remembering without ceasing your work of faith and labor of love and perseverance of hope in our Lord Jesus Christ, before our God and Father. We know, brothers[a] loved by God, that you are chosen, and that our Good News came to you not in word only, but also in power, and in the Holy Spirit, and with much assurance.

You know what kind of men we showed ourselves to be among you for your sake. You became imitators of us and of the Lord, having received the word in much affliction, with joy of the Holy Spirit, so that you became an example to all who believe in Macedonia and in Achaia. For from you the word of the Lord has been declared, not only in Macedonia and Achaia, but also in every place your faith toward God has gone out, so that we need not to say anything.

---

341. Paul's wording in 1 Thessalonians 5:27 is unique to the closing of Paul's other letters and uses a strong verb choice which means to put under oath to have the epistle read to all the brothers and sisters. Personal correspondence with Jeffrey Weima, 6/12/22. Paul's letters "were meant to be read out loud to the assembled congregation." Richard Horsley, et al., *The Message and the Kingdom*, 147; David Capes, et al., *Rediscovering Paul*, 117; N.T. Wright, *Paul: A Biography*, xii.

342. Gordon Fee, *The First and Second Epistles to the Thessalonians*, NICNT (Grand Rapids, MI: Eerdmans, 2009), 13.

343. This is a plausible scenario since the church in Thessalonica knew Timothy. He could also interpret the letter and answer any questions. For details on the genre, style, structure, and background of the epistle, see Nijay Gupta, *1 & 2 Thessalonians*, chaps. 1-2.

For they themselves report concerning us what kind of a reception we had from you, and how you turned to God from idols, to serve a living and true God, and to wait for his Son from heaven, whom he raised from the dead: Jesus, who delivers us from the wrath to come.

For you yourselves know, brothers, our visit to you wasn't in vain, but having suffered before and been shamefully treated, as you know, at Philippi, we grew bold in our God to tell you the Good News of God in much conflict. For our exhortation is not of error, nor of uncleanness, nor in deception. But even as we have been approved by God to be entrusted with the Good News, so we speak: not as pleasing men, but God, who tests our hearts.

For neither were we at any time found using words of flattery, as you know, nor a cloak of covetousness (God is witness), nor seeking glory from men (neither from you nor from others), when we might have claimed authority as apostles of Christ. But we were gentle among you, like a nursing mother cherishes her own children.

Even so, affectionately longing for you, we were well pleased to impart to you, not the Good News of God only, but also our own souls, because you had become very dear to us. For you remember, brothers, our labor and travail; for working night and day, that we might not burden any of you, we preached to you the Good News of God.

You are witnesses with God how holy, righteously, and blamelessly we behaved ourselves toward you who believe. As you know, we exhorted, comforted, and implored every one of you, as a father does his own children, to the end that you should walk worthily of God, who calls you into his own Kingdom and glory.

For this cause we also thank God without ceasing, that when you received from us the word of the message of God, you accepted it not as the word of men, but as it is in truth, the word of God, which also works in you who believe.

For you, brothers, became imitators of the assemblies of God which are in Judea in Christ Jesus; for you also suffered the same things from your own countrymen, even as they did from the Jews who killed both the Lord Jesus and their own prophets, and drove us out, and don't please God, and are contrary to all men, forbidding us to speak to the Gentiles that they may be saved, to fill up their sins always. But wrath has come on them to the uttermost.

But we, brothers, being bereaved of you for a short season, in presence, not in heart, tried even harder to see your face with great desire, because we wanted to come to you—indeed, I, Paul, once and again—but Satan hindered us. For what is our hope, or joy, or crown of rejoicing? Isn't it even you, before our Lord Jesus[b] at his coming? For you are our glory and our joy.

Therefore when we couldn't stand it any longer, we thought it good to be left behind at Athens alone, and sent Timothy, our brother and God's servant in the Good News of Christ, to establish you, and to comfort you concerning your faith, that no one would be moved by these afflictions. For you know that we are appointed to this task. For most certainly, when we were with you, we told you beforehand that we are to suffer affliction, even as it happened, and you know.

For this cause I also, when I couldn't stand it any longer, sent that I might know your faith, for fear that by any means the tempter had tempted you, and our labor would have been in vain. But when Timothy came just now to us from you, and brought us glad news of your faith and love, and that you have good memories of us always, longing to see us, even as we also long to see you, for this cause, brothers, we were comforted over you in all our distress and affliction through your faith.

For now we live, if you stand fast in the Lord. For what thanksgiving can we render again to God for you, for all the joy with which we rejoice for your sakes before our God, night and day praying exceedingly that we may see your face, and may perfect that which is lacking in your faith?

Now may our God and Father himself, and our Lord Jesus Christ, direct our way to you. May the Lord make you to increase and abound in love toward one another, and toward all men, even as we also do toward you, to the end he may establish your hearts blameless in holiness before our God and Father at the coming of our Lord Jesus with all his saints.

Finally then, brothers, we beg and exhort you in the Lord Jesus, that as you received from us how you ought to walk and to please God, that you abound more and more. For you know what instructions we gave you through the Lord Jesus. For this is the will of God: your sanctification, that you abstain from sexual immorality, that each one of you know how to control his own body[c] in sanctification and honor, not in the passion of lust, even as the Gentiles who don't know God, that no one should take advantage of and wrong a brother or sister in this matter; because the Lord is an avenger in all these things, as also we forewarned you and testified. For God called us not for uncleanness, but in sanctification. Therefore he who rejects this doesn't reject man, but God, who has also given his Holy Spirit to you.

But concerning brotherly love, you have no need that one write to you. For you yourselves are taught by God to love one another, for indeed you do it toward all the brothers who are in all Macedonia. But we exhort you, brothers, that you abound more and more; and that you make it your ambition to lead a quiet life, and to do your own business, and to work with your own hands, even as we instructed you; that you may walk properly toward those who are outside, and may have need of nothing.

But we don't want you to be ignorant, brothers, concerning those who have fallen asleep, so that you don't grieve like the rest, who have no hope. For if we believe that Jesus died and rose again, even so God will bring with him those who have fallen asleep in Jesus. For this we tell you by the word of the Lord, that we who are alive, who are left until the coming of the Lord, will in no way precede those who have fallen asleep. For the Lord himself will descend from heaven with a shout, with the voice of the archangel and with God's trumpet. The dead in Christ will rise first, then we who are alive, who are left, will be caught up together with them in the clouds, to meet the Lord in the air. So we will be with the Lord forever. Therefore comfort one another with these words.

But concerning the times and the seasons, brothers, you have no need that anything be written to you. For you yourselves know well that the day of the Lord comes like a thief in the night. For when they are saying, "Peace and safety," then sudden destruction will come on them, like birth pains on a pregnant woman. Then they will in no way escape.

But you, brothers, aren't in darkness, that the day should overtake you like a thief. You are all children of light and children of the day. We don't belong to the night, nor to darkness, so then let's not sleep, as the rest do, but let's watch and be sober.

For those who sleep, sleep in the night; and those who are drunk are drunk in the night. But since we belong to the day, let's be sober, putting on the breastplate of faith and love, and for a helmet, the hope of salvation.

For God didn't appoint us to wrath, but to the obtaining of salvation through our Lord Jesus Christ, who died for us, that, whether we wake or sleep, we should live together with him. Therefore exhort one another, and build each other up, even as you also do. But we beg you, brothers, to know those who labor among you, and are over you in the Lord, and admonish you, and to respect and honor them in love for their work's sake.

Be at peace among yourselves. We exhort you, brothers: Admonish the disorderly; encourage the faint-hearted; support the weak; be patient toward all. See that no one returns evil for evil to anyone, but always follow after that which is good for one another and for all. Always rejoice. Pray without ceasing. In everything give thanks, for this is the will of God in Christ Jesus toward you. Don't quench the Spirit. Don't despise prophecies. Test all things, and hold firmly that which is good. Abstain from every form of evil.

May the God of peace himself sanctify you completely. May your whole spirit, soul, and body be preserved blameless at the coming of our Lord Jesus Christ.

He who calls you is faithful, who will also do it. Brothers, pray for us. Greet all the brothers with a holy kiss. I solemnly command you by the Lord that this letter be read to all the holy brothers. The grace of our Lord Jesus Christ be with you. Amen.

a. 1:4 The word for "brothers" here and where context allows may also be correctly translated "brothers and sisters" or "siblings."

b. 2:19 TR adds "Christ."

c. 4:4 literally, possess his own vessel.

* * *

Paul has been visiting the Corinthian synagogue every Sabbath, preaching Christ persuasively to both Jews and God-fearers.[344] As he cites the Hebrew Scriptures, the apostle argues that the divine promises point to Jesus of Nazareth. Paul does this for weeks.[345] As he devotes himself to preaching Christ in the synagogue, the Jewish leaders oppose and revile him. So he leaves the synagogue, shaking off the dust from his clothes and exclaiming, "Your blood be on your own heads! I am innocent of it. From now on I will go to the Gentiles!"[346]

Paul persuades Stephanas and his household to trust in Jesus the Christ.[347] As a result, they become the first converts in Corinth.[348] Erastus, a man of substantial wealth and the

344. Acts 18:1ff.

345. F.F. Bruce, *New Testament History*, 314-315.

346. Acts 18:6, NIV. Compare with Matthew 10:14 and Luke 10:11.

347. Stephanas was well-to-do. John Barclay, *Pauline Churches and Diaspora Jews*, 189. The word "household" in 1 Corinthians 1:16 and 16:15 supports this conclusion. Personal correspondence with Jeffrey Weima, 2/10/22

348. 1 Corinthians 16:15. Paul previously made individual converts in Athens, but this text mentions the first converted *household* in Achaia. Craig Keener, *Acts*, 3:2677-2678. In addition, during this time, Athens

city treasurer, as well as Quartus, are also converted.[349] A Roman citizen named Gaius Titius Justus believes on Christ as well.[350] Gaius is a well-to-do God-fearer[351] with a large home located next door to the synagogue.[352] The home holds between forty and fifty people, the typical size of a large house in the first century.[353] Gaius opens his house for Paul to minister and for the new believers to gather.[354]

---

was not regarded as part of Achaia from the perspective of Roman administration. So it's also possible that Paul didn't regard the converts made in Athens to be part of Achaia.

349. According to Romans 16:23 (which was written from Corinth), Erastus was the city treasurer (NLT, NKJV, ESV) or the director of public works (NIV). So he was likely a man of substantial wealth. Bruce Winter, *Seek the Welfare of the City*, 196; Craig Keener, *Acts*, 3:2864. I side with those scholars who regard Erastus to be a freedman (former slave), and he was the same person mentioned in Acts 19:22, Romans 16:23, and 2 Timothy 4:20. This connection is not unreasonable. Clinton Arnold, ed., *Zondervan Illustrated Bible Backgrounds Commentary*, 3:94. Erastus was also a Roman citizen. Eckhard Schnabel, *Acts*, 766.

350. Gaius' name indicates that he was a Roman citizen. James D.G. Dunn, *Beginning from Jerusalem*, 699.

351. Bruce points out that Gaius is the same man Luke calls "Titius Justus" (Acts 18:7; 1 Corinthians 1:14; Romans 16:23). F.F. Bruce, *Paul: Apostle of the Heart Set Free*, 251; *Jesus and Paul*, 104. Some manuscripts add "Titius" or "Titus" to "Justus" in Acts 18:7 (see the ESV and NASB). See also Peter Lampe, *From Paul to Valentinus*, 192. Gaius was well-to-do. John Barclay, *Pauline Churches and Diaspora Jews*, 189.

352. Acts 18:7.

353. Again, regarding the size of the churches that met in homes in the first century, "the best estimates run up to fifty" individuals in a single ekklesia. James D.G. Dunn, *Beginning from Jerusalem*, 607. However, most of the churches in the first century were smaller, from a dozen to twenty people in all. James D.G. Dunn, *Jesus, Paul, and the Gospels*, 171. Many scholars believe the church in Corinth, as well as most of the other ekklesias in the first century, was made up of forty-five to fifty people. Jerome Murphy-O'Connor, *St. Paul's Corinth*, 182; Eckhard Schnabel, *Paul the Missionary*, 303; James Papandrea, *A Week in the Life of Rome*, 51; Marcus Borg, *Evolution of the Word*, 12-13. According to Jeffrey Weima, fourteen men were connected with the church in Corinth. Assuming each was married, that comes to twenty-eight people. Three members were wealthy and had households. Therefore, an educated guess is that the Corinthian church had between forty and fifty members. Personal correspondence with Weima, 4/21/22. Sixteen specific individuals are named as part of the ekklesia in Corinth. Jerome Murphy-O'Connor, *St. Paul's Corinth*, 182. All told, the size of most of the assemblies in the first century ran from a dozen to fifty people. The exceptions would be large assemblies like those in Syrian Antioch, Jerusalem, and Ephesus, though those churches met in homes throughout the city. For more on Greek and Italian homes, see David deSilva, *Honor, Patronage, Kinship & Purity*, 193.

354. See Romans 16:23. Paul wrote Romans from Corinth. Banks points out that the whole church came together in Gaius' home. This isn't surprising since he was an eminent man in the city, like Erastus. His home may have had an upper room as well. Robert Banks, *Paul's Idea of Community*, 30.

Crispus (the synagogue ruler) is highly respected and a man of wealth.[355] Crispus and his household are converted, and Paul baptizes them in the name of Jesus along with Gaius and the household of Stephanas.[356] Priscilla, Aquila, and some of the other members of the ekklesia baptize the other converts.[357]

After sparring with the philosophers in Athens earlier, Paul made a decision to shoot a straight arrow pointing to Jesus and His cross alone without reliance on Greek rhetorical devices or wisdom.[358]

When I came to you, brothers, I didn't come with excellence of speech or of wisdom, proclaiming to you the testimony of God. For I determined not to know anything among you except Jesus Christ and him crucified. (1 Corinthians 2:1-2)

Paul tells the new converts in Corinth that they are called into the fellowship of God's Son.[359] As he ministers to the new ekklesia, he boasts about the church in Thessalonica, praising it for how the believers there are persevering under their afflictions.[360] The body of

---

355. Acts 18:8. Alan Bandy, *An Illustrated Guide to the Apostle Paul*, 113. As the synagogue ruler, Crispus was responsible for synagogue services. It also demonstrates that he possessed status and wealth. "Crispus" (which means curly-haired) is a Latin name in origin and Roman in usage. Jews often took Latin names. Craig Keener, *The IVP Bible Background Commentary: New Testament*, 380.

356. In 1 Corinthians 1:13-16, Paul states these individuals weren't baptized into his name, the implication being that they were baptized in the name of Jesus. As the *archisynagogos*, Crispus had a household and was a wealthy community patron. Douglas Campbell, *Paul: An Apostle's Journey*, 72; James D.G. Dunn, *Beginning from Jerusalem*, 627.

357. This is an educated assumption based on 1 Corinthians 1:14-17 along with how highly Paul regarded Priscilla and Aquila. Dunn lists the key players in the Corinthian assembly, explaining they were patrons and benefactors who helped Paul. James D.G. Dunn, *Beginning from Jerusalem*, 627-628.

358. According to Keener, "Paul's letters are saturated with Greek rhetorical devices—more than typical ancient letters, even from members of the elite—and popular philosophic language. Paul certainly continued to contextualize, without compromise of the gospel. Proper contextualization (vs. syncretism) makes the meaning all the more intelligible by using relevant language, without altering the meaning itself." Personal correspondence with Craig Keener, 12/4/23. While this is true, when Paul preached and taught the Corinthians in person, it appears he didn't employ polished Greco-Roman oratory (1 Corinthians 2:1-2). For this reason, the Corinthians would later criticize his speaking skills as "contemptible" (2 Corinthians 10:10, NASB).

359. 1 Corinthians 1:9.

360. 2 Thessalonians 1:4. Paul would sometimes boast to other churches about God's work in a particular assembly, holding that assembly up as a model that would urge the believers to a higher level of spiritual

Jesus Christ is now present in Corinth, expressing God's image and manifesting His reign in the city. While a number of the converts in the assembly are well-to-do and have high standing in Corinth, most are uneducated and poor.[361]

As Paul continues to lay the foundation of the Corinthian assembly, the Lord Jesus appears to him in a night vision and encourages him. He tells the apostle the following:

Do not be afraid, but go on speaking and do not be silent, for I am with you, and no one will attack you to harm you, for I have many in this city who are my people. (Acts 18:9-10, ESV)

Consequently, Paul decides to stay in Corinth for eighteen months, planting the new kingdom community and evangelizing the city.[362] Signs, wonders, and miracles follow his ministry.[363] He teaches the things of Jesus Christ and delivers several apostolic traditions to the new converts.[364] As a token of thanksgiving to God for His promise of protection, Paul lets his hair grow long as part of a voluntary Nazirite vow.[365] During his lengthy

---

faith and life. See also 2 Corinthians 7:14; 9:2. Charles Wanamaker, *The Epistle to the Thessalonians,* 217; Ben Witherington III, *1 and 2 Thessalonians,* 190.

361. 1 Corinthians 1:26-27. The ekklesia in Corinth was made up predominantly of lower-status individuals (slaves, women, freedmen) along with some well-to-do people and some with social and political influence. James D.G. Dunn, *Beginning from Jerusalem,* 699. This was true for most of the kingdom communities Paul founded. Lydia in Philippi, many of "the leading women" of Thessalonica, Dionysius of Athens, Erastus, Stephanas, Crispus, Gaius Titius Justus, and Sosthenes of Corinth all belonged to the higher social strata of Greece.

362. Acts 18:11.

363. While Luke doesn't mention any of these things in Acts regarding Paul's time in Corinth, Paul mentions them in 2 Corinthians 12:12.

364. 1 Corinthians 11:2. These traditions included how husbands and wives were to pray and prophesy in the church meetings (1 Corinthians 11:2-16), the Lord's Supper (1 Corinthians 11:23-25), and the resurrection of Jesus (1 Corinthians 15:3-8). For details, see Paul Barnett, *A Short Book about Paul,* 99-100; F.F. Bruce, *Paul: Apostle of the Heart Set Free,* 264-265.

365. Numbers 6:1ff. James D.G. Dunn, *The Acts of the Apostles,* 246-247; Ben Witherington III, *The Acts of the Apostles,* 557. Most scholars agree that Paul wasn't against the Law or against Jewish customs. However, he was vehemently against the idea that either can save or sanctify a person. "Dr. Craig Keener on the Historicity of the Book of Acts," video interview. As a Jesus-follower, Paul observed some Jewish devotional practices for spiritual reasons. N.T. Wright, *Paul: A Biography,* 351.

stay in Corinth, the gospel spreads to the surrounding communities (Cenchreae, for example).[366]

Timothy returns to Corinth from Thessalonica and brings Paul good news. The faith of the believers is increasing despite their opposition, and so is their love for one another.[367] The Thessalonians are constantly on Paul's heart, and he prays that God will grant them His power to accomplish every good act of faith they have purposed to carry out for the glory of Christ.[368]

A short time later, someone from another church visits Corinth and gives Paul a report about the church in Thessalonica.[369] The person informs the apostle that the Thessalonians misunderstood what he wrote about the Lord's return in his first epistle. The church has received misguided teaching through some form of communication alleging to have come from Paul.[370] As a result, some of the believers have been deceived into thinking the

366. This point is clear from the reference to Phoebe who is an important person from the ekklesia in Cenchreae, the eastern port of Corinth (Romans 16:1-2). In addition, 2 Corinthians 1:1 refers to "all the saints who are in the whole of Achaia." Cenchreae was in Achaia. Personal correspondence with Jeffrey Weima, 12/28/23.

367. 2 Thessalonians 1:3.

368. 2 Thessalonians 1:11-12.

369. We don't know how this news got to Paul. It's unlikely that Timothy observed it when he brought Paul's first letter to the church because the timeline is too tight. Timothy returned to Thessalonica to give Paul a report on how the church was doing (1 Thessalonians 3:6), and he was with Paul when 2 Thessalonians was written (2 Thessalonians 1:1). Plausibly, someone else traveled from Thessalonica to Corinth and reported to Paul what was going on with the believers in Thessalonica. Wanamaker makes a strong case that the information was given to Paul from someone in the church in Philippi. Charles Wanamaker, *The Epistle to the Thessalonians,* 58-59. While I don't agree with Wanamaker's view that 2 Thessalonians was written before 1 Thessalonians, his proposal of where Paul received his information about the Thessalonians is plausible. The apostle is also hazy on the details of the crisis he addresses in 2 Thessalonians 2, indicating that the information came to him from someone who wasn't part of the church.

370. Paul is unaware of the source of their misconception that the day of the Lord had come, a misconception he calls deception (2 Thessalonians 2:3). See Ben Witherington III, *1 and 2 Thessalonians,* 214; Andy Johnson, *1 & 2 Thessalonians,* 184; Gene Green, *The Letters to the Thessalonians,* 303. Some scholars believe "the letter from us" in 2 Thessalonians 2:2 refers to 1 Thessalonians, while others do not. If the letter mentioned in that text is a reference to 1 Thessalonians (rather than a forgery), it means the church misunderstood Paul's teaching on the day of the Lord. If, on the other hand, Paul is referring to a forged letter, this explains his signature of authenticity in 2 Thessalonians 3:17.

day of the Lord has arrived.[371] They are alarmed and unsettled by the news.[372] The Thessalonians are wondering, "If the day of the Lord is here, what happened to the resurrection and our being translated into the Lord's presence that Paul told us about? And does this mean our persecutions are going to increase?"[373]

Paul is also informed that the "rebelliously idle" (as he calls them) continue to defy his exhortation to work for a living.[374] The idle believers are scrounging off others in the assembly who earn their income.[375] (This was already a problem in the church, but it has escalated.[376]) With too much time on their hands, the rebelliously idle are acting as

371. 2 Thessalonians 2:2, NIV, NASB, ESV, NKJV. Some commentators believe the Thessalonians thought the day of the Lord was imminent. However, the argument that they believed the day of the Lord had already arrived is stronger. For details, see Jeffrey Weima, *1-2 Thessalonians*, 502; Leon Morris, *The First and Second Epistles to the Thessalonians*, 216; Charles Wanamaker, *The Epistle to the Thessalonians*, 239-240; Ben Witherington III, *1 and 2 Thessalonians*, 205, 213-215. Their understanding likely came through a misguided prophetic word that was wrongly attributed to Paul. Or it came from a forged letter alleged to have been authored by Paul, and/or the Thessalonians misinterpreted Paul's first letter. For details on the source of the misconception, see Jeffrey Weima, *1-2 Thessalonians*, 501-506; Leon Morris, *The First and Second Epistles to the Thessalonians*, 216-217; F.F. Bruce, *1 & 2 Thessalonians*, 164-166, 209; John Stott, *The Message of 1 & 2 Thessalonians*, 158; Craig Keener, *The IVP Bible Background Commentary: New Testament*, 596; David deSilva, *An Introduction to the New Testament*, 475-477.

372. The Greek text of 2 Thessalonians 2:2 can be translated "quickly shaken out of your wits." F.F. Bruce, *1 & 2 Thessalonians*, 163. Weima believes it's likely that a false prophecy claiming that the day of the Lord had arrived caused the Thessalonians to be shaken. Jeffrey Weima, *1-2 Thessalonians*, 408.

373. For this argument and others, see F.F. Bruce, *1 & 2 Thessalonians*, 164-166; Charles Wanamaker, *The Epistle to the Thessalonians*, 240; Jeffrey Weima, *1-2 Thessalonians*, 502-504. In the minds of the Thessalonians, the day of the Lord was complex and extended over a period of time. Christ's return was only part of it. Charles Wanamaker, *The Epistle to the Thessalonians*, 240; Leon Morris, *The First and Second Epistles to the Thessalonians*, 216; N.T. Wright and Michael Bird, *The New Testament in Its World*, 427.

374. 2 Thessalonians 3:11.

375. Scholars disagree over whether the rebelliously idle were using their misled belief that the day of the Lord had come as an excuse to refuse work. Even though Paul doesn't make this connection overtly, it's a possibility. For the arguments, see Clinton Arnold, ed., *Zondervan Illustrated Bible Backgrounds Commentary*, 3:439; David deSilva, *An Introduction to the New Testament*, 477-480; N.T. Wright and Michael Bird, *The New Testament in Its World*, 429; Ben Witherington III, *Invitation to the New Testament*, 203.

376. The failure to work (idleness) was a problem the Thessalonian assembly had from the beginning (2 Thessalonians 3:10; 1 Thessalonians 4:11-12; 5:14). It could be said to be a "birth defect" in the ekklesia.

"busybodies" in the lives of others. Upon hearing the report, Paul writes a second letter to address their misunderstandings and resolve the church's problems.[377]

PAUL WRITES 2 THESSALONIANS

Year: A.D. 51[378]

From: Corinth[379]

To: The assembly in Thessalonica (which is about eleven or twelve months old)[380]

Author: Paul[381]

377. I give more detail on what provoked Paul to write 2 Thessalonians as well as provide a deep dive into the epistle in my master class *Ultimate Fury: 2 Thessalonians in 3D*. Refer to thedeeperchristianlife.com/classes.

378. The letter was most likely written a few months after 1 Thessalonians. F.F. Bruce, *New Testament History*, 308; N.T. Wright and Michael Bird, *The New Testament in Its World*, 427. A few scholars believe 2 Thessalonians was written before 1 Thessalonians. Leon Morris lays out the pros and cons for this viewpoint, but argues 2 Thessalonians is Pauline and was written *after* 1 Thessalonians. Leon Morris, *1 and 2 Thessalonians*, 33-37. See also Donald Guthrie, *New Testament Introduction*, 588-603; Nijay Gupta, *1 & 2 Thessalonians*, 85-88; F.F. Bruce, *1 & 2 Thessalonians*, xli-xlvii.

379. "Corinth is more probable." Ben Witherington III, *1 and 2 Thessalonians*, 30. See also Paul Barnett, *A Short Book about Paul*, 12.

380. If Bruce is right and the letter was written a few months after 1 Thessalonians (see earlier note), then the assembly would have been approximately eleven to twelve months old.

381. I agree with those scholars who believe 2 Thessalonians was authored by Paul. Weima says, "The majority opinion within biblical scholarship has always been that the author of 2 Thessalonians is Paul; that opinion, despite facing strong challenge in recent decades, is still the widespread view held today." Jeffrey Weima, *1-2 Thessalonians*, 46. See also Ben Witherington III, *Invitation to the New Testament*, 253-255; N.T. Wright and Michael Bird, *The New Testament in Its World*, 421; D. Michael Martin, *1 & 2 Thessalonians*, 29; David deSilva, *An Introduction to the New Testament*, 472, 474-476. Like 1 Thessalonians, Paul is the "primary voice" with "some collaboration by his associates in ministry" (Silas and Timothy). Gene Green, *The Letters to the Thessalonians*, 59. For the debate over authorship, genre, style, structure, and background of 2 Thessalonians, see Nijay Gupta, *1 & 2 Thessalonians*, chaps. 5-6. Gupta affirms the epistle is authentically Pauline (219-220). Timothy and Silas were still with Paul at the time, and they are listed as co-senders (2 Thessalonians 1:1). This fact confirms the letter was written shortly after 1 Thessalonians. Jeffrey Weima, *1-2 Thessalonians*, 436-437. Adding Silas and Timothy as co-senders added further weight to the letter, showing the church that Paul was well informed of the situation and his two co-workers were in agreement with his exhortations (435).

Contextual Summary: Paul addresses three groups that are disturbing the lives of the Thessalonian believers. First, there are the persecutors; second, the false teachers; third, the idlers. Paul structures his letter around addressing each problem.[382] He encourages the believers in their persecution (1:3-12), enlightens them on the Lord's return (2:1-17), and exhorts them to live disciplined lives (3:1-15).

The letter begins almost exactly like 1 Thessalonians.[383] Paul thanks God for the assembly and encourages the believers, recognizing that their faith and love are increasing. He comforts them in their continued affliction, assuring them that God will bring vengeance on those who are causing them harm. The Father will give them relief from their tribulation when the Lord Jesus is revealed from heaven in blazing fire.

Paul encourages the Thessalonians that they will be counted worthy of God's kingdom[384] for which they are suffering, thus they ought to stand firm and hold fast to the teachings they received from the apostle. He corrects their misunderstanding about the day of the Lord and Christ's return, clarifying what he taught on the subject when he was with them. The "royal appearing" (*parousia*) of Christ is sure to come, but there will be specific signs preceding it.[385] The believers are secure, chosen,

382. Stott summarizes each group. He equates the false teachers with those who either forged a document allegedly from Paul or misinterpreted Paul's words about the day of the Lord. John Stott, *The Message of 1 & 2 Thessalonians*, 140-141.

383. Gene Green, *The Letters to the Thessalonians*, 277ff.; Jeffrey Weima, *1-2 Thessalonians*, 435.

384. Paul mentions the kingdom fourteen times in his epistles. However, every time he uses the terms "Lord Jesus" and "Lord Jesus Christ" (about eighty times combined), he has the kingdom in view. Stating that Jesus is Lord is a reference to God's kingdom. The kingdom was central to Paul's ministry, mirroring its importance in Jesus' ministry. Note also that Paul never uses the word "disciple" in his letters, yet every time he uses words like "brethren," "holy ones," and those who "believe," he's referring to disciples (followers) of Jesus.

385. The term *parousia* literally means "presence," "arrival," or "coming," and it is used in Matthew and the New Testament epistles to refer to the second coming (or advent) of Christ. Ben Witherington III, *Matthew*, 449; N.T. Wright, *Paul for Everyone: Galatians and Thessalonians*, 171. According to some scholars, 2 Thessalonians 2:1-17 is possibly the most obscure and difficult passage in the entire Pauline corpus. Clinton Arnold, ed., *Zondervan Illustrated Bible Backgrounds Commentary*, 3:436.

loved by God, and saved by the sanctifying work of the Spirit and belief in the truth. Therefore, they don't have to be unsettled by rumors of divine wrath or increased persecution.[386]

Paul ends the epistle by asking the church to pray that God will deliver him from wicked men so he and his co-workers can continue to spread the Lord's word swiftly.[387] He assures the believers that the Lord is faithful to establish them in Christ's love and patience as well as protect them from the evil one.[388] The apostle then launches into a strong correction to the believers who refuse to work, instructing the ekklesia not to associate with them as long as they are living undisciplined lives.[389] He encourages the whole assembly to never tire in doing good.[390] God's peace is theirs at all times and in every way.[391]

The letter can be organized into the coming revelation of Christ (chapter 1), the rebellion of the antichrist (chapter 2), and the responsibility of the believers (chapter 3).[392] Timothy likely brings the letter to the assembly.[393]

2 Thessalonians

Paul, Silvanus, and Timothy, to the assembly of the Thessalonians in God our Father, and the Lord Jesus Christ: Grace to you and peace from God our Father and the Lord Jesus Christ.

---

386. Paul also opens the letter by mentioning the triad of faith, love, and hope, just he does in 1 Thessalonians. Compare 1 Thessalonians 1:3 with 2 Thessalonians 1:3-4 (perseverance points to hope).

387. 2 Thessalonians 3:1-2, NKJV. Compare with Psalm 147:15; Acts 13:48; Romans 15:31.

388. 2 Thessalonians 3:3-5, NKJV.

389. 2 Thessalonians 3:6-14.

390. 2 Thessalonians 3:13.

391. 2 Thessalonians 3:16.

392. John Stott, *The Message of 1 & 2 Thessalonians*, 141.

393. This is an educated guess supported by Jeffrey Weima. Personal correspondence with Weima, 4/21/22.

We are bound to always give thanks to God for you, brothers,[ᵃ] even as it is appropriate, because your faith grows exceedingly, and the love of each and every one of you toward one another abounds, so that we ourselves boast about you in the assemblies of God for your perseverance and faith in all your persecutions and in the afflictions which you endure. This is an obvious sign of the righteous judgment of God, to the end that you may be counted worthy of God's Kingdom, for which you also suffer.

Since it is a righteous thing with God to repay affliction to those who afflict you, and to give relief to you who are afflicted with us, when the Lord Jesus is revealed from heaven with his mighty angels in flaming fire, punishing those who don't know God, and to those who don't obey the Good News of our Lord Jesus, who will pay the penalty: eternal destruction from the face of the Lord and from the glory of his might, when he comes in that day to be glorified in his saints and to be admired among all those who have believed, because our testimony to you was believed.

To this end we also pray always for you, that our God may count you worthy of your calling, and fulfill every desire of goodness and work of faith with power, that the name of our Lord Jesus[ᵇ] may be glorified in you, and you in him, according to the grace of our God and the Lord Jesus Christ.

Now, brothers, concerning the coming of our Lord Jesus Christ and our gathering together to him, we ask you not to be quickly shaken in your mind, and not be troubled, either by spirit, or by word, or by letter as if from us, saying that the day of Christ has already come.

Let no one deceive you in any way. For it will not be, unless the rebellion[ᶜ] comes first, and the man of sin is revealed, the son of destruction, he who opposes and exalts himself against all that is called God or that is worshiped, so that he sits as God in the temple of God, setting himself up as God. Don't you remember that, when I was still with you, I told you these things?

Now you know what is restraining him, to the end that he may be revealed in his own season. For the mystery of lawlessness already works. Only there is one who restrains now, until he is taken out of the way.

Then the lawless one will be revealed, whom the Lord will kill with the breath of his mouth, and destroy by the manifestation of his coming; even he whose coming is according to the working of Satan with all power and signs and lying wonders, and with all deception of wickedness for those who are being lost, because they didn't receive the love of the truth, that they might be saved.

Because of this, God sends them a working of error, that they should believe a lie; that they all might be judged who didn't believe the truth, but had pleasure in unrighteousness. But we are bound to always give thanks to God for you, brothers loved by the Lord, because God chose you from the beginning for salvation through sanctification of the Spirit and belief in the truth, to which he called you through our Good News, for the obtaining of the glory of our Lord Jesus Christ. So then, brothers, stand firm and hold the traditions which you were taught by us, whether by word or by letter.

Now our Lord Jesus Christ himself, and God our Father, who loved us and gave us eternal comfort and good hope through grace, comfort your hearts and establish you in every good work and word. Finally, brothers, pray for us, that the word of the Lord may spread rapidly and be glorified, even as also with you, and that we may be delivered from unreasonable and evil men; for not all have faith.

But the Lord is faithful, who will establish you and guard you from the evil one. We have confidence in the Lord concerning you, that you both do and will do the things we command. May the Lord direct your hearts into God's love, and into the perseverance of Christ.

Now we command you, brothers, in the name of our Lord Jesus Christ, that you withdraw yourselves from every brother who walks in rebellion, and not after the tradition which they received from us. For you know how you ought to imitate us.

For we didn't behave ourselves rebelliously among you, neither did we eat bread from anyone's hand without paying for it, but in labor and travail worked night and day, that we might not burden any of you, not because we don't have the right, but to make ourselves an example to you, that you should imitate us.

For even when we were with you, we commanded you this: "If anyone is not willing to work, don't let him eat." For we hear of some who walk among you in rebellion, who don't work at all, but are busybodies. Now those who are that way, we command and exhort in the Lord Jesus Christ, that they work with quietness and eat their own bread.

But you, brothers, don't be weary in doing what is right. If any man doesn't obey our word in this letter, note that man, that you have no company with him, to the end that he may be ashamed. Don't count him as an enemy, but admonish him as a brother.

Now may the Lord of peace himself give you peace at all times in all ways. The Lord be with you all. The greeting of me, Paul, with my own hand, which is the sign in every letter: this is how I write. The grace of our Lord Jesus Christ be with you all. Amen.

a. 1:3 The word for "brothers" here and where context allows may also be correctly translated "brothers and sisters" or "siblings."
b. 1:12 TR adds "Christ."
c. 2:3 or, *falling away*, or, *defection*.

* * *

Paul continues to evangelize in Corinth. Timothy and Silas share in the ministry.[394] Sosthenes, the new synagogue ruler,[395] is converted under their preaching.[396] The money Silas brought to Paul from Philippi has run out. Consequently, the apostle resumes his work as a leatherworker alongside Priscilla and Aquila. The toil is difficult, and it wearies the apostle.[397]

We work wearily with our own hands to earn our living.... (1 Corinthians 4:12, NLT)

As is his custom, Paul refuses to take money from the Corinthian believers. He doesn't want to burden them and stands by his personal conviction to offer his gospel free of

394. 2 Corinthians 1:19. In that text, Paul calls Silas by his Roman name, Silvanus.

395. The head, or ruler, of a synagogue (*archisynagogos*) enjoyed a position of authority and respect. A ruler was also the patron of the synagogue. Women also held this position in antiquity. Personal correspondence with Amy-Jill Levine and Joseph Sievers, 3/8/22. The title was often honorary and sometimes given to the highest donors. Craig Keener, "Lessons on Acts," Session 23. Diaspora synagogues were open to everyone, including pious Greeks interested in Judaism, children, and women. Calvin Roetzel, *The World That Shaped the New Testament*, 95-96. For how the synagogues were organized in the first century, see Clinton Arnold, ed., *Zondervan Illustrated Bible Backgrounds Commentary*, 2b:127.

396. Sosthenes appears to be the successor to Crispus as the synagogue ruler (Acts 18:17). Clinton Arnold, ed., *Zondervan Illustrated Bible Backgrounds Commentary,* 2b:185. In 1 Corinthians 1:1, Paul calls Sosthenes "our brother." This could also explain why he was beaten by the Jews, which takes place shortly thereafter in our story.

397. Artisans like Paul typically worked seven days a week, without holiday breaks. Clyde Fant, et al., *A Guide to Biblical Sites in Greece and Turkey*, 51. "As Jews, though, Aquila, Priscilla, and Paul would undoubtedly stop on the Sabbath. Otherwise Paul couldn't have been reasoning in the synagogue on Sabbaths even before Silas and Timothy came (Acts 18:4)." Personal correspondence with Craig Keener, 12/4/23.

charge.[398] The Jewish leaders in the city are upset that Paul is "stealing sheep" from the synagogue, so they make a united attack upon him, bringing him to the place of judgment (the local tribunal).[399] There they accuse the apostle of propagating an illegal religion.

"This man," they charged, "is persuading the people to worship God in ways contrary to the law." (Acts 18:13, NIV)

Summer 51[400]

Judaism is protected under Roman law. However, the Jewish leaders argue that the message Paul preaches is a completely new religion. As Paul is about to defend himself, Lucius Junius Gallio,[401] the governor (proconsul) of Southern Greece, stops the proceedings.[402] Gallio refuses to take the case. He deems it an internal dispute within the Jewish community, a matter of differences in religious interpretation.[403] Gallio tells the Jews to settle the matter among themselves and drives everyone from his tribunal.[404]

398. 1 Corinthians 9; 2 Corinthians 11:7-9; 12:13-18.

399. The *bema* (tribunal) in Corinth was the largest tribunal in the empire. Craig Keener, "Lessons on Acts," Session 22. It was located in the middle of the large agora. It was good-sized and ornate. It can still be seen today in the agora. This is where Paul was brought. He will use the *bema* as an image for the judgment seat of Christ in 2 Corinthians 5:10. According to Weima, "up till this time the Jewish community simply engaged in personal attacks on Paul (Acts 18:6, 'they opposed and reviled him,' ESV). Now they had escalated their attack on the apostle by making a united assault and bringing a formal charge against him to the proconsul, Gallio." Personal correspondence with Jeffrey Weima, 12/28/23.

400. Bruce says this incident occurred in either summer or early winter A.D. 51. F.F. Bruce, *The Book of the Acts*, 355.

401. Gallio's period of office is dated from A.D. 51-52 (or A.D. 52-53). James D.G. Dunn, *Beginning from Jerusalem*, 695. Gallio was probably anti-Jewish, as were the other Greek leaders. (Greeks were notorious for being hostile to Jews.) Craig Keener, "Lessons on Acts," Session 30.

402. For details on Paul and Gallio, see Rainer Riesner, *Paul's Early Period*, chap. 11.

403. Gallio believed the message Paul preached was a type of Judaism; hence, it wasn't forbidden by Roman law. F.F. Bruce, *Paul: Apostle of the Heart Set Free*, 366. Judaism, as a recognized ancestral tradition, enjoyed legal protection throughout much of the Roman Empire. James D.G. Dunn, *Beginning from Jerusalem*, 692-693.

404. Acts 18:12-16. Gallio was the brother of Seneca, the famous Roman Stoic philosopher who tutored Emperor Nero. Otto F.A. Meinardus, *St. Paul in Greece*, 76.

Immediately, some Greek bystanders seize Sosthenes, the synagogue ruler, and beat him in front of the tribunal.[405] Gallio turns a blind eye. (This reveals the general scorn with which Jews were held in Corinth, since Sosthenes receives no protection in the very presence of the governor.) Even though Paul spends eighteen months laying the foundation of the ekklesia in Corinth, he is unable to teach the believers the meat of God's word. They are too unspiritual.

> *Brothers, I couldn't speak to you as to spiritual, but as to fleshly, as to babies in Christ. I fed you with milk, not with meat; for you weren't yet ready.... (1 Corinthians 3:1-2)*[406]

Spring 52

Paul stays in Corinth for many more days.[407] Timothy returns from Thessalonica.[408] Paul leaves the brothers and sisters in Corinth and crosses the Aegean Sea to Syria.[409] Timothy, Priscilla, and Aquila are with him, and they all head to Ephesus.[410] But Paul leaves behind

405. Sosthenes was probably beaten because he was a Jesus-follower and/or he was blamed for not doing enough to bring formal charges against Paul. Personal correspondence with Jeffrey Weima, 12/28/23. "Unless, as seems equally plausible, it is the Gentile bystanders who rough him up for clogging up the day's docket with stupid charges." Personal correspondence with David deSilva, 1/18/24.

406. Some scholars believe this statement by Paul could be a rhetorical trope to goad the Cōrinthians into taking what Paul is about to say seriously. Personal correspondence with David deSilva, 1/18/24.

407. Acts 18:18. According to Bandy, that could mean anything from a few weeks to half a year. Alan Bandy, *An Illustrated Guide to the Apostle Paul*, 115.

408. As already mentioned, Timothy likely brought 2 Thessalonians to the church in Thessalonica. Guthrie says it's reasonable to conclude that Timothy left Thessalonica to join Paul, Priscilla, and Aquila as they traveled to Ephesus, though Luke doesn't specifically mention it. Donald Guthrie, *The Apostles*, 170. We know Timothy was in Ephesus with Paul from Acts 19:22. Paul will also send him from Ephesus to Corinth (1 Corinthians 4:17; 16:10).

409. The New Testament doesn't inform us about the movements of Silas after this point. The next time we see Silas will be years later when he assists Peter with the writing of 1 Peter.

410. Acts 18:18-19. Bruce believes this journey probably took place in the spring of A.D. 52. F.F. Bruce, *Paul: Apostle of the Heart Set Free*, 255. Bandy asserts that Paul left Corinth in October A.D. 51 or early March A.D. 52. Sailing came to a stop during the winter months. Alan Bandy, *An Illustrated Guide to the Apostle Paul*, 115. For a detailed description of first-century Ephesus, see Otto F.A. Meinardus, *St. Paul in Ephesus*, 58ff.

a multiethnic kingdom community in Corinth.[411] The ekklesia is made up of simple people, as well as several educated and well-to-do individuals.[412]

For you see your calling, brothers, that not many are wise according to the flesh, not many mighty, and not many noble.... (1 Corinthians 1:26)

As Paul, Timothy, Priscilla, and Aquila head toward Ephesus, they stop at a little town seven miles east of Corinth called Cenchreae, Corinth's seaport. Before traveling on to Ephesus, Paul cuts his hair and ends his temporary Nazirite vow.[413] The four set sail to Ephesus, located in Roman Asia.[414] Priscilla and Aquila settle in Ephesus, setting up their leatherworking business in the city. Paul briefly visits the synagogue, preaching Christ to the Jews. The Jews ask him to stay longer, but he cannot, so he tells them he plans to return if God wills. Timothy stays in Ephesus with Priscilla and Aquila.

From Ephesus, Paul sails to Caesarea. (It is on this long voyage that the apostle may have had his third shipwreck. He might have also spent a night and a day in the open sea, suffering hunger, thirst, and experiencing the cold waters in nakedness.[415])

411. As well as others in the surrounding area, such as Cenchreae.

412. Otto F.A. Meinardus, *St. Paul in Greece*, 74.

413. Paul did not make a formal Nazirite vow, which could not have been properly undertaken outside the Holy Land. Rather, it was a private vow of thanksgiving.

414. "Roman Asia" refers to the Roman province of Asia that occupied the westernmost part of what is now Turkey. It was used to distinguish this particular province from the larger region of "Asia Minor" and, of course, the continent of Asia as a whole. For a detailed analysis of Paul's apostolic work in the Roman province of Asia, see Eckhard Schnabel, *Early Christian Mission*, 2:1197-1257. For details on the Jews in the province of Asia, see John Barclay, *Jews in the Mediterranean Diaspora*, chap. 9.

415. The trip from Ephesus to Caesarea was over 500 sea miles, a likely stretch for a shipwreck. See my earlier notes on the likely places for Paul's first and second shipwrecks (Paphos to Perga; Attalia to Syrian Antioch). It's plausible to conclude that during one of these shipwrecks, Paul spent a full day in the open sea (2 Corinthians 11:25). In 2 Corinthians 11:27, the apostle says he suffered being naked and cold. Survivors of shipwrecks often found themselves naked or partially unclothed after having to abandon ship and swim to safety. Paul's mention of being "cold" in the same text could allude to a shipwreck as well. Again, the only shipwreck Luke mentions in Acts took place *after* 2 Corinthians was written. It's also possible that one of Paul's three shipwrecks occurred when he was sent from Caesarea to Tarsus (Acts 9:30). Personal correspondence with Craig Keener, 6/21/24. Additionally, the trips to/from Jerusalem from Antioch for the famine relief and later the Jerusalem council could have involved some travel by boat rather than by land. Personal correspondence with Jeffrey Weima, 6/21/24.

...three times I was shipwrecked, I spent a night and a day in the open sea.... (2 Corinthians 11:25, NIV)

...I have known hunger and thirst and have often gone without food; I have been cold and naked. (2 Corinthians 11:27, NIV)

From Caesarea, Paul visits the ekklesia in Jerusalem.[416] The apostle greets the Jerusalem assembly, then returns to his home base in Antioch of Syria where he spends time resting.[417]

416. Acts 18:22 says, "he went up and greeted the assembly." People always "go up" to Jerusalem since it's in the hills. Craig Keener, *The IVP Bible Background Commentary: New Testament*, 381. Therefore, it seems evident that Paul visited and greeted the assembly in Jerusalem at this time. Donald Guthrie, *The Apostles*, 170-171. This was Paul's fourth post-conversion visit to Jerusalem. To see a table of all five of Paul's post-conversion visits to Jerusalem, see Eckhard Schnabel, *Acts*, 455.

417. Acts 18:19-23. It's possible that Timothy remained in Ephesus to wait for Paul to return. Also, Silas may have returned to Jerusalem from Corinth during this time. We last saw Silas/Silvanus in Corinth with Paul (Acts 18:5; 2 Thessalonians 1:1).

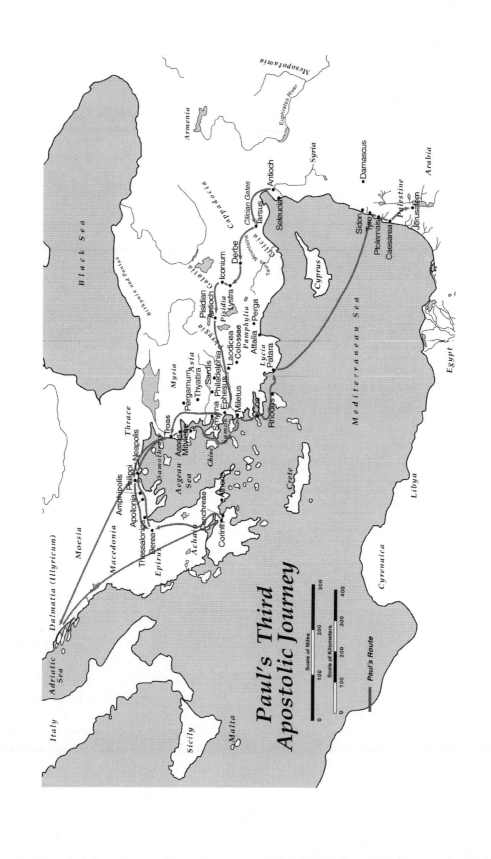

Paul's Third Apostolic Journey

Scale of Miles

0   100   200   300

Scale of Kilometers

0   100   200   300   400

▬▬▬ Paul's Route

CHAPTER 11

THE EPHESIAN CHRONICLE

A.D. 53 – A.D. 57

While Apollos was at Corinth, Paul, having passed through the upper country, came to Ephesus and found certain disciples. (Acts 19:1)

PREVIEW OF PAUL'S THIRD APOSTOLIC JOURNEY[1]

Duration: Four years[2]

Dates: A.D. 53-57[3]

Kingdom Communities Planted: (11+) Paul raises up a church in Ephesus. Epaphras, one of Paul's apprentices, plants kingdom communities in Laodicea, Colossae, and

---

1. Some scholars estimate that Paul traveled 2,700 miles on this apostolic trip. Rose Publishing, *Rose Chronological Guide to the Bible*, 155. For Paul's route, which closely matches the third journey map in this book, see Craig Keener, et al., *Journeys of the Apostle Paul*, 86-87.

2. The notes in this section will support the timeline. For details on Paul's third apostolic journey, see Craig Keener, *Acts*, 3:2779-2945; James D.G. Dunn, *Beginning from Jerusalem*, chap. 32; W.J. Conybeare and J.S. Howson, *The Life & Epistles of St. Paul*, 361-433.

3. Ben Witherington III, *The New Testament Story*, 277. Beginning with the first apostolic journey to the third, Paul spent ten years (A.D. 47 to 57) preaching the gospel and raising up ekklesias east and west of the Aegean Sea. F.F. Bruce, *Romans*, 13. Eckhard Schnabel gives his timeline of this period in *Acts*, 792-793.

Hierapolis.[4] Paul's other co-workers found assemblies throughout the Roman province of Asia.[5] Namely, Smyrna, Pergamum, Thyatira, Sardis, and Philadelphia.[6]

Paul establishes an assembly of Christ in Troas and in Illyricum.[7] He also transplants a new multiethnic kingdom community in the city of Rome, and he does so in a most ingenious way.[8]

Time Planting:

Ephesus = Three years[9]

4. F.F. Bruce, *Paul: Apostle of the Heart Set Free*, 384; R.C. Lucas, *The Message of Colossians & Philemon: Fullness and Freedom* (Downers Grove, IL: InterVarsity Press, 1980), 19. These three cities are often referred to as the "tri-cities" of the Lycus valley.

5. Co-working is written in the bloodstream of God's work. See Frank Viola, *48 Laws of Spiritual Power* (Carol Stream, IL: Tyndale, 2022), 155-158. For details on Paul's co-workers, see F.F. Bruce, *The Pauline Circle*, 81-90. The apostle had about thirty male co-workers and eleven female co-workers. Lars Kierspel, *Charts on the Life, Letters, and Theology of Paul*, 45. James D.G. Dunn provides an annotated list of all Paul's co-workers in *Beginning from Jerusalem*, 566-572. In addition, Ellis has written a superb article on the apostle's co-workers. See E.E. Ellis, "Paul and His Co-Workers," *NTS* 17 (1970-71): 437-452. See also Paul Barnett, *A Short Book about Paul,* chap. 10. For a table of Paul's co-workers, including biblical texts and the terms by which they were called (e.g., partner, co-worker, apostle, brother, minister, etc.), see Gerald Hawthorne, et al., eds., *Dictionary of Paul and His Letters*, 184. While Paul understood gender differences, he endorsed the "Jesus tradition" of full equality of men and women in Christ (Galatians 3:28). Leland Ryken, et al., eds., *Dictionary of Biblical Imagery*, 962.

6. For a historical outline of each of these churches, including Ephesus, see Otto F.A. Meinardus, *St. John of Patmos and the Seven Churches of the Apocalypse* (Athens, Greece: Lycabettus Press, 1974), 23-133.

7. F.F. Bruce, *Paul: Apostle of the Heart Set Free*, 316ff. Keener believes Paul's visit to the Roman province of Illyricum likely took place in the period mentioned in Acts 20:1-3. Craig Keener, *Acts*, 3:2560; *The IVP Bible Background Commentary: New Testament*, 454.

8. This will be explained later. The Jewish presence of Christians in Rome by the Jewish pilgrims returning from Pentecost in A.D. 30 had dwindled after Claudius expelled the Jews in A.D. 49. Around A.D. 55, Paul founded a brand-new ekklesia made up of Jews and Gentiles in the city through transplantation. Details forthcoming.

9. According to Bruce, Paul was in Ephesus the better part of three years. F.F. Bruce, *Paul: Apostle of the Heart Set Free*, 288. Witherington agrees and argues that Paul's time in Ephesus, according to Luke, was two years, three months, and "awhile longer" (Acts 19:22) which comes to about three years. Ben Witherington III, *The Acts of the Apostles*, 576.

> The kingdom communities in the Roman province of Asia = Unknown
>
> Troas = Unknown
>
> Illyricum = Unknown
>
> Rome = Unknown

While in Antioch of Syria, Paul plans three things that will set the course for the rest of his ministry:

- He decides to begin a collection fund to help the poor believers in the Jerusalem assembly, showing solidarity among all Christ-followers.[10] Paul does this to mend the rift between the Jewish and Gentile believers. The fund will also fulfill a promise he made to Peter, James, and John years earlier.[11] Paul wants to remind the Gentile assemblies of their debt to the Jewish people and the Jerusalem ekklesia. His desire is to show that the Gentile and Jewish believers are part of the same family, and members of a family help one another when in need.[12]

- Paul is approximately fifty years old. Not knowing how much time he has left to live, he decides to train apostolic workers in Ephesus, just like Jesus trained apostolic workers in Galilee.[13] Most of the men Paul trains are Gentiles, and they will represent the Gentile assemblies when they deliver the collection to the Jerusalem ekklesia.[14]

10. Donald Guthrie, *The Apostles,* 229.
11. Galatians 2:10.
12. N.T. Wright, *Paul: A Biography,* 340.
13. For insights into how Jesus trained the Twelve, see Robert Coleman, *The Master Plan of Evangelism* (Grand Rapids, MI: Fleming Revell), 1993. Simply substitute "evangelism" with "church planting" when reading the book, because that's what Jesus trained the Twelve to do (plant kingdom communities). See also A.B. Bruce, *The Training of the Twelve: Timeless Principles for Leadership Development* (Grand Rapids, MI: Kregel, 2000).
14. I argue that Paul trained the following men (of mixed races) in Ephesus: Titus (a Gentile), Timothy (half Jew, half Gentile), Aristarchus (a Jew), Secundus (a Gentile), Sopater (a Jew), Gaius (a Gentile), Tychicus (a Gentile), and Trophimus (a Gentile). Paul duplicated the training of workers that Jesus conducted in

- Paul wants to bring the gospel message as far west as possible, so he plans to preach in Rome and then Spain.[15] He decides to accomplish this on his fourth apostolic trip after he plants the assembly in Ephesus and brings the relief collection to Jerusalem.[16]

With these three goals in mind, Paul leaves Syrian Antioch with Titus. The two men head up through Tarsus and pass the Cilician Gates to Galatia.[17] After they make the long, arduous journey over the rugged Taurus Mountains, they visit and encourage the four Galatian assemblies,[18] strengthening them in the faith.[19] The Galatian ekklesias have not seen Paul in about three years. While there, the apostle gives each assembly specific

---

Galilee when the Lord trained the Twelve. Acts 20:4 lists most of the workers who were with Paul at this time. (We are positive that Aristarchus, Gaius, and Timothy were in Ephesus with Paul because they are explicitly mentioned in Acts 19:22, 29.) According to David deSilva, "Titus appears to have been with Paul in Ephesus as the latter ironed out his relations with the Corinthians (Titus is the smooth go-between bearing the lost 'tearful letter' and our 2 Corinthians)." Personal correspondence with deSilva, 7/18/22. Scholars typically assert that the men listed in Acts 20:4 were only delegates to help Paul bring the relief fund to Jerusalem. But this assertion has just as much evidence as the thesis that Paul trained them for the Lord's work. One would think that if they were only delegates for the relief fund, they would all be Gentiles, but they were not. Luke never says the men were representatives for the relief fund. This is educated conjecture. I contend, therefore, that both theories are true. These men were trained by Paul in Ephesus, *and* they represented the Gentile ekklesias in bringing the relief fund to Jerusalem. (If this is the case, Luke may have represented the ekklesia in Philippi and Titus may have represented the ekklesia in Corinth. John Stott, *The Message of Acts*, 318; Richard Longenecker, *Luke-Acts*, 1022; Ben Witherington III, *The Acts of the Apostles*, 603; Darrell Bock, *Acts*, 618.) Titus is never mentioned in Acts, but he's clearly present as the epistles indicate. Richard Longenecker, *Luke-Acts*, 1014. Since I believe Paul trained these men in Ephesus and sent them out, it's not surprising that Luke lists most of them in twos (Acts 20:4), just as Matthew does the Lord's disciples when Jesus sent them out (Matthew 10:1-5). See also Craig Keener, *Acts*, 3:2952. In a later footnote, I will list numerous sources confirming that Paul trained workers in Ephesus.

15. Spain = Tarshish, a location listed in the Table of Nations in Genesis 10. Richard Plummer, et al., *Paul's Missionary Methods*, 21. Paul sought to recover to God the nations listed in Genesis 10. This explains why he moved from east to west. Michael Heiser, *The Unseen Realm*, 298-306; Frank Viola, *Insurgence*, 360ff.

16. Romans 15:24ff.

17. Witherington believes this took place in the summer of A.D. 53.

18. The four assemblies are in Derbe, Lystra, Iconium, and Pisidian Antioch.

19. Acts 18:23. Alan Bandy, *An Illustrated Guide to the Apostle Paul*, 117. The trip from the Cilician Gates to Ephesus was a long, difficult trek of about 1,500 miles on foot. Ben Witherington III, *The Acts of the Apostles*, 559-560.

instructions concerning the Jerusalem relief collection.[20] As they leave Galatia, they take Gaius (of Derbe) with them.

Back in Ephesus, Priscilla and Aquila begin visiting the synagogue to locate any Jewish or God-fearing seekers who may be open to the gospel. They also follow up with those who were previously impressed with Paul's message. The couple shares the gospel with a man named Epaenetus who receives the message and becomes the first convert to Jesus Christ in Ephesus.[21]

Apollos

An educated man named Apollos visits Ephesus.[22] (He is from Alexandria, Egypt.[23]) Apollos is a Hellenistic Jew who knows the Hebrew Scriptures well.[24] He's also an impressive orator, stunningly eloquent and charismatic.[25] Apollos is a Jesus-follower, but there's a gap in his knowledge of the Lord.[26]

Apollos preaches Jesus as the Messiah in the Ephesian synagogue with the glow of the Holy Spirit. His ability to tell the story of Christ from the Hebrew Scriptures is

20. 1 Corinthians 16:1-3.

21. According to Romans 16:5, Epaenetus was "the first convert to Christ from Asia" (NASB). See Reta Halteman Finger, *Roman House Churches for Today*, 16. While Paul could have shared the gospel with Epaenetus during his earlier time in Ephesus (Acts 18), I cite Lampe later in the notes for my reconstruction, which according to Keener, "is quite plausible." Personal correspondence with Craig Keener, 12/4/23.

22. The story of Apollos is told in Acts 18:24 through Acts 19:1. He is also mentioned in 1 Corinthians 1:12; 3:4-6, 22; 4:6; 16:12.

23. First-century Alexandria is a metropolis. It's the second largest city in the empire, with a population of over half a million. Its population at this time was about 600,000. It had a large Jewish population of around 200,000. James Hope Moulton and George Milligan, *The Vocabulary of the Greek Testament*, Logos edition (Sydney: Hodder and Stoughton Australia, 1930), 306. For details on the Jews in Egypt during this period, see John Barclay, *Jews in the Mediterranean Diaspora*, chap. 3.

24. For details on Apollos, see F.F. Bruce, *The Pauline Circle*, 51-57.

25. Acts 18:24. Apollos may have been schooled in the allegorical style of expositing the Hebrew Scriptures pioneered by Philo of Alexandria, the famed Jewish philosopher. This theory has led some scholars to suggest that Apollos wrote Hebrews, which they believe resonates with Philo's style of allegorical interpretation. Other scholars disagree.

26. According to the Western text, Apollos came to the Lord in his home city of Alexandria. There was a Jewish Christian community in Alexandria as early as A.D. 41.

remarkable.[27] However, he knows nothing about water baptism in the name of Jesus. He only knows the baptism of John the Baptist.[28] Priscilla and Aquila hear Apollos preach. They are so impressed they invite him to their home. During their meeting, the couple instructs Apollos more accurately in the gospel and the truths of Jesus.[29]

Some of the believers from Corinth come to Ephesus and visit Priscilla and Aquila. When they meet Apollos, they too are impressed, so they invite him to visit the Corinthian assembly.[30] Apollos wants to go, so Priscilla and Aquila (along with some other believers) write Corinth a letter of commendation, asking the church to welcome him.[31] Shortly after, Apollos leaves Ephesus for Corinth with the letter of commendation.[32]

Corinth Has Visitors

When Apollos arrives in Corinth, he argues with the local Jewish leaders in the synagogue, refuting them with his apologetic savvy, piercing logic, and powerful rhetoric. He also visits the Corinthian assembly and encourages the believers in their faith. The Corinthians are spellbound by Apollos' masterful oratorical skills. As a result, some of them, mostly Greeks in the assembly, begin rallying around Apollos. Because Apollos is such a gifted speaker, they begin criticizing Paul as a less capable orator and a less spiritual person.[33] (Greeks are known for equating knowledge and impressive oratory with spirituality.[34])

27. It's possible that the gospel reached Alexandria after Pentecost by those who lived there, came to Jerusalem, and returned. This may have been the way Apollos heard the good news.

28. Acts 18:25.

29. While Luke never mentions it, it's plausible to assume that Priscilla and Aquila baptized Apollos in the name of Jesus.

30. This is the story told in Acts 18:27 of the Western text. Some scholars avoid the Western text when it differs from the oldest codices, while others find it credible in certain instances, such as this one.

31. Acts 18:27, NIV. Given the context in Acts 18, it's likely that Priscilla and Aquila had a major hand in crafting the letter.

32. "Apollos sailed across the Aegean Sea from Ephesus, landing at Corinth's eastern port city of Cenchreae and walking the short distance to Corinth." Personal correspondence with Jeffrey Weima, 1/6/24. It's possible that Apollos planned to preach the gospel to the Jewish communities in other cities beyond Corinth in Achaia. Eckhard Schnabel, *Acts*, 786.

33. Acts 18:24ff.; 1 Corinthians 1:12 through 3:22.

34. See 1 Corinthians 1:17-25. This was the case in the first century, which is the setting of this narrative.

When Apollos leaves the assembly, Barnabas pays a visit to the Corinthian church to strengthen the disciples.[35] Peter and his wife also visit the ekklesia.[36] Peter is known for his impressive signs and wonders. While he is with the Corinthians, he prays for some of the sick and they are healed.[37] Consequently, a new party in the church, mostly Jews in the assembly, develops around Peter.[38] (Jews are known for being awed by signs and wonders.[39])

In reaction to the growing divide in the ekklesia (some elevating Apollos and others extolling Peter), a number of the Corinthians declare that Paul is their only apostle. Others in the church claim that they don't follow any man, but Jesus only. The assembly in Corinth is fracturing into four parties. Each party develops around the different apostolic workers who have visited the church. Some claim, "We are of Peter." Others claim, "We are of Apollos." Others claim they are of Paul, while another group claims they are only of Christ.[40]

---

35. According to 1 Corinthians 9:6, the Corinthians were familiar with Barnabas, so I infer that he visited them. Bandy says it's possible that while Apollos was still in Corinth, Paul headed through the interior of Asia Minor to go to Ephesus (Acts 19:1), which was his next move. Alan Bandy, *An Illustrated Guide to the Apostle Paul*, 119.

36. Implied from 1 Corinthians 1:12; 3:22; 9:5. Clearly, the Corinthian believers knew Barnabas, Peter, and Apollos. They also knew that Jude and the other brothers of Jesus were married and traveled for the Lord's work (1 Corinthians 9:5-6). Witherington and Barnett confirm Peter's visit to Corinth. Ben Witherington III, *Letters and Homilies for Hellenized Christians*, 2:67; Paul Barnett, *Bethlehem to Patmos,* 212. See also Clinton Arnold, ed., *Zondervan Illustrated Bible Backgrounds Commentary*, 4:154.

37. This is a reasonable conjecture based on the fact that Peter's ministry, from its inception in the book of Acts, was marked by profound healings (even healing the palsy and raising the dead). Peter's ministry was so powerful that people believed his shadow could heal. Add to this the fact that some of the Corinthians were awed by signs and wonders and claimed they were "of Peter." Therefore, it makes perfect sense to infer that Peter healed people while he was among the Corinthians.

38. 1 Corinthians 1:12; 3:22. Peter is called "Cephas" in these passages, as he is known also in Galatians 1:18; 2:9-14.

39. "Jews demand signs and Greeks look for wisdom…." (1 Corinthians 1:22, NIV). This was the case in the first century, which is the setting of this narrative.

40. 1 Corinthians 1:12-13; 3:4-9, 21-23. Paul wasn't pleased with the slogan "I am of Paul." Gordon Fee, *The First Epistle to the Corinthians*, NICNT (Grand Rapids, MI: Eerdmans, 1987), 54-55. According to some scholars, the biggest "camps" seem to be Paul and Apollos. Personal correspondence with Craig Keener, 12/4/23.

A New Work in Ephesus
Summer 53[41]

Paul, Titus, and Gaius travel a route from the highlands and make their way by land to Ephesus in the Roman province of Asia.[42] The men pass through a gate near the southeast corner of the city wall to enter Ephesus.[43] They come to the civic forum, the center of the city's governmental life, and behold the open courtyard surrounded by columned porches.[44] When they arrive in Ephesus, they meet four brothers in Christ who have been waiting for Paul in the city: Sopater[45] (of Berea), Aristarchus and Secundus (of Thessalonica),[46] and Timothy (of Lystra).

These accompanied him as far as Asia: Sopater of Beroea; Aristarchus and Secundus of the Thessalonians; Gaius of Derbe; Timothy; and Tychicus and Trophimus of Asia. (Acts 20:4)

41. Ben Witherington III, *The Acts of the Apostles*, 506. Bruce dates Paul's ministry a year earlier, A.D. 52 to 55. F.F. Bruce, *Paul: Apostle of the Heart Set Free*, 288, 407.

42. Acts 19:1. Translations differ on where they passed to reach Ephesus. Some have "the road through the interior" (NIV), "through the interior regions" (NLT), "through the inland country" (ESV), "through the upper regions" (NKJV), "through the upper country" (NASB). Bandy believes the translation that renders the text: "traveled a route from the highlands" is accurate. Personal correspondence with Alan Bandy, 12/15/23. For details on this part of the journey, see Mark Wilson, "The 'Upper Regions' and the Route of Paul's Third Journey from Apamea to Ephesus," *Scriptura* 117 (2018): 1-21. As often was his custom, Luke doesn't mention the men who were with Paul in this opening text. Witherington has Paul leaving Corinth, sailing to Syria, then landing in the port city of Ephesus briefly in the spring of A.D. 53. Ben Witherington III, *Invitation to the New Testament*, 167. The ministry of Paul rehearsed in Acts 19:21 through 28:20 focuses on his journey to Jerusalem and then to Rome. Throughout these chapters, Paul didn't evangelize any new regions. Instead, he strengthened the existing kingdom communities he raised up on his first three apostolic trips. David Bauer, *The Book of Acts as Story*, 53. According to Bruce, Luke doesn't appear to have been with Paul at any point during his Ephesian trip. F.F. Bruce, *Paul: Apostle of the Heart Set Free*, 288-289.

43. Modern archaeologists call it the "Magnesian Gate" because the road leads to the city of Magnesia on the Meander River, approximately eight to eighteen miles southeast of Ephesus.

44. Barry Beitzel, *Lexham Geographic Commentary on Acts through Revelation*, 540. The courtyard was about 525 by 190 feet.

45. In certain Greek texts, Sopater is said to be the son of Pyrrhus.

46. Paul probably asked the three men from Macedonia to meet him in Ephesus. Timothy was already there.

Paul will train these six men in Ephesus for the work of preaching the explosive gospel of the kingdom and raising up kingdom communities.[47] This mission reaches back to God's eternal purpose[48] from before time—a purpose with an objective to expand the community of the Godhead so God's nature (image) and His reign (authority) will be expressed visibly in the earth by founding assemblies that live by the indwelling life of Christ.[49]

The six men will also serve as delegates from their respective assemblies when they deliver the relief collection to the church in Jerusalem.[50] All six have experienced the life of the body of Christ for at least three years in their respective cities, and they will now be trained as apostolic workers under the tutelage of Paul, a master apostle.[51] The six men Paul trains in Ephesus are:

47. The six men were Gaius, Timothy, Titus, Sopater, Aristarchus, and Secundus. Two men will be added later (Trophimus and Tychicus). These men, minus Titus who Luke never mentions, are named in Acts 20:4. For the strategic reasons why Paul chose Ephesus to be his mission base, see Jerome Murphy-O'Connor, *St. Paul's Corinth*, 170-171.

48. I offer details and biblical support on the eternal purpose (God's grand mission) in my books *From Eternity to Here*, *Reimagining Church*, *Finding Organic Church*, and *Insurgence*.

49. For details on Paul's understanding of living by the indwelling life of Christ throughout his letters, see my course "Living by the Indwelling Life of Christ" at thedeeperjourney.com.

50. While Luke doesn't explicitly say Paul had these men go with him to Ephesus, we know they were in Ephesus with him. The following passages put all eight men in the city during the time that Paul was there: Acts 19:22; 20:4; 21:29; 1 Corinthians 4:17; 16:10, 20 (Paul wrote 1 Corinthians from Ephesus). One can infer from 2 Corinthians that Titus was there also. A case can be made from 2 Corinthians 8 that Titus represented Corinth in the Jerusalem collection. See F.F. Bruce, *Paul: Apostle of the Heart Set Free*, 339. It is clear from the New Testament letter called "Titus" that Paul trained him. Schnabel correctly states that "Paul had several co-workers from the province of Asia during his mission to Ephesus." Eckhard Schnabel, *Early Christian Mission*, 2:1220. Note that moving the relief fund was fraught with hazards and dangers. For speculation on how the men could have transported the money, see N.T. Wright, *Paul: A Biography*, 343-344.

51. For a discussion on the biblical and historical evidence supporting the thesis that Paul trained these men as apostolic workers in Ephesus, see David Shenk and Ervin Stutzman, *Creating Communities of the Kingdom* (Scottdale, PA: Herald, 1988), 152-158; Mark Fairchild, *Christian Origins in Ephesus & Asia Minor*, 58; Alan Bandy, *An Illustrated Guide to the Apostle Paul*, 122; Eckhard Schnabel, *Paul the Missionary*, 248ff.; Richard Plummer, et al., *Paul's Missionary Methods*, 227-233; Frank Viola, *Finding Organic Church*, 71-92. The fact that Paul paid for all their needs while they were in Ephesus supports the idea that he trained them (Acts 20:34). Bandy agrees, saying, "Paul would not have been idle or *only* doing evangelistic work in Ephesus. Paul was intent on discipleship and equipping believers for ministry. His letters themselves give us ample enough evidence that he was focused on discipling and training." Personal correspondence with Alan

- Titus from Syrian Antioch[52]
- Timothy from Lystra[53]
- Gaius from Derbe[54]
- Sopater from Berea[55]
- Aristarchus from Thessalonica[56]
- Secundus from Thessalonica[57]

Sharpening the Focus: Ephesus is a free Greek city.[58] It is located at the mouth of the Cayster River, which flows into the Aegean Sea. It's the largest city in the Roman

---

Bandy, 6/27/23. John Stott confirms saying these men were not only the fruits of Paul's mission, but "they then became the agents of mission." John Stott, *The Message of Acts*, 318. Speaking of Paul's daily discussions in the hall of Tyrannus, another scholar states, "In Ephesus, Paul opened a school of theology to train future leaders for the developing church in the province of Asia." Simon Kistemaker, *Exposition of the Acts of the Apostles*, 684. Again, Luke didn't "spell out" the training any more than he "spelled out" the Jerusalem relief fund. He hardly mentions the fund, yet we know from Paul's letters that it existed.

52. Paul regarded Titus as a spiritual son (Titus 1:4). Ramsay rightly observes that "it is hardly open to doubt that he [Titus] had been in Paul's company on the whole of the third journey." William Ramsay, *St. Paul the Traveler and Roman Citizen*, 219.

53. Like Titus, Paul regarded Timothy as his true son in the faith (1 Corinthians 4:17; Philippians 2:22; 1 Timothy 1:2; 2 Timothy 1:2).

54. Aristarchus and Gaius are mentioned in Acts 19:29. In that text, Gaius is said to be from Macedonia. I believe the Gaius of Derbe is the same Gaius mentioned in Acts 19. Keener remarks that this is "more likely," and Gaius probably came to Ephesus from Derbe "by way of ministry in Macedonia, alongside Aristarchus." Craig Keener, *Acts*, 3:2906, n. 5993. Stott points out that one reading of Acts 19:29 makes only Aristarchus (and not Gaius) a Macedonian. John Stott, *The Message of Acts*, 317-318. It's possible that Gaius moved to Macedonia from Derbe at some point, which would resolve the confusion. Wright confirms that Timothy was from Lystra, and the "Gaius" mentioned in Acts 20:4 was the Gaius from Derbe. N.T. Wright, *Paul: A Biography*, 342.

55. Acts 20:4.

56. Acts 19:29; 20:4.

57. Acts 20:4.

58. As a free city, Ephesus was not a Roman colony. For details on first-century Ephesus, see Ben Witherington III, *The Acts of the Apostles*, 563ff.; Mark Fairchild, *Christian Origins in Ephesus & Asia Minor*, chaps. 1-2.

province of Asia.[59] (It is estimated that of the four million people living in Roman Asia, about 300,000 are Jews.)

The population of Ephesus is about 250,000, making it the fourth largest city in the Roman Empire.[60] The city has a large Jewish population, yet Gentiles significantly outnumber them.[61] Ephesus is Hellenized in its culture. It's considered a Greek city in Asia.[62] The city is a seaport and the first ranking city of Asia Minor in commerce, wealth, politics, and religion. It maintains its population through a steady flow of immigrants.

It's the New York of the ancient world. The city connects the eastern world with the western world, making it a magnificent city of wealth. For this reason, the historian Pliny called it "the ornament of Asia" and "the vanity fair of Asia."

Ephesus is also the communications hub for virtually every part of Asia. The emperor's college of messengers is based in the city. The city's wealth is reflected everywhere, from its marble-paved main street to the mosaic floors in its aristocratic homes.

Official business typically ends by midday, and many people take a break for a meal and a brief rest in the early afternoon. Educational lectures often finish by 11 a.m.[63] Common meals include figs, olives, nuts, baked bread, and wine.[64]

59. Wright and Bird state that only Rome and Alexandria surpassed Ephesus in size and grandeur. N.T. Wright and Michael Bird, *The New Testament in Its World*, 455.

60. Clinton Arnold, ed., *Zondervan Illustrated Bible Backgrounds Commentary*, 2b:190. Others estimate around 200,000. Barry Beitzel, *Lexham Geographic Commentary on Acts through Revelation*, 539. Some have more recently estimated 50,000 to 60,000. J.W. Hanson, *An Urban Geography of the Roman World, 100 BC to AD 300*, 67. Towner estimates 100,000 when Paul arrived. Philip Towner, *The Letters to Timothy and Titus*, NICNT (Grand Rapids, MI: Eerdmans, 2006), 37. While some would say Ephesus is the fifth largest city in the empire, most believe it was the fourth. Personal correspondence with Jeffrey Weima, 1/6/24.

61. Barry Beitzel, *Lexham Geographic Commentary on Acts through Revelation*, 539-553. Some have estimated there were as many as 10,000 Jews in the city during this time. Peter Walker, *In the Steps of Paul*, 137. Josephus makes at least ten references to Jews in Ephesus, which signifies a large presence. Alan Bandy, *An Illustrated Guide to the Apostle Paul*, 121. For details on the Jewish community in Ephesus, see David deSilva, *A Week in the Life of Ephesus* (Downers Grove, IL: InterVarsity Press, 2020), 62-63.

62. Craig Keener, "Lessons on Acts," Session 25.

63. Craig Keener, *The IVP Bible Background Commentary: New Testament*, 521. This is significant because Paul may have used the hall of Tyrannus after Tyrannus (or his renters) occupied the hall for their lectures in the mornings.

64. David deSilva, *A Week in the Life of Ephesus*, 44.

As a port city on the Aegean Sea, Ephesus attracts transients. Many sailors come to trade goods. The city also has two agoras (marketplaces).[65] One of the seven wonders of the world is located just outside the city of Ephesus[66]—the great temple of Artemis (in Latin her name is Diana). She is a nature-fertility goddess and the local patron deity.[67]

It took a little over 200 years to construct the temple of Artemis. Built from pure white marble, it's the largest building in existence at the time, and it's known world-wide. The temple is four times as large as the Parthenon in Athens. It is 220 feet by 425 feet, supported by 127 columns (each sixty feet high), and it's adorned by some of the greatest sculptures of the age.[68]

A meteorite, which the Ephesians revere as a heaven-sent sacred representation of Artemis, resides in the temple (Acts 19:35). Ephesus is also a center for magical arts and the occult in Asia. The ekklesia Paul plants in Ephesus is similar to the ekklesia in Corinth, both in makeup and size. Both churches are mostly populated by Gentiles, some Jews, and a few wealthy members who own slaves.[69] Each church is a miniature of its respective city.

A Kingdom Community Is Planted in Ephesus

When Paul arrives in Ephesus, he meets twelve disciples of John the Baptist.[70] These disciples were previously baptized for repentance (known as "John's baptism"), but they are

65. John Byron, *A Week in the Life of a Slave*, 40-41.

66. Personal correspondence with Jeffrey Weima, 1/6/24.

67. Craig Keener, "Lessons on Acts," Session 30. For a detailed study on Artemis, see Sandra Glahn, *Nobody's Mother: Artemis of the Ephesians in Antiquity and the New Testament* (Downers Grove, IL: InterVarsity Press, 2023). "The Artemis worshipped at Ephesus was decidedly different in appearance than the Artemis worshipped elsewhere throughout the ancient world. Notice that in the Acts account, the 25,000-person crowd doesn't simply shout 'Great is Artemis.' They shout 'Great is Artemis of the Ephesians.'" Personal correspondence with Jeffrey Weima, 1/6/24.

68. F.F. Bruce, *Paul: Apostle of the Heart Set Free*, 287-288; Holly Beers, *A Week in the Life of a Greco-Roman Woman*, 17. Some scholars give slightly different dimensions. See Alan Bandy, *An Illustrated Guide to the Apostle Paul*, 120, n. 19.

69. Jerome Murphy-O'Connor, *Paul: His Story*, 126-127.

70. The number twelve reminds us of the Twelve who made up the foundation for the first Jewish church. The twelve Ephesians would make up the foundation of the Gentile ekklesia in Ephesus. Craig Keener, *Acts*, 3:2824.

unaware of the Holy Spirit. Paul discovers this by asking them, "Have you received the Holy Spirit?" When they respond saying, "No," Paul in effect says, "Well, you're about to!"[71] The apostle presents Christ to them and baptizes them in the name of Jesus. He then lays hands on them, and the Holy Spirit falls on each one.

The twelve men begin speaking in tongues and prophesying. These twelve men, along with Priscilla, Aquila, and Epaenetus, form the nucleus of the new Ephesian ekklesia.[72] Two male converts become part of the assembly also. In time, these two men will be added to the six men Paul trains to be apostolic workers, making a total of eight workers in training.[73] These two converts are:

- Tychicus from Ephesus[74]
- Trophimus from Ephesus[75]

There is now a kingdom community in the great city of Ephesus, a new assembly expressing God's image and bearing His authority. The body of Christ is born in Roman Asia!

The Hall of Tyrannus

For three months, Paul is allowed to preach Christ in the Ephesian synagogue. He ministers boldly and persuasively about the reality of God's kingdom.[76]

---

71. This is my contemporary rendering of Acts 19:1-5.

72. Acts 19:5-7.

73. Schnabel affirms that Timothy, Epaphras, Gaius, Tychicus, Trophimus, etc. were "Paul's many coworkers during this period." Eckhard Schnabel, *Acts*, 794.

74. According to the Western text (Acts 20:4), Tychicus was an Ephesian. J.D. Douglas, et al., eds., *New Bible Dictionary*, 1226; personal correspondence with Mark Fairchild, 8/4/23. Tychicus is mentioned in Ephesians 6:21; Colossians 4:7; 2 Timothy 4:12; Titus 3:12. Paul regarded him to be "a dear brother, a faithful minister." Eckhard Schnabel, *Acts*, 833. Tychicus means "luck" or "fortune." Personal correspondence with Weima, 4/21/22.

75. Trophimus is mentioned in 2 Timothy 4:20. According to Acts 21:29, he was an Ephesian. This Asian pair (Tychicus and Trophimus) were non-Jewish, and their names suggest past (or present) servile status. C.K. Barrett, *A Critical and Exegetical Commentary on the Acts of the Apostles*, Logos edition (New York, NY: T&T Clark, 2004), 909.

76. Schnabel translates Acts 19:8 as "the reality of the kingdom of God." Eckhard Schnabel, *Acts*, 790. Paul's message of the kingdom and his preaching that Jesus is Messiah and Lord is the same message. It's

And he [Paul] entered the synagogue and for three months spoke boldly, reasoning and persuading them about the kingdom of God. (Acts 19:8, ESV)

After this short period, however, the pattern Paul has witnessed for years repeats itself. Most of the Jews reject him, malign his message, and expel him from the synagogue.[77] (This may be the fifth time Paul incurs synagogue discipline, the horrific forty lashes minus one.[78]) After splitting the synagogue,[79] Paul moves his ministry base to the hall of Tyrannus—a lecture hall he rents.[80] Every day, from 11 a.m. to 4 p.m., Paul preaches Christ and the kingdom of God in the hall.[81] He teaches and dialogues, evangelizing the lost as well as equipping the believers.[82] At the same time, he trains his eight apprentices.[83]

---

the message he preached on his first two apostolic journeys and what he ended up preaching in Rome (Acts 28:31). I. Howard Marshall, *Acts*, 308-309. In my book *Insurgence*, I argue that there is only one gospel in the New Testament, but it is described by different names (the gospel of grace, the gospel of Christ, the gospel of the kingdom, etc.). In Galatians 1:8-9, Paul makes plain that there's only one true gospel.

77. Acts 19:8-9. F.F. Bruce, *Paul: Apostle of the Heart Set Free*, 290; James D.G. Dunn, *The Acts of the Apostles*, 157; John Stott, *The Message of Acts*, 305.

78. 2 Corinthians 11:24. N.T. Wright, *Paul: A Biography*, 244-245.

79. Paul's preaching stirred up trouble as some of the Jews hardened their hearts toward him and his message. C.K. Barrett, *A Critical and Exegetical Commentary on the Acts of the Apostles*, 904.

80. Acts 19:9-10. According to Meeks, the hall of Tyrannus may have been a guild hall of a trade association. Wayne Meeks, *The First Urban Christians*, 26. Alternatively, it may have been a lecture hall where Tyrannus was either the landlord or customary lecturer. Craig Keener, *The IVP Bible Background Commentary: New Testament*, 383. For details on the hall of Tyrannus, see Ben Witherington III, *The Acts of the Apostles*, 574-575.

81. According to the Western text, Paul had use of the building for these hours, "from the fifth hour to the tenth hour" (11 a.m. to 4 p.m.). These hours were when public affairs such as schooling and judicial activities came to a halt in all Greco-Roman cities. During that span of time, Tyrannus' hall was not in use, so Paul could employ it for his ministry. F.F. Bruce, *Paul: Apostle of the Heart Set Free*, 290; James D.G. Dunn, *The Acts of the Apostles*, 258. Paul probably spent his mornings mending tents, since the city shut down by noon. Mark Wilson, *Biblical Turkey*, 213. Tyrannus himself may have lectured in the morning, while Paul used the hall in the afternoon. In the Greco-Roman world, the business day ended at 11 a.m. The 11 a.m. meal was typically followed by a nap. F.F. Bruce, *Paul: Apostle of the Heart Set Free*, 290-291; Ben Witherington III, *The Acts of the Apostles*, 574-575. Dunn suggests Paul must have gained "wealthy backers" to be able to fund the lecture hall. For more on Paul's ministry in the lecture hall of Tyrannus, see Eckhard Schnabel, *Acts*, 792; *Paul the Missionary*, 109, 297.

82. John Stott, *The Message of Acts*, 305.

83. They "were soon trained and equipped to be his associates in spreading the gospel far and wide." R.C. Lucas, *The Message of Colossians & Philemon*, 19. Paul's desire was to train these eight men and (eventually) have them train other faithful believers in the future (2 Timothy 2:2).

The apostle continues to lay the foundation for the new Ephesian ekklesia, and his apprentices learn by observing him. Paul resumes his leatherworking business in the morning, starting before sunrise. He ministers in the afternoon and continues his leatherwork in the evening.[84] With his own hands, Paul supports himself and the eight men he trains. For this reason, he often goes hungry and thirsty.[85]

You yourselves know that these hands served my necessities, and those who were with me. (Acts 20:34)

...in labor and travail, in watchings often, in hunger and thirst, in fastings often, and in cold and nakedness. (2 Corinthians 11:27)[86]

Even to this present hour we hunger, thirst, are naked, are beaten, and have no certain dwelling place. We toil, working with our own hands.... (1 Corinthians 4:11-12)

While Paul holds meetings in the hall of Tyrannus, the Christians in Ephesus meet from house to house.[87] And they often gather in the home of Priscilla and Aquila.[88] For two years, Paul preaches and teaches in the hall of Tyrannus, unfolding the "whole purpose of God" in his messages.[89] He also counsels the believers on a regular basis, sometimes

---

84. F.F. Bruce, *Paul: Apostle of the Heart Set Free*, 291; Otto F.A. Meinardus, *St. Paul in Ephesus*, 69; Clinton Arnold, ed., *Zondervan Illustrated Bible Backgrounds Commentary*, 2b:191-192.

85. Clinton Arnold, ed., *Zondervan Illustrated Bible Backgrounds Commentary*, 2b:210-211.

86. Interestingly, Paul considered his manual labor part of the price he paid for the gospel. Gerald Hawthorne, et al., eds., *Dictionary of Paul and His Letters*, 926.

87. Acts 20:20. The meetings in the Hall of Tyrannus were for *the work*, while the house-to-house meetings were for *the church*. Clinton Arnold, ed., *Zondervan Illustrated Bible Backgrounds Commentary*, 2b:208. For the distinction between the church and the work in the New Testament, see Frank Viola, *Finding Organic Church*, Part 1; Robert Banks, *Paul's Idea of Community,* chap. 16.

88. 1 Corinthians 16:19. It's possible that when Paul wrote 1 Corinthians, the whole church in Ephesus met in one large house. And other converts from Ephesus may have become part of the other new assemblies in Asia Minor to help strengthen them. Paul was a master at sending people to aid new church plants.

89. See Acts 20:24-27, NASB. In this text, Paul uses "whole purpose of God," "the gospel of God's grace," and "preaching the kingdom" as synonyms. In short, Paul declared God's eternal purpose in Ephesus, as he did everywhere else.

admonishing them with tears.[90]

Many from Asia, both Jew and Greek, visit the new work in Ephesus and hear Paul proclaim the revolutionary gospel of the kingdom.[91] One such person is Philemon, a well-to-do businessman from the wealthy town of Colossae (about one hundred miles east of Ephesus).[92] Philemon's wife, Apphia,[93] and a slave named Onesimus are with him.[94]

While in Ephesus, Philemon and Apphia receive Paul's message and give their believing allegiance to Jesus.[95] Philemon also becomes a help to Paul. After their short stay, Philemon, his wife Apphia, and Onesimus head back to their home in Colossae. Around the same time, a man named Epaphras visits Ephesus. Epaphras is also from Colossae.[96] Paul

90. Acts 20:31.

91. Paul and his team convinced many, not only in Ephesus, but in "the whole province of Asia" that gods made by human hands were not real deities. Acts 19:26, NIV.

92. Colossae is also spelled Colosse. The NLT and NKJV use "Colosse" while the ESV, NASB, NIV, and NRSV use "Colossae." Colossae is a small town, overshadowed by Laodicea and Hierapolis. F.F. Bruce, *Paul: Apostle of the Heart Set Free*, 407; John Barry, et al., "Letter to the Colossians," *The Lexham Bible Dictionary*. Witherington says it was "the least important and influential city to which Paul ever directed a letter." Ben Witherington III, *The Letters to Philemon, the Colossians, and the Ephesians*, 34. Even so, Bandy says all the towns in the Lycus valley (Laodicea, Hierapolis, Colossae, etc.) had wealth. Personal correspondence with Alan Bandy, 12/6/23. Colossae was primarily a Gentile city, although some Jews were present. Scot McKnight, *The Letter to the Colossians*, NICNT (Grand Rapids, MI: Eerdmans 2018), 20. The city was known for producing figs and olives, as well as "Colossian" black wool. Gary Burge, et al., *The New Testament in Antiquity*, 339.

93. Apphia is "almost universally recognized to be Philemon's wife." N.T. Wright, *Colossians and Philemon*, 173.

94. While this cannot be proven, it's plausible that Philemon brought Onesimus with him, as owners were known for bringing their slaves with them on their travels. Slaves didn't choose their own names, and they couldn't use the name of their father. They were instead named in connection with their master. Onesimus, therefore, would have been called "Onesimus, slave of Philemon." John Byron, *A Week in the Life of a Slave*, 68.

95. In Philemon 19, Paul says, "…not to mention that you owe me your very self." This statement indicates that Paul was responsible for converting Philemon to Christ. Wright and Bird agree and also believe Paul led Apphia to the Lord as well. N.T. Wright and Michael Bird, *The New Testament in Its World*, 452.

96. Colossians 4:12. See also F.F. Bruce, *Paul: Apostle of the Heart Set Free*, 408. Epaphras means "lovely" or "charming." Alan Bandy, *An Illustrated Guide to the Apostle Paul*, 122.

proclaims Christ to Epaphras, and Epaphras believes.[97] Epaphras shows strong signs of having an apostolic call, so he stays in Ephesus for a time to be trained by Paul along with Paul's other apprentices.[98]

Throughout the two years he is in the city, Paul sends his eight apprentices throughout the nearby cities. These men will plant new kingdom communities all over the Roman province of Asia. (Some of the assemblies are listed in the first two chapters of Revelation.[99]) Paul's apprentices establish ekklesias in the following cities:

- Smyrna[100]
- Pergamum[101]
- Thyatira[102]

97. N.T. Wright, *Paul: A Biography*, 286-287.

98. Eckhard Schnabel, *Paul the Missionary*, 254. For more on how workers were raised up in the first century and how the pattern can be recovered today, see Frank Viola, "The Way God Raises Up Workers," at frankviola.org/raises.

99. See F.F. Bruce, *Paul: Apostle of the Heart Set Free*, 407-408. "While Paul stayed in Ephesus, several of his colleagues carried out missionary activity in neighboring cities. During those years his colleague Epaphras appears to have evangelized the cities of the Lycus valley, Colossae, Laodicea, and Hierapolis—cities which Paul evidently did not visit in person (Colossians 1:7-8; 2:1; 4:12-13). Likely, all seven of the churches of Asia addressed in the Revelation of John were also founded about this time. The province was intensively evangelized and remained one of the leading centers of Christianity." F.F. Bruce, *The Book of the Acts*, 366. Bandy confirms, saying, "It's likely that Paul discipled, trained, and sent out messengers to spread the gospel throughout the region." Alan Bandy, *An Illustrated Guide to the Apostle Paul*, 122. Guthrie confirms that the churches in the Lycus valley were planted during this time, Laodicea being one of them. Donald Guthrie, *The Apostles*, 176. Fairchild affirms the same saying, "Paul trained his disciples at the school of Tyrannus (Acts 19:9-10). These disciples in turn traveled to the nearby towns and shared the gospel message." Mark Fairchild, *Christian Origins in Ephesus & Asia Minor*, 58.

100. The population of Smyrna was around 200,000. Bruce Longenecker, *In Stone and Story*, 22. Some estimate the population was 100,000 at its peak. Mark Wilson, *Biblical Turkey*, 302. Others say it was 75,000. Ben Witherington III, *Revelation*, NCBC (New York, NY: Cambridge University Press, 2003), 23.

101. Some estimate the population of Pergamum to be 120,000. Ben Witherington III, *Revelation*, 23. For the history of the city, see Clyde Fant, et al., *A Guide to Biblical Sites in Greece and Turkey*, 273-276.

102. Lydia may have had a helping hand in founding this church along with the apostolic workers, since she was originally from Thyatira. Jerome Murphy-O'Connor, *Paul: His Story*, 128. For further details on Thyatira, see Mark Wilson, *Biblical Turkey*, 311-313.

- Sardis[103]
- Philadelphia[104]

Epaphras heads back to Colossae and begins planting seeds of the gospel to those he knows in the city.[105] As a result of Paul's ministry in Ephesus, along with his decision to send out his eight apprentices to the neighboring towns, Jews and Gentiles in the Roman province of Asia will hear the word of Jesus Christ.[106]

The body of Christ—the community that bears God's image and authority—is growing in Ephesus as well as throughout Roman Asia.[107] Before he leaves the city, Paul will have spent about three years in Ephesus,[108] the longest period of time he will ever remain in a city to do God's work.[109]

October 13[110]
A.D. 54

Back in Rome, Emperor Claudius dies,[111] and Nero assumes the throne at age sixteen.[112] Emperor Nero allows the ban against the Jews to lapse, so the Jews who were expelled

---

103. Sardis was a wealthy city with a population between 60,000 to 100,000. Eckhard Schnabel, *Paul the Missionary*, 269; Ben Witherington III, *Revelation*, 23; Mark Wilson, *Biblical Turkey*, 289-291.

104. For details on ancient Philadelphia, see Mark Wilson, *Biblical Turkey*, 286-289.

105. Later in the story, Epaphras will plant a church in Colossae, Hierapolis, and Laodicea, one assembly per city.

106. Acts 19:9-10, NIV. Witherington confirms that the residents of Asia, both Jew and Gentile, heard the word of God during this time because it was carried "to nearby places being undertaken by Paul's coworkers while he remained and worked in Ephesus itself." Ben Witherington III, *The Acts of the Apostles*, 576. See also Eckhard Schnabel, *Acts,* 794. Demetrius, one of Paul's opponents, attributed the gospel spreading to "almost throughout all Asia" (Acts 19:26) to Paul's influence. Since Paul was the leader of his apprentices who traveled and shared the gospel throughout the region, this attribution is not surprising.

107. The cities mentioned in Revelation 2 and 3 were located in this area.

108. Acts 20:31.

109. For further details on Paul's ministry in Ephesus and the Roman province of Asia, see William Ramsay, *St. Paul the Traveler and Roman Citizen*, chap. 12.

110. F.F. Bruce, *Paul: Apostle of the Heart Set Free*, 295.

111. Claudius possibly died from poisoning by his wife, Agrippina.

112. F.F. Bruce, *The Spreading Flame*, 133. Although there is some minor dispute about Nero's exact birthdate, historians generally agree that he was around sixteen or seventeen years old when he assumed power,

from Rome under Claudius begin returning to the city.[113] Nero's first five years as emperor are relatively moderate. But his pretense of morality and fairness will begin to fade around A.D. 59 when he orders his mother to be killed.[114]

Power Encounters in Ephesus

As Paul continues to labor for the gospel in Ephesus, he performs extraordinary miracles.[115] Astonishingly, people take handkerchiefs and aprons that have contacted his body and use them to heal the sick and cast out demons.[116] Upon seeing the miracles that Paul performs by invoking the name of Jesus, some itinerant Jewish exorcists try to cast out demons using the Lord's name.

Seven sons of a leading Jewish priest named Sceva attempt this.[117] But when they seek to employ the name of Jesus to cast out a demon, the evil spirit says to them, "Jesus I know, and Paul I know, but who are you?"[118] Immediately, the demon-possessed man brutally beats the sons of Sceva, leaving them naked and wounded. The news of the incident spreads throughout the city to both Jews and Gentiles, and the people are filled with fear. But the name of Jesus is magnified as something to be respected.[119]

---

making him one of the youngest emperors in Roman history.

113. Rainer Riesner, *Paul's Early Period*, 300; Reta Halteman Finger, *Roman House Churches for Today*, 15.

114. James D.G. Dunn, *Beginning from Jerusalem*, 1055-1057. Like Genghis Khan and Hitler, Nero was one of the greatest monsters in human history. Early in his reign, Nero's madness was mostly kept in check by the guidance of the philosophers Seneca (philosopher and tutor) and Burrus (head of the Praetorian Guard). Ben Witherington III, *The Acts of the Apostles*, 726. In A.D. 62, Seneca retired, Burrus died, and Nero's madness was fully unleashed. In A.D. 65, Nero ordered Seneca to commit suicide. F.F. Bruce, *Paul: Apostle of the Heart Set Free*, 295. For a compilation of what the early church fathers said about Nero, see David Bercot, ed., *A Dictionary of Early Christian Beliefs* (Peabody, MA: Hendrickson, 1998), 470.

115. For details on Paul's relationship to miracles, see Graham Twelftree, *Paul and the Miraculous: A Historical Reconstruction* (Grand Rapids, MI: Baker, 2013).

116. Acts 19:12.

117. It appears they were invoking the name of Jesus as a magical incantation. For details on Jewish magic in antiquity, see Clinton Arnold, ed., *Zondervan Illustrated Bible Backgrounds Commentary*, 2b:193.

118. Acts 19:15.

119. Acts 19:11-17.

Through his preaching in the hall of Tyrannus and the extraordinary miracles he performs, God gives Paul a wide-open door to proclaim the gospel of the kingdom.[120] At the same time, he encounters many adversaries.[121]

> *But I will stay in Ephesus until Pentecost, for a wide door for effective work has opened to me, and there are many adversaries. (1 Corinthians 16:8-9, ESV)*

Crisis in Corinth

Apollos completes his visit to Corinth and returns to Ephesus. He brings Sosthenes with him, the former ruler of the synagogue.[122] Apollos and Sosthenes meet with Paul, informing him about the problems within the Corinthian ekklesia.[123] Apollos explains to Paul that some in the Corinthian church are reverting to their heathen lifestyles. They're committing

---

120. 1 Corinthians 16:8-9. Some scholars think the wide-open door took place during the annual festival of Artemisia (or Ephesia) to honor Artemis. Otto F.A. Meinardus, *St. Paul in Ephesus*, 95-96. This is possible, but it's difficult to fit it into the timeline during Paul's time in Ephesus, so I believe the open door Paul mentions took place *before* the festival. The riot, however, appears to have taken place *during* the festival.

121. Bruce believes the adversaries were influential men in the Jewish community. F.F. Bruce, *Paul: Apostle of the Heart Set Free*, 297. David deSilva thinks it makes far more sense to consider pagan supporters of Artemis and other local cults to be the source of adversity, as they were so prominently featured in the Acts narrative as a source of real trouble for Paul. Personal correspondence with David deSilva, 2/8/24. Some scholars (like N.T. Wright) believe Paul was imprisoned in Ephesus. N.T. Wright, *Paul: A Biography*, 239-240, 264-269, 280-284. This is possible, and if it did happen, it's likely that Andronicus and Junia may have been imprisoned with him. See Alan Bandy, *An Illustrated Guide to the Apostle Paul*, 128-129. However, as Bruce points out, there is no direct evidence Paul was imprisoned in Ephesus, though "the possibility cannot be excluded." F.F. Bruce, *Paul: Apostle of the Heart Set Free*, 298. Ben Witherington attempts to refute an Ephesian imprisonment in "The Case of the Imprisonment That Did Not Happen: Paul at Ephesus," *JETS* 60, no. 3 (2017): 525-532. One of his arguments is that Paul was on good terms with the provincial officials. Ben Witherington III, *The Letters to Philemon, the Colossians, and the Ephesians*, 23.

122. Sosthenes was present with Paul when the apostle wrote 1 Corinthians (1 Corinthians 1:1).

123. We've already established that Apollos visited the Corinthian church (Acts 19:1). This reconstruction makes the most sense. It explains how Paul heard about the problems he addressed in Corinthians A (a letter we no longer have).

fornication, worshipping idols, and stealing from one another.[124] Paul decides to write a letter to the assembly to address the problems.

PAUL WRITES CORINTHIANS A

(This letter is lost to us.[125])

Year: A.D. 54[126]

From: Ephesus[127]

To: The assembly in Corinth (which is about four years old)

Author: Paul[128]

Contextual Summary: Provoked by Apollos' report, Paul urges the Corinthians to no longer keep company with fornicators, idolaters, and thieves in the assembly. He also shares his plan to create a relief fund for the assembly in Jerusalem and invites them to participate.

Titus brings Paul's letter to Corinth and helps the Corinthian believers collect money for the Jerusalem relief fund.[129] Afterward, Titus rejoins Paul back in Ephesus. In the meantime, the doctrine of Hellenistic dualism[130] begins to gain ground in Corinth. According to

---

124. 1 Corinthians 5:9-13. Gordon Fee, *The First Epistle to the Corinthians*, 6-7.

125. Paul mentions this lost letter in 1 Corinthians 5:9. Note that some other letters (by Paul and John) also haven't survived. For example, see Colossians 4:16 and 3 John 9. Bruce Longenecker, ed., *The New Cambridge Companion to St. Paul*, 6 and n. 8.

126. Ben Witherington III, *Conflict and Community in Corinth*, 352. According to Witherington, it could have been written earlier in A.D. 53.

127. Gordon Fee, *The First Epistle to the Corinthians*, 6.

128. Paul authored the letter (1 Corinthians 5:9).

129. 2 Corinthians 8:6 indicates that Titus helped with the collection. See also John Stott, *The Message of Acts*, 318; Craig Keener, *The IVP Bible Background Commentary: New Testament*, 513; F.F. Bruce, *1 and 2 Corinthians*, 223; Donald Guthrie, *The Apostles*, 218.

130. Hellenistic dualism refers to the belief that spiritual things like the soul and spirit are eternal and good while physical things like the body are temporal and bad. Consequently, many advocates of this belief

301

this doctrine, if a person has the Spirit of God, they will live above the earthly plane. What they do with their physical bodies has no bearing on their spiritual state. The material world is temporary, so it doesn't matter what kinds of physical activity a person practices. According to the doctrine, sexual immorality is perfectly acceptable. And since God is not interested in the physical world, there will be no resurrection of the dead. Some of the Corinthian believers embrace the false teaching and begin acting on it.

A.D. 55

In Ephesus, a sizeable group of magicians are converted as a result of the miraculous exploits of Paul.[131] These magicians believe on the Lord Jesus and confess their deeds. In an act of repentance, they burn their magical scrolls (an action that dispels their secrets).[132] The value of all the magical documents that go up in smoke amounts to 50,000 drachmas.[133] Among the books burned are the so-called "Ephesian letters" which were used as charms to make its bearers invincible.[134]

---

either deny the pleasures of the body like food and sex or adopt the other extreme of believing that whatever one does with their body has no real eternal significance, which then gives them license to engage in all sorts of sexual immorality.

131. According to Keener, "These practitioners of magic were probably not all considered magicians or sorcerers. A lot of people apparently practiced curse invocations, bought amulets, etc. from dealers. But it is all 'occult' in today's language." Personal correspondence with Craig Keener, 12/4/23.

132. The effectiveness of a spell was tied to its secret. If the secret was revealed, the spell would be ineffective. F.F. Bruce, *The Book of the Acts*, 369; Craig Keener, "Lessons on Acts," Session 30.

133. The Greek drachma (silver coin) was the value of a day's wage, the equivalent of the Roman denarius. Craig Keener, "Lessons on Acts," Session 30. The total price of what they burned was about fifty thousand days' wages for an average worker. Craig Keener, *The IVP Bible Background Commentary: New Testament*, 384.

134. Otto F.A. Meinardus, *St. Paul in Ephesus*, 92. They were also called "the Ephesian writings" (*Ephesia grammata*). "Ephesus was world famous as a center for pagan superstition and magic. There were six words in the Greek language that had no meaning (somewhat similar to our 'hocus pocus'), but if spoken in the right combination, they were believed to have power over the spiritual realm. Strikingly, these six magical words were referred to in Paul's day as 'Ephesian letters.'" Personal correspondence with Jeffrey Weima, 1/6/24. For details on the Ephesian Letters, see Craig Keener, *Acts*, 3:2844-2859; Clinton Arnold, *Power and Magic: The Concept of Power in Ephesians*, second edition (Grand Rapids, MI: Baker, 1997), 15-16.

Through Paul's ministry, the word of the Lord continues to spread, and it is confirmed by the mighty power of God.[135] Around the same time, several believers in Corinth employed by a Christian businesswoman named Chloe pay a visit to Ephesus.[136] When Chloe's people meet Paul, they singe his ears with the horrors taking place in the Corinthian assembly. They tell him about the division, jealousy, and strife among the believers. The community is still fracturing into four parties.[137]

Some of the Greeks show exclusive loyalty to Apollos.[138] They equate his Greek oratory with "higher" wisdom and knowledge.[139] Some of the Jews show exclusive loyalty to Peter. They chase signs and wonders. Still others make the elitist claim that they exclusively follow Christ and have no need of any apostle.[140] Finally, some pledge exclusive loyalty to Paul, putting him in competition with the other workers. Chloe's people also inform him about the following:

- Some in the church are ambitiously acting as "tutors" and "instructors" to the assembly. They have grown arrogant toward Paul's apostolic ministry, confidently asserting that he will not visit the church again.[141]

- One of the brothers in the assembly is committing incest, and the rest of the church is ignoring it. Some even boast in their Christian "liberty" while this is happening.

135. Acts 19:18-20; 1 Corinthians 4:20.

136. Chloe was probably an independent and wealthy businesswoman. Her associates (or servants) may have been followers of Christ who had contact with Paul in Ephesus. N.T. Wright, *Paul: A Biography*, 248. Her business agents probably traveled between Ephesus and Corinth. Gordon Fee, *The First Epistle to the Corinthians*, 54-55. Some, like Weima, think Chloe may have lived in Ephesus and some of her household workers traveled to Corinth and then returned to Ephesus where they informed Paul of what was happening in the Corinthian church. Personal correspondence with Jeffrey Weima, 1/6/24.

137. Or four "sects" or "denominations."

138. Although this wasn't his intention, Apollos was *unwittingly* one of the causes of the schism. However, Paul fully supported his ministry (1 Corinthians 16:12). Eckhard Schnabel, *Acts*, 786, n. 18.

139. Paul's words in 1 Corinthians 1:17-18 (NIV) reflect what he learned during his time in Athens. Since the Corinthians are Greeks located close to Athens, their native mindset was the same, and this is why they were so attracted to the "wisdom and eloquence" of Apollos. Since there was a faction of the church who exalted Apollos, I'm of the opinion that Paul had Apollos in mind when he penned 1 Corinthians 1:17 and 1 Corinthians 2:1-4.

140. They probably said, "You all are all following a man, but we follow Christ and no one else!"

141. 1 Corinthians 4:15-18. In verse 15, the WEB uses "tutors," and the NKJV uses "instructors."

- Some of the wealthier brothers are taking one another to the civil law courts. Some are participating in parties and feasts in the dining rooms of pagan temples.[142]

- Some of the men are visiting prostitutes and engaging in gluttony, thinking that what they do with their bodies has no bearing on their spirits. (Their slogans are, "everything is permissible and lawful for me," and, "food for the stomach, and the stomach for food.")

Around the same time, three respected brothers from the Corinthian assembly—Stephanas, Fortunatus, and Achaicus—visit Paul.[143] Erastus also comes with them.[144] The four men scorch Paul's ears with *more* troubling news about the church. They report the following:

- Some of the believers are dangerously sick. And a few have recently died.

- The slaves in the assembly work late and cannot make the church meetings on time. The well-to-do brothers don't wait for them and eat the Lord's Supper ahead of their poorer brethren.[145]

- Still worse, the well-to-do brethren treat the Lord's Supper as if it were a private dinner party. They are gorging themselves on the food and getting drunk on the wine.[146]

142. John Barclay, *Pauline Churches and Diaspora Jews*, 189.

143. Fortunatus means "Lucky," while Achaicus means "the Greek" or "one who is from Achaia." Gordon Fee, *The First Epistle to the Corinthians*, 831. Some scholars believe they were both Stephanas' freedmen or slaves. Richard Horsley, et al., *The Message and the Kingdom*, 171. According to Barclay, those who had influence in the Corinthian assembly (like Stephanas) also had high social standing. John Barclay, *Pauline Churches and Diaspora Jews*, 198.

144. Later, Paul will send Timothy and Erastus to Macedonia (Acts 19:22). See Richard Longenecker, *Luke-Acts*, 1014. Therefore, Erastus had to have been in Ephesus before that took place. This scenario, therefore, makes sense.

145. In the first century, the Lord's Supper was taken as a celebratory, communal meal. It was a "bring-and-share" supper. David and Pat Alexander, eds., *Handbook to the Bible*, 701; Robert Banks, *Paul's Idea of Community*, 70-74; Leon Morris, *1 Corinthians: An Introduction and Commentary*, TNTC, revised edition (Grand Rapids, MI: Eerdmans, 1988), 156, 162; Ben Witherington III, *Making a Meal of It*, chap. 3; Tom Wright, *The Meal Jesus Gave Us*, chap. 7; Frank Viola, *Reimagining Church*, chap. 3; James White, *The Worldliness of Worship* (New York, NY: Oxford University Press, 1967), 85. The higher status believers in Corinth may have kept the best food for their high-status peers, providing lower quality food for the poor believers. For details on the situation in Corinth and Greco-Roman dinner practices, see James D.G. Dunn, *The Theology of Paul the Apostle*, 609ff.

146. Like all Romans, the Corinthians ate while reclining on couches, usually situated in a U shape around a low table. (Corinth was a Roman colony, so Roman customs were observed.) Diners supported

- There is quarreling over the marriage veil. Some of the wives in the church remove their veils when they pray and prophesy in the meetings. This has caused some visitors to accuse them of being immoral.[147] Their husbands have asked them to wear the veil in the meetings, but the women argue that they are at liberty to do as they wish.

Stephanas, Fortunatus, and Achaicus share all these things with Paul. They also hand him a letter from the church,[148] a letter packed with questions. The letter was mainly written by a group of well-to-do Gentile male converts in the church.[149] Some of the questions in the letter are:

---

their body weight with their left elbows and ate with their right fingers. The common banquet etiquette of the first century was to separate those who ate by social class. The wealthy merchants were fed with one kind of food in the dining room. About nine to twelve people could fit there. The leftovers and inferior foods were given to the poor and slaves in the courtyard (*atrium*). For details on this problem and more in Corinth, see John Barclay, *Pauline Churches and Diaspora Jews*, 188-196. For more on the Roman banquet, see James Papandrea, *A Week in the Life of Rome*, 100-101.

147. When a woman married, she wore a veil in public. The veil was a social indicator that a woman was married. An unveiled woman signified to others that she was unmarried. Thus, for married women to wear veils in public was a matter of decorum and supreme importance in Roman society. Married women who did not wear veils in public settings were viewed as shaming their husbands and portraying themselves as promiscuous wives; i.e., unashamed adulteresses. In 44 B.C., a "new" type of woman emerged in Rome. By the first century, these "new women" had spread throughout the Roman Empire. The "new women" were liberated married women who pursued their social lives at the expense of their families and defied previously accepted norms of marriage fidelity and chastity. They were sexually promiscuous and dressed in a seductive manner. Because Paul was a liberator of women, it is not difficult to see that some Christian women associated his views on a woman's freedom with the immoral ideals of the "new women." For a detailed discussion on the cultural meaning of the marriage veil in the first century and "the new Roman women," see Bruce Winter, *After Paul Left Corinth: The Influence of Secular Ethics and Social Change* (Grand Rapids, MI: Eerdmans, 2000), chap. 6; *Roman Wives, Roman Widows: The Appearance of New Women and the Pauline Communities* (Grand Rapids, MI: Eerdmans, 2003), chap. 5; E. Randolph Richards, et al., *Misreading Scripture with Western Eyes*, 43.

148. The three men "almost certainly" carried the church's letter to Paul. Gordon Fee, *The First Epistle to the Corinthians*, 54-55.

149. Witherington believes this group was likely the source of many of the problems Paul addresses in 1 Corinthians (Corinthians B). He asserts they defended the right to attend pagan temples and participate in Greco-Roman society, as well as causing the other troubles mentioned in 1 Corinthians 3 through 15. Ben Witherington III, *Conflict and Community in Corinth*, 313.

- In your previous letter, you told us not to associate with sexually immoral people. But such people are everywhere in our city. How can we do this without quitting our jobs and staying at home?

- Some in the assembly who read your last letter about abstaining from sexual immorality are practicing sexual abstinence in their marriages. They have adopted the slogan: "It is not good for a man to touch a woman." Do you agree with this?

- Some of the brothers and sisters have unsaved spouses, and their marriages are full of conflict. Should they divorce them or stay married?

- Some of the men who are betrothed (engaged) to women in the assembly are not sure if they should marry them. What's your opinion?

- Is it wrong to eat meat that was previously sacrificed to idols? Can we buy meat from the meat-markets?[150] Is it wrong to dine in the pagan temples?[151] Some in the assembly believe this is a social necessity.[152] Pagan gods don't exist anyway, so how could it be wrong? Others believe the consecration to idols does something to the meat, therefore, they cannot partake with a clear conscience.[153]

150. According to Bruce, in 1 Corinthians 10:25, Paul had the Greek meat-markets in mind. He details this problem as well as the issue of eating at the table of a pagan neighbor or in the dining room at a pagan temple in F.F. Bruce, *Paul: Apostle of the Heart Set Free,* 217, including n. 35.

151. Those with a higher social status did not typically dine in the *tabernae* (taverns). They instead dined in the pagan temples.

152. This sentiment was held among the wealthier members of the church. For details, see Craig Keener, *The IVP Bible Background Commentary: New Testament,* 476-482.

153. Craig Keener gives details on the problem of meat sacrificed to idols in *The IVP Bible Background Commentary: New Testament,* 476-477, 480-482. According to Weima, "The issue of meat/food sacrificed to idols was a serious one, evident in the fact that Paul takes up no less than three chapters to deal with it (8:1-11:1). The main problem dealt with meat/food eaten in a pagan temple. The religious component of these meals stemmed from their location. By eating in a dining room located in a temple devoted to a particular deity, one had 'koinonia' with the god or goddess that made the person guilty of idolatry. These cultic meals were very popular in the ancient world and the temptation to continue to participate in them after converting to the Christian faith was great. That this was a huge problem in the early church is clear from the fact that the Jerusalem council had to deal with the problem (Acts 15), and two of the seven letters of Revelation deal with it (letters to Pergamum and Thyatira)." Personal correspondence with Jeffrey Weima, 1/6/24.

- Some are critical of you, Paul. They are raising questions about the genuineness of your apostolic calling. They're asking why you don't take money like the other workers (Peter and Apollos, for example) as well as the traveling philosophers.[154]

- Our open-participatory meetings have been chaotic. The gift of tongues is exalted by some because it's the language of the angels. Many speak in tongues at the same time during the meetings, and it's creating confusion.[155] In addition, some of the married women are challenging those who prophesy with off-topic questions.[156] This creates both confusion and disruption in our gatherings.[157] What should we do about it?

- Some in the church believe only the soul and spirit will live after death. They think the idea of a dead body coming back to life is crazy. They don't believe we will be resurrected bodily after we die. Can you address this?

- There's a general reluctance among many in the church with respect to contributing to the relief collection you asked us to participate in.

Stephanas, Fortunatus, and Achaicus refresh Paul's spirit, and Paul is impressed by their character.[158] Upon hearing the questions in the church's letter, along with the report from Chloe's people, he is disheartened. The apostle responds to all of it by

154. Well-to-do Greeks despised common labor and looked down on those who engaged in it. This would include those who worked as leatherworkers/tentmakers. In the eyes of such, Paul lost credibility because he worked with his hands. Jeffrey Weima, *1-2 Thessalonians*, 297-298; Craig Keener, *The IVP Bible Background Commentary: New Testament,* 477-478.

155. Like many other scholars, Keener is in agreement that the open-participatory church meeting described in 1 Corinthians 14:26 was "Paul's ideal," and Paul's instructions were designed to "ensure order" in that gathering. For abundant scholarly support for this interpretation, see Frank Viola, "When You Come Together…" at frankviola.org/1cor14. See also Craig Keener, *1–2 Corinthians*, 117; Frank Viola, *Reimagining Church*, chap. 2.

156. Craig Keener, *1–2 Corinthians*, 119.

157. The women were also interrupting the meetings by correcting the men. And some noisily asked questions in a disruptive manner. Personal correspondence with Nijay Gupta, 6/6/23. I give details on what I believe was happening in Corinth with the women, and the meaning of 1 Corinthians 14:34-35 in my article "Rethinking a Woman's Role in the Church" at frankviola.org/role.pdf.

158. 1 Corinthians 16:18.

crafting a detailed epistle. We will call it CORINTHIANS B. It's what we know as 1 Corinthians.[159]

As Paul concludes his lengthy letter, he strongly urges Apollos to visit the assembly in Corinth with some of the other brothers. Apollos, however, declines, feeling it's not the right time.[160] Before Paul ends the letter, he sends Timothy to Corinth. He wants his young apprentice to encourage the assembly and report back to him concerning how his long letter was received.[161] Erastus accompanies him, but the two men visit Macedonia first.[162]

159. Weima notes, "Paul received two reports. One was oral from those of Chloe's household (1 Corinthians 1:11; also 5:1) which informed Paul of some shocking behavior within the Corinthian church. Around the same time Paul received a written report—a letter from the Corinthians in which they raised a number of questions. Paul took up the oral report first, since they dealt with a number of serious problems which caused the apostle to become quite upset with his converts in Corinth. These topics from the oral report are taken up in chapters 1-6. Paul then takes up the issues in the Corinthians' letter in chapters 7-16—indicated by his words in 7:1 and the repeated phrase ('Now about…') which introduces each topic (7:1, 25; 8:1, 4; 12:1; 16:1; 16:12). Here in the second half of the letter, Paul's tone is less strident and angry because, in contrast to the first half topics which are clearly wrong, here the Corinthians were taking true teachings—many of which came directly from Paul himself—and were misinterpreting or misapplying them. So Paul had to be more nuanced in his response in the second half." Personal correspondence with Jeffrey Weima, 1/6/24. For an explanation of the transitional formula ("Now about…" and "But concerning…") in Paul's letters, see Jeffrey Weima, *Paul the Ancient Letter Writer.*

160. 1 Corinthians 16:12. According to Witherington, "some Corinthians asked Paul to send Apollos to them again. This means that Apollos must have been working with or near Paul in Ephesus at the time, after having made an initial visit to Corinth…. Paul makes it clear that he himself did not impede Apollos from returning. Indeed, he strongly urged it. In Paul's view, he and Apollos are not at odds but are coworkers in the same cause." Ben Witherington III, *Conflict and Community in Corinth,* 316-317.

161. 1 Corinthians 4:17 in the ESV, NKJV, NASB, NLT, WEB, etc. says Paul *sent* (past tense) Timothy to the Corinthian church. Some argue that the translation should be "I am sending you Timothy" (New American Bible, revised edition). See also 1 Corinthians 16:10.

162. Speaking of 1 Corinthians 16:10, Leon Morris writes, "Paul spoke earlier of sending Timothy to Corinth (4:17). It seems that Timothy was accompanied by Erastus, and that they went to Macedonia first (Acts 19:22)." Leon Morris, *1 Corinthians,* 236. Paul resolved to go to Macedonia and Achaia before traveling to Jerusalem with the collection (Acts 19:21). Timothy and Erastus went ahead of Paul to visit the churches in Macedonia, perhaps to help with the collection as well as encourage them. Eckhard Schnabel, *Acts,* 801-802.

PAUL WRITES CORINTHIANS B

(This is our 1 Corinthians.[163])

Year: Spring 55[164]

From: Ephesus[165]

To: The assembly in Corinth (which is about five years old)

Author: Paul[166]

Contextual Summary: In chapters 1 through 6, Paul addresses the oral report that he's heard from Chloe's people. This includes the divisions, sexual immorality, and civil litigations. In chapters 7 through 16, he answers the ekklesia's list of questions.

Paul then gives the assembly his new travel plans, which had recently changed. Instead of traveling by sea across the Aegean from Ephesus to Corinth, to Macedonia, then back to Corinth as he first planned—he will travel by land from Ephesus to Macedonia and make one long visit to Corinth.[167]

163. Support for my reconstruction of Paul's Corinthian correspondence can be found in F.F. Bruce, *Paul: Apostle of the Heart Set Free*, 264-285.

164. John A.T. Robinson, *Redating the New Testament*, 54; F.F. Bruce, *1 and 2 Corinthians*, 25. Witherington dates it between A.D. 54 and 55. Ben Witherington III, *The New Testament Story*, 277. Most scholars believe the letter was written in the early A.D. 50s. Leon Morris, *The First and Second Epistles to the Thessalonians*, 4. Bernier dates it later at A.D. 56. Jonathan Bernier, *Rethinking the Dates of the New Testament*, 150.

165. In 1 Corinthians 16:19 (NIV), Paul sends greetings from "the church" in Ephesus that meets in the home of Priscilla and Aquila as well as from "the churches in the province of Asia," which refers to the ekklesias raised up by Paul's co-workers. See Gordon Fee, *The First Epistle to the Corinthians*, 835; F.F. Bruce, *1 and 2 Corinthians*, 25, 161.

166. Paul's authorship of 1 Corinthians is undisputed. Paul Gardner, *1 Corinthians: Zondervan Exegetical Commentary on the New Testament* (Grand Rapids, MI: Zondervan, 2018), 18; Walter Elwell, et al., eds., *Tyndale Bible Dictionary*, 312-313.

167. Weima observes, "This change of travel plans is due to the growing tension between Paul and his Corinthian congregation which suggests to the apostle that he might not be very welcome in their midst." Personal correspondence with Jeffrey Weima, 1/6/24.

Throughout the letter, Paul employs irony and quotes the Corinthian's slogans along with his response.[168] He exhorts the church to humility, a virtue that Greeks regard as a fault, characteristic of slaves.[169] He also reminds the Corinthians of what he taught when he was among them ("do you not know" appears ten times in the epistle).[170]

Paul responds to the "tutors" who have alleged that the apostle will never return to Corinth to hold them accountable. He says they are arrogant ("puffed up") and informs them of his intent to come soon and deal with the situation directly (if the Lord wills). The apostle will evaluate their boastful speech and determine whether they possess legitimate spiritual power to back it up. He may also need to use a "rod" (a metaphor for discipline) when he is present.[171]

The apostle tells the church he plans to visit them after he leaves Ephesus. He will then visit the churches in Macedonia and return again to Corinth to collect the relief fund and bring it to Jerusalem.[172] Paul closes the letter by commending Timothy, whom he expects to visit the Corinthian assembly soon.[173] He also exhorts the believers to submit to Stephanas and some others during their present crisis.[174]

168. Examples of these slogans are found in 1 Corinthians 6:12-13. Paul's irony is exemplified in 1 Corinthians 4:10. These all point to the growing tension between Paul and his Corinthian converts.

169. *The NKJV Study Bible*, 1710.

170. The phrase "do you not know" or "don't you know" appears in chapters 3, 5, 6, and 9 in the NIV in the form of a question.

171. 1 Corinthians 4:18-21. *The ESV Study Bible*, 2196; *The NKJV Study Bible*, 1711.

172. 1 Corinthians 16:3-5; 2 Corinthians 1:15-16 (note that Jerusalem was in Judea). For a helpful discussion of Paul's Corinthian correspondence, see John Drane, *Paul: An Illustrated Documentary*, 78-89.

173. When he sent this letter, Paul expected to follow it with an in-person visit. Instead, he sent Timothy ahead of him and exhorted the Corinthian believers to receive him. 1 Corinthians 16:5-11; Acts 19:22. Given the tensions in the ekklesia, Paul was concerned that Timothy would be treated disrespectfully by some of the men in the church, since he was Paul's representative. Ben Witherington III, *Conflict and Community in Corinth*, 316; Gordon Fee, *The First Epistle to the Corinthians*, 821-822.

174. 1 Corinthians 16:15-16.

He sends greetings from the assemblies in Roman Asia,[175] Priscilla, Aquila, the church in Ephesus (which meets in Priscilla and Aquila's house),[176] and the brothers Paul is training.[177]

As he does in most of his letters, Paul weaves into his epistle imperial remarks demonstrating that God's ultimate reign will destroy every other kind of authority and ruler.[178] Paul ends the letter with a summary, the mark of a skilled speaker in the ancient world.[179]

1 Corinthians

Paul, called to be an apostle of Jesus Christ through the will of God, and our brother Sosthenes, to the assembly of God which is at Corinth—those who are sanctified in Christ Jesus, called saints, with all who call on the name of our Lord Jesus Christ in every place, both theirs and ours: Grace to you and peace from God our Father and the Lord Jesus Christ.

I always thank my God concerning you, for the grace of God which was given you in Christ Jesus; that in everything you were enriched in him, in all speech and all knowledge; even as the testimony of Christ was confirmed in you: so that you come behind in no gift; waiting for the revelation of our Lord Jesus Christ; who will also confirm you until the end, blameless

175. "The churches of Asia send you greetings," 1 Corinthians 16:19, ESV.

176. 1 Corinthians 16:19.

177. "All the brothers send you greetings…" 1 Corinthians 16:20, ESV. For an overview of Paul's Corinthian correspondence, see David deSilva, *An Introduction to the New Testament*, chap. 14; N.T. Wright and Michael Bird, *The New Testament in Its World*, chap. 21; Clinton Arnold, ed., *Zondervan Illustrated Bible Backgrounds Commentary*, 3:101-263.

178. Richard Horsley, ed., *Paul and Politics*, 105. For a detailed treatment of the imperial divine honors and the influence they had on Paul and the Corinthian church, see D. Clint Burnett, *Paul and Imperial Divine Honors*, chap. 4.

179. Craig Keener, *The IVP Bible Background Commentary: New Testament*, 497. I give more detail on what provoked Paul to write 1 Corinthians as well as provide a deep dive into the letter in my master class, *Platinum Soul: 1 Corinthians in 3D*. Refer to thedeeperchristianlife.com/classes.

in the day of our Lord Jesus Christ. God is faithful, through whom you were called into the fellowship of his Son, Jesus Christ, our Lord.

Now I beg you, brothers,[a] through the name of our Lord, Jesus Christ, that you all speak the same thing, and that there be no divisions among you, but that you be perfected together in the same mind and in the same judgment. For it has been reported to me concerning you, my brothers, by those who are from Chloe's household, that there are contentions among you.

Now I mean this, that each one of you says, "I follow Paul," "I follow Apollos," "I follow Cephas," and, "I follow Christ." Is Christ divided? Was Paul crucified for you? Or were you baptized into the name of Paul? I thank God that I baptized none of you, except Crispus and Gaius, so that no one should say that I had baptized you into my own name. (I also baptized the household of Stephanas; besides them, I don't know whether I baptized any other.)

For Christ sent me not to baptize, but to preach the Good News—not in wisdom of words, so that the cross of Christ wouldn't be made void. For the word of the cross is foolishness to those who are dying, but to us who are being saved it is the power of God. For it is written, "I will destroy the wisdom of the wise. I will bring the discernment of the discerning to nothing." Isaiah 29:14

Where is the wise? Where is the scribe? Where is the lawyer of this world? Hasn't God made foolish the wisdom of this world? For seeing that in the wisdom of God, the world through its wisdom didn't know God, it was God's good pleasure through the foolishness of the preaching to save those who believe.

For Jews ask for signs, Greeks seek after wisdom, but we preach Christ crucified: a stumbling block to Jews, and foolishness to Greeks, but to those who are called, both Jews and Greeks, Christ is the power of God and the wisdom of God; because the foolishness of God is wiser than men, and the weakness of God is stronger than men.

For you see your calling, brothers, that not many are wise according to the flesh, not many mighty, and not many noble; but God chose the foolish things of the world that he might put to shame those who are wise. God chose the weak things of the world that he might put to shame the things that are strong.

God chose the lowly things of the world, and the things that are despised, and the things that don't exist, that he might bring to nothing the things that exist, that no flesh should boast before God. Because of him, you are in Christ Jesus, who was made to us wisdom from God, and righteousness and sanctification, and redemption: that, as it is written, "He who boasts, let him boast in the Lord." Jeremiah 9:24

When I came to you, brothers, I didn't come with excellence of speech or of wisdom, proclaiming to you the testimony of God. For I determined not to know anything among you except Jesus Christ and him crucified. I was with you in weakness, in fear, and in much trembling. My speech and my preaching were not in persuasive words of human wisdom, but in demonstration of the Spirit and of power, that your faith wouldn't stand in the wisdom of men, but in the power of God.

We speak wisdom, however, among those who are full grown, yet a wisdom not of this world nor of the rulers of this world who are coming to nothing. But we speak God's wisdom in a mystery, the wisdom that has been hidden, which God foreordained before the worlds for our glory, which none of the rulers of this world has known. For had they known it, they wouldn't have crucified the Lord of glory. But as it is written, "Things which an eye didn't see, and an ear didn't hear, which didn't enter into the heart of man, these God has prepared for those who love him." Isaiah 64:4

But to us, God revealed them through the Spirit. For the Spirit searches all things, yes, the deep things of God. For who among men knows the things of a man, except the spirit of the man, which is in him? Even so, no one knows the things of God, except God's Spirit. But we received not the spirit of the world, but the Spirit which is from God, that we might know the things that were freely given to us by God. We also speak these things, not in words which man's wisdom teaches, but which the Holy Spirit teaches, comparing spiritual things with spiritual things.

Now the natural man doesn't receive the things of God's Spirit, for they are foolishness to him, and he can't know them, because they are spiritually discerned. But he who is spiritual discerns all things, and he himself is judged by no one. "For who has known the mind of the Lord, that he should instruct him?" Isaiah 40:13 But we have Christ's mind.

Brothers, I couldn't speak to you as to spiritual, but as to fleshly, as to babies in Christ. I fed you with milk, not with meat; for you weren't yet ready. Indeed, you aren't ready even now, for you are still fleshly. For insofar as there is jealousy, strife, and factions among you, aren't you fleshly, and don't you walk in the ways of men?

For when one says, "I follow Paul," and another, "I follow Apollos," aren't you fleshly? Who then is Apollos, and who is Paul, but servants through whom you believed, and each as the Lord gave to him? I planted. Apollos watered. But God gave the increase. So then neither he who plants is anything, nor he who waters, but God who gives the increase. Now he who plants and he who waters are the same, but each will receive his own reward according to his own labor. For we are God's fellow workers. You are God's farming, God's building.

According to the grace of God which was given to me, as a wise master builder I laid a foundation, and another builds on it. But let each man be careful how he builds on it. For no one can lay any other foundation than that which has been laid, which is Jesus Christ. But if anyone builds on the foundation with gold, silver, costly stones, wood, hay, or stubble, each man's work will be revealed. For the Day will declare it, because it is revealed in fire; and the fire itself will test what sort of work each man's work is. If any man's work remains which he built on it, he will receive a reward. If any man's work is burned, he will suffer loss, but he himself will be saved, but as through fire.

Don't you know that you are a temple of God, and that God's Spirit lives in you? If anyone destroys God's temple, God will destroy him; for God's temple is holy, which you are. Let no one deceive himself. If anyone thinks that he is wise among you in this world, let him become a fool, that he may become wise. For the wisdom of this world is foolishness with God.

For it is written, "He has taken the wise in their craftiness." Job 5:13 And again, "The Lord knows the reasoning of the wise, that it is worthless." Psalm 94:11 Therefore let no one boast in men. For all things are yours, whether Paul, or Apollos, or Cephas, or the world, or life, or death, or things present, or things to come. All are yours, and you are Christ's, and Christ is God's.

So let a man think of us as Christ's servants, and stewards of God's mysteries. Here, moreover, it is required of stewards that they be found faithful. But with me it is a very small thing that I should be judged by you, or by man's judgment. Yes, I don't judge my own self. For I know nothing against myself. Yet I am not justified by this, but he who judges me is the Lord. Therefore judge nothing before the time, until the Lord comes, who will both bring to light the hidden things of darkness, and reveal the counsels of the hearts. Then each man will get his praise from God.

Now these things, brothers, I have in a figure transferred to myself and Apollos for your sakes, that in us you might learn not to think beyond the things which are written, that none of you be puffed up against one another. For who makes you different? And what do you have that you didn't receive? But if you did receive it, why do you boast as if you had not received it? You are already filled. You have already become rich.

You have come to reign without us. Yes, and I wish that you did reign, that we also might reign with you. For I think that God has displayed us, the apostles, last of all, like men sentenced to death. For we are made a spectacle to the world, both to angels and men. We are fools for Christ's sake, but you are wise in Christ.

We are weak, but you are strong. You have honor, but we have dishonor. Even to this present hour we hunger, thirst, are naked, are beaten, and have no certain dwelling place. We toil, working with our own hands. When people curse us, we bless. Being persecuted, we endure. Being defamed, we entreat. We are made as the filth of the world, the dirt wiped off by all, even until now.

I don't write these things to shame you, but to admonish you as my beloved children. For though you have ten thousand tutors in Christ, you don't have many fathers. For in Christ Jesus, I became your father through the Good News.

I beg you therefore, be imitators of me. Because of this I have sent Timothy to you, who is my beloved and faithful child in the Lord, who will remind you of my ways which are in Christ, even as I teach everywhere in every assembly. Now some are puffed up, as though I were not coming to you. But I will come to you shortly, if the Lord is willing. And I will know, not the word of those who are puffed up, but the power. For God's Kingdom is not in word, but in power. What do you want? Shall I come to you with a rod, or in love and a spirit of gentleness?

It is actually reported that there is sexual immorality among you, and such sexual immorality as is not even named among the Gentiles, that one has his father's wife. You are arrogant, and didn't mourn instead, that he who had done this deed might be removed from among you.

For I most certainly, as being absent in body but present in spirit, have already, as though I were present, judged him who has done this thing. In the name of our Lord Jesus Christ, you being gathered together, and my spirit, with the power of our Lord Jesus Christ, are to deliver such a one to Satan for the destruction of the flesh, that the spirit may be saved in the day of the Lord Jesus.

Your boasting is not good. Don't you know that a little yeast leavens the whole lump? Purge out the old yeast, that you may be a new lump, even as you are unleavened. For indeed Christ, our Passover, has been sacrificed in our place. Therefore let's keep the feast, not with old yeast, neither with the yeast of malice and wickedness, but with the unleavened bread of sincerity and truth.

I wrote to you in my letter to have no company with sexual sinners; yet not at all meaning with the sexual sinners of this world, or with the covetous and extortionists, or with idolaters; for then you would have to leave the world. But as it is, I wrote to you not to associate with anyone who is called a brother who is a sexual sinner, or covetous, or an idolater, or a slanderer, or a drunkard, or an extortionist.

Don't even eat with such a person. For what do I have to do with also judging those who are outside? Don't you judge those who are within? But those who are outside, God judges. "Put away the wicked man from among yourselves." Deuteronomy 17:7; 19:19; 21:21; 22:21; 24:7

Dare any of you, having a matter against his neighbor, go to law before the unrighteous, and not before the saints? Don't you know that the saints will judge the world? And if the world is judged by you, are you unworthy to judge the smallest matters? Don't you know that we will judge angels? How much more, things that pertain to this life? If then you have to judge things pertaining to this life, do you set them to judge who are of no account in the assembly? I say this to move you to shame. Isn't there even one wise man among you who would be able to decide between his brothers? But brother goes to law with brother, and that before unbelievers!

Therefore it is already altogether a defect in you, that you have lawsuits one with another. Why not rather be wronged? Why not rather be defrauded? No, but you yourselves do wrong and defraud, and that against your brothers. Or don't you know that the unrighteous will not inherit God's Kingdom? Don't be deceived. Neither the sexually immoral, nor idolaters, nor adulterers, nor male prostitutes, nor homosexuals, nor thieves, nor covetous, nor drunkards, nor slanderers, nor extortionists, will inherit God's Kingdom. Some of you were such, but you were washed. But you were sanctified. But you were justified in the name of the Lord Jesus, and in the Spirit of our God.

"All things are lawful for me," but not all things are expedient. "All things are lawful for me," but I will not be brought under the power of anything. "Foods for the belly, and the belly for foods," but God will bring to nothing both it and them. But the body is not for sexual immorality, but for the Lord; and the Lord for the body.

Now God raised up the Lord, and will also raise us up by his power. Don't you know that your bodies are members of Christ? Shall I then take the members of Christ and make them members of a prostitute? May it never be! Or don't you know that he who is joined to a prostitute is one body? For, "The two," he says, "will become one flesh." Genesis 2:24 But he who is joined to the Lord is one spirit.

Flee sexual immorality! "Every sin that a man does is outside the body," but he who commits sexual immorality sins against his own body. Or don't you know that your body is a temple of the Holy Spirit who is in you, whom you have from God? You are not your own, for you were bought with a price. Therefore glorify God in your body and in your spirit, which are God's.

Now concerning the things about which you wrote to me: it is good for a man not to touch a woman. But, because of sexual immoralities, let each man have his own wife, and let each woman have her own husband.

Let the husband give his wife the affection owed her,[b] and likewise also the wife her husband. The wife doesn't have authority over her own body, but the husband. Likewise also the husband doesn't have authority over his own body, but the wife. Don't deprive one another, unless it is by consent for a season, that you may give yourselves to fasting and prayer, and may be together again, that Satan doesn't tempt you because of your lack of self-control.

But this I say by way of concession, not of commandment. Yet I wish that all men were like me. However each man has his own gift from God, one of this kind, and another of that kind. But I say to the unmarried and to widows, it is good for them if they remain even as I am. But if they don't have self-control, let them marry. For it's better to marry than to burn. But to the married I command—not I, but the Lord—that the wife not leave her husband (but if she departs, let her remain unmarried, or else be reconciled to her husband), and that the husband not leave his wife.

But to the rest I—not the Lord—say, if any brother has an unbelieving wife, and she is content to live with him, let him not leave her. The woman who has an unbelieving husband, and he is content to live with her, let her not leave her husband. For the unbelieving husband is sanctified in the wife, and the unbelieving wife is sanctified in the husband. Otherwise your children would be unclean, but now they are holy.

Yet if the unbeliever departs, let there be separation. The brother or the sister is not under bondage in such cases, but God has called us in peace. For how do you know, wife, whether you will save your husband? Or how do you know, husband, whether you will save your wife? Only, as the Lord has distributed to each man, as God has called each, so let him walk. So I command in all the assemblies.

Was anyone called having been circumcised? Let him not become uncircumcised. Has anyone been called in uncircumcision? Let him not be circumcised. Circumcision is nothing, and uncircumcision is nothing, but the keeping of the commandments of God. Let each man stay in that calling in which he was called.

Were you called being a bondservant? Don't let that bother you, but if you get an opportunity to become free, use it. For he who was called in the Lord being a bondservant is the Lord's free man. Likewise he who was called being free is Christ's bondservant. You were bought with a price. Don't become bondservants of men. Brothers, let each man, in whatever condition he was called, stay in that condition with God.

Now concerning virgins, I have no commandment from the Lord, but I give my judgment as one who has obtained mercy from the Lord to be trustworthy. Therefore I think that because of the distress that is on us, that it's good for a man to remain as he is. Are you bound to a wife? Don't seek to be freed. Are you free from a wife? Don't seek a wife. But if you marry, you have not sinned. If a virgin marries, she has not sinned. Yet such will have oppression in the flesh, and I want to spare you.

But I say this, brothers: the time is short, that from now on, both those who have wives may be as though they had none; and those who weep, as though they didn't weep; and those who rejoice, as though they didn't rejoice; and those who buy, as though they didn't possess; and those who use the world, as not using it to the fullest. For the mode of this world passes away. But I desire to have you to be free from cares.

He who is unmarried is concerned for the things of the Lord, how he may please the Lord; but he who is married is concerned about the things of the world, how he may please his wife. There is also a difference between a wife and a virgin. The unmarried woman cares about the things of the Lord, that she may be holy both in body and in spirit. But she who is married cares about the things of the world—how she may please her husband.

This I say for your own profit; not that I may ensnare you, but for that which is appropriate, and that you may attend to the Lord without distraction. But if any man thinks that he is behaving inappropriately toward his virgin, if she is past the flower of her age, and if need so requires, let him do what he desires. He doesn't sin. Let them marry.

But he who stands steadfast in his heart, having no urgency, but has power over his own will, and has determined in his own heart to keep his own virgin, does well. So then both he who gives his own virgin in marriage does well, and he who doesn't give her in marriage does better. A wife is bound by law for as long as her husband lives; but if the husband is dead, she is free to be married to whomever she desires, only in the Lord. But she is happier if she stays as she is, in my judgment, and I think that I also have God's Spirit.

Now concerning things sacrificed to idols: We know that we all have knowledge. Knowledge puffs up, but love builds up. But if anyone thinks that he knows anything, he doesn't yet know as he ought to know. But if anyone loves God, the same is known by him. Therefore concerning the eating of things sacrificed to idols, we know that no idol is anything in the world, and that there is no other God but one. For though there are things that are called "gods," whether in the heavens or on earth; as there are many "gods" and many "lords"; yet to us there is one God, the Father, of whom are all things, and we for him; and one Lord, Jesus Christ, through whom are all things, and we live through him. However, that knowledge isn't in all men.

But some, with consciousness of the idol until now, eat as of a thing sacrificed to an idol, and their conscience, being weak, is defiled. But food will not commend us to God. For neither, if we don't eat, are we the worse; nor, if we eat, are we the better. But be careful that by no means does this liberty of yours become a stumbling block to the weak. For if a man sees you who have knowledge sitting in an idol's temple, won't his conscience, if he is weak, be emboldened to eat things sacrificed to idols? And through your knowledge, he who is weak perishes, the brother for whose sake Christ died.

Thus, sinning against the brothers, and wounding their conscience when it is weak, you sin against Christ. Therefore if food causes my brother to stumble, I will eat no meat forever more, that I don't cause my brother to stumble. Am I not free? Am I not an apostle? Haven't I seen Jesus Christ, our Lord? Aren't you my work in the Lord? If to others I am not an apostle, yet at least I am to you; for you are the seal of my apostleship in the Lord.

My defense to those who examine me is this: Have we no right to eat and to drink? Have we no right to take along a wife who is a believer, even as the rest of the apostles, and the brothers of the Lord, and Cephas? Or have only Barnabas and I no right to not work? What soldier ever serves at his own expense? Who plants a vineyard, and doesn't eat of its fruit? Or who feeds a flock, and doesn't drink from the flock's milk? Do I speak these things according to the ways of men? Or doesn't the law also say the same thing? For it is written in the law of Moses, "You shall not muzzle an ox while it treads out the grain." Deuteronomy 25:4 Is it for the oxen that God cares, or does he say it assuredly for our sake?

Yes, it was written for our sake, because he who plows ought to plow in hope, and he who threshes in hope should partake of his hope. If we sowed to you spiritual things, is it a great thing if we reap your fleshly things? If others partake of this right over you, don't we yet more?

Nevertheless we didn't use this right, but we bear all things, that we may cause no hindrance to the Good News of Christ. Don't you know that those who serve around sacred things eat from the things of the temple, and those who wait on the altar have their portion with the altar? Even so the Lord ordained that those who proclaim the Good News should live from the Good News.

But I have used none of these things, and I don't write these things that it may be done so in my case; for I would rather die, than that anyone should make my boasting void. For if I preach the Good News, I have nothing to boast about; for necessity is laid on me; but woe is to me if I don't preach the Good News. For if I do this of my own will, I have a reward. But if not of my own will, I have a stewardship entrusted to me.

What then is my reward? That when I preach the Good News, I may present the Good News of Christ without charge, so as not to abuse my authority in the Good News. For though I was free from all, I brought myself under bondage to all, that I might gain the more.

To the Jews I became as a Jew, that I might gain Jews; to those who are under the law, as under the law,[c] that I might gain those who are under the law; to those who are without law, as without law (not being without law toward God, but under law toward Christ), that I might win those who are without law. To the weak I became as weak, that I might gain the weak. I have become all things to all men, that I may by all means save some. Now I do this for the sake of the Good News, that I may be a joint partaker of it.

Don't you know that those who run in a race all run, but one receives the prize? Run like that, that you may win. Every man who strives in the games exercises self-control in all things. Now they do it to receive a corruptible crown, but we an incorruptible. I therefore run like that, not aimlessly. I fight like that, not beating the air, but I beat my body and bring it into submission, lest by any means, after I have preached to others, I myself should be rejected.

Now I would not have you ignorant, brothers, that our fathers were all under the cloud, and all passed through the sea; and were all baptized into Moses in the cloud and in the sea; and all ate the same spiritual food; and all drank the same spiritual drink.

For they drank of a spiritual rock that followed them, and the rock was Christ. However with most of them, God was not well pleased, for they were overthrown in the wilderness. Now these things were our examples, to the intent we should not lust after evil things, as they also lusted. Don't be idolaters, as some of them were.

As it is written, "The people sat down to eat and drink, and rose up to play." Exodus 32:6 Let's not commit sexual immorality, as some of them committed, and in one day twenty-three thousand fell. Let's not test Christ,[d] as some of them tested, and perished by the serpents. Don't grumble, as some of them also grumbled, and perished by the destroyer.

Now all these things happened to them by way of example, and they were written for our admonition, on whom the ends of the ages have come. Therefore let him who thinks he stands be careful that he doesn't fall.

No temptation has taken you except what is common to man. God is faithful, who will not allow you to be tempted above what you are able, but will with the temptation also make the way of escape, that you may be able to endure it.

Therefore, my beloved, flee from idolatry. I speak as to wise men. Judge what I say. The cup of blessing which we bless, isn't it a sharing of the blood of Christ? The bread which we break, isn't it a sharing of the body of Christ? Because there is one loaf of bread, we, who are many, are one body; for we all partake of the one loaf of bread. Consider Israel according to the flesh. Don't those who eat the sacrifices participate in the altar?

What am I saying then? That a thing sacrificed to idols is anything, or that an idol is anything? But I say that the things which the Gentiles sacrifice, they sacrifice to demons, and not to God, and I don't desire that you would have fellowship with demons. You can't both drink the cup of the Lord and the cup of demons. You can't both partake of the table of the Lord and of the table of demons. Or do we provoke the Lord to jealousy? Are we stronger than he?

"All things are lawful for me," but not all things are profitable. "All things are lawful for me," but not all things build up. Let no one seek his own, but each one his neighbor's good. Whatever is sold in the butcher shop, eat, asking no question for the sake of conscience, for "the earth is the Lord's, and its fullness." Psalm 24:1

But if one of those who don't believe invites you to a meal, and you are inclined to go, eat whatever is set before you, asking no questions for the sake of conscience. But if anyone says to you, "This was offered to idols," don't eat it for the sake of the one who told you, and for the sake of conscience. For "the earth is the Lord's, with all its fullness."

Conscience, I say, not your own, but the other's conscience. For why is my liberty judged by another conscience? If I partake with thankfulness, why am I denounced for something I give thanks for? Whether therefore you eat, or drink, or whatever you do, do all to the glory of God. Give no occasion for stumbling, whether to Jews, or to Greeks, or to the assembly of God; even as I also please all men in all things, not seeking my own profit, but the profit of the many, that they may be saved. Be imitators of me, even as I also am of Christ.

Now I praise you, brothers, that you remember me in all things, and hold firm the traditions, even as I delivered them to you. But I would have you know that the head[e] of every man is Christ, and the head[f] of the woman is man, and the head[g] of Christ is God.

Every man praying or prophesying, having his head covered, dishonors his head. But every woman praying or prophesying with her head uncovered dishonors her head. For it is one and the same thing as if she were shaved. For if a woman is not covered, let her hair also be cut off. But if it is shameful for a woman to have her hair cut off or be shaved, let her be covered. For a man indeed ought not to have his head covered, because he is the image and glory of God, but the woman is the glory of the man. For man is not from woman, but woman from man; for man wasn't created for the woman, but woman for the man. For this cause the woman ought to have authority over her own head, because of the angels.

Nevertheless, neither is the woman independent of the man, nor the man independent of the woman, in the Lord. For as woman came from man, so a man also comes through a woman; but all things are from God. Judge for yourselves. Is it appropriate that a woman pray to God unveiled? Doesn't even nature itself teach you that if a man has long hair, it is a dishonor to him? But if a woman has long hair, it is a glory to her, for her hair is given to her for a covering. But if any man seems to be contentious, we have no such custom, neither do God's assemblies.

But in giving you this command, I don't praise you, that you come together not for the better but for the worse. For first of all, when you come together in the assembly, I hear that divisions exist among you, and I partly believe it. For there also must be factions among you, that those who are approved may be revealed among you.

When therefore you assemble yourselves together, it is not the Lord's supper that you eat. For in your eating each one takes his own supper first. One is hungry, and another is drunken. What, don't you have houses to eat and to drink in? Or do you despise God's assembly and put them to shame who don't have enough? What shall I tell you? Shall I praise you? In this I don't praise you.

For I received from the Lord that which also I delivered to you, that the Lord Jesus on the night in which he was betrayed took bread. When he had given thanks, he broke it and said, "Take, eat. This is my body, which is broken for you. Do this in memory of me." In the same way he also took the cup, after supper, saying, "This cup is the new covenant in my blood. Do this, as often as you drink, in memory of me."

For as often as you eat this bread and drink this cup, you proclaim the Lord's death until he comes. Therefore whoever eats this bread or drinks the Lord's cup in a way unworthy of the Lord will be guilty of the body and the blood of the Lord. But let a man examine himself, and so let him eat of the bread, and drink of the cup. For he who eats and drinks in an unworthy way eats and drinks judgment to himself if he doesn't discern the Lord's body. For this cause many among you are weak and sickly, and not a few sleep. For if we discerned ourselves, we wouldn't be judged.

But when we are judged, we are punished by the Lord, that we may not be condemned with the world. Therefore, my brothers, when you come together to eat, wait for one another. But if anyone is hungry, let him eat at home, lest your coming together be for judgment. The rest I will set in order whenever I come.

Now concerning spiritual things, brothers, I don't want you to be ignorant. You know that when you were heathen,[h] you were led away to those mute idols, however you might be led. Therefore I make known to you that no man speaking by God's Spirit says, "Jesus is accursed." No one can say, "Jesus is Lord," but by the Holy Spirit.

Now there are various kinds of gifts, but the same Spirit. There are various kinds of service, and the same Lord. There are various kinds of workings, but the same God, who works all things in all. But to each one is given the manifestation of the Spirit for the profit of all. For to one is given through the Spirit the word of wisdom, and to another the word of knowledge, according to the same Spirit; to another faith, by the same Spirit; and to another gifts of healings, by the same Spirit; and to another workings of miracles; and to another prophecy; and to another discerning of spirits; to another different kinds of languages; and to another the interpretation of languages. But the one and the same Spirit produces all of these, distributing to each one separately as he desires.

For as the body is one, and has many members, and all the members of the body, being many, are one body; so also is Christ. For in one Spirit we were all baptized into one body, whether Jews or Greeks, whether bond or free; and were all given to drink into one Spirit. For the body is not one member, but many.

If the foot would say, "Because I'm not the hand, I'm not part of the body," it is not therefore not part of the body. If the ear would say, "Because I'm not the eye, I'm not part of the body," it's not therefore not part of the body. If the whole body were an eye, where would the hearing be? If the whole were hearing, where would the smelling be?

But now God has set the members, each one of them, in the body, just as he desired. If they were all one member, where would the body be? But now they are many members, but one body. The eye can't tell the hand, "I have no need for you," or again the head to the feet, "I have no need for you." No, much rather, those members of the body which seem to be weaker are necessary.

Those parts of the body which we think to be less honorable, on those we bestow more abundant honor; and our unpresentable parts have more abundant propriety; whereas our presentable parts have no such need. But God composed the body together, giving more abundant honor to the inferior part, that there should be no division in the body, but that the members should have the same care for one another. When one member suffers, all the members suffer with it. When one member is honored, all the members rejoice with it.

Now you are the body of Christ, and members individually. God has set some in the assembly: first apostles, second prophets, third teachers, then miracle workers, then gifts of healings, helps, governments, and various kinds of languages. Are all apostles? Are all prophets? Are all teachers? Are all miracle workers? Do all have gifts of healings? Do all speak with various languages? Do all interpret? But earnestly desire the best gifts. Moreover, I show a most excellent way to you.

If I speak with the languages of men and of angels, but don't have love, I have become sounding brass, or a clanging cymbal. If I have the gift of prophecy, and know all mysteries and all knowledge; and if I have all faith, so as to remove mountains, but don't have love, I am nothing. If I give away all my goods to feed the poor, and if I give my body to be burned, but don't have love, it profits me nothing.

Love is patient and is kind. Love doesn't envy. Love doesn't brag, is not proud, doesn't behave itself inappropriately, doesn't seek its own way, is not provoked, takes no account of evil; doesn't rejoice in unrighteousness, but rejoices with the truth; bears all things, believes all things, hopes all things, and endures all things.

Love never fails. But where there are prophecies, they will be done away with. Where there are various languages, they will cease. Where there is knowledge, it will be done away with. For we know in part and we prophesy in part; but when that which is complete has come, then that which is partial will be done away with.

When I was a child, I spoke as a child, I felt as a child, I thought as a child. Now that I have become a man, I have put away childish things. For now we see in a mirror, dimly, but then face to face. Now I know in part, but then I will know fully, even as I was also fully known. But now faith, hope, and love remain—these three. The greatest of these is love.

Follow after love and earnestly desire spiritual gifts, but especially that you may prophesy. For he who speaks in another language speaks not to men, but to God; for no one understands; but in the Spirit he speaks mysteries. But he who prophesies speaks to men for their edification, exhortation, and consolation.

He who speaks in another language edifies himself, but he who prophesies edifies the assembly. Now I desire to have you all speak with other languages, but rather that you would prophesy. For he is greater who prophesies than he who speaks with other languages, unless he interprets, that the assembly may be built up.

But now, brothers,[1] if I come to you speaking with other languages, what would I profit you, unless I speak to you either by way of revelation, or of knowledge, or of prophesying, or of teaching?

Even things without life, giving a voice, whether pipe or harp, if they didn't give a distinction in the sounds, how would it be known what is piped or harped? For if the trumpet gave an uncertain sound, who would prepare himself for war? So also you, unless you uttered by the tongue words easy to understand, how would it be known what is spoken? For you would be speaking into the air.

There are, it may be, so many kinds of languages in the world, and none of them is without meaning. If then I don't know the meaning of the language, I would be to him who speaks a foreigner, and he who speaks would be a foreigner to me.

So also you, since you are zealous for spiritual gifts, seek that you may abound to the building up of the assembly. Therefore let him who speaks in another language pray that he may interpret. For if I pray in another language, my spirit prays, but my understanding is unfruitful.

What is it then? I will pray with the spirit, and I will pray with the understanding also. I will sing with the spirit, and I will sing with the understanding also. Otherwise if you bless with the spirit, how will he who fills the place of the unlearned say the "Amen" at your giving of thanks, seeing he doesn't know what you say?

For you most certainly give thanks well, but the other person is not built up. I thank my God, I speak with other languages more than you all. However in the assembly I would rather speak five words with my understanding, that I might instruct others also, than ten thousand words in another language.

Brothers, don't be children in thoughts, yet in malice be babies, but in thoughts be mature. In the law it is written, "By men of strange languages and by the lips of strangers I will speak to this people. They won't even hear me that way, says the Lord." Isaiah 28:11-12

Therefore other languages are for a sign, not to those who believe, but to the unbelieving; but prophesying is for a sign, not to the unbelieving, but to those who believe. If therefore the whole assembly is assembled together and all speak with other languages, and unlearned or unbelieving people come in, won't they say that you are crazy?

But if all prophesy, and someone unbelieving or unlearned comes in, he is reproved by all, and he is judged by all. And thus the secrets of his heart are revealed. So he will fall down on his face and worship God, declaring that God is among you indeed.

What is it then, brothers? When you come together, each one of you has a psalm, has a teaching, has a revelation, has another language, or has an interpretation. Let all things be done to build each other up.

If any man speaks in another language, let it be two, or at the most three, and in turn; and let one interpret. But if there is no interpreter, let him keep silent in the assembly, and let him speak to himself, and to God. Let the prophets speak, two or three, and let the others discern. But if a revelation is made to another sitting by, let the first keep silent. For you all can prophesy one by one, that all may learn, and all may be exhorted.

The spirits of the prophets are subject to the prophets, for God is not a God of confusion, but of peace, as in all the assemblies of the saints. Let the wives be quiet in the assemblies, for it has not been permitted for them to be talking except in submission, as the law also says, Deuteronomy 27:9 if they desire to learn anything. "Let them ask their own husbands at home, for it is shameful for a wife to be talking in the assembly." What!? Was it from you that the word of God went out? Or did it come to you alone?

If any man thinks himself to be a prophet, or spiritual, let him recognize the things which I write to you, that they are the commandment of the Lord. But if anyone is ignorant, let him be ignorant. Therefore, brothers, desire earnestly to prophesy, and don't forbid speaking with other languages. Let all things be done decently and in order. Now I declare to you, brothers, the Good News which I preached to you, which also you received, in which you also stand, by which also you are saved, if you hold firmly the word which I preached to you—unless you believed in vain.

For I delivered to you first of all that which I also received: that Christ died for our sins according to the Scriptures, that he was buried, that he was raised on the third day according to the Scriptures, and that he appeared to Cephas, then to the twelve. Then he appeared to over five hundred brothers at once, most of whom remain until now, but some have also fallen asleep.

Then he appeared to James, then to all the apostles, and last of all, as to the child born at the wrong time, he appeared to me also. For I am the least of the apostles, who is not worthy to be called an apostle, because I persecuted the assembly of God. But by the grace of God I am what I am. His grace which was given to me was not futile, but I worked more than all of them; yet not I, but the grace of God which was with me. Whether then it is I or they, so we preach, and so you believed.

Now if Christ is preached, that he has been raised from the dead, how do some among you say that there is no resurrection of the dead? But if there is no resurrection of the dead, neither has Christ been raised. If Christ has not been raised, then our preaching is in vain, and your faith also is in vain.

Yes, we are also found false witnesses of God, because we testified about God that he raised up Christ, whom he didn't raise up, if it is so that the dead are not raised. For if the dead aren't raised, neither has Christ been raised. If Christ has not been raised, your faith is vain; you are still in your sins. Then they also who are fallen asleep in Christ have perished. If we have only hoped in Christ in this life, we are of all men most pitiable.

But now Christ has been raised from the dead. He became the first fruit of those who are asleep. For since death came by man, the resurrection of the dead also came by man. For as in Adam all die, so also in Christ all will be made alive. But each in his own order: Christ the first fruits, then those who are Christ's, at his coming.

Then the end comes, when he will deliver up the Kingdom to God, even the Father, when he will have abolished all rule and all authority and power. For he must reign until he has put all his enemies under his feet. The last enemy that will be abolished is death. For, "He put all things in subjection under his feet." <u>Psalm 8:6</u> But when he says, "All things are put in subjection," it is evident that he is excepted who subjected all things to him.

When all things have been subjected to him, then the Son will also himself be subjected to him who subjected all things to him, that God may be all in all. Or else what will they do who are baptized for the dead? If the dead aren't raised at all, why then are they baptized for the dead? Why do we also stand in jeopardy every hour? I affirm, by the boasting in you which I have in Christ Jesus our Lord, I die daily.

If I fought with animals at Ephesus for human purposes, what does it profit me? If the dead are not raised, then "let's eat and drink, for tomorrow we die." <u>Isaiah 22:13</u> Don't be deceived! "Evil companionships corrupt good morals." Wake up righteously, and don't sin, for some have no knowledge of God. I say this to your shame.

But someone will say, "How are the dead raised?" and, "With what kind of body do they come?" You foolish one, that which you yourself sow is not made alive unless it dies. That which you sow, you don't sow the body that will be, but a bare grain, maybe of wheat, or of some other kind.

But God gives it a body even as it pleased him, and to each seed a body of its own. All flesh is not the same flesh, but there is one flesh of men, another flesh of animals, another of fish, and another of birds. There are also celestial bodies and terrestrial bodies; but the glory of the celestial differs from that of the terrestrial.

There is one glory of the sun, another glory of the moon, and another glory of the stars; for one star differs from another star in glory. So also is the resurrection of the dead. The body is sown perishable; it is raised imperishable. It is sown in dishonor; it is raised in glory. It is sown in weakness; it is raised in power. It is sown a natural body; it is raised a spiritual body. There is a natural body and there is also a spiritual body.

So also it is written, "The first man, Adam, became a living soul." <u>Genesis 2:7</u> The last Adam became a life-giving spirit. However that which is spiritual isn't first, but that which is natural, then that which is spiritual. The first man is of the earth, made of dust. The second man is the Lord from heaven.

As is the one made of dust, such are those who are also made of dust; and as is the heavenly, such are they also that are heavenly. As we have borne the image of those made of dust, let's[j] also bear the image of the heavenly. Now I say this, brothers,[k] that flesh and blood can't inherit God's Kingdom; neither does the perishable inherit imperishable.

Behold,[l] I tell you a mystery. We will not all sleep, but we will all be changed, in a moment, in the twinkling of an eye, at the last trumpet. For the trumpet will sound and the dead will be raised incorruptible, and we will be changed. For this perishable body must become imperishable, and this mortal must put on immortality. But when this perishable body will have become imperishable, and this mortal will have put on immortality, then what is written will happen: "Death is swallowed up in victory." Isaiah 25:8 "Death, where is your sting? Hades,[m] where is your victory?" Hosea 13:14 The sting of death is sin, and the power of sin is the law. But thanks be to God, who gives us the victory through our Lord Jesus Christ. Therefore, my beloved brothers, be steadfast, immovable, always abounding in the Lord's work, because you know that your labor is not in vain in the Lord.

Now concerning the collection for the saints, as I commanded the assemblies of Galatia, you do likewise. On the first day of every week, let each one of you save, as he may prosper, that no collections are made when I come.

When I arrive, I will send whoever you approve with letters to carry your gracious gift to Jerusalem. If it is appropriate for me to go also, they will go with me. But I will come to you when I have passed through Macedonia, for I am passing through Macedonia.

But with you it may be that I will stay, or even winter, that you may send me on my journey wherever I go. For I do not wish to see you now in passing, but I hope to stay a while with you, if the Lord permits. But I will stay at Ephesus until Pentecost, for a great and effective door has opened to me, and there are many adversaries.

Now if Timothy comes, see that he is with you without fear, for he does the work of the Lord, as I also do. Therefore let no one despise him. But set him forward on his journey in peace, that he may come to me; for I expect him with the brothers. Now concerning Apollos, the brother, I strongly urged him to come to you with the brothers; and it was not at all his desire to come now; but he will come when he has an opportunity. Watch! Stand firm in the faith! Be courageous! Be strong! Let all that you do be done in love.

Now I beg you, brothers—you know the house of Stephanas, that it is the first fruits of Achaia, and that they have set themselves to serve the saints—that you also be in subjection to such, and to everyone who helps in the work and labors. I rejoice at the coming of

Stephanas, Fortunatus, and Achaicus; for that which was lacking on your part, they supplied. For they refreshed my spirit and yours. Therefore acknowledge those who are like that.

The assemblies of Asia greet you. Aquila and Priscilla greet you much in the Lord, together with the assembly that is in their house. All the brothers greet you. Greet one another with a holy kiss.

This greeting is by me, Paul, with my own hand. If any man doesn't love the Lord Jesus Christ, let him be cursed.[n] Come, Lord![o] The grace of the Lord Jesus Christ be with you. My love to all of you in Christ Jesus. Amen.

a. 1:10 The word for "brothers" here and where context allows may also be correctly translated "brothers and sisters" or "siblings."

b. 7:3 NU and TR have "what is owed her" instead of "the affection owed her."

c. 9:20 NU adds: though I myself am not under the law.

d. 10:9 NU reads "the Lord" instead of "Christ."

e. 11:3 or, origin.

f. 11:3 or, origin.

g. 11:3 or, origin.

h. 12:2 or Gentiles.

i. 14:6 The word for "brothers" here and where context allows may also be correctly translated "brothers and sisters" or "siblings."

j. 15:49 NU, TR read "we will" instead of "let's."

k. 15:50 The word for "brothers" here and where context allows may also be correctly translated "brothers and sisters" or "siblings."

l. 15:51 "Behold," from "ἰδοὺ," means look at, take notice, observe, see, or gaze at. It is often used as an interjection.

m. 15:55 or, Hell.

n. 16:22 Greek: anathema.

o. 16:22 Aramaic: Maranatha!

Stephanas, Fortunatus, and Achaicus bring Paul's letter to the Corinthians.[180] Shortly after, Timothy (along with Erastus) makes his way to Corinth.[181]

A Church Is Transplanted in Rome

When Paul gets wind of the news that the ban against the Jews is no longer in force and they can return to Rome, he sends Priscilla and Aquila back to the Eternal City.[182] Because there is still a strong backlash against the Jews in Rome, Priscilla and Aquila risk their necks for the apostle by returning to the city.[183]

180. 1 Corinthians 16:15-18 makes it plausible to surmise that Paul entrusted the letter to Stephanas and his company to bring it back to Corinth on their return, as well as oversee the church's response to it. John Barry, et al., "Stephanas," *The Lexham Bible Dictionary;* F.F. Bruce, *1 and 2 Corinthians,* 24.

181. I agree with Witherington who says,"the wording suggests that Timothy is not the bearer of this letter...." Ben Witherington III, *Conflict and Community in Corinth*, 316, n. 9. Instead, the three Corinthian brothers carried the letter back to Corinth. Paul appears to have hoped the letter would arrive *before* Timothy came to Corinth (1 Corinthians 16:10). Weima believes the letter *did* arrive before Timothy made it to Corinth. Personal correspondence with Jeffrey Weima, 1/6/24. Guthrie agrees that Stephanas, Fortunatus, and Achaicus delivered the letter to the Corinthians. Donald Guthrie, *The Apostles,* 204.

182. Paul sends Priscilla and Aquila ahead of him to Rome, just as Jesus sent His disciples in pairs ahead of Him to the towns He would later visit (Luke 10:1). See Peter Lampe, "The Roman Christians in Romans 16," published in Karl Donfried, *The Romans Debate* (Grand Rapids, MI: Baker Academic, 1991), 220. Lampe notes it's easy to imagine Paul sent the couple back to Rome as a "vanguard" of himself, just as he did when he left them in Ephesus before he arrived (Acts 18:19, NIV). Per Romans 16:3-5, Lampe infers that Epaenetus may have moved to Rome from Ephesus with Priscilla and Aquila, as he is listed right after them. Epaenetus was also from Asia Minor (Romans 16:5). Lampe, "The Roman Christians in Romans 16," 221. Other scholars share my theory that Paul sent Priscilla and Aquila to Rome. See William Sanday and Arthur Headlam, *A Critical and Exegetical Commentary on the Epistle to the Romans* (New York, NY: Charles Scribner's Sons, 1905), xxvii.

183. Romans 16:3-4. There is much speculation on what Paul means when he says the couple "risked their necks" for him (ESV). Wright, who believes Paul was imprisoned in Ephesus, thinks they may have gone to the magistrates to argue that Paul was being held on false charges. N.T. Wright, *Paul: A Biography*, 266. It is my belief that their act of returning to Rome shortly after Nero took power is more likely. They may not have wanted to return given the risk, but they did so because they loved Paul and wanted to see a fresh kingdom community established in Rome. With the death of Claudius, the expulsion edict became a dead letter, and Rome eventually became as full of Jews as it ever was. F.F. Bruce, *Jesus and the Christian Origins of the New Testament* (Grand Rapids, MI: Eerdmans, 1974), 20-21. But in the beginning, there was risk involved. Bandy agrees with my scenario. Personal correspondence with Alan Bandy, 12/15/23.

The couple secures a home in the Aventine district, a wealthy part of the city.[184] Paul wants a Gentile kingdom community in the Eternal City, and he wants it to begin before the Jews start trickling back in. For this reason, Paul sends word to the Gentile assemblies and asks some of the believers in each church to move to the unhappy city of Rome. He also asks a few of his Jewish kin from Jerusalem to move there as well.[185]

184. Peter Lampe, *From Paul to Valentinus*, 20-21, 44-45, 65. Aventine Hill was less than two miles away from the Trastevere district (the Jewish quarter), about a twenty- or thirty-minute walk. In the first century, the Aventine was a mixed area of both wealthy and working-class residents with a diverse population. It was popular among merchants and traders from various parts of the empire. Everyone was represented in the Aventine, "from consul to slave." Reta Halteman Finger, *Roman House Churches for Today*, 18-19.

185. I'll explain who Paul's "kin" are in another note. Barnett observes that the people who came to Rome that Paul mentions in Romans 16 were the "fruits of Paul's mission in the eastern provinces" dating back to his earlier years of church planting. Paul Barnett, *From Jerusalem to Illyricum,* 127. In contrast to most scholars, I contend that Paul founded the church in Rome through what I call "inverted transplantation." For a discussion on the biblical and historical evidence supporting this perspective, see Frank Viola, *Finding Organic Church*, 40-43. This viewpoint, which I will give further evidence for in later notes, has never been refuted. Several points to consider: (1) If Paul wasn't the father of the Roman church, he'd be violating his own standard of not building on another man's foundation (Romans 15:20; 2 Corinthians 10:13-16). Some scholars think Paul was saying that he was making an exception and that he was hinting that Peter had laid the foundation for the Roman church, but that idea doesn't follow. Bruce is right when he says, "There is no direct reference to the Roman church or to its founder." F.F. Bruce, *Romans,* 248. (2) The way Paul pens the letter indicates he has a fatherly, spiritual relationship with the believers, not a distant one. Compare his opening of the letter to the opening of his other epistles. (3) While some Romans heard the gospel previous to Paul (in Jerusalem on the day of Pentecost—Acts 2:11), after Claudius expelled the Jewish Christians from the city, Rome was "virgin territory" where the kingdom of God was concerned. Bruce confirms the "re-establishing" of the Roman church after Claudius' decree lapsed. Bruce, *The Spreading Flame,* 144-145. (4) If Paul didn't plant the church in Rome (through inverted transplantation), his comment in Romans 1:13 is strange. Paul writes, "I do not want you to be unaware, brothers, that I have often intended to come to you (but thus far have been prevented), in order that I may reap some harvest among you as well as among the rest of the Gentiles" (ESV). There is no reference to anyone else "sowing" in Rome, so John 4:38 wouldn't apply. Paul is seeking to reap what he himself has sown. Again, most of the people he greets in Romans 16 are the fruit of his ministry, not someone else's. (5) Paul asserts his apostolic credentials in the beginning of the letter precisely because he's never been to Rome and some of the believers in the church don't know him personally. There are also detractors present, as we will see. In the same way, Paul asserts his apostolic credentials in most of his other epistles to churches. (6) Paul's stated goal to preach the gospel where Christ hasn't been named doesn't discount my proposition. Remember, there were few if any Christians

In effect, Paul wants to transplant a number of his Gentile converts to Rome, along with some Jewish believers, creating a cosmopolitan assembly to match the cosmopolitan capital.[186] Some of the believers Paul sends to Rome are:[187]

- Priscilla from Ephesus
- Aquila from Ephesus
- Epaenetus from Ephesus
- Rufus from Syrian Antioch

---

in Rome after Claudius' decree went into force. The inverted transplant was a fresh beginning, and it now included Gentiles in the ekklesia. (7) Just because Paul had some of his own converts in the church didn't ensure there would be no tensions between Jews and Gentiles who became part of the church over the next few years.

186. Most of the names listed in Romans 16 are Gentiles. Throughout *From Paul to Valentinus*, Lampe argues that the Christians were geographically dispersed throughout Rome with a heavy centralization in the poorer areas of the city. In contrast, Watchman Nee effectively argues that whenever a church (singular) is mentioned in the New Testament, it refers to the whole city, not a single house. Watchman Nee, *The Normal Christian Church Life*, chap. 4. According to Nee, when Paul wrote Romans, the ekklesia in Rome met in Priscilla and Aquila's large house (Romans 16:5). For Nee's reasoning, see Watchman Nee, *Further Talks on the Church Life* (Anaheim, CA: Living Stream Ministry, 1974), 31-34. Nee's analysis is supported by Greek Orthodox theologian John Zizioulas in *Eucharist, Bishop, Church: The Unity of the Church in the Divine Eucharist and the Bishop During the First Three Centuries* (Brookline, MA: Holy Cross Orthodox Press, 2001). Zizioulas makes the same distinction that Nee makes between "church" and "churches" in the New Testament (one church per city, multiple churches in a region or province). Zizioulas breaks from many scholars and argues that the whole church in Rome met in the house of Priscilla and Aquila at the time Paul wrote Romans (45-47). Zizioulas is correct in saying, "Nowhere in the sources, however, do we find more than one 'household Church' in each city" (90). While I don't agree with Zizioulas' high ecclesiastical leadership structure, his argument (along with Nee's) regarding one ekklesia per city is compelling. Moo argues that the tradition asserting Peter founded the church in Rome cannot be true. Douglas Moo, *Epistle to the Romans*, 4. This, of course, doesn't mean that a church in the city always met in a single home. The church in Jerusalem was a single assembly, but it met in homes throughout the city. The same with the church in Ephesus at one point. But when the New Testament says an entire church in a city met in a single home, it means it was small enough to gather in one house. The ekklesia in Corinth is an example.

187. According to Romans 16, Paul greets twenty-six individuals and five households that gathered in Rome. Even though Paul had not yet visited the city, he knew them all by name. And he knew at least twelve of them personally. Peter Lampe, *From Paul to Valentinus*, 168. This buttresses the conjecture that Paul sent them all to Rome.

- Andronicus from Jerusalem[188]
- Junia from Jerusalem[189]
- Urbanus from Macedonia
- Apelles from Asia Minor[190]

188. Andronicus and Junia are said to have been "relatives" of Paul (or at least "fellow Jews"). They were also said to be Paul's "fellow prisoners" (Romans 16:7). Paul may have used "kin" to refer to the fact that they were fellow Jews, not necessary blood relatives. Craig Keener, *Romans*, 187. Gupta says "fellow Jews" is much closer to the original meaning, and that "fellow prisoner" could mean they shared space with Paul in a prison cell, or they were simply honored for sharing the same scars of incarceration for the gospel. Personal correspondence with Nijay Gupta, 6/6/23. If they did share prison space with Paul, we do not know when or where this would have happened. Ben Witherington notes there are many possibilities. For example, "Lystra, Iconium, Pisidian Antioch, but more probably Philippi or Thessalonica. Note 'imprisonment' is plural in 2 Corinthians 11:23 which was written before Romans in the mid-50s." Personal correspondence with Witherington, 8/6/22. Andronicus is a Greek name, and Junia is Latin. This may point to the fact that they hailed from Diaspora families in Jerusalem. Junia may have descended from freed slaves.

189. Some scholars identify Junia with Joanna, the wife of Chuza, who followed Jesus during His earthly ministry (Luke 8:3). "Junia" could be the Latin equivalent of "Joanna," who was the wife of Herod's administrator. Amy-Jill Levine and Ben Witherington III, *The Gospel of Luke*, 223-224. Paul calls Junia and Andronicus "apostles." The text says they were not only known to the apostles, but they were eminent apostles themselves and were Jesus-followers before Paul, possibly even witnessing the resurrected Christ. F.F. Bruce, *The Pauline Circle*, 83. Some scholars believe they were husband and wife. C.E.B. Cranfield, *Romans*, 377; Clinton Arnold, ed., *Zondervan Illustrated Bible Backgrounds Commentary*, 3:92. The fact that Junia was also an apostle is clear from the text. Eldon Jay Epp, *Junia: The First Woman Apostle* (Minneapolis, MN: Fortress Press, 2005); Scot McKnight, *Junia is Not Alone* (Englewood, CO: Patheos Press, 2011); Richard Bauckham, *Gospel Women: Studies of the Named Women in the Gospels* (Grand Rapids, MI: Eerdmans, 2002); Lynn Cohick, *Women in the World of the Earliest Christians: Illuminating Ancient Ways of Life* (Grand Rapids, MI: Baker Academic, 2009); David Balch, et al., *Early Christian Families in Context*, 163-164. Andronicus and Junia may have traveled as a married missionary couple, a "husband-wife apostolic team." Craig Keener, *Romans*, 186. They were both outstanding apostolic workers in the eyes of the original apostles. Peter Lampe, "The Roman Christians in Romans 16," published in Karl Donfried's *The Romans Debate*, 223-224; Scot McKnight, *Reading Romans Backwards: A Gospel of Peace in the Midst of Empire* (Waco, TX: Baylor University Press, 2019), 13; Nijay Gupta, *Tell Her Story*, chap. 9. According to Origen, Junia was a disciple of the earthly Jesus and possibly was sent out as part of the seventy (or seventy-two) in Luke 10. Origen, *Commentary on Romans,* 10.21.1-27.

190. Of the twenty-six individuals mentioned in Romans 16, eighteen are men and eight are women. Four are free-born, and at least nine are of slave origin (meaning, they used to be slaves). Peter Lampe, *From Paul to Valentinus*, 165ff., 183.

Sharpening the Focus: First-century Rome is a cosmopolitan city—the melting pot of the entire world. The city is a microcosm of the empire, with representatives of every race, ethnic group, social status, and religion.

Geographically, Rome is a square—about two and a half miles by two and a half miles. (Many of the poor live in densely populated areas outside the city walls.) The city sits on seven hills and contains fourteen districts.[191] It has 1,790 mansions (villas) and 46,602 tenement apartments called *insulae*, where the majority of the population lives in crowded conditions.[192]

The population of Rome is about one million.[193] Inhabitants range from the miserably poor to the lavishly rich. Half the population is made up of slaves, which makes it the "slave capital of the world."[194] Rome is viewed as "favored by the gods" since

191. Most of the poor live in the Trastevere (Trans-Tiber), which was made up of two of the fourteen districts. But the most densely populated areas were within the walls. Personal correspondence with James Papandrea, 8/31/22. For further details on the layout of Rome, see Alan Bandy, *An Illustrated Guide to the Apostle Paul*, 165-166.

192. Reta Halteman Finger, *Roman House Churches for Today*, 25-26. For details on Roman housing, see David Balch, et al., *Early Christian Families in Context*, 10-43. Some estimate that 90 percent of free citizens, and an even greater percentage of slaves and the rest of the empire's population, lived in apartment buildings. The freedmen and their families lived in small rooms measuring twelve square yards. Eckhard Schnabel, *Paul the Missionary*, 300. For details on the various living locations in ancient Rome, see Alberto Angela, *A Day in the Life of Ancient Rome*, 28-41, 80-105.

193. Craig Evans, et al., eds., *Dictionary of New Testament Background*, 1013; Howard Frederic Vos, *Nelson's New Illustrated Bible Manners & Customs: How the People of the Bible Really Lived*, Logos edition (Nashville, TN: Thomas Nelson, 1999), 637; Gerald Hawthorne, et al., eds., *Dictionary of Paul and His Letters*, 851; Clinton Arnold, ed., *Zondervan Illustrated Bible Backgrounds Commentary*, 2b:266. Some scholars estimate around 200,000 family units, calculating to an overall population of one million. David deSilva, *Discovering Revelation: Content, Interpretation, Reception* (Grand Rapids, MI: Baker Academic, 2021), 51. Other scholars believe the population may have been lower. According to James Papandrea, "the estimates range from less than half a million up to one million." Personal correspondence with Papandrea, 8/6/22. Other scholars estimate between a quarter of a million to a million. Craig Keener, *Romans*, 10. It appears most experts estimate the population to be between 850,000 and one million. J.W. Hanson, *An Urban Geography of the Roman World, 100 BC to AD 300*, 67.

194. "One-half the population of the city of Rome was servile." David Fiensy, *The College Press NIV Commentary: New Testament Introduction*, Logos edition (Joplin, MO: College Press, 1997), 229-230. That Rome was the slave capital of the world, see Ben Witherington III, *The Letters to Philemon, the Colossians, and the Ephesians*, 23. A conservative estimate suggests at least one-third, if not half the population of Rome was made up of slaves. Ben Witherington III, *New Testament History*, 321.

the whole world has been brought under its dominion.[195]

Divorce is common and easy.[196] It is rarely initiated over infidelity, since sex with slaves and prostitutes is not considered infidelity.[197] Immorality is so prevalent that Seneca calls Rome "a cesspool of iniquity" and Juvenal said it is "as the filthy sewer into which flowed the abominable dregs of every Syrian and Achaean stream."[198] In Rome, "all of the horrors and abominations of the whole world flow together."[199]

The basic Roman garment is the tunic. (Romans mostly used linen instead of wool.) Wealthy Romans rarely left the house without a toga,[200] and Roman women wore elaborate, folded shawls.[201] Common people eat bread, beans, eggs, olives, lentils, and fish.[202] They cannot afford meat most of the time, but when they can, they consume chicken, sausage, or pork.

The wealthy eat beef and organ meats. They also consume fruits, including apples, dates, pears, plums, and grapes. During high-end banquets, the wealthiest roast small

195. Bruce Longenecker, et al., *Thinking Through Paul*, 338.

196. Under Roman law, children typically stayed with the father. It was said among first-century writers that "only a coward would fail to divorce a troublesome wife." Craig Evans, et al., eds., *Dictionary of New Testament Background*, 6.

197. "For a married man to sleep with a single woman as a mistress or hire a prostitute, it would not constitute the kind of adultery that would necessarily lead to divorce. But a married woman sleeping with another man would be considered adultery, and if caught, her husband would probably divorce her. Divorce was only necessary for those who had a legally registered marriage, and most people did not have that." Personal correspondence with James Papandrea, 8/31/22. For more details, see Papandrea's *A Week in the Life of Rome*, 34-35.

198. William Barclay, *The Gospel of Mark: The New Daily Study Bible* (Edinburgh: Saint Andrew Press, 2001), 12; F.W. Farrar, *The Life and Work of St. Paul* (New York, NY: E.P. Dutton and Company, 1902), 187.

199. Tacitus, *Annals*, 15.44. Other translators render the quote, "all things horrible or shameful in the world collect and find a vogue." According to Lampe, this was a reference to the Christians. Peter Lampe, *From Paul to Valentinus*, 66.

200. There were strict rules about when a man was required to wear a toga. For example, senators when the Senate was in session, etc. Personal correspondence with James Papandrea, 8/31/22.

201. For details on Roman attire, see Alberto Angela, *A Day in the Life of Ancient Rome*, 45-55.

202. "They were also dependent on the daily dole of grain. Something the emperor did to gain the support of the masses. The grain came mostly from Alexandria, which is why there were so many grain ships." Personal correspondence with Alan Bandy, 12/6/23.

birds or mice dipped in honey and rolled in poppy seeds.[203] Romans use salt, but pepper is unavailable. They eat with spoons, knives, and toothpicks.[204] The poor eat whatever they can and often it is not enough. The aristocrats eat well. Breakfast is among the biggest meals of the day, and lunch is meager. (Coffee and hot chocolate do not exist.[205])

The city's economy is based on taxation rather than production. Rome, therefore, must import virtually all its products.[206] The average workday for a wealthy Roman, or Romans in certain businesses, lasts six hours. Poor people and slaves generally work from dawn to dusk.[207]

The Romans do not have minute divisions of the hours. Their time is marked by water clocks and sun dials. For this reason, people are often late for appointments.[208] Virtually everyone in every class uses the Roman baths. Most people take their baths during the afternoon rest time, and most Romans bathe daily.[209] Only uber-wealthy Romans can afford private baths in their homes.[210]

The city's Jewish population is large, standing between 20,000-50,000, with most of them being slaves or freedmen.[211] The Jews are also successful in converting some

203. These were considered delicacies. James Papandrea, *A Week in the Life of Rome*, 90.

204. James Papandrea, *A Week in the Life of Rome*, 90.

205. Alberto Angela, *A Day in the Life of Ancient Rome*, 63.

206. James Papandrea, *A Week in the Life of Rome*, 27.

207. Personal correspondence with James Papandrea, 8/31/22. The major meal for both Romans and Jews was taken during the day. However, evening meals were also common. Personal correspondence with Gary Burge, 7/12/22.

208. No one expected a person to show up on the dot at a certain time. If the appointment was at the third hour, a person aimed for the top of the hour. Personal correspondence with James Papandrea, 8/31/22. For more details, see Papandrea's *A Week in the Life of Rome*, 22.

209. Craig Keener, *Acts*, 3:2752.

210. For details on Roman baths, see James Papandrea, *A Week in the Life of Rome*, 60-61.

211. Craig Keener, *Romans*, 10; James D.G. Dunn, *The Acts of the Apostles*, 351; Ben Witherington III, *Paul's Letter to the Romans*, 12. Freedmen often had it better than the free poor. Freedmen of citizens received citizenship with manumission and become the clients of their former masters. Slavery, ironically, carried with it an access to upward mobility that the free poor did not have. Personal correspondence with James Papandrea, 8/31/22. Bruce estimates 40,000-60,000 Jews lived in Rome at the beginning of the first century, probably as many as lived in Jerusalem. F.F. Bruce, *Paul: Apostle of the Heart Set Free*, 30. See also Eckhard

Romans to Jewish faith and practice.[212] The Jews are spread across the city, but a majority live in a pocket of the city called the Trastevere area.[213] The Trans-Tiber is among the poorest and most densely populated areas of Rome. It was the home of many Judeans before Claudius expelled the Jews from Rome.

Many of the Jews remained in the city during the expulsion, especially slaves owned by non-Jews.[214] The city has between ten and thirteen synagogues.[215] A high percentage of the Jews have Roman citizenship, but most Christians don't.[216]

Not counting the homeless, everyone but the rich lives in *insulas*. A typical *insula* in the empire contains rows of shops facing the street on the ground floor. Owners live above them or in the rear.[217] *Insulas* could rise as high as seven or eight stories and often spanned an entire block. The first floor of the *insula* is used for shops. The second floor is very expensive. The poor live on the third floor or above. Heat and light are also inadequate. The typical *insula* is poorly built and sometimes collapses, killing the tenants inside. An *insula* is made mostly of timber, so it's a fire hazard in the dry season.[218]

The city is unbearably noisy. From dawn to dusk, there is constant babbling in the streets, as well as from the apartments. It's hard for people to sleep because of

Schnabel, *Acts*, 756. With the entire population of Rome ranging from 500,000 to over one million, the Jewish community was a small minority in the city in the first century. Craig Keener, *Romans*, 10.

212. Martin Hengel, et al., *Paul Between Damascus and Antioch*, 63. For details on the Jews in Rome during this period, see John Barclay, *Jews in the Mediterranean Diaspora*, chap. 10.

213. F.F. Bruce, *Paul: Apostle of the Heart Set Free*, 30, 380; James D.G. Dunn, *The Acts of the Apostles*, 351. Keener says many of the Jewish Christians "probably lived in tenements in Trastevere, across the Tiber and safe from the fire that burned much of the city in 64." Craig Keener, *1 Peter*, 31. James Papandrea agrees, suggesting that most of the Jews were free persons living in the Trastevere. Personal correspondence with Papandrea, 8/13/22. For further details on the Jewish community in Rome, see Bruce Winter, et al., eds., *The Book of Acts in Its First Century Setting*, vol. 5, chap. 11; Clinton Arnold, ed., *Zondervan Illustrated Bible Backgrounds Commentary*, 2b:269.

214. James Papandrea, *A Week in the Life of Rome*, 99.

215. James D.G. Dunn, *The Acts of the Apostles*, 351.

216. Peter Lampe, *From Paul to Valentinus*, 83.

217. Leon Morris, *The First and Second Epistles to the Thessalonians*, 5.

218. For a discussion on Roman living spaces, see James Papandrea, *A Week in the Life of Rome*, 49-51.

the racket. (The wealthy areas are an exception.[219]) Merchants yell out their products. Prostitutes, fortune tellers, and sellers of potions swell the city and call out their wares.[220] Then, from dusk to dawn, the racket of carts transporting goods fills the night hours so as not to compete with the daytime pedestrian and carriage traffic.

There is no public transportation and no street lighting (these things don't appear in Rome until the fourth century). The main concourses of the city are attractive, but the back streets are dirty, unlit, pitiful, and stink of human waste and rotting trash. Few homes have running water or private toilets. For human waste, chamber pots are used and then dumped into cesspits or directly onto the streets, which are sometimes covered with human excrement.[221]

The streets are littered with garbage and covered with flies, and the garbage is never removed. The residents must wait for a heavy downpour to flush the refuse into the Tiber River. In the pits along the sides of the roads, a person can see the bodies of the poor who could not afford burials. If you are poor, Rome is one of the worst places on planet Earth to live.[222] Average life expectancy is about twenty years. If infancy is survived, the average life expectancy rises to about forty years of age.[223]

The believers Paul sends to Rome begin entering the city. Consequently, the body of Jesus Christ in its complete form—comprised of Jew and Gentile—is now in Rome.[224] A kingdom community that reflects the fellowship of the Godhead is reborn on Caesar's doorstep. The ekklesia in Rome initially meets in the house of Priscilla and Aquila.[225]

---

219. James Papandrea, *A Week in the Life of Rome*, 24.

220. James Papandrea, *A Week in the Life of Rome*, 24-25.

221. Holly Beers, *A Week in the Life of a Greco-Roman Woman*, 53.

222. Personal correspondence with Mark Philip Reasoner, 4/17/99.

223. Bruce Malina and Richard Rohrbaugh, *Social-Science Commentary on the Synoptic Gospels* (Minneapolis, MI: Fortress Press, 1992), 7.

224. I've supported this conclusion in some of the other notes. While there were already Christians in Rome before Claudius' edict, at this point in the story, there's a full-fledged ekklesia in the city made up of Jews and Gentiles.

225. Romans 16:5. See my previous note on this point. Lampe suggests that the ekklesia in Rome had at least eight separate houses, in which they gathered in different parts of the city. Peter Lampe, "The Roman

Timothy returns from Corinth and tells Paul that his letter (CORINTHIANS B) has been challenged by the assembly. Unfortunately, a strong-willed brother in the church defies Paul's apostolic authority, and he has persuaded most of the assembly to follow his rebellion.[226]

An Urgent Visit to Corinth
Spring 55

Upon hearing the troubling news, Paul pays an urgent visit to Corinth.[227] But the visit turns out to be painful.[228] The strong-willed brother defies Paul's apostolic authority in

---

Christians in Romans 16," in Karl Donfried's *The Romans Debate*, 230. I believe this growth took place *after* Paul wrote his famous letter to the Romans (more on this later). After the Christians spread throughout the city, a high number lived in the Trastevere district. The Trastevere was the traditional Jewish quarter in Rome. It's likely the Jewish Christians (who converted through Peter's message at Pentecost) were living in this district before Claudius's edict. Peter Lampe, *From Paul to Valentinus*, 38-39. The area was known for its bad stench, high population density, and low income. Peter Lampe, *From Paul to Valentinus*, 50-59. According to Lampe, most of the Christians lived in the lowest social strata in Rome (52-54). However, some of the believers were well-to-do, like Priscilla and Aquila. Such texts as Romans 12:13; 15:24, 28; Acts 28:30 give us a hint that a number of Christians had the means to be hospitable and support Paul. For details on the home gatherings and the Christian households in Rome, see Scot McKnight, *Reading Romans Backwards*, 10-14.

226. Donald Guthrie, *The Apostles*, 207. Bruce sketches out the situation in detail in *Paul: Apostle of the Heart Set Free*, 274-279. Paul's spiritual authority in Corinth had severely eroded at this point. Gordon Fee, *The First Epistle to the Corinthians*, 7.

227. "This visit was almost certainly by boat, sailing across the Aegean from Ephesus to Corinth (more precisely, the city's east port of Cenchreae). Though this visit is not recorded in Acts, it was foreshadowed in his second letter to them (1 Corinthians 4:21, 'Shall I come to you with a rod of discipline...?' and confirmed by two references in 2 Corinthians where Paul refers to a future 'third' visit to them. Since this visit is not recorded in Acts, it unfortunately is omitted in all biblical maps outlining Paul's travels." Personal correspondence with Jeffrey Weima, 1/6/24.

228. Bruce lays out his timeline from Paul's painful visit to Corinth to Paul's return to Corinth two years later (spring A.D. 55 to March A.D. 57). Bruce believes Paul wrote Corinthians C in the spring of A.D. 55. F.F. Bruce, *Paul: Apostle of the Heart Set Free*, 317-318. The visit is not successful. His opponents appear to have even taunted him with being humble in person, but bold when he was away (2 Corinthians 10:10). Richard Longenecker, *The Ministry and Message of Paul*, 73; Otto F.A. Meinardus, *St. Paul in Ephesus*, 77ff. Keener is less convinced by 2 Corinthians 2:1 about an actual intervening painful visit and might date 2 Corinthians earlier than Bruce—another example of how scholars disagree with each other.

Paul's presence. Even worse, the other believers in the assembly do not defend Paul against the man's opposition.

Paul leaves Corinth angry and humiliated.[229] But out of his love for the believers, he wants to visit Corinth again to try to correct the problem. However, he chooses to let it go, lest he experience sorrow a second time.[230] In haste,[231] he writes a severe letter and gives it to Titus to read to the assembly.[232] We will call this letter CORINTHIANS C. It no longer exists.[233]

PAUL WRITES CORINTHIANS C

(This letter is lost to us.[234])

Year: A.D. 55[235]

229. Barnett sketches out the scenario brilliantly using the pertinent texts. Paul Barnett, *The Second Epistle to the Corinthians*, 28-33.

230. 2 Corinthians 1:22-2:4; 12:21.

231. It seems Paul wrote the letter too quickly and without thinking carefully through what he wrote. Despite his recent rejection and humiliation, Paul did not want to "wash his hands" of the Corinthians and the whole messy situation. Instead, the apostle still loved his spiritual children and wasn't willing to give up on them, so he wrote this new letter to them, albeit a strongly written and rebuking letter. Personal correspondence with Jeffrey Weima, 1/6/24.

232. Instead of coming to them in person, Paul wrote the letter out of love for the believers to "spare" them (2 Corinthians 1:23-2:4). Craig Keener, *The IVP Bible Background Commentary: New Testament*, 515; Donald Guthrie, *The Apostles*, 208. According to Keener, public readings in the first century were usually done at dinner parties. So readings in the ekklesias may have been during the Lord's Supper. Craig Keener, "Lessons on Acts," Session 3.

233. 2 Corinthians 2:4ff.; 7:8ff. This lost epistle is often called "the painful letter." N.T. Wright, *Paul: A Biography*, 259. It's also called "the tearful letter." Bruce Malina, et al., *Social-Science Commentary on the Letters of Paul*, 150; F.F. Bruce, *Paul: Apostle of the Heart Set Free*, 274; Donald Guthrie, *The Apostles*, 208.

234. For further details on my reconstruction of Paul's Corinthian correspondence, see F.F. Bruce, *Paul: Apostle of the Heart Set Free*, 264-285; David deSilva, *Introduction to the New Testament*, chap. 14. In 2 Corinthians 10:9-10, Paul alludes to more than one letter he sent to the Corinthians (some of which are lost to us, as we have already established).

235. Based on previous events and the timelines I've documented, this date is plausible. According to deSilva, A.D. 54-55 is pretty standard among scholars. Personal correspondence with David deSilva, 2/8/24.

From: Ephesus[236]

To: The assembly in Corinth (which is about five years old)

Author: Paul

Contextual Summary: After returning from Corinth in frustration, Paul composes this stinging letter to the Corinthians. He writes it in pure agony, bathing it in bitter tears. In the letter, the apostle asks the assembly to prove its love for him by disciplining the man who defied his spiritual authority.[237]

Paul chooses to write the letter instead of visiting the Corinthians in person. The letter reflects his affection for them. His goal is to cauterize the wound. To Paul's mind, an in-person meeting may prove too confrontational for them. However, some in the assembly who value in-person forceful speeches mistake Paul's meekness when he was among them to be a sign of weakness. So they complain that he is bold in his letters, but weak in person.[238]

As soon as Titus heads off to Corinth with the letter, Paul regrets writing it.[239] He fears that his tone is too severe, and it may exacerbate the situation. Paul is heartbroken and worried about the Corinthian assembly.

236. F.F. Bruce, *Paul: Apostle of the Heart Set Free*, 274. There is also a possibility that Paul sent this "stinging letter" as he was passing through Macedonia. F.F. Bruce, *1 and 2 Corinthians*, 164-165.

237. For further details on Paul's thorny relationship with the Corinthians, see Paul Barnett, *Paul: Missionary of Jesus*, 160-180.

238. Craig Keener, *The IVP Bible Background Commentary: New Testament*, 515. Paul's critics saw meekness as an indicator of low status and weak character. For a detailed conversation on Paul's critics, see Patrick Gray, *Paul as a Problem in History and Culture: The Apostle and His Critics through the Centuries* (Grand Rapids, MI: Baker Academic, 2016).

239. Later Paul will write that, despite his initial regrets, he was glad he wrote the severe letter because of its positive results. 2 Corinthians 7:8-12.

Opposition in Ephesus

While waiting for Titus to return to him in Ephesus, Paul plots his next move. He plans to leave Ephesus after Pentecost and travel north by land to visit the kingdom communities in Macedonia (Philippi, Thessalonica, and Berea), before heading south to Corinth in Achaia.[240] He wants to encourage the believers and also collect the relief fund from these predominantly Gentile assemblies.[241]

Paul has high hopes that the relief collection will erase the concerns the Jewish Christians have about him and the legitimacy of his gospel. After that, he hopes to visit Rome. While Paul is in Ephesus, Peter travels to Western Anatolia, including the provinces of Pontus and Bithynia.[242]

March/April 55[243]

It is spring, and the annual festival held in honor of Artemis begins. As a result, the city of Ephesus swells with people from all over Asia Minor. Paul's powerful influence in Ephesus persuades many in the city to forsake their idols. As a result, the silversmiths who make their living selling miniature statues of Artemis' temple begin losing customers.[244]

240. 1 Corinthians 16:8. Pentecost fell on May 25 in A.D. 55. F.F. Bruce, *The Book of the Acts*, 381; Clinton Arnold, ed., *Zondervan Illustrated Bible Backgrounds Commentary*, 2b:203.

241. Alan Bandy, *An Illustrated Guide to the Apostle Paul*, 130. Again, the relief fund was for the Jerusalem believers in Judea.

242. Ben Witherington III, *Letters and Homilies for Hellenized Christians*, 2:67. The area Peter probably covered was at least 129,000 square miles. He will address the believers in this region later by letter when he writes 1 Peter. Recall that years earlier Paul was prevented from going to Bithynia to preach the gospel (Acts 16:7).

243. According to Bruce, it's plausible that the riot broke out during the Ephesian festival of Artemisia, held annually in March/April. F.F. Bruce, *The Book of the Acts*, 381.

244. Artemis is the goddess of fertility. She's also called Diana. Most Bible translations use "Artemis," but the KJV and NKJV use "Diana." Weima states, "The evidence strongly suggests that the silver models were not of the goddess, but of her temple in Ephesus, one of the seven wonders of the ancient world." Personal correspondence with Jeffrey Weima, 1/6/24. For more on the guild of the silversmiths in Ephesus, see Clinton Arnold, ed., *Zondervan Illustrated Bible Backgrounds Commentary*, 2b:199-200.

Demetrius, one of the silversmiths, brings his fellow craftsmen together and spearheads a mob protest against Paul.[245] Demetrius convinces the other silversmiths that Paul is hurting their business by discrediting the temple of the great Artemis.[246] Upon hearing this report, the mob is filled with fury and screams out, "Great is Artemis of the Ephesians!" The protest bleeds through the entire city, causing a huge uproar. The protesters move their way into the massive Ephesian theater.[247]

In a violent rage, the mob seizes Aristarchus and Gaius,[248] two of Paul's apostolic apprentices. Paul wants to enter the theater to confront the mob, but the Ephesian believers prevent him. Some of Paul's friends who are officials of the province (*asiarchs*) beg him not to go into the theater. The Jews from Ephesus want to dissociate themselves from Paul, so they have Alexander speak on their behalf.[249] When the Ephesian citizens realize that Alexander is a Jew (knowing that Jews do not worship the pagan gods), the crowd shouts continually for two hours, "Great is Artemis of the Ephesians!"[250]

After hours of mayhem, the town clerk calms the mob and suggests that those who have a complaint against Paul go through the proper governmental channels to resolve their grievances. The clerk then dismisses the crowd.[251] At this very moment, Paul drops to the

---

245. Acts 19:23ff. Bruce says Demetrius may have been the president of the local guild of silversmiths. F.F. Bruce, *Paul: Apostle of the Heart Set Free*, 293.

246. According to Weima, "The start of the protest was small and was located either in the commercial agora or main harbor street situated very close to the theater. The protest then moved to the theater where it took on much greater force." Personal correspondence with Jeffrey Weima, 1/6/24.

247. The theater held approximately 24,000 people. James D.G. Dunn, *The Acts of the Apostles*, 263.

248. It is my view that the Gaius here is the same Gaius from Derbe (Acts 20:4). Some manuscripts refer to Aristarchus and Gaius as "men from Macedonia" while others use the singular form, Gaius and Aristarchus, "a man from Macedonia."

249. Both Bruce and Ramsay point out that Alexander the coppersmith (or metalworker who may have used bronze), the man who did Paul great harm, may be identical with Alexander the silversmith mentioned in this part of the story. Compare Acts 19:33 with 2 Timothy 4:14. William Ramsay, *St. Paul the Traveler and Roman Citizen*, 214; F.F. Bruce, *Paul: Apostle of the Heart Set Free*, 297. This is possible, but Alexander was also a common name in the first century.

250. Guthrie agrees that Paul wrote 1 Corinthians (Corinthians B) *before* the riot. Donald Guthrie, *The Apostles*, 204-207.

251. Acts 19:23-41. David deSilva points out that "the assembly in the theater was only dispersed, and the issue was never resolved." Personal correspondence with deSilva, 2/8/24.

lowest point of his life. The opposition from Ephesian "wild beasts" (as he metaphorically calls them) is so great that Paul falls into despair.[252]

The relentless opposition has severely tested his faith, even bringing him to tears.[253] He describes himself as feeling "pressed out of measure," "despairing even of life," "having the sentence of death" upon him.[254] The human hostility from Paul's adversaries is so tumultuous that the apostle comes close to dying. But God in His mercy delivers him.

Paul is universally viewed as a dangerous social and cultural threat by the pagans and the Jews.[255] His revolutionary message is an affront to Gentile and Jewish worldviews. Despite the opposition he receives in Ephesus, Paul experiences the resurrection power of Christ to rescue him, even while he's at his wits' end.

We are pressed on every side, yet not crushed; perplexed, yet not to despair; pursued, yet not forsaken; struck down, yet not destroyed; always carrying in the body the putting to death of the Lord Jesus, that the life of Jesus may also be revealed in our body. For we who live are always delivered to death for Jesus' sake, that the life also of Jesus may be revealed in our mortal flesh. So then death works in us, but life in you. (2 Corinthians 4:8-12)

Back in nearby Colossae, Epaphras plants three kingdom communities in the south banks of the Lycus valley: one in Colossae (his hometown), one in Laodicea, and another

252. 1 Corinthians 15:32. While Paul already sent 1 Corinthians by the time of the riot, he was opposed in Ephesus before the riot broke out. The riot was simply the culmination. The reference to "wild beasts" probably refers to human opposition. Ben Witherington III, *The New Testament Story*, 64-65. However, there is a longstanding tradition among Greek writers where human passions and pleasures of the flesh are described as beasts that fight against man. Richard Longenecker, *The Ministry and Message of Paul*, 72. Nevertheless, philosophers more *often* designated unreasoning humans as beasts rather than passions. Personal correspondence with Craig Keener, 12/4/23. Paul "died daily" throughout his Christian life, but especially when under the oppression and distress he faced in Ephesus (1 Corinthians 15:31). See also Eckhard Schnabel, *Paul the Missionary*, 111.

253. Acts 20:19.

254. 2 Corinthians 1:8-11.

255. N.T. Wright, *Paul: A Biography*, 260. Details on the social, cultural, and religious life across the ancient Mediterranean can be found in Richard Ascough, Philip Harland, and John Kloppenborg, *Associations in the Greco-Roman World: A Sourcebook* (Waco, TX: Baylor University Press, 2023).

in Hierapolis.[256] Laodicea has a population of about 45,000.[257] Hierapolis has a population of about 20,000.[258] Colossae is a city with a much smaller population, less than 4,000 residents.[259] All three cities are known for their wool production, and each is within walking distance from each other.[260]

From Ephesus to Troas

After the uproar in Ephesus finally dissipates, Paul sends for the Ephesian believers to meet him in an inconspicuous location.[261] During the gathering, the apostle speaks words of encouragement, bids them farewell and heads north to Macedonia.[262] Paul's apprentices

256. That Epaphras evangelized the Lycus valley, see Colossians 1:7; 4:12-13. See also Jerome Murphy-O'Connor, *Paul: His Story*, 127. Neither Colossae, Laodicea, nor Hierapolis are Roman colonies. The Lycus valley had a large Jewish population. It was part of Phrygia Asiana, as opposed to Phrygia Galatica (where the four Galatian churches Paul and Barnabas planted were located).

257. Mark Wilson estimates the urban population of Laodicea to be 45,000. Personal correspondence with Mark Wilson, 5/16/23. Laodicea was known for its raven-black wool as well as its developments in medicine. For details on ancient Laodicea, see Mark Wilson, *Biblical Turkey*, 242-249.

258. Based on the demographic studies of Andrew Wilson and J.W. Hansen, Wilson estimates the urban population (excluding the chora) of Hierapolis to be around 20,000. Personal correspondence with Mark Wilson, 4/11/23. N.T. Wright and Michael Bird estimate the populations of Laodicea and Hierapolis to be less, around 10,000 each. *The New Testament in Its World*, 456. Hierapolis had hot springs located around the city, which also led to its success. John Byron, *A Week in the Life of a Slave*, 30, 52. Both Colossae and Hierapolis were known for their reddish-purple wool.

259. Based on the demographic studies of Andrew Wilson and J.W. Hansen, Wilson estimates the urban population (excluding the chora) of Colossae to be 3,500. Personal correspondence with Mark Wilson, 4/11/23. Wright and Bird point out that the population of Colossae was "dwarfed" by Laodicea and Hierapolis. N.T. Wright and Michael Bird, *The New Testament in Its World*, 456. Nevertheless, Colossae was still an important city during Paul's day. For details on the city, see *Colossae in Space and Time: Linking to an Ancient City*, eds. Alan Cadwallader and Michael Trainor (Göttingen: Vandenhoeck & Ruprecht, 2011).

260. John Byron, *A Week in the Life of a Slave*, 52; N.T. Wright and Michael Bird, *The New Testament in Its World*, 456.

261. According to Bandy, "There is a cave church on the hillside in Ephesus. Its current structure and art was located in the third century, but it is believed to have been used as a cave church in the first century. It overlooks the harbor, and it is a difficult hike to get to. I can't help of thinking about that cave as a possible location for this meeting." Personal correspondence with Alan Bandy, 12/6/23.

262. Acts 19:21; 20:1-2. Donald Guthrie, *The Apostles*, 207. The Thessalonians haven't seen Paul in about five years. Jeffrey Weima, *1-2 Thessalonians*, 39. For a highly detailed treatment of Paul's journey from Macedonia to Jerusalem, see Craig Keener, *Acts*, 3:2945-3348.

leave Ephesus with him.[263] On his way to Macedonia, Paul stops in Troas where he's given an open door to preach the high-voltage gospel of the kingdom. As a result, he plants a new assembly of Jesus Christ in the city.[264]

Now when I went to Troas to preach the gospel of Christ and found that the Lord had opened a door for me... (2 Corinthians 2:12, NIV)

However, Paul's mind is still unsettled about the Corinthian assembly. He desperately hopes to see Titus and find out how the Corinthians reacted to his "severe letter." Time crawls by for the apostle as he fights off worst-case scenarios that assault his mind. So he takes action and searches for Titus throughout Troas, but he fails to find him.[265] Deeply concerned about the church in Corinth, the apostle leaves Troas, forsaking the promising opportunity God has granted him there, and embarks on a journey to Macedonia in hopes of encountering Titus.

I still had no peace of mind, because I did not find my brother Titus there. So I said goodbye to them and went on to Macedonia. (2 Corinthians 2:13, NIV)

October 55[266]

As Paul leaves Troas and arrives in Macedonia, he fights internal fears regarding the Corinthians. Paul visits the ekklesias he planted on his second apostolic journey in Macedonia, namely, Philippi, Thessalonica,[267] and Berea. With respect to seeing the Thessalonians, the prayer Paul offered to God four years earlier is now answered:

263. This becomes apparent throughout the narrative. The notes will confirm.

264. Luke omits this visit, but Paul mentions it in 2 Corinthians 2:12. Richard Longenecker, *The Ministry and Message of Paul*, 73. While it's possible that Paul planted the assembly in Troas on his second apostolic trip, we don't have evidence for it. To my mind, it's more likely that the church was planted at this time given his words in 2 Corinthians 12:12-13.

265. Donald Guthrie, *The Apostles*, 208.

266. F.F. Bruce, *Paul: Apostle of the Heart Set Free*, 318.

267. The ban was lifted and Paul was allowed to return to Thessalonica. Keener observes, "Once the politarchs who ruled against Paul were out of office, their order was no longer in effect." Personal correspondence with Craig Keener, 12/4/23.

Now may our God and Father himself and our Lord Jesus clear the way for us to come to you. (1 Thessalonians 3:11, NIV)

While in Macedonia, Paul receives opposition.

For when we came into Macedonia, we had no rest, but we were harassed at every turn—conflicts on the outside, fears within. (2 Corinthians 7:5, NIV)

The apostle daily battles anxiety over the state of all the churches he's raised up, not just Corinth.

Besides those things that are outside, there is that which presses on me daily: anxiety for all the assemblies. (2 Corinthians 11:28)

He also wants to visit the believers in Rome, but circumstances prevent him.[268] Despite how he feels, the apostle encourages each of the Macedonian assemblies with many words. He also exhorts each church to complete the collection for the Jerusalem ekklesia.[269] As Paul shares with the believers in Macedonia, he boasts in the example set by the assembly in Corinth because they have been zealous in laying aside their money for the relief fund over the past year.[270] Through some of the believers, the Holy Spirit reveals that tribulation and imprisonment await Paul in Jerusalem.[271]

268. Romans 1:13; 15:22-23.

269. In Acts 24:17, Paul says, "Now after some years, I came to bring gifts for the needy to my nation, and offerings." The gifts and offerings in this text are not the same. The offerings refer to the sacrificial offerings associated with the Nazirite vow, where Paul paid the expenses of four men to purchase grain, bread, animals, etc. Beyond this one time, there's no evidence that Paul ever engaged in offerings associated with temple worship. The gifts refer to the Jerusalem relief fund. Craig Keener, *The IVP Bible Background Commentary: New Testament*, 387; Clinton Arnold, ed., *Zondervan Illustrated Bible Backgrounds Commentary*, 2b:238.

270. See 2 Corinthians 9:2. This isn't what it seems. When Paul writes these words to the Corinthians, he lets them know he's been bragging to the believers in Macedonia about their involvement in the collection. But he does this to motivate the Corinthians to live up to the task and complete the collection. When it came to the relief fund, the Macedonians were generous, but the Corinthians were tardy. Donald Guthrie, *The Apostles,* 229; David deSilva, *Introduction to the New Testament*, 511.

271. Acts 20:23.

At last, Paul finds Titus,[272] and to his grateful delight, Titus bears good news from Corinth. Paul rejoices in relief.

Nevertheless, he who comforts the lowly, God, comforted us by the coming of Titus, and not by his coming only, but also by the comfort with which he was comforted in you while he told us of your longing, your mourning, and your zeal for me, so that I rejoiced still more. (2 Corinthians 7:6-7)

Titus informs Paul that his severe letter was well received. The Corinthians sorrowfully regretted the way they treated him. They apologized, repented, and acted accordingly.[273] The Corinthians disciplined the man who defied Paul's spiritual authority. However, they were too extreme in their discipline.[274]

Titus tells Paul that the church treated him (Titus) with great respect and humility while he was among the believers. He also informs Paul that the assembly has slacked off in collecting money for the Jerusalem fund.[275] Even so, Paul is comforted by the report,[276]

---

272. Paul probably finds Titus in Philippi (which is in Macedonia). Richard Longenecker, *The Ministry and Message of Paul*, 73.

273. 2 Corinthians 7:8-16. Wright claims they were "falling over themselves to apologize." N.T. Wright, *Paul: A Biography*, 307. Some scholars, including Craig Keener, think the rebellious man was the same person who had an illicit relationship with his stepmom in 1 Corinthians 5 (the incestuous man). Personal correspondence with Craig Keener, 12/4/23. According Barnett, "Paul crossed the Northern Aegean to Macedonia (i.e., Neapolis) to wait for Titus who eventually arrived. Titus's news was mixed. There was strong resentment against Paul's 'painful' letter, as reported by Titus ('His letters are weighty and strong, but his bodily presence is weak, and his speech of no account'—2 Corinthians 10:10). Regarding the incestuous man...Paul argued for his reinstatement (2 Corinthians 2:6-7)." Personal correspondence with Paul Barnett, 1/12/24.

274. 2 Corinthians 2:1-11; 7:6-7. Donald Guthrie, *The Apostles*, 209; F.F. Bruce, *Paul: Apostle of the Heart Set Free*, 275.

275. 2 Corinthians 8:6-11. Interestingly, Paul never mentions the word "money" in those chapters. Instead, he uses terms like "grace," "service," and "partnership." N.T. Wright, *Paul: A Biography*, 308. Weima observes, "Despite Paul's surprise and joy at Titus' good news, he still harbors concerns about the Corinthians, wondering if their change of heart is genuine. Thus, the material in 2 Corinthians 8 through 9 is where Paul challenges the church to 'put their money where their mouth is' by becoming more committed to supporting the financial collection." Personal correspondence with Jeffrey Weima, 1/6/24.

276. 2 Corinthians 7:13-16.

and he begins deliberating over penning another letter to the assembly. We will call it CORINTHIANS D. We know it as 2 Corinthians.[277]

Paul has all eight apprentices with him as he pens this letter.[278] As the apostle writes the epistle, he receives word that the assembly in Corinth faces a new problem. Not long after Titus left Corinth, the assembly was visited by Jewish "super apostles" (as Paul sarcastically calls them).[279] They are from the Jerusalem assembly.[280] These pseudo-apostles sought to undermine Paul's authority and bring the Corinthians under the authority of the Jerusalem church.[281] They are the same men who came to Syrian Antioch,

277. Most scholars, even those who believe 2 Corinthians is a composite letter, believe Paul authored the epistle. Ben Witherington III, *The New Testament Story*, 62. Wright believes Paul cheered up and wrote the letter on the road around northern Greece (Macedonia) on his way to Corinth from Ephesus. N.T. Wright, *Paul: A Biography*, 239.

278. Acts 20:3-4. Luke compresses his narrative as usual.

279. James D.G. Dunn, *Unity and Diversity in the New Testament*, 255. Paul refers to these men sardonically as "super apostles" because they were self-aggrandizing posers. They were dishonest deceivers who were themselves deceived. Ben Witherington III, *Conflict and Community in Corinth*, 449. C.K. Barrett, "Paul's Opponents in II Corinthians," *NTS* 17 (1971): 233-254. Barrett's article is superb. The only disagreement I have with it involves Barrett's distinction between the "super apostles" as Paul's ironic reference to the original apostles and the "false apostles" (Paul's reference to those who came to Corinth to hijack the church). To my mind, Paul was referring to the same group of visitors in Corinth when speaking of the "super apostles" and the "false apostles." See Paul Barnett, *The Message of 2 Corinthians*, 21; Craig Keener, *1–2 Corinthians*, 145. It appears that the Judaizers simply modified their strategy slightly from their visit to Galatia. P.W. Barnett, "Opposition in Corinth," *JSNT* 22 (1984): 3-17. For further details on the identity, mission, method, and attacks of the false apostles, see Paul Barnett, *The Second Epistle to the Corinthians*, 33-40. In *Identifying Paul's Opponents: The Question of Method in 2 Corinthians* (New York, NY: Bloomsbury Academic, 2015), Jerry Sumney summarizes the arguments of C.K. Barrett and F.C. Baur (and others) who are representative of the statement: "The majority of interpreters conclude that the opponents of 2 Corinthians are Judaizers" (15). According to Baur, the opponents in every genuine letter of Paul are Judaizers. Although Sumney doesn't fully agree, his summarization is valuable. Paul didn't have to use the same lines he used in Galatians with the same people. Since their tactics changed, Paul's response to them changed also. But as Barnett and others have demonstrated, there are enough similarities to conclude these are the same agitators. Paul's language in 2 Corinthians 3 is just one example.

280. It's highly likely these men came from the Jerusalem assembly, or at least "the Judaean milieu" (as Barnett calls it). Paul Barnett, *Bethlehem to Patmos,* 187. Paul's designations of them in 2 Corinthians 3 and 11 make this plain. Also, I'm following the timeline of F.F. Bruce who believes the super apostles came to Corinth *after* Paul's painful visit and not before. See F.F. Bruce, *Paul: Apostle of the Heart Set Free*, 273-279.

281. This was a clear breach of the agreement that Paul and Barnabas made with Peter, James, and John (see Galatians 2:8-9). Although the original apostles from Jerusalem didn't sanction these visitors, it still

Galatia, and Greece years earlier to overturn Paul's work and put the believers under the Mosaic Law.[282]

It is at this time that Paul begins to refer to the man who leads these opponents as his "thorn in the flesh."[283] The "thorn" is one of the "super apostles" who has worked overtime

---

reflects the growing rift between Paul and the Jerusalem ekklesia. James D.G. Dunn, *Unity and Diversity in the New Testament*, 255.

282. Murphy-O'Connor supports this conclusion calling these men "Judaizers" and identifies them as the delegation headed up by one man who caused trouble in Antioch and Galatia. Jerome Murphy-O'Connor, *Paul: His Story*, 169-171, 176, 190-192. See also Paul Barnett, *Paul: Missionary of Jesus*, 148-149; 171-175; C.K. Barrett, "Paul's Opponents in II Corinthians," 233-254. The similarities between how Paul described these men in Galatians and in 2 Corinthians could hardly be more striking. They were Jews, they preached "another Jesus" and "another gospel," they were "false brethren," and they corrupted the word of God. James D.G. Dunn, *Unity and Diversity in the New Testament*, 24. They also contended that Moses and the Law were still applicable and must be obeyed (see 2 Corinthians 3). Barnett, Murphy, and Barrett agree that just because Paul didn't specifically mention circumcision in 2 Corinthians doesn't mean these false apostles were a different group from those who came to Galatia. The Law is mentioned in 2 Corinthians 3, which covers circumcision and the rest of the 613 laws of Moses. In that chapter, Paul argues that the new covenant of the Spirit and righteousness has displaced the old covenant of condemnation and death. The righteousness of God is through Christ alone (2 Corinthians 5:21), not through the works of the Law. Wright agrees that the opponents Paul addressed in 2 Corinthians 1 through 6 were the same men he addressed in chapters 10 through 13. N.T. Wright, *Paul for Everyone: 2 Corinthians* (Louisville, KY: Westminster John Knox Press, 2004), 114. In another work, Wright aptly says, "2 Corinthians 3 through 5 demonstrate that Paul is quite capable of mounting a full-dress argument about the old and new covenants in which the words 'law' and 'commandment' do not appear." N.T. Wright, *Colossians and Philemon: An Introduction and Commentary*, TNTC (Grand Rapids, MI: Eerdmans, 1986), 26. Schnabel also identifies these men as the same people who pushed the Law on the believers in Antioch of Syria and Galatia. Eckhard Schnabel, *Early Christian Mission*, 2:1004. Drane underscores the similarities between Galatians and 2 Corinthians 3, which supports the idea that Paul was addressing the same problem. John Drane, *Paul: Libertine or Legalist?*, 73. See also Ben Witherington III, *Conflict and Community in Corinth*, 346, n. 49, where Witherington references an unpublished lecture by C.K. Barrett. Barrett argues that the agenda and strategy of the Judaizers wasn't the same in all the churches they sought to influence; for that reason, it's not an issue for Paul not to have directly mentioned circumcision in 2 Corinthians. Again, 2 Corinthians 3 covers food laws, circumcision, and the Sabbath without mentioning them by name. The false apostles appealed to Moses and the Mosaic covenant. Ben Witherington III, *Conflict and Community in Corinth*, 350.

283. 2 Corinthians 12:7. Speaking about the thorn in the flesh, Keener agrees that "opposition is more likely," and it is "possible that the opposition includes the agents of Satan against whom Paul has been railing." Craig Keener, *1–2 Corinthians*, 240. Witherington confirms that Paul's rivals in Corinth were led by "one person" who was their "ringleader." Ben Witherington III, *Conflict and Community in Corinth*, 447.

to discredit Paul in the eyes of the Corinthians, as well as in the other ekklesias.[284] The "super apostles" are telling the Corinthian believers the following:

- Paul cannot be trusted. He's not a man of his word. For example, he changed his mind regarding his travel plans. He says one thing but does another. Therefore, his "yes" does not mean "yes," and his "no" doesn't mean "no." Paul is fickle.[285]

- When Paul preached to you, he left out the most glorious, life-giving part of the gospel—the Law of Moses.

- Paul doesn't have a letter of commendation like we do.[286] He wasn't sent from Jerusalem (the Mecca of the apostles). He's a traitor, an upstart, and a false teacher.[287]

- He doesn't receive money for himself. If he were a real apostle, he would take your money to support his ministry just as all real apostles do.

- Paul is standoffish, and he doesn't love you.[288]

- He is ignorant.[289]

- He exploits you by asking you to collect money for a "supposed" relief fund. But there's something off about this request. Don't trust it. Despite what he appears to be, Paul is a peddler of God's word. He's in the ministry for personal gain, even though he pretends not to profit from God's people.[290]

---

284. Some of Paul's scathing epithets for his opponents in 2 Corinthians are: those who "peddle God's word" (2:17), "super-apostles" (11:5, 12:11), "pseudo-apostles" (11:13), "deceitful workmen" (11:13), "servants of Satan" (11:15) who "proclaim a different Jesus" (11:4) and bring "a different gospel" (11:4).

285. Inferred from 2 Corinthians 1:15-24. Paul planned to visit Corinth on his way both to and from Macedonia (1 Corinthians 16:5-8). However, he changed his plan and did not visit the Corinthians on his return trip from Macedonia because the visit on the outbound trip went so poorly. The opponents argued that because Paul says one thing, yet does another, he is not a real apostle. Ben Witherington III, *Conflict and Community in Corinth*, 340-341.

286. According to Witherington, they might have claimed the support of James and Peter with some kind of general letter of reference. Ben Witherington III, *Conflict and Community in Corinth*, 347.

287. James D.G. Dunn, *Unity and Diversity in the New Testament*, 255.

288. N.T. Wright, *Paul: A Biography*, 313.

289. 2 Corinthians 10:10; 11:6. Craig Keener, *The IVP Bible Background Commentary: New Testament*, 518.

290. 2 Corinthians 2:17 appears to be a response to an accusation against Paul himself. The opponents accused the apostle of peddling the word of God for profit, something they were guilty of. This is the same

- Whenever Paul is among you, he is weak, humble, and unimpressive in his speaking. But when he is away from you, he becomes bold, fierce, and forceful in his letters. Some of you have already made this observation.

- Paul doesn't have supernatural experiences like we have, which is another proof that God hasn't called him.

- Paul doesn't possess the impeccable Israelite pedigree that we do.[291]

Regrettably, some of the Corinthians received these men and believed their false gospel—which is a gospel of bondage to the Law. Some of the well-do-do believers in the assembly want an apostle they can be proud of. They desire an apostle who is part of high society who doesn't work for a living, but who accepts their money and becomes their client (or dependent).[292]

PAUL WRITES CORINTHIANS D

(This is our 2 Corinthians.[293])

accusation they brought against him in Thessalonica (1 Thessalonians 2:5). Bruce Malina, et al., *Social-Science Commentary on the Letters of Paul*, 137.

291. Keener observes that "they certainly claimed an impeccable pedigree; whether they denied Paul's or not is less clear. Maybe they were Levites vs. his Benjamite ancestry, or maybe because he was likely descended from freed slaves, they questioned the purity of his line." Personal correspondence with Craig Keener, 12/4/23. The scenario I've presented was aided by the reconstructive work in F.F. Bruce's *Paul: Apostle of the Heart Set Free*, chaps. 23-24.

292. In 2 Corinthians 12:13, Paul responds with irony, saying he accepted the financial support of others instead of them. Craig Keener, *The IVP Bible Background Commentary: New Testament*, 521. Again, my reconstruction of what provoked Paul to write 2 Corinthians (Corinthians D) is largely based on F.F. Bruce, *1 and 2 Corinthians*, 164-174.

293. Because of the abrupt changes in tone and content throughout 2 Corinthians, some scholars hold to the idea that 2 Corinthians 1 through 9 was pieced together from as many as five originally separate letters and that 2 Corinthians 10 through 13 is another separate letter entirely. Craig Keener, *The IVP Bible Background Commentary: New Testament*, 515. Therefore, Bruce and other scholars think there was also a Corinthians E, which they believe to be 2 Corinthians chaps. 10 through 13. According to this view, Corinthians D contains only chaps. 1 through 9. F.F. Bruce, *Paul: Apostle of the Heart Set Free*, 264-285. Bruce may be correct, but I side with those scholars who view 2 Corinthians as a single letter. According to Longenecker,

Year: A.D. 56[294]

From: Macedonia[295]

To: The assembly in Corinth (which is about six years old)

Author: Paul[296]

Contextual Summary: Paul is faced with the possibility of losing the Corinthian ekklesia. It's a desperate situation so the apostle writes this epistle to repair the damage.[297]

   The letter can be broken in the following way: Chapters 1:1 through 2:13 (the apostle addresses internal Corinthian issues). Chapters 2:14 through 6:13 (he addresses his opponents). Chapters 6:14 through 10:12 (he addresses internal Corinthian issues).

"Many have proposed that Second Corinthians 10-13, the 'Severe Letter,' preceded the writing of Second Corinthians 1-9 (with or without 6:14-7:1), the 'Conciliatory Letter.' Although this is possible, there is little that requires such a view." Richard Longenecker, *The Ministry and Message of Paul*, 74. "Evidently, Paul understood that he had to win the Corinthians' hearts and minds if he was to defeat and discredit the teachings of the newly arrived counter-mission. This would explain the apparently fractured nature of the letter." Personal correspondence with Paul Barnett, 1/12/24. See also Paul Barnett, *The Second Epistle to the Corinthians*, 17-33. For details on the various "partition theories" of 2 Corinthians along with arguments in favor of reading it as a literary unity, see Ben Witherington III, *Conflict and Community in Corinth*, 328-333; David deSilva, *Introduction to the New Testament*, 504-506, 510-513.

   294. Ben Witherington III, *The Acts of the Apostles*, 601; *Conflict and Community in Corinth*, 352; Gary Burge, et al., *The New Testament in Antiquity*, 319; Jonathan Bernier, *Rethinking the Dates of the New Testament*, 152-154; F.F. Bruce, *Paul: Apostle of the Heart Set Free*, 134.

   295. Donald Guthrie, *The Apostles*, 228; Ben Witherington III, *The Acts of the Apostles*, 601; *The ESV Study Bible*, 2219. Wright and Bird make a case that it's plausible that Paul penned 2 Corinthians over a period of time while in Macedonia. N.T. Wright and Michael Bird, *The New Testament in Its World*, 484-485.

   296. Craig Keener, *1-2 Corinthians*, 143. 2 Corinthians is one of Paul's undisputed letters. Aside from Galatians, it's more autobiographical than any other Paul wrote. The letter reveals a great deal about Paul himself and his emotions, tensions, and aspirations. Donald Guthrie, *The Apostles*, 208.

   297. According to Barnett, "Paul was already criticised for his handling of the disciplinary matter, for failure to return and instead sending a harsh letter. He must repair the damage in Corinth to have any hope of persuading the members to reaffirm his teachings against the challenge of the pseudo-apostles. This he sought to do in the first, third, and fifth parts of the letter. He then concentrates his defensive apologetic in the second and fourth parts. This explains the anatomy of the letter and its various purposes." Personal correspondence with Paul Barnett, 1/12/24.

Chapters 10:13 through 12:13 (he addresses his opponents). Chapters 12:14 through 13:14 (he addresses internal Corinthian issues).[298]

Looking at the epistle more broadly, in chapters 1 through 7, Paul is thankful for the good report that Titus brought him in response to his severe letter.[299] In chapters 8 through 9, the apostle regards the church's willingness to contribute to the collection as a litmus test, an opportunity for them to demonstrate their repentance from previously rejecting Paul's authority and their renewed commitment to supporting the apostle and his ministry.[300]

In chapters 10 through 13, the tone changes. Paul is more negative and concerned about the Corinthians. (Some scholars talk about a "long night" or pause between his writing of chapters 1 through 9 and chapters 10 through 13 which accounts for this change.[301]) More specifically, Paul encourages the assembly to forgive the man who defied him.

He responds to the charge that he is inconsistent and his word cannot be trusted. He clarifies why he changed his travel plans (chapters 1 through 2). The letter digresses into a parenthesis from 2:14 to 7:4. The apostle replies to the accusation that he has no letter of commendation. He then compares his life-giving gospel of grace with the death-producing gospel of his opponents (chapters 3 through 4).

He exhorts the Corinthians not to yoke themselves with unbelievers. He then becomes autobiographical about his emotions behind writing the severe letter. In so

---

298. Paul Barnett, *From Jerusalem to Illyricum*, 117. Again, Barnett refers to Paul's opponents (the circumcision party) as the Jerusalem-based countermission.

299. The Titus mentioned in 2 Corinthians (Corinthians D) is the same Titus of Galatians 2:1. William Ramsay, *St. Paul the Traveler and Roman Citizen*, 218.

300. Personal correspondence with Jeffrey Weima, 1/6/24. Paul equates the church in Corinth's zeal for the collection with zeal for himself as their apostle. Craig Keener, *1–2 Corinthians*, 211.

301. I owe this breakdown of sections in the letter to Jeffrey Weima. Personal correspondence with Weima, 1/6/24. For a detailed explanation of this rhetorical strategy behind the alleged "seams" in 2 Corinthians, see David deSilva, "Measuring Penultimate against Ultimate Reality: An Investigation of the Integrity and Argumentation of 2 Corinthians," *JSNT* 52 (1993) 41-70; *idem*, "Meeting the Exigency of a Complex Rhetorical Situation: Paul's Strategy in 2 Corinthians 1 through 7," *Andrews University Seminary Studies* 34 (1996) 5-22.

doing, he exhorts the assembly to be fully reconciled to him and the Lord (chapters 5 through 7).

Paul goes on to encourage the believers to resume the collection they began for the Jerusalem ekklesia (chapters 8 through 9). He urges Titus to visit the assembly along with two other brothers in Christ, one "whose praise in the Good News is known throughout all the assemblies," and another "whom we have many times proved earnest in many things."[302] These men are to help the Corinthian believers complete the collection.

In the last four chapters (chapters 10 through 13), which Paul likely began writing when he heard the news about his opponents in Corinth, the apostle addresses the major charges that the Jewish "super apostles" have leveled against him.

To Paul, the process of defending his apostleship is utter foolishness. So instead of boasting about his great achievements, he boasts about his sufferings.[303] He does all this to save the ekklesia from accepting a false gospel.

302. 2 Corinthians 8:18-22. Paul regarded Titus as his fellow worker and the other two brothers as representatives of the churches (v. 23-24). Some think that one of the brothers alluded to is Luke. F.F. Bruce, *The Book of the Acts*, 383. Witherington speculates that the two brothers were Timothy and Apollos. Ben Witherington III, *Conflict and Community in Corinth*, 422. David deSilva thinks Apollos is the best candidate for the brother "whose fame in the things of the gospel has spread through all the churches" (2 Corinthians 8:19, NASB). Personal correspondence with David deSilva, 2/8/24. This is possible, but I think it's just as likely that the two men are Aristarchus and Secundus. They are both mentioned in Acts 20:4, and they are from Macedonia. In addition, both are described as *apostolos*, which one can take to mean representatives (or messengers) of the churches or apostles or both. My opinion is shared by J. Gillman, "Aristarchus" (Person) and J.F. Watson "Secundus" (Person) in D.N. Freedman, ed., *The Anchor Yale Bible Dictionary*. Interestingly, the term "travel companion" (*sunekdemos*) is only used twice in the New Testament. In Acts 19:29 (where Aristarchus is mentioned) and in 2 Corinthians 8:19.

303. Corinth was a Roman colony. Roman officials commonly boasted about their achievements and benefactions. The Corinthians looked up to these kinds of people. But instead of boasting about his great deeds, Paul displayed the gospel by boasting about all the wrong things. His résumé of greatness is really a résumé of shame. N.T. Wright, *Paul: A Biography*, 313-315. According to Barnett, "Paul implies that the counter-missionaries have not suffered during their mission, but that Paul has, abundantly so. In fact, their easy ride implies that they didn't preach the crucified Christ and moreover were reticent to do so. By contrast, Paul's missionary suffering validates his claimed proclamation of the suffering, crucified Christ." Personal correspondence with Paul Barnett, 1/12/24.

> Paul exposes the fleshliness of the Judaizing "super apostles" in strong terms. He also links them with his "thorn in the flesh."[304] Titus accepts Paul's request that he visit the Corinthians, and Paul sends the letter with him.[305] Titus is accompanied by two other men.[306]

Paul's love for the Corinthian believers is unmistakable. He authors his incredible letter (2 Corinthians) out of a heart of unwavering compassion, underpinned by firm love. The apostle plans to visit the Corinthian assembly again, and as his pattern has always been, he will not burden the church financially. He cherishes the believers for who they are, not for what they can give him.[307]

2 Corinthians

Paul, an apostle of Christ Jesus through the will of God, and Timothy our brother, to the assembly of God which is at Corinth, with all the saints who are in the whole of Achaia: Grace to you and peace from God our Father and the Lord Jesus Christ.

Blessed be the God and Father of our Lord Jesus Christ, the Father of mercies and God of all comfort; who comforts us in all our affliction, that we may be able to comfort those who are in any affliction, through the comfort with which we ourselves are comforted by God.

---

304. Keener says the "thorn" (a "messenger of Satan") may be an ironic insult against Paul's opponents themselves. Craig Keener, *The IVP Bible Background Commentary: New Testament*, 521.

305. I derive this conclusion from 2 Corinthians 8:10-24. See also F.F. Bruce, *1 and 2 Corinthians*, 223. The fact that 8:16-18 is a "letter of recommendation for Titus" supports this idea. Craig Keener, *The IVP Bible Background Commentary: New Testament*, 513.

306. See my previous note on the identity of these two men. I give more detail on what provoked Paul to write 2 Corinthians as well as provide a deep dive into the letter in my master class, *Glorious Triumph: 2 Corinthians in 3D*. Refer to thedeeperchristianlife.com/classes.

307. 2 Corinthians 12:14-15.

For as the sufferings of Christ abound to us, even so our comfort also abounds through Christ. But if we are afflicted, it is for your comfort and salvation. If we are comforted, it is for your comfort, which produces in you the patient enduring of the same sufferings which we also suffer.

Our hope for you is steadfast, knowing that, since you are partakers of the sufferings, so you are also of the comfort. For we don't desire to have you uninformed, brothers,[a] concerning our affliction which happened to us in Asia, that we were weighed down exceedingly, beyond our power, so much that we despaired even of life.

Yes, we ourselves have had the sentence of death within ourselves, that we should not trust in ourselves, but in God who raises the dead, who delivered us out of so great a death, and does deliver; on whom we have set our hope that he will also still deliver us; you also helping together on our behalf by your supplication; that, for the gift given to us by means of many, thanks may be given by many persons on your behalf.

For our boasting is this: the testimony of our conscience, that in holiness and sincerity of God, not in fleshly wisdom but in the grace of God we behaved ourselves in the world, and more abundantly toward you. For we write no other things to you than what you read or even acknowledge, and I hope you will acknowledge to the end, as also you acknowledged us in part, that we are your boasting, even as you also are ours, in the day of our Lord Jesus.

In this confidence, I was determined to come first to you, that you might have a second benefit, and by you to pass into Macedonia, and again from Macedonia to come to you, and to be sent forward by you on my journey to Judea. When I therefore was thus determined, did I show fickleness? Or the things that I purpose, do I purpose according to the flesh, that with me there should be the "Yes, yes" and the "No, no?"

But as God is faithful, our word toward you was not "Yes and no." For the Son of God, Jesus Christ, who was preached among you by us, by me, Silvanus, and Timothy, was not "Yes and no," but in him is "Yes." For however many are the promises of God, in him is the "Yes." Therefore also through him is the "Amen," to the glory of God through us.

Now he who establishes us with you in Christ and anointed us is God, who also sealed us, and gave us the down payment of the Spirit in our hearts. But I call God for a witness to my soul, that I didn't come to Corinth to spare you. We don't control your faith, but are fellow workers with you for your joy. For you stand firm in faith.

But I determined this for myself, that I would not come to you again in sorrow. For if I make you grieve, then who will make me glad but he who is made to grieve by me? And I wrote this very thing to you, so that, when I came, I wouldn't have sorrow from them of whom I ought to rejoice; having confidence in you all, that my joy would be shared by all of you.

For out of much affliction and anguish of heart I wrote to you with many tears, not that you should be made to grieve, but that you might know the love that I have so abundantly for you. But if any has caused sorrow, he has caused sorrow, not to me, but in part (that I not press too heavily) to you all. This punishment which was inflicted by the many is sufficient for such a one; so that on the contrary you should rather forgive him and comfort him, lest by any means such a one should be swallowed up with his excessive sorrow.

Therefore I beg you to confirm your love toward him. For to this end I also wrote, that I might know the proof of you, whether you are obedient in all things. Now I also forgive whomever you forgive anything. For if indeed I have forgiven anything, I have forgiven that one for your sakes in the presence of Christ, that no advantage may be gained over us by Satan, for we are not ignorant of his schemes.

Now when I came to Troas for the Good News of Christ, and when a door was opened to me in the Lord, I had no relief for my spirit, because I didn't find Titus, my brother, but taking my leave of them, I went out into Macedonia.

Now thanks be to God, who always leads us in triumph in Christ, and reveals through us the sweet aroma of his knowledge in every place. For we are a sweet aroma of Christ to God, in those who are saved and in those who perish: to the one a stench from death to death, to the other a sweet aroma from life to life. Who is sufficient for these things? For we are not as so many, peddling the word of God. But as of sincerity, but as of God, in the sight of God, we speak in Christ.

Are we beginning again to commend ourselves? Or do we need, as do some, letters of commendation to you or from you? You are our letter, written in our hearts, known and read by all men, being revealed that you are a letter of Christ, served by us, written not with ink, but with the Spirit of the living God; not in tablets of stone, but in tablets that are hearts of flesh. Such confidence we have through Christ toward God, not that we are sufficient of ourselves, to account anything as from ourselves; but our sufficiency is from God, who also made us sufficient as servants of a new covenant, not of the letter, but of the Spirit. For the letter kills, but the Spirit gives life.

But if the service of death, written engraved on stones, came with glory, so that the children of Israel could not look steadfastly on the face of Moses for the glory of his face, which was passing away, won't service of the Spirit be with much more glory? For if the service of condemnation has glory, the service of righteousness exceeds much more in glory. For most certainly that which has been made glorious has not been made glorious in this respect, by reason of the glory that surpasses. For if that which passes away was with glory, much more that which remains is in glory.

Having therefore such a hope, we use great boldness of speech, and not as Moses, who put a veil on his face, that the children of Israel wouldn't look steadfastly on the end of that which was passing away. But their minds were hardened, for until this very day at the reading of the old covenant the same veil remains, because in Christ it passes away.

But to this day, when Moses is read, a veil lies on their heart. But whenever someone turns to the Lord, the veil is taken away. Now the Lord is the Spirit and where the Spirit of the Lord is, there is liberty. But we all, with unveiled face seeing the glory of the Lord as in a mirror, are transformed into the same image from glory to glory, even as from the Lord, the Spirit.

Therefore seeing we have this ministry, even as we obtained mercy, we don't faint. But we have renounced the hidden things of shame, not walking in craftiness, nor handling the word of God deceitfully, but by the manifestation of the truth commending ourselves to every man's conscience in the sight of God.

Even if our Good News is veiled, it is veiled in those who are dying, in whom the god of this world has blinded the minds of the unbelieving, that the light of the Good News of the glory of Christ, who is the image of God, should not dawn on them. For we don't preach ourselves, but Christ Jesus as Lord, and ourselves as your servants for Jesus' sake, seeing it is God who said, "Light will shine out of darkness," Genesis 1:3 who has shone in our hearts to give the light of the knowledge of the glory of God in the face of Jesus Christ.

But we have this treasure in clay vessels, that the exceeding greatness of the power may be of God, and not from ourselves. We are pressed on every side, yet not crushed; perplexed, yet not to despair; pursued, yet not forsaken; struck down, yet not destroyed; always carrying in the body the putting to death of the Lord Jesus, that the life of Jesus may also be revealed in our body. For we who live are always delivered to death for Jesus' sake, that the life also of Jesus may be revealed in our mortal flesh. So then death works in us, but life in you.

But having the same spirit of faith, according to that which is written, "I believed, and therefore I spoke." Psalm 116:10 We also believe, and therefore we also speak; knowing that he who raised the Lord Jesus will raise us also with Jesus, and will present us with you. For all things are for your sakes, that the grace, being multiplied through the many, may cause the thanksgiving to abound to the glory of God.

Therefore we don't faint, but though our outward person is decaying, yet our inward person is renewed day by day. For our light affliction, which is for the moment, works for us more and more exceedingly an eternal weight of glory, while we don't look at the things which are seen, but at the things which are not seen. For the things which are seen are temporal, but the things which are not seen are eternal.

For we know that if the earthly house of our tent is dissolved, we have a building from God, a house not made with hands, eternal, in the heavens. For most certainly in this we groan, longing to be clothed with our habitation which is from heaven, if indeed being clothed, we will not be found naked. For indeed we who are in this tent do groan, being burdened, not that we desire to be unclothed, but that we desire to be clothed, that what is mortal may be swallowed up by life. Now he who made us for this very thing is God, who also gave to us the down payment of the Spirit.

Therefore we are always confident and know that while we are at home in the body, we are absent from the Lord; for we walk by faith, not by sight. We are courageous, I say, and are willing rather to be absent from the body and to be at home with the Lord. Therefore also we make it our aim, whether at home or absent, to be well pleasing to him. For we must all be revealed before the judgment seat of Christ that each one may receive the things in the body according to what he has done, whether good or bad.

Knowing therefore the fear of the Lord, we persuade men, but we are revealed to God, and I hope that we are revealed also in your consciences. For we are not commending ourselves to you again, but speak as giving you occasion of boasting on our behalf, that you may have something to answer those who boast in appearance, and not in heart. For if we are beside ourselves, it is for God. Or if we are of sober mind, it is for you.

For the love of Christ constrains us; because we judge thus, that one died for all, therefore all died. He died for all, that those who live should no longer live to themselves, but to him who for their sakes died and rose again.

Therefore we know no one after the flesh from now on. Even though we have known Christ after the flesh, yet now we know him so no more. Therefore if anyone is in Christ, he is a new creation. The old things have passed away. Behold,[b] all things have become new. But all things are of God, who reconciled us to himself through Jesus Christ, and gave to us the ministry of reconciliation; namely, that God was in Christ reconciling the world to himself, not reckoning to them their trespasses, and having committed to us the word of reconciliation.

We are therefore ambassadors on behalf of Christ, as though God were entreating by us: we beg you on behalf of Christ, be reconciled to God. For him who knew no sin he made to be sin on our behalf; so that in him we might become the righteousness of God. Working together, we entreat also that you do not receive the grace of God in vain, for he says, "At an acceptable time I listened to you. In a day of salvation I helped you." Isaiah 49:8

Behold, now is the acceptable time. Behold, now is the day of salvation. We give no occasion of stumbling in anything, that our service may not be blamed, but in everything commending ourselves, as servants of God, in great endurance, in afflictions, in hardships, in distresses, in beatings, in imprisonments, in riots, in labors, in watchings, in fastings; in pureness, in knowledge, in perseverance, in kindness, in the Holy Spirit, in sincere love, in the word of truth, in the power of God; by the armor of righteousness on the right hand and on the left, by glory and dishonor, by evil report and good report; as deceivers, and yet true; as unknown, and yet well known; as dying, and behold, we live; as punished, and not killed; as sorrowful, yet always rejoicing; as poor, yet making many rich; as having nothing, and yet possessing all things. Our mouth is open to you, Corinthians. Our heart is enlarged. You are not restricted by us, but you are restricted by your own affections. Now in return, I speak as to my children: you also open your hearts.

Don't be unequally yoked with unbelievers, for what fellowship do righteousness and iniquity have? Or what fellowship does light have with darkness? What agreement does Christ have with Belial? Or what portion does a believer have with an unbeliever? What agreement does a temple of God have with idols? For you are a temple of the living God. Even as God said, "I will dwell in them and walk in them. I will be their God and they will be my people." Leviticus 26:12; Jeremiah 32:38; Ezekiel 37:27

Therefore "'Come out from among them, and be separate,' says the Lord. 'Touch no unclean thing. I will receive you. Isaiah 52:11; Ezekiel 20:34,41 I will be to you a Father. You will be to me sons and daughters,' says the Lord Almighty." 2 Samuel 7:14; 7:8 Having therefore these promises, beloved, let's cleanse ourselves from all defilement of flesh and spirit, perfecting holiness in the fear of God.

Open your hearts to us. We wronged no one. We corrupted no one. We took advantage of no one. I say this not to condemn you, for I have said before that you are in our hearts to die together and live together. Great is my boldness of speech toward you. Great is my boasting on your behalf. I am filled with comfort. I overflow with joy in all our affliction.

For even when we had come into Macedonia, our flesh had no relief, but we were afflicted on every side. Fightings were outside. Fear was inside. Nevertheless, he who comforts the lowly, God, comforted us by the coming of Titus, and not by his coming only, but also by the comfort with which he was comforted in you while he told us of your longing, your mourning, and your zeal for me, so that I rejoiced still more.

For though I grieved you with my letter, I do not regret it, though I did regret it. For I see that my letter made you grieve, though just for a while. I now rejoice, not that you were grieved, but that you were grieved to repentance. For you were grieved in a godly way, that you might suffer loss by us in nothing. For godly sorrow produces repentance to salvation, which brings no regret.

But the sorrow of the world produces death. For behold, this same thing, that you were grieved in a godly way, what earnest care it worked in you. Yes, what defense, indignation, fear, longing, zeal, and vengeance! In everything you demonstrated yourselves to be pure in the matter. So although I wrote to you, I wrote not for his cause that did the wrong, nor for his cause that suffered the wrong, but that your earnest care for us might be revealed in you in the sight of God.

Therefore we have been comforted. In our comfort we rejoiced the more exceedingly for the joy of Titus, because his spirit has been refreshed by you all. For if in anything I have boasted to him on your behalf, I was not disappointed. But as we spoke all things to you in truth, so our glorying also which I made before Titus was found to be truth. His affection is more abundantly toward you, while he remembers all of your obedience, how with fear and trembling you received him. I rejoice that in everything I am confident concerning you.

Moreover, brothers, we make known to you the grace of God which has been given in the assemblies of Macedonia, how in much proof of affliction, the abundance of their joy and their deep poverty abounded to the riches of their generosity. For according to their power, I testify, yes and beyond their power, they gave of their own accord, begging us with much entreaty to receive this grace and the fellowship in the service to the saints. This was not as we had expected, but first they gave their own selves to the Lord, and to us through the will of God. So we urged Titus, that as he had made a beginning before, so he would also complete in you this grace. But as you abound in everything, in faith, utterance, knowledge, all earnestness, and in your love to us, see that you also abound in this grace.

I speak not by way of commandment, but as proving through the earnestness of others the sincerity also of your love. For you know the grace of our Lord Jesus Christ, that though he was rich, yet for your sakes he became poor, that you through his poverty might become rich. I give a judgment in this: for this is expedient for you who were the first to start a year ago, not only to do, but also to be willing. But now complete the doing also, that as there was the readiness to be willing, so there may be the completion also out of your ability.

For if the readiness is there, it is acceptable according to what you have, not according to what you don't have. For this is not that others may be eased and you distressed, but for equality. Your abundance at this present time supplies their lack, that their abundance also may become a supply for your lack; that there may be equality. As it is written, "He who gathered much had nothing left over, and he who gathered little had no lack." Exodus 16:18

But thanks be to God, who puts the same earnest care for you into the heart of Titus. For he indeed accepted our exhortation, but being himself very earnest, he went out to you of his own accord. We have sent together with him the brother whose praise in the Good News is known throughout all the assemblies.

Not only so, but he was also appointed by the assemblies to travel with us in this grace, which is served by us to the glory of the Lord himself, and to show our readiness. We are avoiding this, that any man should blame us concerning this abundance which is administered by us. Having regard for honorable things, not only in the sight of the Lord, but also in the sight of men.

We have sent with them our brother, whom we have many times proved earnest in many things, but now much more earnest, by reason of the great confidence which he has in you. As for Titus, he is my partner and fellow worker for you. As for our brothers, they are the apostles of the assemblies, the glory of Christ. Therefore show the proof of your love to them before the assemblies, and of our boasting on your behalf.

It is indeed unnecessary for me to write to you concerning the service to the saints, for I know your readiness, of which I boast on your behalf to those of Macedonia, that Achaia has been prepared for the past year. Your zeal has stirred up very many of them. But I have sent the brothers that our boasting on your behalf may not be in vain in this respect, that, just as I said, you may be prepared, lest by any means, if anyone from Macedonia comes there with me and finds you unprepared, we (to say nothing of you) would be disappointed in this confident boasting.

I thought it necessary therefore to entreat the brothers that they would go before to you and arrange ahead of time the generous gift that you promised before, that the same might be ready as a matter of generosity, and not of greediness. Remember this: he who sows sparingly will also reap sparingly. He who sows bountifully will also reap bountifully. Let each man give according as he has determined in his heart, not grudgingly or under compulsion, for God loves a cheerful giver. And God is able to make all grace abound to you, that you, always having all sufficiency in everything, may abound to every good work. As it is written, "He has scattered abroad. He has given to the poor. His righteousness remains forever." Psalm 112:9

Now may he who supplies seed to the sower and bread for food, supply and multiply your seed for sowing, and increase the fruits of your righteousness, you being enriched in everything to all generosity, which produces thanksgiving to God through us. For this service of giving that you perform not only makes up for lack among the saints, but abounds also through much giving of thanks to God, seeing that through the proof given by this service, they glorify God for the obedience of your confession to the Good News of Christ and for the generosity of your contribution to them and to all, while they themselves also, with supplication on your behalf, yearn for you by reason of the exceeding grace of God in you. Now thanks be to God for his unspeakable gift!

Now I Paul, myself, entreat you by the humility and gentleness of Christ, I who in your presence am lowly among you, but being absent am bold toward you. Yes, I beg you that I may not, when present, show courage with the confidence with which I intend to be bold against some, who consider us to be walking according to the flesh.

For though we walk in the flesh, we don't wage war according to the flesh; for the weapons of our warfare are not of the flesh, but mighty before God to the throwing down of strongholds, throwing down imaginations and every high thing that is exalted against the knowledge of God and bringing every thought into captivity to the obedience of Christ, and being in readiness to avenge all disobedience when your obedience is made full.

Do you look at things only as they appear in front of your face? If anyone trusts in himself that he is Christ's, let him consider this again with himself, that even as he is Christ's, so we also are Christ's. For even if I boast somewhat abundantly concerning our authority, which the Lord gave for building you up, and not for casting you down, I will not be ashamed, that I may not seem as if I desire to terrify you by my letters.

For, "His letters," they say, "are weighty and strong, but his bodily presence is weak, and his speech is despised." Let such a person consider this, that what we are in word by letters when we are absent, such are we also in deed when we are present. For we are not bold to number or compare ourselves with some of those who commend themselves. But they themselves, measuring themselves by themselves, and comparing themselves with themselves, are without understanding. But we will not boast beyond proper limits, but within the boundaries with which God appointed to us, which reach even to you. For we don't stretch ourselves too much, as though we didn't reach to you.

For we came even as far as to you with the Good News of Christ, not boasting beyond proper limits in other men's labors, but having hope that as your faith grows, we will be abundantly enlarged by you in our sphere of influence, so as to preach the Good News even to the parts beyond you, not to boast in what someone else has already done. But "he who boasts, let him boast in the Lord." Jeremiah 9:24 For it isn't he who commends himself who is approved, but whom the Lord commends.

I wish that you would bear with me in a little foolishness, but indeed you do bear with me. For I am jealous over you with a godly jealousy. For I married you to one husband, that I might present you as a pure virgin to Christ. But I am afraid that somehow, as the serpent deceived Eve in his craftiness, so your minds might be corrupted from the simplicity that is in Christ. For if he who comes preaches another Jesus, whom we didn't preach, or if you receive a different spirit, which you didn't receive, or a different "good news," which you didn't accept, you put up with that well enough. For I reckon that I am not at all behind the very best apostles.

But though I am unskilled in speech, yet I am not unskilled in knowledge. No, in every way we have been revealed to you in all things. Or did I commit a sin in humbling myself that you might be exalted, because I preached to you God's Good News free of charge? I robbed other assemblies, taking wages from them that I might serve you. When I was present with you and was in need, I wasn't a burden on anyone, for the brothers, when they came from Macedonia, supplied the measure of my need.

In everything I kept myself from being burdensome to you, and I will continue to do so. As the truth of Christ is in me, no one will stop me from this boasting in the regions of Achaia. Why? Because I don't love you? God knows. But what I do, that I will do, that I may cut off occasion from those who desire an occasion, that in which they boast, they may be found even as we. For such men are false apostles, deceitful workers, masquerading as Christ's apostles. And no wonder, for even Satan masquerades as an angel of light. It is no great thing therefore if his servants also masquerade as servants of righteousness, whose end will be according to their works.

I say again, let no one think me foolish. But if so, yet receive me as foolish, that I also may boast a little. That which I speak, I don't speak according to the Lord, but as in foolishness, in this confidence of boasting. Seeing that many boast after the flesh, I will also boast. For you bear with the foolish gladly, being wise. For you bear with a man if he brings you into bondage, if he devours you, if he takes you captive, if he exalts himself, or if he strikes you on the face.

I speak by way of disparagement, as though we had been weak. Yet in whatever way anyone is bold (I speak in foolishness), I am bold also. Are they Hebrews? So am I. Are they Israelites? So am I. Are they the offspring[c] of Abraham? So am I. Are they servants of Christ? (I speak as one beside himself.) I am more so: in labors more abundantly, in prisons more abundantly, in stripes above measure, and in deaths often.

Five times I received forty stripes minus one from the Jews. Three times I was beaten with rods. Once I was stoned. Three times I suffered shipwreck. I have been a night and a day in the deep. I have been in travels often, perils of rivers, perils of robbers, perils from my countrymen, perils from the Gentiles, perils in the city, perils in the wilderness, perils in the sea, perils among false brothers; in labor and travail, in watchings often, in hunger and thirst, in fastings often, and in cold and nakedness.

Besides those things that are outside, there is that which presses on me daily: anxiety for all the assemblies. Who is weak, and I am not weak? Who is caused to stumble, and I don't burn with indignation? If I must boast, I will boast of the things that concern my weakness. The God and Father of the Lord Jesus Christ, he who is blessed forever more, knows that I don't lie. In Damascus the governor under King Aretas guarded the Damascenes' city, desiring to arrest me. I was let down in a basket through a window by the wall, and escaped his hands.

It is doubtless not profitable for me to boast. For I will come to visions and revelations of the Lord. I know a man in Christ who was caught up into the third heaven fourteen years ago—whether in the body, I don't know, or whether out of the body, I don't know; God knows. I know such a man (whether in the body, or outside of the body, I don't know; God knows), how he was caught up into Paradise, and heard unspeakable words, which it is not lawful for a man to utter.

On behalf of such a one I will boast, but on my own behalf I will not boast, except in my weaknesses. For if I would desire to boast, I will not be foolish; for I will speak the truth. But I refrain, so that no man may think more of me than that which he sees in me or hears from me. By reason of the exceeding greatness of the revelations, that I should not be exalted excessively, a thorn in the flesh was given to me: a messenger of Satan to torment me, that I should not be exalted excessively.

Concerning this thing, I begged the Lord three times that it might depart from me. He has said to me, "My grace is sufficient for you, for my power is made perfect in weakness." Most gladly therefore I will rather glory in my weaknesses, that the power of Christ may rest on me.

Therefore I take pleasure in weaknesses, in injuries, in necessities, in persecutions, and in distresses, for Christ's sake. For when I am weak, then am I strong. I have become foolish in boasting. You compelled me, for I ought to have been commended by you, for I am in no way inferior to the very best apostles, though I am nothing. Truly the signs of an apostle were worked among you in all perseverance, in signs and wonders and mighty works. For what is there in which you were made inferior to the rest of the assemblies, unless it is that I myself was not a burden to you? Forgive me this wrong.

Behold, this is the third time I am ready to come to you, and I will not be a burden to you; for I seek not your possessions, but you. For the children ought not to save up for the parents, but the parents for the children. I will most gladly spend and be spent for your souls. If I love you more abundantly, am I loved the less? Even so, I myself didn't burden you. "But, being crafty, I caught you with deception." Did I take advantage of you by anyone of those whom I have sent to you? I exhorted Titus, and I sent the brother with him. Did Titus take any advantage of you? Didn't we walk in the same spirit? Didn't we walk in the same steps?

Again, do you think that we are excusing ourselves to you? In the sight of God we speak in Christ. But all things, beloved, are for your edifying. For I am afraid that by any means, when I come, I might find you not the way I want to, and that I might be found by you as you don't desire, that by any means there would be strife, jealousy, outbursts of anger, factions, slander, whisperings, proud thoughts, or riots, that again when I come my God would humble me before you, and I would mourn for many of those who have sinned before now, and not repented of the uncleanness, sexual immorality, and lustfulness which they committed.

This is the third time I am coming to you. "At the mouth of two or three witnesses shall every word be established." Deuteronomy 19:15 I have said beforehand, and I do say before-hand, as when I was present the second time, so now, being absent, I write to those who have sinned before now, and to all the rest, that, if I come again, I will not spare; seeing that you seek a proof of Christ who speaks in me; who toward you is not weak, but is powerful in you.

For he was crucified through weakness, yet he lives through the power of God. For we also are weak in him, but we will live with him through the power of God toward you. Examine your own selves, whether you are in the faith. Test your own selves. Or don't you know about your own selves, that Jesus Christ is in you?—unless indeed you are disqualified. But I hope that you will know that we aren't disqualified.

Now I pray to God that you do no evil; not that we may appear approved, but that you may do that which is honorable, though we are as reprobate. For we can do nothing against the truth, but for the truth. For we rejoice when we are weak and you are strong. We also pray for this: your becoming perfect. For this cause I write these things while absent, that I may not deal sharply when present, according to the authority which the Lord gave me for building up, and not for tearing down.

Finally, brothers, rejoice! Be perfected. Be comforted. Be of the same mind. Live in peace, and the God of love and peace will be with you. Greet one another with a holy kiss. All the saints greet you. The grace of the Lord Jesus Christ, God's love, and the fellowship of the Holy Spirit be with you all. Amen.

a. 1:8 The word for "brothers" here and where context allows may also be correctly translated "brothers and sisters" or "siblings."

b. 5:17 "Behold," from "ἰδοὺ," means look at, take notice, observe, see, or gaze at. It is often used as an interjection.

c. 11:22 or, seed.

* * *

Paul leaves Macedonia and takes with him Jason, Aristarchus, Secundus, and Sopater (from Berea).[308] Timothy, Titus, Trophimus, and Tychicus also go with him.[309] They head north to Illyricum where Paul preaches the gospel of the kingdom in new territory.[310]

308. Acts 20:1-4. This is the same Jason who was part of the ekklesia in Thessalonica. It's also possible that Paul took Jason with him to Illyricum, but we cannot be sure. Jason, along with Sopater, spent three months with Paul in Corinth. Gene Green, *The Letters to the Thessalonians*, 7. In Romans 16:21, Paul mentions Jason and Sosipater (also called Sopater) who were with him in Corinth (where he went after Macedonia and Illyricum). Ben Witherington III, *1 and 2 Thessalonians*, 36-37. It's possible that Paul passed through Macedonia after he traveled to Illyricum to pick up these men, but I think it's more reasonable to assume they accompanied him there.

309. Bruce confirms that these men were with Paul in Corinth before he went back through Macedonia. Acts 20:2-5. Paul wrote Romans from Corinth, and Romans 16:16 is a reference to these men because they represented "all the churches of Christ." F.F. Bruce, *The Book of the Acts*, 382. Aside from Titus, the other men have the collection from their respective churches. This is a plausible guess because most of the men were in Macedonia and will later go ahead to Troas with the relief fund (Acts 20:4). Timothy and Gaius may have already received it from the churches in Galatia. Wright speculates that Gaius represented Galatia while Timothy represented the church in Ephesus and the other churches in Asia with Tychicus and Trophimus. N.T. Wright, *Paul: A Biography*, 342-343. It's possible that the church in Corinth entrusted its contribution to Titus when he and Paul were with the Corinthians. F.F. Bruce, *The Book of the Acts*, 382-383. Some have conjectured that Luke represented Philippi. Ben Witherington III, *The Acts of the Apostles*, 603; N.T. Wright, *Paul: A Biography*, 342-343. Because Acts is short on details, one must reconstruct the scenario from remarks in the epistles.

310. Romans 15:19. This part of the trip is based on reasonable conjecture by a number of scholars. Paul may have gone through Illyricum from Macedonia's Via Egnatia to bring the gospel. If this happened, many months passed before he reached Corinth in Achaia. Craig Keener, *The IVP Bible Background Commentary: New Testament*, 387; *Acts*, 3:2949-2951; Richard Longenecker, *The Ministry and Message of Paul*, 74;

Illyricum is a large mountainous region northwest of Macedonia on the east of the Adriatic Sea.[311] After founding a new kingdom community in Illyricum, Paul and his companions head to Southern Greece (Achaia) together.[312]

Three Months in Corinth
Winter 57[313]

Now in Greece, Paul and his apprentices visit the assembly in Corinth.[314] This is Paul's third visit to the church.[315] He and his companions will spend three winter months with the believers.[316] Paul will stay in the home of Gaius Titius Justus.[317] The apostle is pleased to learn that the Corinthians received his last letter (CORINTHIANS D), and they've even completed their collection for the Jerusalem ekklesia.[318]

Paul is still in contact with Priscilla and Aquila in Rome. Even though the ban has been lifted against the Jews in the city, the ekklesia in Rome still doesn't contain many Jews.[319]

Witherington III, *The Acts of the Apostles*, 601; Clinton Arnold, ed., *Zondervan Illustrated Bible Backgrounds Commentary*, 2b:203. Schnabel sets the date for Paul's ministry in Illyricum at A.D. 56. Eckhard Schnabel, *Paul the Missionary*, 112. Bruce suggests Paul went to Illyricum during the period covered by Acts 20:2 in the summer of A.D. 56. F.F. Bruce, *Paul: Apostle of the Heart Set Free*, 318; *The Book of the Acts*, 381. See also Eckhard Schnabel, *Early Christian Mission*, 2:1250-1257. For a timeline confirming Paul went to Illyricum after Macedonia and a comparison of Paul's itinerary in Acts and Paul's letters, see *Dictionary of Paul and His Letters*, 455.

311. Illyricum covered the modern regions of Albania and Yugoslavia. Herbert Lockyer, ed., *Nelson's Illustrated Bible Dictionary*, 502.

312. Acts 20:2-4.

313. Many scholars believe Paul and his companions spent the winter months (January to March) in Corinth. Craig Keener, *The IVP Bible Background Commentary: New Testament*, 387.

314. Luke makes reference to this visit in Acts 20:2-3. Paul will mention some of the men in Romans 16:21. Bruce agrees that the apprentices were with Paul in Corinth during this time. F.F. Bruce, *Paul: Apostle of the Heart Set Free*, 339.

315. 2 Corinthians 12:14; 13:1. Even though Luke doesn't record Paul's emergency visit, this was his third visit to Corinth. For the timeline, see F.F. Bruce, *Paul: Apostle of the Heart Set Free*, 318.

316. Some of Paul's companions who are with him in Corinth are listed in Romans 16:21-23.

317. Romans 16:23. F.F. Bruce, *The Book of the Acts*, 381.

318. 2 Corinthians 8:6ff.

319. David Fiensy, *The College Press NIV Commentary*, 229-230.

The apostle has received word that the faith and witness of the Roman assembly is spreading all over the empire.[320] Many travelers who have visited the Eternal City have believed in the Lord Jesus, and they've taken their new faith back to their homelands. Paul longs to see the assembly in Rome. He has tried to visit the city on many occasions, but he's been hindered each time.

Paul receives the following pieces of news regarding the church in Rome:[321]

- There is tension between the Jewish and Gentile believers in the assembly. The two groups are disputing over several issues.

- Some of the Jews in the assembly are "weak in conscience" and believe eating certain foods is sinful.[322]

- They also feel that all believers must keep certain days holy, as prescribed in the Law of Moses.

- The "weak" scrupulous believers (Jewish Christians) judge and criticize their emancipated brothers and sisters (Gentile Christians) who have liberty in these areas.

- The emancipated believers (some of the Gentiles), who have a "strong" conscience, look down on and despise their weaker scrupulous brethren.

- Behind some of these divisions is the influence of the circumcision party which asserts that Paul's gospel of liberty encourages sin. According to the circumcision party, Paul is a renegade Jew who holds to a supersessionistic belief that God is finished with Israel.[323]

---

320. Paul likely received such reports about the Christians in Rome at different times and locations. Personal correspondence with Jeffrey Weima, 1/6/24.

321. My conjecture is that Priscilla and Aquila sent him this news, a plausible scenario since the apostle had a very close relationship with the couple and they were instrumental in founding the Roman *ekklesia*. Barnett supports this idea. Paul Barnett, *From Jerusalem to Illyricum,* 128.

322. According to Weima, "The food issue in Romans was different from the food issue in 1 Corinthians. In Romans, it was a matter of Jewish law with regard to clean and unclean food/animals. In 1 Corinthians, it was a matter of participating in cultic meals and thus becoming guilty of idolatry. Not surprisingly, Paul had a different position to each of these differing situations." Personal correspondence with Jeffrey Weima, 1/6/24. See also Craig Keener, *The IVP Bible Background Commentary: New Testament,* 451-452.

323. Barnett confirms the theory that the influence of the circumcision party had reached Rome. Paul Barnett, *Paul: Missionary of Jesus,* 144-153, 157, 183-186.

Paul decides to pen a full proclamation of the gospel for the Jesus-followers in Rome. One of his primary objectives is to explain the gospel in such a way that it will resolve the tension between the Gentile and Jewish believers in the ekklesia.[324]

PAUL WRITES ROMANS

Year: A.D. 57[325]

From: Corinth[326]

To: The assembly in Rome (which is two to three years old). The ekklesia is made up of a majority of Gentiles with a minority of Jews.[327]

Author: Paul[328]

Contextual Summary: This letter has three purposes:

324. Personal correspondence with Jeffrey Weima, 1/6/24.

325. F.F. Bruce, *Paul: Apostle of the Heart Set Free*, 316, 324, 392. Bruce believes Paul wrote Romans early in A.D. 57. F.F. Bruce, *The Book of the Acts*, 506. Witherington believes the letter was written in late A.D. 56 or early 57. It was likely composed during Paul's three-month winter stay in Corinth before his trip to Jerusalem in the spring of A.D. 57. Ben Witherington III, *Paul's Letter to the Romans*, 6-7.

326. According to Romans 16:23, Paul was with Gaius and the Corinthian ekklesia when he penned the letter. See also Ben Witherington III, *The New Testament Story*, 277; Paul Barnett, *A Short Book about Paul*, 12. More specifically, Paul wrote the letter as a guest in Gaius' home. F.F. Bruce, *Paul: Apostle of the Heart Set Free*, 316, 324.

327. Ben Witherington III, *Invitation to the New Testament*, 336; Stephen Westerholm, *Romans: Texts, Readers, and the History of Interpretation* (Grand Rapids, MI: Eerdmans, 2022), 47; Craig Keener, *Romans*, 12; Douglas Moo, *Epistle to the Romans*, 11. The majority of the names in Romans 16 are Gentile, indicating that Gentiles made up the majority of the church. Clinton Arnold, ed., *Zondervan Illustrated Bible Backgrounds Commentary*, 3:91. For the debate over the audience of Romans, see Ben Witherington III, *Paul's Letter to the Romans*, 7-8. Witherington also believes Paul was addressing Gentile Christians, mainly.

328. Paul Achtemeier, *Romans: Interpretation* (Atlanta, GA: John Knox Press, 1985), 4; Craig Keener, *1-2 Corinthians*, 1. Romans is one of Paul's undisputed letters. "There has been no serious challenge to this claim." Douglas Moo, *Epistle to the Romans*, 1. See also Richard Longenecker, *The Epistle to the Romans*, 4ff.

1) *An apostolic purpose:* To gain support from the assembly for Paul's desired trip to Spain.[329]

2) *An apologetic purpose:* To provide a clear presentation of the gospel of grace and craft a defense of God's righteousness through the gospel, which is currently under attack.[330]

3) *A pastoral purpose:* To deal with the problems of division within the assembly between Jewish and Gentile believers.[331]

The "weak" believers (weak in conscience) want only kosher food, while the "strong" believers (strong in conscience) have no scruples concerning food. The two groups also disagree on which days to hold sacred.[332] One of Paul's goals is to encourage the Gentile believers in the church to embrace the Jewish minority.[333]

329. This proposed purpose is often presented as parallel to the Syrian Antioch church. As the Antioch church sponsored Paul's apostolic journeys as far west as Greece, Paul hopes the Roman believers will sponsor his future apostolic journeys west, as far as Spain. Personal correspondence with Jeffrey Weima, 1/6/24. While it's likely that many of the Roman believers weren't well off financially, not all of them were impoverished. Paul expected some of them to offer hospitality (Romans 12:13), to help Phoebe with her needs (Romans 16:1-2), and to sponsor his trip to Spain (Romans 15:24). According to Keener, Paul's logic is that if the eastern churches supported Paul's Jerusalem mission (to help the poor believers), then the believers in Rome should support his Spanish mission. Craig Keener, *Romans*, 178.

330. Paul calls the good news "my gospel" in Romans 2:16; 16:25; 2 Timothy 2:8 (NIV and NKJV). In Romans, he expounds his gospel to confirm and deepen his supporters in the truth and answer the circumcision party (the Jerusalem-based countermission) who are influencing the assembly. Paul Barnett, *Paul: Missionary of Jesus*, 184. The focus and central thrust of the letter is found in 5:1 through 8:39. Richard Longenecker, *The Epistle to the Romans*, 16. A related reason why the apostle wrote Romans was to "set the record right about what Paul actually believed and taught, in particular, that he was not against the law of God nor against the Jews." Paul Barnett, *Bethlehem to Patmos*, 192.

331. For a crystal-clear description of the issues Paul was addressing along with a general analysis of the letter, see Paul Barnett, *Paul: Missionary of Jesus*, 181-197. To learn more about Paul's purposes in writing Romans, see John Stott, *The Message of Romans: Good News for the World* (Downers Grove, IL: InterVarsity Press, 1994), 31ff.; Richard Longenecker, *The Epistle to the Romans*, 9ff.; Douglas Moo, *Epistle to the Romans*, 16ff.

332. Scot McKnight, *Reading Romans Backwards*, 17-23, 179-181.

333. For alternative theories on Paul's argument in Romans, particularly that he sought to persuade the Gentile believers from viewing themselves as superior to a vanquished Israel, see Richard Horsley, ed., *Paul and Politics*, 35-71.

Romans has been called "the purest Gospel" and "the quintessence and perfection of saving doctrine."[334] Most of the letter is written as a treatise or tractate, with parts of it in the form of rhetoric called "diatribe," a style of writing where the author raises objections and answers them.[335]

In chapters 1 through 5, Paul masterfully presents the gospel of Jesus Christ as it relates to justification by faith and the forgiveness of sins.[336] In chapters 6 through 8, he discusses sanctification and deliverance from sin and the Law. He demonstrates that there is no condemnation hanging over the heads of the believers. Jesus has not only provided forgiveness by His blood, but He has given His followers hope and power to overcome the disordered desires of the physical body.

In chapters 9 through 11, Paul explains the role of Israel in God's plan.[337] In chapters 12 through 15, he brings the epistle to its climax, applying the theological arguments he made in the previous chapters to bear on the present situation in Rome. The apostle urges the believers to offer their bodies as a living sacrifice to God, resist following the world system, and renew their minds.

334. Douglas Moo, *Epistle to the Romans*, 1. This doesn't imply that Romans is a kind of "systematic theology." It's not. It's another Pauline letter that addresses specific problems a believing community faced. At the same time, as Paul addresses those problems, he unveils the gospel of saving grace in a remarkable way.

335. Douglas Moo, *Epistle to the Romans*, 14-15. By contrast, Longenecker calls it a "protreptic message" of instruction and exhortation, a "letter essay" similar to other Greco-Roman letters of instruction. Richard Longenecker, *The Epistle to the Romans*, 41. It can be argued that it's all these things.

336. For comparisons between Romans and Galatians regarding the theme of God's righteousness, see Ben Witherington III, *Invitation to the New Testament*, 219ff.

337. Goldingay shows how Romans employs the Old Testament to tell the Gospel story. John Goldingay, *Reading Jesus's Bible*, 13-28, 134-147. Some commentators believe this section is best understood as a parenthesis. Compare the last paragraphs in Romans 8 with the first paragraphs in Romans 12:1. They seamlessly flow together. Others, however, view Romans 9 through 11 as an integral part of Paul's overall argument rather than a parenthetical break. "In any event, just as chapters 1 through 4 negate Jewish privilege before God, chapters 9 through 11 negate Gentile arrogance in regard to the Jewish people; both are foundational to Paul's exhortation to all the believers in Rome to 'welcome one another as Christ has welcomed you' (15:7)." Personal correspondence with David deSilva, 2/7/24. Both ideas can be true. A parenthesis doesn't equal unimportant. It's simply a change in a person's flow of thought.

He addresses the problems the Gentile believers have with the Jewish believers about meat-eating and holy days.[338] In addition, Paul discusses the various giftings in the body of Christ. He lists most of the problems kingdom communities have struggled with throughout his long experience as an apostolic worker, along with their solutions.[339]

He shares his desire to bring the gospel to the westernmost country in the Roman Empire—Spain. (Spain is the oldest Roman province in the West.[340] It's also referred to as "the limits of the West" and the Western "end of the earth."[341] The province is part of the Latin West, and it's closely related to Rome.[342])

On his way to Spain, the apostle hopes to visit the ekklesia in Rome. But before he does, he intends to visit Jerusalem to deliver the relief collection. He asks for the prayers of the church because he knows he will face danger in the holy city, and he doesn't want his plans to visit the Roman Christians thwarted. He prays to God that his service (that is, the relief collection) is acceptable to the assembly in Jerusalem.[343]

---

338. For a detailed discussion on the Jewish and Gentile problem in the Roman ekklesia, see Peter Lampe, *From Paul to Valentinus*, chap. 5.

339. Some of the most helpful works on Romans are those written by C.E.B. Cranfield (*Romans*); Watchman Nee (*The Normal Christian Life*); Tom Westwood (*Romans: A Courtroom Drama*); Stephen Westerholm (*Romans: Texts, Readers, and the History of Interpretation*); F.F. Bruce (*The Letter of Paul to the Romans: An Introduction and Commentary*); Scot McKnight (*Reading Romans Backwards*); Frederick Dale Bruner (*The Letter to the Romans: A Short Commentary*); Richard Longenecker (*The Epistle to the Romans*); John Stott (*The Message of Romans*).

340. F.F. Bruce, *Paul: Apostle of the Heart Set Free*, 315.

341. Eckhard Schnabel, *Paul the Missionary*, 116; *Early Christian Mission*, 2:1271-1283. Regarding Paul's apostolic strategy stated in Romans 15:18-23, some scholars link this text with Isaiah 66:19-20. They argue Paul sought to reclaim the Table of Nations (listed in Genesis 10) with the gospel. James D.G. Dunn, *Beginning from Jerusalem*, 541-544. Wright agrees that the "farthest limits of the west" means Spain. N.T. Wright, *Paul: A Biography*, 393.

342. Paul would have had to break new ground in Spain, since there's little evidence of a significant population of Jews living there. Therefore, the city may not have had a synagogue, Paul's usual starting place for preaching the gospel. Craig Keener, *Romans*, 177.

343. Romans 15:30-31.

Finally, Paul greets many of the believers in the church by name (chapter 16).[344] He calls the circumcision party out as those who have caused division in the assembly.[345] To Paul's mind, they are slaves to their fleshly appetites and deceivers who speak against the true gospel.

Paul extends warm greetings not only from himself but also on behalf of the Corinthian believers.[346] In addition, he sends greetings from some of his esteemed apostolic co-workers who are with him in Corinth, namely Timothy, Jason, Sopater,

344. Keener breaks down the names of the people Paul greeted in the letter. For instance, Ampliatus (also called Amplias) and Urbanus were slave names and probably freedmen at this point. Herodian was from the Herodian family. Narcissus was a wealthy imperial freedman. Tryphaena and Tryphosa were probably twin sisters. Persis was a slave name from those imported from Persia, so she was either a slave or a freedwoman, etc. Craig Keener, *Romans*, 184-189. A number of scholars working in the field of epistolography (like Gamble, Jervis, and Weima) conclude that Paul sent the greetings to make evident the nature of his relationship with such a large group in Rome and thus to establish his apostolic authority there. Personal correspondence with Runar Thorsteinsson, 5/6/03. Some scholars in the past were troubled by the many people Paul greets in Romans 16, since the apostle had never been to Rome. These same scholars went on to hypothesize that the ending of Romans was originally an ending to another letter written to a different church (perhaps Ephesus) and was later added to the Roman letter. Anthony Thiselton, *Discovering Romans*, 58-61. However, Lampe makes a strong case that Romans 16 is part of Paul's epistle to the Romans. Karl Donfried, *The Romans Debate*, 217-222. See also Douglas Moo, *Epistle to the Romans*, 5-9; Jeffrey Weima, *Paul the Ancient Letter Writer*. According to Witherington, "There is no basis for seeing Romans 16 as addressed to some other church than Rome." Personal correspondence with Witherington, 8/6/22. Weima adds, "I am convinced that the many greetings in Romans 16 are part of Paul's strategy of convincing his unknown and somewhat skeptical readers in Rome that he and his gospel are legitimate. Thus, Paul mentions not only Priscila and Aquila who can testify from firsthand experience the effectiveness of Paul's ministry, but he also mentions quickly Epaenetus as a living, breathing convert due to his (Paul's and not Priscila and Aquila's) ministry." Personal correspondence with Jeffrey Weima, 1/6/24. In short, I side with scholars like F.F. Bruce, N.T. Wright, Weima, Moo, Lampe, Cranfield, Jewett, et al. who argue convincingly that Paul wrote Romans 1 through 16 as a single epistle.

345. Paul Barnett, *Paul: Missionary of Jesus*, 152, 183-186. The scenario I've described is derived from mirror-reading Paul's words in Romans, particularly Romans 3, 6, 9 through 11, and 16:17-18. Note that these are the same people who followed Paul's work in Galatia and Corinth. For details on this argument, see P.W. Barnett, "Opposition in Corinth," 6-9.

346. Gaius, Erastus, and Quartus are among them. Romans 16:23.

and Lucius.[347] Throughout the letter, Paul generously uses the words "therefore" and "because," indicating that he is making an argument leading up to a practical, life-giving conclusion.[348] The epistle also contains many echoes from and allusions to the teachings of Jesus.[349]

Tertius, a brother in the Corinthian assembly, scribes the letter.[350] He also greets the church directly. The epistle is delivered by Phoebe,[351] a patron and ministry provider

347. Romans 16:21. See my previous note on Lucius where I state my agreement with F.F. Bruce that he is *not* to be equated with Luke. F.F. Bruce has written a superb chapter summarizing Romans in F.F. Bruce, *Paul: Apostle of the Heart Set Free*, chap. 29. For an overview of Romans, see David deSilva, *An Introduction to the New Testament*, chap. 15; N.T. Wright and Michael Bird, *The New Testament in Its World*, chap. 22; Clinton Arnold, ed., *Zondervan Illustrated Bible Backgrounds Commentary*, 3:3-99. For an impressive discussion of how Romans has been understood by Christians throughout the centuries, see Richard Longenecker, *Paul, Apostle of Liberty*, 267-373.

348. In the ESV, Paul uses "therefore" seventeen times and "because" twenty-five times.

349. Paul Barnett lists them in *From Jerusalem to Illyricum,* 135-137.

350. Paul regularly used an amanuensis (secretary) to pen his letters, but Tertius is the only one he mentions by name. Tertius' greeting "in the Lord" makes plain that he was a Christian (Romans 16:22). F.F. Bruce, *Romans*, 265. Keener believes it's likely that Paul wrote Romans chapter 16 himself, without the aid of his scribe. Craig Keener, *Romans*, 192.

351. In Romans 16:1-2, Phoebe is described as a *diakonos* (deacon), implying she was a "ministry provider." Some scholars believe Phoebe visited Rome (from Cenchreae) on business. She is also described as a generous, wealthy patron. Personal correspondence with Jeffrey Weima, 1/6/24. Phoebe was a Gentile, likely a free person and a woman of wealth. C.E.B. Cranfield, *Romans: A Shorter Commentary* (Grand Rapids, MI: Eerdmans, 1985), 374; Scot McKnight, *Reading Romans Backwards*, chap. 1. For details on how Pheobe helped Paul in his ministry, see David Balch, et al., *Early Christian Families in Context*, 166; Nijay Gupta, *Tell Her Story*, chap. 7. Hylen points out that women involved in business traveled, so this may have been the case with Phoebe. Or she may have been traveling to visit family. Personal correspondence with Susan Hylen, 6/5/23. Other scholars like Robert Jewett and Nijay Gupta believe Phoebe was in Rome long-term to help establish the ekklesia as a key base of operations for Paul's Gentile mission. Personal correspondence with Nijay Gupta, 6/6/23. Paul also speaks about "deacons" in Romans 16:1 (NIV); 1 Timothy 3:8-12 (NIV); Philippians 1:1 (NIV). Martin believes deacons were responsible for various welfare duties in the believing community. Ralph Martin, *Philippians: An Introduction and Commentary*, revised edition, TNTC (Grand Rapids, MI: Eerdmans, 1987), 59. According to deSilva, "it appears that some believers were specially set apart as 'recognized' servants/ministers." Personal correspondence with David deSilva, 6/22/23. Martin and deSilva, along with other scholars, believe deacons handled administrative tasks like those mentioned in Acts 6:1-6 (even though the term "deacon" isn't used in that text).

in the assembly in Cenchreae.[352] She will bring the letter to the assembly (at her own expense)[353] and read it out loud to the believers.[354] Phoebe probably interprets the letter as well.[355]

Romans

Paul, a servant of Jesus Christ, called to be an apostle, set apart for the Good News of God, which he promised before through his prophets in the holy Scriptures, concerning his Son, who was born of the offspring[a] of David according to the flesh, who was declared to be the Son of God with power, according to the Spirit of holiness, by the resurrection from the dead, Jesus Christ our Lord, through whom we received grace and apostleship for obedience of faith among all the nations for his name's sake; among whom you are also called to belong

352. Cenchreae (sometimes spelled Cenchrea) was the eastern port of Corinth. We've already established that the assembly in Cenchreae, being so close to Corinth (a mere seven miles east), was probably born as a natural outgrowth of the Corinthian assembly. Because Phoebe was a woman of means, it's possible that the ekklesia in Cenchreae met in her house.

353. Richard Longenecker, *The Epistle to the Romans*, 1064.

354. N.T. Wright, *Paul: A Biography*, 327; Bruce Longenecker, ed., *The New Cambridge Companion to St. Paul*, 10, n. 22. For a discussion on the uniqueness of Romans 16, see Anthony Thiselton, *Discovering Romans*, chap. 25. As previously noted, some commentators believe the entire assembly in Rome met in the house of Priscilla and Aquila. Others believe the assembly in Rome met in different houses throughout the city, in which case Phoebe may have carried the letter from one house fellowship to another. F.F. Bruce, *Paul: Apostle of the Heart Set Free*, 384, 389. Reta Halteman Finger gives a comprehensive reconstruction of the situation in Rome based on her reading of the available scholarship. *Roman House Churches for Today*, chaps. 1-8.

355. Scot McKnight, *Reading Romans Backwards*, 5; Richard Longenecker, *The Epistle to the Romans*, 1064-1065. According to Weima, "The letter carrier was sometimes authorized not just to read the letter, but to interpret the intention or meaning of the author. Example: the references to Tychicus at the end of the letters to the Colossians and Ephesians where Paul seems to authorize this letter carrier to fill in the audience the other details related to Paul's life." Personal correspondence with Jeffrey Weima, 1/6/24. The letter to the Romans functions as a speech, rather than a typical letter. Reta Halteman Finger, *Roman House Churches for Today*, 61.

to Jesus Christ; to all who are in Rome, beloved of God, called to be saints: Grace to you and peace from God our Father and the Lord Jesus Christ.

First, I thank my God through Jesus Christ for all of you, that your faith is proclaimed throughout the whole world. For God is my witness, whom I serve in my spirit in the Good News of his Son, how unceasingly I make mention of you always in my prayers, requesting, if by any means now at last I may be prospered by the will of God to come to you. For I long to see you, that I may impart to you some spiritual gift, to the end that you may be established; that is, that I with you may be encouraged in you, each of us by the other's faith, both yours and mine.

Now I don't desire to have you unaware, brothers, that I often planned to come to you, and was hindered so far, that I might have some fruit among you also, even as among the rest of the Gentiles. I am debtor both to Greeks and to foreigners, both to the wise and to the foolish. So as much as is in me, I am eager to preach the Good News to you also who are in Rome.

For I am not ashamed of the Good News of Christ, because it is the power of God for salvation for everyone who believes, for the Jew first, and also for the Greek. For in it is revealed God's righteousness from faith to faith. As it is written, "But the righteous shall live by faith." Habakkuk 2:4 For the wrath of God is revealed from heaven against all ungodliness and unrighteousness of men who suppress the truth in unrighteousness, because that which is known of God is revealed in them, for God revealed it to them.

For the invisible things of him since the creation of the world are clearly seen, being perceived through the things that are made, even his everlasting power and divinity, that they may be without excuse. Because knowing God, they didn't glorify him as God, and didn't give thanks, but became vain in their reasoning, and their senseless heart was darkened.

Professing themselves to be wise, they became fools, and traded the glory of the incorruptible God for the likeness of an image of corruptible man, and of birds, four-footed animals, and creeping things. Therefore God also gave them up in the lusts of their hearts to uncleanness, that their bodies should be dishonored among themselves; who exchanged the truth of God for a lie, and worshiped and served the creature rather than the Creator, who is blessed forever. Amen.

For this reason, God gave them up to vile passions. For their women changed the natural function into that which is against nature. Likewise also the men, leaving the natural function of the woman, burned in their lust toward one another, men doing what is inappropriate with men, and receiving in themselves the due penalty of their error.

Even as they refused to have God in their knowledge, God gave them up to a reprobate mind, to do those things which are not fitting; being filled with all unrighteousness, sexual immorality, wickedness, covetousness, malice; full of envy, murder, strife, deceit, evil habits, secret slanderers, backbiters, hateful to God, insolent, arrogant, boastful, inventors of evil things, disobedient to parents, without understanding, covenant breakers, without natural affection, unforgiving, unmerciful; who, knowing the ordinance of God, that those who practice such things are worthy of death, not only do the same, but also approve of those who practice them.

Therefore you are without excuse, O man, whoever you are who judge. For in that which you judge another, you condemn yourself. For you who judge practice the same things. We know that the judgment of God is according to truth against those who practice such things.

Do you think this, O man who judges those who practice such things, and do the same, that you will escape the judgment of God? Or do you despise the riches of his goodness, forbearance, and patience, not knowing that the goodness of God leads you to repentance? But according to your hardness and unrepentant heart you are treasuring up for yourself wrath in the day of wrath, revelation, and of the righteous judgment of God; who "will pay back to everyone according to their works:" Psalm 62:12; Proverbs 24:12 to those who by perseverance in well-doing seek for glory, honor, and incorruptibility, eternal life; but to those who are self-seeking, and don't obey the truth, but obey unrighteousness, will be wrath, indignation, oppression, and anguish on every soul of man who does evil, to the Jew first, and also to the Greek.

But glory, honor, and peace go to every man who does good, to the Jew first, and also to the Greek. For there is no partiality with God. For as many as have sinned without the law will also perish without the law. As many as have sinned under the law will be judged by the law.

For it isn't the hearers of the law who are righteous before God, but the doers of the law will be justified (for when Gentiles who don't have the law do by nature the things of the law, these, not having the law, are a law to themselves, in that they show the work of the law written in their hearts, their conscience testifying with them, and their thoughts among themselves accusing or else excusing them) in the day when God will judge the secrets of men, according to my Good News, by Jesus Christ.

Indeed you bear the name of a Jew, rest on the law, glory in God, know his will, and approve the things that are excellent, being instructed out of the law, and are confident that you yourself are a guide of the blind, a light to those who are in darkness, a corrector of the foolish, a teacher of babies, having in the law the form of knowledge and of the truth.

You therefore who teach another, don't you teach yourself? You who preach that a man shouldn't steal, do you steal? You who say a man shouldn't commit adultery, do you commit adultery? You who abhor idols, do you rob temples? You who glory in the law, do you dishonor God by disobeying the law? For "the name of God is blasphemed among the Gentiles because of you," Isaiah 52:5; Ezekiel 36:22 just as it is written. For circumcision indeed profits, if you are a doer of the law, but if you are a transgressor of the law, your circumcision has become uncircumcision. If therefore the uncircumcised keep the ordinances of the law, won't his uncircumcision be accounted as circumcision?

Won't the uncircumcision which is by nature, if it fulfills the law, judge you, who with the letter and circumcision are a transgressor of the law? For he is not a Jew who is one outwardly, neither is that circumcision which is outward in the flesh; but he is a Jew who is one inwardly, and circumcision is that of the heart, in the spirit not in the letter; whose praise is not from men, but from God.

Then what advantage does the Jew have? Or what is the profit of circumcision? Much in every way! Because first of all, they were entrusted with the revelations of God. For what if some were without faith? Will their lack of faith nullify the faithfulness of God? May it never be! Yes, let God be found true, but every man a liar. As it is written, "that you might be justified in your words, and might prevail when you come into judgment." Psalm 51:4

But if our unrighteousness commends the righteousness of God, what will we say? Is God unrighteous who inflicts wrath? I speak like men do. May it never be! For then how will God judge the world? For if the truth of God through my lie abounded to his glory, why am I also still judged as a sinner? Why not (as we are slanderously reported, and as some affirm that we say), "Let's do evil, that good may come?" Those who say so are justly condemned.

What then? Are we better than they? No, in no way. For we previously warned both Jews and Greeks that they are all under sin. As it is written, "There is no one righteous; no, not one. There is no one who understands. There is no one who seeks after God. They have all turned away. They have together become unprofitable. There is no one who does good, no, not so much as one." Psalm 14:1-3; 53:1-3; Ecclesiastes 7:20 "Their throat is an open tomb. With their tongues they have used deceit." Psalm 5:9 "The poison of vipers is under their lips." Psalm 140:3 "Their mouth is full of cursing and bitterness." Psalm 10:7 "Their feet are swift to shed blood. Destruction and misery are in their ways. The way of peace, they haven't known." Isaiah 59:7-8 "There is no fear of God before their eyes." Psalm 36:1

Now we know that whatever things the law says, it speaks to those who are under the law, that every mouth may be closed, and all the world may be brought under the judgment of God. Because by the works of the law, no flesh will be justified in his sight; for through the law comes the knowledge of sin. But now apart from the law, a righteousness of God has been revealed, being testified by the law and the prophets; even the righteousness of God through faith in Jesus Christ to all and on all those who believe.

For there is no distinction, for all have sinned, and fall short of the glory of God; being justified freely by his grace through the redemption that is in Christ Jesus; whom God sent to be an atoning sacrifice,[b] through faith in his blood, for a demonstration of his righteousness through the passing over of prior sins, in God's forbearance; to demonstrate his righteousness at this present time; that he might himself be just, and the justifier of him who has faith in Jesus.

Where then is the boasting? It is excluded. By what kind of law? Of works? No, but by a law of faith. We maintain therefore that a man is justified by faith apart from the works of the law. Or is God the God of Jews only? Isn't he the God of Gentiles also? Yes, of Gentiles also, since indeed there is one God who will justify the circumcised by faith, and the uncircumcised through faith.

Do we then nullify the law through faith? May it never be! No, we establish the law. What then will we say that Abraham, our forefather, has found according to the flesh? For if Abraham was justified by works, he has something to boast about, but not toward God. For what does the Scripture say? "Abraham believed God, and it was accounted to him for righteousness." Genesis 15:6

Now to him who works, the reward is not counted as grace, but as something owed. But to him who doesn't work, but believes in him who justifies the ungodly, his faith is accounted for righteousness. Even as David also pronounces blessing on the man to whom God counts righteousness apart from works, "Blessed are they whose iniquities are forgiven, whose sins are covered. Blessed is the man whom the Lord will by no means charge with sin." Psalm 32:1-2

Is this blessing then pronounced on the circumcised, or on the uncircumcised also? For we say that faith was accounted to Abraham for righteousness. How then was it counted? When he was in circumcision, or in uncircumcision? Not in circumcision, but in uncircumcision. He received the sign of circumcision, a seal of the righteousness of the faith which he had while he was in uncircumcision, that he might be the father of all those who believe, though they might be in uncircumcision, that righteousness might also be accounted to them.

He is the father of circumcision to those who not only are of the circumcision, but who also walk in the steps of that faith of our father Abraham, which he had in uncircumcision. For the promise to Abraham and to his offspring that he should be heir of the world wasn't through the law, but through the righteousness of faith. For if those who are of the law are heirs, faith is made void, and the promise is made of no effect.

For the law produces wrath, for where there is no law, neither is there disobedience. For this cause it is of faith, that it may be according to grace, to the end that the promise may be sure to all the offspring, not to that only which is of the law, but to that also which is of the faith of Abraham, who is the father of us all. As it is written, "I have made you a father of many nations." Genesis 17:5

This is in the presence of him whom he believed: God, who gives life to the dead, and calls the things that are not, as though they were. Besides hope, Abraham in hope believed, to the end that he might become a father of many nations, according to that which had been spoken, "So will your offspring be." Genesis 15:5

Without being weakened in faith, he didn't consider his own body, already having been worn out, (he being about a hundred years old), and the deadness of Sarah's womb. Yet, looking to the promise of God, he didn't waver through unbelief, but grew strong through faith, giving glory to God, and being fully assured that what he had promised, he was also able to perform.

Therefore it also was "credited to him for righteousness." Genesis 15:6 Now it was not written that it was accounted to him for his sake alone, but for our sake also, to whom it will be accounted, who believe in him who raised Jesus, our Lord, from the dead, who was delivered up for our trespasses, and was raised for our justification.

Being therefore justified by faith, we have peace with God through our Lord Jesus Christ; through whom we also have our access by faith into this grace in which we stand. We rejoice in hope of the glory of God. Not only this, but we also rejoice in our sufferings, knowing that suffering produces perseverance; and perseverance, proven character; and proven character, hope: and hope doesn't disappoint us, because God's love has been poured into our hearts through the Holy Spirit who was given to us.

For while we were yet weak, at the right time Christ died for the ungodly. For one will hardly die for a righteous man. Yet perhaps for a good person someone would even dare to die. But God commends his own love toward us, in that while we were yet sinners, Christ died for us.

Much more then, being now justified by his blood, we will be saved from God's wrath through him. For if while we were enemies, we were reconciled to God through the death of his Son, much more, being reconciled, we will be saved by his life.

Not only so, but we also rejoice in God through our Lord Jesus Christ, through whom we have now received the reconciliation. Therefore as sin entered into the world through one man, and death through sin; so death passed to all men, because all sinned. For until the law, sin was in the world; but sin is not charged when there is no law.

Nevertheless death reigned from Adam until Moses, even over those whose sins weren't like Adam's disobedience, who is a foreshadowing of him who was to come. But the free gift isn't like the trespass. For if by the trespass of the one the many died, much more did the grace of God, and the gift by the grace of the one man, Jesus Christ, abound to the many.

The gift is not as through one who sinned; for the judgment came by one to condemnation, but the free gift came of many trespasses to justification. For if by the trespass of the one, death reigned through the one; so much more will those who receive the abundance of grace and of the gift of righteousness reign in life through the one, Jesus Christ. So then as through one trespass, all men were condemned; even so through one act of righteousness, all men were justified to life.

For as through the one man's disobedience many were made sinners, even so through the obedience of the one, many will be made righteous. The law came in that the trespass might abound; but where sin abounded, grace abounded more exceedingly; that as sin reigned in death, even so grace might reign through righteousness to eternal life through Jesus Christ our Lord.

What shall we say then? Shall we continue in sin, that grace may abound? May it never be! We who died to sin, how could we live in it any longer? Or don't you know that all we who were baptized into Christ Jesus were baptized into his death? We were buried therefore with him through baptism into death, that just as Christ was raised from the dead through the glory of the Father, so we also might walk in newness of life.

For if we have become united with him in the likeness of his death, we will also be part of his resurrection; knowing this, that our old man was crucified with him, that the body of sin might be done away with, so that we would no longer be in bondage to sin. For he who has died has been freed from sin. But if we died with Christ, we believe that we will also live with him; knowing that Christ, being raised from the dead, dies no more. Death no longer has dominion over him! For the death that he died, he died to sin one time; but the life that he lives, he lives to God. Thus consider yourselves also to be dead to sin, but alive to God in Christ Jesus our Lord.

Therefore don't let sin reign in your mortal body, that you should obey it in its lusts. Also, do not present your members to sin as instruments of unrighteousness, but present yourselves to God as alive from the dead, and your members as instruments of righteousness to God. For sin will not have dominion over you. For you are not under law, but under grace.

What then? Shall we sin, because we are not under law, but under grace? May it never be! Don't you know that when you present yourselves as servants and obey someone, you are the servants of whomever you obey; whether of sin to death, or of obedience to righteousness? But thanks be to God, that, whereas you were bondservants of sin, you became obedient from the heart to that form of teaching to which you were delivered. Being made free from sin, you became bondservants of righteousness.

I speak in human terms because of the weakness of your flesh, for as you presented your members as servants to uncleanness and to wickedness upon wickedness, even so now present your members as servants to righteousness for sanctification. For when you were servants of sin, you were free from righteousness.

What fruit then did you have at that time in the things of which you are now ashamed? For the end of those things is death. But now, being made free from sin and having become servants of God, you have your fruit of sanctification and the result of eternal life. For the wages of sin is death, but the free gift of God is eternal life in Christ Jesus our Lord.

Or don't you know, brothers[c] (for I speak to men who know the law), that the law has dominion over a man for as long as he lives? For the woman that has a husband is bound by law to the husband while he lives, but if the husband dies, she is discharged from the law of the husband. So then if, while the husband lives, she is joined to another man, she would be called an adulteress.

But if the husband dies, she is free from the law, so that she is no adulteress, though she is joined to another man. Therefore, my brothers, you also were made dead to the law through the body of Christ, that you would be joined to another, to him who was raised from the dead, that we might produce fruit to God. For when we were in the flesh, the sinful passions which were through the law worked in our members to bring out fruit to death. But now we have been discharged from the law, having died to that in which we were held; so that we serve in newness of the spirit, and not in oldness of the letter.

What shall we say then? Is the law sin? May it never be! However, I wouldn't have known sin, except through the law. For I wouldn't have known coveting, unless the law had said, "You shall not covet." Exodus 20:17; Deuteronomy 5:21 But sin, finding occasion through the commandment, produced in me all kinds of coveting. For apart from the law, sin is dead. I was alive apart from the law once, but when the commandment came, sin revived, and I died. The commandment which was for life, this I found to be for death; for sin, finding occasion through the commandment, deceived me, and through it killed me. Therefore the law indeed is holy, and the commandment holy, and righteous, and good.

Did then that which is good become death to me? May it never be! But sin, that it might be shown to be sin, was producing death in me through that which is good; that through the commandment sin might become exceedingly sinful. For we know that the law is spiritual, but I am fleshly, sold under sin. For I don't know what I am doing.

For I don't practice what I desire to do; but what I hate, that I do. But if what I don't desire, that I do, I consent to the law that it is good. So now it is no more I that do it, but sin which dwells in me. For I know that in me, that is, in my flesh, dwells no good thing. For desire is present with me, but I don't find it doing that which is good. For the good which I desire, I don't do; but the evil which I don't desire, that I practice.

But if what I don't desire, that I do, it is no more I that do it, but sin which dwells in me. I find then the law that, to me, while I desire to do good, evil is present. For I delight in God's law after the inward person, but I see a different law in my members, warring against the law of my mind, and bringing me into captivity under the law of sin which is in my members.

What a wretched man I am! Who will deliver me out of the body of this death? I thank God through Jesus Christ, our Lord! So then with the mind, I myself serve God's law, but with the flesh, sin's law. There is therefore now no condemnation to those who are in Christ Jesus, who don't walk according to the flesh, but according to the Spirit.[d] For the law of the Spirit of life in Christ Jesus made me free from the law of sin and of death. For what the law couldn't do, in that it was weak through the flesh, God did, sending his own Son in the likeness of sinful flesh and for sin, he condemned sin in the flesh; that the ordinance of the law might be fulfilled in us, who walk not after the flesh, but after the Spirit.

For those who live according to the flesh set their minds on the things of the flesh, but those who live according to the Spirit, the things of the Spirit. For the mind of the flesh is death, but the mind of the Spirit is life and peace; because the mind of the flesh is hostile toward God; for it is not subject to God's law, neither indeed can it be. Those who are in the flesh can't please God. But you are not in the flesh but in the Spirit, if it is so that the Spirit of God dwells in you.

But if any man doesn't have the Spirit of Christ, he is not his. If Christ is in you, the body is dead because of sin, but the spirit is alive because of righteousness. But if the Spirit of him who raised up Jesus from the dead dwells in you, he who raised up Christ Jesus from the dead will also give life to your mortal bodies through his Spirit who dwells in you.

So then, brothers, we are debtors, not to the flesh, to live after the flesh. For if you live after the flesh, you must die; but if by the Spirit you put to death the deeds of the body, you will live. For as many as are led by the Spirit of God, these are children of God. For you didn't receive the spirit of bondage again to fear, but you received the Spirit of adoption, by whom we cry, "Abba![e] Father!"

The Spirit himself testifies with our spirit that we are children of God; and if children, then heirs: heirs of God and joint heirs with Christ, if indeed we suffer with him, that we may also be glorified with him. For I consider that the sufferings of this present time are not worthy to be compared with the glory which will be revealed toward us. For the creation waits with eager expectation for the children of God to be revealed.

For the creation was subjected to vanity, not of its own will, but because of him who subjected it, in hope that the creation itself also will be delivered from the bondage of decay into the liberty of the glory of the children of God. For we know that the whole creation groans and travails in pain together until now.

Not only so, but ourselves also, who have the first fruits of the Spirit, even we ourselves groan within ourselves, waiting for adoption, the redemption of our body. For we were saved in hope, but hope that is seen is not hope. For who hopes for that which he sees? But if we hope for that which we don't see, we wait for it with patience.

In the same way, the Spirit also helps our weaknesses, for we don't know how to pray as we ought. But the Spirit himself makes intercession for us with groanings which can't be uttered. He who searches the hearts knows what is on the Spirit's mind, because he makes intercession for the saints according to God.

We know that all things work together for good for those who love God, for those who are called according to his purpose. For whom he foreknew, he also predestined to be conformed to the image of his Son, that he might be the firstborn among many brothers.[f] Whom he predestined, those he also called. Whom he called, those he also justified. Whom he justified, those he also glorified.

What then shall we say about these things? If God is for us, who can be against us? He who didn't spare his own Son, but delivered him up for us all, how would he not also with him freely give us all things? Who could bring a charge against God's chosen ones? It is God who justifies. Who is he who condemns? It is Christ who died, yes rather, who was raised from the dead, who is at the right hand of God, who also makes intercession for us.

Who shall separate us from the love of Christ? Could oppression, or anguish, or persecution, or famine, or nakedness, or peril, or sword? Even as it is written, "For your sake we are killed all day long. We were accounted as sheep for the slaughter." Psalm 44:22

No, in all these things, we are more than conquerors through him who loved us. For I am persuaded that neither death, nor life, nor angels, nor principalities, nor things present, nor things to come, nor powers, nor height, nor depth, nor any other created thing will be able to separate us from God's love which is in Christ Jesus our Lord.

I tell the truth in Christ. I am not lying, my conscience testifying with me in the Holy Spirit that I have great sorrow and unceasing pain in my heart. For I could wish that I myself were accursed from Christ for my brothers' sake, my relatives according to the flesh who are Israelites; whose is the adoption, the glory, the covenants, the giving of the law, the service, and the promises; of whom are the fathers, and from whom is Christ as concerning the flesh, who is over all, God, blessed forever. Amen.

But it is not as though the word of God has come to nothing. For they are not all Israel that are of Israel. Neither, because they are Abraham's offspring, are they all children. But, "your offspring will be accounted as from Isaac." <u>Genesis 21:12</u> That is, it is not the children of the flesh who are children of God, but the children of the promise are counted as heirs.

For this is a word of promise, "At the appointed time I will come, and Sarah will have a son." <u>Genesis 18:10,14</u> Not only so, but Rebekah also conceived by one, by our father Isaac. For being not yet born, neither having done anything good or bad, that the purpose of God according to election might stand, not of works, but of him who calls,[g] it was said to her, "The elder will serve the younger." <u>Genesis 25:23</u> Even as it is written, "Jacob I loved, but Esau I hated." <u>Malachi 1:2-3</u>

What shall we say then? Is there unrighteousness with God? May it never be! For he said to Moses, "I will have mercy on whom I have mercy, and I will have compassion on whom I have compassion." <u>Exodus 33:19</u> So then it is not of him who wills, nor of him who runs, but of God who has mercy. For the Scripture says to Pharaoh, "For this very purpose I caused you to be raised up, that I might show in you my power, and that my name might be proclaimed in all the earth." <u>Exodus 9:16</u> So then, he has mercy on whom he desires, and he hardens whom he desires. You will say then to me, "Why does he still find fault? For who withstands his will?" But indeed, O man, who are you to reply against God? Will the thing formed ask him who formed it, "Why did you make me like this?" <u>Isaiah 29:16</u>; <u>45:9</u> Or hasn't the potter a right over the clay, from the same lump to make one part a vessel for honor, and another for dishonor?

What if God, willing to show his wrath and to make his power known, endured with much patience vessels of wrath prepared for destruction, and that he might make known the riches of his glory on vessels of mercy, which he prepared beforehand for glory, us, whom he also called, not from the Jews only, but also from the Gentiles? As he says also in Hosea, "I will call them 'my people,' which were not my people; and her 'beloved,' who was not beloved." Hosea 2:23 "It will be that in the place where it was said to them, 'You are not my people,' there they will be called 'children of the living God.'" Hosea 1:10

Isaiah cries concerning Israel, "If the number of the children of Israel are as the sand of the sea, it is the remnant who will be saved; for He will finish the work and cut it short in righteousness, because the LORD will make a short work upon the earth." Isaiah 10:22-23 As Isaiah has said before, "Unless the Lord of Armies[h] had left us a seed, we would have become like Sodom, and would have been made like Gomorrah." Isaiah 1:9

What shall we say then? That the Gentiles, who didn't follow after righteousness, attained to righteousness, even the righteousness which is of faith; but Israel, following after a law of righteousness, didn't arrive at the law of righteousness. Why? Because they didn't seek it by faith, but as it were by works of the law. They stumbled over the stumbling stone; even as it is written, "Behold,['] I lay in Zion a stumbling stone and a rock of offense; and no one who believes in him will be disappointed." Isaiah 8:14; 28:16

Brothers, my heart's desire and my prayer to God is for Israel, that they may be saved. For I testify about them that they have a zeal for God, but not according to knowledge. For being ignorant of God's righteousness, and seeking to establish their own righteousness, they didn't subject themselves to the righteousness of God. For Christ is the fulfillment[j] of the law for righteousness to everyone who believes.

For Moses writes about the righteousness of the law, "The one who does them will live by them." Leviticus 18:5 But the righteousness which is of faith says this, "Don't say in your heart, 'Who will ascend into heaven?' Deuteronomy 30:12 (that is, to bring Christ down); or, 'Who will descend into the abyss?' Deuteronomy 30:13 (that is, to bring Christ up from the dead.)" But what does it say? "The word is near you, in your mouth, and in your heart;" Deuteronomy 30:14 that is, the word of faith which we preach: that if you will confess with your mouth that Jesus is Lord, and believe in your heart that God raised him from the dead, you will be saved. For with the heart, one believes resulting in righteousness; and with the mouth confession is made resulting in salvation.

For the Scripture says, "Whoever believes in him will not be disappointed." Isaiah 28:16 For there is no distinction between Jew and Greek; for the same Lord is Lord of all, and is rich to all who call on him. For, "Whoever will call on the name of the Lord will be saved."

<u>Joel 2:32</u> How then will they call on him in whom they have not believed? How will they believe in him whom they have not heard? How will they hear without a preacher? And how will they preach unless they are sent? As it is written: "How beautiful are the feet of those who preach the Good News of peace, who bring glad tidings of good things!" <u>Isaiah 52:7</u>

But they didn't all listen to the glad news. For Isaiah says, "Lord, who has believed our report?" <u>Isaiah 53:1</u> So faith comes by hearing, and hearing by the word of God. But I say, didn't they hear? Yes, most certainly, "Their sound went out into all the earth, their words to the ends of the world." <u>Psalm 19:4</u> But I ask, didn't Israel know? First Moses says, "I will provoke you to jealousy with that which is no nation. I will make you angry with a nation void of understanding." <u>Deuteronomy 32:21</u> Isaiah is very bold and says, "I was found by those who didn't seek me. I was revealed to those who didn't ask for me." <u>Isaiah 65:1</u> But about Israel he says, "All day long I stretched out my hands to a disobedient and contrary people." <u>Isaiah 65:2</u>

I ask then, did God reject his people? May it never be! For I also am an Israelite, a descendant of Abraham, of the tribe of Benjamin. God didn't reject his people, which he foreknew. Or don't you know what the Scripture says about Elijah? How he pleads with God against Israel: "Lord, they have killed your prophets, they have broken down your altars. I am left alone, and they seek my life." <u>1 Kings 19:10,14</u> But how does God answer him? "I have reserved for myself seven thousand men who have not bowed the knee to Baal." <u>1 Kings 19:18</u> Even so then at this present time also there is a remnant according to the election of grace. And if by grace, then it is no longer of works; otherwise grace is no longer grace. But if it is of works, it is no longer grace; otherwise work is no longer work.

What then? That which Israel seeks for, that he didn't obtain, but the chosen ones obtained it, and the rest were hardened. According as it is written, "God gave them a spirit of stupor, eyes that they should not see, and ears that they should not hear, to this very day." <u>Deuteronomy 29:4</u>; <u>Isaiah 29:10</u> David says, "Let their table be made a snare, a trap, a stumbling block, and a retribution to them. Let their eyes be darkened, that they may not see. Always keep their backs bent." <u>Psalm 69:22-23</u>

I ask then, did they stumble that they might fall? May it never be! But by their fall salvation has come to the Gentiles, to provoke them to jealousy. Now if their fall is the riches of the world, and their loss the riches of the Gentiles; how much more their fullness? For I speak to you who are Gentiles. Since then as I am an apostle to Gentiles, I glorify my ministry; if by any means I may provoke to jealousy those who are my flesh, and may save some of them. For if the rejection of them is the reconciling of the world, what would their acceptance be, but life from the dead? If the first fruit is holy, so is the lump.

If the root is holy, so are the branches. But if some of the branches were broken off, and you, being a wild olive, were grafted in among them and became partaker with them of the root and of the richness of the olive tree, don't boast over the branches. But if you boast, it is not you who support the root, but the root supports you. You will say then, "Branches were broken off, that I might be grafted in." True; by their unbelief they were broken off, and you stand by your faith.

Don't be conceited, but fear; for if God didn't spare the natural branches, neither will he spare you. See then the goodness and severity of God. Toward those who fell, severity; but toward you, goodness, if you continue in his goodness; otherwise you also will be cut off. They also, if they don't continue in their unbelief, will be grafted in, for God is able to graft them in again. For if you were cut out of that which is by nature a wild olive tree, and were grafted contrary to nature into a good olive tree, how much more will these, which are the natural branches, be grafted into their own olive tree?

For I don't desire you to be ignorant, brothers,[ᵏ] of this mystery, so that you won't be wise in your own conceits, that a partial hardening has happened to Israel, until the fullness of the Gentiles has come in, and so all Israel will be saved. Even as it is written, "There will come out of Zion the Deliverer, and he will turn away ungodliness from Jacob. This is my covenant with them, when I will take away their sins." Isaiah 59:20-21; 27:9; Jeremiah 31:33-34

Concerning the Good News, they are enemies for your sake. But concerning the election, they are beloved for the fathers' sake. For the gifts and the calling of God are irrevocable. For as you in time past were disobedient to God, but now have obtained mercy by their disobedience, even so these also have now been disobedient, that by the mercy shown to you they may also obtain mercy. For God has bound all to disobedience, that he might have mercy on all.

Oh the depth of the riches both of the wisdom and the knowledge of God! How unsearchable are his judgments, and his ways past tracing out! "For who has known the mind of the Lord? Or who has been his counselor?" Isaiah 40:13 "Or who has first given to him, and it will be repaid to him again?" <u>Job 41:11</u> For of him, and through him, and to him are all things. To him be the glory for ever! Amen.

Therefore I urge you, brothers, by the mercies of God, to present your bodies a living sacrifice, holy, acceptable to God, which is your spiritual service. Don't be conformed to this world, but be transformed by the renewing of your mind, so that you may prove what is the good, well-pleasing, and perfect will of God. For I say through the grace that was given me, to every man who is among you, not to think of himself more highly than he ought to think; but to think reasonably, as God has apportioned to each person a measure of faith.

For even as we have many members in one body, and all the members don't have the same function, so we, who are many, are one body in Christ, and individually members of one another, having gifts differing according to the grace that was given to us: if prophecy, let's prophesy according to the proportion of our faith; or service, let's give ourselves to service; or he who teaches, to his teaching; or he who exhorts, to his exhorting; he who gives, let him do it with generosity; he who rules, with diligence; he who shows mercy, with cheerfulness.

Let love be without hypocrisy. Abhor that which is evil. Cling to that which is good. In love of the brothers be tenderly affectionate to one another; in honor preferring one another; not lagging in diligence; fervent in spirit; serving the Lord; rejoicing in hope; enduring in troubles; continuing steadfastly in prayer; contributing to the needs of the saints; given to hospitality.

Bless those who persecute you; bless, and don't curse. Rejoice with those who rejoice. Weep with those who weep. Be of the same mind one toward another. Don't set your mind on high things, but associate with the humble. Don't be wise in your own conceits. Repay no one evil for evil. Respect what is honorable in the sight of all men. If it is possible, as much as it is up to you, be at peace with all men. Don't seek revenge yourselves, beloved, but give place to God's wrath. For it is written, "Vengeance belongs to me; I will repay, says the Lord." <u>Deuteronomy 32:35</u> Therefore "If your enemy is hungry, feed him. If he is thirsty, give him a drink; for in doing so, you will heap coals of fire on his head." <u>Proverbs 25:21-22</u> Don't be overcome by evil, but overcome evil with good.

Let every soul be in subjection to the higher authorities, for there is no authority except from God, and those who exist are ordained by God. Therefore he who resists the authority withstands the ordinance of God; and those who withstand will receive to themselves judgment. For rulers are not a terror to the good work, but to the evil. Do you desire to have no fear of the authority? Do that which is good, and you will have praise from the authority, for he is a servant of God to you for good.

But if you do that which is evil, be afraid, for he doesn't bear the sword in vain; for he is a servant of God, an avenger for wrath to him who does evil. Therefore you need to be in subjection, not only because of the wrath, but also for conscience' sake. For this reason you also pay taxes, for they are servants of God's service, continually doing this very thing. Therefore give everyone what you owe: if you owe taxes, pay taxes; if customs, then customs; if respect, then respect; if honor, then honor.

Owe no one anything, except to love one another; for he who loves his neighbor has fulfilled the law. For the commandments, "You shall not commit adultery," "You shall not murder," "You shall not steal,"['] "You shall not covet," Exodus 20:13-15,17; Deuteronomy 5:17-19,21 and whatever other commandments there are, are all summed up in this saying, namely, "You shall love your neighbor as yourself." Leviticus 19:18 Love doesn't harm a neighbor. Love therefore is the fulfillment of the law.

Do this, knowing the time, that it is already time for you to awaken out of sleep, for salvation is now nearer to us than when we first believed. The night is far gone, and the day is near. Let's therefore throw off the deeds of darkness, and let's put on the armor of light. Let's walk properly, as in the day; not in reveling and drunkenness, not in sexual promiscuity and lustful acts, and not in strife and jealousy. But put on the Lord Jesus Christ, and make no provision for the flesh, for its lusts.

Now accept one who is weak in faith, but not for disputes over opinions. One man has faith to eat all things, but he who is weak eats only vegetables. Don't let him who eats despise him who doesn't eat. Don't let him who doesn't eat judge him who eats, for God has accepted him. Who are you who judge another's servant? To his own lord he stands or falls. Yes, he will be made to stand, for God has power to make him stand.

One man esteems one day as more important. Another esteems every day alike. Let each man be fully assured in his own mind. He who observes the day, observes it to the Lord; and he who does not observe the day, to the Lord he does not observe it. He who eats, eats to the Lord, for he gives God thanks. He who doesn't eat, to the Lord he doesn't eat, and gives God thanks. For none of us lives to himself, and none dies to himself. For if we live, we live to the

Lord. Or if we die, we die to the Lord. If therefore we live or die, we are the Lord's. For to this end Christ died, rose, and lived again, that he might be Lord of both the dead and the living.

But you, why do you judge your brother? Or you again, why do you despise your brother? For we will all stand before the judgment seat of Christ. For it is written, "'As I live,' says the Lord, 'to me every knee will bow. Every tongue will confess to God.'" Isaiah 45:23 So then each one of us will give account of himself to God.

Therefore let's not judge one another anymore, but judge this rather, that no man put a stumbling block in his brother's way, or an occasion for falling. I know, and am persuaded in the Lord Jesus, that nothing is unclean of itself; except that to him who considers anything to be unclean, to him it is unclean. Yet if because of food your brother is grieved, you walk no longer in love.

Don't destroy with your food him for whom Christ died. Then don't let your good be slandered, for God's Kingdom is not eating and drinking, but righteousness, peace, and joy in the Holy Spirit. For he who serves Christ in these things is acceptable to God and approved by men. So then, let's follow after things which make for peace, and things by which we may build one another up.

Don't overthrow God's work for food's sake. All things indeed are clean, however it is evil for that man who creates a stumbling block by eating. It is good to not eat meat, drink wine, nor do anything by which your brother stumbles, is offended, or is made weak. Do you have faith? Have it to yourself before God. Happy is he who doesn't judge himself in that which he approves. But he who doubts is condemned if he eats, because it isn't of faith; and whatever is not of faith is sin.

Now to him who is able to establish you according to my Good News and the preaching of Jesus Christ, according to the revelation of the mystery which has been kept secret through long ages, but now is revealed, and by the Scriptures of the prophets, according to the commandment of the eternal God, is made known for obedience of faith to all the nations; to the only wise God, through Jesus Christ, to whom be the glory forever! Amen.[m]

Now we who are strong ought to bear the weaknesses of the weak, and not to please ourselves. Let each one of us please his neighbor for that which is good, to be building him up. For even Christ didn't please himself. But, as it is written, "The reproaches of those who reproached you fell on me." Psalm 69:9 For whatever things were written before were written for our learning, that through perseverance and through encouragement of the Scriptures we might have hope. Now the God of perseverance and of encouragement grant you to be of the same mind with one another according to Christ Jesus, that with one accord you may with one mouth glorify the God and Father of our Lord Jesus Christ.

Therefore accept one another, even as Christ also accepted you,[n] to the glory of God. Now I say that Christ has been made a servant of the circumcision for the truth of God, that he might confirm the promises given to the fathers, and that the Gentiles might glorify God for his mercy. As it is written, "Therefore I will give praise to you among the Gentiles and sing to your name." 2 Samuel 22:50; Psalm 18:49 Again he says, "Rejoice, you Gentiles, with his people." Deuteronomy 32:43 Again, "Praise the Lord, all you Gentiles! Let all the peoples praise him." Psalm 117:1 Again, Isaiah says, "There will be the root of Jesse, he who arises to rule over the Gentiles; in him the Gentiles will hope." Isaiah 11:10

Now may the God of hope fill you with all joy and peace in believing, that you may abound in hope, in the power of the Holy Spirit. I myself am also persuaded about you, my brothers,[o] that you yourselves are full of goodness, filled with all knowledge, able also to admonish others. But I write the more boldly to you in part, as reminding you, because of the grace that was given to me by God, that I should be a servant of Christ Jesus to the Gentiles, serving as a priest of the Good News of God, that the offering up of the Gentiles might be made acceptable, sanctified by the Holy Spirit.

I have therefore my boasting in Christ Jesus in things pertaining to God. For I will not dare to speak of any things except those which Christ worked through me, for the obedience of the Gentiles, by word and deed, in the power of signs and wonders, in the power of God's Spirit; so that from Jerusalem, and around as far as to Illyricum, I have fully preached the Good News of Christ; yes, making it my aim to preach the Good News, not where Christ was already named, that I might not build on another's foundation. But, as it is written, "They will see, to whom no news of him came. They who haven't heard will understand." Isaiah 52:15

Therefore also I was hindered these many times from coming to you, but now, no longer having any place in these regions, and having these many years a longing to come to you, whenever I travel to Spain, I will come to you. For I hope to see you on my journey, and to be helped on my way there by you, if first I may enjoy your company for a while. But now, I say, I am going to Jerusalem, serving the saints.

For it has been the good pleasure of Macedonia and Achaia to make a certain contribution for the poor among the saints who are at Jerusalem. Yes, it has been their good pleasure, and they are their debtors. For if the Gentiles have been made partakers of their spiritual things, they owe it to them also to serve them in fleshly things. When therefore I have accomplished this, and have sealed to them this fruit, I will go on by way of you to Spain. I know that when I come to you, I will come in the fullness of the blessing of the Good News of Christ.

Now I beg you, brothers, by our Lord Jesus Christ and by the love of the Spirit, that you strive together with me in your prayers to God for me, that I may be delivered from those who are disobedient in Judea, and that my service which I have for Jerusalem may be acceptable to the saints, that I may come to you in joy through the will of God, and together with you, find rest. Now the God of peace be with you all. Amen.

I commend to you Phoebe, our sister, who is a servant[p] of the assembly that is at Cenchreae, that you receive her in the Lord, in a way worthy of the saints, and that you assist her in whatever matter she may need from you, for she herself also has been a helper of many, and of my own self.

Greet Prisca and Aquila, my fellow workers in Christ Jesus, who risked their own necks for my life, to whom not only I give thanks, but also all the assemblies of the Gentiles. Greet the assembly that is in their house. Greet Epaenetus, my beloved, who is the first fruits of Achaia to Christ. Greet Mary, who labored much for us. Greet Andronicus and Junia, my relatives and my fellow prisoners, who are notable among the apostles, who were also in Christ before me.

Greet Amplias, my beloved in the Lord. Greet Urbanus, our fellow worker in Christ, and Stachys, my beloved. Greet Apelles, the approved in Christ. Greet those who are of the household of Aristobulus. Greet Herodion, my kinsman. Greet them of the household of Narcissus, who are in the Lord. Greet Tryphaena and Tryphosa, who labor in the Lord. Greet Persis, the beloved, who labored much in the Lord. Greet Rufus, the chosen in the Lord, and his mother and mine.

Greet Asyncritus, Phlegon, Hermes, Patrobas, Hermas, and the brothers[q] who are with them. Greet Philologus and Julia, Nereus and his sister, and Olympas, and all the saints who are with them. Greet one another with a holy kiss. The assemblies of Christ greet you.

Now I beg you, brothers, look out for those who are causing the divisions and occasions of stumbling, contrary to the doctrine which you learned, and turn away from them.

For those who are such don't serve our Lord, Jesus Christ, but their own belly; and by their smooth and flattering speech, they deceive the hearts of the innocent. For your obedience has become known to all. I rejoice therefore over you. But I desire to have you wise in that which is good, but innocent in that which is evil. And the God of peace will quickly crush Satan under your feet. The grace of our Lord Jesus Christ be with you.

Timothy, my fellow worker, greets you, as do Lucius, Jason, and Sosipater, my relatives. I, Tertius, who write the letter, greet you in the Lord. Gaius, my host and host of the whole assembly, greets you. Erastus, the treasurer of the city, greets you, as does Quartus, the brother. The grace of our Lord Jesus Christ be with you all! Amen.[r]

a. 1:3 or, seed.

b. 3:25 or, a propitiation.

c. 7:1 The word for "brothers" here and where context allows may also be correctly translated "brothers and sisters" or "siblings."

d. 8:1 NU omits "who don't walk according to the flesh, but according to the Spirit."

e. 8:15 Abba is an Aramaic word for "Father" or "Daddy," which can be used affectionately and respectfully in prayer to our Father in heaven.

f. 8:29 The word for "brothers" here and where context allows may also be correctly translated "brothers and sisters" or "siblings."

g. 9:11 NU puts the phrase "not of works, but of him who calls" at the beginning of verse 12 instead of the end of verse 11.

h. 9:29 Greek: Sabaoth (for Hebrew: Tze'va'ot).

i. 9:33 "Behold," from "ἰδού," means look at, take notice, observe, see, or gaze at. It is often used as an interjection.

j. 10:4 or, completion, or end.

k. 11:25 The word for "brothers" here and where context allows may also be correctly translated "brothers and sisters" or "siblings."

l. 13:9 TR adds "You shall not give false testimony."

m. 14:26 TR places verses 24-26 after Romans 16:24 as verses 25-27.

n. 15:7 TR reads "us" instead of "you."

o. 15:14 The word for "brothers" here and where context allows may also be correctly translated "brothers and sisters" or "siblings."

p. 16:1 or, deacon.

q. 16:14 The word for "brothers" here and where context allows may also be correctly translated "brothers and sisters" or "siblings."

r. 16:25 TR places Romans 14:24-26 at the end of Romans instead of at the end of chapter 14, and numbers these verses 16:25-27.

Macedonia to Miletus
April 57[356]

After spending three months in Corinth, Paul is poised to head east toward Antioch of Syria,[357] but the Jews hatch a plot to kill him.[358] As a result, he heads back north to Philippi in Macedonia with his apprentices.[359] The trip takes him two weeks by foot.[360] While he is in Philippi, he warns the believers about those who are enemies of the cross of Christ, a warning he has given them more than once.

> *For many walk, of whom I told you often, and now tell you even weeping, as the enemies of the cross of Christ, whose end is destruction, whose god is the belly, and whose glory is in their shame, who think about earthly things. (Philippians 3:18-19)*[361]

While in Philippi, he meets with Luke[362] and sends his eight co-workers ahead of him to Troas.[363] From Philippi, Paul and Luke sail to Troas[364] with the collection from the

356. Clinton Arnold, ed., *Zondervan Illustrated Bible Backgrounds Commentary*, 2b:204.

357. Acts 20:3. It was Paul's plan all along to leave Corinth and travel east, ultimately to Syrian Antioch, but with an important previous stop in Jerusalem to deliver the collection for the needy Jewish believers there. Personal correspondence with Jeffrey Weima, 1/6/24.

358. Paul's Jewish opponents caught wind of his trip and sought to stop him. Donald Guthrie, *The Apostles*, 229-230.

359. Acts 20:3-4. It was this plot that led to a change of plans. Rather than sailing from Corinth to Syria, Paul traveled by foot north through Macedonia and from there to Troas in Asia Minor, while others evidently sailed from Corinth to Troas where they waited for Paul (20:4-6). Eckhard Schnabel, *Early Christian Mission*, 1:122; personal correspondence with Schnabel, 8/25/23.

360. Craig Keener, *The IVP Bible Background Commentary: New Testament*, 387.

361. Paul would pen these words years later in his letter to the Philippians, reflecting back on this warning. Note the words "of whom I told you often."

362. Acts 20:5-6, 13-14. The "we" and "us" included Luke along with the men mentioned in Acts 20:4. Luke had been ministering in Philippi for the past seven years. While Luke was an itinerant physician, his "normal orbit" was to move back and forth between Troas and Philippi. Ben Witherington III, *Letters and Homilies for Hellenized Christians*, 1:67. Many doctors were itinerant during this period. Ben Witherington III, *The Acts of the Apostles*, 490.

363. Acts 20:4-5.

364. Acts 20:5ff. Luke uses "us" and "we" in this section of Acts. According to Bandy, while Paul's apprentices went on foot to Troas, Paul and Luke waited to sail there until after celebrating Passover (Acts 20:6). Alan Bandy, *An Illustrated Guide to the Apostle Paul,* 130.

Philippian church. This takes place after the feast of Unleavened Bread.[365] Because of unfavorable winds, the trip takes them five days. When the men arrive at Troas, Paul's eight apprentices are waiting for him. Paul and his companions spend a full week with the assembly in Troas.[366] The kingdom community in Troas gathers in one of the believer's apartments, two floors above the ground floor.[367]

Paul gathers with the assembly on Sunday evening to break bread (the Lord's Supper).[368] In this third-floor apartment, they gather together for the meeting. Since it's evening, there are many lamps in the room. The air is smoky and stuffy. The apostle is pressed for time. He wants to leave the next day, but he has a lot to say, so he ministers[369] until midnight.[370] The heat from the lamps causes drowsiness.[371]A young boy between the ages of eight and fourteen, Eutychus, sits on a ledge. He's doing his best to stay awake to hear the apostle's entire message. As Paul continues to speak, Eutychus falls asleep and drops out of the window to meet his death.[372]

Paul rushes to the boy and throws himself on his body. He puts his arms around him and exhorts everyone to remain calm, announcing that the boy is alive. Miraculously,

---

365. The feast fell during the week of April 7-14, A.D. 57. Paul was in Philippi during the feast. F.F. Bruce, *The Book of the Acts*, 383.

366. Acts 20:5-6. Luke rejoined Paul in Philippi. The "we/us" narrative picks back up in Acts 20:5. Donald Guthrie, *The Apostles*, 230.

367. Some scholars assert that believers met on the third floor of an *insula* in a large upper room lit with many torches (Acts 20:8). Robert Banks, *Paul's Idea of Community*, 32. In the ancient Mediterranean world, meetings held in the evenings were deeply suspect. Bruce Malina, et al., *Social-Science Commentary on the Book of Acts*, 144. For the time of this gathering (Acts 20:7), whether Saturday or Sunday evening (depending on Jewish or Roman reckoning) and the type of dwelling used, see Ben Witherington III, *The Acts of the Apostles*, 606-607.

368. Acts 20:7-9. Alan Bandy, *An Illustrated Guide to the Apostle Paul*, 131. The "breaking of bread," that is, the Lord's Supper, was taken as part of the Greco-Roman meal. Ben Witherington III, *The Acts of the Apostles*, 606.

369. Paul may have been preaching, teaching, and dialoguing. The NASB refers to it as a "message." The KJV uses "preaching." The ESV uses "speech."

370. Mark Fairchild, *Christian Origins in Ephesus & Asia Minor*, 105. According to Bruce, Paul's last day in Troas was probably April 24, A.D. 57. F.F. Bruce, *The Book of the Acts*, 384.

371. Acts 20:8. For the details on the lamps and their influence, see Craig Keener, *The IVP Bible Background Commentary: New Testament*, 388.

372. Windows were large during this era, large enough for a human to fall through. Craig Keener, "Lessons on Acts," Session 30.

Eutychus rises up. Paul walks back inside and breaks bread with the assembly. Following the meal, Paul continues to speak to the church until dawn.[373]

A divine miracle has just taken place, but Paul and the others don't focus on it nor stop what they are doing. They are completely absorbed with Christ and the message of the kingdom that Paul has been declaring. The next morning, Paul's eight co-workers set sail ahead of the apostle to Assos. Luke sails with them. Surprisingly, Paul chooses not to sail, but to travel by land alone. He wants time alone with his God. Knowing what awaits him in Jerusalem, this walk is Paul's "Gethsemane."[374]

He catches up with them all in Assos where they sail together to Mitylene. The following day, they arrive at the island of Chios, and the day after that, they come to the island of Samos. The following day, they harbor at Miletus, located on the coast about thirty miles south of Ephesus.[375] Paul chooses to sail past Ephesus because he wants to arrive in Jerusalem for the day of Pentecost. But he sends word to the Ephesian elders to meet him in Miletus.[376]

The Ephesian elders make the trip, and Paul gives them an incredibly moving farewell speech. He tells the elders about his plans to visit the assembly in Jerusalem, not knowing what his fate will be. All he knows is that he's committed to bringing the relief fund to the church, despite the prophetic words given that he will suffer in Jerusalem.

---

373. Acts 20:4-12.

374. Acts 20:13. Bandy says that just as they were about to board the ship, Paul told them to leave ahead of him. The apostle decided to walk to Assos himself; he wanted time alone. Perhaps he wanted to pray since he knew that trouble awaited him in Jerusalem, including the threat of imprisonment. Alan Bandy, *An Illustrated Guide to the Apostle Paul*, 131. I believe this was Paul's "Gethsemane" where he surrendered himself to God's perfect will, even though it meant suffering and possibly death. For details on Assos and the significance of Paul's walk there, see Mark Wilson, *Biblical Turkey*, 354-355; Mark Fairchild, *Christian Origins in Ephesus & Asia Minor*, 111-116; Clinton Arnold, ed., *Zondervan Illustrated Bible Backgrounds Commentary*, 2b:206.

375. Alan Bandy, *An Illustrated Guide to the Apostle Paul*, 132. The population of Miletus in the second century B.C. is estimated at 100,000. It is doubtful if the size of the city increased greatly under the Roman Empire. For details on first-century Miletus, see Mark Fairchild, *Christian Origins in Ephesus & Asia Minor*, 45-48; Mark Wilson, *Biblical Turkey*, 261-266.

376. Bandy thinks Paul sent some of his co-workers, like Tychicus and Trophimus (who used to be part of the Ephesian church), to Ephesus to fetch the elders. The trip to Ephesus and back would have taken several days. Alan Bandy, *An Illustrated Guide to the Apostle Paul*, 132.

Now, behold, I go bound by the Spirit to Jerusalem, not knowing what will happen to me there; except that the Holy Spirit testifies in every city, saying that bonds and afflictions wait for me. But these things don't count; nor do I hold my life dear to myself, so that I may finish my race with joy, and the ministry which I received from the Lord Jesus, to fully testify to the Good News of the grace of God. (Acts 20:22-24)

Paul warns the Ephesian elders that wolves will emerge from within and outside the ekklesia. These wolves will bring perverse teachings with an aim to draw disciples after themselves. In light of this warning, he charges the elders to both feed and guard the flock of God and to work with their own hands—for it's better to give than to receive (as Jesus taught).[377] With these words, he exhorts the elders to help those who are weak in the church.[378]

As the apostle closes his farewell speech, he tells the elders they will never see his face again. He kneels and prays with the elders, each of whom breaks out into convulsive weeping as they embrace their apostle. The elders cover Paul's face with kisses of brotherly affection. Utterly devastated by Paul's heartbreaking declaration that he will never lay eyes on them again, they struggle to tear themselves away from his embrace.[379]

The elders escort the apostle to the ship.[380] Paul and his company leave Miletus and follow a course that passes through Cos, Rhodes, and Patara. In Patara, they find another ship crossing over to Phoenicia. They board and set sail across the Mediterranean Sea to Tyre in Palestine. The trip from Patara to Tyre lasts five days. Paul and his company meet for a full week with the assembly in Tyre, a Christian community that might have been founded during the Jerusalem dispersion after Stephen's death.[381]

Some of the brethren in Tyre prophesy that tribulation awaits Paul in Jerusalem, so they urge him not to set foot there. The entire assembly in Tyre (including men, women,

377. Acts 20:35.

378. This refers to those who were needy and vulnerable. Just as the Jerusalem leaders urged Paul to remember the poor (Galatians 2:10), Paul passed on the same word to the Ephesian elders (Acts 20:35, NLT). N.T. Wright, *Paul: A Biography*, 348.

379. The wording used in Acts 21:1 (NIV) is comparable to a nursing infant being torn away from its mother's breast. Clinton Arnold, ed., *Zondervan Illustrated Bible Backgrounds Commentary*, 2b:211.

380. The rest of the narrative, including elements in Acts 20 through 21, contain striking parallels with the Lord Jesus' final journey to Jerusalem. Ben Witherington III, *The Acts of the Apostles*, 627-628.

381. F.F. Bruce, *Paul: Apostle of the Heart Set Free*, 343.

and children) escorts Paul and his companions out of the city. They all kneel on the beach and pray, bidding each other a loving farewell.[382]

A Visit to Caesarea

The apostle and his companions board ship and head south to the seaport town of Ptolemais.[383] They spend a day with the kingdom community in that town,[384] then head off to Caesarea, the home of Philip the evangelist. Paul and his company stay with Philip and his four unmarried daughters, all of whom are prophetesses.[385] While in Caesarea, Agabus—a wandering prophet—pays Paul a visit.[386] In Hebrew prophetic fashion, Agabus dramatically takes Paul's belt and binds his own hands and feet with it. With his feet and hands bound, Agabus prophesies that the Jews in Jerusalem will bind Paul and hand him over to the Gentiles.[387]

Upon hearing Agabus' prophetic word, the believers weep and beg Paul not to enter Jerusalem. Paul, however, cannot be persuaded. He tells them that he is ready to die in Jerusalem for the name of Jesus. Just like his Lord who set His face to go to Jerusalem,[388] Paul is determined to paddle into the gale with all his resolve and travel to Jerusalem to deliver the offering, despite the hazards that await. The assembly stops pressing Paul and yields, saying, "The will of the Lord be done."[389] So Paul, Luke, and the eight co-workers

382. Acts 21:5. Similar to Jesus, Paul endeared himself to everyone in the community, including the women and children.

383. The trip from Tyre to Ptolemais was a two-day walk, but they took a ship to cut down the time. Craig Keener, *The IVP Bible Background Commentary: New Testament*, 391.

384. F.F. Bruce, *Paul: Apostle of the Heart Set Free*, 343.

385. Acts 21:8-9.

386. James D.G. Dunn, *The Acts of the Apostles*, 282. We met Agabus, a prophet from Jerusalem, years earlier (Acts 11:27-28).

387. Acts 21:11. Donald Guthrie, *The Apostles*, 265.

388. Luke 9:51.

389. Acts 21:14, NIV. Agabus' prophecy was one among other prophetic words given to Paul regarding his fate in Jerusalem. The Holy Spirit had testified in every city that imprisonment and affliction awaited the apostle (Acts 20:23). F.F. Bruce, *Paul: Apostle of the Heart Set Free*, 344.

head off to Jerusalem with the relief collection. Paul regards this gift as the "priestly service of the gospel of God."[390]

Jerusalem is a sixty-four-mile trip from Caesarea Maritima.[391] Some of the disciples from the ekklesia in Caesarea accompany the men to Jerusalem.[392]

Troubles in Jerusalem
May 57[393]

Paul and his company arrive in Jerusalem for the feast of Pentecost. Due to the reluctance of many Jews in the Jerusalem assembly to host Paul's Gentile companions, the believers from Caesarea escort Paul and his group to the home of Mnason, a substantial house-holder.[394] The men stay overnight in Mnason's home. Despite Paul's fears, the ekklesia in Jerusalem receives him and his companions warmly.[395]

The next day Paul and the men who are with him have a private meeting with James (the Lord's half-brother) along with the Jerusalem elders.[396] After Paul greets them, he passionately testifies, recounting the remarkable works God has accomplished among the Gentiles through his tireless ministry. When the elders hear the report, they praise God.[397]

390. Romans 15:16, ESV.

391. Barry Beitzel, *Lexham Geographic Commentary on Acts through Revelation*, 206.

392. Acts 21:7-16.

393. Ben Witherington III, *The New Testament Story*, 278; F.F. Bruce, *Paul: Apostle of the Heart Set Free*, 340, 475.

394. Acts 21:16. James D.G. Dunn, *The Acts of the Apostles*, 283. Mnason was likely a person of means since he had a house large enough to host this sizeable group. Craig Keener, *The IVP Bible Background Commentary: New Testament*, 392. Although his name is Greek, Mnason appears to have been a Hellenistic Jew from Cyprus. Alan Bandy, *An Illustrated Guide to the Apostle Paul*, 140; Clinton Arnold, ed., *Zondervan Illustrated Bible Backgrounds Commentary*, 2b:215. He was an early disciple, probably since Pentecost. J.D. Douglas, et al., eds., *New Bible Dictionary*, 786.

395. Acts 21:17.

396. Dunn infers this meeting had to be arranged privately. Peter wasn't present, and the meeting was ominous given the hostile environment with the Jewish believers who didn't like Paul. James D.G. Dunn, *The Acts of the Apostles*, 285.

397. Acts 21:17-20.

Paul and his associates then hand the relief collection to the elders. In so doing, Paul makes good on the promise he made to Peter, James, and John years earlier.[398]

> *They only asked us to remember the poor–which very thing I was also zealous to do. (Galatians 2:10)*

The elders inform Paul that the circumcision party has become the dominating factor in the ekklesia.[399] They now make up thousands of Jewish believers, and they are ultra-zealous for the Law of Moses.[400] They have also picked up a false rumor that Paul teaches the Jews living in Gentile lands to disobey the Law and disregard the ancient Hebrew customs.[401] Paul, therefore, is *persona non grata* in the eyes of many believing and unbelieving Jews in Jerusalem. For this reason, his life is in danger.

James and the elders try to dispel the false rumor, but they now ask Paul to do something to demonstrate that he is a faithful Jew. They recommend that he take part in a Nazirite purification ceremony, along with four other Jewish believers in the assembly who have undertaken the Nazirite vow.[402] Paul agrees and shaves his head for the purification

398. According to some scholars, since Luke only mentions the collection once in Acts, and Paul does not mention its effect in his "Captivity Letters" (the epistles he wrote while imprisoned in Rome), we can assume that the fund did not have the kind of effect that Paul wanted—namely, the uniting of the Jewish and Gentile assemblies. Dunn says the Jerusalem leaders may have even rejected it, given the hostility in Jerusalem toward Paul. James D.G. Dunn, *The Acts of the Apostles*, 284. The offering from the Gentile mission to the Jewish mission was designed to increase the unity of God's people, but also (perhaps) to neutralize the efforts of the circumcision party in Jerusalem. Paul Barnett, *Paul: Missionary of Jesus*, 155-158. Regarding the reception of the relief fund, Wright says we don't know what happened because Luke never discusses it. He likens the narrative to watching a sporting event on television that goes off the air the last ten minutes of the game due to a power outage. N.T. Wright, *Paul: A Biography*, 350.

399. For a helpful sketch of the ekklesia in Jerusalem from Acts 2 through Acts 28, see F.F. Bruce, *A Mind for What Matters*, chap. 10.

400. Acts 21:20. Dunn confirms that this is the same group mentioned in Acts 15:1, 5. They've simply grown in size and strength. James D.G. Dunn, *The Acts of the Apostles*, 199. See also Clinton Arnold, ed., *Zondervan Illustrated Bible Backgrounds Commentary*, 2b:216.

401. Paul had been absent from Judea which allowed false rumors about him to spread more easily. Some Jews from Asia Minor, likely from Ephesus, were present and primed to incite a riot against Paul. Craig Keener, "Lessons on Acts," Session 30.

402. The vow normally lasted thirty days, but the four men appear to have taken a temporary Nazirite vow that was shorter. Alan Bandy, *An Illustrated Guide to the Apostle Paul*, 142; Clinton Arnold, ed., *Zondervan Illustrated Bible Backgrounds Commentary*, 2b:217.

rite.[403] He also pays the expenses of the other four men.[404] He does this to squash the false rumor that he's teaching people the Law of Moses has no value.[405]

To the Jews I became as a Jew, in order to win Jews. To those under the law I became as one under the law (though not being myself under the law) that I might win those under the law. (1 Corinthians 9:20, ESV)

Give no occasion for stumbling, whether to Jews, or to Greeks, or to the assembly of God.... (1 Corinthians 10:32)

The next day, Paul purifies himself with the four Jewish brethren, and they all walk to the temple. The massive structure stands at the top of Mount Zion and towers above every other building in the city.[406] After seven days, some Jews from Ephesus who are visiting Jerusalem for Pentecost[407] see Paul in the temple courts with the four men. They remember Paul from the time he was in Ephesus, and they believe he is an enemy of Moses.

Because these Ephesian Jews had seen Paul and Trophimus walk together in Jerusalem earlier,[408] they mistakenly assume that Paul took Trophimus *into* the court of the Jews. Since Trophimus is a Gentile, they conclude that Paul is desecrating the holy temple by bringing an unclean heathen into the sacred space.[409] In a furious rage, the Jews shout out the following:

403. Unlike Paul's Nazirite vow earlier in the story, which appears to have been for personal devotion, here Paul took the vow of purity for harmony and witness (see 1 Corinthians 10:32).

404. The purification rite is the Nazirite vow discussed in Numbers 6:1-21. For details on these events, see F.F. Bruce, *Paul: Apostle of the Heart Set Free*, 346-353.

405. N.T. Wright, *Paul: A Biography*, 351.

406. Alan Bandy, *An Illustrated Guide to the Apostle Paul*, 142.

407. Pentecost fell on May 29 in A.D. 57. F.F. Bruce, *The Book of the Acts*, 387; Ben Witherington III, *The Acts of the Apostles*, 609.

408. Trophimus was from Ephesus, so he was likely known to the group of Jews from Asia (specifically, Ephesus) who were at the temple.

409. Trophimus *was* in the temple complex with Paul. That wasn't a problem as long as he stayed in the court of the Gentiles. The problem was that some accused Paul of bringing Trophimus from the court of the Gentiles into the court of the Jews.

"Men of Israel, help! This is the man who teaches all men everywhere against the people, and the law, and this place. Moreover, he also brought Greeks[410] into the temple, and has defiled this holy place!" (Acts 21:28)

It's a capital offense for a Gentile to enter the temple area.[411] Gentiles are limited to a segment outside the temple proper called "the court of the Gentiles."[412] Anyone who enters the temple unlawfully could be executed on the orders of the Sanhedrin.[413]

Immediately, the city erupts with turmoil, confusion, and anger. In a mad rush, some of the Jews seize Paul, drag him out of the temple, shut the gates, and begin beating him.[414] The Roman commander (*tribune*), Claudius Lysias, receives word and sends soldiers to rescue Paul from the angry mob.[415] When the Jews spot the Roman commander and his soldiers, they stop beating Paul.[416]

The soldiers arrest Paul, chaining both his hands.[417] They ask him who he is and what he's done to create the violent reaction. The crowd begins to shout out different answers, so the soldiers cannot decipher a clear response. The commander orders the soldiers to take Paul to the Antonia (also called "the barracks"), a fortress that overlooks the temple

410. In the New Testament, Greeks are often used as a synonym for Gentiles.

411. Colin Hemer, *The Book of Acts in the Setting of Hellenistic History*, 126.

412. The court of the Gentiles was still in the temple mount and complex, but not in the temple proper. Personal correspondence with Jeffrey Weima, 1/6/24. An inscription on the temple clearly warned that any Gentile—including any Roman citizen—who violated the sacred area would be put to death immediately.

413. Josephus, *The Jewish War*, 6.2.4; John Drane, *Early Christians*, 27. The one automatic death penalty right that Rome granted Judea was for violating the temple. Craig Keener, "Lessons on Acts," Session 31.

414. Keener describes the scene and gives details on the size of the gates in *The IVP Bible Background Commentary: New Testament*, 393-394. The temple gates were between fifty to eighty feet high, and twenty to sixty feet wide. "Reports of temple desecration could lead to uncontrolled riots" (393). Paul was dragged into the outer court and the gates were shut to avoid desecrating the temple with his blood. Craig Keener, "Lessons on Acts," Session 31.

415. Claudius Lysias, according to Luke, was a good commander who valued accuracy, fairness, and justice. Acts 23:26ff.; 24:22. Alan Bandy, *An Illustrated Guide to the Apostle Paul*, 144.

416. Acts 21:30ff. The soldiers saved Paul's life. There is irony here. God's apostle to the Gentiles was shut out of the most sacred place of Judaism, the temple. But the temple was no longer the place where God's grace was received. God's grace was upon the new temple made without human hands, and it included both Jews and Gentiles. Clinton Arnold, ed., *Zondervan Illustrated Bible Backgrounds Commentary*, 2b:219.

417. Paul's trip to Jerusalem had the same consequence as that of Jesus. Like Jesus, Paul was rejected by his own people and left at the mercy of the Roman authorities. James D.G. Dunn, *The Acts of the Apostles*, 280.

and is connected to its outer court by two flights of steps. They carry the apostle into the fortress because of the violence of the crowd. The crowd screams, "Away with him!"

When Paul gets to the Antonia Fortress, he asks the commander for permission to address the hostile audience. When the commander discovers that Paul speaks Greek, he grants him permission.[418] Paul stands on the steps of the fortress and motions with his hands for the crowd to quiet down. When the mass of people falls silent, Paul begins to address his Jewish audience in Aramaic, and they become even quieter.[419]

Paul shares his testimony of life as a Pharisee and how he became a follower of Jesus of Nazareth. The Jews listen intently, until he tells them that God sent him to the Gentiles, at which point they then begin waving their garments, flinging dust into the air and shouting, "Rid the earth of him! He is not fit to live!"[420]

Because they cannot understand Hebrew or Aramaic, the Roman soldiers assume Paul is intentionally instigating the crowd. So they prepare to interrogate him by flogging.[421]

418. The commander was surprised Paul spoke Greek. He wrongly assumed that Paul was the Egyptian revolutionary who was hated by the Jews. Three years previously, an Egyptian revolutionary had come to Jerusalem claiming to be a prophet. He had led a large band of followers to the Mount of Olives and told them to wait for his word of command. The walls of the city would fall flat, and they would overthrow the Roman garrison and take the city. Governor Felix, however, sent troops in and killed some of them while imprisoning others. The Egyptian discreetly escaped and became the object of rage for many of the Jews in Jerusalem. Josephus, *The Jewish War,* 2.261-263; *The Antiquities of the Jews*, 20.169-172. The fact that Paul spoke Greek probably led the tribune to conclude that Paul wasn't a local Judean revolutionary. Clinton Arnold, ed., *Zondervan Illustrated Bible Backgrounds Commentary*, 2b:221.

419. Acts 22:2. The NIV and the CSB say he spoke to the crowd in Aramaic. See also Alan Bandy, *An Illustrated Guide to the Apostle Paul*, 144. Other translations say he spoke to them in Hebrew. Aramaic is a Semitic language related to Hebrew. It was the mother tongue of those living in Palestine during this time. Clinton Arnold, ed., *Zondervan Illustrated Bible Backgrounds Commentary*, 2b:222. Paul's act of speaking in Hebrew or Aramaic was likely a crowd-pleasing technique that played to the majority of homespun Judeans on the site. Personal correspondence with David deSilva, 2/8/24.

420. Acts 22:22.

421. Acts 22:24. The brutal innovation of flogging could result in crippling or even death even before the truth was discovered. The *flagrum* used here was more lethal than the lictor's rods or the lashes inflicted by the Jewish authorities. For details, including photos of Roman scourges, see Ben Witherington III, *The Acts of the Apostles*, 676-677. For the various reasons why Romans scourged people, see Craig Keener, *Acts*, 3:2479. Romans employed rods on free persons, sticks on soldiers, and scourges on slaves or provincials of equivalent status. It was unlawful for a Roman citizen to be flogged before a trial. Craig Keener, "Lessons on Acts," Session 31; Clinton Arnold, ed., *Zondervan Illustrated Bible Backgrounds Commentary*, 2b:159-160, 225.

Paul, however, declares that he is a Roman citizen. The centurion immediately drops his scourge and tells the Roman commander that Paul is a citizen.[422] The commander's reaction is the same as the city officials in Philippi years earlier—fear![423] He had just put a Roman citizen in chains.

The next day, the Roman commander releases Paul and orders the chief priests and Sanhedrin to hold a trial for him (likely in the temple complex).[424] When the Sanhedrin assembles, Paul fixes his eyes on the judges and declares that he has lived all his life in good conscience before God. Ananias, the high priest, takes offense at Paul's opening statement and orders him to be struck across the mouth. Ananias considers Paul's statement blasphemous.[425] Paul retorts that God will strike Ananias and calls him a "whitewashed wall."[426]

Initially, Paul does not recognize that Ananias is the high priest. However, upon realizing his position, the apostle acknowledges his remark was inappropriate and continues his defense.[427] Noting that half the Sanhedrin is made up of Sadducees and the other half Pharisees, Paul throws a theological curve ball in their midst. He declares that he is a Pharisee, the son of a Pharisee, and that he is on trial for believing in the resurrection of the dead! (The Sadducees and Pharisees are bitterly divided over this point of doctrine. The Pharisees believe in the resurrection, while the Sadducees deny it.)

Immediately, a dispute breaks out in the Sanhedrin. The Pharisees claim they find nothing wrong with Paul, asserting that perhaps an angel spoke to him. The Sadducees don't believe in angels or spirits, so the dispute continues.[428] The argument becomes so

422. How did the soldiers verify that Paul was a citizen? In Rome, citizens wore a toga. But Paul probably didn't in this situation. He may have been wearing a wooden badge (*diploma*) to prove his citizenship. N.T. Wright, *Paul: A Biography*, 357.

423. See Acts 22:29.

424. Personal correspondence with Jeffrey Weima, 1/6/24.

425. Ananias was high priest from A.D. 47-58. James D.G. Dunn, *The Acts of the Apostles*, 303. Other sources say he served from A.D. 47-59. Clinton Arnold, ed., *Zondervan Illustrated Bible Backgrounds Commentary*, 2b:227.

426. Acts 23:3. This imagery comes from Ezekiel 13 and denotes something weak and unstable that appears strong. Clinton Arnold, ed., *Zondervan Illustrated Bible Backgrounds Commentary*, 2b:227. Ananias was known to be abusive. Craig Keener, "Lessons on Acts," Session 31.

427. Acts 23:5.

428. This is based on Acts 23:8. Since the Sadducees believed the Torah, one would think they had to believe in angels, particularly "the angel of the Lord." Perhaps they objected to the far more advanced beliefs in a multitude of angels and demons or perhaps they denied the Pharisaic views of an angelic interim state of

heated that the Roman soldiers remove Paul and bring him back to the fortress, fearing that the Sadducees will tear him apart.

The next night, the Lord Jesus appears to a despondent Paul and stands beside him to encourage him.[429] Jesus tells the apostle, "Take courage! As you have testified about me in Jerusalem, so you must also testify in Rome."[430] Around the same time, Peter and Mark visit Rome to encourage the believers in that city.[431]

MARK WRITES HIS GOSPEL (MARK)

Year: mid-to-late A.D. 50s (or 60s)[432]

From: Rome[433]

---

the soul prior to the general resurrection. Personal correspondence with Craig Keener, 12/4/23 and David deSilva, 2/7/24

429. The preceding narrative is based on Acts 21:17 through 23:11.

430. Acts 23:11, NIV.

431. According to Witherington, Peter visited Rome after Paul wrote "Romans." Ben Witherington III, *Letters and Homilies for Hellenized Christians*, 2:68. Bruce reconstructs the narrative differently placing Peter and Mark in Rome shortly after A.D. 54. F.F. Bruce, *Paul: Apostle of the Heart Set Free*, 392.

432. *The ESV Study Bible*, 1889; William Steuart McBirnie, *The Search for the Twelve Apostles* (Carol Stream, IL: Tyndale, 2013), 192-193; Eckhard Schnabel, *Acts*, 27. According to Gundry, "no compelling reason exists to deny an early date, say, A.D. 45-60." Robert Gundry, *A Survey of the New Testament*, 127. The general consensus is that Mark is the earliest Gospel. Ben Witherington III, *The New Testament Story*, 29. While the early church fathers believed Matthew was the first written Gospel, the arguments supporting Markan priority are stronger. See Michael Licona, *Jesus, Contradicted,* chap. 3. Many scholars date Mark later, asserting that he wrote his Gospel to Roman believers during the time of the great persecution in Rome, around A.D. 64. R. Alan Cole, *Mark: An Introduction and Commentary,* revised edition, TNTC (Grand Rapids, MI: Eerdmans, 1989), 29. Witherington dates it around A.D. 68. Ben Witherington III, *Invitation to the New Testament*, 61. Keener is currently writing a commentary on Mark, moving the dating of the Gospel to A.D. 68. Bernier argues for a dating of A.D. 42-45. Jonathan Bernier, *Rethinking the Dates of the New Testament*, 69-77, 84. According to Keener, there is not enough evidence to be very precise. Therefore, "the 40's through 60s is pretty safe!" Personal correspondence with Craig Keener, 12/4/23.

433. R. Alan Cole, *Mark*, 29; Ben Witherington III, *The Gospel of Mark: A Socio-Rhetorical Commentary* (Grand Rapids, MI: Eerdmans, 2001), 27-30; Mark Strauss, *Four Portraits, One Jesus*, 250; *The ESV Study Bible*, 1889.

To: Gentile believers in the western part of the empire[434]

Author: Mark[435]

Contextual Summary: Mark presents Christ as the Suffering Servant of God.[436] He also presents the story of Israel's renewal under Jesus against its own rulers.[437] According to tradition, Mark's Gospel is based on Peter's account.[438]

Mark is noted for its brevity and fast-paced narrative. It is the shortest of the four Gospels. The narrative moves quickly from one episode to the next, often using the word "immediately" to transition between events. The author emphasizes Jesus' actions over His teachings. The Gospel includes a number of Aramaic expressions, reflecting the Aramaic-speaking context of Christ's ministry.[439]

The Gospel covers John the Baptist's ministry, the baptism and temptation of Jesus (1:1-13); Jesus' ministry in Galilee (1:14-9:50); His journey to Jerusalem (10:1-52); His ministry in Jerusalem (11:1-13:37); and His death and resurrection (14:1-16:20).[440]

---

434. Ben Witherington III, *The New Testament Story*, 77.

435. I agree with those scholars who hold that John Mark is the best candidate to have authored the Gospel. See N.T. Wright and Michael Bird, *The New Testament in Its World*, 557; Craig Keener, *The IVP Bible Background Commentary: New Testament*, 126; Ben Witherington III, *The Gospel of Mark*, 18-27.

436. Mark Strauss, *Four Portraits, One Jesus*, 39.

437. Richard Horsley, *Jesus and Empire*, 74-75, 79-104. For the structure of Mark's Gospel, see Ben Witherington III, *The Gospel of Mark*, 36-49.

438. According to the traditional view, Mark was "Peter's interpreter" and wrote down carefully (though not in order) all that Peter could remember about what Jesus said and did. Eusebius, *The History of the Church*, 3.39; Benjamin Laird, *Creating the Canon*, 26ff. Some modern scholars disagree and "deny that the Gospel shows any signs of being based on traditions mediated by Peter." Richard Bauckham, *Jesus and the Eyewitnesses*, 155.

439. For an overview of Mark's Gospel, see Mark Strauss, *Four Portraits, One Jesus*, chap. 7; David deSilva, *An Introduction to the New Testament*, chap. 5; N.T. Wright and Michael Bird, *The New Testament in Its World*, chap. 24; Clinton Arnold, ed., *Zondervan Illustrated Bible Backgrounds Commentary* (Grand Rapids, MI: Zondervan, 2002), 1:205-317.

440. Mark, along with the other three Gospels, was written in the form of ancient biography. However, ancient biographies were different from modern biographies. They were focused on conveying a person's character and significant deeds, often for moral purposes, with less emphasis on chronological order. See Michael Licona, *Jesus, Contradicted*, chap. 4.

Bound to Caesarea

At daybreak, more than forty Jews assemble to hatch a plot to assassinate Paul. They are so dedicated to carry out their plan that they bind themselves with an oath to forfeit food and drink until the apostle is dead. These Jews approach the Sanhedrin with their scheme, and the Sanhedrin supports them. Paul's nephew hears about the plot and heads to the Antonia Fortress to warn Paul.[441]

Upon hearing the news, Paul tells his nephew to inform the Roman commander about the assassination plan.[442] The commander orders 470 heavily armed troops to secretly take Paul to Caesarea in the middle of the night. The 470 is made up of 200 soldiers, 70 horsemen, and 200 spearmen.[443] The Roman commander writes a letter to Felix, the provincial governor, and explains why he's sending Paul (guarded and in chains) into his custody. Paul spends only twelve days in Jerusalem before he is taken to Caesarea.[444]

441. The apostle was guarded by centurions, which means Paul was a high-level prisoner. Craig Keener, "Lessons on Acts," Session 32.

442. Paul's nephew was young. Craig Keener, "Lessons on Acts," Session 31.

443. Given the Roman-Jewish unrest building in Judea at this time, the Roman commander called for a strong military response to stave off any explosive uprising that would result from Paul's ambush.

444. Acts 23:12-35. For further details on Paul's journey to Jerusalem and his time in Caesarea, see William Ramsay, *St. Paul the Traveler and Roman Citizen*, chap. 13.

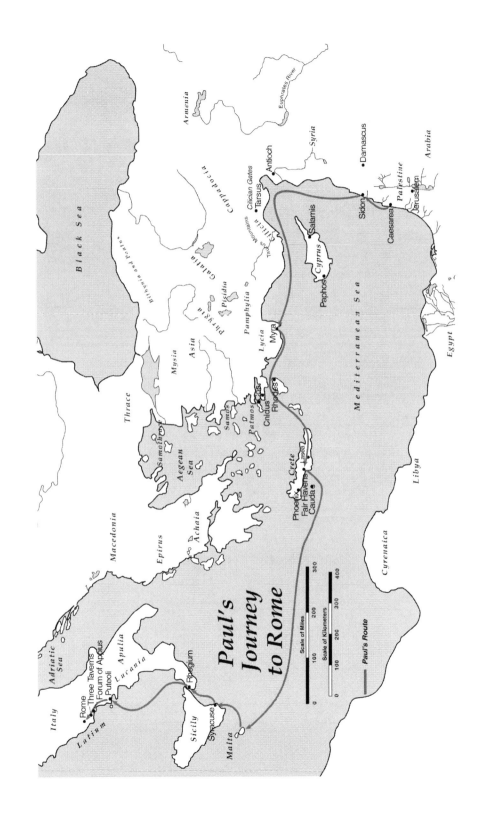

Paul's Journey to Rome

Scale of Miles
0   100   200   300

Scale of Kilometers
0   100   200   300   400

—— Paul's Route

Black Sea

Armenia

Euphrates River

Cappadocia

Syria

Damascus

Cilician Gates
Tarsus
Antioch
Cilicia
Taurus Mountains

Palestine
Jerusalem
Arabia

Salamis
Cyprus
Paphos
Sidon
Caesarea

Galatia

Bithynia and Pontus

Pisidia

Phrygia

Pamphylia

Lycia
Myra

Mysia
Asia

Thrace

Samothrace

Cos
Samos
Patmos
Cnidus
Rhodes

Aegean Sea

Mediterranean Sea

Macedonia

Epirus

Achaia

Crete
Phoenix
Fair Havens
Lasea
Cauda

Libya

Cyrenaica

Egypt

Adriatic Sea

Italy

Rome
Three Taverns
Forum of Appius
Puteoli
Latium
Apulia
Lucania
Rhegium

Sicily
Syracuse

Malta

CHAPTER 12

THE ROMAN CHRONICLE

A.D. 57 – A.D. 62

The following night, the Lord stood by him and said, "Cheer up, Paul, for as you have testified about me at Jerusalem, so you must testify also at Rome." (Acts 23:11)

Paul's Caesarean Imprisonment[1]
A.D. 57 – A.D. 59[2]

Caesarea is predominantly a Gentile city,[3] the Roman capital of the sub-province of Judea. Paul is placed in custody in Herod's palace,[4] which was converted into the Roman governor's praetorium in A.D. 6. He is guarded by a Roman centurion. Paul appears before Felix, the governor of the province. Felix reads the Roman commander's letter about Paul, and he promises the apostle a fair hearing.

---

1. I'm including a very brief treatment of Paul's two-year imprisonment in Caesarea in this chapter. Not a lot took place during those two years with respect to his ministry. Although Acts dedicates more time to this period (Acts 23:23 through 26:32) than Paul's time in Rome (Acts 28:11-31), we know from the epistles that the apostle was far more active in ministry during his Roman imprisonment. Hence, the chapter title, "The Roman Chronicle."

2. Luke may have stayed in Palestine during this time to gather information for his two-volume work, "Luke-Acts." Clinton Arnold, ed., *Zondervan Illustrated Bible Backgrounds Commentary*, 2b:218.

3. F.F. Bruce, *Paul: Apostle of the Heart Set Free*, 354ff. For details on Caesarea, see my previous notes on the city.

4. Acts 23:35, ESV.

Five days later, Paul's court trial begins when Ananias, the high priest, along with some Jewish elders arrive. The Jews bring an orator named Tertullus to prosecute Paul before Felix. As Tertullus begins his prosecution, he flatters Felix.[5] He then accuses Paul of being a troublemaker who stirs up riots among the Jews all over the empire.[6]

Tertullus asserts that Paul is a ringleader of the Nazarene sect, and he even attempted to desecrate the Jewish temple. The Jews who are present affirm the accusations. Felix motions for Paul to respond. Paul defends his actions, pointing out that there are no witnesses present to accuse him. He admits he worships the God of Israel as a "follower of the Way,"[7] and states that he came to Jerusalem to bring his people an offering for the poor.[8]

Felix defers his decision until Claudius Lysias (the Roman commander) arrives. He orders that Paul be kept in guarded custody in the governor's palace, allowing the apostle's friends to care for his needs. On a frequent basis, Felix calls for Paul, hoping the apostle will offer him a bribe.[9] Each time he asks for him, Paul speaks to him about faith in Jesus, righteousness, self-control, and the coming judgment. When Paul talks about the judgment of God, Felix becomes fearful and leaves Paul's presence. He never releases Paul because he wants to gain favor with the Jews.[10] As a result, Paul languishes for two years in one of the cells in the governor's palace in Caesarea.[11]

5. Acts 24:2-4. James D.G. Dunn, *The Acts of the Apostles*, 312.

6. This accusation contains truth. The message of the kingdom is hardly a private individual religious belief or experience. It's highly seditious, touching the material and physical as well as the spiritual. It confronts power of all kinds, both religious and political. The kingdom "coming on earth as it is in heaven" causes chaos and hostility because there are other lords, masters, and kings in the world. N.T. Wright, Lecture 1, The Soularize Conference. See also Andy Johnson, *1 & 2 Thessalonians*, 12.

7. In Acts 24:11, Paul remarks that "twelve days ago" he went to Jerusalem to worship. For a summary of each of the twelve days, see Clinton Arnold, ed., *Zondervan Illustrated Bible Backgrounds Commentary*, 2b:237.

8. Acts 24:17 is the only place where Luke mentions the Jerusalem relief fund. He almost entirely leaves it out of his narrative, even though Paul made a big deal about it in his letters. Craig Keener, "Lessons on Acts," Session 24.

9. "The legal system in the first century was notoriously corrupt." Personal correspondence with Jeffrey Weima, 1/6/24. When Felix heard that Paul had brought "alms and offerings" (Acts 24:17), this may have inspired him to ask for a bribe.

10. According to the Roman historian Tacitus, Felix "practiced every kind of cruelty and lust, wielding the power of a king with all the instincts of a slave." Tacitus, *Histories*, 5.9.1.

11. Acts 23:33-24:27. These texts cover A.D. 57-59. F.F. Bruce, *Paul: Apostle of the Heart Set Free*, 359-362, 475; Clinton Arnold, ed., *Zondervan Illustrated Bible Backgrounds Commentary*, 2b:238-243.

Porcius Festus eventually replaces Felix as governor.[12] Three days after he arrives in the province, Festus pays a visit to Jerusalem. While there, the Jerusalem Jews request that Paul be brought to trial in Jerusalem. (They ask this favor because they plan to ambush Paul and kill him on the way.) Festus tells the Jews to send their leading men to Caesarea and level their accusations against Paul there.

Festus is inclined to gratify the Jewish leaders because he wants to build a good relationship with them. But since Paul is a Roman citizen, Festus must follow the appropriate process. Eight to ten days later, Festus returns to Caesarea and asks that Paul be brought before him. Consequently, Paul's case is reopened. A deputation of the Sanhedrin arrives in Caesarea, and they level accusations against Paul in front of Festus—none of which they can prove.

Paul declares that he has done nothing wrong to the Jews, the temple, the Law of Moses, or Caesar. Wanting to grant the Jews a favor, however, Festus asks Paul if he is willing to go to Jerusalem and stand trial before the Sanhedrin. Paul knows that if he agrees, the Jews will try to take his life. So he exercises his right as a Roman citizen and appeals to Caesar in Rome.[13]

Legally, Festus must comply, and he does. In order for Festus to send Paul to Rome, however, he must write and send a letter with the accused. The letter will outline the nature of the case and the course of events that led up to it. King Agrippa II, ruler of part of Northern Palestine, is visiting Caesarea with his sister, Bernice, at this time. Agrippa is well-versed in the Jewish faith. Since Festus is unclear about Jewish law and unsure how to craft a letter about Paul's case, he rehearses Paul's situation to King Agrippa.

Agrippa requests to hear Paul for himself. The next day, Paul is brought before King Agrippa and Bernice to offer his defense.[14] Paul recounts his background as a devoted Pharisee, his opposition to the name of Jesus, his profound encounter with Christ on the way to Damascus, and his commission to bring the good news of God's kingdom to the Gentiles, urging them to repent and believe the message.

Paul then states emphatically that he's never contradicted Moses and the prophets, but rather, he has echoed what the Law has revealed—namely that the Messiah must suffer

---

12. Festus is believed to have governed Judea from A.D. 59-62. F.F. Bruce, *The Book of the Acts*, 449, n. 44.

13. For details on Paul's appeal to Caesar and the legality of it, see Clinton Arnold, ed., *Zondervan Illustrated Bible Backgrounds Commentary*, 2b:243.

14. Acts 26:1-29. Keener gives a detailed commentary on Paul's brilliant defense in *Acts: An Exegetical Commentary* (Grand Rapids, MI: Baker Academic, 2015), 4:3491ff. See also F.F. Bruce, *The Book of the Acts*, 461-473.

and be the first person to rise from the dead. At this point, Festus shouts out, "Paul, you are crazy! Your great learning is driving you insane!"[15] Paul responds saying that he has spoken sober truth. Agrippa finds Paul's testimony persuasive. He concludes that Paul has done nothing worthy of death or imprisonment. But Festus cannot release Paul because the apostle has already appealed to Caesar.[16]

Paul's Voyage to Rome[17]
September 59[18]

Paul and some other prisoners are placed in the custody of a Roman centurion named Julius. Julius is part of the Imperial Regiment. He is a kind, humane, civilized person and holds Paul in high regard.[19] Paul and the prisoners are guarded by Roman soldiers. Luke and Aristarchus accompany Paul on the voyage to Rome. Luke is approved as the ship's doctor, and Aristarchus passes as Paul's servant.[20] They all board a ship slated to sail for ports along the coast of the province of Syria and Asia.

The next day the ship stops in Sidon, which is about seventy miles from Caesarea.[21] Julius treats Paul kindly and allows him to visit his friends in Sidon who tend to his needs.[22]

15. Acts 26:24. Paul was well aware that his gospel was scandalous blasphemy to the Jews and foolish madness to the Gentiles. N.T. Wright, *Paul: A Biography*, 370, 406.

16. The narrative in this section is taken from Acts 25 through 26. For details, see Clinton Arnold, ed., *Zondervan Illustrated Bible Backgrounds Commentary*, 2b:244-251.

17. Some scholars estimate that Paul's entire journey to Rome (beginning from Jerusalem) spanned 2,250 miles. Rose Publishing, *Rose Chronological Guide to the Bible*, 156. For a highly specific treatment of the events that led up to Paul's visit to Rome, his voyage there, and his time spent imprisoned in the city, see Craig Keener, *Acts*, 4:3349-3780.

18. F.F. Bruce, *Paul: Apostle of the Heart Set Free*, 475.

19. Acts 27:3. Alan Bandy, *An Illustrated Guide to the Apostle Paul*, 155.

20. The other seven apostolic workers probably returned to their homes after Paul was seized in Jerusalem. F.F. Bruce, *Paul: Apostle of the Heart Set Free*, 358. For details on the "we" and "sea" passages in Acts, see Ben Witherington III, *The Acts of the Apostles*, 480-486.

21. Sidon was one of the major cities of Phoenicia. Clinton Arnold, ed., *Zondervan Illustrated Bible Backgrounds Commentary*, 2b:252. Churches were transplanted in Phoenicia after Stephen's martyrdom (Acts 11:19).

22. Acts 27:3. They probably stopped in Sidon for trade. It's possible that Paul made a visit to Sidon on his way to Cilicia when he left Jerusalem after his conversion, when friendships were forged. Personal

From Sidon, the ship sails toward the coast of Asia, encountering strong prevailing winds from the northwest. Therefore, the ship sails along the east coast of Cyprus, using the island as a natural barrier. The progress is slow due to the strong winds.[23]

They then sail across the open sea along the coasts of Cilicia and Pamphylia, making a stop at Myra in Lycia.[24] (The trip from Sidon to Myra is over 400 miles.) In Myra, the centurion finds a grain ship of Alexandria sailing to Italy. The men set sail on the Alexandrian ship which contains a total of 276 passengers.[25]

The Day of Atonement
October 5[26]
A.D. 59

After several days of slow sailing, the ship moves near Cnidus. Because the wind is so unfavorable, they sail to the mountainous island of Crete.[27] With great difficulty, they stop at Fair Havens, a small fishing settlement near the town of Lasea. The trip has now become so dangerous that Paul offers his advice to the ship's officers.[28] He predicts that if the crew sets sail now, the voyage will lead to a shipwreck. The officer in charge of the prisoners ignores Paul's advice. He instead listens to the judgment of the ship's captain, who advises them to set out to sea and stop in Phoenix for the winter. (Phoenix is a harbor farther up the coast of Crete and offers greater protection.)

---

correspondence with Alan Bandy, 7/19/23. On the other hand, churches in Tyre and Sidon (both in Phoenicia) could have been transplanted during the events of Acts 11:19. And Paul may have visited them in Acts 15:3. Craig Keener, *Acts*, 4:3577-3578.

23. Acts 27:4. Alan Bandy, *An Illustrated Guide to the Apostle Paul*, 156.

24. Acts 27:5. According to the Western text, the voyage from Caesarea to Myra took fifteen days. Otto F.A. Meinardus, *St. Paul in Greece*, 106.

25. Acts 27:37. Clinton Arnold, ed., *Zondervan Illustrated Bible Backgrounds Commentary*, 2b:261-264.

26. N.T. Wright, *Paul: A Biography*, 377; F.F. Bruce, *Paul: Apostle of the Heart Set Free*, 370; Ben Witherington III, *The Acts of the Apostles*, 762.

27. J.D. Douglas, et al., eds., *New Bible Dictionary*, 249.

28. The danger was due to the slow progress, which meant that the hazardous weather of the winter season was fast approaching.

The Shipwreck

While they drift along the shore of Crete, a furious northeasterly wind called *Euraquilo* catches the ship. For two weeks the ship is driven along by the storm.[29] During this time, an angel appears to Paul and tells him not to be afraid. The angel assures the apostle that he will stand in the presence of Caesar. The angel also explains that God has granted that Paul and the lives of the entire crew will be spared. Paul encourages the crew with this news and offers some practical direction during the crisis.[30]

At last, the crew spots the island of Malta and tries to make landfall. The bow is stuck in a reef and the pounding waves destroy the ship. The passengers almost lose their lives. Yet they all escape unharmed, just as Paul predicted. Paul shows himself to be a practical and bold man in the midst of major crisis.[31]

Wintering in Malta
A.D. 59 – 60

It is morning. The crew and passengers arrive safely ashore on the island of Malta.[32] Malta is eighteen miles long and eight miles wide, located some sixty miles south of Sicily.[33] The crew is wet, cold, hungry, and sick. The natives of Malta are hospitable and build a fire for the men so they can warm themselves. Paul makes himself useful again, gathering

---

29. To save space, I have intentionally omitted the details of the shipwreck. Luke's description is a classic in ancient literature, a masterpiece of vivid narrative. A good deal of our knowledge of ancient seamanship comes from his account which appears in Acts 27:14-44. N.T. Wright offers an imaginative theological reading of Acts chaps. 27 and 28. He states that the equivalent in Acts to the cross is the shipwreck. If the gospel was going to get to Rome, it had to carry the cross with it. The powers of the deep sea were overcome. Paul came through it on the other side just as Jesus came through the cross on the other side in resurrection. N.T. Wright, Lecture 1, The Soularize Conference.

30. For details, see Clinton Arnold, ed., *Zondervan Illustrated Bible Backgrounds Commentary*, 2b:258ff.

31. Acts 27.

32. Wright's timeline puts the date from November 59 to January or February 60. N.T. Wright, *Paul: A Biography*, 377. See also Clinton Arnold, ed., *Zondervan Illustrated Bible Backgrounds Commentary*, 2b:264.

33. Barry Beitzel, *Lexham Geographic Commentary on Acts through Revelation*, 406. The shortest distance between Malta and Sicily across the Mediterranean Sea is about sixty miles.

brushwood to keep the fire burning. As he does, a venomous snake emerges from the brushwood and bites him on the hand.

The natives conclude that Paul is receiving divine justice for some crime he committed. Paul, however, shakes the snake from his hand unharmed. The natives of Malta are shocked that Paul never swells up, becomes ill, or dies after the snakebite. So they conclude he must be a god. Publius, the chief man on the island, takes Paul, Luke, and Aristarchus into his home for three days. Publius' father is sick with dysentery. Paul lays his hands on the man and prays for God to heal him, and he is miraculously healed. News of the healing spreads throughout the island, and other sick people come to Paul to be healed. And they are!

The entire crew spends three winter months on Malta. When sailing is no longer a hazard, they set sail for Rome on a different Alexandrian ship.[34] Around the same time, the Lycus valley suffers an earthquake, devastating the cities of Laodicea, Colossae, and Hierapolis.[35]

The Roman Christians Greet Paul

The crew stops at Syracuse, the major port city in Sicily, where they stay three days. After that, they arrive in Rhegium. A strong wind propels them to Puteoli, the major port for those traveling to Rome. In Puteoli, Paul and his companions find some Jesus-followers.[36] The brothers and sisters in Puteoli invite Paul to stay with them for seven days. Julius kindly grants Paul permission. From Puteoli, Paul and his companions are escorted on the Via Appia (also called the Appian Way). The Via Appia is a great Roman road known as "the queen of the long roads."

---

34. Acts 28:1-11. For details on the journey from Malta to Rome, see Ben Witherington III, *The Acts of the Apostles*, 783-816.

35. Tacitus dates the earthquake to A.D. 60. *Annals*, 14.27. See also Jonathan Bernier, *Rethinking the Dates of the New Testament*, 164; F.F. Bruce, *Paul: Apostle of the Heart Set Free*, 408, n. 4. Laodicea was rebuilt, but Colossae never completely recovered. John McRay, *Archaeology of the New Testament* (Grand Rapids, MI: Baker Books, 1990), 262.

36. Acts 28:13-14. Luke uses the term that refers to brothers and sisters in Christ, though it's often translated "brothers" in many Bibles. James D.G. Dunn, *The Acts of the Apostles*, 349. We don't know anything about these Jesus-followers or how they heard the gospel, but they could have been converted at Pentecost in Acts 2. Personal correspondence with Alan Bandy, 7/19/23. See also Craig Keener, *Acts*, 4:3703-3704.

According to tradition, Matthew (the apostle) has been traveling through Palestine, Egypt and Ethiopia, proclaiming the gospel. He then travels to Syrian Antioch where he writes his account of the Lord's life.[37]

MATTHEW WRITES HIS GOSPEL (MATTHEW)

Year: mid A.D. 50s to early 60s[38]

From: Antioch of Syria[39]

To: The Jews[40]

Author: Matthew[41]

37. Tradition places him in these various places. See Thomas Schmidt, *The Apostles After Acts,* chap. 21. However, it's impossible to verify these accounts.

38. *The ESV Study Bible,* 1815. Some scholars are certain this Gospel was written before the destruction of Jerusalem in A.D. 70 because the temple was spoken of as still standing (Matthew 24:15). Walter Elwell, et al., eds., *Tyndale Bible Dictionary,* 868; R.T. France, *The Gospel of Matthew,* 19. Bernier dates Matthew A.D. 45-59. Jonathan Bernier, *Rethinking the Dates of the New Testament,* 80-82, 84. Craig Blomberg dates Matthew between A.D. 58-69. Gundry believes Matthew was written later, between A.D. 65-67. Robert Gundry, *Matthew: A Commentary on His Handbook for a Mixed Church under Persecution,* second edition (Grand Rapids, MI: Eerdmans, 1994), 607. Other scholars date it from A.D. 70-100. N.T. Wright and Michael Bird, *The New Testament in Its World,* 584; Joel Green, Jeannine Brown, and Nicholas Perrin, eds., *Dictionary of Jesus and the Gospels,* second edition (Downers Grove, IL: InterVarsity Press, 2013), 576; Mark Strauss, *Four Portraits, One Jesus,* 303-304; Craig Keener, *The IVP Bible Background Commentary: New Testament,* 44.

39. Robert Gundry, *Matthew,* 609. Most interpreters believe Matthew's Gospel was composed in Syria or Palestine, but Syria is the stronger option. Daniel Harrington, *The Gospel of Matthew,* 9-10; Craig Keener, *The IVP Bible Background Commentary: New Testament,* 45. Galilee (specifically Capernaum) has also been suggested. Ben Witherington III, *Invitation to the New Testament,* 88.

40. Mark Strauss, *Four Portraits, One Jesus,* 39. Matthew's Gospel was written in Greek, not Aramaic or Hebrew, and it was penned in the genre of ancient biography. Ben Witherington III, *Matthew,* 7, 11. For an overview of Matthew's Gospel, see Strauss, *Four Portraits, One Jesus,* chap. 8; David deSilva, *An Introduction to the New Testament,* chap. 6; N.T. Wright and Michael Bird, *The New Testament in Its World,* chap. 25; Clinton Arnold, ed., *Zondervan Illustrated Bible Backgrounds Commentary,* 1:3-203.

41. The text doesn't name the author. The words, "According to Matthew" do not appear in the original. Daniel Harrington, *The Gospel of Matthew,* 8. However, church tradition unanimously attributes this Gospel to the authorship of the apostle Matthew, a tax collector. R.T. France, *Matthew: An Introduction and Commentary,* TNTC (Grand Rapids, MI: Eerdmans, 1985), 30. Among Galileans, a tax collector would be the most

Contextual Summary: Matthew presents Christ as the Messiah, King of the Jews.[42] In the beginning of the Gospel, the apostle introduces Jesus as Emmanuel, "God with us." At the end of the Gospel, he quotes Jesus saying, "I am with you always." Everything in between is the story of how God came to dwell with humans in the person of Jesus.[43]

The Gospel is broken up into five discourses (Matthew chapters 5-7, 10, 13, 18, 23-25). Each discourse ends the same ("When Jesus had finished saying these things," etc.).[44] The beatitudes in Matthew 5 (at the beginning of Jesus' ministry) correspond with the woes in Matthew 23 (at the end of His ministry).[45] The climax of Matthew's story is Jesus ruling on earth as He rules in heaven.[46]

February 60

When the assembly in Rome is notified that Paul is near, some of the brothers in the church head to a town thirty-three miles away called Three Taverns. There they meet Paul and escort him on the last part of his journey to Rome. Others from the church walk ten

---

apt to take notes. This buttresses the case that Matthew authored the Gospel. Craig Keener, *The IVP Bible Background Commentary: New Testament*, 44. According to Guthrie, "there is no conclusive reason for rejecting the strong external testimony regarding the authorship of Matthew...." Donald Guthrie, *New Testament Introduction*, 53. See also Mark Strauss, *Four Portraits, One Jesus*, 305. For the various arguments surrounding authorship, see Robert Gundry, *Matthew*, 609-622; Joel Green, et al., eds., *Dictionary of Jesus and the Gospels*, 574-576. Roughly 90 percent of Mark's accounts show up in Matthew's Gospel, and Mark's grammar is much weaker. For this reason, many scholars believe Matthew drew on Mark's material. Craig Keener, et al., *NIV Cultural Backgrounds Study Bible*, 1682. For a detailed discussion on the background of Matthew's Gospel, see Craig Keener, *The Gospel of Matthew*, xxv-71.

42. Matthew also presents Jesus as the giver of God's Law, prophecy, and wisdom. Ben Witherington III, *Matthew*, 15.

43. C.H. Dodd, *The Founder of Christianity*, 173.

44. Some scholars add Matthew 23 to the list, making it six discourses. Ben Witherington III, *Matthew*, 14-15.

45. Ben Witherington III, *Matthew*, 427; Daniel Harrington, *The Gospel of Matthew*, 326.

46. N.T. Wright, Lecture 3, The Soularize Conference. According to Wright, the Gospels tell the story of how the kingdom of God came to earth as it is in heaven and how it was launched in Jesus. Goldingay cleverly shows how Matthew uses the Old Testament in *Reading Jesus's Bible*, chaps. 2-6.

miles farther south and greet the apostle and his companions at a town called the Forum of Appius.[47] As Paul lays eyes on the Roman Christians, he is greatly encouraged and gives thanks to God. (Recall that Paul had written a letter to the Roman assembly three years earlier, where he shared his desire to visit them. But none of the believers ever imagined he would visit as a prisoner.) Finally, Paul arrives in Rome.[48]

While Paul is in Rome, Judas (also called Thaddeus) brings the gospel to the region of modern-day Lebanon, Turkey, Iran, and Syria. He is martyred near the summit of Mount Ararat around A.D. 60.[49]

Paul's First Roman Imprisonment[50]

In Rome, Paul is placed under house arrest.[51] He lives in his own private lodging in a Roman *insula* (apartment), and he's chained by his wrist to a Roman guard.[52] The guard is relieved by another soldier every four hours. Each guard belongs to the Praetorian Guard, the emperor's personal bodyguards.[53] Paul quickly becomes a talking point among the

47. Acts 28:14-15, ESV. The Forum of Appius (or Appii) was a town in Italy about forty miles southeast of Rome on the Appian Way. Herbert Lockyer, ed., *Nelson's Illustrated Bible Dictionary*, 79.

48. F.F. Bruce, *Paul: Apostle of the Heart Set Free*, 475.

49. Richard Orzeck, *The Twelve Apostles of Jesus* (Trumansburg, NY: Purrfect Love Publishing, 2021), 102-107. According to tradition, after Thaddeus baptized the daughter of a king, the king became furious and ordered all Christians to be killed, including his own daughter and the apostle. While this tradition is important in some Christian traditions, particularly Syriac Christianity, its historical reliability is debatable.

50. For further details on Paul's voyage to Rome and his first imprisonment in the city, see William Ramsay, *St. Paul the Traveler and Roman Citizen*, chaps. 14-15.

51. This likely occurred in A.D. 60. Ben Witherington III, *The Acts of the Apostles*, 79, 82, 85. Paul spent two years under house arrest (A.D. 60-62). Ben Witherington III, *Paul's Letter to the Philippians*, 45.

52. According to Witherington, the dwelling was rented at Paul's expense, and it was a temporary dwelling, the kind a person would rent if they weren't staying for a long time. Ben Witherington III, *The Acts of the Apostles*, 813. According to Philippians 4:22, some of the emperor's household were converted, probably those from among the slaves and freedmen who worked for Caesar's household. Eckhard Schnabel, *Paul the Missionary*, 115.

53. Philippians 1:13.

guards. On the third day of his house arrest, the apostle invites the local leaders of the Jewish community to visit him. He does so because he cannot attend the synagogues to visit them.[54]

When the Jewish leaders arrive, Paul introduces himself and summarizes the course of events that brought him to Rome. The Jewish leaders have never heard of Paul or his case. No one from Judea wrote letters about him, and no Jew living in Rome who visited Judea brought back a bad report about him.[55] However, the Jewish leaders are aware of the Christians, for the "new sect" is spoken against everywhere.[56] Consequently, the Jewish leaders are eager to hear Paul's views about the new faith.

On a scheduled day, the leaders visit Paul again to hear him present the gospel. It is a marathon session, stretching from morning to evening. When Paul finishes, the response is mixed. Some of the leaders give serious heed to his words, finding them persuasive. Others reject his message outright. Paul quotes Isaiah 6, exposing their stubborn and callous hearts for rejecting the salvation God has graciously offered them.[57] The apostle then

54. According to Bandy, there may have been up to five synagogues in Rome at this time, although there may have been more. So Paul would have had to send a note of invitation to each one. Alan Bandy, *An Illustrated Guide to the Apostle Paul*, 167. See also Clinton Arnold, ed., *Zondervan Illustrated Bible Backgrounds Commentary*, 2b:270-271. Interestingly, Paul greeted the leaders with the term "brothers," indicating his Jewish connection with them (Acts 28:17). He was not calling them spiritual brothers in Christ, however.

55. Acts 28:21. Some may wonder if this text contradicts my proposal that Romans 16:7 refers to the influence of the circumcision party from Jerusalem. I agree with Barnett on this point who says, "Paul wrote Romans c. 57 and arrived in Rome c. 60. Do we assume that the Jewish leaders in Rome belonged to or knew about the Jerusalem based anti-Paul 'Judaizers'? On the contrary, I think they were just mainstream Jews who knew little if anything about the Jewish Jerusalem-based anti-Paul movement. There were, I believe, tens of thousands of Jews in Rome, many of whom may not have been aware of Paul and the mission against him. Also, to illustrate the point about varying Jewish responses to Paul, the synagogue in Berea welcomed Paul and appeared to have gone over *en masse* to him. I don't think there is a contradiction here." Personal correspondence with Paul Barnett, 2/10/24.

56. Acts 28:22.

57. Paul boldly quotes this bone-chilling text from Isaiah 6:9-10: "Go to this people and say, in hearing, you will hear, but will in no way understand. In seeing, you will see, but will in no way perceive. For this people's heart has grown callous. Their ears are dull of hearing. Their eyes they have closed. Lest they should see with their eyes, hear with their ears, understand with their heart, and would turn again, then I would heal them."

announces he will hereafter preach to the Gentiles, because they (unlike the Jews) will receive the good news about the Messiah Jesus and His kingdom.[58]

The Jewish leaders dispute what Paul has said, but they cannot arrive at a consensus. After hearing him quote Isaiah 6, they all leave.[59] And for the next two years, Paul carries on the work of proclaiming the life-transforming gospel of the kingdom[60] and teaching the Lord Jesus Christ from his *insula,* where he is confined.

> *Paul stayed two whole years in his own rented house and received all who were coming to him, preaching God's Kingdom, and teaching the things concerning the Lord Jesus Christ with all boldness, without hindrance. (Acts 28:30-31)*[61]

While imprisoned in Rome, Paul's detractors from many different cities travel to the Eternal City. The fact that Paul is permitted to live in a rented house with only one guard indicates the officials expect him to be acquitted.[62] Although he remains under house arrest, he welcomes everyone who visits him and enjoys complete freedom of speech.[63] For this reason, Paul's imprisonment causes the gospel to advance in multiple ways.

---

58. While Paul believed there would be a massive turning of Jews to the faith in the future (Romans 11:25-32), it was at this point that he departed from his standard practice of preaching the gospel "to the Jew first." He now focused fully on the Gentiles. Clinton Arnold, ed., *Zondervan Illustrated Bible Backgrounds Commentary*, 2b:272-273.

59. Acts 28:12-29. For a discussion on why the book of Acts ends with Paul awaiting trial, see Thomas Schmidt, *The Apostles After Acts: A Sequel* (Eugene, OR: Cascade Books, 2013), 189-195.

60. Paul's message of Christ and His kingdom is not distinct from the message that Jesus preached. Acts 28 ends with Paul fulfilling Scripture, while Luke 24 ends with Jesus fulfilling Scripture. Bruce Malina, et al., *Social-Science Commentary on the Book of Acts*, 180; James D.G. Dunn, *The Acts of the Apostles*, 356. For details on the continuity between the message of Jesus and Paul, see my book *Insurgence.*

61. These are the last words in Acts. The book leaves readers with a cliffhanger. For a discussion on Luke's ending of Acts and the issues that surround it, see Ben Witherington III, ed., *History, Literature and Society in the Book of Acts*, chap. 14. Acts 28:31 matches Acts 1:3. Both include the kingdom of God as the subject. Bruce Malina, et al., *Social-Science Commentary on the Book of Acts*, 180. Luke ends his narrative on a happy note. He demonstrates that the case against Paul was baseless (just as the case against Jesus was baseless). Craig Keener, "Lessons on Acts," Session 32.

62. Alan Bandy, *An Illustrated Guide to the Apostle Paul*, 169.

63. Acts 28:30-31. Paul's apartment was likely modest or less than modest. He was still chained by his wrist to a guard. This was probably the time when he asked the believers in Asia Minor to pray for him to

First, his personal guards hear the message directly from Paul. Second, his imprisonment encourages others to boldly proclaim the word of God without fear. These individuals support Paul's message and work. Third, some of Paul's detractors are jealous of his success in spreading the good news to so many places in such a brief period of time. And now that the apostle is confined, they see his detention as an opportunity to spread the gospel to the churches Paul planted, hoping to take over his work. Paul's response to these ill-motivated souls is that he is happy Christ is proclaimed, regardless of their ungodly intentions.[64]

Paul is "aged" now.[65] He's about fifty-six, an old man by first-century standards.[66] He must pay rent for his *insula*. (Ancient prisons didn't provide meals or do laundry, so this was typically done by a prisoner's friends.) Luke and Aristarchus remain with Paul, tending to his needs.[67]

LUKE WRITES HIS GOSPEL (LUKE)

Year: A.D. 59-62[68]

---

preach the gospel boldly (Ephesians 6:19-20). Clinton Arnold, ed., *Zondervan Illustrated Bible Backgrounds Commentary*, 2b:273.

64. Philippians 1:12-18. I agree with the opinion of David deSilva: "I favor the possibility that they [those stirring up trouble for Paul] regarded themselves as taking advantage of Paul's detention to spread their own influence, which they believed would irk Paul and cause him trouble insofar as they were pursuing a rival mission and, perhaps, seeking to draw away some of Paul's own converts." Personal correspondence with David deSilva, 11/17/23. See also Ben Witherington III, *Friendship and Finance in Philippi: The Letter of Paul to the Philippians* (Harrisburg, PA: Trinity Press International, 1994), 45.

65. Philemon 9, NKJV. The ESV, NIV, and NLT say "an old man."

66. In the ancient world, a man in his mid-fifties was considered elderly. If Paul was born in A.D. 5, and Philemon was written in A.D. 61, this would make him fifty-five or fifty-six. See also Paul Barnett, *Paul: Missionary of Jesus*, 24-25. Paul was probably frail and weary at this time, given the sufferings his mind and body faced throughout the years. Johannes Weiss, *Earliest Christianity*, 392-393.

67. Colossians 4:10, 14.

68. Clinton Arnold, ed., *Zondervan Illustrated Bible Backgrounds Commentary*, 1:322; Leon Morris, *Luke*, 25; *The ESV Study Bible*, 1935; Mark Strauss, *Four Portraits, One Jesus,* 348. Bernier dates this Gospel at A.D. 59. Jonathan Bernier, *Rethinking the Dates of the New Testament*, 77-80, 84. Still others believe Luke and Acts were written after A.D. 70. N.T. Wright and Michael Bird, *The New Testament in Its World*, 612. Many scholars take issue with a date earlier than A.D. 70 for Luke (as well as for Mark and Matthew) based on the idea that Jesus

From: Rome[69]

To: Theophilus and the Gentiles[70]

Author: Luke[71]

Contextual Summary: Luke presents the humanity of Christ. Jesus is the true human and the Savior of all people.[72] Luke shares how the gospel, incarnated in Jesus of Nazareth, moved from Galilee to Jerusalem. The Gospel contains the strongest polemic against the abuse of wealth among all the New Testament authors, and this emphasis is clearly seen throughout the document.[73]

Luke's Gospel can be outlined as follows: The infancy narrative (chapters 1:5 through 2:52); the beginnings of John and Jesus (chapters 3:1 through 4:13); the Galilean ministry (chapters 4:14 through 9:50); the journey to Jerusalem (chapters 9:51

couldn't foretell the Roman siege of Jerusalem and/or the way the Gospel writers "recast" the event. See David deSilva, *Introduction to the New Testament*, 176-177, 269-270. Others find this objection unconvincing.

69. Irenaeus, *Against Heresies*, 3.1.1 and 3.1.14; Eusebius, *The History of the Church*, 2.22.6. Rome, Greece, Caesarea, and Alexandria have also been suggested. Clinton Arnold, ed., *Zondervan Illustrated Bible Backgrounds Commentary*, 1:322.

70. Theophilus appears to have been a wealthy Roman familiar with the Christian faith. He was probably Luke's patron who financed his two-volume work (Luke-Acts). Luke seems to have written Luke-Acts for recent converts of high status (like Theophilus) to confirm the authenticity of what they had been taught about Jesus and the movement He spawned. Ben Witherington III, *The New Testament Story*, 80. If Theophilus underwrote the expense of writing and producing Luke-Acts, Luke probably dedicated the work to him. Luke's intended audience appears to be mostly Gentiles acquainted with the Hebrew Scriptures. Ben Witherington III, *Invitation to the New Testament*, 106-107; personal correspondence with David Bauer, 3/19/22. Theophilus means "lover of God," so Luke could have created the name to represent anyone who loves God and desires to know what God. N.T. Wright, *Luke for Everyone*, 3. But this is unlikely as "symbolic dedicatees were virtually known." Craig Keener, *The IVP Bible Background Commentary: New Testament*, 319.

71. The available evidence (both internal and external) favors the unanimous tradition attributing this Gospel to Luke. Craig Keener, *The IVP Bible Background Commentary: New Testament*, 176; Leon Morris, *Luke*, 16-18; Mark Strauss, *Four Portraits, One Jesus*, 347.

72. For an overview of Luke's Gospel, see Mark Strauss, *Four Portraits, One Jesus*, chap. 9; David deSilva, *An Introduction to the New Testament*, chap. 7; N.T. Wright and Michael Bird, *The New Testament in Its World*, chap. 26; Clinton Arnold, ed., *Zondervan Illustrated Bible Backgrounds Commentary*, 1:319-515.

73. Craig Keener, "Lessons on Acts," Session 1; Thomas Schmidt, *Hostility to Wealth in the Synoptics*, chap. 8.

through 19:44); ministry in Jerusalem, crucifixion, resurrection, and ascension (chapters 19:45 through 24:53).[74]

Luke is generally believed to be the only Gospel written by a Gentile author. His Gospel provides one of the most comprehensive accounts of Jesus' life, starting from before His birth and ending with His ascension. Luke includes more stories involving women than the other Gospels, highlighting their role in Jesus' ministry. He also emphasizes Jesus' concern for the poor, outcasts, and sinners. Luke also emphasizes Jesus' prayer life more than the other Gospels. There's also a strong emphasis on the role of the Holy Spirit throughout the narrative.

As Luke was not an eyewitness to Jesus' life, he acknowledges his sources at the outset of his Gospel. Luke carefully investigated everything from the beginning, consulting eyewitnesses to compile his orderly account (Luke 1:1-4). In addition, many scholars believe Luke used three main sources for his gospel: the Gospel of Mark, a hypothetical collection of Jesus' sayings called the Q source, and unique material derived from firsthand witnesses not found in the other Gospels. Luke spent considerable time with Paul, which likely provided him access to early Christian traditions and eyewitness accounts.

The Synoptic Gospels (Matthew, Mark, and Luke)[75] tell the end of Israel's story and its climax in Jesus.[76] They all present Jesus as the One who proclaims God's kingdom, which means "judgment on oppressive rulers and promised blessings for the poor and hungry."[77]

74. For details on this outline, see Gary Burge, et al., *The New Testament in Antiquity*, 199ff. Luke's vocabulary reveals a higher level of education than the other Gospel writers. David deSilva, *An Introduction to the New Testament*, 261-262.

75. Matthew, Mark, and Luke are called the Synoptics because they share a common viewpoint and similar perspectives. The Gospel of John doesn't share those similarities. Ben Witherington III, *Invitation to the New Testament*, 134.

76. James D.G. Dunn, *Neither Jew Nor Greek: A Contested Identity* (Grand Rapids, MI: Eerdmans, 2015), 187-371; N.T. Wright, *Interpreting Jesus: Essays on the Gospels* (Grand Rapids, MI: Zondervan, 2020); *The New Testament and the People of God*, chaps. 13-14.

77. Richard Horsley, *Jesus and Empire*, 136. Matthew, Mark, and Luke revolve around the death and resurrection of Jesus in the context of encountering the power of the Roman Empire. The disciples followed Jesus by taking up their own crosses in discipleship. James Aageson, *After Paul*, 129.

Despite the shame associated with supporting a Roman prisoner, the following men visit Paul while he is under house arrest in Rome:[78]

- Epaphras from the tri-cities of the Lycus valley[79]
- Tychicus from Ephesus[80]
- Timothy from Lystra[81]
- Demas from Thessalonica[82]
- Mark from Jerusalem[83]

Crisis in Colossae

The assembly in Colossae faces a crisis. Some of the believers in the church are having conflicts, and false teachers have come into the assembly to subvert the gospel of grace. The teachers have introduced a bizarre form of Jewish legalism mixed with counterfeit spirituality.[84] They are teaching the Colossian believers the following:

78. Being in Roman custody in chains was shameful. So Paul's "guilt" spread to the Gentile churches and the Diaspora. For this reason, some believers wanted to dissociate with him while he was imprisoned. But those who were faithful to Paul and the gospel stood with him during his confinement. Luke's narrative (Acts) shows that Paul, like Jesus before him, was innocent. The book of Acts works to vindicate Paul. It's a legal apologetic, among other things. Craig Keener, "Lessons on Acts," Session 31.

79. Colossians 4:12; Philemon 1:23.

80. Ephesians 6:21; Colossians 4:7.

81. Colossians 1:1; Philippians 1:1; 2:19.

82. Colossians 4:14; Philemon 24.

83. Philemon 24; Colossians 4:10. Obviously, Paul reconciled with Mark after their falling out on the first apostolic journey. 2 Timothy 4:11; *The NKJV Study Bible*, 1799. According to Wright, "Mark is clearly rehabilitated both as a worker for the gospel and as a companion to Paul." N.T. Wright, *Colossians and Philemon*, 156.

84. Bruce believes the heresy was Jewish, since it involved new moons, the Sabbath, food regulations, etc. It appears to have been a fusion of Judaism and an early form of gnosticism. F.F. Bruce, *Paul: Apostle of the Heart Set Free*, 413. McKnight says the false teachers operated with a Jewish set of ideas and practices that Paul calls vain "philosophy" and "wisdom." Scot McKnight, *The Letter to the Colossians*, 29-30. Wright agrees that the opponents in Colossae were seeking to push Judaism on the believers. Paul's masterstroke was to associate the religion of Judaism with a form of pagan religion (Colossians 2:8, 22). N.T. Wright, *Colossians*

- You cannot share in the inheritance of Israel unless you observe certain rules.[85]

- To experience God's "fullness," you must observe all the ceremonies in the Law of Moses. You must observe special "holy" days and only eat "clean" foods. Also, the men in the assembly must be circumcised.[86]

- Union with God is evidenced by mystical visions and angelic visitations. If you don't have these operating in your life, you're falling short.

- What you handle, taste, and/or touch can either help or harm your relationship with God. If you handle, taste, or touch what is "unclean," you will lose your union with God, and you'll never experience His fullness.[87]

The false teaching has also spread beyond Colossae to the assembly in Laodicea. Epaphras, the founder of the Colossian and Laodicean assemblies (as well as the church in Hierapolis)[88] is troubled by the new spiritual assault. Therefore, he sails to Rome to receive advice from Paul.[89] At the same time, Onesimus (Philemon's slave) runs away.[90]

---

and Philemon, 24-30. Gundry holds that the "Colossian heresy" was a blending of Jewish legalism, Greek philosophy, and eastern mysticism. These features would appear in full-blown form years later in gnosticism. Robert Gundry, *A Survey of the New Testament*, 395.

85. Scot McKnight, *The Letter to the Colossians*, 30.

86. In this regard, the false teachers who were active in Colossae weren't too different from those who opposed Paul's message in Galatia, etc. Eckhard Schnabel, *Early Christian Mission*, 2:1027-1028; Mark Fairchild, *Christian Origins in Ephesus & Asia Minor*, 74.

87. References to circumcision, fasting, new moons, sabbaths, and angels in Colossians 2:8-18 show that the brand of Judaism being promoted was mixed with pre-gnostic overtones. It doesn't appear this was the influence of "Paul's thorn" (the Jerusalem-based countermission), but rather, a localized heresy. Paul Barnett, *Paul: Missionary of Jesus*, 151.

88. For details on the church in Hierapolis, see Mark Fairchild, *Christian Origins in Ephesus & Asia Minor*, 76ff.; F.F. Bruce, *The Epistles to the Colossians, to Philemon, and to the Ephesians*, 8-17.

89. Many scholars assert that Epaphras visited Paul in Rome during the time he wrote the two letters that mention him as present (Colossians 4:12; Philemon 23). The trip from Colossae to Rome is a long one, from 1,000 to 1,300 miles depending on how one calculates.

90. For details on slave resistance in the first century and the common treatment of slaves, see John Byron, *A Week in the Life of a Slave*, 54-55, 61.

But he doesn't run away empty-handed. He steals money from Philemon, a capital offense.[91]

Epaphras gets word that Onesimus has run away. He locates the runaway slave and takes him to Rome, believing Paul can help him.[92] Onesimus is not a follower of Jesus, but he recalls Paul as a compassionate man and believes the apostle will help extricate him from his precarious situation. With Onesimus accompanying him to Rome to visit Paul, Epaphras (also called Epaphroditus)[93] stops at Philippi to visit the assembly there.

Epaphras/Epaphroditus spends time ministering to the kingdom community in Philippi, and the church is greatly encouraged by him. In fact, the believers fall in love with him. After a time, the Philippians send him off to Rome with a small fortune to hand

91. This is the traditional view based on Philemon 18 and 19. Scholars like N.T. Wright, Craig Keener, and Jeffrey Weima agree it's plausible. N.T. Wright, *Colossians and Philemon*, 166; Craig Keener, *The IVP Bible Background Commentary: New Testament,* 633; personal correspondence with Jeffrey Weima, 1/6/24. See also *The ESV Study Bible,* 2356. Alternative theories can be found in David deSilva, *An Introduction to the New Testament*, 591-593. Slaves who ran away were commonly punished by crucifixion, and harboring runaway slaves was a serious criminal offense. N.T. Wright, *Paul: A Biography*, 280.

92. According to Keener, "That Epaphras took Onesimus is a reconstruction; this could have gotten Epaphras arrested. But again, it is plausible; it makes sense of how Onesimus got to Paul." Personal correspondence with Craig Keener, 12/4/23.

93. I agree with those scholars who believe Epaphras and Epaphroditus were the same person. Epaphras is a shortened form of Epaphroditus. Alan Bandy, *An Illustrated Guide to the Apostle Paul*, 122; John McKenzie, *Dictionary of the Bible* (New York, NY: The Macmillan Company, 1965), 239. According to Lightfoot, "The name occurs very frequently in inscriptions both Greek and Latin, whether at full length Epaphroditus, or in its contracted form Epaphras." J.B. Lightfoot, *Saint Paul's Epistle to the Philippians*, Logos edition (New York, NY: The Macmillan Company, 1913), 123. Both Epaphroditus (Philippians 2:25; 4:18) and Epaphras (Philemon 23; Colossians 1:7; 4:12) were co-workers with Paul, and both were with him during the same Roman imprisonment. (Paul uses similar language in those texts.) Epaphras planted churches, and Paul calls Epaphroditus an *apostolos* (Philippians 2:25). This all suggests that they were the same person. Witherington acknowledges that my theory is possible, in which case the Asians called him Epaphras while the Latins knew him as Epaphroditus. Personal correspondence with Ben Witherington III, 1/3/06. While Epaphras was from Colossae and planted a church there, when he visited Philippi, he fell in love with the assembly and became their "apostle," sent by Paul. Though he may understand the term differently than I do, Witherington rightly calls Epaphroditus an "apostle" numerous times in his commentary on Philippians. Ben Witherington III, *Paul's Letter to the Philippians*, 173, 175, 178. People like Priscilla, Aquila, Timothy, Titus, Luke, et al. all traveled extensively. It is plausible to conclude that Epaphras/Epaphroditus spent time in Colossae first and Philippi afterward.

to Paul as a love offering to care for his needs.[94] Once again, the assembly in Philippi has provided financial support to Paul.

The Philippians are deeply concerned for Paul and ask Epaphras to let them know about the apostle's state when he visits him. Epaphras and Onesimus continue toward Rome, but Epaphras becomes deathly ill on the way. Despite his illness, Epaphras persists on to Rome for the Lord's sake.[95] A message is sent to the assembly in Philippi, informing them about Epaphras' sickness and requesting prayer for him.[96] When the assembly in Philippi hears that Epaphras is sick, they write Paul a letter inquiring about Epaphras' health.

By God's mercy, Epaphras arrives in Rome with Onesimus.[97] He greets Paul with a warm embrace and a holy kiss,[98] and he hands him the financial gift from the Philippian assembly. Epaphras tells Paul about the love the Philippians have for the apostle and gives him an update on their progress. He also informs Paul about the believing community in Colossae. He joyfully tells the aged worker about the love the Colossians have for one another. But he also shares a report on the problems they are facing, along with the issues in the ekklesias at Laodicea and Philippi.

Epaphras informs Paul that Archippus—the son of Philemon and Apphia[99]—is spiritually gifted and regularly ministers to the believers.[100] But Archippus is discouraged and

---

94. Philippians 2:25 with 4:10-19.

95. Ben Witherington III, *Paul's Letter to the Philippians*, 175-176.

96. Witherington suggests they could have met a fellow Christian traveling east and tasked him with sending the message about Epaphras/Epaphroditus to the church in Philippi. Ben Witherington III, *Paul's Letter to the Philippians*, 176.

97. Fee is right in saying that Epaphroditus likely didn't travel alone, especially given the large sum of money he carried. Based on piecing the narrative together, and equating Epaphroditus with Epaphras, I believe Onesimus is the most plausible option for the person who traveled with him. Gordon Fee, *Paul's Letter to the Philippians*, NICNT (Grand Rapids, MI: Eerdmans, 1995), 278.

98. The holy kiss was the customary greeting among the believers. See my previous notes on the holy kiss with biblical references.

99. Philemon 1:1-2. "He is addressed with Philemon and Apphia in a manner suggesting that he may have been their son." J.D. Douglas, et al., eds., *New Bible Dictionary*, 78. See also F.F. Bruce, *Paul: Apostle of the Heart Set Free*, 405; R.C. Lucas, *The Message of Colossians & Philemon*, 184-185; Craig Keener, *The IVP Bible Background Commentary: New Testament*, 580. Archippus appears to have had a leadership role in the ekklesia. Colossians 4:17; N.T. Wright and Michael Bird, *The New Testament in Its World*, 453. Perhaps he was one of the overseers. He is called our "fellow soldier" in Philemon 2, NIV.

100. N.T. Wright, *Colossians and Philemon*, 161-162.

needs inspiration to continue God's work in the assemblies at Colossae and Laodicea.[101] Hearing all the bad news, Paul struggles in prayer for the assemblies in Colossae, Laodicea, Hierapolis, and Philippi. Onesimus is with Epaphras, and Paul shares the gospel with the slave. The Holy Spirit opens his heart, and Onesimus believes on the Lord Jesus Christ. As the days pass by, Onesimus turns out to be an excellent assistant to Paul, and Paul grows to depend upon him.

PAUL WRITES COLOSSIANS

Year: A.D. 60-62[102]

From: Rome[103]

To: The church in Colossae (which is five to seven years old)

Author: Paul[104]

101. Colossians 4:17. Paul's encouragement to "complete" his ministry must have a context behind it. My scenario constitutes a plausible context.

102. Many scholars date the letter within this timeframe. *The ESV Study Bible*, 2289; Clinton Arnold, ed., *Zondervan Illustrated Bible Backgrounds Commentary*, 3:371; Ben Witherington III, *Invitation to the New Testament*, 171; David deSilva, *An Introduction to the New Testament*, 623; F.F. Bruce, *The Epistles to the Colossians, to Philemon, and to the Ephesians*, 32. Those who believe Colossians was written from Ephesus date the epistle earlier (mid-to-late 50s). Scot McKnight, *The Letter to the Colossians*, 39. While I agree with Weima and others who believe Colossians was written from Rome, the Ephesian imprisonment theory has become very popular these days among many New Testament scholars. Personal correspondence with Jeffrey Weima, 1/6/24.

103. F.F. Bruce, *Paul: Apostle of the Heart Set Free*, 398-399, 412; *The Epistles to the Colossians, to Philemon, and to the Ephesians*, 32. Like many scholars, Schnabel believes Paul wrote Colossians and Ephesians as a prisoner in Rome. Eckhard Schnabel, *Paul the Missionary*, 143. See also Mark Fairchild, *Christian Origins in Ephesus & Asia Minor*, 53. Others, like N.T. Wright, believe all four "prison letters" (Ephesians, Philippians, Colossians, and Philemon) were penned in Ephesus. N.T. Wright, *Paul: A Biography*, 268.

104. Ben Witherington III, *Invitation to the New Testament*, 231-233; N.T. Wright and Michael Bird, *The New Testament in Its World*, 458-459; N.T. Wright, *Paul: A Biography*, 285. Wright concludes, "There is therefore no need to reject Pauline authorship of Colossians…." N.T. Wright, *Colossians and Philemon*, 34. Barnett also believes Paul authored Ephesians, Colossians, and Philemon. Paul Barnett, *Paul: Missionary of Jesus*, 216ff. F.F. Bruce agrees that Paul penned Colossians. F.F. Bruce, *Paul: Apostle of the Heart Set Free*, 408ff. McKnight believes Colossians as well as Ephesians and the rest of the letters attributed to Paul were Pauline in the sense that Paul was "behind the letter" and made use of scribes to pen them. Scot McKnight, *The*

Contextual Summary: Paul addresses the heretical gospel introduced in Colossae by false teachers. He does so by giving the Colossian Christians a peerless unveiling of the cosmic Christ, the head of the body (the ekklesia) and the fullness of the Godhead in bodily form.

Within his seismic revealing of Christ, he portrays Jesus to be the incarnation of God's wisdom, which is a subtext in much of the letter.[105] Paul combats the heresy[106] by declaring that the Colossian believers *already* have union with God through Christ, apart from religious works or mystical experiences.

He takes dead aim at the false doctrine that asserts the Colossians must observe the ceremonial laws of Moses, pointing out that Christ is the substance and fulfillment of those laws. Paul ends the letter by exhorting the believers to walk in the new humanity, bearing with one another in love, forgiveness, and respect.[107]

In his closing, the apostle sends greetings from some of the believers who are with him in Rome, specifically six of his friends: Aristarchus, Mark, and Jesus Justus (all of Jewish birth) as well as Epaphras, Luke, and Demas (all of Gentile birth).[108] The

---

Letter to the Colossians, 18, 34-35. According to McKnight, when Paul wrote a letter, it was according to the process identified in Randolph Richards' *Paul and First-Century Letter Writing: Secretaries, Composition, and Collection* (Downers Grove, IL: InterVarsity Press, 2004). Personal correspondence with McKnight, 11/12/22. For details on the authorship of Colossians as a genuine work of Paul, see Ben Witherington III, *The Letters to Philemon, the Colossians, and the Ephesians*, 100ff.; Donald Guthrie, *New Testament Introduction*, 572-577.

105. N.T. Wright, *Paul: A Biography*, 287.

106. In context, "heresy" refers to a doctrine, usually a false teaching, that divides God's people. For details, see Frank Viola, *ReGrace: What the Shocking Beliefs of the Great Christians Can Teach Us Today* (Grand Rapids, MI: Baker, 2019), chap. 24.

107. For an overview of Colossians, see David deSilva, *An Introduction to the New Testament*, 610-630; N.T. Wright and Michael Bird, *The New Testament in Its World*, chap. 20; Clinton Arnold, ed., *Zondervan Illustrated Bible Backgrounds Commentary*, 3:371-403. For an insightful but short commentary on Colossians and the majority of Paul's other epistles, see T. Austin-Sparks, *The Gospel According to Paul* (Bethesda, MD: Testimony Book Ministry, 1988); *The Mission, the Meaning, and the Message of Jesus Christ*, chaps. 6-12.

108. Colossians 4:10-14. F.F. Bruce, *The Epistles to the Colossians, to Philemon, and to the Ephesians*, 178. In Colossians 4:10, Paul sent the church instructions about Mark, but we have no idea what they were. Although Bruce, following Lightfoot, thinks they have to do with the church welcoming Mark (180). Mark is also mentioned as the cousin of Barnabas, indicating that the Colossians knew who Barnabas was.

apostle asks the assembly to read his letter to the Laodicean assembly, which gathers in the home of Nympha.[109]

The letter of Laodicea will also be sent to Colossae, and Paul asks that it be read by the Colossian assembly.[110] (The Laodicean letter is lost to us.[111]) Colossians is written differently than Paul's earlier epistles because they contain the Asiatic style of rhetoric.[112] Timothy is the co-sender of the letter.[113]

Colossians

Paul, an apostle of Christ Jesus through the will of God, and Timothy our brother, to the saints and faithful brothers[a] in Christ at Colossae: Grace to you and peace from God our Father and the Lord Jesus Christ.

We give thanks to God the Father of our Lord Jesus Christ, praying always for you, having heard of your faith in Christ Jesus and of the love which you have toward all the saints, because of the hope which is laid up for you in the heavens, of which you heard before in the

109. Colossians 4:15. N.T. Wright and Michael Bird, *The New Testament in Its World*, 453. Meeks believes the entire ekklesia met in Nympha's home. I agree. Wayne Meeks, *The First Urban Christians*, 143. Gupta believes Nympha was a highly influential leader in the church in Laodicea. Nijay Gupta, *Tell Her Story*, 109-110.

110. Colossians 4:16.

111. Some scholars have suggested that the letter to the Laodiceans is our Ephesians. Craig Keener, *The IVP Bible Background Commentary: New Testament*, 579. Weima points out that only a small minority thinks this. Personal correspondence with Jeffrey Weima, 1/6/24.

112. This explains the difference in style and how Colossians (and Ephesians) can be genuinely Pauline. Ben Witherington III, *Invitation to the New Testament*, 231-233.

113. Colossians 1:1. Bruce says a "natural explanation" for this is that Timothy served as Paul's amanuensis in penning the letter, and he served the same function in writing Philemon. F.F. Bruce, *Paul: Apostle of the Heart Set Free*, 408. Timothy was with Paul in Rome when Colossians, Philemon, and Philippians were written. F.F. Bruce, *The Epistle to the Hebrews*, revised edition, NICNT (Grand Rapids, MI: Eerdmans, 1990), 390. I give more detail on what provoked Paul to write Colossians as well as provide a deep dive into the letter in my master class, *Immortal Mystery: Colossians in 3D*. Refer to thedeeperchristianlife.com/classes.

word of the truth of the Good News which has come to you, even as it is in all the world and is bearing fruit and growing, as it does in you also, since the day you heard and knew the grace of God in truth, even as you learned of Epaphras our beloved fellow servant, who is a faithful servant of Christ on your[b] behalf, who also declared to us your love in the Spirit.

For this cause, we also, since the day we heard this, don't cease praying and making requests for you, that you may be filled with the knowledge of his will in all spiritual wisdom and understanding, that you may walk worthily of the Lord, to please him in all respects, bearing fruit in every good work and increasing in the knowledge of God, strengthened with all power, according to the might of his glory, for all endurance and perseverance with joy, giving thanks to the Father, who made us fit to be partakers of the inheritance of the saints in light, who delivered us out of the power of darkness, and translated us into the Kingdom of the Son of his love, in whom we have our redemption,[c] the forgiveness of our sins.

He is the image of the invisible God, the firstborn of all creation. For by him all things were created in the heavens and on the earth, visible things and invisible things, whether thrones or dominions or principalities or powers. All things have been created through him and for him.

He is before all things, and in him all things are held together. He is the head of the body, the assembly, who is the beginning, the firstborn from the dead, that in all things he might have the preeminence. For all the fullness was pleased to dwell in him, and through him to reconcile all things to himself by him, whether things on the earth or things in the heavens, having made peace through the blood of his cross.

You, being in past times alienated and enemies in your mind in your evil deeds, yet now he has reconciled in the body of his flesh through death, to present you holy and without defect and blameless before him, if it is so that you continue in the faith, grounded and steadfast, and not moved away from the hope of the Good News which you heard, which is being proclaimed in all creation under heaven, of which I, Paul, was made a servant.

Now I rejoice in my sufferings for your sake, and fill up on my part that which is lacking of the afflictions of Christ in my flesh for his body's sake, which is the assembly, of which I was made a servant according to the stewardship of God which was given me toward you to fulfill the word of God, the mystery which has been hidden for ages and generations.

But now it has been revealed to his saints, to whom God was pleased to make known what are the riches of the glory of this mystery among the Gentiles, which is Christ in you, the hope of glory. We proclaim him, admonishing every man and teaching every man in all wisdom, that we may present every man perfect in Christ Jesus; for which I also labor, striving according to his working, which works in me mightily.

For I desire to have you know how greatly I struggle for you, and for those at Laodicea, and for as many as have not seen my face in the flesh; that their hearts may be comforted, they being knit together in love, and gaining all riches of the full assurance of understanding, that they may know the mystery of God, both of the Father and of Christ, in whom all the treasures of wisdom and knowledge are hidden.

Now I say this that no one may delude you with persuasiveness of speech. For though I am absent in the flesh, yet I am with you in the spirit, rejoicing and seeing your order, and the steadfastness of your faith in Christ. As therefore you received Christ Jesus, the Lord, walk in him, rooted and built up in him, and established in the faith, even as you were taught, abounding in it in thanksgiving.

Be careful that you don't let anyone rob you through his philosophy and vain deceit, after the tradition of men, after the elements of the world, and not after Christ. For in him all the fullness of the Deity dwells bodily, and in him you are made full, who is the head of all principality and power.

In him you were also circumcised with a circumcision not made with hands, in the putting off of the body of the sins of the flesh, in the circumcision of Christ, having been buried with him in baptism, in which you were also raised with him through faith in the working of God, who raised him from the dead. You were dead through your trespasses and the uncircumcision of your flesh.

He made you alive together with him, having forgiven us all our trespasses, wiping out the handwriting in ordinances which was against us. He has taken it out of the way, nailing it to the cross. Having stripped the principalities and the powers, he made a show of them openly, triumphing over them in it.

Let no one therefore judge you in eating, or in drinking, or with respect to a feast day or a new moon or a Sabbath day, which are a shadow of the things to come; but the body is Christ's. Let no one rob you of your prize by self-abasement and worshiping of the angels, dwelling in the things which he has not seen, vainly puffed up by his fleshly mind, and not holding firmly to the Head, from whom all the body, being supplied and knit together through the joints and ligaments, grows with God's growth.

If you died with Christ from the elements of the world, why, as though living in the world, do you subject yourselves to ordinances, "Don't handle, nor taste, nor touch" (all of which perish with use), according to the precepts and doctrines of men? These things indeed appear like wisdom in self-imposed worship, humility, and severity to the body; but aren't of any value against the indulgence of the flesh.

If then you were raised together with Christ, seek the things that are above, where Christ is, seated on the right hand of God. Set your mind on the things that are above, not on the things that are on the earth. For you died, and your life is hidden with Christ in God. When Christ, our life, is revealed, then you will also be revealed with him in glory.

Put to death therefore your members which are on the earth: sexual immorality, uncleanness, depraved passion, evil desire, and covetousness, which is idolatry. For these things' sake the wrath of God comes on the children of disobedience. You also once walked in those, when you lived in them; but now you also put them all away: anger, wrath, malice, slander, and shameful speaking out of your mouth.

Don't lie to one another, seeing that you have put off the old man with his doings, and have put on the new man, who is being renewed in knowledge after the image of his Creator, where there can't be Greek and Jew, circumcision and uncircumcision, barbarian, Scythian, bondservant, or free person; but Christ is all, and in all.

Put on therefore, as God's chosen ones, holy and beloved, a heart of compassion, kindness, lowliness, humility, and perseverance; bearing with one another, and forgiving each other, if any man has a complaint against any; even as Christ forgave you, so you also do.

Above all these things, walk in love, which is the bond of perfection. And let the peace of God rule in your hearts, to which also you were called in one body, and be thankful. Let the word of Christ dwell in you richly; in all wisdom teaching and admonishing one another with psalms, hymns, and spiritual songs, singing with grace in your heart to the Lord.

Whatever you do, in word or in deed, do all in the name of the Lord Jesus, giving thanks to God the Father, through him. Wives, be in subjection to your husbands, as is fitting in the Lord. Husbands, love your wives, and don't be bitter against them. Children, obey your parents in all things, for this pleases the Lord. Fathers, don't provoke your children, so that they won't be discouraged.

Servants, obey in all things those who are your masters according to the flesh, not just when they are looking, as men pleasers, but in singleness of heart, fearing God. And whatever you do, work heartily, as for the Lord, and not for men, knowing that from the Lord you will receive the reward of the inheritance; for you serve the Lord Christ. But he who does wrong will receive again for the wrong that he has done, and there is no partiality. Masters, give to your servants that which is just and equal, knowing that you also have a Master in heaven.

Continue steadfastly in prayer, watching in it with thanksgiving, praying together for us also, that God may open to us a door for the word, to speak the mystery of Christ, for which I am also in bonds, that I may reveal it as I ought to speak. Walk in wisdom toward those who are outside, redeeming the time. Let your speech always be with grace, seasoned with salt, that you may know how you ought to answer each one.

All my affairs will be made known to you by Tychicus, the beloved brother, faithful servant, and fellow bondservant in the Lord. I am sending him to you for this very purpose, that he may know your circumstances and comfort your hearts, together with Onesimus, the faithful and beloved brother, who is one of you. They will make known to you everything that is going on here.

Aristarchus, my fellow prisoner, greets you, and Mark, the cousin of Barnabas (concerning whom you received commandments, "if he comes to you, receive him"), and Jesus who is called Justus. These are my only fellow workers for God's Kingdom who are of the circumcision, men who have been a comfort to me. Epaphras, who is one of you, a servant of Christ, salutes you, always striving for you in his prayers, that you may stand perfect and complete in all the will of God.

For I testify about him that he has great zeal for you, and for those in Laodicea, and for those in Hierapolis. Luke the beloved physician and Demas greet you. Greet the brothers who are in Laodicea, and Nymphas, and the assembly that is in his house.

When this letter has been read among you, cause it to be read also in the assembly of the Laodiceans, and that you also read the letter from Laodicea. Tell Archippus, "Take heed to the ministry which you have received in the Lord, that you fulfill it." The salutation of me, Paul, with my own hand: remember my bonds. Grace be with you. Amen.

a. 1:2 The word for "brothers" here and where context allows may also be correctly translated "brothers and sisters" or "siblings."

b. 1:7 NU reads our.

c. 1:14 TR adds "through his blood."

PAUL WRITES PHILEMON

Year: A.D. 60-62[114]

From: Rome[115]

To: Philemon and the Colossian assembly that gathers in his home[116]

Author: Paul[117]

Contextual Summary: After greeting Philemon, his wife Apphia, and his son Archippus, Paul—the aged prisoner of Jesus Christ[118]—commends Philemon on his love and faith for Jesus and toward all the believers. He then informs Philemon that Onesimus is with him and has converted to Christ.

Because Onesimus has run away and stolen from his master (Philemon), Onesimus is subject to severe punishment. Runaway slaves are branded with the letter "F" for

114. *The ESV Study Bible,* 2353; F.F. Bruce, *Paul: Apostle of the Heart Set Free,* 403; Clinton Arnold, ed., *Zondervan Illustrated Bible Backgrounds Commentary,* 3:513; *The KJV Study Bible,* 1850. Those who believe in an Ephesian imprisonment date the letter between A.D. 52 and 55. N.T. Wright, *Colossians and Philemon,* 36-37.

115. *The ESV Study Bible,* 2353; F.F. Bruce, *Paul: Apostle of the Heart Set Free,* 399; Clinton Arnold, ed., *Zondervan Illustrated Bible Backgrounds Commentary,* 3:513; Donald Guthrie, *New Testament Introduction,* 664; *The KJV Study Bible,* 1850. Others believe it was written from Ephesus. N.T. Wright, *Colossians and Philemon,* 36-37.

116. For a detailed epistolary analysis of Paul's letter to Philemon, see Jeffrey Weima, *Paul the Ancient Letter Writer,* chap. 6. According to Towner, out of the thirteen canonical Pauline letters, ten were written to ekklesias, and only three were written to individuals (1 Timothy, Titus, 2 Timothy). Towner doesn't count Philemon to be a purely individual letter because it includes the names of other individuals and the church as a whole. Philip Towner, *The Letters to Timothy and Titus,* 85-86, n. 159.

117. Most scholars accept that Paul wrote Philemon. N.T. Wright and Michael Bird, *The New Testament in Its World,* 458; John A.T. Robinson, *Redating the New Testament,* 61.

118. Some scholars believe Paul mentions that he's an old man (v. 9) to induce respect and submission to what he requests in the letter. Jeffrey Weima, *Paul the Ancient Letter Writer,* 223-224.

"fugitive" and treated harshly. Paul appeals to Philemon to forgive Onesimus and receive him as a brother in Christ on equal footing (rather than a slave).[119] He also hints that he wants Philemon to send Onesimus back to Paul to help the apostle while he's still under house arrest.[120]

Paul promises to pay back any money that Onesimus owes Philemon while mentioning (quite deliberately) that Philemon owes the apostle his own life since Paul led him to Christ.[121] Paul is confident that Philemon will do what he requests. He also believes he will be released from prison, so he asks Philemon to prepare a room for him when he is able to visit the assembly in Colossae.[122]

At the end of the letter, Paul sends greetings from his co-workers, namely Epaphras, Mark, Aristarchus, Demas, and Luke.[123] Timothy is the co-sender of the letter.[124]

119. F.F. Bruce, *The Epistles to the Colossians, to Philemon, and to the Ephesians*, 200. Wright argues that Paul's chief aim in the letter is reconciliation, his larger concern being unity among those in Christ across traditional boundaries (slave and free, etc.). N.T. Wright, *Colossians and Philemon*, 166-170, 186.

120. According to Weima, "Many scholars believe that Paul is asking the slave owner to free his slave. I disagree with this position. I instead believe Paul is asking the slave owner to do a very difficult thing, namely forgive his runaway slave. Also, Paul is hinting for Philemon to send his forgiven slave back to the apostle so he can continue to help Paul in his captivity." Personal correspondence with Jeffrey Weima, 2/17/24. See also N.T. Wright and Michael Bird, *The New Testament in Its World*, 467-468. On the rhetorical constraints Paul places upon Philemon to do the right thing, see David deSilva, *An Introduction to the New Testament*, 594-597.

121. Philemon 19. Bruce points out that Philemon granted Paul's request and freed Onesimus. The evidence for this is that the letter survived. F.F. Bruce, *The Epistles to the Colossians, to Philemon, and to the Ephesians*, 200. See also N.T. Wright, *Colossians and Philemon*, 170.

122. For an overview of Philemon, see David deSilva, *An Introduction to the New Testament*, chap. 17; N.T. Wright and Michael Bird, *The New Testament in Its World*, chap. 20; Clinton Arnold, ed., *Zondervan Illustrated Bible Backgrounds Commentary*, 3:513-519. I give more detail on what provoked Paul to write Philemon as well as provide a deep dive into the letter in my master class, *Enduring Liberty: Philemon in 3D*. Refer to thedeeperchristianlife.com/classes.

123. Philemon 23-24. According to Weima, Paul's act of mentioning his co-workers put persuasive pressure on Philemon to yield to Paul's requests. Jeffrey Weima, *Paul the Ancient Letter Writer*, 212. See also F.F. Bruce, *The Epistles to the Colossians, to Philemon, and to the Ephesians*, 199 for how Paul used persuasion in this epistle.

124. Philemon 1:1. See my previous note on Timothy being the co-sender of Colossians.

Philemon

Paul, a prisoner of Christ Jesus, and Timothy our brother, to Philemon, our beloved fellow worker, to the beloved Apphia, to Archippus our fellow soldier, and to the assembly in your house: Grace to you and peace from God our Father and the Lord Jesus Christ.

I thank my God always, making mention of you in my prayers, hearing of your love and of the faith which you have toward the Lord Jesus, and toward all the saints, that the fellowship of your faith may become effective in the knowledge of every good thing which is in us in Christ Jesus. For we have much joy and comfort in your love, because the hearts of the saints have been refreshed through you, brother.

Therefore though I have all boldness in Christ to command you that which is appropriate, yet for love's sake I rather beg, being such a one as Paul, the aged, but also a prisoner of Jesus Christ. I beg you for my child, whom I have become the father of in my chains, Onesimus,[a] who once was useless to you, but now is useful to you and to me. I am sending him back.

Therefore receive him, that is, my own heart, whom I desired to keep with me, that on your behalf he might serve me in my chains for the Good News. But I was willing to do nothing without your consent, that your goodness would not be as of necessity, but of free will.

For perhaps he was therefore separated from you for a while, that you would have him forever, no longer as a slave, but more than a slave, a beloved brother, especially to me, but how much rather to you, both in the flesh and in the Lord. If then you count me a partner, receive him as you would receive me. But if he has wronged you at all or owes you anything, put that to my account.

I, Paul, write this with my own hand: I will repay it (not to mention to you that you owe to me even your own self besides). Yes, brother, let me have joy from you in the Lord. Refresh my heart in the Lord. Having confidence in your obedience, I write to you, knowing that you will do even beyond what I say.

Also, prepare a guest room for me, for I hope that through your prayers I will be restored to you. Epaphras, my fellow prisoner in Christ Jesus, greets you, as do Mark, Aristarchus, Demas, and Luke, my fellow workers. The grace of our Lord Jesus Christ be with your spirit. Amen.

a. 1:10 Onesimus means "useful."

PAUL WRITES EPHESIANS[125]

Year: A.D. 60-62[126]

From: Rome[127]

To: The kingdom communities in Roman Asia, particularly those in the Lycus valley. The earliest manuscripts omit the words "in Ephesus," and there are no personal greetings in the epistle.[128] These facts lend credence to the belief that "Ephesians" is a circular (encyclical) letter.[129]

125. Most scholars think Colossians was written before Ephesians, a conclusion with which I agree. Ben Witherington III, *Invitation to the New Testament*, 232.

126. Clinton Arnold, ed., *Zondervan Illustrated Bible Backgrounds Commentary*, 3:301; Ben Witherington III, *Invitation to the New Testament*, 171; F.F. Bruce, *Paul: Apostle of the Heart Set Free*, 475; *The ESV Study Bible*, 2257. My ordering of Colossians, Philemon, and Ephesians maps to F.F. Bruce's ordering in his *The Letters of Paul: An Expanded Paraphrase*, revised edition (Grand Rapids, MI: Eerdmans, 1965), 7. At the time of that publication, Bruce believed Philippians was written earlier (after 2 Corinthians).

127. *The ESV Study Bible,* 2257. Witherington (along with many other scholars) thinks Ephesians is Pauline and written from Rome. He also argues that it was a "circular homily" written to a group of Christians (mostly Gentile) in Asia using the style of Asiatic rhetoric, rather than the style of a typical Pauline epistle. Ben Witherington III, *The Letters to Philemon, the Colossians, and the Ephesians*, 24-25, 215-223. Asiatic rhetoric accounts for the super long sentences. In keeping with the Asiatic style, Ephesians chapter 1 goes on for twenty-six lines. It's the longest sentence in the entire New Testament. Personal correspondence with Ben Witherington III, 1/6/06 and 1/20/06. Keener agrees, but points out that Paul knew how to write super-long sentences earlier, as in Romans chapter 1. Personal correspondence with Craig Keener, 12/4/23. Guthrie agrees that the letter was written during Paul's Roman imprisonment. Donald Guthrie, *New Testament Introduction*, 536. See also Constantine Campbell, *The Letter to the Ephesians*, PNTC (Grand Rapids, MI: Eerdmans, 2023), 18.

128. F.F. Bruce, *Paul: Apostle of the Heart Set Free*, 426, n. 11. The name "Ephesus" became attached to the letter because it was the main city in Asia to have received the letter. Personal correspondence with Ben Witherington III, 12/27/05. See also F.F. Bruce, *The Epistles to the Colossians, to Philemon, and to the Ephesians*, 245; John Stott, *The Message of Ephesians: God's New Society* (Downers Grove, IL: InterVarsity Press, 1979), 24; Constantine Campbell, *The Letter to the Ephesians*, 13. Martin affirms that most scholars conclude that no name stood in the original text, but it was a circular letter intended to be passed around a group of ekklesias. Ralph Martin, *Ephesians, Colossians, and Philemon: Interpretation* (Louisville, KY: John Knox Press, 1991), 3-4. Other scholars, like Hoehner, believe "in Ephesus" was part of the original reading. Philip Comfort, ed., *Cornerstone Biblical Commentary* (Carol Stream, IL: Tyndale, 2008), vol. 16:15-16.

129. F.F. Bruce, *Paul: Apostle of the Heart Set Free*, 425-426; *The Epistles to the Colossians, to Philemon, and to the Ephesians*, 230; Otto F.A. Meinardus, *St. John of Patmos and the Seven Churches of the Apocalypse*, 43; N.T.

Author: Paul[130]

Contextual Summary: Ephesians is "the crown of Paulinism,"[131] "the divinest composition of man."[132] While the theme of Colossians is Christ's headship, the theme of Ephesians is Christ's body.[133] Colossians and Ephesians are the two highest mountain peaks of Scripture. Colossians is K2; Ephesians is Everest.

In Ephesians, Paul crafts a matchless presentation of God's eternal purpose and the unsearchable riches all believers have inherited in Christ.[134] Throughout the epistle,

---

Wright, *Paul: A Biography*, 295; David deSilva, *An Introduction to the New Testament*, 638-639; Clinton Arnold, *Ephesians*, 29.

130. The vast majority of prominent evangelical scholars are convinced of Pauline authorship. Clinton Arnold, *Ephesians*, 46; Craig Keener, *The IVP Bible Background Commentary: New Testament*, 541; F.F. Bruce, *The Epistle to the Ephesians* (London: Fleming H. Revell, 1961), 11-12; Donald Guthrie, *New Testament Introduction*, 509-528. Witherington rightly argues that pseudonymity creates more problems than it solves. Ben Witherington III, *The Letters to Philemon, the Colossians, and the Ephesians*, 223-224. According to Stott, the alternatives to Pauline authorship are unsatisfactory. John Stott, *The Message of Ephesians*, 15-22. Wright and Bird believe it's just as possible that Paul wrote Ephesians, Colossians, and Philemon himself. N.T. Wright and Michael Bird, *The New Testament in Its World*, 459. In a lengthy conversation I had with N.T. Wright in 2007 at The Soularize Conference where we both spoke, he stated that he personally believes Paul wrote Ephesians. Harold Hoehner argues persuasively that Paul authored the letter in Philip Comfort, ed., *Cornerstone Biblical Commentary*, vol. 16:3-13. For details on the Pauline authorship of Ephesians, see Constantine Campbell, *The Letter to the Ephesians*, 3-11.

131. N.T. Wright, *Paul: A Biography*, 295. The letter has also been called "the quintessence of Paulinism." F.F. Bruce, *The Epistles to the Colossians, to Philemon, and to the Ephesians*, 229.

132. A description from Samuel Taylor Coleridge, F.F. Bruce, *Paul: Apostle of the Heart Set Free*, 425. These superlative descriptions of Ephesians do not preclude that Ephesians is an epistle and should be treated as such.

133. We can also say Colossians presents "Christ the Head," while Ephesians presents "Christ the body." By this statement, I do not mean that there is no distinction between Christ our Lord and His church. Rather, the church is the corporate expression of Christ (see Acts 9:1-5; 1 Corinthians 12:12, etc.). While Christ and His body are distinct, they are not separate. See my book *From Eternity to Here*, Part 3 for details and biblical support.

134. Recent scholarship agrees that the *missio Dei* (mission or purpose of God) is the central motif of Paul's epistles, especially Ephesians. Constantine Campbell, *The Letter to the Ephesians*, 29. I give more detail on what provoked Paul to write Ephesians as well as provide a deep dive into the letter in my master class, *Untraceable Riches: Ephesians in 3D*. Refer to thedeeperchristianlife.com/classes.

Paul displays the immensity of Christ and the superlative calling of the believers who are in Him.[135]

The letter opens with a stunning presentation of the church's *wealth*. The ekklesia is *seated* with Christ in heavenly places (chapters 1 through 3). It goes on to exhort the church in its *walk* in this world (chapters 4 through 5). It ends with a discussion on the church's *warfare* as it *stands* against God's enemy (chapter 6).[136]

In short, Paul encourages the Gentile believers to appreciate and embrace their high calling in Christ and learn afresh their commitment to God's eternal purpose.[137]

Ephesians

Paul, an apostle of Christ Jesus through the will of God, to the saints who are at Ephesus, and the faithful in Christ Jesus: Grace to you and peace from God our Father and the Lord Jesus Christ.

Blessed be the God and Father of our Lord Jesus Christ, who has blessed us with every spiritual blessing in the heavenly places in Christ, even as he chose us in him before the foundation of the world, that we would be holy and without defect before him in love, having predestined us for adoption as children through Jesus Christ to himself, according to the good pleasure of his desire, to the praise of the glory of his grace, by which he freely gave us favor in the Beloved, in whom we have our redemption through his blood, the forgiveness of our trespasses, according to the riches of his grace, which he made to abound toward us in

---

135. For an overview of Ephesians, see N.T. Wright and Michael Bird, *The New Testament in Its World*, chap. 20; Clinton Arnold, ed., *Zondervan Illustrated Bible Backgrounds Commentary*, 3:301-341; *Ephesians*, 21-61; David deSilva, *An Introduction to the New Testament*, chap. 18; *Ephesians*, NCBC (New York, NY: Cambridge University Press, 2022), 1-39. For the debate among scholars regarding the dating, destination, and authenticity of Ephesians, see Donald Guthrie, *New Testament Introduction*, 496-540.

136. Some of the most helpful works on Ephesians are written by T. Austin-Sparks (*The Stewardship of the Mystery: vol. 2*); Watchman Nee (*Sit, Walk, Stand: The Process of Christian Maturity*); Ruth Paxson (*The Wealth, Walk and Warfare of the Christian*); John Kennedy (*Secret of His Purpose*).

137. F.F. Bruce, *The Epistles to the Colossians, to Philemon, and to the Ephesians*, 245.

all wisdom and prudence, making known to us the mystery of his will, according to his good pleasure which he purposed in him to an administration of the fullness of the times, to sum up all things in Christ, the things in the heavens and the things on the earth, in him.

We were also assigned an inheritance in him, having been foreordained according to the purpose of him who does all things after the counsel of his will, to the end that we should be to the praise of his glory, we who had before hoped in Christ. In him you also, having heard the word of the truth, the Good News of your salvation—in whom, having also believed, you were sealed with the promised Holy Spirit, who is a pledge of our inheritance, to the redemption of God's own possession, to the praise of his glory.

For this cause I also, having heard of the faith in the Lord Jesus which is among you, and the love which you have toward all the saints, don't cease to give thanks for you, making mention of you in my prayers, that the God of our Lord Jesus Christ, the Father of glory, may give to you a spirit of wisdom and revelation in the knowledge of him, having the eyes of your hearts[a] enlightened, that you may know what is the hope of his calling, and what are the riches of the glory of his inheritance in the saints, and what is the exceeding greatness of his power toward us who believe, according to that working of the strength of his might which he worked in Christ, when he raised him from the dead and made him to sit at his right hand in the heavenly places, far above all rule, authority, power, dominion, and every name that is named, not only in this age, but also in that which is to come.

He put all things in subjection under his feet, and gave him to be head over all things for the assembly, which is his body, the fullness of him who fills all in all. You were made alive when you were dead in transgressions and sins, in which you once walked according to the course of this world, according to the prince of the power of the air, the spirit who now works in the children of disobedience. We also all once lived among them in the lusts of our flesh, doing the desires of the flesh and of the mind, and were by nature children of wrath, even as the rest.

But God, being rich in mercy, for his great love with which he loved us, even when we were dead through our trespasses, made us alive together with Christ—by grace you have been saved—and raised us up with him, and made us to sit with him in the heavenly places in Christ Jesus, that in the ages to come he might show the exceeding riches of his grace in kindness toward us in Christ Jesus; for by grace you have been saved through faith, and that not of yourselves; it is the gift of God, not of works, that no one would boast.

For we are his workmanship, created in Christ Jesus for good works, which God prepared before that we would walk in them. Therefore remember that once you, the Gentiles in the flesh, who are called "uncircumcision" by that which is called "circumcision" (in the flesh, made by hands), that you were at that time separate from Christ, alienated from the commonwealth of Israel, and strangers from the covenants of the promise, having no hope and without God in the world. But now in Christ Jesus you who once were far off are made near in the blood of Christ.

For he is our peace, who made both one, and broke down the middle wall of separation, having abolished in his flesh the hostility, the law of commandments contained in ordinances, that he might create in himself one new man of the two, making peace, and might reconcile them both in one body to God through the cross, having killed the hostility through it.

He came and preached peace to you who were far off and to those who were near. For through him we both have our access in one Spirit to the Father. So then you are no longer strangers and foreigners, but you are fellow citizens with the saints and of the household of God, being built on the foundation of the apostles and prophets, Christ Jesus himself being the chief cornerstone; in whom the whole building, fitted together, grows into a holy temple in the Lord; in whom you also are built together for a habitation of God in the Spirit.

For this cause I, Paul, am the prisoner of Christ Jesus on behalf of you Gentiles, if it is so that you have heard of the administration of that grace of God which was given me toward you, how that by revelation the mystery was made known to me, as I wrote before in few words, by which, when you read, you can perceive my understanding in the mystery of Christ, which in other generations was not made known to the children of men, as it has now been revealed to his holy apostles and prophets in the Spirit, that the Gentiles are fellow heirs and fellow members of the body, and fellow partakers of his promise in Christ Jesus through the Good News, of which I was made a servant according to the gift of that grace of God which was given me according to the working of his power.

To me, the very least of all saints, was this grace given, to preach to the Gentiles the unsearchable riches of Christ, and to make all men see what is the administration[b] of the mystery which for ages has been hidden in God, who created all things through Jesus Christ, to the intent that now through the assembly the manifold wisdom of God might be made known to the principalities and the powers in the heavenly places, according to the eternal purpose which he accomplished in Christ Jesus our Lord. In him we have boldness and access in confidence through our faith in him. Therefore I ask that you may not lose heart at my troubles for you, which are your glory.

For this cause, I bow my knees to the Father of our Lord Jesus Christ, from whom every family in heaven and on earth is named, that he would grant you, according to the riches of his glory, that you may be strengthened with power through his Spirit in the inner person, that Christ may dwell in your hearts through faith, to the end that you, being rooted and grounded in love, may be strengthened to comprehend with all the saints what is the width and length and height and depth, and to know Christ's love which surpasses knowledge, that you may be filled with all the fullness of God.

Now to him who is able to do exceedingly abundantly above all that we ask or think, according to the power that works in us, to him be the glory in the assembly and in Christ Jesus to all generations forever and ever. Amen.

I therefore, the prisoner in the Lord, beg you to walk worthily of the calling with which you were called, with all lowliness and humility, with patience, bearing with one another in love, being eager to keep the unity of the Spirit in the bond of peace. There is one body and one Spirit, even as you also were called in one hope of your calling, one Lord, one faith, one baptism, one God and Father of all, who is over all and through all, and in us all.

But to each one of us, the grace was given according to the measure of the gift of Christ. Therefore he says, "When he ascended on high, he led captivity captive, and gave gifts to people." Psalm 68:18 Now this, "He ascended," what is it but that he also first descended into the lower parts of the earth? He who descended is the one who also ascended far above all the heavens, that he might fill all things.

He gave some to be apostles; and some, prophets; and some, evangelists; and some, shepherds[c] and teachers; for the perfecting of the saints, to the work of serving, to the building up of the body of Christ, until we all attain to the unity of the faith and of the knowledge of the Son of God, to a full grown man, to the measure of the stature of the fullness of Christ, that we may no longer be children, tossed back and forth and carried about with every wind of doctrine, by the trickery of men, in craftiness, after the wiles of error; but speaking truth in love, we may grow up in all things into him who is the head, Christ, from whom all the body, being fitted and knit together through that which every joint supplies, according to the working in measure of each individual part, makes the body increase to the building up of itself in love.

This I say therefore, and testify in the Lord, that you no longer walk as the rest of the Gentiles also walk, in the futility of their mind, being darkened in their understanding, alienated from the life of God because of the ignorance that is in them, because of the hardening of their hearts. They, having become callous, gave themselves up to lust, to work all uncleanness with greediness.

But you didn't learn Christ that way, if indeed you heard him, and were taught in him, even as truth is in Jesus: that you put away, as concerning your former way of life, the old man that grows corrupt after the lusts of deceit, and that you be renewed in the spirit of your mind, and put on the new man, who in the likeness of God has been created in righteousness and holiness of truth.

Therefore putting away falsehood, speak truth each one with his neighbor. For we are members of one another. "Be angry, and don't sin." <u>Psalm 4:4</u> Don't let the sun go down on your wrath, and don't give place[d] to the devil. Let him who stole steal no more; but rather let him labor, producing with his hands something that is good, that he may have something to give to him who has need. Let no corrupt speech proceed out of your mouth, but only what is good for building others up as the need may be, that it may give grace to those who hear.

Don't grieve the Holy Spirit of God, in whom you were sealed for the day of redemption. Let all bitterness, wrath, anger, outcry, and slander be put away from you, with all malice. And be kind to one another, tender hearted, forgiving each other, just as God also in Christ forgave you. Be therefore imitators of God, as beloved children. Walk in love, even as Christ also loved us and gave himself up for us, an offering and a sacrifice to God for a sweet-smelling fragrance.

But sexual immorality, and all uncleanness or covetousness, let it not even be mentioned among you, as becomes saints; nor filthiness, nor foolish talking, nor jesting, which are not appropriate, but rather giving of thanks. Know this for sure, that no sexually immoral person, nor unclean person, nor covetous man, who is an idolater, has any inheritance in the Kingdom of Christ and God.

Let no one deceive you with empty words. For because of these things, the wrath of God comes on the children of disobedience. Therefore don't be partakers with them. For you were once darkness, but are now light in the Lord. Walk as children of light, for the fruit of the Spirit is in all goodness and righteousness and truth, proving what is well pleasing to the Lord. Have no fellowship with the unfruitful deeds of darkness, but rather even reprove them. For it is a shame even to speak of the things which are done by them in secret. But all things, when they are reproved, are revealed by the light, for everything that reveals is light. Therefore he says, "Awake, you who sleep, and arise from the dead, and Christ will shine on you."

Therefore watch carefully how you walk, not as unwise, but as wise, redeeming the time, because the days are evil. Therefore don't be foolish, but understand what the will of the Lord is. Don't be drunken with wine, in which is dissipation, but be filled with the Spirit, speaking to one another in psalms, hymns, and spiritual songs; singing and making melody in your heart to the Lord; giving thanks always concerning all things in the name of our Lord Jesus Christ, to God, even the Father; subjecting yourselves to one another in the fear of Christ.

Wives, be subject to your own husbands, as to the Lord. For the husband is the head of the wife, as Christ also is the head of the assembly, being himself the savior of the body. But as the assembly is subject to Christ, so let the wives also be to their own husbands in everything. Husbands, love your wives, even as Christ also loved the assembly, and gave himself up for it; that he might sanctify it, having cleansed it by the washing of water with the word, that he might present the assembly to himself gloriously, not having spot or wrinkle or any such thing; but that it should be holy and without defect.

Even so husbands also ought to love their own wives as their own bodies. He who loves his own wife loves himself. For no man ever hated his own flesh; but nourishes and cherishes it, even as the Lord also does the assembly; because we are members of his body, of his flesh and bones. "For this cause a man will leave his father and mother, and will be joined to his wife. Then the two will become one flesh." <u>Genesis 2:24</u> This mystery is great, but I speak concerning Christ and of the assembly. Nevertheless each of you must also love his own wife even as himself; and let the wife see that she respects her husband.

Children, obey your parents in the Lord, for this is right. "Honor your father and mother," which is the first commandment with a promise: "that it may be well with you, and you may live long on the earth." <u>Deuteronomy 5:16</u> You fathers, don't provoke your children to wrath, but nurture them in the discipline and instruction of the Lord.

Servants, be obedient to those who according to the flesh are your masters, with fear and trembling, in singleness of your heart, as to Christ, not in the way of service only when eyes are on you, as men pleasers, but as servants of Christ, doing the will of God from the heart, with good will doing service as to the Lord, and not to men, knowing that whatever good thing each one does, he will receive the same good again from the Lord, whether he is bound or free. You masters, do the same things to them, and give up threatening, knowing that he who is both their Master and yours is in heaven, and there is no partiality with him.

Finally, be strong in the Lord, and in the strength of his might. Put on the whole armor of God, that you may be able to stand against the wiles of the devil. For our wrestling is not against flesh and blood, but against the principalities, against the powers, against the world's rulers of the darkness of this age, and against the spiritual forces of wickedness in the heavenly places.

Therefore put on the whole armor of God, that you may be able to withstand in the evil day, and having done all, to stand. Stand therefore, having the utility belt of truth buckled around your waist, and having put on the breastplate of righteousness, and having fitted your feet with the preparation of the Good News of peace, above all, taking up the shield of faith, with which you will be able to quench all the fiery darts of the evil one.

And take the helmet of salvation, and the sword of the Spirit, which is the word[e] of God; with all prayer and requests, praying at all times in the Spirit, and being watchful to this end in all perseverance and requests for all the saints: on my behalf, that utterance may be given to me in opening my mouth, to make known with boldness the mystery of the Good News, for which I am an ambassador in chains; that in it I may speak boldly, as I ought to speak.

But that you also may know my affairs, how I am doing, Tychicus, the beloved brother and faithful servant in the Lord, will make known to you all things. I have sent him to you for this very purpose, that you may know our state and that he may comfort your hearts. Peace be to the brothers, and love with faith, from God the Father and the Lord Jesus Christ. Grace be with all those who love our Lord Jesus Christ with incorruptible love. Amen.

a. 1:18 TR reads "understanding" instead of "hearts."
b. 3:9 TR reads "fellowship" instead of "administration."
c. 4:11 or, pastors.
d. 4:27 or, opportunity.
e. 6:17 from the Greek "ῥῆμα" (rhema), which means "spoken word."

LUKE WRITES ACTS

Year: A.D. 62[138]

From: Rome[139]

To: Theophilus and the Gentiles[140]

Author: Luke[141]

Contextual Summary: Acts is the second volume of Luke's two-part work (Luke-Acts). The Gospel of Luke tells the story of what Jesus *began* to do and teach[142] while

138. Jonathan Bernier, *Rethinking the Dates of the New Testament*, 54-67, 84; Colin Hemer, *The Book of Acts in the Setting of Hellenistic History*, chap. 9; Thomas Schmidt, *The Apostles After Acts*, 193; Eckhard Schnabel, *Acts*, 28; *The ESV Study Bible*, 2073; Mark Strauss, *Four Portraits, One Jesus,* 348. Burge dates the composition of Acts in the early 60s as most likely. Gary Burge, etc., *The New Testament in Antiquity*, 210. See also *The NKJV Study Bible,* 1617; Clinton Arnold, ed., *Zondervan Illustrated Bible Backgrounds Commentary*, 1:322; 2b:7. Gundry and Longenecker date the writing of Acts around A.D. 63 or 64. Robert Gundry, *A Survey of the New Testament*, 128, 210, 298; Richard Longenecker, *Luke-Acts*, 698-701. Bock suggests Acts was written before A.D. 70. Darrell Bock, *Acts*, 25-27. On the contrary, most scholars today date the book after A.D. 70. N.T. Wright and Michael Bird, *The New Testament in Its World*, 612; Ben Witherington III, *The Acts of the Apostles*, 61-62; Donald Guthrie, *New Testament Introduction*, 362. According to Craig Keener, F. F Bruce popularized the 60ish date, but later dated Acts after 70." Personal correspondence with Craig Keener, 12/4/23. For a detailed treatment of the various arguments for the dating of Acts, see Craig Keener, *Acts*, 1:383-401.

139. Eckhard Schnabel, *Acts*, 28; Clinton Arnold, ed., *Zondervan Illustrated Bible Backgrounds Commentary*, 2b:7; Irenaeus, *Against Heresies,* 3.1.1 and 3.1.14; Eusebius, *The History of the Church*, 2.22.6. Since the location isn't certain, some have suggested Ephesus along with Rome. I. Howard Marshall, *Acts,* 48-49. Other suggestions have been Corinth and Caesarea. Darrell Bock, *Acts,* 27.

140. See my notes on the Gospel of Luke.

141. Keener argues that Acts is a historical monograph that's historically accurate, and that Luke is the author of both Acts and the Gospel that bears his name. Luke was probably a Gentile, the only Gentile author of the New Testament. He knew the Septuagint extremely well and was immersed in the Jewish Scriptures. Craig Keener, "Lessons on Acts," Session 1.

142. In the opening of Acts, Luke references his Gospel (Luke) saying, "The first book I wrote, Theophilus, concerned all that Jesus *began* both to do and to teach, until the day in which he was received up, after he had given commandment through the Holy Spirit to the apostles whom he had chosen" (Acts 1:1-2, italics mine). For a discussion on the preface of Acts, see Ben Witherington III, ed., *History, Literature and Society in the Book of Acts*, chap. 4.

Acts tells the story of what Jesus *continued* to do and teach through His body on earth.[143]

The kingdom of God is the overarching theme of the book. Acts begins with the risen Jesus talking about the kingdom of God and ends with Paul in Rome on Caesar's doorstep, preaching and teaching the kingdom. Luke is in effect saying, "This is the story of how the kingdom of God breaks into the world and spreads."[144]

Acts traces the rise and progress of the gospel of Jesus Christ in its first thirty years. Luke wrote Acts to legitimize the early Christian movement (refuting current objections to it), showing how it spread to the Eternal City. The author also shows how the Christian faith is the fulfillment of ancient Judaism and is entitled to share in the liberty that the empire accords the Jewish faith.

He also writes for the edification of the believing communities throughout the empire. He tells the story from Jesus' resurrection to Paul's arrival in Rome—around thirty years compressed into one volume. For this reason, Luke abridges his narrative.

Chapters 1 through 12 chronicle how Jesus was proclaimed King of the Jews in the face of Jewish authorities like Herod. These chapters mostly concentrate on Israel and Judaism. Jesus is announced as Messiah despite opposition from the temple authorities.

Chapters 13 through 28 chronicle how Jesus was proclaimed Lord of the world in the face of Gentile authorities like Claudius and Nero. These chapters mostly focus on Jesus being announced as the new emperor despite opposition from pagan authorities.[145]

The apostles of Jesus—including the Twelve and other apostolic workers like Paul, Barnabas, and Silas—have been called and sent by Jesus as heralds of the true King,

---

143. Acts 1:1-2. For an overview of the book of Acts, see David deSilva, *An Introduction to the New Testament*, chap. 8; I. Howard Marshall, *Acts*, 17-50; N.T. Wright and Michael Bird, *The New Testament in Its World*, chap. 26; Richard Longenecker, *Luke-Acts*, 665-712; Clinton Arnold, ed., *Zondervan Illustrated Bible Backgrounds Commentary*, 2b.

144. N.T. Wright, Lecture 1, The Soularize Conference.

145. Their pagan temples were upstaged by Jesus as Lord of the world. N.T. Wright, Lecture 1, The Soularize Conference.

bringing the gospel of the kingdom to the entire world, including the uppermost tiers of society.[146]

Luke sketches out his primary program for his narrative in Acts 1:8.[147] The story focuses on the witness to Jesus Christ, a witness that moves from Jerusalem (chapters 1 through 7), to all Judea and Samaria (chapters 8 through 12), to the ends of the earth (chapters 13 through 28).[148] From the very opening of Acts, Luke tells the story of how the rule of Jesus is "being launched on earth as in heaven."[149]

Acts comes to its climax with the proclamation of the gospel in Rome, the capital of the empire (chapter 28).[150] Some scholars believe Acts was based on a case file for Paul's trial in Rome.[151]

Luke leaves Rome and travels to Philippi, where he spends time with the Philippian assembly.[152] Titus travels[153] to the island of Crete where he plants several kingdom communi-

146. According to Keener, "Luke likes to report converts of status when possible" (see Acts 8:27, 38; 13:12; 17:12; 18:8, etc.). Craig Keener, *Acts*, 3:2678.

147. The literary form of Acts points to an apologetic intention. It begins with Acts 1:8 revealing that the gift at Pentecost would be carried to the uttermost parts of the world. This was foreshadowed by the gospel being preached to "every nation under heaven" (Acts 2:5, NIV), then producing the conversions of an Ethiopian statesman, a Jewish religious leader, and a Roman army officer. Edwin Judge, *The Social Pattern of the Christian Groups in the First Century*, 50.

148. Personal correspondence with David Bauer, 3/19/22. The theme of "witness" repeats itself throughout Acts.

149. N.T. Wright, *The Gospel According to Acts*, 7.

150. For the most exhaustive introduction to Acts, see Craig Keener, *Acts*, 1:43-638.

151. Wright believes Acts was written as a document for Paul's trial. N.T. Wright, Lecture 1, The Soularize Conference. According to Keener, one of the reasons for Luke's purposes in writing Acts, especially the latter part, is to be an apologetic for Paul. Craig Keener, "Lessons on Acts," Session 4.

152. As previously noted, Luke spent seven years with the assembly in Philippi during much of Paul's second and third apostolic journeys. When Paul wrote to the church in Philippi, he addressed someone he called "true yokefellow" or "true companion" (Philippians 4:3, KJV and ESV). Many scholars believe this is a reference to Luke. For this reasoning, see Gordon Fee, *Paul's Letter to the Philippians*, 393-395; F.F. Bruce, *Philippians*, 138. However, Witherington believes "the most plausible conjecture" is that the "yokefellow" is a reference to Epaphroditus, the bearer of the letter. Ben Witherington III, *Paul's Letter to the Philippians*, 239.

153. We aren't sure where Titus was shortly before this. He likely traveled with Paul to Corinth where the apostle wrote Romans, but we lack information on where he went after that.

ties.[154] According to tradition, Barnabas is stoned and burned by the Jews in Salamis. He is a victim of his zeal for the gospel and his undying devotion to Christ.[155]

Crisis in Philippi
A.D. 62

Paul decides to address the problems in the Philippian ekklesia that Epaphras/Epaphroditus told him about. Namely:

- The Philippians are experiencing persecution at the hands of their pagan neighbors.[156]
- The opposition from the outside is creating tension within the community. There are contentions, grumblings, and disputes among the believers, all of which are rooted in pride and petty jealousy.[157]

154. Crete is an island south of Greece. Schnabel offers some theories on how the assemblies in Crete were founded, one of them being that Titus planted the ekklesias on the island. Eckhard Schnabel, *Early Christian Mission*, 2:1284. Some surmise that Paul planted the churches there.

155. Omer Engelbert, *The Lives of the Saints* (New York, NY: Barnes and Noble, 1951), 226. One tradition says he was stoned at Salamis in A.D. 61 while holding a copy of the Gospel of Matthew, which he had written out by hand. Rodney Castleden, *The Book of Saints* (London: Quercus Publishing, 2006), 74, electronic edition; Thomas Schmidt, *The Apostles After Acts*, 132, 197. Note that many of the stories regarding the deaths of the apostolic workers are based on later traditions, which are less certain. Others are based on more reliable traditions. For details, consult the sources in the notes.

156. Philippians 1:28-30. The opposition was likely "the direct result of the Roman character of the city." Gordon Fee, *Paul's Letter to the Philippians*, 31. The Christians were defying the decrees of the emperor by not paying homage to the gods or the cult of the emperor. This infuriated their pagan neighbors (167, 172).

157. Inferred from Philippians 2:1-18; 4:2. If the complaining and arguing were left unchecked, it could lead to division. Fee says this may be why Paul felt compelled to address the problem and why he sent Timothy to look into it before the apostle himself came to Philippi. Gordon Fee, *Paul's Letter to the Philippians*, 33.

- Two sisters in particular, Euodia and Syntyche,[158] are fiercely quarreling with each other. These two women, along with Clement,[159] have helped Paul labor in the gospel.

Paul gets word that the circumcision party, led by his "thorn in the flesh," will soon be in Philippi. And as these agitators have done elsewhere, they will seek to persuade the believers to be circumcised[160] and put themselves under the Law of Moses.[161] Since the Philippian believers are under great pressure from the pagans, "being Jewish" looks attractive since Judaism is considered a legitimate religion in the empire.[162]

158. Philippians 4:2, NKJV. These women were probably on the ground floor of the Philippian church along with Lydia. F.F. Bruce, *Philippians,* 138. Their names suggest they were Gentiles or God-fearers. Paul Barnett, *From Jerusalem to Illyricum,* 75. Macedonian women played a large role in religious affairs. Even though the empire was patriarchal, the status of women was on the rise during this period. Since Euodia and Syntyche have Greek names (rather than Roman names), it suggests they were from Macedonia rather than from Roman families. Respectively, their names mean "good journey" and "with luck." They could have helped Paul financially (as did Lydia) or they could have defended him when he was persecuted in Philippi. Ben Witherington III, *Paul's Letter to the Philippians,* 235-238. Keener suggests they also could have been merchants like Lydia. Craig Keener, *The IVP Bible Background Commentary: New Testament,* 565.

159. Paul calls Clement a "fellow worker" (Philippians 4:3, NKJV). The early church fathers associated him with Clement of Rome who wrote *1 Clement* in the late first century. But according to most scholars, this belief is highly unlikely. Clement was a common Roman name at the time. Herbert Lockyer, ed., *Nelson's Illustrated Bible Dictionary,* 240; Craig Keener, *The IVP Bible Background Commentary: New Testament,* 565; Ben Witherington III, *Paul's Letter to the Philippians,* 240. Since his name is Latin, Clement may have been a citizen of Philippi. F.F. Bruce, *Philippians,* 139.

160. The men in the church, of course.

161. While I disagree with his timeline, Jerome Murphy-O'Connor rightly argues that Paul was combating the Judaizers in his letter to the Philippians. Jerome Murphy-O'Connor, *Paul: His Story,* 146. Philippians 3:4-8 contains echoes of Galatians 1; Philippians 3:9 contains echoes of Galatians 2:16. Barnett has come to the same conclusion. Paul Barnett, *Paul: Missionary of Jesus,* 149-151. Barnett points out that Philippians 3:2-3 and 3:17-19 refer to the same people, and "point to members of the Jewish Christian counter-mission who have come to the city" (149). For other supporting scholars, see P.T. O'Brien, *Commentary on Philippians,* NIGTC (Grand Rapids, MI: Eerdmans, 1991), 26-35; Gordon Fee, *Paul's Letter to the Philippians,* 294; Ben Witherington III, *Friendship and Finance in Philippi,* 29, 89. These false brethren do not appear to be in Philippi yet, but Paul knows they are coming and is warning against them in advance. Personal correspondence with Craig Keener, 12/4/23. See also David deSilva, *An Introduction to the New Testament,* 580-581.

162. Gordon Fee, *Paul's Letter to the Philippians,* 33, 289.

Epaphras/Epaphroditus fully recovers from his illness, which is a great relief to Paul, for he deeply loves the young worker. Epaphras longs to see the Philippian believers again and wants them to know he is no longer sick. So Paul makes plans to send him back to Philippi.[163]

Paul also plans to send Timothy to Philippi after he discovers the results of his upcoming trial.[164] He wants Timothy to look into the problems the church is facing as well as bring back a report on the assembly's progress.[165] Paul is optimistic that he will be released and plans to visit the Philippian community also when he is free.[166]

Before Paul sends Epaphras back to Philippi, he begins writing a letter to the church. The letter we know as "Philippians" will be Paul's last letter to a kingdom community recorded in the New Testament. Paul is ready to die for his Savior, but he has confidence that the Lord will not take him yet because his service hasn't been completed.[167]

PAUL WRITES PHILIPPIANS

Year: A.D. 62[168]

From: Rome[169]

To: The assembly in Philippi (which is about twelve years old)

163. Philippians 2:25-30.
164. Philippians 2:19-23.
165. Gordon Fee, *Paul's Letter to the Philippians*, 33.
166. Philippians 2:22-23.
167. Philippians 1:21-26; 2:17.
168. A.D. 62 is the opinion among scholars who believe Paul wrote the letter from Rome. Ben Witherington III, *Invitation to the New Testament*, 240-241; Paul Barnett, *From Jerusalem to Illyricum*, 127. Those who believe Paul wrote the epistle from Ephesus place it earlier (A.D. 53, etc.). Clinton Arnold, ed., *Zondervan Illustrated Bible Backgrounds Commentary*, 3:343.
169. There is good reason to believe Paul wrote this epistle from Rome. This is the majority view among scholars. Craig Keener, *The IVP Bible Background Commentary: New Testament*, 556; Eckhard Schnabel, *Paul the Missionary*, 115; Ben Witherington III, *Paul's Letter to the Philippians*, 9-11; Paul Barnett, *From Jerusalem to Illyricum*, 77. References to the "Praetorian Guard" and "Caesar's household" lend credence to the idea. Otto F.A. Meinardus, *St. Paul in Ephesus*, 85; Gordon Fee, *Paul's Letter to the Philippians*, 1, 34-37. Other scholars have argued for Ephesus or Caesarea. F.F. Bruce, *Philippians*, 11-16.

Author: Paul[170]

Contextual Summary: In response to the assembly's questions, which came from Epaphras, Paul wants the Philippian believers to know how he is holding up during his imprisonment. He opens the letter by joyfully thanking them for their partnership in supporting the gospel and his ministry. With familial affection, he longs to see them again.

News regarding Paul's subversive message has spread to the Praetorian Guard (the emperor's cohort of bodyguards) where he is located.[171] He rejoices that his imprisonment has encouraged some to proclaim the gospel out of sincere motives and others out of envy. The latter are motivated by self-interested partisanship. Their aim in preaching is to harm the apostle and possibly prejudice the outcome of his upcoming trial.[172] But he is thankful they are proclaiming Christ, nonetheless.

Torn between departing to be with the Lord and remaining for the sake of the believers, Paul is confident that through the prayers of the assembly, he will be released from house arrest and see the church again. Regardless of the outcome, he exhorts the Philippians to continue in the faith and not be frightened by those who oppose them.

He gives them an update on Epaphras/Epaphroditus, reporting that he has recovered from his sickness. Paul goes out of his way to explain why he's sending him back to Philippi so soon.[173] The apostle wants the Philippian believers to honor Epaphras

---

170. Philippians is one of Paul's undisputed letters. F.F. Bruce, *Philippians*, 8

171. N.T. Wright, *Paul for Everyone: The Prison Letters* (Louisville, KY: Westminster John Knox Press, 2004), 89.

172. Philippians 1:12-18. Bruce Winter, *Seek the Welfare of the City*, 94, 97. Due to their envy and jealousy of Paul, they were emboldened to kick a man when he was down. To their minds, Paul's imprisonment was their opportunity to preach Jesus "accurately." Gordon Fee, *Paul's Letter to the Philippians*, 119-120. These individuals may be the same people Paul warned about in Romans 16:17. If so, they represented the influence of "conservative members of the Jewish mission in Jerusalem." Paul Barnett, *Paul: Missionary of Jesus*, 153.

173. Paul didn't want Epaphroditus to be shamed. Ben Witherington III, *Paul's Letter to the Philippians*, 171.

for his valiant service and accept his spiritual authority.[174] He also asks them to prepare for Timothy's possible visit.[175] Additionally, he requests they prepare for his own visit when he is released from house arrest.[176]

The apostle encourages the assembly to stand firm in the Lord despite its struggles. He addresses the church's internal conflicts by presenting Christ, especially His humility and lack of self-preservation. Paul's desire is for the believers to love each other and have one spirit and mind.

He speaks directly to Luke ("true companion") and asks him to help two sisters in the church to reconcile and live in harmony.[177] The apostle puts the believing community on guard against the Judaizers ("the mutilation party," "dogs," and "troublemakers," as he calls them). These are the same people who caused trouble in Syrian Antioch, Galatia, Corinth, etc.[178] He writes with tears when he warns the church against the enemies of the cross. Several times, he thanks the assembly for sending its generous financial gift.[179]

---

174. Paul calls Epaphroditus his brother, co-worker, fellow soldier, and "your apostle." Ben Witherington III, *Paul's Letter to the Philippians*, 174-175; Gordon Fee, *Paul's Letter to the Philippians*, 275.

175. Paul wanted Timothy to visit Philippi and return to him with a report. Ben Witherington III, *Paul's Letter to the Philippians*, 173.

176. F.F. Bruce, *Philippians*, 19-20.

177. For details on this interpretation, see Gordon Fee, *Paul's Letter to the Philippians*, 393-395.

178. F.F. Bruce, *Paul: Apostle of the Heart Set Free*, 179; Ben Witherington III, *Friendship and Finance in Philippi*, 89; Craig Keener, *The IVP Bible Background Commentary: New Testament*, 562. Paul refers to these people as "those who mutilate the flesh," speaking of their demand to circumcise people for salvation (Philippians 3:2, ESV). In the same verse, the apostle calls the rival missionaries "dogs" and "evil workers." "Dog" is a derogatory, insulting term used by Jews for Gentiles. Paul reverses it and calls the Judaizers "dogs." Ralph Martin, *Philippians*, 141; Ben Witherington III, *Paul's Letter to the Philippians,* 181. "Evil workers" is similar to "deceitful workers," a term Paul calls these same people in 2 Corinthians 11:13. According to Witherington, Paul is addressing "those who had dogged his steps one too many times on the mission field—Jewish Christians whose agenda was to make Gentile believers Jewish—get circumcised, observe the Sabbath, keep kosher, and in short keep the whole of the Mosaic covenant, all 613 commandments." Ben Witherington III, *Paul's Letter to the Philippians,* 181.

179. Paul references the gift in Philippians 1:5; 4:14-20. Philippians is a "hortatory letter of friendship." For a discussion on this style of letter-writing, see Gordon Fee, *Paul's Letter to the Philippians*, 2-7, 24, 37-39.

A highlight of the letter is found in chapter 2:6-11, which may be Paul's own composition or represent an early Christian hymn about the incarnation of Christ.[180] The hymn reveals that what is honorable to God is opposite of what is honorable in the Greco-Roman world. In God's eyes, living as a slave who serves others like Christ did is honorable rather than displaying military power like Caesar.[181]

Similar to 1 Thessalonians, Paul uses imperial language to describe the kingdom of God.[182] A major theme that runs throughout the letter is God's sovereignty over the Roman authorities.[183] According to Paul, the Philippian ekklesia is a colonial outpost of Jesus' empire, just as Philippi is a colonial outpost of Caesar's empire.[184] Paul sends the letter with Epaphras/Epaphroditus to take to Philippi.[185]

180. I give more detail on what provoked Paul to write Philippians as well as provide a deep dive into the letter in my master class, *Subversive Colony: Philippians in 3D*. Refer to thedeeperchristianlife.com/classes.

181. Ben Witherington III, *Friendship and Finance in Philippi*, 46.

182. For a detailed treatment of the imperial divine honors and the influence they had on Paul and the Philippian church, see D. Clint Burnett, *Paul and Imperial Divine Honors,* chap. 2.

183. Peter Oakes, *Empire, Economics, and the New Testament*, chaps. 7 and 10. For an overview of Philippians, see David deSilva, *An Introduction to the New Testament*, chap. 16; N.T. Wright and Michael Bird, *The New Testament in Its World*, chap. 19; Clinton Arnold, ed., *Zondervan Illustrated Bible Backgrounds Commentary*, 3:343-369. Educated prisoners would read and write from prison. Since Paul's custody in Rome was light, he could write letters including Philippians, Colossians, Philemon, etc. without any problem. Craig Keener, *Acts*, 4:3727.

184. Richard Horsley, ed., *Paul and Politics*, 173ff. Paul's words "our citizenship in heaven" in Philippians 3:20 have traditionally been misunderstood. Citizens of Rome were expected to promote the interests of its mother city. In the same way, citizens of God's heavenly kingdom were to express and promote the culture of heaven on earth. The church in Philippi, therefore, was a colonial outpost of Jesus' empire. For an exposition of this text along these lines, see F.F. Bruce, *Philippians*, 133; N.T. Wright, *Paul for Everyone: The Prison Letters*, 126-127; Frank Viola, *Insurgence*, 380ff.

185. Ben Witherington III, *Paul's Letter to the Philippians*, 171, 174, 178, 239; Gordon Fee, *Paul's Letter to the Philippians*, 272. The trip between Philippi and Rome would typically take between four and seven weeks spanning around 740 miles. Ben Witherington III, *Friendship and Finance in Philippi*, 25.

Philippians

Paul and Timothy, servants of Jesus Christ; To all the saints in Christ Jesus who are at Philippi, with the overseers[a] and servants:[b] Grace to you, and peace from God our Father and the Lord Jesus Christ.

I thank my God whenever I remember you, always in every request of mine on behalf of you all, making my requests with joy, for your partnership[c] in furtherance of the Good News from the first day until now; being confident of this very thing, that he who began a good work in you will complete it until the day of Jesus Christ.

It is even right for me to think this way on behalf of all of you, because I have you in my heart, because both in my bonds and in the defense and confirmation of the Good News, you all are partakers with me of grace. For God is my witness, how I long after all of you in the tender mercies of Christ Jesus.

This I pray, that your love may abound yet more and more in knowledge and all discernment, so that you may approve the things that are excellent, that you may be sincere and without offense to the day of Christ, being filled with the fruits of righteousness, which are through Jesus Christ, to the glory and praise of God.

Now I desire to have you know, brothers,[d] that the things which happened to me have turned out rather to the progress of the Good News, so that it became evident to the whole palace[e] guard, and to all the rest, that my bonds are in Christ, and that most of the brothers in the Lord, being confident through my bonds, are more abundantly bold to speak the word of God without fear.

Some indeed preach Christ even out of envy and strife, and some also out of good will. The former insincerely preach Christ from selfish ambition, thinking that they add affliction to my chains; but the latter out of love, knowing that I am appointed for the defense of the Good News. What does it matter? Only that in every way, whether in pretense or in truth, Christ is proclaimed. I rejoice in this, yes, and will rejoice. For I know that this will turn out to my salvation, through your prayers and the supply of the Spirit of Jesus Christ, according to my earnest expectation and hope, that I will in no way be disappointed, but with all boldness, as always, now also Christ will be magnified in my body, whether by life or by death.

For to me to live is Christ, and to die is gain. But if I live on in the flesh, this will bring fruit from my work; yet I don't know what I will choose. But I am hard pressed between the two, having the desire to depart and be with Christ, which is far better. Yet to remain in the flesh is more needful for your sake. Having this confidence, I know that I will remain, yes, and remain with you all for your progress and joy in the faith, that your rejoicing may abound in Christ Jesus in me through my presence with you again.

Only let your way of life be worthy of the Good News of Christ, that whether I come and see you or am absent, I may hear of your state, that you stand firm in one spirit, with one soul striving for the faith of the Good News; and in nothing frightened by the adversaries, which is for them a proof of destruction, but to you of salvation, and that from God.

Because it has been granted to you on behalf of Christ, not only to believe in him, but also to suffer on his behalf, having the same conflict which you saw in me and now hear is in me. If therefore there is any exhortation in Christ, if any consolation of love, if any fellowship of the Spirit, if any tender mercies and compassion, make my joy full by being like-minded, having the same love, being of one accord, of one mind; doing nothing through rivalry or through conceit, but in humility, each counting others better than himself; each of you not just looking to his own things, but each of you also to the things of others.

Have this in your mind, which was also in Christ Jesus, who, existing in the form of God, didn't consider equality with God a thing to be grasped, but emptied himself, taking the form of a servant, being made in the likeness of men. And being found in human form, he humbled himself, becoming obedient to the point of death, yes, the death of the cross. Therefore God also highly exalted him, and gave to him the name which is above every name, that at the name of Jesus every knee should bow, of those in heaven, those on earth, and those under the earth, and that every tongue should confess that Jesus Christ is Lord, to the glory of God the Father.

So then, my beloved, even as you have always obeyed, not only in my presence, but now much more in my absence, work out your own salvation with fear and trembling. For it is God who works in you both to will and to work, for his good pleasure.

Do all things without complaining and arguing, that you may become blameless and harmless, children of God without defect in the middle of a crooked and perverse generation, among whom you are seen as lights in the world, holding up the word of life, that I may have something to boast in the day of Christ, that I didn't run in vain nor labor in vain. Yes, and if

I am poured out on the sacrifice and service of your faith, I rejoice, and rejoice with you all. In the same way, you also rejoice, and rejoice with me.

But I hope in the Lord Jesus to send Timothy to you soon, that I also may be cheered up when I know how you are doing. For I have no one else like-minded, who will truly care about you. For they all seek their own, not the things of Jesus Christ. But you know the proof of him, that as a child serves a father, so he served with me in furtherance of the Good News. Therefore I hope to send him at once, as soon as I see how it will go with me. But I trust in the Lord that I myself also will come shortly.

But I counted it necessary to send to you Epaphroditus, my brother, fellow worker, fellow soldier, and your apostle and servant of my need, since he longed for you all, and was very troubled because you had heard that he was sick. For indeed he was sick, nearly to death, but God had mercy on him, and not on him only, but on me also, that I might not have sorrow on sorrow.

I have sent him therefore the more diligently, that when you see him again, you may rejoice, and that I may be the less sorrowful. Receive him therefore in the Lord with all joy, and hold such people in honor, because for the work of Christ he came near to death, risking his life to supply that which was lacking in your service toward me.

Finally, my brothers, rejoice in the Lord! To write the same things to you, to me indeed is not tiresome, but for you it is safe. Beware of the dogs; beware of the evil workers; beware of the false circumcision. For we are the circumcision, who worship God in the Spirit, and rejoice in Christ Jesus, and have no confidence in the flesh; though I myself might have confidence even in the flesh.

If any other man thinks that he has confidence in the flesh, I yet more: circumcised the eighth day, of the stock of Israel, of the tribe of Benjamin, a Hebrew of Hebrews; concerning the law, a Pharisee; concerning zeal, persecuting the assembly; concerning the righteousness which is in the law, found blameless. However, I consider those things that were gain to me as a loss for Christ.

Yes most certainly, and I count all things to be a loss for the excellency of the knowledge of Christ Jesus, my Lord, for whom I suffered the loss of all things, and count them nothing but refuse, that I may gain Christ and be found in him, not having a righteousness of my own, that which is of the law, but that which is through faith in Christ, the righteousness which is from God by faith, that I may know him, and the power of his resurrection, and the fellowship of his sufferings, becoming conformed to his death, if by any means I may attain to the resurrection from the dead. Not that I have already obtained, or am already made perfect; but I press on, that I may take hold of that for which also I was taken hold of by Christ Jesus.

Brothers, I don't regard myself as yet having taken hold, but one thing I do: forgetting the things which are behind, and stretching forward to the things which are before, I press on toward the goal for the prize of the high calling of God in Christ Jesus. Let us therefore, as many as are perfect, think this way. If in anything you think otherwise, God will also reveal that to you. Nevertheless, to the extent that we have already attained, let's walk by the same rule. Let's be of the same mind.

Brothers, be imitators together of me, and note those who walk this way, even as you have us for an example. For many walk, of whom I told you often, and now tell you even weeping, as the enemies of the cross of Christ, whose end is destruction, whose god is the belly, and whose glory is in their shame, who think about earthly things.

For our citizenship is in heaven, from where we also wait for a Savior, the Lord Jesus Christ, who will change the body of our humiliation to be conformed to the body of his glory, according to the working by which he is able even to subject all things to himself. Therefore, my brothers, beloved and longed for, my joy and crown, stand firm in the Lord in this way, my beloved.

I exhort Euodia, and I exhort Syntyche, to think the same way in the Lord. Yes, I beg you also, true partner, help these women, for they labored with me in the Good News with Clement also, and the rest of my fellow workers, whose names are in the book of life.

Rejoice in the Lord always! Again I will say, "Rejoice!" Let your gentleness be known to all men. The Lord is at hand. In nothing be anxious, but in everything, by prayer and petition with thanksgiving, let your requests be made known to God. And the peace of God, which surpasses all understanding, will guard your hearts and your thoughts in Christ Jesus.

Finally, brothers, whatever things are true, whatever things are honorable, whatever things are just, whatever things are pure, whatever things are lovely, whatever things are of good report: if there is any virtue and if there is any praise, think about these things. The things which you learned, received, heard, and saw in me: do these things, and the God of peace will be with you.

But I rejoice in the Lord greatly, that now at length you have revived your thought for me; in which you did indeed take thought, but you lacked opportunity. Not that I speak because of lack, for I have learned in whatever state I am, to be content in it. I know how to be humbled, and I also know how to abound. In everything and in all things I have learned the secret both to be filled and to be hungry, both to abound and to be in need. I can do all things through Christ, who strengthens me.

However you did well that you shared in my affliction. You yourselves also know, you Philippians, that in the beginning of the Good News, when I departed from Macedonia, no assembly shared with me in the matter of giving and receiving but you only. For even in Thessalonica you sent once and again to my need. Not that I seek for the gift, but I seek for the fruit that increases to your account.

But I have all things and abound. I am filled, having received from Epaphroditus the things that came from you, a sweet-smelling fragrance, an acceptable and well-pleasing sacrifice to God. My God will supply every need of yours according to his riches in glory in Christ Jesus. Now to our God and Father be the glory forever and ever! Amen.

Greet every saint in Christ Jesus. The brothers who are with me greet you. All the saints greet you, especially those who are of Caesar's household. The grace of the Lord Jesus Christ be with you all. Amen.

a. 1:1 or, superintendents, or bishops.
b. 1:1 Or, deacons.
c. 1:5 The word translated "partnership" (κοινωνία) also means "fellowship" and "sharing."
d. 1:12 The word for "brothers" here and where context allows may also be correctly translated "brothers and sisters" or "siblings."
e. 1:13 or, praetorian.

James (the Lord's Half-Brother) Is Martyred[186]

While Paul is facing opposition for his faith in Rome, other Christian leaders are also suffering for their faith, with some experiencing martyrdom. In far off Judea, Porcius Festus

---

186. This took place in A.D. 62. Herbert Lockyer, ed., *Nelson's Illustrated Bible Dictionary*, 227; Ben Witherington III, *Invitation to the New Testament*, 280.

dies in office.[187] Ananus, the high priest, convenes the Sanhedrin and brings "James the Just" (the half-brother of Jesus), along with some others in Jerusalem, before the council.[188] In the presence of the Sanhedrin, Ananus accuses James of blaspheming the Law of Moses. Ananus is known for making rash judgments. He is a more heartless Sadducee than other Jewish leaders and unusually daring.[189]

As a result of the procedure, James is brought to the pinnacle of the temple, thrown down, stoned and clubbed to death.[190] The half-brother of Jesus leaves this earth and graduates to his eternal destiny. Since James is held in high regard in Jerusalem as a "Torah-true Jew," the fair-minded Jews in the city are highly offended by his execution. Not long after this tragedy, Albinus takes office, and Ananus is deposed for illegally convening the Sanhedrin.[191]

187. Festus died in A.D. 62. F.F. Bruce, *Paul: Apostle of the Heart Set Free*, 359.

188. Ananus was also called Annas. He was the son of the high priest who bore the same name (John 18:13, 24).

189. Josephus, *The Antiquities of the Jews*, 20.199-202; James VanderKam, *An Introduction to Early Judaism*, 194; David Rhoads, *Israel in Revolution 6-74 C.E.*, 92.

190. Eusebius, *The History of the Church*, 2.23.

191. Josephus, *The Antiquities of the Jews*, 20.9.1.

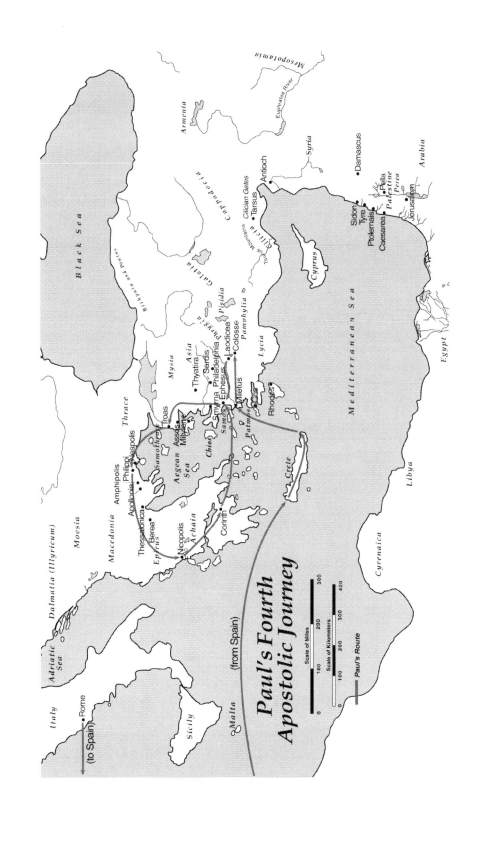

Paul's Fourth
Apostolic Journey

CHAPTER 13

THE ASIAN CHRONICLE

A.D. 62 – A.D. 70

For I am already being offered, and the time of my departure has come. I have fought the good fight. I have finished the course. I have kept the faith. From now on, the crown of righteousness is stored up for me, which the Lord, the righteous judge, will give to me on that day; and not to me only, but also to all those who have loved his appearing. (2 Timothy 4:6-8)

PREVIEW OF PAUL'S FOURTH APOSTOLIC JOURNEY[1]

Duration: Four years

Dates: A.D. 62-65[2]

Kingdom Communities Planted: (2) Nicopolis and Miletus[3]

---

1. The notes in this chapter reference works by Pauline scholars who explain why they postulate a fourth apostolic journey, including the basis for the second imprisonment theory.

2. During these years, Paul moved to Asia Minor (perhaps in the spring of A.D. 63) and remained there until A.D. 64. Later, he would visit Spain and travel to Crete with Titus. Herbert Lockyer, ed., *Nelson's Illustrated Bible Dictionary*, 227.

3. According to a number of scholars, on Paul's fourth journey, he went to Spain (Romans 15:24, 28), Crete (Titus 1:5), Miletus (2 Timothy 4:20), Colossae (Philemon 22), Ephesus (1 Timothy 1:3), and Nicopolis (Titus 3:12). It appears that he also visited Macedonia (1 Timothy 1:3), Corinth (2 Timothy 4:20), Ephesus again (1 Timothy 3:14-15), Troas (2 Timothy 4:13), and finally ended up in Rome (2 Timothy 1:17). See John Stott, *The Message of 2 Timothy*, 17; *The NKJV Study Bible*, 1826; William Ramsay, *St. Paul the Traveler and Roman Citizen*, 285. There is great debate among scholars concerning the timeline for Paul's apostolic labors (which included evangelization, church planting, and training). In this connection, we can't be sure of the

> *Time Planting:*
>
> Miletus = Unknown
>
> Nicopolis = Unknown

Peter and Silas have been traveling in northwest Turkey, specifically the regions of Asia, Pontus, Galatia, Cappadocia, and Bithynia. In these regions, the assemblies are a mix of Jewish and Gentile believers.[4] Peter and Silas come to Rome where they join Mark.[5]

Late 62[6]

After spending two years under house arrest in Rome, Paul is released from prison.[7] The apostle now makes his long-awaited trip to Spain.[8] There is no Jewish settlement there so

---

exact sequence of the visits mentioned in the main narrative nor if Paul planted any other churches beyond those in Miletus and Nicopolis. Barnett rightly says, "It's impossible to work out a precise sequence." Paul Barnett, *A Short Book about Paul*, 47.

4. The association of Peter and Silas in these regions is largely an inference based on 1 Peter 1:1 and 5:12 coupled with the fact that Jesus commanded His disciples to travel in pairs. They also end up in Rome together. Recall that the Lord did not permit Paul to minister in some of these regions years earlier (Acts 16:6-10). Pontus-Bithynia formed a single province, but they are separate in 1 Peter 1:1. Peter's list represents the travel route he (probably with Silas) took when visiting these assemblies. For details, see Mark Fairchild, *Christian Origins in Ephesus & Asia Minor*, 117-121.

5. 1 Peter 5:12-13. Peter viewed John Mark as a son.

6. What I present in this part of the book is a plausible reconstruction of the events. But again, we cannot be certain about most of it. Sources from scholars who agree with the various pieces of this timeline are cited in the notes.

7. Paul wasn't prosecuted for two years, possibly because those in Judea dropped the case. The Sanhedrin may have decided not to send a delegation to Rome (due to the expense) and withdrew the case entirely. Normally, if the accusers didn't show up after two years, a prisoner would be released. Craig Keener, "Lessons on Acts," Session 32; Ben Witherington III, *The Acts of the Apostles*, 791. For details on Paul's release, see Ben Witherington III, *Letters and Homilies for Hellenized Christians*, 1:65. Witherington believes Paul lived two years under house arrest from around A.D. 60 to 62. Ben Witherington III, *The Acts of the Apostles*, 791-793, 812. Bruce notes that this scenario of Paul's release is "the most plausible" reconstruction, after which the apostle is imprisoned a second time years later. F.F. Bruce, *Paul: Apostle of the Heart Set Free*, 444. More on this later.

8. Romans 15:24-28. There is good reason to believe Paul traveled to Spain after his release from his first Roman imprisonment. (I will cite the sources in another note.) Paul may have also returned to Illyricum.

Paul must speak to people who know nothing about the Hebrew Scriptures.[9] He must also speak Latin or use interpreters as most people in Spain cannot understand Greek.[10] The visit is brief, and we have no evidence that any kingdom communities are planted in the country.[11]

Paul then travels southeast and meets Titus on the island of Crete.[12] Both men minister to the kingdom communities on the island. These assemblies have undergone an assault of false teaching by ungodly teachers. As a result, the assemblies are beginning to fall apart. Paul leaves Titus on the island of Crete to strengthen the believing communities and select elders (overseers). The elders are to care for the assemblies when Titus leaves Crete.[13]

The apostle travels northeast and spends time in Asia Minor. He visits Miletus where he begins preaching the life-changing gospel of the kingdom. While there, Paul sends a message to Trophimus in Ephesus to meet him in Miletus and help him with the work. Trophimus eventually joins him, and a kingdom community is planted in Miletus. But Trophimus falls ill. Paul must leave so he heads off to Colossae as he promised,[14] leaving Trophimus behind in Miletus.[15] Timothy, who is now in Ephesus,[16] sends word to Paul that

---

Jerome Murphy-O'Connor, *Paul: His Story*, 218ff. See also traditions from Hippolytus, Jerome, Chrysostom, et al. Lars Kierspel, *Charts on the Life, Letters, and Theology of Paul*, 73; Eckhard Schnabel, *Paul the Missionary*, 117-120; Alan Bandy, *An Illustrated Guide to the Apostle Paul*, 170-172; Thomas Schmidt, *The Apostles After Acts*, chap. 1.

9. Craig Keener, *The IVP Bible Background Commentary: New Testament*, 454.

10. Craig Keener, *Romans*, 177; *The IVP Bible Background Commentary: New Testament*, 454.

11. By going to Spain, Paul fulfilled Christ's commission to him in Acts 13:47. He took the gospel of the kingdom to the "ends of the earth" (NIV). Throughout his ministry, Paul continuously traveled west. David Capes, et al., *Rediscovering Paul*, 122-123. For an explanation of why Paul moved from east to west to bring the gospel of the kingdom to the world, see Frank Viola, *Insurgence*, 360-362. Schnabel argues that the "ends of the earth" refers to Spain. Eckhard Schnabel, *Early Christian Mission*, 1:372-376.

12. Inferred from Titus 1:5. While Titus established churches in Crete, there may have already been Jewish believers there from the day of Pentecost in A.D. 30. (Acts 2:11 refers to people from Crete.) Eckhard Schnabel, *Paul the Missionary*, 121. But again, a group of converts doesn't necessarily constitute an established ekklesia. Alan Bandy pieces together Paul's trip to Crete in *An Illustrated Guide to the Apostle Paul*, 172-173.

13. Titus 1:5.

14. Philemon 22.

15. 2 Timothy 4:20.

16. During his imprisonment in Rome, Paul expressed to the Philippians his desire to send Timothy to them (Philippians 2:19-23). While it's unclear whether this plan came to fruition, we do know that Timothy journeyed to Ephesus at some point after Paul's release from captivity.

the Ephesian assembly is being ravaged by false teachers.[17] So Paul leaves Colossae and meets Timothy in Ephesus.

While in Ephesus, Paul excommunicates two men from the church. Their names are Hymenaeus and Alexander, and they've been blaspheming.[18] The men refuse to repent, so Paul has no other choice but to put them out of the assembly. Unfortunately, they have damaged the faith of some of the believers. Alexander, a metalworker, retaliates by opposing Paul's message and causing him great harm.[19] Thankfully, a brother in the assembly in Ephesus named Onesiphorus is of great help to Paul.[20]

Paul leaves Timothy in Ephesus, instructing him to remain in the city and combat the false teachers in the church.[21] Timothy is reluctant to stay in Ephesus, but he yields to Paul's instruction.[22] The false teachers are ambitious to be instructors of the Law of Moses, even though they know little about it. They are also teaching myths that pervert the creation account and debating over genealogies.[23] Paul is ready to head off to Macedonia.

17. The heresy that plagued the church in Ephesus was similar, if not the same, as the heresy plaguing the assemblies in Crete. Any distinctions were minor. Donald Guthrie, *The Pastoral Epistles: An Introduction and Commentary*, revised edition, TNTC (Grand Rapids, MI: Eerdmans, 1990), 42.

18. 1 Timothy 1:19-20. The idea of delivering someone over to satan implies excommunication from the assembly. See 1 Corinthians 5:4-13. Hymenaeus is mentioned again in 2 Timothy 2:17-18.

19. 2 Timothy 4:14-15. Again, some scholars believe this Alexander is the same person mentioned in Acts 19:33. Otto F.A. Meinardus, *St. Paul in Ephesus*, 98; Craig Keener, et al., *NIV Cultural Backgrounds Study Bible*, 2124. It's also possible to equate him with the Alexander Paul describes as having been handed over to satan in 1 Timothy 1:20. Craig Keener, *The IVP Bible Background Commentary: New Testament*, 623-624; Philip Towner, *The Letters to Timothy and Titus*, 630-631; *The NKJV Study Bible*, 1841. The word translated "coppersmith" (NKJV) or "metalworker" (NIV) in 2 Timothy 4:14 refers to all kinds of metal work, so it could signify that Alexander was the "silversmith" in Acts 19. J.D. Douglas, et al., eds., *New Bible Dictionary*, 24. Even so, the harm the Alexander mentioned in 2 Timothy caused Paul was likely either done in Ephesus or Troas, where he may have brought false charges against Paul that eventually led to his arrest in Troas. See also Ben Witherington III, *Letters and Homilies for Hellenized Christians*, 1:379-380.

20. 2 Timothy 1:18. See also F.F. Bruce, *Paul: Apostle of the Heart Set Free*, 445; Philip Towner, *The Letters to Timothy and Titus,* 486.

21. 1 Timothy 1:3ff. "Timothy stayed in Ephesus while Paul traveled northwest through Troas (2 Tim. 4:13) and across into Macedonia." Craig Keener, *The IVP Bible Background Commentary: New Testament*, 603.

22. Donald Guthrie, *The Pastoral Epistles*, 67.

23. 1 Timothy 1:3-7; 2 Timothy 4:4. For a plausible sequence of these events, see Gerald Hawthorne, et al., eds. *Dictionary of Paul and His Letters*, 661-662; J.D. Douglas, et al., eds., *New Bible Dictionary*, 1202.

As I urged you when I was going into Macedonia, stay at Ephesus that you might command certain men not to teach a different doctrine.... (1 Timothy 1:3)

Before Paul departs, he embraces Timothy. The situation is so hot for the Christians throughout the empire that Timothy doesn't know if he will ever see his mentor again, so he weeps in Paul's presence. Several years later, Paul will pen these words to Timothy:

...How unceasing is my memory of you in my petitions, night and day longing to see you, remembering your tears.... (2 Timothy 1:3-4)

On his way to Macedonia, Paul visits the assembly in Troas and stays in the home of a man named Carpus. While there, he ministers to the believing community.[24] When Paul exits Troas, he leaves behind his winter coat, some scrolls and parchments at Carpus' home.[25] The apostle arrives in Macedonia and visits the assembly in Philippi as he had planned when he was under house arrest in Rome.[26]

Crisis in Ephesus

Despite Timothy's attempt to recenter the assembly in Ephesus on Christ, the problems worsen. Five years earlier, Paul forewarned the Ephesian elders that wolves

---

24. For a sketch of the movements of Titus and Timothy during this period, see Philip Towner, *The Letters to Timothy and Titus*, 13-14. Bandy agrees that Paul planted the church in Troas the second time he was in the city (2 Corinthians 2:12), rather than on his second apostolic journey (Acts 16). Alan Bandy, *An Illustrated Guide to the Apostle Paul*, 174.

25. These scrolls may have been Old Testament books and the parchments notebooks. Parchments were made from animal skins, and they were costly. The parchments probably contained notes that Paul used when he ministered in the various churches. They may also have been copies of previous letters he wrote to the assemblies since it was the normal practice of the day to retain copies of epistles that were dispatched. It's possible that the letter of Ephesians was written on "the new writing material, parchment." Otto F.A. Meinardus, *St. Paul in Ephesus*, 72. The term "parchments" was already in use to refer to codices, an early form of the modern book which the Christians quickly popularized. Craig Keener, *The IVP Bible Background Commentary: New Testament*, 623.

26. 1 Timothy 1:3; Philippians 2:24.

would invade the ekklesia and draw disciples after themselves with perverse teachings.[27]

Take heed, therefore, to yourselves, and to all the flock, in which the Holy Spirit has made you overseers, to shepherd the assembly of the Lord and God which he purchased with his own blood. For I know that after my departure, vicious wolves will enter in among you, not sparing the flock. Men will arise from among your own selves, speaking perverse things, to draw away the disciples after them. (Acts 20:28-30)

The apostle's warning to the elders in Ephesus is now coming to pass. The wolves have appeared,[28] and the heresy they are spreading is an odd brand of Jewish proto-gnosticism.[29] The false teachers preach that the Law of Moses is binding on all believers, along

27. Elders and overseers weren't two different groups in the first century. They, along with shepherds, were descriptive terms for the same function and role. Clinton Arnold, ed., *Zondervan Illustrated Bible Backgrounds Commentary*, 2b:209-210.

28. 1 Timothy 1:3-7; 6:3-5.

29. By "proto-gnosticism," I mean a species of teaching that would later develop into gnosticism. According to E.E. Ellis, the false teaching was a kind of "Judaism cross with Gnosticism." It began with the circumcision party years earlier, but later developed in the Diaspora to take on Greek mystical elements. Gerald Hawthorne, et al., eds. *Dictionary of Paul and His Letters*, 662-663. Developed gnosticism would make its appearance in the second century, though some of the church fathers claim it was present in the first century. Mark Fairchild, *Christian Origins in Ephesus & Asia Minor*, 76. According to gnosticism, full salvation comes through special knowledge (*gnosis*) that only the initiated possess. In Ephesus, an embryonic form of this heresy had emerged. Paul refers to the heresy when he says to Timothy, "Timothy, guard that which is committed to you, turning away from the empty chatter and oppositions of what is falsely called knowledge [*gnosis*]" (1 Timothy 6:20). According to another scholar, while fully developed gnosticism cannot be demonstrated before A.D. 135, a number of the emerging streams of its teaching converged in the first century to form the beginning of gnosticism. Clinton Arnold, *Ephesians: Power and Magic* (Eugene, OR: Wipf & Stock, 1989), 12. In Titus 1:10, Paul wasn't saying that the teaching was influenced by Jewish thought, but rather, it was being promoted by Jewish teachers. There was a Jewish community in Crete. Donald Guthrie, *The Pastoral Epistles*, 199; Philip Towner, *The Letters to Timothy and Titus*, 696.

with emphasizing myths and genealogies.[30] They also teach that it is sinful to eat meat and participate in marriage.[31] In addition to these things, they believe:

- Eve was both a mediator and a redeemer figure who existed before Adam.[32]

- Man came into existence because of a woman, and man was given enlightenment through the woman. Since Eve was the first to take a bite from the Tree of Knowledge, she is the bearer of a special spiritual knowledge (called *gnosis*).[33]

- Women are called to lead people to the illuminating *gnosis*, which is represented by the Tree of Knowledge. Redemption completely reversed the effects of the Fall. Therefore, men are no longer subject to earthly authorities and women now have authority over their husbands.[34]

Those in the Ephesian church who accept this heresy prefer the leadership of women over men.[35] The teaching finds fertile ground among the women in the assembly.[36] Consequently, the homes of the Ephesian sisters also provide a network by which the false

---

30. 1 Timothy 1:3-11. Proponents of this teaching transformed the stories and genealogies in Genesis into new tales ("myths"). The speculations led them into a rabbit hole that kept going deeper with more genealogies, creating more tales without the support of the biblical witness. Overall, these teachings led people away from Jesus rather than toward Him. As one scholar says, "Judaism was at this time capable of spawning rich theological speculation." J.L. Houlden, *The Pastoral Epistles: I and II Timothy, Titus,* The Pelican New Testament Commentaries (Harmondsworth, UK: Penguin, 1976), 55-56.

31. 1 Timothy 4:1-3. Paul says these teachings came from demons (4:1).

32. Paul appears to refute this concept in 1 Timothy 2:5, 13-14.

33. The second-century gnostics taught this. So it appears at this point to be a pre-gnostic teaching.

34. Paul refutes this concept in 1 Timothy 2:9-15.

35. The heretical teaching could have been propagated by women as well as men. 1 Timothy 1:20 and 2 Timothy 2:17 mention men. But in 1 Timothy 1:3, the Greek could be translated "certain people" rather than "certain men." See the NIV and NASB. According to one scholar, "Historically, older women are often the story bearers of the culture, and they transmit the culture from generation to generation through myths, fairy tales, and lore that are repeated in front of the hearth and at bedtime." Cynthia Long Westfall, *Paul and Gender: Reclaiming the Apostle's Vision for Men and Women in Christ* (Grand Rapids, MI: Baker Academic, 2016), 302-303.

36. 1 Timothy 4:7; 2 Timothy 3:6-9.

doctrine rapidly spreads.[37] Some of the stronger women are teaching the heresy in the church gatherings, and they are lording over (dominating) the men.[38]

They have also accepted the ideals of the "new women" of the Roman Empire. Specifically, they dress in an immodest and exploitive way. They also defy other accepted norms regarding marriage and family.[39] There is also a problem with how the widows in the assembly are being cared for. Some of them have adopted the heresy, and others have no family members who are able to care for their needs. Still worse, a number of the younger widows who refuse to remarry are acting promiscuously. Consequently, Timothy wants Paul to tell him which widows the assembly should care for.

On top of all these problems, some of the rich brethren in the assembly are influencing their poorer brethren to lust for wealth. The assembly in Ephesus is wildly deteriorating, and a concerned Timothy writes to Paul about it. Upon hearing the bad report, Paul wants to return to Ephesus, but he cannot. So he responds to Timothy by letter.

PAUL WRITES 1 TIMOTHY[40]

Year: A.D. 62-63[41]

---

37. 1 Timothy 3:11; 5:13-15.

38. Some scholars believe the keyword in 1 Timothy 2:12, *authentein*, means wielding a harmful and destructive power, i.e., dominating others. In this case, some of the women in the church were domineering over the men. Personal correspondence with Nijay Gupta, 6/6/23; Louw & Nida, *Greek-English Lexicon of the New Testament: Based on Semantic Domains,* second edition, 1996: vol. 1, 473.

39. Under ancient Roman law, you were what you wore. The way wives dressed in public sent clear signals to other men that the wife was either modest or promiscuous. See Bruce Winter's *Roman Wives, Roman Widows,* chaps. 6-7.

40. 1 Timothy along with Titus and 2 Timothy have been dubbed the "Pastoral Epistles" (or the "Pastorals") since the eighteenth century. *New Testament of the New American Bible: Giant Print Edition* (Totowa, NJ: Catholic Book Pub Company, 1987), 469. The term may trace back to Paul Anton during that century. Philip Towner, *The Letters to Timothy and Titus,* 88. However, these letters were not written to pastors (shepherds). They were written to traveling apostolic workers. Timothy and Titus were itinerant men, not local shepherds.

41. Given my timeline in this book, the proposed time frame is plausible. Keener thinks the letter was written between A.D. 62 and 64. Craig Keener, *The IVP Bible Background Commentary: New Testament,* 601. See also Aida Besancon Spencer, *1 Timothy: A New Covenant Commentary,* NCCS (Havertown, UK: The Lutterworth Press, 2014), 5. According to Knight, the idea that 1 Timothy was written A.D. 62-63 is plausible.

From: Philippi[42]

To: Timothy who is in Ephesus

Author: Paul[43]

Contextual Summary: Paul wants to visit Timothy soon, but he writes so that if he is delayed, Timothy knows how to proceed with his work and encourage the assemblies to live out the faith.[44]

George Knight, *The Pastoral Epistles,* 54-55. Witherington believes it was written later in A.D. 64-65. Ben Witherington III, *Letters and Homilies for Hellenized Christians,* 1:66. See also Gerald Hawthorne, et al., eds., *Dictionary of Paul and His Letters,* 661. Some scholars reconstruct the narrative differently, claiming that Paul wrote 1 Timothy and Titus during his third apostolic journey (Acts 18-21). Philip Towner, *The Letters to Timothy and Titus,* 13-14. For a detailed sketch on the scholarly debate regarding the historical reconstruction of the Pastoral Epistles (including authorship, provenance, etc.), see William Mounce, *Pastoral Epistles,* WBC (Nashville, TN: Thomas Nelson, 2000), intro.; Donald Guthrie, *The Pastoral Epistles,* intro.; Philip Towner, *The Letters to Timothy and Titus,* intro.; George Knight, *The Pastoral Epistles: A Commentary on the Greek Text,* NIGTC (Grand Rapids, MI: Eerdmans, 1992), intro.

42. Gerald Hawthorne, et al., eds. *Dictionary of Paul and His Letters,* 448; Clinton Arnold, ed., *Zondervan Illustrated Bible Backgrounds Commentary,* 3:445; Alan Bandy, *An Illustrated Guide to the Apostle Paul,* 174.

43. 1 Timothy, as well as Titus and 2 Timothy, are widely considered by Pauline scholars as pseudonymous, that is, not having been written by Paul. Although I and many other scholars (including Jeffrey Weima) disagree with this widely held view, the main reason why these letters aren't considered Pauline is due to the differences in style from Paul's uncontested works. But I stand with those scholars who make a case that Luke was Paul's secretary for the Pastorals, which would account for the stylistic differences and the commonalities with the style used in Luke-Acts. See Ben Witherington III, *Invitation to the New Testament,* 255ff.; Craig Keener, *The IVP Bible Background Commentary: New Testament,* 600. For the argument that Paul was the author of 1 Timothy (as well as the two other Pastorals), see Philip Towner, *The Letters to Timothy and Titus,* 86-88; Donald Guthrie, *New Testament Introduction,* 607-649; *The Pastoral Epistles,* 55-62; 224-240; George Knight, *The Pastoral Epistles,* 4-52; Clinton Arnold, ed., *Zondervan Illustrated Bible Backgrounds Commentary,* 3:445-447; Eckhard Schnabel, "Paul, Timothy, and Titus: The Assumption of a Pseudonymous Author and of Pseudonymous Recipients in the Light of Literary, Theological, and Historical Evidence," *Do Historical Matters Matter to Faith? A Critical Appraisal of Modern and Postmodern Approaches to Scripture,* eds., James Hoffmeier and Dennis Magary (Wheaton, IL: Crossway, 2012), 383-403. Stott interacts with what Pauline scholars have argued on both sides and ends up supporting Pauline authorship. John Stott, *The Message of 1 Timothy & Titus: Guard the Gospel* (Downers Grove, IL: InterVarsity Press, 1996), 21-34.

44. 1 Timothy 3:14-15, ESV. Alan Bandy, *An Illustrated Guide to the Apostle Paul,* 174.

Paul exhorts his younger apprentice to give attention to the public reading of the Scriptures in the gatherings, to exhortation, and to teaching. He urges Timothy not to neglect his spiritual gift that was bestowed on him by the laying on of hands. Paul also exhorts him to permit no one to disregard him because of his youth.[45]

The apostle encourages his apprentice to be faithful to the ministry to which God has called him, exhorting him to combat the proto-gnostic heresy that's spreading like cancer in the church. Salvation is for everyone, Paul affirms, not for a select few who possess secret knowledge (as the false teachers proclaim). The false teachers have corrupt minds and are motivated by dishonest gain.[46] Paul gives Timothy practical instructions on how to fight the heresy. One solution is to forbid the women peddling the false doctrine from teaching in the meetings.

He also addresses the problem of the Ephesian women who have accepted the ideals of the "new women" in their dress. In addition, he calls for the need to select new elders (overseers) and exhorts the ekklesia to give respect to those who oversee well.

Paul exposes the spirit behind the present heresy and predicts that it will increase in the future. He exhorts Timothy to boldly proclaim the truth in the face of error. He gives his apprentice practical instruction on how to treat the older men, the younger men, the older women, the younger women, and the widows in the church. Paul closes the letter by admonishing the contentious and the rich.[47]

Luke, who is still in Philippi, serves as the apostle's amanuensis and scribes the letter.[48] This letter, along with Titus and 2 Timothy, is written to Paul's co-workers rather than to a believing community. This fact, along with Luke's penmanship, accounts for the uniqueness of vocabulary and style in the so-called "Pastoral Epistles." While Paul is responsible for the content, Luke helps shape the style and vocabulary.[49]

45. 1 Timothy 4:12-14.

46. 1 Timothy 6:5.

47. For an overview of 1 Timothy, see Clinton Arnold, ed., *Zondervan Illustrated Bible Backgrounds Commentary*, 3:445-477; David deSilva, *An Introduction to the New Testament*, chap. 19; N.T. Wright and Michael Bird, *The New Testament in Its World*, 23.

48. See F.F. Bruce, *Paul: Apostle of the Heart Set Free*, 443.

49. Gary Burge, et al., *The New Testament in Antiquity*, 371. According to Witherington, with respect to the Pastorals (including 1 Timothy), the "voice is the voice of Paul, but the hands are the hands of Luke."

1 Timothy

Paul, an apostle of Jesus Christ according to the commandment of God our Savior and the Lord Jesus Christ[a] our hope; to Timothy, my true child in faith: Grace, mercy, and peace, from God our Father and Christ Jesus our Lord.

As I urged you when I was going into Macedonia, stay at Ephesus that you might command certain men not to teach a different doctrine, and not to pay attention to myths and endless genealogies, which cause disputes, rather than God's stewardship, which is in faith— but the goal of this command is love, out of a pure heart and a good conscience and sincere faith, from which things some, having missed the mark, have turned away to vain talking, desiring to be teachers of the law, though they understand neither what they say, nor about what they strongly affirm.

But we know that the law is good, if a person uses it lawfully, as knowing this, that law is not made for a righteous person, but for the lawless and insubordinate, for the ungodly and sinners, for the unholy and profane, for murderers of fathers and murderers of mothers, for manslayers, for the sexually immoral, for homosexuals, for slave-traders, for liars, for perjurers, and for any other thing contrary to the sound doctrine, according to the Good News of the glory of the blessed God, which was committed to my trust.

I thank him who enabled me, Christ Jesus our Lord, because he counted me faithful, appointing me to service; although I used to be a blasphemer, a persecutor, and insolent. However, I obtained mercy, because I did it ignorantly in unbelief. The grace of our Lord abounded exceedingly with faith and love which is in Christ Jesus. The saying is faithful and worthy of all acceptance, that Christ Jesus came into the world to save sinners, of whom I am chief.

However, for this cause I obtained mercy, that in me first, Jesus Christ might display all his patience for an example of those who were going to believe in him for eternal life. Now to the King eternal, immortal, invisible, to God who alone is wise, be honor and glory forever and ever. Amen.

Ben Witherington III, *Invitation to the New Testament*, 254. See also Witherington's *Letters and Homilies for Hellenized Christians*, 1:23-85.

I commit this instruction to you, my child Timothy, according to the prophecies which were given to you before, that by them you may wage the good warfare, holding faith and a good conscience, which some having thrust away made a shipwreck concerning the faith, of whom are Hymenaeus and Alexander, whom I delivered to Satan, that they might be taught not to blaspheme.

I exhort therefore, first of all, that petitions, prayers, intercessions, and givings of thanks be made for all men: for kings and all who are in high places, that we may lead a tranquil and quiet life in all godliness and reverence.

For this is good and acceptable in the sight of God our Savior, who desires all people to be saved and come to full knowledge of the truth. For there is one God, and one mediator between God and men, the man Christ Jesus, who gave himself as a ransom for all, the testimony in its own times, to which I was appointed a preacher and an apostle—I am telling the truth in Christ, not lying—a teacher of the Gentiles in faith and truth.

I desire therefore that the men in every place pray, lifting up holy hands without anger and doubting. In the same way, that women also adorn themselves in decent clothing, with modesty and propriety, not just[b] with braided hair, gold, pearls, or expensive clothing, but with good works, which is appropriate for women professing godliness.

Let a woman learn in quietness with full submission. But I don't permit a woman to teach, nor to exercise authority over a man, but to be in quietness. For Adam was formed first, then Eve. Adam wasn't deceived, but the woman, being deceived, has fallen into disobedience; but she will be saved through her childbearing, if they continue in faith, love, and sanctification with sobriety.

This is a faithful saying: someone who seeks to be an overseer[c] desires a good work. The overseer therefore must be without reproach, the husband of one wife, temperate, sensible, modest, hospitable, good at teaching; not a drinker, not violent, not greedy for money, but gentle, not quarrelsome, not covetous; one who rules his own house well, having children in subjection with all reverence; (but how could someone who doesn't know how to rule one's own house take care of God's assembly?) not a new convert, lest being puffed up he fall into the same condemnation as the devil. Moreover he must have good testimony from those who are outside, to avoid falling into reproach and the snare of the devil.

Servants,[d] in the same way, must be reverent, not double-tongued, not addicted to much wine, not greedy for money, holding the mystery of the faith in a pure conscience. Let them also first be tested; then let them serve[e] if they are blameless. Their wives in the same way must be reverent, not slanderers, temperate, and faithful in all things. Let servants[f] be husbands of one wife, ruling their children and their own houses well. For those who have served well[g] gain for themselves a good standing, and great boldness in the faith which is in Christ Jesus.

These things I write to you, hoping to come to you shortly; but if I wait long, that you may know how men ought to behave themselves in God's house, which is the assembly of the living God, the pillar and ground of the truth. Without controversy, the mystery of godliness is great: God[h] was revealed in the flesh, justified in the spirit, seen by angels, preached among the nations, believed on in the world, and received up in glory.

But the Spirit says expressly that in later times some will fall away from the faith, paying attention to seducing spirits and doctrines of demons, through the hypocrisy of men who speak lies, branded in their own conscience as with a hot iron, forbidding marriage and commanding to abstain from foods which God created to be received with thanksgiving by those who believe and know the truth. For every creature of God is good, and nothing is to be rejected, if it is received with thanksgiving. For it is sanctified through the word of God and prayer.

If you instruct the brothers of these things, you will be a good servant of Christ Jesus, nourished in the words of the faith, and of the good doctrine which you have followed. But refuse profane and old wives' fables.

Exercise yourself toward godliness. For bodily exercise has some value, but godliness has value in all things, having the promise of the life which is now, and of that which is to come. This saying is faithful and worthy of all acceptance. For to this end we both labor and suffer reproach, because we have set our trust in the living God, who is the Savior of all men, especially of those who believe. Command and teach these things.

Let no man despise your youth; but be an example to those who believe, in word, in your way of life, in love, in spirit, in faith, and in purity. Until I come, pay attention to reading, to exhortation, and to teaching. Don't neglect the gift that is in you, which was given to you by prophecy, with the laying on of the hands of the elders. Be diligent in these things. Give yourself wholly to them, that your progress may be revealed to all. Pay attention to yourself and to your teaching. Continue in these things, for in doing this you will save both yourself and those who hear you.

Don't rebuke an older man, but exhort him as a father; the younger men as brothers; the elder women as mothers; the younger as sisters, in all purity. Honor widows who are widows indeed. But if any widow has children or grandchildren, let them learn first to show piety toward their own family and to repay their parents, for this is[1] acceptable in the sight of God.

Now she who is a widow indeed and desolate, has her hope set on God, and continues in petitions and prayers night and day. But she who gives herself to pleasure is dead while she lives. Also command these things, that they may be without reproach. But if anyone doesn't provide for his own, and especially his own household, he has denied the faith, and is worse than an unbeliever. Let no one be enrolled as a widow under sixty years old, having been the wife of one man, being approved by good works, if she has brought up children, if she has been hospitable to strangers, if she has washed the saints' feet, if she has relieved the afflicted, and if she has diligently followed every good work.

But refuse younger widows, for when they have grown wanton against Christ, they desire to marry, having condemnation, because they have rejected their first pledge. Besides, they also learn to be idle, going about from house to house. Not only idle, but also gossips and busybodies, saying things which they ought not. I desire therefore that the younger widows marry, bear children, rule the household, and give no occasion to the adversary for insulting. For already some have turned away after Satan. If any man or woman who believes has widows, let them relieve them, and don't let the assembly be burdened, that it might relieve those who are widows indeed.

Let the elders who rule well be counted worthy of double honor, especially those who labor in the word and in teaching. For the Scripture says, "You shall not muzzle the ox when it treads out the grain." Deuteronomy 25:4 And, "The laborer is worthy of his wages." Luke 10:7; Leviticus 19:13 Don't receive an accusation against an elder, except at the word of two or three witnesses. Those who sin, reprove in the sight of all, that the rest also may be in fear.

I command you in the sight of God, and the Lord Jesus Christ, and the chosen angels, that you observe these things without prejudice, doing nothing by partiality. Lay hands hastily on no one. Don't be a participant in other people's sins. Keep yourself pure. Be no longer a drinker of water only, but use a little wine for your stomach's sake and your frequent infirmities. Some men's sins are evident, preceding them to judgment, and some also follow later. In the same way also there are good works that are obvious, and those that are otherwise can't be hidden.

Let as many as are bondservants under the yoke count their own masters worthy of all honor, that the name of God and the doctrine not be blasphemed. Those who have believing masters, let them not despise them because they are brothers, but rather let them serve them, because those who partake of the benefit are believing and beloved. Teach and exhort these things.

If anyone teaches a different doctrine, and doesn't consent to sound words, the words of our Lord Jesus Christ, and to the doctrine which is according to godliness, he is conceited, knowing nothing, but obsessed with arguments, disputes, and word battles, from which come envy, strife, insulting, evil suspicions, constant friction of people of corrupt minds and destitute of the truth, who suppose that godliness is a means of gain. Withdraw yourself from such.[¹]

But godliness with contentment is great gain. For we brought nothing into the world, and we certainly can't carry anything out. But having food and clothing, we will be content with that. But those who are determined to be rich fall into a temptation, a snare, and many foolish and harmful lusts, such as drown men in ruin and destruction. For the love of money is a root of all kinds of evil. Some have been led astray from the faith in their greed, and have pierced themselves through with many sorrows.

But you, man of God, flee these things, and follow after righteousness, godliness, faith, love, perseverance, and gentleness. Fight the good fight of faith. Take hold of the eternal life to which you were called, and you confessed the good confession in the sight of many witnesses.

I command you before God, who gives life to all things, and before Christ Jesus, who before Pontius Pilate testified the good confession, that you keep the commandment without spot, blameless, until the appearing of our Lord Jesus Christ, which in its own times he will show, who is the blessed and only Ruler, the King of kings, and Lord of lords. He alone has immortality, dwelling in unapproachable light, whom no man has seen, nor can see: to whom be honor and eternal power. Amen.

Charge those who are rich in this present world that they not be arrogant, nor have their hope set on the uncertainty of riches, but on the living God, who richly provides us with everything to enjoy; that they do good, that they be rich in good works, that they be ready to distribute, willing to share; laying up in store for themselves a good foundation against the time to come, that they may lay hold of eternal life.

Timothy, guard that which is committed to you, turning away from the empty chatter and oppositions of what is falsely called knowledge, which some profess, and thus have wandered from the faith. Grace be with you. Amen.

a. 1:1 NU reads "Christ Jesus" and omits the Lord.

b. 2:9 The word "just" is inserted here in English to preserve the meaning of the whole original Greek sentence in context. The word for "not" is the negative particle "μη" which denies an expected idea, as opposed to the usual word for "not" (ου) which denies a fact. Thus "μη" in this context is denying an expected idea (that women can be properly dressed without good works).

c. 3:1 or, superintendent, or bishop.

d. 3:8 or, Deacons.

e. 3:10 or, serve as deacons.

f. 3:12 or, deacons.

g. 3:13 or, served well as deacons.

h. 3:16 NU replaces "God" with "who."

i. 5:4 TR adds "good and."

j. 6:5 NU omits "Withdraw yourself from such."

* * *

During this time, Matthias—the apostle who replaced Judas Iscariot—has been preaching Christ in Syria and Cappadocia. He is stoned; however, when the stoning fails to kill him, he is beheaded.[50] Sometime after Timothy receives Paul's letter, he finds himself in trouble with the authorities. As a result, he is imprisoned.[51]

50. According to tradition, this allegedly occurred in A.D. 63. Richard Orzeck, *The Twelve Apostles of Jesus*, 172-179. Others date it at A.D. 62 in Jerusalem. Thomas Schmidt, *The Apostles After Acts*, 196.

51. Inferred from Hebrews 13:23. Some believe Timothy was imprisoned in Rome. Craig Keener, *The IVP Bible Background Commentary: New Testament*, 637, 666. Others think he was imprisoned in Ephesus. F.F. Bruce, *The Epistle to the Hebrews*, 390-391, n. 128. Another possibility is that he was arrested in Troas. Ben

In the eyes of imperial Rome, Christianity is still not distinguished from Judaism as an independent religion or separate movement. But this will soon change.[52] The Christians in Rome are experiencing growing oppression. Though they have not yet shed their blood for the faith, the oppression against them is increasing. As a result, some of the Jewish believers begin re-attending the synagogue to circumvent the persecution.[53] A number of them are giving up on the faith entirely, returning to observing the Law because "the secure confines of Judaism" are much safer.[54] Timothy is released from imprisonment.[55]

HEBREWS IS WRITTEN

Year: A.D. 63[56]

Witherington III, *Letters and Homilies for Hellenized Christians: A Socio-Rhetorical Commentary on Hebrews, James and Jude* (Downers Grove, IL: InterVarsity Press, 2007), 3:368-369. It's impossible to be certain.

52. Ben Witherington III, *Invitation to the New Testament*, 272. For a comprehensive treatment of Judaism's shifting political, religious, and geographical boundaries under Roman rule from Pompey to Diocletian, along with the shift from Roman pagan rule to Christian Roman rule and how it influenced Judaism's position, see E. Mary Smallwood, *The Jews under Roman Rule: From Pompey to Diocletian: A Study in Political Relations* (Atlanta, GA: SBL Press, reprint edition 2014).

53. More than a decade earlier, the Jewish Christians in Rome had suffered public abuse and the confiscation of property. This occurred when Claudius expelled them from the city in A.D. 49 (Hebrews 10:32-34). See Ben Witherington III, *Invitation to the New Testament*, 336. But at this time, the Jewish faith was tolerated by many Romans.

54. Raymond Brown, *The Message of Hebrews: Christ Above All* (Downers Grove, IL: InterVarsity Press, 1982), 13-14, 258. One of the key thrusts of the epistle to the Hebrews is endurance. Judaism was protected under Roman law, while Christianity was rapidly being viewed as a separate sect from the Jewish faith.

55. Hebrews 13:23.

56. Bruce thinks the letter was written to Jewish believers in Rome around A.D. 63 before the believers were being killed during the Neronian persecution. This is partly based on Hebrews 12:7. F.F. Bruce, *Paul: Apostle of the Heart Set Free*, 385; *The Epistle to the Hebrews*, 13, 20-22. Blomberg agrees. Craig Blomberg, et al., *From Pentecost to Patmos*, 605. See also *The Chronological Study Bible*, 1380 and *The NKJV Study Bible*, 1856 for support. Witherington, however, believes it was written later in A.D. 67-68 and Hebrews 13:7 is referring to some of the leaders who were being martyred. Ben Witherington III, *Invitation to the New Testament*, 337-338; *Letters and Homilies for Hellenized Christians*, 3:28-30. Keener also believes the letter may have been written in A.D. 68. Craig Keener, *The IVP Bible Background Commentary: New Testament*, 637.

From: In or around Italy[57]

To: The Hellenistic Jewish believers in Rome[58]

Author: Unknown (perhaps Apollos)[59]

Contextual Summary: The believers in Rome are in social distress. They are tempted to abandon their allegiance to Jesus as well as forsake the gatherings of the assembly.[60] For this reason, the writer encourages the Jewish believers in their persecution and warns that they cannot have one foot in the Jewish camp and one foot in Christ's camp.

Some of the leading believers in the assembly have had their property confiscated and their homes plundered. Others have been cast into prison.[61] The author

57. Ben Witherington III, *Invitation to the New Testament*, 332; F.F. Bruce, *The Epistle to the Hebrews*, 13, 391. Bernier makes a case that it was written outside Italy in the company of Italian Christians. Bruce agrees saying, "our author is writing outside Italy to a community in Italy." F.F. Bruce, *The Epistle to the Hebrews*, 391.

58. Ben Witherington III, *Letters and Homilies for Hellenized Christians*, 3:19; Raymond Brown, *The Message of Hebrews*, 17. David deSilva argues that Gentiles were included in the intended audience in *Perseverance in Gratitude: A Socio-rhetorical Commentary on the Epistle "to the Hebrews"* (Grand Rapids, MI: Eerdmans, 2000), 2-7. The consensus among scholars today is that Rome was the letter's destination. Alan Mitchell, *Hebrews*, Sacra Pagina (Collegeville, MN: Liturgical Press, 2007), 7. See also F.F. Bruce's discussion in *The Epistle to the Hebrews*, 10-14. For a superb analysis of Hebrews, including date, authorship, audience, structure, occasion, etc., see Sigurd Grindheim, *The Letter to the Hebrews*, PNTC (Grand Rapids, MI: Eerdmans, 2023), 1-71.

59. Possibilities offered by scholars have been Apollos, Barnabas, Silas, Philip, and Priscilla. Amy Peeler, *Hebrews* (Grand Rapids, MI: Eerdmans, 2024), 16-20; Craig Blomberg, et al., *From Pentecost to Patmos*, 602-603; Alan Mitchell, *Hebrews*, 2-6; F.F. Bruce, *The Epistle to the Hebrews*, 18-19. A reasonable case can be made that Apollos penned the letter. Ben Witherington III, *The New Testament Story*, 68; Raymond Brown, *The Message of Hebrews*, 15-16. An early tradition says Barnabas authored the epistle. Craig Keener, *Acts*, 3:2310. The idea that Paul wrote Hebrews was only championed in the West by Jerome and Augustine before it formed deep roots. David deSilva, *An Introduction to the New Testament*, 695; Alan Mitchell, *Hebrews*, 2-3. The earliest advocate of Pauline authorship was Pantaenus of Alexandria (in the East) in the second century. Like Witherington, I favor Apollos as the most likely option. For specific arguments supporting this conclusion, see Ben Witherington III, *Letters and Homilies for Hellenized Christians*, 3:21-24; Sigurd Grindheim, *The Letter to the Hebrews*, 6-17.

60. Ben Witherington III, *Letters and Homilies for Hellenized Christians*, 3:28-33.

61. Hebrews 10:34; 13:3. Ben Witherington III, *Invitation to the New Testament*, 336-337; Raymond Brown, *The Message of Hebrews*, 13. Apparently, some of the believers were still in prison at the time the epistle was written. Amy Peeler, *Hebrews*, 24.

encourages the Christians to visit their brethren who are in prison (even though it will risk their lives).[62] The letter contains five warnings against apostasy—i.e., leaving Christ and returning to the ungodly modes of belief and behavior that their neighbors find acceptable. The parenthetical warnings are found in Hebrews 2:14; 3:7–4:13; 5:11–6:20; 10:26-39; 12:15-29.[63]

A beautiful theme runs consistently through the letter, the theme of Jesus as our high priest. Christ is the supreme and only effective mediator between God and people. He is also the author of a new covenant, which is far superior to the old covenant. The new covenant is a "better" covenant that produces a "better" hope, "better" promises, and a "better" sacrifice in a "more perfect" tabernacle.[64]

The writer ends the letter with an exhortation to submit to those who care for their souls,[65] and to take note of Timothy, who was recently released from prison.[66] The author sends greetings from the Italian Christians.[67]

62. These conclusions are inferred from Hebrews 10:32-35; 13:3, 13.

63. If one reads Hebrews without these five passages, the epistle flows smoothly, indicating that the warnings are parenthetical. But parenthetical doesn't mean unimportant. They are essential to the author's argument. For a discussion of the warning texts, see Amy Peeler, *Hebrews*, 29-32.

64. For an overview of Hebrews, see David deSilva, *An Introduction to the New Testament*, chap. 20; N.T. Wright and Michael Bird, *The New Testament in Its World*, chap. 30; Clinton Arnold, ed., *Zondervan Illustrated Bible Backgrounds Commentary*, vol. 4 (Grand Rapids, MI: Zondervan, 2002), 3-85. The fact that Hebrews and 1 John do not open with an identifying sender indicates they may not have been letters, but homilies (messages). Personal correspondence with Jeffrey Weima, 1/6/24. Hebrews appears to be written as a message in the form of a "word of exhortation." David deSilva, *An Introduction to the New Testament*, 697-698; Alan Mitchell, *Hebrews*, 14-16; Ben Witherington III, *Letters and Homilies for Hellenized Christians*, 3:20-21. Given the similarities between Hebrews and Mark, it seems likely that the author knew the Gospel of Mark. Alan Mitchell, *Hebrews*, 10-11.

65. Some scholars regard Hebrews "the high point of the New Testament" in terms of writing style. Sigurd Grindheim, *The Letter to the Hebrews*, 1.

66. If Timothy visits the author, they can both visit the church together.

67. Some of the most helpful works on Hebrews are those written by T. Austin-Sparks (*The Letter to the Hebrews*); Andrew Murray (*The Holiest of All: The Exposition of the Epistle to the Hebrews*); G.H. Lang (*The Epistle to the Hebrews: A Practical Treatise for Plain and Serious Readers*); and F.F. Bruce (*The Epistle to the Hebrews*).

Hebrews

God, having in the past spoken to the fathers through the prophets at many times and in various ways, has at the end of these days spoken to us by his Son, whom he appointed heir of all things, through whom also he made the worlds. His Son is the radiance of his glory, the very image of his substance, and upholding all things by the word of his power, who, when he had by himself purified us of our sins, sat down on the right hand of the Majesty on high, having become as much better than the angels as the more excellent name he has inherited is better than theirs.

For to which of the angels did he say at any time, "You are my Son. Today I have become your father?" Psalm 2:7 and again, "I will be to him a Father, and he will be to me a Son?" 2 Samuel 7:14; 1 Chronicles 17:13 When he again brings in the firstborn into the world he says, "Let all the angels of God worship him." Deuteronomy 32:43 Of the angels he says, "He makes his angels winds, and his servants a flame of fire." Psalm 104:4 But of the Son he says, "Your throne, O God, is forever and ever. The scepter of uprightness is the scepter of your Kingdom. You have loved righteousness and hated iniquity; therefore God, your God, has anointed you with the oil of gladness above your fellows." Psalm 45:6-7

And, "You, Lord, in the beginning, laid the foundation of the earth. The heavens are the works of your hands. They will perish, but you continue. They all will grow old like a garment does. You will roll them up like a mantle, and they will be changed; but you are the same. Your years won't fail." Psalm 102:25-27 But which of the angels has he told at any time, "Sit at my right hand, until I make your enemies the footstool of your feet?" Psalm 110:1 Aren't they all serving spirits, sent out to do service for the sake of those who will inherit salvation?

Therefore we ought to pay greater attention to the things that were heard, lest perhaps we drift away. For if the word spoken through angels proved steadfast, and every transgression and disobedience received a just penalty, how will we escape if we neglect so great a salvation—which at the first having been spoken through the Lord, was confirmed to us by those who heard, God also testifying with them, both by signs and wonders, by various works of power and by gifts of the Holy Spirit, according to his own will?

For he didn't subject the world to come, of which we speak, to angels. But one has somewhere testified, saying, "What is man, that you think of him? Or the son of man, that you care for him? You made him a little lower than the angels. You crowned him with glory and honor. [ᵃ] You have put all things in subjection under his feet." Psalm 8:4-6 For in that he subjected all things to him, he left nothing that is not subject to him. But now we don't see all things subjected to him, yet. But we see him who has been made a little lower than the angels, Jesus, because of the suffering of death crowned with glory and honor, that by the grace of God he should taste of death for everyone.

For it became him, for whom are all things, and through whom are all things, in bringing many children to glory, to make the author of their salvation perfect through sufferings. For both he who sanctifies and those who are sanctified are all from one, for which cause he is not ashamed to call them brothers,[ᵇ] saying, "I will declare your name to my brothers. Among the congregation I will sing your praise." Psalm 22:22 Again, "I will put my trust in him." Again, "Behold, here I am with the children whom God has given me." Isaiah 8:18

Since then the children have shared in flesh and blood, he also himself in the same way partook of the same, that through death he might bring to nothing him who had the power of death, that is, the devil, and might deliver all of them who through fear of death were all their lifetime subject to bondage. For most certainly, he doesn't give help to angels, but he gives help to the offspring[ᶜ] of Abraham. Therefore he was obligated in all things to be made like his brothers, that he might become a merciful and faithful high priest in things pertaining to God, to make atonement for the sins of the people. For in that he himself has suffered being tempted, he is able to help those who are tempted.

Therefore, holy brothers, partakers of a heavenly calling, consider the Apostle and High Priest of our confession: Jesus, who was faithful to him who appointed him, as also Moses was in all his house. For he has been counted worthy of more glory than Moses, because he who built the house has more honor than the house. For every house is built by someone; but he who built all things is God. Moses indeed was faithful in all his house as a servant, for a testimony of those things which were afterward to be spoken, but Christ is faithful as a Son over his house. We are his house, if we hold fast our confidence and the glorying of our hope firm to the end.

Therefore, even as the Holy Spirit says, "Today if you will hear his voice, don't harden your hearts, as in the rebellion, in the day of the trial in the wilderness, where your fathers tested me and tried me, and saw my deeds for forty years. Therefore I was displeased with that generation, and said, 'They always err in their heart, but they didn't know my ways.' As I swore in my wrath, 'They will not enter into my rest.'" <u>Psalm 95:7-11</u>

Beware, brothers, lest perhaps there might be in any one of you an evil heart of unbelief, in falling away from the living God; but exhort one another day by day, so long as it is called "today," lest any one of you be hardened by the deceitfulness of sin. For we have become partakers of Christ, if we hold the beginning of our confidence firm to the end, while it is said, "Today if you will hear his voice, don't harden your hearts, as in the rebellion." <u>Psalm 95:7-8</u>

For who, when they heard, rebelled? Wasn't it all those who came out of Egypt led by Moses? With whom was he displeased forty years? Wasn't it with those who sinned, whose bodies fell in the wilderness? To whom did he swear that they wouldn't enter into his rest, but to those who were disobedient? We see that they weren't able to enter in because of unbelief.

Let's fear therefore, lest perhaps anyone of you should seem to have come short of a promise of entering into his rest. For indeed we have had good news preached to us, even as they also did, but the word they heard didn't profit them, because it wasn't mixed with faith by those who heard. For we who have believed do enter into that rest, even as he has said, "As I swore in my wrath, they will not enter into my rest;" <u>Psalm 95:11</u> although the works were finished from the foundation of the world. For he has said this somewhere about the seventh day, "God rested on the seventh day from all his works;" <u>Genesis 2:2</u> and in this place again, "They will not enter into my rest." <u>Psalm 95:11</u>

Seeing therefore it remains that some should enter into it, and they to whom the good news was preached before failed to enter in because of disobedience, he again defines a certain day, today, saying through David so long a time afterward (just as has been said), "Today if you will hear his voice, don't harden your hearts." <u>Psalm 95:7-8</u> For if Joshua had given them rest, he would not have spoken afterward of another day. There remains therefore a Sabbath rest for the people of God. For he who has entered into his rest has himself also rested from his works, as God did from his. Let's therefore give diligence to enter into that rest, lest anyone fall after the same example of disobedience.

For the word of God is living and active, and sharper than any two-edged sword, piercing even to the dividing of soul and spirit, of both joints and marrow, and is able to discern the thoughts and intentions of the heart. There is no creature that is hidden from his sight, but all things are naked and laid open before the eyes of him to whom we must give an account.

Having then a great high priest who has passed through the heavens, Jesus, the Son of God, let's hold tightly to our confession. For we don't have a high priest who can't be touched with the feeling of our infirmities, but one who has been in all points tempted like we are, yet without sin. Let's therefore draw near with boldness to the throne of grace, that we may receive mercy and may find grace for help in time of need.

For every high priest, being taken from among men, is appointed for men in things pertaining to God, that he may offer both gifts and sacrifices for sins. The high priest can deal gently with those who are ignorant and going astray, because he himself is also surrounded with weakness. Because of this, he must offer sacrifices for sins for the people, as well as for himself. Nobody takes this honor on himself, but he is called by God, just like Aaron was. So also Christ didn't glorify himself to be made a high priest, but it was he who said to him, "You are my Son. Today I have become your father." Psalm 2:7 As he says also in another place, "You are a priest forever, after the order of Melchizedek." Psalm 110:4

He, in the days of his flesh, having offered up prayers and petitions with strong crying and tears to him who was able to save him from death, and having been heard for his godly fear, though he was a Son, yet learned obedience by the things which he suffered. Having been made perfect, he became to all of those who obey him the author of eternal salvation, named by God a high priest after the order of Melchizedek.

About him we have many words to say, and hard to interpret, seeing you have become dull of hearing. For although by this time you should be teachers, you again need to have someone teach you the rudiments of the first principles of the revelations of God. You have come to need milk, and not solid food. For everyone who lives on milk is not experienced in the word of righteousness, for he is a baby. But solid food is for those who are full grown, who by reason of use have their senses exercised to discern good and evil.

Therefore leaving the teaching of the first principles of Christ, let's press on to perfection—not laying again a foundation of repentance from dead works, of faith toward God, of the teaching of baptisms, of laying on of hands, of resurrection of the dead, and of eternal judgment. This will we do, if God permits. For concerning those who were once enlightened and tasted of the heavenly gift, and were made partakers of the Holy Spirit, and tasted the good word of God and the powers of the age to come, and then fell away, it is impossible to renew them again to repentance; seeing they crucify the Son of God for themselves again, and put him to open shame.

For the land which has drunk the rain that comes often on it and produces a crop suitable for them for whose sake it is also tilled, receives blessing from God; but if it bears thorns and thistles, it is rejected and near being cursed, whose end is to be burned. But, beloved, we are persuaded of better things for you, and things that accompany salvation, even though we speak like this. For God is not unrighteous, so as to forget your work and the labor of love which you showed toward his name, in that you served the saints, and still do serve them.

We desire that each one of you may show the same diligence to the fullness of hope even to the end, that you won't be sluggish, but imitators of those who through faith and perseverance inherited the promises. For when God made a promise to Abraham, since he could swear by no one greater, he swore by himself, saying, "Surely blessing I will bless you, and multiplying I will multiply you." <u>Genesis 22:17</u> Thus, having patiently endured, he obtained the promise.

For men indeed swear by a greater one, and in every dispute of theirs the oath is final for confirmation. In this way God, being determined to show more abundantly to the heirs of the promise the immutability of his counsel, interposed with an oath, that by two immutable things, in which it is impossible for God to lie, we may have a strong encouragement, who have fled for refuge to take hold of the hope set before us. This hope we have as an anchor of the soul, a hope both sure and steadfast and entering into that which is within the veil; where as a forerunner Jesus entered for us, having become a high priest forever after the order of Melchizedek.

For this Melchizedek, king of Salem, priest of God Most High, who met Abraham returning from the slaughter of the kings and blessed him, to whom also Abraham divided a tenth part of all (being first, by interpretation, "king of righteousness," and then also "king of Salem," which means "king of peace," without father, without mother, without genealogy, having neither beginning of days nor end of life, but made like the Son of God), remains a priest continually.

Now consider how great this man was, to whom even Abraham, the patriarch, gave a tenth out of the best plunder. They indeed of the sons of Levi who receive the priest's office have a commandment to take tithes of the people according to the law, that is, of their brothers, though these have come out of the body of Abraham, but he whose genealogy is not counted from them has accepted tithes from Abraham, and has blessed him who has the promises.

But without any dispute the lesser is blessed by the greater. Here people who die receive tithes, but there one receives tithes of whom it is testified that he lives. We can say that through Abraham even Levi, who receives tithes, has paid tithes, for he was yet in the body of his father when Melchizedek met him.

Now if perfection was through the Levitical priesthood (for under it the people have received the law), what further need was there for another priest to arise after the order of Melchizedek, and not be called after the order of Aaron? For the priesthood being changed, there is of necessity a change made also in the law.

For he of whom these things are said belongs to another tribe, from which no one has officiated at the altar. For it is evident that our Lord has sprung out of Judah, about which tribe Moses spoke nothing concerning priesthood. This is yet more abundantly evident, if after the likeness of Melchizedek there arises another priest, who has been made, not after the law of a fleshly commandment, but after the power of an endless life; for it is testified, "You are a priest forever, according to the order of Melchizedek." Psalm 110:4

For there is an annulling of a foregoing commandment because of its weakness and use-lessness (for the law made nothing perfect), and a bringing in of a better hope, through which we draw near to God. Inasmuch as he was not made priest without the taking of an oath (for they indeed have been made priests without an oath), but he with an oath by him that says of him, "The Lord swore and will not change his mind, 'You are a priest forever, according to the order of Melchizedek.'" Psalm 110:4

By so much, Jesus has become the collateral of a better covenant. Many, indeed, have been made priests, because they are hindered from continuing by death. But he, because he lives forever, has his priesthood unchangeable. Therefore he is also able to save to the uttermost those who draw near to God through him, seeing that he lives forever to make intercession for them.

For such a high priest was fitting for us: holy, guiltless, undefiled, separated from sin-ners, and made higher than the heavens; who doesn't need, like those high priests, to offer up sacrifices daily, first for his own sins, and then for the sins of the people. For he did this once for all, when he offered up himself. For the law appoints men as high priests who have weakness, but the word of the oath which came after the law appoints a Son forever who has been perfected.

Now in the things which we are saying, the main point is this. We have such a high priest, who sat down on the right hand of the throne of the Majesty in the heavens, a servant of the sanctuary and of the true tabernacle, which the Lord pitched, not man. For every high priest is appointed to offer both gifts and sacrifices. Therefore it is necessary that this high priest also have something to offer.

For if he were on earth, he would not be a priest at all, seeing there are priests who offer the gifts according to the law, who serve a copy and shadow of the heavenly things, even as Moses was warned by God when he was about to make the tabernacle, for he said, "See, you shall make everything according to the pattern that was shown to you on the mountain." Exodus 25:40 But now he has obtained a more excellent ministry, by so much as he is also the mediator of a better covenant, which on better promises has been given as law.

For if that first covenant had been faultless, then no place would have been sought for a second. For finding fault with them, he said, "Behold,[d] the days come," says the Lord, "that I will make a new covenant with the house of Israel and with the house of Judah; not according to the covenant that I made with their fathers, in the day that I took them by the hand to lead them out of the land of Egypt; for they didn't continue in my covenant, and I disregarded them," says the Lord. "For this is the covenant that I will make with the house of Israel. After those days," says the Lord; "I will put my laws into their mind, I will also write them on their heart. I will be their God, and they will be my people. They will not teach every man his fellow citizen,[e] and every man his brother, saying, 'Know the Lord,' for all will know me, from their least to their greatest. For I will be merciful to their unrighteousness. I will remember their sins and lawless deeds no more." Jeremiah 31:31-34 In that he says, "A new covenant," he has made the first old. But that which is becoming old and grows aged is near to vanishing away.

Now indeed even the first[f] covenant had ordinances of divine service and an earthly sanctuary. For a tabernacle was prepared. In the first part were the lamp stand, the table, and the show bread; which is called the Holy Place. After the second veil was the tabernacle which is called the Holy of Holies, having a golden altar of incense, and the ark of the covenant overlaid on all sides with gold, in which was a golden pot holding the manna, Aaron's rod that budded, and the tablets of the covenant; and above it cherubim of glory overshadowing the mercy seat, of which things we can't speak now in detail.

Now these things having been thus prepared, the priests go in continually into the first tabernacle, accomplishing the services, but into the second the high priest alone, once in the year, not without blood, which he offers for himself, and for the errors of the people. The Holy Spirit is indicating this, that the way into the Holy Place wasn't yet revealed while the first tabernacle was still standing. This is a symbol of the present age, where gifts and sacrifices are offered that are incapable, concerning the conscience, of making the worshiper perfect, being only (with meats and drinks and various washings) fleshly ordinances, imposed until a time of reformation.

But Christ having come as a high priest of the coming good things, through the greater and more perfect tabernacle, not made with hands, that is to say, not of this creation, nor yet through the blood of goats and calves, but through his own blood, entered in once for all into the Holy Place, having obtained eternal redemption. For if the blood of goats and bulls, and the ashes of a heifer sprinkling those who have been defiled, sanctify to the cleanness of the flesh, how much more will the blood of Christ, who through the eternal Spirit offered himself without defect to God, cleanse your conscience from dead works to serve the living God?

For this reason he is the mediator of a new covenant, since a death has occurred for the redemption of the transgressions that were under the first covenant, that those who have been called may receive the promise of the eternal inheritance. For where a last will and testament is, there must of necessity be the death of him who made it. For a will is in force where there has been death, for it is never in force while he who made it lives. Therefore even the first covenant has not been dedicated without blood. For when every commandment had been spoken by Moses to all the people according to the law, he took the blood of the calves and the goats, with water and scarlet wool and hyssop, and sprinkled both the book itself and all the people, saying, "This is the blood of the covenant which God has commanded you." Exodus 24:8

Moreover he sprinkled the tabernacle and all the vessels of the ministry in the same way with the blood. According to the law, nearly everything is cleansed with blood, and apart from shedding of blood there is no remission. It was necessary therefore that the copies of the things in the heavens should be cleansed with these, but the heavenly things themselves with better sacrifices than these.

For Christ hasn't entered into holy places made with hands, which are representations of the true, but into heaven itself, now to appear in the presence of God for us; nor yet that he should offer himself often, as the high priest enters into the holy place year by year with blood not his own, or else he must have suffered often since the foundation of the world.

But now once at the end of the ages, he has been revealed to put away sin by the sacrifice of himself. Inasmuch as it is appointed for men to die once, and after this, judgment, so Christ also, having been offered once to bear the sins of many, will appear a second time, without sin, to those who are eagerly waiting for him for salvation.

For the law, having a shadow of the good to come, not the very image of the things, can never with the same sacrifices year by year, which they offer continually, make perfect those who draw near. Or else wouldn't they have ceased to be offered, because the worshipers, having been once cleansed, would have had no more consciousness of sins? But in those sacrifices there is a yearly reminder of sins. For it is impossible that the blood of bulls and goats should take away sins.

Therefore when he comes into the world, he says, "You didn't desire sacrifice and offering, but you prepared a body for me. You had no pleasure in whole burnt offerings and sacrifices for sin. Then I said, 'Behold, I have come (in the scroll of the book it is written of me) to do your will, O God.'" Psalm 40:6-8 Previously saying, "Sacrifices and offerings and whole burnt offerings and sacrifices for sin you didn't desire, neither had pleasure in them" (those which are offered according to the law), then he has said, "Behold, I have come to do your will." He takes away the first, that he may establish the second, by which will we have been sanctified through the offering of the body of Jesus Christ once for all.

Every priest indeed stands day by day serving and offering often the same sacrifices which can never take away sins, but he, when he had offered one sacrifice for sins forever, sat down on the right hand of God, from that time waiting until his enemies are made the footstool of his feet. For by one offering he has perfected forever those who are being sanctified. The Holy Spirit also testifies to us, for after saying, "This is the covenant that I will make with them: 'After those days,' says the Lord, 'I will put my laws on their heart, I will also write them on their mind;'" Jeremiah 31:33 then he says, "I will remember their sins and their iniquities no more." Jeremiah 31:34

Now where remission of these is, there is no more offering for sin. Having therefore, brothers, boldness to enter into the holy place by the blood of Jesus, by the way which he dedicated for us, a new and living way, through the veil, that is to say, his flesh, and having a great priest over God's house, let's draw near with a true heart in fullness of faith, having our hearts sprinkled from an evil conscience, and having our body washed with pure water, let's hold fast the confession of our hope without wavering; for he who promised is faithful.

Let's consider how to provoke one another to love and good works, not forsaking our own assembling together, as the custom of some is, but exhorting one another, and so much the more as you see the Day approaching. For if we sin willfully after we have received the knowledge of the truth, there remains no more a sacrifice for sins, but a certain fearful expectation of judgment, and a fierceness of fire which will devour the adversaries. A man who disregards Moses' law dies without compassion on the word of two or three witnesses.

How much worse punishment do you think he will be judged worthy of who has trodden under foot the Son of God, and has counted the blood of the covenant with which he was sanctified an unholy thing, and has insulted the Spirit of grace? For we know him who said, "Vengeance belongs to me. I will repay," says the Lord. Deuteronomy 32:35 Again, "The Lord will judge his people." Deuteronomy 32:36; Psalm 135:14 It is a fearful thing to fall into the hands of the living God.

But remember the former days, in which, after you were enlightened, you endured a great struggle with sufferings; partly, being exposed to both reproaches and oppressions; and partly, becoming partakers with those who were treated so. For you both had compassion on me in my chains, and joyfully accepted the plundering of your possessions, knowing that you have for yourselves a better possession and an enduring one in the heavens.

Therefore don't throw away your boldness, which has a great reward. For you need endurance so that, having done the will of God, you may receive the promise. "In a very little while, he who comes will come, and will not wait. But the righteous will live by faith. If he shrinks back, my soul has no pleasure in him." Habakkuk 2:3-4 But we are not of those who shrink back to destruction, but of those who have faith to the saving of the soul.

Now faith is assurance of things hoped for, proof of things not seen. For by this, the elders obtained testimony. By faith, we understand that the universe has been framed by the word of God, so that what is seen has not been made out of things which are visible. By faith, Abel offered to God a more excellent sacrifice than Cain, through which he had testimony given to him that he was righteous, God testifying with respect to his gifts; and through it he, being dead, still speaks.

By faith, Enoch was taken away, so that he wouldn't see death, and he was not found, because God translated him. For he has had testimony given to him that before his translation he had been well pleasing to God. Without faith it is impossible to be well pleasing to him, for he who comes to God must believe that he exists, and that he is a rewarder of those who seek him.

By faith, Noah, being warned about things not yet seen, moved with godly fear,[g] prepared a ship for the saving of his house, through which he condemned the world, and became heir of the righteousness which is according to faith.

By faith, Abraham, when he was called, obeyed to go out to the place which he was to receive for an inheritance. He went out, not knowing where he went. By faith, he lived as an alien in the land of promise, as in a land not his own, dwelling in tents with Isaac and Jacob, the heirs with him of the same promise. For he looked for the city which has the foundations, whose builder and maker is God.

By faith, even Sarah herself received power to conceive, and she bore a child when she was past age, since she counted him faithful who had promised. Therefore as many as the stars of the sky in multitude, and as innumerable as the sand which is by the sea shore, were fathered by one man, and him as good as dead.

These all died in faith, not having received the promises, but having seen[h] them and embraced them from afar, and having confessed that they were strangers and pilgrims on the earth. For those who say such things make it clear that they are seeking a country of their own. If indeed they had been thinking of that country from which they went out, they would have had enough time to return. But now they desire a better country, that is, a heavenly one. Therefore God is not ashamed of them, to be called their God, for he has prepared a city for them.

By faith, Abraham, being tested, offered up Isaac. Yes, he who had gladly received the promises was offering up his one and only son, to whom it was said, "Your offspring will be accounted as from Isaac," Genesis 21:12 concluding that God is able to raise up even from the dead. Figuratively speaking, he also did receive him back from the dead. By faith, Isaac blessed Jacob and Esau, even concerning things to come. By faith, Jacob, when he was dying, blessed each of the sons of Joseph, and worshiped, leaning on the top of his staff. By faith, Joseph, when his end was near, made mention of the departure of the children of Israel, and gave instructions concerning his bones.

By faith, Moses, when he was born, was hidden for three months by his parents, because they saw that he was a beautiful child, and they were not afraid of the king's commandment. By faith, Moses, when he had grown up, refused to be called the son of Pharaoh's daughter, choosing rather to share ill treatment with God's people than to enjoy the pleasures of sin for a time, considering the reproach of Christ greater riches than the treasures of Egypt; for he looked to the reward. By faith, he left Egypt, not fearing the wrath of the king; for he endured, as seeing him who is invisible. By faith, he kept the Passover, and the sprinkling of the blood, that the destroyer of the firstborn should not touch them.

By faith, they passed through the Red Sea as on dry land. When the Egyptians tried to do so, they were swallowed up. By faith, the walls of Jericho fell down, after they had been encircled for seven days. By faith, Rahab the prostitute didn't perish with those who were disobedient, having received the spies in peace.

What more shall I say? For the time would fail me if I told of Gideon, Barak, Samson, Jephthah, David, Samuel, and the prophets, who through faith subdued kingdoms, worked out righteousness, obtained promises, stopped the mouths of lions, Daniel 6:22-23 quenched the power of fire, Daniel 3:1-30 escaped the edge of the sword, 1 Kings 19:1-3; 2 Kings 6:31–7:20 from weakness were made strong, grew mighty in war, and caused foreign armies to flee.

Women received their dead by resurrection. 1 Kings 17:17-23; 2 Kings 4:32-37 Others were tortured, not accepting their deliverance, that they might obtain a better resurrection. Others were tried by mocking and scourging, yes, moreover by bonds and imprisonment. They were stoned. 2 Chronicles 24:20-21 They were sawn apart. They were tempted. They were slain with the sword. Jeremiah 26:20-23; 1 Kings 19:10 They went around in sheep skins and in goat skins; being destitute, afflicted, ill-treated—of whom the world was not worthy—wandering in deserts, mountains, caves, and the holes of the earth.

These all, having had testimony given to them through their faith, didn't receive the promise, God having provided some better thing concerning us, so that apart from us they should not be made perfect. Therefore let's also, seeing we are surrounded by so great a cloud of witnesses, lay aside every weight and the sin which so easily entangles us, and let's run with perseverance the race that is set before us, looking to Jesus, the author and perfecter of faith, who for the joy that was set before him endured the cross, despising its shame, and has sat down at the right hand of the throne of God.

For consider him who has endured such contradiction of sinners against himself, that you don't grow weary, fainting in your souls. You have not yet resisted to blood, striving against sin. You have forgotten the exhortation which reasons with you as with children, "My son, don't take lightly the chastening of the Lord, nor faint when you are reproved by him; for whom the Lord loves, he disciplines, and chastises every son whom he receives." Proverbs 3:11-12

It is for discipline that you endure. God deals with you as with children, for what son is there whom his father doesn't discipline? But if you are without discipline, of which all have been made partakers, then you are illegitimate, and not children. Furthermore, we had the fathers of our flesh to chasten us, and we paid them respect. Shall we not much rather be in subjection to the Father of spirits, and live? For they indeed, for a few days, punished us as seemed good to them; but he for our profit, that we may be partakers of his holiness. All chastening seems for the present to be not joyous but grievous; yet afterward it yields the peaceful fruit of righteousness to those who have been trained by it. Therefore lift up the hands that hang down and the feeble knees, Isaiah 35:3 and make straight paths for your feet, Proverbs 4:26 so what is lame may not be dislocated, but rather be healed.

Follow after peace with all men, and the sanctification without which no man will see the Lord, looking carefully lest there be any man who falls short of the grace of God, lest any root of bitterness springing up trouble you, and many be defiled by it, lest there be any sexually immoral person, or profane person, like Esau, who sold his birthright for one meal. For you know that even when he afterward desired to inherit the blessing, he was rejected, for he found no place for a change of mind though he sought it diligently with tears.

For you have not come to a mountain that might be touched, and that burned with fire, and to blackness, darkness, storm, the sound of a trumpet, and the voice of words; which those who heard it begged that not one more word should be spoken to them, for they could not stand that which was commanded, "If even an animal touches the mountain, it shall be stoned."[¹] Exodus 19:12-13 So fearful was the appearance that Moses said, "I am terrified and trembling." Deuteronomy 9:19

But you have come to Mount Zion, and to the city of the living God, the heavenly Jerusalem, and to innumerable multitudes of angels, to the festal gathering and assembly of the firstborn who are enrolled in heaven, to God the Judge of all, to the spirits of just men made perfect, to Jesus, the mediator of a new covenant, Jeremiah 31:31 and to the blood of sprinkling that speaks better than that of Abel.

See that you don't refuse him who speaks. For if they didn't escape when they refused him who warned on the earth, how much more will we not escape who turn away from him who warns from heaven, whose voice shook the earth then, but now he has promised, saying, "Yet once more I will shake not only the earth, but also the heavens." Haggai 2:6

This phrase, "Yet once more" signifies the removing of those things that are shaken, as of things that have been made, that those things which are not shaken may remain. Therefore, receiving a Kingdom that can't be shaken, let's have grace, through which we serve God acceptably, with reverence and awe, for our God is a consuming fire. Deuteronomy 4:24

Let brotherly love continue. Don't forget to show hospitality to strangers, for in doing so, some have entertained angels without knowing it. Remember those who are in bonds, as bound with them, and those who are ill-treated, since you are also in the body. Let marriage be held in honor among all, and let the bed be undefiled; but God will judge the sexually immoral and adulterers.

Be free from the love of money, content with such things as you have, for he has said, "I will in no way leave you, neither will I in any way forsake you." Deuteronomy 31:6 So that with good courage we say, "The Lord is my helper. I will not fear. What can man do to me?" Psalm 118:6-7

Remember your leaders, men who spoke to you the word of God, and considering the results of their conduct, imitate their faith. Jesus Christ is the same yesterday, today, and forever. Don't be carried away by various and strange teachings, for it is good that the heart be established by grace, not by food, through which those who were so occupied were not benefited.

We have an altar from which those who serve the holy tabernacle have no right to eat. For the bodies of those animals, whose blood is brought into the holy place by the high priest as an offering for sin, are burned outside of the camp. <u>Leviticus 16:27</u> Therefore Jesus also, that he might sanctify the people through his own blood, suffered outside of the gate. Let's therefore go out to him outside of the camp, bearing his reproach.

For we don't have here an enduring city, but we seek that which is to come. Through him, then, let's offer up a sacrifice of praise to God <u>Psalm 50:23</u> continually, that is, the fruit of lips which proclaim allegiance to his name. But don't forget to be doing good and sharing, for with such sacrifices God is well pleased.

Obey your leaders and submit to them, for they watch on behalf of your souls, as those who will give account, that they may do this with joy, and not with groaning, for that would be unprofitable for you. Pray for us, for we are persuaded that we have a good conscience, desiring to live honorably in all things. I strongly urge you to do this, that I may be restored to you sooner.

Now may the God of peace, who brought again from the dead the great shepherd of the sheep with the blood of an eternal covenant, our Lord Jesus, make you complete in every good work to do his will, working in you that which is well pleasing in his sight, through Jesus Christ, to whom be the glory forever and ever. Amen.

But I exhort you, brothers, endure the word of exhortation; for I have written to you in few words. Know that our brother Timothy has been freed, with whom, if he comes shortly, I will see you. Greet all of your leaders and all the saints. The Italians greet you. Grace be with you all. Amen.

a. <u>2:7</u> TR adds "and set him over the works of your hands."

b. <u>2:11</u> The word for "brothers" here and where context allows may also be correctly translated "brothers and sisters" or "siblings."

c. <u>2:16</u> or, seed.

d. <u>8:8</u> "Behold," from "ἰδοὺ," means look at, take notice, observe, see, or gaze at. It is often used as an interjection.

e. <u>8:11</u> TR reads "neighbor" instead of "fellow citizen."

f. <u>9:1</u> TR adds "tabernacle."

g. <u>11:7</u> or, reverence.

h. <u>11:13</u> TR adds "and being convinced of."

i. <u>12:20</u> TR adds "or shot with an arrow."

A Fire Burns in Rome
July 19
A.D. 64

And now, a very dark page in church history opens. In the early hours of July 19, A.D. 64, a shop in the Circus Maximus erupts in flames.[68] For nine days, the fire rages through the city, destroying ten out of the fourteen quarters of Rome.[69] Shops, homes, and temples are demolished throughout the heart of the city. Emperor Nero is blamed,[70] so he looks for a scapegoat to deflect attention away from himself.

Since the Christians are despised throughout Rome, Nero blames them for the fire.[71] He claims they burned the city to fulfill their own prophecy of the earth's destruction by fire. The Christians were already disliked for their antisocial attitudes,[72] but this new accusation causes them to be viewed as outcasts by the citizens of Rome, and they are relentlessly harassed.

The Neronian Persecution

Nero's massacre of the Christians begins.[73] The emperor brutalizes those who trust in Christ in such unspeakable ways that the Romans themselves have pity on

68. It may have been during the night of July 18/19 in the northeast end of the Circus Maximus. Tacitus, *Annals*, 15.38ff.; F.F. Bruce, *Paul: Apostle of the Heart Set Free*, 441.

69. Jerome Murphy-O'Connor, *Paul: His Story*, 226.

70. Nero was in the process of building himself a "golden house"—a massive new palace. Therefore, many Romans believed Nero deliberately started the fire in certain city districts in order to drive out those living there so he could then appropriate the abandoned land for his new palace. Personal correspondence with Jeffrey Weima, 1/6/24.

71. By this time, Nero distinguished between the Christians and the Jews. Tacitus, *Annals*, 15.44. Before that, the Jesus movement could barely be distinguished from its Jewish beginnings. Rainer Riesner, *Paul's Early Period*, 358. Nero was the first emperor to be the declared enemy of the worship of the true God. Eusebius, *The History of the Church*, 2.25. "Nero was even more vicious than Domitian, although his persecution was more limited in geographic scope (probably restricted to Rome and its environs)." Craig Keener, *1 Peter*, 33. The fire may have begun in either A.D. 64 or A.D. 65. For further details on these events, see also Alan Bandy, *An Illustrated Guide to the Apostle Paul*, 176-177.

72. F.F. Bruce, *Paul: Apostle of the Heart Set Free*, 442.

73. F.F. Bruce, *Paul: Apostle of the Heart Set Free*, 444; *The Epistle to the Hebrews*, 21. The persecution began in A.D. 64-65. For details, see Thomas Schmidt, *The Apostles After Acts*, chap. 3; Philip Schaff, *History of the Christian Church* (Grand Rapids, MI: Eerdmans, 1910, reprint edition 1994), vol. 1, 376-390.

them.[74] His hatred and cruelty is inexplicable. He has some of the Christians sewn up in the skins of wild beasts to be preyed upon by dogs until they expire. Others he dresses up in shirts of stiff wax, fixes them to trees and crosses in his expansive garden, and lights them up as human torches.[75] Due to the violent murders, the ekklesia in Rome dwindles.[76]

Priscilla and Aquila escape the onslaught and move back to Ephesus to help Timothy care for the assembly there.[77] This remarkable couple is beloved by Paul, who regards them as his co-workers. They are also esteemed by the Gentiles churches Paul raised up.[78]

Crisis in Crete

Paul is still in Macedonia,[79] and Apollos,[80] along with a lawyer named Zenas, visits him there. Paul receives word from Titus in Crete that the ekklesias on the island remain in crisis. The influence of the false teachers grows stronger, and they are spreading the same heresy Timothy

74. Nero's plan to blame the Christians for the fire ultimately failed. "The cruelty exacted upon the Christians in Rome in the Colosseum (Christians thrown to the lions, used as human torches, covered with animal skins and thrown into the arena to be attacked by a variety of wild animals) was so great that they gained the sympathy of many Roman citizens." Personal correspondence with Jeffrey Weima, 1/6/24.

75. The Roman historian Tacitus graphically describes the bloodbath. Tacitus, *Annals*, 15.44. See also *1 Clement*, 6.1; Peter Lampe, *From Paul to Valentinus*, 82-84; Alan Bandy, *An Illustrated Guide to the Apostle Paul*, 176; John Drane, *Early Christians*, 112.

76. The persecution of the Christians spread throughout the city and lasted until A.D. 68 when Nero was banished from Rome and committed suicide. F.F. Bruce, *The Spreading Flame,* 166; D. Clint Burnett, *Paul and Imperial Divine Honors,* 234.

77. Inferred from 2 Timothy 4:19. We know Priscilla and Aquila were in Rome in A.D. 57 when Paul wrote Romans, and we also know they were alive around A.D. 67 when Paul wrote 2 Timothy to his apprentice in Ephesus. Therefore, it's a logical inference to conclude the couple escaped Nero's persecution.

78. Consider Paul's words in Romans 16:3-4 (NIV), "Greet Priscilla and Aquila, my co-workers in Christ Jesus. …Not only I but all the churches of the Gentiles are grateful to them."

79. See the note in the coming section on the letter to Titus and the sources cited affirming that Paul was likely in Macedonia when he penned the epistle. The apostle probably visited the Macedonian assemblies in Thessalonica (and possibly Berea) after he spent time with the Philippian believers. Alan Bandy, *An Illustrated Guide to the Apostle Paul*, 174.

80. This is the same Apollos we met earlier in the story, the Alexandrian Jew mentioned in Acts 18 through 19 and 1 Corinthians. Clinton Arnold, ed., *Zondervan Illustrated Bible Backgrounds Commentary*, 3:509.

combated in Ephesus. Jewish false teachers[81] are raising foolish controversies, teaching about genealogies, and creating quarrels over the Law of Moses.[82] At the same time, some pagan influencers are encouraging rebellion and immorality in the church. (The Cretans, as a culture, are noted for lying, engaging in wild parties, gluttony, and uncontrolled greed.[83])

As a result of these problems, several families in the assembly are shaken in their faith. Specifically, the old and young men are being influenced by the old Cretan lifestyle, and they are struggling with self-control. Some are rebelling against local authorities, and a number of the older women in the assemblies are engaging in slander and the abuse of wine.

Paul feels the need to write Titus to give him further instruction on how to handle the growing crisis.[84]

PAUL WRITES TITUS

Year: A.D. 65[85]

---

81. In Titus 1:10, Paul says the false teachers are of the "circumcision group" (NIV). This may *not* be the "circumcision party" described earlier in this book, but instead, a reference that they are simply Jews. (It's used this way in Acts 10:45; 11:2; Colossians 4:11, NKJV.) See John Stott, *The Message of 1 Timothy & Titus*, 180. While these teachers may not have pushed circumcision, they did hold to some "Judaizing" beliefs contrary to Paul's gospel. Philip Towner, *The Letters to Timothy and Titus*, 695. It's also possible they belonged to the same group of agitators called "the circumcision party" (the wording of the ESV). For this idea, see Gerald Hawthorne, et al., eds., *Dictionary of Paul and His Letters*, 662-663. Barclay is correct when he says the churches Paul raised up didn't adopt the significant Jewish customs and identity markers (circumcision, Sabbath-keeping, food laws, etc.). John Barclay, *Pauline Churches and Diaspora Jews*, 27. They managed to resist the pressure placed upon them by the Judaizers.

82. Titus 3:9.

83. In his letter to Titus, Paul quotes the Cretan prophet Epimenides, who said, "Cretans are always liars, evil beasts, lazy gluttons" (Titus 1:12, ESV). For details on the way of life in Crete, see Donald Guthrie, *The Pastoral Epistles*, 200; Philip Towner, *The Letters to Timothy and Titus*, 40.

84. The scenario I've described is derived from mirror-reading Paul's words in Titus and 2 Timothy 4 as well as gleaning material from Philip Towner, *The Letters to Timothy and Titus;* Clinton Arnold, ed., *Zondervan Illustrated Bible Backgrounds Commentary*, 3; Donald Guthrie, *The Pastoral Epistles;* John Stott, *The Message of 1 Timothy & Titus;* Craig Keener, *The IVP Bible Background Commentary: New Testament;* Ben Witherington III, *Letters and Homilies for Hellenized Christians*, 1.

85. Gerald Hawthorne, et al., eds., *Dictionary of Paul and His Letters*, 661. The traditional dating is A.D. 64-67. John Barry, et al., "Letter to Titus," *The Lexham Bible Dictionary*. I agree with Towner that Paul likely wrote Titus after 1 Timothy. Philip Towner, *The Letters to Timothy and Titus*, 13. Witherington believes the

From: Macedonia[86]

To: Titus in Crete[87]

Author: Paul[88]

Contextual Summary: Paul encourages his apostolic apprentice to strengthen the positive things that remain in the assemblies on the island of Crete. He gives Titus practical instructions on selecting elders (1:5ff.). He tells Titus, whom he calls his "true son" in the faith,[89] how to silence and rebuke those who are spreading heresy in Crete, as well as how to encourage the believers with the eternal truths of Christ.

Paul describes the false teachers as rebellious, empty-talkers, deceivers, lazy, gluttons, detestable, and disobedient. He exhorts his young apprentice to take a strong hand with this group and rebuke them sharply.[90]

Just as he did with Timothy, Paul exhorts Titus on how to treat the older men, the older women, the young women, and the young men.[91] The apostle closes the letter by telling Titus that he plans to send either Tychicus or Artemas to replace him in

---

letter was written in A.D. 64-65, but earlier than 1 Timothy. Ben Witherington III, *Letters and Homilies for Hellenized Christians*, 1:65-66. See also Rose Publishing, *Rose Chronological Guide to the Bible*, 167.

86. Some believe it could have been written from Nicopolis. Favoring Macedonia, see Ben Witherington III, *Letters and Homilies for Hellenized Christians*, 1:65. Favoring in (or on his way to) Nicopolis, see Gerald Hawthorne, et al., eds., *Dictionary of Paul and His Letters*, 448; Clinton Arnold, ed., *Zondervan Illustrated Bible Backgrounds Commentary*, 3:499. Towner believes Paul hadn't yet reached Nicopolis when he wrote the letter. Philip Towner, *The Letters to Timothy and Titus*, 800-801.

87. Titus was one of Paul's most faithful co-workers. Ben Witherington III, *Letters and Homilies for Hellenized Christians*, 1:88-89.

88. Witherington believes Paul penned 1 Timothy, Titus, and 2 Timothy with the help of Luke. Ben Witherington III, *Letters and Homilies for Hellenized Christians*, 1:67. See also my notes in the "Paul Writes 1 Timothy" box.

89. Titus 1:4, NIV.

90. Titus 1:10-16.

91. For an overview of Titus, see Clinton Arnold, ed., *Zondervan Illustrated Bible Backgrounds Commentary*, 3:499-511; David deSilva, *An Introduction to the New Testament*, chap. 19; N.T. Wright and Michael Bird, *The New Testament in Its World*, 23.

Crete.[92] When that takes place, he asks Titus to meet him in Nicopolis,[93] where Paul plans to spend the winter.[94]

The apostle charges Titus to "diligently help" Apollos and Zenas (the lawyer)[95] when they leave Crete so their needs are met.[96] Apollos and Zenas bring Paul's letter to Titus. The letter is not just for Titus, it's also for the believers in Crete.[97] Luke scribes the letter.[98]

Titus

Paul, a servant of God, and an apostle of Jesus Christ, according to the faith of God's chosen ones, and the knowledge of the truth which is according to godliness, in hope of eternal life, which God, who can't lie, promised before time began; but in his own time revealed his word in the message with which I was entrusted according to the commandment of God our Savior; to Titus, my true child according to a common faith: Grace, mercy, and peace from God the Father and the Lord Jesus Christ our Savior.

I left you in Crete for this reason, that you would set in order the things that were lacking and appoint elders in every city, as I directed you, if anyone is blameless, the husband of one wife,

92. Paul hadn't yet decided which one to send. Philip Towner, *The Letters to Timothy and Titus*, 799.

93. Nicopolis was located on the Greek side of the Adriatic coast, around 200 miles east of Italy. (It was on the western side of Greece itself.) Traveling by sea wasn't possible during the winter so Paul waited in Nicopolis for Titus. Craig Keener, *The IVP Bible Background Commentary: New Testament*, 631; Clinton Arnold, ed., *Zondervan Illustrated Bible Backgrounds Commentary*, 3:509.

94. Titus 3:12.

95. Zenas could have been a Roman jurist or a "scribe" (an expert in Mosaic Law). Clinton Arnold, ed., *Zondervan Illustrated Bible Backgrounds Commentary*, 3:509.

96. Titus 3:13, NASB.

97. "Apparently Zenas and Apollos were leaving Paul on a journey that would take them through Crete. Presumably they brought the epistle to Titus...." William Mounce, *Pastoral Epistles*, 458. Keener agrees. Craig Keener, *The IVP Bible Background Commentary: New Testament*, 631.

98. This conjecture is plausible. F.F. Bruce, *Paul: Apostle of the Heart Set Free*, 443. See also the sources I cite in my notes on the "Paul Writes 1 Timothy" box.

having children who believe, who are not accused of loose or unruly behavior. For the overseer must be blameless, as God's steward, not self-pleasing, not easily angered, not given to wine, not violent, not greedy for dishonest gain; but given to hospitality, a lover of good, sober minded, fair, holy, self-controlled, holding to the faithful word which is according to the teaching, that he may be able to exhort in the sound doctrine, and to convict those who contradict him.

For there are also many unruly men, vain talkers and deceivers, especially those of the circumcision, whose mouths must be stopped: men who overthrow whole houses, teaching things which they ought not, for dishonest gain's sake. One of them, a prophet of their own, said, "Cretans are always liars, evil beasts, and idle gluttons."

This testimony is true. For this cause, reprove them sharply, that they may be sound in the faith, not paying attention to Jewish fables and commandments of men who turn away from the truth. To the pure, all things are pure; but to those who are defiled and unbelieving, nothing is pure; but both their mind and their conscience are defiled. They profess that they know God, but by their deeds they deny him, being abominable, disobedient, and unfit for any good work.

But say the things which fit sound doctrine, that older men should be temperate, sensible, sober minded, sound in faith, in love, and in perseverance: and that older women likewise be reverent in behavior, not slanderers nor enslaved to much wine, teachers of that which is good, that they may train the young wives to love their husbands, to love their children, to be sober minded, chaste, workers at home, kind, being in subjection to their own husbands, that God's word may not be blasphemed.

Likewise, exhort the younger men to be sober minded. In all things show yourself an example of good works. In your teaching, show integrity, seriousness, incorruptibility, and soundness of speech that can't be condemned, that he who opposes you may be ashamed, having no evil thing to say about us. Exhort servants to be in subjection to their own masters and to be well-pleasing in all things, not contradicting, not stealing, but showing all good fidelity, that they may adorn the doctrine of God, our Savior, in all things.

For the grace of God has appeared, bringing salvation to all men, instructing us to the intent that, denying ungodliness and worldly lusts, we would live soberly, righteously, and godly in this present age; looking for the blessed hope and appearing of the glory of our great God and Savior, Jesus Christ, who gave himself for us, that he might redeem us from all iniquity, and purify for himself a people for his own possession, zealous for good works.

Say these things and exhort and reprove with all authority. Let no one despise you. Remind them to be in subjection to rulers and to authorities, to be obedient, to be ready for every good work, to speak evil of no one, not to be contentious, to be gentle, showing all humility toward all men. For we were also once foolish, disobedient, deceived, serving various lusts and pleasures, living in malice and envy, hateful, and hating one another.

But when the kindness of God our Savior and his love toward mankind appeared, not by works of righteousness which we did ourselves, but according to his mercy, he saved us through the washing of regeneration and renewing by the Holy Spirit, whom he poured out on us richly, through Jesus Christ our Savior; that being justified by his grace, we might be made heirs according to the hope of eternal life.

This saying is faithful, and concerning these things I desire that you affirm confidently, so that those who have believed God may be careful to maintain good works. These things are good and profitable to men; but shun foolish questionings, genealogies, strife, and disputes about the law; for they are unprofitable and vain. Avoid a factious man after a first and second warning, knowing that such a one is perverted and sins, being self-condemned.

When I send Artemas to you, or Tychicus, be diligent to come to me to Nicopolis, for I have determined to winter there. Send Zenas, the lawyer, and Apollos on their journey speedily, that nothing may be lacking for them. Let our people also learn to maintain good works for necessary uses, that they may not be unfruitful. All who are with me greet you. Greet those who love us in faith. Grace be with you all. Amen.

* * *

Paul travels to Nicopolis in the far western coast of Greece and spends the winter there.[99] He plants a kingdom community in Nicopolis. He then sends Artemas to replace Titus in Crete.[100] When Artemas arrives, Titus joins Paul in Nicopolis and both men nurture the new kingdom community.[101]

99. Because wintertime was unsafe for travel, Paul always chose a place to winter. This also accounts for his urgent plea to Timothy to "do your best to come before winter" (2 Timothy 4:21, ESV).

100. Titus 3:12. According to Keener, "Because Paul later sent Tychicus from Rome to Timothy (2 Tim 4:12), it was probably Artemas he sent to Titus." Craig Keener, *The IVP Bible Background Commentary: New Testament*, 631.

101. Inferred from Titus 3:12.

Winter ends and Paul heads to Corinth to check on the Corinthian ekklesia.[102] After spending time in Corinth, he leaves for Ephesus.[103] Paul invites Erastus to accompany him, but Erastus remains in Corinth, unable to join him.[104] Paul spends time ministering in Ephesus.

Paul's Second Roman Imprisonment[105]
A.D. 66[106]

After a while, Paul leaves Ephesus and heads to Troas where he is arrested.[107]

---

102. 2 Timothy 4:20. Gerald Hawthorne, et al., eds., *Dictionary of Paul and His Letters*, 448. Titus possibly stayed in Nicopolis, or as Ramsay asserts, he accompanied Paul. William Ramsay, *St. Paul the Traveler and Roman Citizen*, 285.

103. According to Stott, "It is safe to assume that he [Paul] later kept his promise to revisit Timothy in Ephesus" (1 Timothy 1:3; 3:14-15). John Stott, *The Message of 2 Timothy*, 17. Ramsay agrees. William Ramsay, *St. Paul the Traveler and Roman Citizen*, 285. Ramsay presumes Titus went with him. If the apostle traveled to Ephesus from Corinth, he probably sailed.

104. 2 Timothy 4:20. For a reconstruction of these events, see Alan Bandy, *An Illustrated Guide to the Apostle Paul*, 174-175. Again, we cannot be certain about the sequence, and all who hold to a fourth apostolic journey disagree on the details.

105. The hypothesis of Paul's acquittal after his first Roman imprisonment creates space for Paul's other ministry trips that are mentioned in the Pastorals, but which are absent from Acts. His acquittal and trip to Spain is attested in such early works as the Muratorian Canon; *1 Clement* 5.7; Eusebius, *The History of Church*, 2.22; 3.1; Polycarp, *Letter to the Philippians*, 9.1-2; Irenaeus, *Against Heresies*, 3.1.1. See also Harry Tajra, *The Martyrdom of St. Paul*, vol. 3 (Tübingen: Mohr Siebeck, 1994). Even critics of the second imprisonment theory admit that the tradition "is strong, although we have no authentic testimony of it from Paul himself." John-Christian Eurell, "The Second Imprisonment of Paul: Fiction or Reality?," *Scottish Journal of Theology* (2023), vol. 76, 230–239. See also John Macpherson, "Was there a Second Imprisonment of Paul in Rome," *American Journal of Theology* 4 (1900), 23-40; Philip Towner, *The Letters to Timothy and Titus*, 11-12; Gerald Hawthorne, et al., eds., *Dictionary of Paul and His Letters*, 661-662; F.F. Bruce, *Paul: Apostle of the Heart Set Free,* chap. 37; Alan Bandy, *An Illustrated Guide to the Apostle Paul*, 169-170; Richard Longenecker, *The Ministry and Message of Paul*, 85-86.

106. According to Pollock, the arrest took place in the summer of A.D. 66. John Pollock, *The Apostle: A Life of Paul* (Wheaton, IL: Victor Books, 1985), 303.

107. It is uncertain whether Paul was arrested in Troas (2 Timothy 4:13), Ephesus, or Miletus (2 Timothy 4:20). Eckhard Schnabel, *Early Christian Mission*, 1:122. In favor of Troas, see Philip Towner, *The Letters to Timothy and Titus*, 631; Gerald Hawthorne, et al., eds., *Dictionary of Paul and His Letters*, 448. We don't know what the charges were, but the Christians were accused of horrid crimes against the state, like atheism (because they denied the gods), cannibalism (because they "eat the body and blood" of Christ in the Lord's

He is taken back to Rome where he experiences his second Roman imprisonment.[108] Unfortunately, he is not enjoying house arrest as he did during his first imprisonment.[109] Confined in Rome, the apostle awaits trial.[110] Although Paul can receive visitors, people have a difficult time locating him. Onesiphorus (from Ephesus)[111] hunts for Paul and finally locates him.[112] Onesiphorus refreshes Paul's spirit; he is not ashamed of the apostle's imprisonment.[113] Tychicus, Demas, Titus, and a man named Crescens also find Paul and stay in Rome with him for a time.[114]

Anticipating that war is on the horizon, Jewish believers from the ekklesias in Judea plan to migrate to the Christian assemblies in other places. This impulse is confirmed by a divine revelation warning them to leave the city of Jerusalem. So the believers begin dispersing into the Gentile ekklesias outside Israel. Many flee to Pella in Perea.[115] Others flee to Asia.[116]

Supper), and hatred of the human race (because they live distinct lives from the rest of the world). John Stott, *The Message of 2 Timothy*, 122-123.

108. Witherington agrees that Paul was released from his first imprisonment, taken captive again and put to death during Nero's reign. Ben Witherington III, *The Acts of the Apostles*, 815.

109. Paul's second confinement is "more rigorous" than his first. William Ramsay, *St. Paul the Traveler and Roman Citizen*, 284.

110. One tradition says Paul was confined in the Mamertine dungeon (Rome's state prison). However, Weima thinks this is highly improbable. Personal correspondence with Jeffrey Weima, 1/6/24. Interestingly, Paul spent as much as 25 percent of his apostolic ministry in prison or house arrest.

111. 2 Timothy 4:19.

112. 2 Timothy 1:16.

113. 2 Timothy 1:16-17. First-century Roman culture was dominated by honor and shame. There was a huge stigma that went with being imprisoned. The public exposure of being charged as a criminal was both degrading and lifelong. For Paul's shame concerns, see Philippians 1:12-20; 2 Timothy 1:8, 11-12, 16; 2:9. Paul may have been under military watch at the Campus Martius on the edge of Rome awaiting trial. Roman soldiers would not provide food or drink for prisoners, so perhaps Onesiphorus literally "refreshed" Paul in this way. Ben Witherington III, *Letters and Homilies for Hellenized Christians*, 324-325.

114. 2 Timothy 4:10-12.

115. Eusebius wrote that the Christians were supernaturally warned by the Lord to flee Jerusalem before the bloodbath began. Many of them fled to the city of Pella in the Decapolis before the destruction of Jerusalem in A.D. 70. Pella was located east of the Jordan River (in the Transjordan), in what is now modern-day Jordan. Eusebius, *The History of the Church*, 3.5. See also Epiphanius of Salamis, *On Weights and Measures*, 15. The account is also mentioned in the writings of Remigius of Reims.

116. According to church tradition, a community of Christians migrated to Asia from Judea in A.D. 66. Clinton Arnold, ed., *Zondervan Illustrated Bible Backgrounds Commentary*, 4:246.

False prophets in the unbelieving Jewish community promise swift messianic deliverance, thus many of the Jews remain in the city.[117]

Crisis in the Kingdom Communities in Western Anatolia[118]

Peter receives word that the ekklesias in Western Anatolia are distressed by persecution and in need of encouragement.[119] The opposition has become so intense that the Gentile believers find themselves tempted to revert to their past pagan lifestyles to alleviate the pressure. Some of the believers even rebel against local authorities because of the mistreatment they're receiving. Marital discord has become common in the households of many believers. Some of the elders are exercising too much control in their attempt to keep the assembly faithful under the weight of the pressure.

117. Craig Keener, *The Gospel of Matthew*, 251. All of this took place A.D. 66 which was a dark year for the Jewish people. Ananias the high priest was murdered by the Zealots, and 10,000-18,000 Jews were massacred in Damascus. F.F. Bruce, *Paul: Apostle of the Heart Set Free*, 77, 351.

118. "Western Anatolia" is an appropriate term for the five Roman provinces addressed in 1 Peter 1:1. Personal correspondence with David deSilva, 2/15/24. Keener says not all the provinces were equally or heavily inhabited or Romanized. Craig Keener, *1 Peter,* 43. The five provinces are "geographically connected." The southern coastal regions of Asia Minor are omitted. Craig Keener, *The IVP Bible Background Commentary: New Testament*, 687. The term Dispersion (Diaspora) in 1 Peter 1:1, ESV is to be taken metaphorically, referring to the fact that the Christians were "resident aliens" on the earth (1 Peter 1:17; 2:11). Craig Keener, *1 Peter,* 45; *The IVP Bible Background Commentary: New Testament*, 690; Wayne Grudem, *1 Peter,* 49; Peter Davids, *The First Epistle of Peter*, 46-47.

119. The kind of persecution Peter describes in his letter includes suffering in the form of ridicule, slander, stigmatization, and false accusations. These are the same assaults that the Christians will face some fifty years later and beyond, a persecution instigated by their neighbors. *The SBL Study Bible*, 2133-2134. The blood-letting against the Christians was limited in time and location—just in Rome and for a small period of Nero's reign. There was no official empire-wide judgment against Christianity at this time, and thus none of the torture that took place in Rome occurred elsewhere. Instead, the opposition to the early Christians involved things like social harassment, ostracization, and financial suffering (loss of job and business). Personal correspondence with Jeffrey Weima, 1/6/24.

PETER WRITES 1 PETER

Year: A.D. 66[120]

From: Rome[121]

To: The kingdom communities in Western Anatolia: Pontus, Galatia, Cappadocia, Asia, and Bithynia[122] (all of which are predominantly Gentile)[123]

Author: Peter[124]

120. Witherington believes the letter was written A.D. 65-66. Ben Witherington III, *Invitation to the New Testament*, 321. Keener agrees it was written during the time of Nero's persecution (mid-to-late 60s). Craig Keener, *1 Peter*, 30. See also Clinton Arnold, ed., *Zondervan Illustrated Bible Backgrounds Commentary*, 4:121; Peter Davids, *The First Epistle of Peter*, NICNT (Grand Rapids, MI: Eerdmans, 1990), 10. Other scholars date it between A.D. 62 and 64. Wayne Grudem, *1 Peter: An Introduction and Commentary*, TNTC (Grand Rapids, MI: Eerdmans, 1988), 37; Donald Guthrie, *New Testament Introduction*, 787; *The ESV Study Bible*, 2401.

121. Babylon mentioned in 1 Peter 5:13 is a reference to Rome, the location where the letter was penned. Craig Keener, *1 Peter*, 31, 403-404; Wayne Grudem, *1 Peter*, 35, 201; Peter Davids, *The First Epistle of Peter*, 202; Ben Witherington III, *Letters and Homilies for Hellenized Christians*, 2:248.

122. The five Roman provinces "encompass parts of western, northern, and central Asia Minor (modern-day Turkey)." N.T. Wright and Michael Bird, *The New Testament in Its World*, 760; David deSilva, *An Introduction to the New Testament*, 744-745. Witherington believes Peter evangelized these areas in the A.D. 40s and returned to those regions after the Jerusalem council in A.D. 50. Ben Witherington III, *Invitation to the New Testament*, 315, 321. "Two of the provinces, Galatia and Asia, had been the scene of Paul's ministry, but the others had not." Donald Guthrie, *The Apostles*, 364.

123. It is without doubt that Gentile Christians were mainly in view. John Drane, *Early Christians*, 106. Texts including 1 Peter 2:10 and 4:3 confirm this conclusion. See Walter Elwell, et al., eds., *Tyndale Bible Dictionary*, 1016; David deSilva, *An Introduction to the New Testament*, 745; Ralph Martin and Peter Davids, eds., *Dictionary of the Later New Testament & Its Development* (Downers Grove, IL: InterVarsity Press, 1997), 917. Keener points out that scholars disagree on this. Some believe the letter was written to mostly Gentiles, others to mostly Jews, and others a mixture of both. Craig Keener, *1 Peter*, 31. According to Keener, many Jews lived in each of the regions named in 1 Peter 1:1. For an exploration of how these believing communities may have been founded, see Keener, *1 Peter*, 43-48. The population of Asia Minor during this time was around four million. And about 300,000 of them were Jews. Ben Witherington III, *Letters and Homilies for Hellenized Christians*, 2:25; *Invitation to the New Testament*, 311.

124. This is disputed among scholars, but I agree with Keener that the burden of proof is upon those who contest the authorial claim made in 1 Peter 1:1. Craig Keener, *1 Peter*, 9, 30. Witherington agrees and provides a compelling argument that Peter wrote the letter with the help of Silas (Silvanus). Ben Witherington III, *Letters and Homilies for Hellenized Christians*, 2:49-54. Grudem says "the objections to authorship by Peter

Contextual Summary: Peter encourages his Jewish and Gentile brothers and sisters in the midst of their suffering—a suffering shared by their fellow siblings in Christ everywhere.

He exhorts the Gentile believers against reverting to the lifestyle they lived as pagans. He encourages the assembly to submit to its local authorities and gives practical instruction to family members on how to treat one another. The apostle also charges the elders to lead by example rather than by force.

Peter conveys the idea that the Gentile Christians are now the true successors to ancient Israel, and they have achieved this position by divine inheritance through faith.[125] Throughout the letter, he uses the general Greek verb "to suffer" (*pascho*) twelve times—more than any other New Testament letter.

The epistle strongly reflects the reality of Christ the Suffering Servant as the pattern for all believers to follow in their affliction. The letter contains many citations and allusions to the Old Testament.[126] Given its excellent Greek style, the letter is likely scribed by Silas (Silvanus) who is with Peter in Rome.[127]

Peter closes the letter by sending greetings from Mark, whom he calls his "son,"[128] as well as from the ekklesia in Rome. He calls Rome by its code name "Babylon,"

---

remain unpersuasive." Wayne Grudem, *1 Peter*, 33. (Grudem lays out his argument in 21-33.) Barnett agrees, pointing out that Peter (an Aramaic-speaking fisherman from Galilee) received the help of Silas in crafting the letter. Paul Barnett, *Bethlehem to Patmos*, 217.

125. John Drane, *Early Christians*, 106.

126. For a listing of them, see Peter Davids, *The First Epistle of Peter*, 24.

127. 1 Peter 5:12. I agree with those scholars who believe this is the same Silas who traveled with Paul on the second apostolic journey. Peter Davids, *The First Epistle of Peter*, 6, 198-199; Craig Keener, *1 Peter*, 392. The idea that Silas helped compose the letter would account for the elegant Greek that marks it. As a former Galilean fisherman, Peter could speak and write a little Greek for business purposes, but his Greek skills were limited. The elegant and sophisticated Greek in 1 Peter is beyond what Peter could have produced. F.F. Bruce, *The Pauline Circle*, 28; Gary Burge, et al., *The New Testament in Antiquity*, 347; Craig Keener, *1 Peter*, 10-11, 392-402; Ben Witherington III, *Letters and Homilies for Hellenized Christians*, 2:41-45. Peter refers to the cross of Christ as a tree (1 Peter 2:24), a term he uses in his messages to the Jewish rulers (Acts 5:30) and to Cornelius (Acts 10:39). This observation also points to Peter's authorship of the letter. John Drane, *Early Christians*, 109.

128. 1 Peter 5:13. This reference could indicate that Mark was converted by Peter's preaching in the A.D. 30s. Ben Witherington III, *Letters and Homilies for Hellenized Christians*, 2:247.

and he speaks of a "king" (rather than the emperor). The explanation: Peter writes during a time of persecution. He's a marginalized Jew so he uses coded language to describe Rome and Nero.[129] The apostle sends the letter with Silas, who reads it to the kingdom communities.[130]

1 Peter

Peter, an apostle of Jesus Christ, to the chosen ones who are living as foreigners in the Dispersion in Pontus, Galatia, Cappadocia, Asia, and Bithynia, according to the foreknowledge of God the Father, in sanctification of the Spirit, that you may obey Jesus Christ and be sprinkled with his blood: Grace to you and peace be multiplied.

Blessed be the God and Father of our Lord Jesus Christ, who according to his great mercy caused us to be born again to a living hope through the resurrection of Jesus Christ from the dead, to an incorruptible and undefiled inheritance that doesn't fade away, reserved in Heaven for you, who by the power of God are guarded through faith for a salvation ready to be revealed in the last time.

Wherein you greatly rejoice, though now for a little while, if need be, you have been grieved in various trials, that the proof of your faith, which is more precious than gold that perishes even though it is tested by fire, may be found to result in praise, glory, and honor at the revelation of Jesus Christ—whom, not having known, you love. In him, though now you don't see him, yet believing, you rejoice greatly with joy that is unspeakable and full of glory, receiving the result of your faith, the salvation of your souls. Concerning this salvation, the prophets sought and searched diligently.

---

129. Ben Witherington III, *Invitation to the New Testament*, 315.

130. 1 Peter 5:12. Wayne Grudem, *1 Peter*, 200; Ben Witherington III, *Letters and Homilies for Hellenized Christians*, 2:245. For an overview of 1 Peter, see David deSilva, *An Introduction to the New Testament*, chap. 22; N.T. Wright and Michael Bird, *The New Testament in Its World*, chap. 32; Clinton Arnold, ed., *Zondervan Illustrated Bible Backgrounds Commentary*, 4:121-151.

They prophesied of the grace that would come to you, searching for who or what kind of time the Spirit of Christ, which was in them, pointed to, when he predicted the sufferings of Christ, and the glories that would follow them. To them it was revealed, that they served not themselves, but you, in these things, which now have been announced to you through those who preached the Good News to you by the Holy Spirit sent out from heaven; which things angels desire to look into.

Therefore prepare your minds for action.[a] Be sober, and set your hope fully on the grace that will be brought to you at the revelation of Jesus Christ—as children of obedience, not conforming yourselves according to your former lusts as in your ignorance, but just as he who called you is holy, you yourselves also be holy in all of your behavior; because it is written, "You shall be holy; for I am holy." Leviticus 11:44-45

If you call on him as Father, who without respect of persons judges according to each man's work, pass the time of your living as foreigners here in reverent fear, knowing that you were redeemed, not with corruptible things, with silver or gold, from the useless way of life handed down from your fathers, but with precious blood, as of a lamb without blemish or spot, the blood of Christ, who was foreknown indeed before the foundation of the world, but was revealed in this last age for your sake, who through him are believers in God, who raised him from the dead, and gave him glory, so that your faith and hope might be in God.

Seeing you have purified your souls in your obedience to the truth through the Spirit in sincere brotherly affection, love one another from the heart fervently, having been born again, not of corruptible seed, but of incorruptible, through the word of God, which lives and remains forever. For, "All flesh is like grass, and all of man's glory like the flower in the grass. The grass withers, and its flower falls; but the Lord's word endures forever." Isaiah 40:6-8

This is the word of Good News which was preached to you. Putting away therefore all wickedness, all deceit, hypocrisies, envies, and all evil speaking, as newborn babies, long for the pure milk of the Word, that with it you may grow, if indeed you have tasted that the Lord is gracious: coming to him, a living stone, rejected indeed by men, but chosen by God, precious. You also, as living stones, are built up as a spiritual house, to be a holy priesthood, to offer up spiritual sacrifices, acceptable to God through Jesus Christ. Because it is contained in Scripture, "Behold,[b] I lay in Zion a chief cornerstone, chosen and precious: He who believes in him will not be disappointed." Isaiah 28:16 For you who believe therefore is the honor, but for those who are disobedient, "The stone which the builders rejected has become the chief cornerstone," Psalm 118:22 and, "a stumbling stone and a rock of offense." Isaiah 8:14

For they stumble at the word, being disobedient, to which also they were appointed. But you are a chosen race, a royal priesthood, a holy nation, a people for God's own possession, that you may proclaim the excellence of him who called you out of darkness into his marvelous light. In the past, you were not a people, but now are God's people, who had not obtained mercy, but now have obtained mercy.

Beloved, I beg you as foreigners and pilgrims, to abstain from fleshly lusts, which war against the soul; having good behavior among the nations, so in that of which they speak against you as evildoers, they may by your good works, which they see, glorify God in the day of visitation.

Therefore subject yourselves to every ordinance of man for the Lord's sake: whether to the king, as supreme; or to governors, as sent by him for vengeance on evildoers and for praise to those who do well. For this is the will of God, that by well-doing you should put to silence the ignorance of foolish men: as free, and not using your freedom for a cloak of wickedness, but as bondservants of God. Honor all men. Love the brotherhood. Fear God. Honor the king.

Servants, be in subjection to your masters with all respect: not only to the good and gentle, but also to the wicked. For it is commendable if someone endures pain, suffering unjustly, because of conscience toward God. For what glory is it if, when you sin, you patiently endure beating? But if, when you do well, you patiently endure suffering, this is commendable with God. For you were called to this, because Christ also suffered for us, leaving you[c] an example, that you should follow his steps, who didn't sin, "neither was deceit found in his mouth." Isaiah 53:9 When he was cursed, he didn't curse back.

When he suffered, he didn't threaten, but committed himself to him who judges righteously. He himself bore our sins in his body on the tree, that we, having died to sins, might live to righteousness. You were healed by his wounds.[d] For you were going astray like sheep; but now you have returned to the Shepherd and Overseer[e] of your souls.

In the same way, wives, be in subjection to your own husbands; so that, even if any don't obey the Word, they may be won by the behavior of their wives without a word, seeing your pure behavior in fear. Let your beauty be not just the outward adorning of braiding the hair, and of wearing jewels of gold, or of putting on fine clothing; but in the hidden person of the heart, in the incorruptible adornment of a gentle and quiet spirit, which is very precious in the sight of God.

For this is how in the past, the holy women who hoped in God also adorned themselves, being in subjection to their own husbands. So Sarah obeyed Abraham, calling him lord, whose children you now are, if you do well, and are not put in fear by any terror. You husbands, in the same way, live with your wives according to knowledge, giving honor to the woman, as to the weaker vessel, as also being joint heirs of the grace of life, that your prayers may not be hindered.

Finally, all of you be like-minded, compassionate, loving as brothers, tenderhearted, courteous, not rendering evil for evil, or insult for insult; but instead blessing, knowing that you were called to this, that you may inherit a blessing. For, "He who would love life and see good days, let him keep his tongue from evil and his lips from speaking deceit. Let him turn away from evil and do good. Let him seek peace and pursue it. For the eyes of the Lord are on the righteous, and his ears open to their prayer; but the face of the Lord is against those who do evil." Psalm 34:12-16

Now who will harm you if you become imitators of that which is good? But even if you should suffer for righteousness' sake, you are blessed. "Don't fear what they fear, neither be troubled." Isaiah 8:12 But sanctify the Lord God in your hearts. Always be ready to give an answer to everyone who asks you a reason concerning the hope that is in you, with humility and fear, having a good conscience. Thus, while you are spoken against as evildoers, they may be disappointed who curse your good way of life in Christ.

For it is better, if it is God's will, that you suffer for doing well than for doing evil. Because Christ also suffered for sins once, the righteous for the unrighteous, that he might bring you to God, being put to death in the flesh, but made alive in the Spirit, in whom he also went and preached to the spirits in prison, who before were disobedient, when God waited patiently in the days of Noah, while the ship was being built.

In it, few, that is, eight souls, were saved through water. This is a symbol of baptism, which now saves you—not the putting away of the filth of the flesh, but the answer of a good conscience toward God, through the resurrection of Jesus Christ, who is at the right hand of God, having gone into heaven, angels and authorities and powers being made subject to him.

Therefore, since Christ suffered for us in the flesh, arm yourselves also with the same mind; for he who has suffered in the flesh has ceased from sin, that you no longer should live the rest of your time in the flesh for the lusts of men, but for the will of God. For we have spent enough of our past time doing the desire of the Gentiles, and having walked in lewdness, lusts, drunken binges, orgies, carousings, and abominable idolatries.

They think it is strange that you don't run with them into the same excess of riot, blaspheming. They will give account to him who is ready to judge the living and the dead. For to this end the Good News was preached even to the dead, that they might be judged indeed as men in the flesh, but live as to God in the spirit.

But the end of all things is near. Therefore be of sound mind, self-controlled, and sober in prayer. And above all things be earnest in your love among yourselves, for love covers a multitude of sins. Be hospitable to one another without grumbling. As each has received a gift, employ it in serving one another, as good managers of the grace of God in its various forms. If anyone speaks, let it be as it were the very words of God. If anyone serves, let it be as of the strength which God supplies, that in all things God may be glorified through Jesus Christ, to whom belong the glory and the dominion forever and ever. Amen.

Beloved, don't be astonished at the fiery trial which has come upon you to test you, as though a strange thing happened to you. But because you are partakers of Christ's sufferings, rejoice, that at the revelation of his glory you also may rejoice with exceeding joy. If you are insulted for the name of Christ, you are blessed; because the Spirit of glory and of God rests on you. On their part he is blasphemed, but on your part he is glorified.

For let none of you suffer as a murderer, or a thief, or an evil doer, or a meddler in other men's matters. But if one of you suffers for being a Christian, let him not be ashamed; but let him glorify God in this matter. For the time has come for judgment to begin with the household of God. If it begins first with us, what will happen to those who don't obey the Good News of God? "If it is hard for the righteous to be saved, what will happen to the ungodly and the sinner?" <u>Proverbs 11:31</u> Therefore let them also who suffer according to the will of God in doing good entrust their souls to him, as to a faithful Creator.

Therefore I exhort the elders among you, as a fellow elder, and a witness of the sufferings of Christ, and who will also share in the glory that will be revealed: Shepherd the flock of God which is among you, exercising the oversight, not under compulsion, but voluntarily, not for dishonest gain, but willingly; not as lording it over those entrusted to you, but making yourselves examples to the flock. When the chief Shepherd is revealed, you will receive the crown of glory that doesn't fade away.

Likewise, you younger ones, be subject to the elder. Yes, all of you clothe yourselves with humility, to subject yourselves to one another; for "God resists the proud, but gives grace to the humble." <u>Proverbs 3:34</u> Humble yourselves therefore under the mighty hand of God, that he may exalt you in due time, casting all your worries on him, because he cares for you.

Be sober and self-controlled. Be watchful. Your adversary, the devil, walks around like a roaring lion, seeking whom he may devour. Withstand him steadfast in your faith, knowing that your brothers who are in the world are undergoing the same sufferings. But may the God of all grace, who called you to his eternal glory by Christ Jesus, after you have suffered a little while, perfect, establish, strengthen, and settle you. To him be the glory and the power forever and ever. Amen.

Through Silvanus, our faithful brother, as I consider him, I have written to you briefly, exhorting, and testifying that this is the true grace of God in which you stand. She who is in Babylon, chosen together with you, greets you. So does Mark, my son. Greet one another with a kiss of love. Peace be to all of you who are in Christ Jesus. Amen.

a. <u>1:13</u> literally, "gird up the waist of your mind" or "put on the belt of the waist of your mind."

b. <u>2:6</u> "Behold," from "הִנֵּה" or "ἰδοὺ," means look at, take notice, observe, see, or gaze at. It is often used as an interjection.

c. <u>2:21</u> TR reads "us" instead of "you."

d. <u>2:24</u> or, stripes.

e. <u>2:25</u> "Overseer" is from the Greek ἐπίσκοπον, which can mean overseer, curator, guardian, or superintendent.

* * *

After Silas delivers the letter, he brings the gospel to the island of Rhodes. He later moves to Greece, where he is martyred.[131] Philip, one of the Twelve apostles, travels to Phrygia and Hierapolis. According to tradition, he is imprisoned, scourged, and crucified in Hierapolis.[132] Tragically, two firebrand apostles leave the earth.

131. While traditions vary, Schmidt puts the death of Silas in Macedonia during the mid-60s. Thomas Schmidt, *The Apostles After Acts*, 132-134, 197.

132. According to Eusebius, Philip and two of his daughters migrated to Hierapolis in Asia Minor where they died. Another daughter was presumably married and rests in Ephesus. Eusebius, *The History of the*

War in Jerusalem
Spring 66

The Jewish revolt against Rome begins.[133] For the next four years, a bloody battle rages between Jewish revolutionaries and Roman soldiers.[134] The revolt begins in Judea and spreads throughout Palestine. Turmoil and strife pervade Jerusalem.[135]

A group of terrorists called the Sicarii (dagger-men) actively engage their violent tactics.[136] They are part of a larger group called "Zealots" who oppose the Roman occupation of Judea, believing it to be godless.[137] The Sicarii are known for showing up at festivals and other public places, stabbing Jews who are sympathetic to Rome.[138]

Church, 3.31; 5.24. The tomb of Philip (the apostle), which was recently discovered, confirms that he died in Hierapolis. Personal correspondence with Jeffrey Weima, 1/6/24. Most traditions date Philip's death between A.D. 80-90. Schmidt, however, places it around A.D. 66 in Hierapolis by crucifixion. Thomas Schmidt, *The Apostles After Acts*, 144, 196. Like some of the other traditions about the death of the apostles, they are in conflict. So we cannot be certain.

133. The revolt was initiated by the Zealots, and it stopped the Judaizing mission in Paul's field of labor. It also led to the destruction of the temple, the city of Jerusalem, and the dispersing of the ekklesia in Jerusalem. F.F. Bruce, *Paul: Apostle of the Heart Set Free*, 27-28, 174, 232, 278, 361, 464.

134. David Rhoads, *Israel in Revolution 6-74 C.E.*, 94-174. Rhoads provides a detailed account, including the major players in the war and the motives behind their activities.

135. By this time, contact between the ekklesia in Jerusalem and the other Gentile assemblies had reduced to a minimum. F.F. Bruce, *Paul: Apostle of the Heart Set Free*, 464. Christian Jews were no longer welcome in the synagogues during this period. While many of the churches in Judea existed after the war of A.D. 66-70, its membership continued to be exclusively Jewish. But the future of the Christian faith was with the Gentiles. Paul Barnett, *Bethlehem to Patmos*, 206.

136. The Sicarii actually arose earlier in the fifties, but by this time they had gained prominence. Josephus, *The Jewish War*, 2.258-259.

137. The land of Judea was regarded as sacred by the Jews since it was God's gift to them. Therefore, the Gentiles (particularly the Romans) had made it impure by living there. The Jews prayed urgently that the Messiah would cleanse the land from those who trampled it. Gary Burge, *A Week in the Life of a Roman Centurion*, 130.

138. The Zealots eventually took over from November A.D. 67 to the spring of AD. 68, and they allowed criminals to murder people in the temple. Ben Witherington III, *Matthew*, 447. For details on the Zealots and the Sicarii, see Calvin Roetzel, *The World That Shaped the New Testament*, 28-36, 57-59; Mark Brighton, "The Sicarii in Acts: A New Perspective," *JETS* 54.3 (2011), 547-558; F.F. Bruce, *Paul: Apostle of the Heart Set Free*, 355; David Rhoads, *Israel in Revolution 6-74 C.E.*, 56ff., 78ff.; Richard Horsley, *Jesus and Empire*, 42-45;

John Moves to Ephesus

While Paul is in prison, John (the apostle) relocates to Ephesus.[139] From Ephesus, he travels throughout Roman Asia.[140] He also sends some of his co-workers to minister to the ekklesias in the region. In one of these assemblies, a self-appointed demagogue named Diotrephes rejects John's ministry. Diotrephes' ambition to have first place in the church is so extreme that he accuses John with wicked words. He will not receive the workers John sent and excommunicates the believers who have given them hospitality. Gaius, a brother in Christ, resists Diotrephes' attempts at dominating the believers.[141] And he acts in the opposite manner, providing hospitality to John's co-workers.[142]

The heresy that teaches liberty as license to sin has crept into many of the ekklesias in Roman Asia. False prophets have risen up, and they are spreading the teaching. These false prophets are "antichrists," and they're undermining the foundational elements of the gospel of Christ. Though they have left the assemblies, they remain in contact with the believers, leading some astray with their deviant gospel. They are proclaiming the following:

- God has made us (the false prophets) teachers of truth, so we exist to teach you the right way.[143]

Ben Witherington III, *A Week in the Fall of Jerusalem*, 10-11. The Sicarii are mentioned in Acts 21:38 (often translated "assassins" or "terrorists").

139. "There is a strong tradition that he [John] went to Ephesus and exercised a wide ministry among the churches in Asia." Donald Guthrie, *The Apostles*, 278. This reportedly took place shortly before A.D. 67. *The ESV Study Bible*, 2425. For details, see Iranaeus, *Against Heresies,* 3.1.1; Thomas Schmidt, *The Apostles After Acts*, 135; Clinton Arnold, ed., *Zondervan Illustrated Bible Backgrounds Commentary*, 4:246; Mark Fairchild, *Christian Origins in Ephesus & Asia Minor*, 121-133; Mark Wilson, *Biblical Turkey*, 221.

140. For confirmation that John traveled in this region, see 2 John 12 and 3 John 10 where he speaks about visiting the believers.

141. It's possible that Gaius was excommunicated by Diotrephes, or he was part of a nearby assembly. John Painter, *1, 2, and 3 John*, Sacra Pagina (Collegeville, MN: Liturgical Press, 2002), 19.

142. 3 John 5-8.

143. 1 John 2:26-28. The false prophets' teaching ran against the spiritual instincts of the believers. For this reason, John reminds the believers that it is the anointing (the indwelling Spirit) who gives them spiritual instincts to test the spirit of truth from the spirit of error. They don't need the false teachers to teach them anything.

- The material world of matter is evil. Therefore, the divine and holy Christ could not have come to earth in human flesh. Instead, He came in spirit and only *appeared* in human flesh.[144]

- The man, Jesus, was not the Son of God.

- Since salvation means deliverance in or from the physical world, it doesn't matter how a person behaves in his or her physical body.

- Since sin is part of the material world, sin does not exist for the Christian. We (the false prophets) are sinless.

- We (the false prophets) also have special insight from God's Spirit to see these deeper truths.

Regrettably, some of the believers embrace the false gospel. As a result, they begin exhibiting hatred toward one another. Others claim they have never sinned and sin doesn't exist. John decides to write a Gospel that emphasizes the *divinity* of Jesus Christ. In it, he demonstrates that Jesus truly is the Son of God who took on human flesh.[145]

JOHN WRITES HIS GOSPEL (JOHN)[146]

Year: late A.D. 60s (or 90s)[147]

144. This denial of the Lord's incarnation later came to be known as *docetism*. Docetism is the belief that Christ could not possibly dwell in a human body. The physical body of Jesus, therefore, just seemed (Greek, *dokeo*) to be human.

145. R.V.C. Tasker, *John: An Introduction and Commentary*, TNTC, revised edition (Grand Rapids, MI: Eerdmans, 1960), 30.

146. Also known as the "Fourth Gospel."

147. For the early dating, see Jonathan Bernier, *Rethinking the Dates of the New Testament*, 87-111; John A.T. Robinson, *Redating the New Testament*, 276; Leon Morris, *The Gospel According to John*, 26-30. According to Craig Keener, most who accept John's authorship date the Gospel and his three letters in the 90s. Personal correspondence with Craig Keener, 12/4/23. Other scholars have argued that a date much earlier than the reigns of Domitian and Trajan (A.D. 81-117) is "possible and even preferable." N.T. Wright and Michael Bird, *The New Testament in Its World*, 661. For details on the debate regarding the dating of John, see Donald Guthrie, *New Testament Introduction*, 297-303; Mark Strauss, *Four Portraits, One Jesus*, 402-404; Clinton

From: Ephesus[148]

To: Christians throughout the Diaspora[149]

Author: John the apostle[150]

Arnold, ed., *Zondervan Illustrated Bible Backgrounds Commentary* (Grand Rapids, MI: Zondervan, 2019), vol. 2a.

148. Irenaeus, *Against Heresies,* 3.1.1. Early tradition unanimously suggests the Gospel was written from Ephesus. N.T. Wright and Michael Bird, *The New Testament in Its World,* 662; Donald Guthrie, *The Apostles,* 378. This tradition is as likely as any other. David deSilva, *An Introduction to the New Testament,* 344. By contrast, some scholars believe John wrote the Gospel in Palestine but circulated a more finished version from Ephesus. Joel Green, et al., eds., *Dictionary of Jesus and the Gospels,* 422-423.

149. N.T. Wright and Michael Bird, *The New Testament in Its World,* 662; Craig Keener, *The Gospel of John,* 175ff. Keener believes the Gospel was written to encourage Jewish Christians that their faith was genuinely Jewish and their opponents were misrepresenting biblical Judaism. Craig Keener, *The IVP Bible Background Commentary: New Testament,* 246-247. The Gospel writer adds a lot of Judean content and some unique material from Samaria and Galilee as well. Ben Witherington III, *Invitation to the New Testament,* 153.

150. The Fourth Gospel is anonymous. F.F. Bruce, *The Gospel of John* (Grand Rapids, MI: Eerdmans, 1983), 1. The title "According to John," wasn't attached to the Gospel until at least the end of the second century. N.T. Wright and Michael Bird, *The New Testament in Its World,* 653. However, many scholars believe John the apostle (son of Zebedee) wrote the Gospel. This is the traditional view, and according to some scholars, it's "the best solution" to the problem of who authored this Gospel. Gary Burge, et al., *The New Testament in Antiquity,* 225-226. According to Keener, the author was an eyewitness, and the internal evidence supports the idea that the "beloved disciple" fits John, the apostle, most closely. Craig Keener, *The IVP Bible Background Commentary: New Testament,* 245-246; *The Gospel of John,* 1:139. Morris confirms. Leon Morris, *The Gospel According to John,* revised, NICNT (Grand Rapids, MI: Eerdmans, 1995), 24. Other scholars, such as Ben Witherington, believe Lazarus was the "beloved disciple" who wrote this Gospel. Ben Witherington III, *Invitation to the New Testament,* 134-140, 352-353. Others argue that an unknown disciple of Jesus authored it. Bauckham, for instance, believes a disciple of Jesus who lived longer than the rest of the disciples and died in Ephesus wrote it. Richard Bauckham, *The Testimony of the Beloved Disciple: Narrative, History, and Theology in the Gospel of John* (Grand Rapids, MI: Baker Academic, 2007), 12, 15; *Jesus and the Eyewitnesses,* chaps. 16 and 20. In his book *The Johannine Circle* (Philadelphia, PA: Westminster Press, 1975), Oscar Cullmann argues that the "beloved disciple" in John's Gospel was not the son of Zebedee, nor was he one of the Twelve. For details on the scholarly debate over who wrote the Gospel of John (as well as the Johannine epistles and the book of Revelation), see Craig Keener, *The Gospel of John,* 1:81-139. For details on the discussion surrounding the identity of John and the style of his writings as a storyteller and evangelist, see Sherri Brown, et al., *Interpreting the Gospel and Letters of John,* chaps. 5-6.

Contextual Summary: John presents Jesus as the heavenly, divine, eternal Son of God, the One who reveals the Father.[151] John's Gospel includes information about Christ's early Judean ministry which is absent from the synoptic Gospels (Matthew, Mark, and Luke).[152] John pays special attention to the feasts of Israel as he traces the Lord's life.[153]

The Gospel contains many unique features compared to the other Gospels. For example, it has a distinctive prologue. John begins with a poetic introduction about the Word (*Logos*) becoming flesh. He emphasizes Jesus as the divine Son of God more explicitly than the other Gospels. The seven "I am" statements are contained in the Gospel.

John does not contain the traditional narrative parables found in the Synoptic Gospels. However, He does include figurative language and metaphorical teachings that some scholars consider parabolic in nature. Some of Jesus' teachings in John are more allegorical, blending metaphor with direct explanation.

The Gospel includes lengthy messages by Jesus, such as the "Farewell Discourse" in chapters 14 through 17. John also records miracles not found in other Gospels, like

151. For an overview of John's Gospel, see Mark Strauss, *Four Portraits, One Jesus*, chap. 10; David deSilva, *An Introduction to the New Testament*, chap. 9; N.T. Wright and Michael Bird, *The New Testament in Its World*, chap. 27; Clinton Arnold, ed., *Zondervan Illustrated Bible Backgrounds Commentary*, vol. 2a.

152. Like the Synoptic Gospels, John's Gospel is a biography of Jesus in the Greco-Roman sense. Richard Bauckham, *The Testimony of the Beloved Disciple*, 13. Keener argues that the genre is "historical biography," just like the Synoptics, with some differences. Craig Keener, *The Gospel of John*, 1:33-34. For a discussion of the ancient media contexts of the Gospels, see Nicholas Elder, *Gospel Media*. This work includes a fresh look at silent and vocalized reading in the ancient world, solitary and communal reading, and the publication and circulation of the Gospels.

153. John's Gospel contains historical information about the geography of Palestine that's reliable and supports the author's theological vision. James Riley Strange, *Excavating the Land of Jesus*, 86-87. Some of the most helpful works on John's Gospel are those written by T. Austin-Sparks (*We Beheld His Glory*); F.B. Meyer (*Gospel of John*); Craig Keener (*The Gospel of John*); and Richard Bauckham (*Gospel of Glory* and *The Testimony of the Beloved Disciple*). For a social analysis of John's Gospel, see Bruce Malina and Richard Rohrbaugh, *Social-Science Commentary on the Gospel of John* (Minneapolis, MN: Fortress Press, 1998). For two concise, but valuable introductions to the Gospel, see F.F. Bruce, *The Gospel of John*, 1-27 and R.V.C. Tasker, *John*, 1-40. For the scholarly debate about the Gospel including date, authorship, genre, destination, social contexts, motifs, style, etc., see Craig Keener, *The Gospel of John*, 3-330.

turning water into wine and raising Lazarus from the dead. In addition, he provides more teaching about the role of the Holy Spirit, especially in chapters 14 through 16.

John's Gospel is organized as follows: Prologue: The Word Becomes Flesh (1:1-18); John the Baptist and Jesus' Early Ministry (1:19-4:54); Jesus' Public Ministry (5:1-12:50); Last Supper and Farewell Discourse (13:1-17:26); Passion Narrative (18:1-19:42); Resurrection and Appearances (20:1-21:25).

Taken together, the four Gospels in the New Testament present a compelling picture of the life, ministry, and message of Jesus Christ including His death, burial, resurrection, and ascension.[154]

Jewish believers are being expelled from the synagogues in Smyrna, Philadelphia, and elsewhere in Asia.[155] As a result, some have denied Jesus as Messiah so they can return to synagogue worship. John is concerned for the believers who are in cities other than the locations he addressed in his Gospel. He wants to minister to the Christians who have been

154. For a discussion of the Gospels as ancient biography, see Wayne Meeks, ed., *Library of Early Christianity*, 8:63-69; Craig Keener, *The Gospel of John: A Commentary*, 1:11-33; *The Historical Jesus of the Gospels*, chap. 5. The four canonical Gospels are theologically distinct from the noncanonical "gospels" that were written later. Simon Gathercole, *The Gospel and the Gospels: Christian Proclamation and Early Jesus Books* (Grand Rapids, MI: Eerdmans, 2022). For a deep analysis into the source material behind the Gospels, including questions of provenance, authorship, and dates, see James D.G. Dunn, *Neither Jew Nor Greek*, 43-80; *Jesus Remembered*, chaps. 7-8; Craig Keener, *The Historical Jesus of the Gospels*, chaps. 9-10. For a scholarly discussion of how the four Gospels were written and the surrounding controversies over them, including the question of canonicity, see Francis Watson's two works, *What Is a Gospel?* (Grand Rapids, MI: Eerdmans, 2022) and *Gospel Writing: A Canonical Perspective* (Grand Rapids, MI: Eerdmans, 2013); Alan Kirk's *Jesus Tradition, Early Christian Memory, and Gospel Writing: The Long Search for the Authentic Source* (Grand Rapids, MI: Eerdmans, 2023); Martin Hengel, *The Four Gospels and the One Gospel of Jesus Christ: An Investigation of the Collection and Origin of the Canonical Gospels* (Harrisburg, PA: Trinity Press International, 2000). For a discussion of the social and cultural context of the Gospels, including their theology, Eckhard Schnabel, *New Testament Theology*, 657-762; James D.G. Dunn, *Neither Jew Nor Greek*, 187-371; N.T. Wright, *Interpreting Jesus* and *The New Testament and the People of God*, chaps. 13-14; David Wenham, et al., *Exploring the New Testament*, 1:2021; Darrell Bock, *Jesus According to the Scripture: Restoring the Portrait of the Gospels* (Grand Rapids, MI: Baker Academic, 2002); Mark Strauss, *Four Portraits, One Jesus*; Craig Blomberg, *Jesus and the Gospels: An Introduction and Survey*, third edition (Nashville, TN: B&H Academic, 2022); David deSilva, *An Introduction to the New Testament*, chaps. 4-7 and 9.

155. Craig Keener, *The IVP Bible Background Commentary: New Testament*, 707.

expelled from the synagogues but who haven't denied the Lord. His aim is to encourage them to stay true to the faith. These believers are being tempted to compromise and accept false doctrines.

John also wants to encourage Gaius in his dealings with Diotrephes and the problems he has created. The apostle will write three letters that specifically deal with the crisis in Roman Asia.[156] In those letters, he will emphasize the full *humanity* of Christ.[157]

JOHN WRITES 1 JOHN

Year: A.D. late 60s (or 90s)[158]

From: Ephesus[159]

To: Kingdom communities throughout Roman Asia[160]

156. For this reconstruction, see Craig Keener, *The IVP Bible Background Commentary: New Testament,* 707-708. According to Witherington, various Jews came to visit the congregations that were part of the Johannine community, which was a Jewish Christian community that reached out to Jews in and around Ephesus. Some of these visitors had a different view of Jesus. There was a schism as a result, and those who caused the division brought some godly members of the congregation with them. 1 John (along with the other letters of John) was written to address the crisis. Ben Witherington III, *Invitation to the New Testament,* 362-363.

157. The heresy denied the full humanity of Jesus as well as the fact that Jesus was the Son of God. For this reason, John's letters stress the humanity of Christ, especially 1 John and 2 John, while John's Gospel stresses Jesus as God's divine Son.

158. Some scholars date 1 John after A.D. 67. *The NKJV Study Bible,* 1915. It is difficult to determine the precise date of John's three epistles. Scholars range from the mid-to-late 60s to the 90s. I. Howard Marshall, *The Epistles of John,* NICNT (Grand Rapids, MI: Eerdmans, 1978), 48; Jonathan Bernier, *Rethinking the Dates of the New Testament,* 113-129. Based on my analysis of the historical timeline and the migration patterns of Judean Christians to Asia Minor, I estimate these texts were written in the mid-to-late 60s.

159. Donald Guthrie, *The Apostles,* 378.

160. Witherington argues that these weren't the ekklesias that Paul or his co-workers founded. Rather, they were primarily Hellenized Jewish congregations that were part of the "Johannine community." Ben Witherington III, *Letters and Homilies for Hellenized Christians,* 1:399-402. This isn't inconceivable since both John and Peter traveled, proclaimed the gospel, and raised up ekklesias (which is the role of the apostolic ministry). According to Burge, John's believing community "lived on the frontiers of Judaism." But it was heterogeneous containing Jewish Christians with little knowledge of Greek living alongside Greeks who knew little of the Old Testament. Gary Burge, et al., *The New Testament in Antiquity,* 412.

Author: John the apostle[161]

Contextual Summary: Jesus Christ is divine. He is the embodiment of perfect light, infinite love, and eternal life (1:5; 4:8; 5:20). In Christ, God has come to us in the flesh and was seen, heard, and handled by the author and the other apostles (1:1-3; 4:2).

John refutes the heresy that has spread in Roman Asia by revealing God's true nature in Christ. The fruit of that nature is love for the brothers and sisters in Christ and the refusal to habitually practice sin.

The believers do not need the false teachers because all Christians have received insight ("knowledge") from the Holy Spirit, and all have the anointing of the Spirit to teach them truth from error (2:20-27). John warns against the antichrist and affirms that many antichrists are currently in the world (2:18, 22; 4:3). Those who left the assembly were never truly part of it (2:19). He exhorts the fathers, the young men, and the children in the ekklesia to abide in Christ and His teaching.

He closes the letter by exhorting the believers to guard themselves against false conceptions about God, which are actually idols.[162] Except for 2:12-14, the epistle is written more like a homily (message) than a letter.[163]

1 John

That which was from the beginning, that which we have heard, that which we have seen with our eyes, that which we saw, and our hands touched, concerning the Word of life (and the life

---

161. Keener believes it's highly probable that the Gospel of John and the epistles (of John) are from the same author. Craig Keener, *The Gospel of John*, 1:139; *The IVP Bible Background Commentary: New Testament*, 706. In contrast to many scholars, Witherington believes Lazarus wrote 1 John. Ben Witherington III, *Invitation to the New Testament*, 353. For the debate among scholars on who wrote the three epistles that bear John's name, including their relationship to the Gospel of John, see John Painter, *1, 2, and 3 John*, 44-108; Gary Burge, et al., *The New Testament in Antiquity*, 415. Marshall points out that most scholars have regarded the three Johannine letters as stemming from one author. I. Howard Marshall, *The Epistles of John*, 31.

162. For an overview of John's three epistles, see David deSilva, *An Introduction to the New Testament*, chap. 10; N.T. Wright and Michael Bird, *The New Testament in Its World*, chap. 33; Clinton Arnold, ed., *Zondervan Illustrated Bible Backgrounds Commentary*, 4:177-227.

163. Craig Keener, *The IVP Bible Background Commentary: New Testament*, 706.

was revealed, and we have seen, and testify, and declare to you the life, the eternal life, which was with the Father, and was revealed to us); that which we have seen and heard we declare to you, that you also may have fellowship with us.

Yes, and our fellowship is with the Father, and with his Son, Jesus Christ. And we write these things to you, that our joy may be fulfilled. This is the message which we have heard from him and announce to you, that God is light, and in him is no darkness at all. If we say that we have fellowship with him and walk in the darkness, we lie, and don't tell the truth.

But if we walk in the light, as he is in the light, we have fellowship with one another, and the blood of Jesus Christ, his Son, cleanses us from all sin. If we say that we have no sin, we deceive ourselves, and the truth is not in us. If we confess our sins, he is faithful and righteous to forgive us the sins, and to cleanse us from all unrighteousness. If we say that we haven't sinned, we make him a liar, and his word is not in us.

My little children, I write these things to you so that you may not sin. If anyone sins, we have a Counselor[a] with the Father, Jesus Christ, the righteous. And he is the atoning sacrifice[b] for our sins, and not for ours only, but also for the whole world.

This is how we know that we know him: if we keep his commandments. One who says, "I know him," and doesn't keep his commandments, is a liar, and the truth isn't in him. But God's love has most certainly been perfected in whoever keeps his word. This is how we know that we are in him: he who says he remains in him ought himself also to walk just like he walked.

Brothers, I write no new commandment to you, but an old commandment which you had from the beginning. The old commandment is the word which you heard from the beginning. Again, I write a new commandment to you, which is true in him and in you; because the darkness is passing away and the true light already shines.

He who says he is in the light and hates his brother is in the darkness even until now. He who loves his brother remains in the light, and there is no occasion for stumbling in him. But he who hates his brother is in the darkness, and walks in the darkness, and doesn't know where he is going, because the darkness has blinded his eyes.

I write to you, little children, because your sins are forgiven you for his name's sake. I write to you, fathers, because you know him who is from the beginning. I write to you, young men, because you have overcome the evil one. I write to you, little children, because you know the

Father. I have written to you, fathers, because you know him who is from the beginning. I have written to you, young men, because you are strong, and the word of God remains in you, and you have overcome the evil one.

Don't love the world or the things that are in the world. If anyone loves the world, the Father's love isn't in him. For all that is in the world, the lust of the flesh, the lust of the eyes, and the pride of life, isn't the Father's, but is the world's. The world is passing away with its lusts, but he who does God's will remains forever.

Little children, these are the end times, and as you heard that the Antichrist is coming, even now many antichrists have arisen. By this we know that it is the final hour. They went out from us, but they didn't belong to us; for if they had belonged to us, they would have continued with us. But they left, that they might be revealed that none of them belong to us. You have an anointing from the Holy One, and you all have knowledge.[c] I have not written to you because you don't know the truth, but because you know it, and because no lie is of the truth.

Who is the liar but he who denies that Jesus is the Christ? This is the Antichrist, he who denies the Father and the Son. Whoever denies the Son doesn't have the Father. He who confesses the Son has the Father also. Therefore, as for you, let that remain in you which you heard from the beginning. If that which you heard from the beginning remains in you, you also will remain in the Son, and in the Father. This is the promise which he promised us, the eternal life. These things I have written to you concerning those who would lead you astray.

As for you, the anointing which you received from him remains in you, and you don't need for anyone to teach you. But as his anointing teaches you concerning all things, and is true, and is no lie, and even as it taught you, you will remain in him. Now, little children, remain in him, that when he appears, we may have boldness, and not be ashamed before him at his coming. If you know that he is righteous, you know that everyone who practices righteousness has been born of him.

See how great a love the Father has given to us, that we should be called children of God! For this cause the world doesn't know us, because it didn't know him. Beloved, now we are children of God. It is not yet revealed what we will be; but we know that when he is revealed, we will be like him; for we will see him just as he is.

Everyone who has this hope set on him purifies himself, even as he is pure. Everyone who sins also commits lawlessness. Sin is lawlessness. You know that he was revealed to take away our sins, and no sin is in him. Whoever remains in him doesn't sin. Whoever sins hasn't seen him and doesn't know him.

Little children, let no one lead you astray. He who does righteousness is righteous, even as he is righteous. He who sins is of the devil, for the devil has been sinning from the beginning. To this end the Son of God was revealed: that he might destroy the works of the devil.

Whoever is born of God doesn't commit sin, because his seed remains in him, and he can't sin, because he is born of God. In this the children of God are revealed, and the children of the devil. Whoever doesn't do righteousness is not of God, neither is he who doesn't love his brother. For this is the message which you heard from the beginning, that we should love one another; unlike Cain, who was of the evil one, and killed his brother. Why did he kill him? Because his deeds were evil, and his brother's righteous.

Don't be surprised, my brothers, if the world hates you. We know that we have passed out of death into life, because we love the brothers. He who doesn't love his brother remains in death. Whoever hates his brother is a murderer, and you know that no murderer has eternal life remaining in him.

By this we know love, because he laid down his life for us. And we ought to lay down our lives for the brothers. But whoever has the world's goods and sees his brother in need, then closes his heart of compassion against him, how does God's love remain in him?

My little children, let's not love in word only, or with the tongue only, but in deed and truth. And by this we know that we are of the truth, and persuade our hearts before him, because if our heart condemns us, God is greater than our heart, and knows all things. Beloved, if our hearts don't condemn us, we have boldness toward God; so whatever we ask, we receive from him, because we keep his commandments and do the things that are pleasing in his sight.

This is his commandment, that we should believe in the name of his Son, Jesus Christ, and love one another, even as he commanded. He who keeps his commandments remains in him, and he in him. By this we know that he remains in us, by the Spirit which he gave us.

Beloved, don't believe every spirit, but test the spirits, whether they are of God, because many false prophets have gone out into the world. By this you know the Spirit of God: every spirit who confesses that Jesus Christ has come in the flesh is of God, and every spirit who doesn't confess that Jesus Christ has come in the flesh is not of God, and this is the spirit of the Antichrist, of whom you have heard that it comes.

Now it is in the world already. You are of God, little children, and have overcome them; because greater is he who is in you than he who is in the world. They are of the world. Therefore they speak of the world, and the world hears them. We are of God. He who knows God listens to us. He who is not of God doesn't listen to us. By this we know the spirit of truth, and the spirit of error.

Beloved, let's love one another, for love is of God; and everyone who loves has been born of God, and knows God. He who doesn't love doesn't know God, for God is love. By this God's love was revealed in us, that God has sent his one and only Son into the world that we might live through him. In this is love, not that we loved God, but that he loved us, and sent his Son as the atoning sacrifice[d] for our sins. Beloved, if God loved us in this way, we also ought to love one another. No one has seen God at any time. If we love one another, God remains in us, and his love has been perfected in us.

By this we know that we remain in him and he in us, because he has given us of his Spirit. We have seen and testify that the Father has sent the Son as the Savior of the world. Whoever confesses that Jesus is the Son of God, God remains in him, and he in God. We know and have believed the love which God has for us.

God is love, and he who remains in love remains in God, and God remains in him. In this, love has been made perfect among us, that we may have boldness in the day of judgment, because as he is, even so we are in this world. There is no fear in love; but perfect love casts out fear, because fear has punishment.

He who fears is not made perfect in love. We love him, because he first loved us. If a man says, "I love God," and hates his brother, he is a liar; for he who doesn't love his brother whom he has seen, how can he love God whom he has not seen? This commandment we have from him, that he who loves God should also love his brother.

Whoever believes that Jesus is the Christ has been born of God. Whoever loves the Father also loves the child who is born of him. By this we know that we love the children of God, when we love God and keep his commandments. For this is loving God, that we keep his commandments. His commandments are not grievous. For whatever is born of God overcomes the world. This is the victory that has overcome the world: your faith.

Who is he who overcomes the world, but he who believes that Jesus is the Son of God? This is he who came by water and blood, Jesus Christ; not with the water only, but with the water and the blood. It is the Spirit who testifies, because the Spirit is the truth. For there are three who testify:[c] the Spirit, the water, and the blood; and the three agree as one. If we receive the witness of men, the witness of God is greater; for this is God's testimony which he has testified concerning his Son.

He who believes in the Son of God has the testimony in himself. He who doesn't believe God has made him a liar, because he has not believed in the testimony that God has given concerning his Son. The testimony is this, that God gave to us eternal life, and this life is in his Son. He who has the Son has the life. He who doesn't have God's Son doesn't have the life.

These things I have written to you who believe in the name of the Son of God, that you may know that you have eternal life, and that you may continue to believe in the name of the Son of God.

This is the boldness which we have toward him, that if we ask anything according to his will, he listens to us. And if we know that he listens to us, whatever we ask, we know that we have the petitions which we have asked of him.

If anyone sees his brother sinning a sin not leading to death, he shall ask, and God will give him life for those who sin not leading to death. There is a sin leading to death. I don't say that he should make a request concerning this. All unrighteousness is sin, and there is a sin not leading to death.

We know that whoever is born of God doesn't sin, but he who was born of God keeps himself, and the evil one doesn't touch him. We know that we are of God, and the whole world lies in the power of the evil one. We know that the Son of God has come, and has given us an understanding, that we know him who is true, and we are in him who is true, in his Son Jesus Christ. This is the true God and eternal life. Little children, keep yourselves from idols.

a. 2:1 Greek παρακλητον: Counselor, Helper, Intercessor, Advocate, and Comforter.

b. 2:2 "atoning sacrifice" is from the Greek "ιλασμος," an appeasing, propitiating, or the means of appeasement or propitiation—the sacrifice that turns away God's wrath because of our sin.

c. 2:20 Or, "know what is true," or, "know all things."

d. <u>4:10</u> "atoning sacrifice" is from the Greek "ιλασμος," an appeasing, propitiating, or the means of appeasement or propitiation—the sacrifice that turns away God's wrath because of our sin.

e. <u>5:7</u> Only a few recent manuscripts add "in heaven: the Father, the Word, and the Holy Spirit; and these three are one. And there are three that testify on earth."

JOHN WRITES 2 JOHN

Year: A.D. late 60s (or 90s)[164]

From: Ephesus[165]

To: An unnamed local ekklesia in Roman Asia

Author: John the apostle[166]

Contextual Summary: John addresses the believing community as a woman ("the elect lady") and its members as her children.[167]

He warns the assembly against receiving itinerant teachers who bring a false gospel that denies the humanity of Jesus.[168] He exhorts the believers not to admit false teachers into the assembly (which meets in a home), nor greet them. He closes with a greeting from the believers in Ephesus, whom he describes as the "children" of a "sister" church.

164. See my notes on the dating of 1 John in the "John Writes 1 John" box. "This epistle was probably written soon after 1 John, for it assumes that the readers will understand what is meant by 'antichrist' in verse 7." *The NKJV Study Bible,* 1926.

165. Donald Guthrie, *The Apostles,* 378.

166. Some scholars believe "John the Elder" is a different person from John, son of Zebedee, and the former person wrote 2 and 3 John. Ben Witherington III, *Invitation to the New Testament,* 353. Others believe they are the same John, and he is the John who also wrote Revelation (John of Patmos). Jonathan Bernier, *Rethinking the Dates of the New Testament,* 126-127. For the debate among scholars on the author of 2 John and 3 John, see David deSilva, *An Introduction to the New Testament,* 391-394. See also my notes in the "John Writes 1 John" box.

167. I. Howard Marshall, *The Epistles of John,* 60-61; Mark Fairchild, *Christian Origins in Ephesus & Asia Minor,* 128-129; N.T. Wright, *The Early Christian Letters for Everyone,* 174. Since the ekklesia is the bride of Jesus Christ, it makes perfect sense to speak of an assembly as a "chosen lady."

168. In 1 and 2 John, the false teachers are called "adversaries," "antichrists," "deceivers," "false prophets," and "heretics." John Painter, *1, 2, and 3 John,* 5.

2 John

The elder, to the chosen lady and her children, whom I love in truth, and not I only, but also all those who know the truth, for the truth's sake, which remains in us, and it will be with us forever: Grace, mercy, and peace will be with us, from God the Father, and from the Lord Jesus Christ, the Son of the Father, in truth and love.

I rejoice greatly that I have found some of your children walking in truth, even as we have been commanded by the Father. Now I beg you, dear lady, not as though I wrote to you a new commandment, but that which we had from the beginning, that we love one another.

This is love, that we should walk according to his commandments. This is the commandment, even as you heard from the beginning, that you should walk in it. For many deceivers have gone out into the world, those who don't confess that Jesus Christ came in the flesh. This is the deceiver and the Antichrist. Watch yourselves, that we don't lose the things which we have accomplished, but that we receive a full reward.

Whoever transgresses and doesn't remain in the teaching of Christ, doesn't have God. He who remains in the teaching has both the Father and the Son. If anyone comes to you, and doesn't bring this teaching, don't receive him into your house, and don't welcome him, for he who welcomes him participates in his evil deeds.

Having many things to write to you, I don't want to do so with paper and ink, but I hope to come to you, and to speak face to face, that our joy may be made full. The children of your chosen sister greet you. Amen.

JOHN WRITES 3 JOHN

Year: A.D. late 60s (or 90s)[169]

From: Ephesus[170]

---

169. See my previous note on the dating of 1 John.
170. Donald Guthrie, *The Apostles*, 378.

To: Gaius in Roman Asia[171]

Author: John the apostle[172]

Contextual Summary: John commends Gaius for receiving the apostolic workers he (John) sent. But he warns Gaius about Diotrephes, who didn't receive John or any of his co-workers. (Gaius is part of a nearby ekklesia, to which Diotrephes belongs.)

John praises Gaius for his hospitality and exhorts him not to imitate evil (referring to Diotrephes). He deplores Diotrephes for his overlordship and religious ambition. John sends the letter with Demetrius, one of his co-workers and a man he highly commends.[173]

3 John

The elder to Gaius the beloved, whom I love in truth. Beloved, I pray that you may prosper in all things and be healthy, even as your soul prospers. For I rejoiced greatly when brothers

171. Gaius is a typical Latin name. He probably owned a home large enough to accommodate the itinerant workers associated with John as well as the ekklesia. Birger Olsson, *A Commentary on the Letters of John: An Intra-Jewish Approach* (Eugene, OR: Pickwick, 2013), 4. Gaius appears to be one of John's converts and a shepherd in the church, possibly the same church John addresses in 1 John 2. Mark Fairchild, *Christian Origins in Ephesus & Asia Minor*, 130-131.

172. According to Stott, the three epistles of John and the Gospel of John were all authored by the same person—John the apostle. John Stott, *The Letters of John*, 29-30, 44. While other scholars are reluctant to attribute 3 John (as well as 1 and 2 John) to the son of Zebedee, I agree with Stott and others. Daniel Akin states that "evidence both internal and external favors the view that the apostle John is the author of the three letters Christian tradition has attributed to him." Akin goes on to argue that the writing style is strikingly similar to the Fourth Gospel and the early church was unanimous in its verdict that John the apostle wrote the Gospel of John. Daniel Akin, *1, 2, 3 John*, NAC (Nashville, TN: Broadman & Holman, 2001), 26-27. See also Gary Burge, *Letters of John, The NIV Application Commentary* (Grand Rapids, MI: Zondervan, 1996), 38-40 and my notes in the "John Writes 1 John" box.

173. According to Keener, 3 John is a "letter of recommendation" for Demetrius, a traveling worker. Craig Keener, *The IVP Bible Background Commentary: New Testament*, 718. That Demetrius was the carrier of the letter is probable. F.F. Bruce, *The Epistles of John* (Grand Rapids, MI: Eerdmans, 1979), 154; John Stott, *The Letters of John*, 233. Demetrius had a good testimony from everyone. John may have wanted him to confront Diotrephes as it seems that Gaius was too meek to do so. Mark Fairchild, *Christian Origins in Ephesus & Asia Minor*, 132-133.

came and testified about your truth, even as you walk in truth. I have no greater joy than this: to hear about my children walking in truth.

Beloved, you do a faithful work in whatever you accomplish for those who are brothers and strangers. They have testified about your love before the assembly. You will do well to send them forward on their journey in a way worthy of God, because for the sake of the Name they went out, taking nothing from the Gentiles. We therefore ought to receive such, that we may be fellow workers for the truth.

I wrote to the assembly, but Diotrephes, who loves to be first among them, doesn't accept what we say. Therefore if I come, I will call attention to his deeds which he does, unjustly accusing us with wicked words. Not content with this, neither does he himself receive the brothers, and those who would, he forbids and throws out of the assembly.

Beloved, don't imitate that which is evil, but that which is good. He who does good is of God. He who does evil hasn't seen God. Demetrius has the testimony of all, and of the truth itself; yes, we also testify, and you know that our testimony is true.

I had many things to write to you, but I am unwilling to write to you with ink and pen; but I hope to see you soon. Then we will speak face to face. Peace be to you. The friends greet you. Greet the friends by name.

* * *

Paul remains imprisoned in Rome. Priscilla and Aquila labor in Ephesus, trying to save the assembly there from the constant threat of heresy.[174] The false teachers appear to have a winning edge and contribute to a serious departure from Paul's ministry in the Roman province of Asia.[175]

174. We know the false teachers were still in Ephesus from 2 Timothy 4:19.

175. *The ESV Study Bible*, 2339; Donald Guthrie, *The Pastoral Epistles*, 147. The term "all" in antiquity often means "most," as it does in 2 Timothy 1:15 (ESV) according to the context. Craig Keener, *The IVP Bible Background Commentary: New Testament*, 618. Bruce calls this "a wholesale defection from loyalty to him [Paul] in proconsular Asia." F.F. Bruce, *Paul: Apostle of the Heart Set Free*, 445. The defection was serious and may have been due to Paul's arrest. Ben Witherington III, *Letters and Homilies for Hellenized Christians*, 1:323. However, not everyone departed from Paul (the loyal Onesiphorus and his household were among those who stood with him, not fearing his chains—2 Timothy 1:16). Timothy, of course, didn't forsake the apostle either. He was in or near Ephesus at the time. Philip Towner, *The Letters to Timothy and Titus*, 480-481. But key people failed to support Paul during his imprisonment and many were departing from the truth. For this

This you know, that all who are in Asia turned away from me.... (2 Timothy 1:15)

Because Paul is imprisoned, many Christians no longer want to associate with him out of fear that they too will be imprisoned. Two brothers in Christ whom Paul once trusted—Phygelus and Hermogenes—turn away from him.[176] Demas also forsakes Paul. Because of his love for the world, Demas no longer supports the apostle and returns to Thessalonica.[177] Paul is afflicted with piercing loneliness, yet he knows the Lord is still with him.[178]

A handful of workers have remained true to the gospel and to Paul. The apostle sends a man named Crescens to Galatia[179] and Titus to Dalmatia[180] to work with the Christians there. He also sends Tychicus and Onesiphorus back to Ephesus to help Priscilla and Aquila. Paul's preliminary hearing (*prima actio*) occurs, but no one comes to support him.[181] While the apostle feels deserted,[182] he is not embittered: "May it not be held against them," he writes to Timothy.[183]

The trial moves forward. Upon hearing the news, Luke travels to Rome and visits Paul in prison. Some of the survivors from Nero's persecution of the Roman ekklesia also visit Paul to check on him, including Eubulus, Pudens, Linus, and Claudia.[184] Paul is burdened with the future of the assemblies, and he senses that his time of departure is drawing near. But he is fully prepared to meet his Lord.

---

reason, Paul exhorts Timothy to "hold fast the pattern of sound words" (2 Timothy 1:13, NKJV) and "guard the good deposit" (2 Timothy 1:14, NIV). John Stott, *The Message of 2 Timothy,* 45. The Roman province of Asia was a source of great trouble for Paul about a decade earlier (2 Corinthians 1:8).

176. 2 Timothy 1:15.

177. 2 Timothy 4:10.

178. Stott draws some fascinating parallels between Jesus' last days and Paul's last days with respect to feeling deserted. Compare Mark 14:50 and John 16:32 with 2 Timothy 4:16-17. John Stott, *The Message of 2 Timothy*, 123.

179. Galatia was likely the same region where Paul and Barnabas planted churches and to whom "Galatians" was written. Craig Keener, *The IVP Bible Background Commentary: New Testament*, 624.

180. Dalmatia was near Nicopolis. Craig Keener, *The IVP Bible Background Commentary: New Testament*, 623. Some believe it was identical with Illyricum. J.D. Douglas, et al., eds., *New Bible Dictionary*, 259.

181. 2 Timothy 4:16. F.F. Bruce, *Paul: Apostle of the Heart Set Free*, 446; Philip Towner, *The Letters to Timothy and Titus*, 637-638.

182. John Stott, *The Message of 2 Timothy*, 117.

183. See Donald Guthrie, *The Pastoral Epistles*, 188.

184. The last three are Latin names. This could suggest that the faith was "making inroads into the new sectors of Roman society." Craig Keener, *The IVP Bible Background Commentary: New Testament*, 624.

For I am already being offered, and the time of my departure has come. I have fought the good fight. I have finished the course. I have kept the faith. From now on, the crown of righteousness is stored up for me, which the Lord, the righteous judge, will give to me on that day; and not to me only, but also to all those who have loved his appearing. (2 Timothy 4:6-8)

Paul longs to see Timothy and prays for him day and night.[185] He desires to encourage his apprentice in his calling and exhort him to stay strong and optimistic in the face of detractors. He also wants to warn Timothy of the coming apostasy (falling away) and remind him of those intangible things that he (Paul) deposited in him over the years.

The false teachers continue to plague the ekklesias in Roman Asia and Crete.[186] Their teachings have even become more developed. Because Paul's opponents have spread throughout Asia, the situation is now worse than when he penned his first letter to Timothy.[187] While Paul previously excommunicated Hymenaeus, his sphere of activity continues in Ephesus.[188] Hymenaeus and a man named Philetus are subverting the faith of some of the believers, teaching that the future resurrection of the dead has already passed.[189]

PAUL WRITES 2 TIMOTHY

Year: A.D. 67[190]

185. 2 Timothy 1:3-4.

186. The false teachers are referenced in 1 Timothy 1:7; 4:3; Titus 1:10, 15; 2 Timothy 3:6-7. See also Gerald Hawthorne, et al., eds., *Dictionary of Paul and His Letters*, 662-663.

187. Craig Keener, *The IVP Bible Background Commentary: New Testament*, 616.

188. Hymenaeus and Philetus were excommunicated previously (1 Timothy 1:20), but they "still retained a pervasive influence and probably a significant following." Craig Keener, *The IVP Bible Background Commentary: New Testament,* 619.

189. 2 Timothy 2:17-18. Like some of the Corinthians (1 Corinthians 15:12), Hymenaeus and Philetus were denying that the resurrection was a physical reality and taught it was a spiritual experience instead. Donald Guthrie, *The Pastoral Epistles*, 161. A future, physical resurrection of the body held no appeal to the Greek mind, thus the idea of a spiritual resurrection in Christ was more palatable to Greek tastes and culture. Craig Keener, *The IVP Bible Background Commentary: New Testament*, 619.

190. Gerald Hawthorne, et al., eds., *Dictionary of Paul and His Letters*, 662; Samuel Ngewa, *1 & 2 Timothy and Titus*, ABC (Grand Rapids, MI: Zondervan/HippoBooks, 2009), 3; Herbert Lockyer, ed., *Nelson's Illustrated Bible Dictionary*, 227. 2 Timothy was "probably written around A.D. 67." *The NKJV Study Bible,*

From: Rome[191]

To: Timothy in Ephesus

Author: Paul[192]

Contextual Summary: "2 Timothy is the testament of a dying man."[193] A lonely Paul encourages Timothy and reminds him about the perils and responsibilities of an apostolic worker. He exhorts Timothy, whom he calls "my dear son,"[194] to train others who are called to God's work, just as he (Paul) trained Timothy.[195]

He gives his apprentice instructions on how to deal with those who have turned away from the truth. He exhorts Timothy to warn God's people against quarreling over words and engaging with the false teachers, as such activities are fruitless.[196]

Paul exhorts Timothy to care for the household of God, encourages him to endure suffering, charges him to be faithful to his calling, and warns him of what lies ahead. The apostle entrusts Timothy with a "good treasure" (or "good deposit") which is to be guarded.[197] He encourages his apprentice to kindle afresh the gift of God that Paul imparted to him through the laying on of his hands.

1832. Some scholars date the book earlier. For an overview of 2 Timothy, see Clinton Arnold, ed., *Zondervan Illustrated Bible Backgrounds Commentary*, 3:479-497; David deSilva, *An Introduction to the New Testament*, chap. 19; N.T. Wright and Michael Bird, *The New Testament in Its World*, 23.

191. Ben Witherington III, *Letters and Homilies for Hellenized Christians*, 1:66.

192. The abundance of personal notes strongly suggests Pauline authorship. Craig Keener, *The IVP Bible Background Commentary: New Testament*, 617; Ben Witherington III, *Letters and Homilies for Hellenized Christians*, 1:378. See also my notes in the "Paul Writes 1 Timothy" box.

193. William Ramsay, *St. Paul the Traveler and Roman Citizen*, 284.

194. 2 Timothy 1:2, NLT. In 1 Corinthians 4:17, Paul calls Timothy his "beloved and faithful child in the Lord."

195. 2 Timothy 2:2. The NIV uses "reliable people." The ESV and NKJV have "faithful men." Workers who steward the things of God must be faithful (1 Corinthians 4:1).

196. 2 Timothy 2:14-17, 23.

197. 2 Timothy 1:12-14; James Aageson, *After Paul*, 45.

The apostle exhorts Timothy to be diligent to live as a man approved of God. This includes shunning youthful passions. (Timothy is probably still in his thirties.[198]) Paul names some of the people who have turned away from the gospel, as well as from him.

As the letter closes, Paul testifies that he has run the race of Christian service and discipleship well, and he has a clear conscience. He is not ashamed of his imprisonment for preaching the gospel, and he is ready to be offered up to his Lord in death.

Anticipating Timothy's travel to Rome, Paul warns him against Alexander the metalworker, a man who caused Paul great harm. Alexander may do the same to Timothy by bringing false charges against the younger worker.[199]

Paul longs to see Timothy and closes the letter by asking him to visit before winter. He requests that he bring Mark with him. Paul asks for his winter cloak (indicating that it's cold where he is), his scrolls and parchments, all of which Paul left behind in Troas.[200]

The apostle sends greetings to Priscilla and Aquila and the household of Onesiphorus.[201] He sends greetings to Timothy from Eubulus, Pudens, Linus, Claudia, and the rest of the ekklesia in Rome. Luke scribes the letter.[202]

198. John Stott, *The Message of 2 Timothy*, 19; Ben Witherington III, *Letters and Homilies for Hellenized Christians*, 1:74; 1 Timothy 4:12.

199. 2 Timothy 4:14. Philip Towner, *The Letters to Timothy and Titus*, 633-634; John Stott, *The Message of 2 Timothy*, 122. Alexander was in the vicinity since Paul told Timothy to stay away from him. According to 2 Timothy 4:15, Alexander violently opposed Paul's message. See also Ben Witherington III, *Letters and Homilies for Hellenized Christians*, 1:379-380.

200. 2 Timothy 4:13. Regarding the parchments, since Paul was a leatherworker, he could have used animal skins to keep notes or copies of his letters. Ben Witherington III, *Letters and Homilies for Hellenized Christians*, 1:378-379.

201. Because Onesiphorus had a household, he was probably a man of means. Philip Towner, *The Letters to Timothy and Titus*, 482. The fact that Onesiphorus' household is mentioned, rather than Onesiphorus himself, has caused some to speculate that he was dead and his visit to Paul (who was regarded a serious criminal) was what got him killed. Ben Witherington III, *Letters and Homilies for Hellenized Christians*, 1:325. Others like Stott believe this is an unwarranted assumption. It's possible that Onesiphorus was still in Rome while his household was at home in Ephesus. John Stott, *The Message of 2 Timothy*, 45-46; Philip Towner, *The Letters to Timothy and Titus*, 482-484.

202. F.F. Bruce, *Paul: Apostle of the Heart Set Free*, 443. Luke was the only real co-worker and companion who stayed with Paul during this time (2 Timothy 4:11). Ben Witherington III, *Letters and Homilies for*

2 Timothy

Paul, an apostle of Jesus Christ through the will of God, according to the promise of the life which is in Christ Jesus, to Timothy, my beloved child: Grace, mercy, and peace, from God the Father and Christ Jesus our Lord.

I thank God, whom I serve as my forefathers did, with a pure conscience. How unceasing is my memory of you in my petitions, night and day longing to see you, remembering your tears, that I may be filled with joy; having been reminded of the sincere faith that is in you, which lived first in your grandmother Lois, and your mother Eunice, and, I am persuaded, in you also.

For this cause, I remind you that you should stir up the gift of God which is in you through the laying on of my hands. For God didn't give us a spirit of fear, but of power, love, and self-control.

Therefore don't be ashamed of the testimony of our Lord, nor of me his prisoner; but endure hardship for the Good News according to the power of God, who saved us and called us with a holy calling, not according to our works, but according to his own purpose and grace, which was given to us in Christ Jesus before times eternal, but has now been revealed by the appearing of our Savior, Christ Jesus, who abolished death, and brought life and immortality to light through the Good News.

For this I was appointed as a preacher, an apostle, and a teacher of the Gentiles. For this cause I also suffer these things. Yet I am not ashamed, for I know him whom I have believed, and I am persuaded that he is able to guard that which I have committed to him against that day.

Hold the pattern of sound words which you have heard from me, in faith and love which is in Christ Jesus. That good thing which was committed to you, guard through the Holy Spirit who dwells in us.

This you know, that all who are in Asia turned away from me, of whom are Phygelus and Hermogenes. May the Lord grant mercy to the house of Onesiphorus, for he often refreshed me, and was not ashamed of my chain, but when he was in Rome, he sought me diligently

---

Hellenized Christians, 1:378; Richard Longenecker, *The Ministry and Message of Paul*, 86. Paul's second letter to Timothy is his last extant epistle. For a scholarly discussion on Paul and his entire catalog of surviving letters, see N.T. Wright, *Interpreting Paul: Essays on the Apostle and His Letters* (Grand Rapids, MI: Zondervan, 2020).

and found me (the Lord grant to him to find the Lord's mercy in that day); and in how many things he served at Ephesus, you know very well.

You therefore, my child, be strengthened in the grace that is in Christ Jesus. The things which you have heard from me among many witnesses, commit the same things to faithful men, who will be able to teach others also. You therefore must endure hardship as a good soldier of Christ Jesus. No soldier on duty entangles himself in the affairs of life, that he may please him who enrolled him as a soldier. Also, if anyone competes in athletics, he isn't crowned unless he has competed by the rules. The farmer who labors must be the first to get a share of the crops. Consider what I say, and may the Lord give you understanding in all things.

Remember Jesus Christ, risen from the dead, of the offspring[a] of David, according to my Good News, in which I suffer hardship to the point of chains as a criminal. But God's word isn't chained. Therefore I endure all things for the chosen ones' sake, that they also may obtain the salvation which is in Christ Jesus with eternal glory. This saying is trustworthy: "For if we died with him, we will also live with him. If we endure, we will also reign with him. If we deny him, he also will deny us. If we are faithless, he remains faithful; for he can't deny himself." Remind them of these things, charging them in the sight of the Lord, that they don't argue about words, to no profit, to the subverting of those who hear.

Give diligence to present yourself approved by God, a workman who doesn't need to be ashamed, properly handling the Word of Truth. But shun empty chatter, for it will go further in ungodliness, and those words will consume like gangrene, of whom is Hymenaeus and Philetus: men who have erred concerning the truth, saying that the resurrection is already past, and overthrowing the faith of some.

However God's firm foundation stands, having this seal, "The Lord knows those who are his," Numbers 16:5 and, "Let every one who names the name of the Lord[b] depart from unrighteousness." Now in a large house there are not only vessels of gold and of silver, but also of wood and of clay. Some are for honor, and some for dishonor. If anyone therefore purges himself from these, he will be a vessel for honor, sanctified, and suitable for the master's use, prepared for every good work.

Flee from youthful lusts; but pursue righteousness, faith, love, and peace with those who call on the Lord out of a pure heart. But refuse foolish and ignorant questionings, knowing that they generate strife. The Lord's servant must not quarrel, but be gentle toward all, able to teach, patient, in gentleness correcting those who oppose him: perhaps God may give them repentance leading to a full knowledge of the truth, and they may recover themselves out of the devil's snare, having been taken captive by him to his will.

But know this: that in the last days, grievous times will come. For men will be lovers of self, lovers of money, boastful, arrogant, blasphemers, disobedient to parents, unthankful, unholy, without natural affection, unforgiving, slanderers, without self-control, fierce, not lovers of good, traitors, headstrong, conceited, lovers of pleasure rather than lovers of God, holding a form of godliness, but having denied its power.

Turn away from these, also. For some of these are people who creep into houses and take captive gullible women loaded down with sins, led away by various lusts, always learning, and never able to come to the knowledge of the truth. Even as Jannes and Jambres opposed Moses, so these also oppose the truth, men corrupted in mind, who concerning the faith are rejected. But they will proceed no further. For their folly will be evident to all men, as theirs also came to be. But you followed my teaching, conduct, purpose, faith, patience, love, steadfastness, persecutions, and sufferings: those things that happened to me at Antioch, Iconium, and Lystra.

I endured those persecutions. The Lord delivered me out of them all. Yes, and all who desire to live godly in Christ Jesus will suffer persecution. But evil men and impostors will grow worse and worse, deceiving and being deceived. But you remain in the things which you have learned and have been assured of, knowing from whom you have learned them. From infancy, you have known the holy Scriptures which are able to make you wise for salvation through faith, which is in Christ Jesus. Every Scripture is God-breathed and[c] profitable for teaching, for reproof, for correction, and for instruction in righteousness, that each person who belongs to God may be complete, thoroughly equipped for every good work.

I command you therefore before God and the Lord Jesus Christ, who will judge the living and the dead at his appearing and his Kingdom: preach the word; be urgent in season and out of season; reprove, rebuke, and exhort with all patience and teaching. For the time will come when they will not listen to the sound doctrine, but having itching ears, will heap up for themselves teachers after their own lusts, and will turn away their ears from the truth, and turn away to fables. But you be sober in all things, suffer hardship, do the work of an evangelist, and fulfill your ministry.

For I am already being offered, and the time of my departure has come. I have fought the good fight. I have finished the course. I have kept the faith. From now on, the crown of righteousness is stored up for me, which the Lord, the righteous judge, will give to me on that day; and not to me only, but also to all those who have loved his appearing.

Be diligent to come to me soon, for Demas left me, having loved this present world, and went to Thessalonica; Crescens to Galatia; and Titus to Dalmatia. Only Luke is with me. Take Mark, and bring him with you, for he is useful to me for service. But I sent Tychicus to Ephesus. Bring the cloak that I left at Troas with Carpus when you come, and the books, especially the parchments. Alexander, the coppersmith, did much evil to me. The Lord will repay him according to his deeds, of whom you also must beware; for he greatly opposed our words.

At my first defense, no one came to help me, but all left me. May it not be held against them. But the Lord stood by me and strengthened me, that through me the message might be fully proclaimed, and that all the Gentiles might hear. So I was delivered out of the mouth of the lion. And the Lord will deliver me from every evil work, and will preserve me for his heavenly Kingdom. To him be the glory forever and ever. Amen.

Greet Prisca and Aquila, and the house of Onesiphorus. Erastus remained at Corinth, but I left Trophimus at Miletus sick. Be diligent to come before winter. Eubulus salutes you, as do Pudens, Linus, Claudia, and all the brothers. The Lord Jesus Christ be with your spirit. Grace be with you. Amen.

a. 2:8 or, seed.
b. 2:19 TR reads "Christ" instead of "the Lord."
c. 3:16 or, Every writing inspired by God is.

Crisis in the Kingdom Communities of the Dispersion A.D. 68

False teachers have subtly infiltrated the dispersed Jewish ekklesias, spreading a heretical doctrine that perverts God's grace into license to sin. These unsound teachers have successfully disguised themselves as true believers, even managing to partake of the Lord's Supper with the assemblies.[203] The false teachers have these qualities:

- They distort the gospel by advocating sexual license under the banner of God's grace.
- They are "dreamers," seeing "visions" that originate from themselves rather than from God.
- They slander celestial beings, and in so doing, despise the Law of Moses because it was delivered by heavenly beings.
- They indulge their own needs when eating the Lord's Supper.
- They are grumblers and malcontents, pursuing their own will rather than God's.
- They are arrogant and employ flattery to take advantage of the Lord's people.
- They are scoffers, laughing at moral purity and mocking divine judgment.
- They are devoid of the Holy Spirit and provoke divisions within the believing communities.

Jude (also known as Judah or Judas), the half-brother of Jesus and brother to James in the church of Jerusalem,[204] is grieved by the outbreak of the libertine teachers and their corrupting influence on the churches. These self-indulgent teachers are antagonistic to God's moral will, insubordinate to spiritual authority, and peddle a perverted view of freedom.[205] So Jude pens an epistle to address the crisis.

JUDE WRITES HIS LETTER (JUDE)

Year: A.D. 68[206]

---

203. Jude describes the Lord's Supper as the "love (*agape*) feast" (Jude 12).

204. Mark 6:3; Matthew 13:55. Ben Witherington III, *The New Testament Story*, 57; *Invitation to the New Testament*, 294-298; *Letters and Homilies for Hellenized Christians*, 3:560-567; David deSilva, *An Introduction to the New Testament*, 767,

205. Michael Green, *2 Peter and Jude*, TNTC (Grand Rapids, MI: Eerdmans, 1987), 55.

206. Scholars disagree on the dating. It's impossible to be confident about it. See Jonathan Bernier, *Rethinking the Dates of the New Testament*, 230-234. Witherington gives reasons to believe Jude had to be

From: Unknown[207]

To: The dispersed Jewish Christian congregations in and outside Palestine, most of which were founded by the other apostles[208]

Author: Jude[209]

Contextual Summary: Jude was eager to draft a letter to believers in Palestine about the salvation they all share. However, he changed his topic and tone when he learned that false teachers had entered the scene and were creating problems in the churches.[210]

---

written before A.D. 70. Ben Witherington III, *Letters and Homilies for Hellenized Christians*, 3:577. Others say it was written between A.D. 66 and 70. M.G. Easton, *Illustrated Bible Dictionary and Treasury of Biblical History, Biography, Geography, Doctrine, and Literature* (New York, NY: Harper & Brothers, 1893), 398; Keith Brooks, *Summarized Bible: Complete Summary of the New Testament*, Logos edition (Bellingham, WA: Logos Bible Software, 2009), 88. Given the brand of false teaching Jude was combating in the letter and its parallels with 2 Peter, A.D. 68 is a reasonable estimate. Schreiner agrees that a date in the 60s is most likely. Thomas Schreiner, *1, 2 Peter, Jude*, NAC (Nashville, TN: Broadman & Holman Publishers, 2003), 276, 409. Some scholars believe the letter is contemporaneous with the letters of Paul or it was written at least before A.D. 80. David deSilva, *An Introduction to the New Testament*, 767-769. Green, on the other hand, indicates the epistle may have been written before A.D. 65. Michael Green, *2 Peter and Jude*, 56.

207. There is no scholarly consensus on the exact location where the letter of Jude was written. Scholars have suggested Palestine, Syria, Asia Minor, and Egypt.

208. Some think Jude was written to Greek-speaking congregations possibly in the territory of Israel, particularly Galilee, the Decapolis, and the coastal plains. Ben Witherington III, *Letters and Homilies for Hellenized Christians*, 3:577; David deSilva, *An Introduction to the New Testament*, 769, 771. The emphasis Jude gives to Jewish traditions is often taken to indicate a Jewish audience, but it's really just a sign of the author's own thought world. It is quite possible that the audience was composed of both Jews and Gentiles.

209. "We conclude, then, that in Jude 1 the author intends to identify himself as that Jude who is listed as the third or fourth of the brothers of Jesus, James always being listed first." Peter Davids, *The Letters of 2 Peter and Jude*, PNTC (Grand Rapids, MI: Eerdmans, 2006), 36, Logos edition. On the authenticity of the letter, see David deSilva, *The Jewish Teachers of Jesus, James, and Jude* (Oxford: Oxford University Press, 2012), 45-54; *An Introduction to the New Testament*, 767-769. "The Epistle of Jude is a vigorous and pointed piece of writing. Scholars have often remarked that the Greek is quite good and that Jude used imagery effectively." Thomas Schreiner, *1, 2 Peter, Jude*, 419.

210. Gary Burge, et al., *The New Testament in Antiquity*, 406.

With just 25 verses, Jude is the shortest book in the New Testament. The letter is also the only New Testament epistle that directly quotes from the non-canonical Jewish work known as the book of Enoch.[211]

A major theme is the strong condemnation of false teachers who have "crept in unnoticed" and are perverting the grace of God. The letter employs vivid and colorful language, using examples from nature (clouds, trees, waves) and imagery of wandering stars and blackest darkness to describe the corrupt teachers.

The key exhortation in verse 3 is "to contend for the faith that was once for all entrusted to God's holy people." Following the salutation and occasion for writing, Jude discusses the condemnation of the ungodly and he calls the godly to persevere.

Jude sounds the alarm that "ungodly people" or false teachers have already infiltrated the church, leading people astray. Due to its brevity, references, themes, and vivid language, the letter of Jude stands out as a unique book in the New Testament.

Jude

Jude,[a] a servant of Jesus Christ, and brother of James, to those who are called, sanctified by God the Father, and kept for Jesus Christ: May mercy, peace, and love be multiplied to you.

Beloved, while I was very eager to write to you about our common salvation, I was constrained to write to you exhorting you to contend earnestly for the faith which was once for all delivered to the saints. For there are certain men who crept in secretly, even those who were long ago written about for this condemnation: ungodly men, turning the grace of our God into indecency, and denying our only Master, God, and Lord, Jesus Christ.

Now I desire to remind you, though you already know this, that the Lord, having saved a people out of the land of Egypt, afterward destroyed those who didn't believe. Angels who didn't keep their first domain, but deserted their own dwelling place, he has kept in everlasting bonds under darkness for the judgment of the great day.

---

211. Jude 14-15.

Even as Sodom and Gomorrah and the cities around them, having in the same way as these given themselves over to sexual immorality and gone after strange flesh, are shown as an example, suffering the punishment of eternal fire.

Yet in the same way, these also in their dreaming defile the flesh, despise authority, and slander celestial beings. But Michael, the archangel, when contending with the devil and arguing about the body of Moses, dared not bring against him an abusive condemnation, but said, "May the Lord rebuke you!"

But these speak evil of whatever things they don't know. They are destroyed in these things that they understand naturally, like the creatures without reason. Woe to them! For they went in the way of Cain, and ran riotously in the error of Balaam for hire, and perished in Korah's rebellion.

These are hidden rocky reefs in your love feasts when they feast with you, shepherds who without fear feed themselves; clouds without water, carried along by winds; autumn trees without fruit, twice dead, plucked up by the roots; wild waves of the sea, foaming out their own shame; wandering stars, for whom the blackness of darkness has been reserved forever.

About these also Enoch, the seventh from Adam, prophesied, saying, "Behold,[b] the Lord came with ten thousands of his holy ones, to execute judgment on all, and to convict all the ungodly of all their works of ungodliness which they have done in an ungodly way, and of all the hard things which ungodly sinners have spoken against him." These are murmurers and complainers, walking after their lusts—and their mouth speaks proud things—showing respect of persons to gain advantage.

But you, beloved, remember the words which have been spoken before by the apostles of our Lord Jesus Christ. They said to you, "In the last time there will be mockers, walking after their own ungodly lusts." These are those who cause divisions and are sensual, not having the Spirit.

But you, beloved, keep building up yourselves on your most holy faith, praying in the Holy Spirit. Keep yourselves in God's love, looking for the mercy of our Lord Jesus Christ to eternal life. On some have compassion, making a distinction, and some save, snatching them out of the fire with fear, hating even the clothing stained by the flesh.

Now to him who is able to keep them[c] from stumbling, and to present you faultless before the presence of his glory in great joy, to God our Savior, who alone is wise, be glory and majesty, dominion and power, both now and forever. Amen.

a. 1:1 or, Judah.
b. 1:14 "Behold," from "ἰδοὺ," means look at, take notice, observe, see, or gaze at. It is often used as an interjection.
c. 1:24 TR and NU read "you."

* * *

Peter knows the end of his time on earth is near. He also sees a need to address the false teachers infecting the ekklesias in the Diaspora. He has it on his heart to remind the Christians about the truths of Jesus Christ. He wants to encourage them to walk steadfastly in the Lord and warn them about the false teachers. Peter possesses a copy of Jude's letter, whose description of the false teachers is vivid and accurate.[212] He is burdened about the problem and decides to confront it in a letter of his own.

PETER WRITES 2 PETER

Year: A.D. 68[213]

From: Rome[214]

To: The kingdom communities in Western Anatolia and beyond[215]

212. When speaking about the false teachers, Peter draws heavily from Jude's epistle (compare Jude 4 through 18 with 2 Peter 2:1 through 3:3). He also enlarges upon it.

213. N.T. Wright, *Paul: A Biography*, 169; Michael Green, *2 Peter and Jude*, 16-17. For details on alternative datings of 2 Peter, see Jonathan Bernier, *Rethinking the Dates of the New Testament*, 224-229. According to Guthrie, the letter wasn't written long after 1 Peter. Donald Guthrie, *New Testament Introduction*, 844. Other scholars suggest it had to be written between A.D. 65 and 68. *The NIV Study Bible*, 2204. Witherington believes 2 Peter is one of the latest documents in the New Testament. Ben Witherington III, *The New Testament Story*, 67.

214. For this conjecture, see N.T. Wright and Michael Bird, *The New Testament in Its World*, 765. Witherington agrees saying, "there is no location more likely for the composition of 2 Peter than the growing church in Rome…." Ben Witherington III, *Invitation to the New Testament*, 385.

215. Based on 2 Peter 3:1, some scholars believe the letter was written to the same audience as that of 1 Peter. Michael Green, *2 Peter and Jude*, 40; Donald Guthrie, *New Testament Introduction*, 842; *The NKJV Study*

Author: Peter[216]

Contextual Summary: Some Christian teachers have been flirting with Greek thought and promoting a mixture of Christian faith with Greek philosophy. This has led them to deny the second coming of Christ and believe that bodily sins are irrelevant.

Peter reminds the churches of the authentic apostolic teaching because false doctrines are endangering the purity of their faith. He encourages the believers to cultivate their spiritual lives and warns about the false teachers and their destructive heresies. He also exposes the true motives of these teachers.

Peter does all this by employing language from Jude's letter (nineteen of Jude's twenty-five verses appear in 2 Peter).[217] He also adds substantial arguments of his own to explain the alleged "delay" of the Lord's return. The apostle informs the assemblies

---

Bible, 1905; Paul Barnett, *Bethlehem to Patmos,* 218. Witherington states that 1 Peter 3:1 "is most naturally taken as an allusion to 1 Peter." Ben Witherington III, *Invitation to the New Testament,* 341. Witherington also believes it was an encyclical letter written to all the existing churches in the empire, even the assemblies that Paul founded. Ben Witherington III, *Invitation to the New Testament,* 382, 385, 387. See also N.T. Wright and Michael Bird, *The New Testament in Its World,* 767-768. 2 Peter 3:15-16 makes plain that Peter's audience was familiar with Paul's letters.

216. Scholars debate Peter's authorship of the letter. Keener says the letter "is one of the most disputed letters in the New Testament." Craig Keener, *The IVP Bible Background Commentary: New Testament,* 698-699. Some believe someone like Mark wrote down Peter's concerns in the epistle. For the style of Asiatic Greek that marks the letter, see Ben Witherington III, *Invitation to the New Testament,* 382. For the problems associated with the authorship of 2 Peter, see I. Howard Marshall, et al., *Exploring the New Testament,* 2:329-332. Barton affirms its authenticity. Bruce Barton, *1 Peter, 2 Peter, Jude* (Wheaton, IL: Tyndale House Publishing, 1995), 150. Other scholars confirm, saying, "no compelling arguments have been put forward against the authenticity of 2 Peter, and doubts that have arisen have reasonable explanations." Gary Burge, et al., *The New Testament in Antiquity,* 406.

217. Ben Witherington III, *Letters and Homilies for Hellenized Christians,* 3:569. Most scholars believe 2 Peter incorporated parts of Jude, making it an expansion of Jude's epistle. Jonathan Bernier, *Rethinking the Dates of the New Testament,* 230-231; Ben Witherington III, *Invitation to the New Testament,* 380-381; David deSilva, *An Introduction to the New Testament,* 782-783; Thomas Schreiner, *1, 2 Peter, Jude,* 418-419. One of the grounds for disputing Peter's authorship is that 2 Peter uses much of Jude. But as other scholars have argued, this isn't proof that the letter isn't Petrine.

that his time on earth is coming to a close.[218] He ends his letter by commending Paul's letters, referring to them as "Scripture."[219]

2 Peter

Simon Peter, a servant and apostle of Jesus Christ, to those who have obtained a like precious faith with us in the righteousness of our God and Savior, Jesus Christ: Grace to you and peace be multiplied in the knowledge of God and of Jesus our Lord, seeing that his divine power has granted to us all things that pertain to life and godliness, through the knowledge of him who called us by his own glory and virtue, by which he has granted to us his precious and exceedingly great promises; that through these you may become partakers of the divine nature, having escaped from the corruption that is in the world by lust.

Yes, and for this very cause adding on your part all diligence, in your faith supply moral excellence; and in moral excellence, knowledge; and in knowledge, self-control; and in self-control perseverance; and in perseverance godliness; and in godliness brotherly affection; and in brotherly affection, love. For if these things are yours and abound, they make you to not be idle or unfruitful in the knowledge of our Lord Jesus Christ.

For he who lacks these things is blind, seeing only what is near, having forgotten the cleansing from his old sins. Therefore, brothers,[ª] be more diligent to make your calling and election sure. For if you do these things, you will never stumble. For thus you will be richly supplied with the entrance into the eternal Kingdom of our Lord and Savior, Jesus Christ.

Therefore I will not be negligent to remind you of these things, though you know them, and are established in the present truth. I think it right, as long as I am in this tent, to stir

---

218. 2 Peter 1:13-15.

219. 2 Peter 3:15-16. This remark reveals that Peter still believed Paul's ministry was approved by God. Mark Fairchild, "The Last Apostle," documentary film. For an overview of Jude and 2 Peter, see David deSilva, *An Introduction to the New Testament*, chap. 23; N.T. Wright and Michael Bird, *The New Testament in Its World*, chaps. 31-32; Clinton Arnold, ed., *Zondervan Illustrated Bible Backgrounds Commentary*, 4:153-243.

you up by reminding you, knowing that the putting off of my tent comes swiftly, even as our Lord Jesus Christ made clear to me.

Yes, I will make every effort that you may always be able to remember these things even after my departure. For we didn't follow cunningly devised fables when we made known to you the power and coming of our Lord Jesus Christ, but we were eyewitnesses of his majesty. For he received from God the Father honor and glory when the voice came to him from the Majestic Glory, "This is my beloved Son, in whom I am well pleased." Matthew 17:5; Mark 9:7; Luke 9:35 We heard this voice come out of heaven when we were with him on the holy mountain.

We have the more sure word of prophecy; and you do well that you heed it, as to a lamp shining in a dark place, until the day dawns, and the morning star arises in your hearts: knowing this first, that no prophecy of Scripture is of private interpretation. For no prophecy ever came by the will of man: but holy men of God spoke, being moved by the Holy Spirit.

But false prophets also arose among the people, as false teachers will also be among you, who will secretly bring in destructive heresies, denying even the Master who bought them, bringing on themselves swift destruction. Many will follow their immoral[b] ways, and as a result, the way of the truth will be maligned. In covetousness they will exploit you with deceptive words: whose sentence now from of old doesn't linger, and their destruction will not slumber.

For if God didn't spare angels when they sinned, but cast them down to Tartarus,[c] and committed them to pits of darkness to be reserved for judgment; and didn't spare the ancient world, but preserved Noah with seven others, a preacher of righteousness, when he brought a flood on the world of the ungodly; and turning the cities of Sodom and Gomorrah into ashes, condemned them to destruction, having made them an example to those who would live in an ungodly way; and delivered righteous Lot, who was very distressed by the lustful life of the wicked (for that righteous man dwelling among them was tormented in his righteous soul from day to day with seeing and hearing lawless deeds): the Lord knows how to deliver the godly out of temptation and to keep the unrighteous under punishment for the day of judgment, but chiefly those who walk after the flesh in the lust of defilement and despise authority.

Daring, self-willed, they are not afraid to speak evil of dignitaries; whereas angels, though greater in might and power, don't bring a railing judgment against them before the Lord. But these, as unreasoning creatures, born natural animals to be taken and destroyed, speaking evil in matters about which they are ignorant, will in their destroying surely be destroyed, receiving the wages of unrighteousness; people who count it pleasure to revel in the daytime, spots and defects, reveling in their deceit while they feast with you; having eyes full of adultery, and who can't cease from sin; enticing unsettled souls; having a heart trained in greed; children of cursing; forsaking the right way, they went astray, having followed the way of Balaam the son of Beor, who loved the wages of wrongdoing; but he was rebuked for his own disobedience.

A mute donkey spoke with a man's voice and stopped the madness of the prophet. These are wells without water, clouds driven by a storm; for whom the blackness of darkness has been reserved forever. For, uttering great swelling words of emptiness, they entice in the lusts of the flesh, by licentiousness, those who are indeed escaping from those who live in error; promising them liberty, while they themselves are bondservants of corruption; for a man is brought into bondage by whoever overcomes him.

For if, after they have escaped the defilement of the world through the knowledge of the Lord and Savior Jesus Christ, they are again entangled in it and overcome, the last state has become worse for them than the first. For it would be better for them not to have known the way of righteousness, than after knowing it, to turn back from the holy commandment delivered to them. But it has happened to them according to the true proverb, "The dog turns to his own vomit again," Proverbs 26:11 and "the sow that has washed to wallowing in the mire."

This is now, beloved, the second letter that I have written to you; and in both of them I stir up your sincere mind by reminding you that you should remember the words which were spoken before by the holy prophets and the commandment of us, the apostles of the Lord and Savior: knowing this first, that in the last days mockers will come, walking after their own lusts and saying, "Where is the promise of his coming? For, from the day that the fathers fell asleep, all things continue as they were from the beginning of the creation."

For this they willfully forget that there were heavens from of old, and an earth formed out of water and amid water by the word of God, by which means the world that existed then, being overflowed with water, perished. But the heavens that exist now and the earth, by the same word have been stored up for fire, being reserved against the day of judgment and destruction of ungodly men.

But don't forget this one thing, beloved, that one day is with the Lord as a thousand years, and a thousand years as one day. The Lord is not slow concerning his promise, as some count slowness; but he is patient with us, not wishing that anyone should perish, but that all should come to repentance. But the day of the Lord will come as a thief in the night; in which the heavens will pass away with a great noise, and the elements will be dissolved with fervent heat, and the earth and the works that are in it will be burned up.

Therefore since all these things will be destroyed like this, what kind of people ought you to be in holy living and godliness, looking for and earnestly desiring the coming of the day of God, which will cause the burning heavens to be dissolved, and the elements will melt with fervent heat? But, according to his promise, we look for new heavens and a new earth, in which righteousness dwells.

Therefore, beloved, seeing that you look for these things, be diligent to be found in peace, without defect and blameless in his sight. Regard the patience of our Lord as salvation; even as our beloved brother Paul also, according to the wisdom given to him, wrote to you, as also in all of his letters, speaking in them of these things. In those, there are some things that are hard to understand, which the ignorant and unsettled twist, as they also do to the other Scriptures, to their own destruction.

You therefore, beloved, knowing these things beforehand, beware, lest being carried away with the error of the wicked, you fall from your own steadfastness. But grow in the grace and knowledge of our Lord and Savior Jesus Christ. To him be the glory both now and forever. Amen.

a. 1:10 The word for "brothers" here and where context allows may also be correctly translated "brothers and sisters" or "siblings."
b. 2:2 TR reads "destructive" instead of "immoral."
c. 2:4 Tartarus is another name for Hell.

Two Great Apostles Are Martyred

Paul finishes his long, arduous race and is beheaded in Rome during Nero's reign.[220] A great light goes out of the world. One of the greatest men who ever breathed oxygen goes

220. Some historians believe Paul was executed in the spring of A.D. 68. Herbert Lockyer, ed., *Nelson's Illustrated Bible Dictionary*, 227. Witherington believes Paul was beheaded under Nero one year earlier in A.D. 67. Ben Witherington III, *Letters and Homilies for Hellenized Christians*, 1:67. By contrast, other scholars date Paul's execution earlier, between A.D. 62 and 64. Robert Jewett, *A Chronology of Paul's Life*, 46. According

home. While heaven is richer, the earth has lost a remarkable man. Paul not only leaves an extraordinary legacy; he leaves behind men he poured himself into and trained to carry on God's work. Summing up the life of the apostle, one scholar writes,

> *I should not disagree with those who maintain that, apart from his Master, he was the greatest man who ever lived. Certainly he was the greatest man the Christian Church has ever known.*[221]

Another says,

> *Paul's greatest achievement, however, was that he fulfilled the vision of Jesus in taking the gospel of the kingdom of God to the Gentile nations.... Paul's gospel to the Gentiles was grace-based and circumcision-free, in defiance of the Pharisaic demands of the 'circumcision party' within the Jerusalem church.*[222]

The influence of Paul's ministry is difficult to capture.[223] As the message of Jesus spread after His resurrection until Paul's death, most people viewed the church as another Jewish sect. But within a generation after Paul's passing, the leaders of the Roman Empire recognized the Christian faith as a predominantly Gentile cult.[224] F.F. Bruce observes,

> *To begin with...there was very little contact between the Church and the Empire. Christianity was regarded as nothing more than a new sect of Judaism. The Jewish religion was a* religio licita, *religion permitted and tolerated by Roman law, and so long as Christianity was regarded as merely one more of the many Jewish sects, it attracted no particular attention. That*

---

to tradition, Paul was beheaded at Aquae Salviae near the third milestone along the Ostian Way south of Rome, below a pine tree. William Ramsay, *St. Paul the Traveler and Roman Citizen*, 286. See also Thomas Schmidt, *The Apostles After Acts*, chap 5.

221. F.F. Bruce, "The Early Church in the Roman Empire," *The Bible Student* 56 (Bangalore, India: March-April 1933): 30-32.

222. Paul Barnett, *Paul: Missionary of Jesus,* 203.

223. For thoughts on the greatness of Paul and his legacy, see Paul Barnett, *A Short Book about Paul*, chaps. 1 and 18.

224. F.F. Bruce, *Paul: Apostle of the Heart Set Free,* 17.

this state of affairs could not last indefinitely was quite clear for a number of reasons. One of these was the universal character of the Church's mission. The apostles were commanded by their Master to make disciples of all nations, and as soon as they began to go outside the Jewish pale with their message their distinctive character became evident. It was Paul who made it his life's work to evangelize the non-Jewish races of the Empire, and all ages have consented to call him the Apostle of the Gentiles par excellence.[225]

During his service to the Lord Jesus, Paul traveled to over forty cities.[226] He stewarded the mystery of God as a chosen instrument, a mystery that the Lord Jesus specially called and equipped him to unveil and proclaim.[227] With impressive humility, Paul sums up his own view of the ministry to which the Lord called him saying,

For I am the least of all the apostles. In fact, I'm not even worthy to be called an apostle after the way I persecuted God's church. But whatever I am now, it is all because God poured out his special favor on me–and not without results. For I have worked harder than any of the other apostles; yet it was not I but God who was working through me by his grace. (1 Corinthians 15:9-10, NLT)

225. F.F. Bruce, "The Early Church in the Roman Empire," *The Bible Student* 56 (Bangalore, India: March-April 1933): 30-32. For a discussion on the last days of Paul and his enduring contributions, see F.F. Bruce, *Paul: Apostle of the Heart Set Free,* chaps. 37-38.

226. Lars Kierspel, *Charts on the Life, Letters, and Theology of Paul,* 46-47. Kierspel leaves out Spain. So counting Spain, the full number of his calculation would be just over forty-four cities. See also Jerome Murphy-O'Connor, "On the Road and on the Sea with St. Paul," *Bible Review* 1:2, Summer 1985. Adding up all Paul's trips, he traveled an estimated 15,000 miles during his apostolic journeys. Of the total, 8,700 miles were by land, which leaves over 6,000 miles by sea. Barry Beitzel, *Lexham Geographic Commentary on Acts through Revelation,* 191; Eckhard Schnabel, *Paul the Missionary,* 122. For a detailed breakdown of Paul's travels, see James D.G. Dunn, *Beginning from Jerusalem,* 512-515. Despite the apostle's extensive travels, Malina writes, "perhaps 99.9 percent of the non-Israelite population of the regions Paul traveled fell far beyond the pale of Paul's outreach and were fully unaware of his activity." Bruce Malina, et al., *Social-Science Commentary on the Letters of Paul,* 7.

227. 1 Corinthians 2:1, NRSV; 4:1, ESV; Ephesians 3:1-11, ESV. For a powerful exposition on the mystery of God, see T. Austin-Sparks, *The Stewardship of the Mystery* (Shippensburg, PA: MercyPlace, 2002). For a detailed analysis of Paul's life and theology, including the world in which he lived, see N.T. Wright's massive two-volume work, *Paul and the Faithfulness of God.*

Around the time of Paul's death,[228] Peter, the great apostle, is taken and scourged. At his request, he is crucified upside down because he doesn't feel worthy to die in the same manner as his Lord.[229] Aside from being faithful to the bitter end, Peter's legacy includes a staggering reality—that a deeply flawed human being who made profound mistakes could be fully forgiven and restored to the point of being regarded as one of the most prominent apostles in the New Testament era.[230] Aristarchus from Thessalonica, Erastus from Corinth, Trophimus from Ephesus, Joseph Barsabbas from Jerusalem, and Ananias of Damascus are all allegedly martyred as well.[231]

As the hemorrhaging continues, more tragedy strikes. According to tradition, Andrew, the apostle and brother of Peter, actively ministers in Macedonia, Achaia, Parthia, and Scythia.[232] But his time on earth comes to an end, and he is crucified in Greece on an

228. "Peter died a martyr around A.D. 68." *The NKJV Study Bible,* 1905. See also Donald Guthrie, *New Testament Introduction,* 844. Some scholars date his death a few years earlier, but not after A.D. 68. *The NIV Study Bible,* 2204.

229. Thomas Schmidt, *The Apostles After Acts,* chap. 6. Note that Jesus predicted the kind of death Peter would have (John 21:18-19). According to Eusebius, Peter was crucified under Nero around the same time that Paul was executed. Eusebius, *The History of the Church,* 2.25. According to Keener, "this tradition seems early enough to be plausible." Personal correspondence with Craig Keener, 12/4/23. In contrast to Paul's means of execution, Peter was not a Roman citizen. Therefore, he suffered the death of a common criminal—death by crucifixion. Personal correspondence with Jeffrey Weima, 1/6/24. Jerome records a tradition that Peter was crucified on the same day Paul was beheaded, but this is disputed. Alan Bandy, *An Illustrated Guide to the Apostle Paul,* 177.

230. I explain and expand this point in episode #38, "Remember Peter: Rethinking the Love of Christ," on the Christ is All podcast at frankviola.org/thechristisallpodcast. Evangelical scholars are in agreement that the New Testament portrays Peter as "the most prominent of Jesus' twelve apostles." Herbert Lockyer, ed., *Nelson's Illustrated Bible Dictionary,* 824. Despite his mistakes, in the Gospels and elsewhere "a primacy among the apostles is ascribed to Peter...." J.D. Douglas, et al., eds., *New Bible Dictionary,* 917. This, of course, shouldn't be confused with the Catholic idea that Peter was the first pope. But Jesus gave Peter the keys of the kingdom (Matthew 16:17-19) to open God's realm to the Jews (Acts 2) and later to the Gentiles (Acts 10). Peter dominates the first part of the book of Acts, and Paul calls him one of the "pillars" of the church (Galatians 2:9, NIV).

231. John Foxe, *Foxe's Christian Martyrs of the World* (Westwood, NJ: Barbour and Company, 1985), 43-44. Again, these accounts are based on tradition, so one cannot evaluate their reliability.

232. Thomas Schmidt, *The Apostles After Acts,* 196. It is impossible to verify this tradition, and some historians dismiss it.

X-shaped cross.[233] Before his death, Andrew traveled throughout Greece and Asia Minor, crossing over to the northern shores of the Black Sea. His life was marked by the miraculous, including raising the dead.[234]

Mark has preached in Greece and Asia Minor. He then brings the gospel to Alexandria, Egypt.[235] While there, he enrages a mob by telling them that the pagan god, Serapis, is worthless. Mark is dragged with a rope around his neck through the streets by horses and then imprisoned for the night. The following morning, the same ordeal is repeated until he dies.[236]

Nero and Vespasian
June 9[237]
A.D. 68

After fourteen years of Nero's reign, the Romans can no longer tolerate their cruel and embarrassing emperor. A series of revolts against the emperor begin in the western provinces. As support for Nero crumbles, the Senate declares him a public enemy of the state. Nero hides in a villa outside of Rome, at the home of one of his freedmen. There, he commits suicide to avoid a far more degrading end. His famous reputed last words are, "What an artist the world is losing!"[238] Galba follows Nero as emperor.

---

233. Thomas Schmidt, *The Apostles After Acts*, 156. An X-shaped cross consists of two diagonal beams or planks that intersect to form an "X" shape, rather than the traditional "t" shape of a Latin cross. Again, it is impossible to verify this tradition, and some historians don't believe it's reliable.

234. One such story is of Andrew resurrecting thirty-nine dead sailors who washed up to shore from a shipwreck. John Drane, *Early Christians*, 57.

235. Thomas Schmidt, *The Apostles After Acts*, 197.

236. According to a Coptic/Egyptian tradition, this took place in A.D. 68. Thomas Schmidt, *The Apostles After Acts*, 171-172.

237. F.F. Bruce, *New Testament History*, 410; D. Clint Burnett, *Paul and Imperial Divine Honors*, 234.

238. Suetonius, *Life of Nero*, 49. "Nero considered himself a great actor and participated in plays and dramas, much to the embarrassment of the leading citizens of Rome who had an extremely low view of actors." Personal correspondence with Jeffrey Weima, 1/6/24.

After preaching the gospel in India, Southern Arabia, Ethiopia, and Armenia, Bartholomew (also called Nathanael)—one of the Twelve—is allegedly beaten and crucified in Albanopolis, Armenia.[239]

A.D. 69

This is the year of the four emperors,[240] plunging the Roman world into civil war on a scale not seen since Octavian defeated Antony at Actium in 31 B.C.[241] With Nero's death and lack of heirs, the Julio-Claudian line ends. Galba's brief reign of about seven months ends with his assassination by the Praetorian Guard, who then proclaims Otho as the new emperor.

At the same time, the legions in Germany declare for their own general, Vitellius, and the legions in Alexandria declare for their commander, Vespasian, the general whom Nero sent, to suppress the Jewish revolt.[242] Vespasian emerges as the last man standing and is officially proclaimed emperor of Rome by the Senate in December of 69.

A.D. 70

Vespasian entrusts Titus, his son, with the task of reasserting Roman control over Judea.[243] John, the beloved apostle, is exiled to the island of Patmos for his testimony of Jesus Christ.[244] (The island of Patmos sits fifty miles southwest of

---

239. Some believe this occurred between A.D. 80 and 90, but Schmidt thinks it took place in A.D. 68. Thomas Schmidt, *The Apostles After Acts*, 144, 196. According to another tradition, Bartholomew was flayed alive by a whip and then crucified with his head downward. As with the other traditions of the apostles' deaths, this account has limited historical reliability.

240. F.F. Bruce, *Paul: Apostle of the Heart Set Free*, 29. The four emperors were Galba, Otho, Vitellius, and Vespasian.

241. N.T. Wright, *Paul: A Biography*, 222.

242. See the full account of this tumultuous year in Tacitus, *Histories*.

243. Titus eventually became emperor and died in A.D. 81 when his brother Domitian succeeded him.

244. Exile was a common punishment for those guilty of subversive teaching against the empire. David deSilva, *Discovering Revelation*, 32. For a historical outline of Patmos, see Otto F.A. Meinardus, *St. John of Patmos and the Seven Churches of the Apocalypse*, 13ff.; Jeffrey Weima, *The Sermons to the Seven Churches of Revelation:*

Ephesus.[245]) The apostle had become a nuisance in Asia, so he is sent to Rome where he is reportedly boiled in oil, but miraculously unhurt.[246] He is then sentenced to exile by a local governor. While on Patmos, God gives John visions concerning the present and future. John is released from exile[247] and returns to Ephesus where he meditates on the visions and records them for the churches in Roman Asia.[248]

JOHN WRITES REVELATION[249]

Year: A.D. 69-70 (or 90s)[250]

A Commentary and Guide (Grand Rapids, MI: Baker Academic, 2021), 15-18. Some early church authors report that this took place later in A.D. 82. Thomas Schmidt, *The Apostles After Acts*, 141.

245. Patmos wasn't a barren island with no inhabitants. It had enough people living in it to support a gym and several pagan temples. David deSilva, *A Week in the Life of Ephesus*, 144. There is compelling literary and archaeological evidence that John wasn't alone on a deserted island. Personal correspondence with Jeffrey Weima on 1/16/23. "Patmos is seven miles long and three miles across at its widest point, but the total land area (about fourteen square miles) is much less than these dimensions suggest." Jeffrey Weima, *The Sermons to the Seven Churches of Revelation*, 13. The highest point of the island is 883 feet. For details, see Barry Beitzel, *Lexham Geographic Commentary on Acts through Revelation*, 619-628.

246. Tertullian, *Prescription Against Heretics*, 36.

247. Those who hold to a later date for Revelation rely on traditions alleging John was exiled in A.D. 82 and released to return to Ephesus in A.D. 96. Thomas Schmidt, *The Apostles After Acts,* 141. The tradition that John was exiled to Patmos during the reign of Domitian is questionable. Patmos was a penal colony, not a military garrison. N.T. Wright and Michael Bird, *The New Testament in Its World*, 818.

248. In their book, Wright and Bird agree that this reconstruction is a "plausible scenario." N.T. Wright and Michael Bird, *The New Testament in Its World,* 818. (However, they don't mention the tradition from Tertullian.)

249. The book of Revelation is also referred to as the "Apocalypse of John."

250. For arguments supporting the earlier dating, see Jonathan Bernier, *Rethinking the Dates of the New Testament*, 118-129; John A.T. Robinson, *Redating the New Testament*, chap. 8; Jon Zens, ed., *Searching Together Magazine*, vol. 33:3-4 & vol. 34:1, 2005-2006; Clinton Arnold, ed., *Zondervan Illustrated Bible Backgrounds Commentary*, 4:246-247. Mark Wilson also holds to an early date for Revelation. See Clinton Arnold, ed., *Zondervan Illustrated Bible Backgrounds Commentary*, 4:245-247. Because church tradition says John was exiled to the island of Patmos during the reign of Domitian, many scholars date Revelation during the period of Domitian's reign as emperor in the 90s. However, Domitian served temporarily as emperor (or more accurately as vice-regent) in A.D. 70 when his father was away from Rome, leading some to contest the value of the tradition for a later date of composition. Also, the idea that Domitian persecuted, or supported the persecution of, Christians has been contested. Leonard Thompson, *The Book of Revelation: Apocalypse and Empire*

From: Ephesus[251]

To: Seven ekklesias in the Roman province of Asia (Ephesus, Smyrna, Pergamum, Thyatira, Sardis, Philadelphia, and Laodicea)[252]

Author: John the apostle[253]

(Oxford: Oxford University Press, 1990), 96-185. According to Bernier, Robinson, Wilson, Zens, et al., the weight of internal evidence in Revelation suggests that the document might have been written *before* the destruction of Jerusalem. Other scholars argue that Revelation was written during the Domitian persecution in the 90s. Ben Witherington III, *Invitation to the New Testament*, 401; David deSilva, *Discovering Revelation*, 35-39. Jeffrey Weima also holds to a dating of A.D. 95. Personal correspondence with Weima on 1/16/23.

251. N.T. Wright and Michael Bird, *The New Testament in Its World*, 818. Others, like Witherington, believe Revelation was written from Patmos. Ben Witherington III, *Invitation to the New Testament*, 401.

252. These seven cities form a horseshoe-shaped circuit, each between a two- to three-day walk from each other. David deSilva, *An Introduction to the New Testament*, 796. The ekklesias in these cities are mentioned in Revelation 2 and 3. While Revelation was clearly written to those specific churches in the first century, Weima believes "the seven churches are representative of the whole church and so John expects his book of Revelation to be read by churches throughout Asia Minor. In other words, the audience is broader than just the seven kingdom communities." Personal correspondence with Jeffrey Weima, 1/6/24. Contrary to popular opinion, the seven churches were not all experiencing persecution during this time. N.T. Wright and Michael Bird, *The New Testament in Its World*, 818. For a detailed analysis of Jesus' words to the seven churches in Revelation 2 through 3, see Jeffrey Weima, *The Sermons to the Seven Churches of Revelation*. Weima calls these words "prophetic oracles" or "sermons." He analyzes each message using the following internal structure: the Christ title, the commendation, the complaint, the correction, and the consequence. Weima, *The Sermons to the Seven Churches of Revelation*, 1-11, 27-267. For more on the turmoil present in Asia Minor at the time, along with the messages to the seven churches, see Mark Fairchild, *Christian Origins in Ephesus & Asia Minor*, chap. 5; David deSilva, *Discovering Revelation*, 44-54. Bauckham argues that Revelation is an "apocalyptic prophecy in the form of a circulate letter to seven churches in the Roman province of Asia." The churches are mentioned in the order in which a messenger would visit them starting from Patmos. The churches, seven in number (which signifies completeness) have been said to represent all the Lord's ekklesias. Richard Bauckham, *The Theology of the Book of Revelation* (New York, NY: Cambridge University Press, 1993), 2, 11-12, 16, 26.

253. Scholars debate the identity of the "John" who wrote the book of Revelation. See the arguments in Donald Guthrie, *New Testament Introduction*, 932-964; Leon Morris, *Revelation: An Introduction and Commentary*, TNTC, revised edition (Grand Rapids, MI: Eerdmans, 1987), 27-35; David deSilva, *Discovering Revelation*, 29-31; *An Introduction to the New Testament*, 792-795; Jeffrey Weima, *The Sermons to the Seven Churches of Revelation*, 12-13. It's plausible to conclude that the same person who wrote the Gospel of John also wrote Revelation. Weima believes the author was John (the apostle), son of Zebedee, which is the traditional view. Personal correspondence with Weima, 1/16/23. Early church literature is unanimous in ascribing Revelation

Contextual Summary: On the isle of Patmos, John is given a dramatic vision of Jesus Christ and the future purpose of God. The Lord Jesus tells John to write down the vision in a book and send it to the seven kingdom communities in Roman Asia (1:10-11).

We call this book "The Revelation of Jesus Christ," and it encompasses the things that John has "seen, and the things which are, and the things which will happen here-after."[254] The letter is to be read aloud by a disciple to an audience of other disciples.[255]

The entire book of Revelation, including the judgments of seals, trumpets, and plagues,[256] echoes material found throughout the Old Testament.[257] Revelation presents Jesus Christ as the One who turns the kingdoms of this world into His own kingdom.[258] The book is a magisterial unveiling of Christ's absolute authority over

---

to John, the apostle. Leon Morris, *Revelation*, 27. However, scholars like David deSilva believe a different John wrote Revelation. David deSilva, *Discovering Revelation*, 29-31. According to Burge, "the evidence garnered by critics is not persuasive enough to overturn tradition's declaration that John the apostle wrote Revelation." Gary Burge, et al., *The New Testament in Antiquity*, 438. In light of the evidence, Mounce concludes, "the wisest course of action is to accept as a reasonable hypothesis that the Apocalypse was written by John the apostle, son of Zebedee and disciple of Jesus." Robert Mounce, *The Book of Revelation*, revised edition, NICNT (Grand Rapids, MI: Eerdmans, 1998), 15. According to Justin Martyr (*Dialogue with Trypho the Jew*, 91), John the apostle was its author. Note that some apostles were also prophets. (Silas was both, see Acts 15:32; 1 Thessalonians 1:1 with 2:6.) I believe this was also the case with John. See also John Drane, *Early Christians*, 124; Walter Elwell, et al., eds., *Tyndale Bible Dictionary*, 1127.

254. Revelation 1:1-2, 19. John describes his writing as a "prophecy" (Revelation 1:3). John was sent to Patmos as a punishment "on account of" his prior activity of testifying to the word of God and the reality of Jesus Christ. Revelation 1:9; David deSilva, *A Week in the Life of Ephesus*, 143. Revelation is a stunning continuation of John's testimony to the word of God which is embodied in Jesus Christ. Leon Morris, *Revelation*, 47. The obvious subversive intent of John's message provides solid evidence for why a local Roman official would think it was beneficial to remove John from his sphere of influence in the seven cities. David deSilva, *Discovering Revelation*, 32.

255. Revelation 1:3. David deSilva, *Discovering Revelation*, 3.

256. For a conversation on whether the judgments should be read in a linear fashion, as a circular plot (recapitulation), or as a combination of both, see David deSilva, *Discovering Revelation*, chap. 8.

257. "Although the book of Revelation contains virtually no explicit quotations from the Old Testament, it nevertheless is saturated with allusions to the Old Testament." Personal correspondence with Jeffrey Weima, 1/6/24.

258. Revelation 11:15.

creation and the forces that oppose God's kingdom. The Dragon, Serpent, and Beast (the anti-trinity) will be overcome in a blistering defeat, and Jesus—the risen, enthroned Lord—will return to earth in triumph.

John calls the churches back to being faithful witnesses to God's kingdom, even to the point of martyrdom. In this regard, Revelation was written to teach Christians how to be dissidents in a world deeply influenced by Babylon.[259]

Chapters 21 and 22 remarkably mirror Genesis chapters 1 and 2.[260] All of the themes found in the first two chapters of Genesis have now been fully developed and find their consummation in the last two chapters of Revelation. The Bible ends where it began. Eden is restored, and the fullness of God's kingdom has arrived on earth.[261]

The timeless message of Revelation is that God's eternal kingdom, while now hidden, opposes all forms of idolatry and human-made kingdoms based on power and exploitation. The book borrows heavily from the Hebrew Scriptures and offers hope that no matter how bad the world becomes, the living God remains on the throne, and He will set all things right in the end.[262]

259. For this argument, see Scot McKnight with Cody Matchett, *Revelation for the Rest of Us: A Prophetic Call to Follow Jesus as a Dissident Disciple* (Grand Rapids, MI: Zondervan, 2023). The authors describe "Babylon" as a murderous, opulent, economically exploitive and arrogant system. The city of Rome was modern Babylon when Revelation was written (61). See also David deSilva, *Unholy Allegiances: Heeding Revelation's Warning* (Peabody, MA: Hendrickson, 2013), 21-76.

260. I explain the significance of these themes in my book *From Eternity to Here,* which seeks to unveil the eternal purpose of God from Genesis to Revelation.

261. The book of Revelation belongs to the ancient literary genre called "apocalypse" which means "uncovering." For details, see David deSilva, *An Introduction to the New Testament*, 788ff.; Wayne Meeks, ed., *Library of Early Christianity*, 8:226ff. For an overview of Revelation, see Ben Witherington III, *Revelation*, 1-64; David deSilva, *An Introduction to the New Testament*, chap. 24; N.T. Wright and Michael Bird, *The New Testament in Its World*, chap. 34; Clinton Arnold, ed., *Zondervan Illustrated Bible Backgrounds Commentary*, 4:245-383.

262. For an overview of the central message of the New Testament, from beginning to end, see F.F. Bruce, *The Message of the New Testament*, 11-116; Eckhard Schnabel, *New Testament Theology*, 789-961; George Ladd, *A Theology of the New Testament*, chap. 45.

The Roman Siege of Jerusalem
May – August 70

The population of Jerusalem swells to around 600,000 as refugees from the Roman assault throughout Galilee and Judea as well as revolutionary gangs pour into the city. Titus, the son of Emperor Vespasian, marches to Jerusalem with four legions (roughly 60,000 troops), laying siege to the city.[263] The Roman army breaches the first and second walls of Jerusalem. A mass execution of the escapees begins. Outside the city, the Romans crucify up to 500 Jews per day.[264]

Because of the infighting among revolutionary groups within the city, famine also besieges Jerusalem. As it takes its toll, some of the Jews resort to infanticide and cannibalism to survive. The Romans destroy the Antonia Fortress and overtake the temple and the city. They enter the Jerusalem temple and set it on fire.[265] The sacred temple is desecrated and destroyed. Hundreds of thousands perish in the siege, and over 90,000 of the able-bodied are led into captivity and sold.[266] During the last month of the war, the Romans crucify so many Jews that they run out of timber.[267] Remembering Jesus' warning recorded in the Gospels,[268] many Christians have already fled the city and avoided the bloodbath.[269]

263. Calvin Roetzel, *The World That Shaped the New Testament*, 32-33.

264. Josephus, *The Jewish War*, 5.11.1. "Josephus's first-hand account of the war from 66 through 74 is a historical source of unparalleled importance, despite the fact that scholars have reason to doubt his complete honesty—not least of all in his portrayal of himself and his patrons' motives (Josephus began the war as a revolutionary general and ended it as Vespasian's pensioner in Rome)." Personal correspondence with David deSilva, 2/8/24.

265. The burning of the city of Jerusalem was carried out by the Romans in A.D. 70 while "the burning of the temple is attributed to Jewish defenders." R.T. France, *The Gospel of Matthew*, 825. David deSilva states that "the reality is that both parties burned various parts of the temple complex, at least if we accept Josephus's account." Personal correspondence with deSilva, 2/8/24.

266. This account of how the Romans attacked Jerusalem comes from the Jewish historian Josephus. See Josephus, *The Jewish War*, 1.10, 12; 6.256-257; 5.566; 6.26. See also Daniel Harrington, *The Gospel of Matthew*, 11; Philip Schaff, *History of the Christian Church* (Grand Rapids, MI: Eerdmans, 1910, reprint edition 1994), vol. 1, 391-404.

267. N.T. Wright, *Paul: A Biography*, 136.

268. Mark 13; Luke 21; Matthew 24.

269. Eusebius, *The History of the Church*, 3.7. Those who remained in Jerusalem when the revolt started came under intense pressure from Jewish nationalists. Eventually, they too left and resettled in Pella. The unbelieving Jews placed curses on the Christians ("Nazarenes") in their synagogue prayers shortly following

But when you see Jerusalem surrounded by armies, then know that its desolation is at hand. Then let those who are in Judea flee to the mountains. Let those who are in the middle of her depart. Let those who are in the country not enter therein. For these are days of vengeance, that all things which are written may be fulfilled. Woe to those who are pregnant and to those who nurse infants in those days! For there will be great distress in the land, and wrath to this people. They will fall by the edge of the sword, and will be led captive into all the nations. Jerusalem will be trampled down by the Gentiles, until the times of the Gentiles are fulfilled. (Luke 21:20-24)

The Jerusalem ekklesia has dispersed again. The Jewish Christians are now forced to sit down and eat with their "unclean" Gentile brothers and sisters in the Gentile ekklesias that Paul and his co-workers planted all over the Roman Empire.[270]

The Kingdom of God after A.D. 70

Given the horrific events that took place in A.D. 70, the ekklesia in Jerusalem is "effectively out of the picture."[271] Between A.D. 30 and 70, the vast majority of Jews have rejected the proclamation that Jesus is the Messiah, though they still regard their fellow Jews who have converted to Christ as Jewish.[272] The apostasy Paul and Peter foresaw continues to flourish.[273]

---

these events. M.A. Smith, *From Christ to Constantine*, 18-19. In addition, Pella was "bitterly hated by the Jews." Hans Leitzmann, *A History of the Early Church*, 1:178. See also Ben Witherington III, *A Week in the Fall of Jerusalem*, 27-28; Thomas Schmidt, *The Apostles After Acts*, 124-126.

270. A few of them took a different path and founded the Ebionite heresy, which rejected Paul's writings, the virgin birth, Christ's divinity, and espoused that all followers of Jesus must follow the Law of Moses. Keener observes that "although Jerusalemites were killed or dispersed, many Galileans and others remained in the holy land, under Roman domination." Personal correspondence with Craig Keener, 12/4/23.

271. M.A. Smith, *From Christ to Constantine*, 20. For a discussion on the significance of A.D. 70 as well as the post-apostolic period, see John A.T. Robinson, *Redating the New Testament*, chaps. 2 and 10.

272. James D.G. Dunn, *Neither Jew Nor Greek*, 609. For the complex question of the relationship between the Christians and the Jews post A.D. 70, see Dunn, 610ff. Some commentators have theorized that the Jesus movement became overwhelmingly Gentile during Paul's lifetime. Witherington, however, argues against this idea in *Invitation to the New Testament*, 271-273.

273. In his book *The Apostles After Acts*, Schmidt provides a reconstruction of what may have taken place in the lives of the apostles after A.D. 70. Thomas Schmidt, *The Apostles After Acts*, 7-47. Again, each tradition regarding how the apostles died has limited historical reliability, but that doesn't make them untrue.

According to tradition, the following tragedies take place. Simon the Zealot, one of the Twelve, actively ministers and spreads the gospel of the kingdom in Samaria, Galilee, Africa, Gaul, Persia, and Britain.[274] But he is martyred in Britain.[275] Jude, half-brother of Jesus, also goes to Africa and Britain for the gospel, and he too is martyred.[276] Matthew (also called Levi), another of the Twelve, preaches the gospel in Judea for nine years and again travels to Egypt and Ethiopia, making many converts. He dies in Ethiopia of natural causes in A.D. 90.[277]

Thomas (also called Didymus), one of the Twelve, brings the gospel to the Parthian empire. He preaches to Parthians, Medes, and Persians. His life ends on the Indian coast near Bombay where he is killed by a lance thrust through his body as he kneels in prayer.[278] James, the apostle and son of Alphaeus, preaches the gospel in Spain, Ireland, and Britain. He is stoned to death by Jews who resist the gospel.[279]

274. Thomas Schmidt, *The Apostles After Acts*, 167-169.

275. George Jowett, *The Drama of the Lost Disciples* (London: Covenant Publishing Company, 1966), chap. 14. Thomas Schmidt, *The Apostles After Acts*, 167-169. Schmidt suggests he was hacked with swords in A.D. 71 (196), though this tradition is of an uncertain date.

276. According to tradition, this occurred between A.D. 50 and 80. Thomas Schmidt, *The Apostles After Acts*, 167-169.

277. The earliest tradition we have alleges that Matthew died of natural causes. Clement of Alexandria, *Stromata*, 4.9. Schmidt believes this account is the most reliable. Thomas Schmidt, *The Apostles After Acts*, 176, 196. Later traditions say he traveled to Parthia where he was slain by the sword. John Foxe, *Foxe's Christian Martyrs of the World*, 28. Western traditions say he was killed by the sword during the time of Domitian on September 21, A.D. 90. Omer Engelbert, *The Lives of the Saints*, 132-133.

278. Herbert Lockyer *All the Apostles of the Bible*, Logos edition (Grand Rapids, MI: Zondervan, 2013), 260. For other accounts of Thomas' ministry and death, see Thomas Schmidt, *The Apostles After Acts*, 177-185, 196. One tradition says he was speared in India in A.D. 72.

279. William Steuart McBirnie, *The Search for the Twelve Apostles* (digital version), 147-148; Herbert Lockyer, *All the Apostles of the Bible*, 250. Some scholars identify this James with "James the Less" or "James the Younger." Some believe he was the brother of Matthew. Richard Losch, *All the People in the Bible: An A–Z Guide to the Saints, Scoundrels, and Other Characters in Scripture*, Logos edition (Grand Rapids, MI: Eerdmans, 2008), 187. One tradition says James the Less was martyred by being beaten to death with a fuller's club.

Luke dies a natural death in Thebes of Boeotia at eighty-four years of age.[280] In A.D. 96, Titus dies on the island of Crete.[281] Timothy dies in Ephesus a year later; he is clubbed to death after protesting an idolatrous celebration.[282] Archippus, Philemon, and Apphia die as martyrs in Colossae.[283] What Jesus warned decades earlier has come to pass.

> *Therefore also the wisdom of God said, "I will send to them prophets and apostles; and some of them they will kill and persecute, that the blood of all the prophets, which was shed from the foundation of the world, may be required of this generation...." (Luke 11:49-50)*

John, the apostle, is still living in Ephesus. The great apostle dies of natural causes at the age of ninety-four in A.D. 100.[284] According to tradition, Philip (the evangelist) preaches in Carthage, Phrygia, and Asia Minor. The wife of a Roman proconsul is converted as a result, but the backlash is fatal. The proconsul has Philip arrested and executed.[285]

The apostolic workers and evangelists of the first century are some of the finest human beings to ever draw breath. They are among those choice vessels of whom the world was not worthy.[286] Following the death of the apostles and their co-workers, the glow of the first-century ekklesia begins to fade. Over the centuries, human-created traditions slowly

---

280. Thomas Schmidt, *The Apostles After Acts*, 157. Another tradition says he died naturally in Bithynia at the age of seventy-four. Later traditions say he was crucified. John Foxe, *Foxe's Christian Martyrs of the World*, 35. However, according to Thomas Schmidt, "Up to A.D. 400, the few sources indicate a natural death. My sense is that martyrdom was retroactively applied in many cases as the cult of martyrdom grew." Personal correspondence with Thomas Schmidt, 1/26/23.

281. Omer Engelbert, *The Lives of the Saints*, 6. Another tradition says he died in A.D. 107 of natural causes. Thomas Schmidt, *The Apostles After Acts*, 197.

282. John Foxe, *Foxe's Christian Martyrs of the World*, 50-51. Another source says he was stoned to death. Omer Engelbert, *The Lives of the Saints*, 32. Still another says he died in Ephesus in A.D. 80. Thomas Schmidt, *The Apostles After Acts*, 197.

283. Eckhard Schnabel, *Early Christian Mission*, 2:1246.

284. Irenaeus, *Against Heresies*, 3.3.4; Jerome, *Illustrious Man*, 9; Eusebius, *The History of the Church*, 3.23, 31; Thomas Schmidt, *The Apostles After Acts*, 141.

285. Mark Water, *The Christian Book of Records*, Logos edition (Alresford, Hants: John Hunt Publishing, Ltd., 2002), 14; Tim Dowley and Nick Rowland, *Atlas of Christian History* (Minneapolis, MN: Fortress Press, 2016), 18.

286. The phrase "of whom the world was not worthy" comes from Hebrews 11:38, ESV.

evolve to dim her light and replace her glory. Yet God does not give up on His eternal purpose. According to Tertullian, the blood of the martyrs is the seed of God's kingdom.

> *But go zealously on, good presidents, you will stand higher with the people if you sacrifice the Christians at their wish, kill us, torture us, condemn us, grind us to dust; your injustice is the proof that we are innocent.... The oftener we are mown down by you, the more in number we grow; the blood of Christians is seed.*[287]

The principle of death and resurrection not only held true for Jesus Himself, but it also holds true for His church. Therefore, the untold story of the New Testament doesn't end on a negative note with the deaths of the apostles. *There is resurrection!* Throughout the centuries, the Lord has progressively worked to restore the pristine simplicity and glory of His body, His house, His bride, and His family—His kingdom community.

In every generation, God has gained a remnant of His people who have been willing to risk life and limb to fight valiantly to recover the precious things of Christ.[288] Those first things of Jesus have been won with sweat, blood, and tears. Even today, the glorious gospel of the kingdom, which shifted the earth from its axis in the first century, continues to be reclaimed all over the globe.[289] This restoration, though slow and steady, will continue until the time when she, the ekklesia—the bride of the Lord Jesus Christ—will make herself ready for her glorious bridegroom.[290]

287. Tertullian, *Apology*, 50.

288. For an interesting perspective on the history of God's restoration work throughout the ages, see John Kennedy's *The Torch of the Testimony* (Fort Washington, PA: Gospel Literature Crusade, 1963) and E.H. Broadbent's *The Pilgrim Church* (London: Pickering & Inglis, 1974). The original editions of both books contain remarkable forewords by F.F. Bruce. Regrettably, newer reprints have removed Bruce's powerful forewords. Another insightful work on this topic is Kim Tan's *Lost Heritage: The Heroic Story of Radical Christianity* (Godalming, Surrey: Highland Books, 1996).

289. For more on the restoration of the gospel of the kingdom, see TheInsurgence.org.

290. Revelation 19:6-9; Matthew 25:1-13.

CHAPTER 14

THE FOURTH MOTION: THE KING RETURNS TO EARTH

The seventh angel sounded, and great voices in heaven followed, saying, "The kingdom of the world has become the Kingdom of our Lord, and of his Christ. He will reign forever and ever!" (Revelation 11:15)

THE APPOINTED HOUR has arrived. The spotless Lamb of God is ready to receive the reward of His suffering.

Behold, he is coming with the clouds, and every eye will see him, including those who pierced him. All the tribes of the earth will mourn over him. Even so, Amen. (Revelation 1:7)

The thin veil that hides the full presence of the Lord Jesus tears asunder, and the long-rejected Savior appears in great glory.[1] The Son of God returns to earth to take His beloved bride, for she has finally made herself ready.[2] In immaculate glory and unapproachable light, the Son presents His beautiful bride to Himself and then to His Father.

Jesus, the Son of man and the second Adam, establishes His kingdom on earth and reigns over all things, putting everything under His feet—even death, the last surviving

---

1. Matthew 24:30. For details on the coming of Christ and the age to come, see George Ladd, *A Theology of the New Testament*, chaps. 15 and 39; Eckhard Schnabel, *New Testament Theology*, chaps. 15 and 26; Leonard Sweet and Frank Viola, *Jesus: A Theography*, chap. 16.

2. Ephesians 5:26-27; Revelation 19:7.

enemy.[3] The Lamb of God has returned as the royal lion to judge humankind and set the world right.[4]

I saw in the night visions, and behold, there came with the clouds of the sky one like a son of man, and he came even to the ancient of days, and they brought him near before him. Dominion was given him, and glory, and a kingdom, that all the peoples, nations, and languages should serve him. His dominion is an everlasting dominion, which will not pass away, and his kingdom one that which will not be destroyed. (Daniel 7:13-14)

The Son of man and Son of God reconciles all creation to Himself and subdues all things under His kingship.[5] The restoration of all things has come.[6] The old heaven and old earth give way to a renewed heaven and renewed earth in which both overlap, just as they did in the Garden of Eden.[7] Jesus Christ, the true Lamb of God, is now King of kings and Lord of lords, absolute possessor of heaven and earth. He is preeminent and supreme over all things. This has been true since His resurrection, but it is now a practical reality that is manifested throughout the universe, unchallenged and undisputed.

---

3. 1 Corinthians 15:24-27.

4. Revelation 5:5; 20:12-15; John 5:21-25; Romans 2:16; Hebrews 9:27-28; 2 Timothy 4:1; 1 Peter 4:5.

5. Ephesians 1:9-10; Colossians 1:19-20.

6. Acts 3:20-21.

7. Revelation 21:1, 9; 2 Peter 3:10-13; Isaiah 66:22. For an explanation on the Garden of Eden being an overlap of two realms, see Frank Viola, "Vantage Point: The Story We Haven't Heard," the Christ is All podcast, episodes #18 and #19 at frankviola.org/thechristisallpodcast. Regarding the old heaven and earth passing away, N.T. Wright observes that Peter (in 2 Peter 3) isn't saying that space, time, and matter will burn up and be destroyed, but God will use fire to purify and dissolve the elements that do not meet the test (similar to the way Paul used the fire of judgment in 1 Corinthians 3). N.T. Wright, *The Early Christian Letters for Everyone*, 119-121. A better reading of 2 Peter 3:10 is that "all the works on it will be disclosed" (117). This text is similar to Paul's words that the children of God will be manifested in the end, an event for which all creation eagerly awaits (Romans 8:19).

CHAPTER 15

THE FINAL MOTION: THE KINGDOM IN ETERNITY FUTURE

When all things have been subjected to him, then the Son will also himself be subjected to him who subjected all things to him, that God may be all in all. (I Corinthians 15:28)

SPACE AND TIME have been transformed. The old creation has passed. The triune God: Father, Son, and Spirit enjoy eternal fellowship. But a new person shall soon join the fellowship—the most beautiful girl in the world, the bride of Jesus Christ.[1]

Then I, John, saw the holy city, New Jerusalem, coming down out of heaven from God, prepared as a bride adorned for her husband. (Revelation 21:2, NKJV)

..."Come, I will show you the bride, the Lamb's wife." And he carried me away in the Spirit to a great and high mountain, and showed me the great city, the holy Jerusalem, descending out of heaven from God, having the glory of God... (Revelation 21:9-11, NKJV)

She, the bride, is made up of the community of the redeemed. She includes all who are part of God's everlasting kingdom throughout the ages, "from every nation, from all tribes and peoples and languages."[2] It is a sublime moment, beautiful beyond words. The Son

---

1. This statement does not mean that the ekklesia will become part of the Godhead. Rather, she will share and participate in the full fellowship, joy, and union of the triune God (Ephesians 5:25-27; 2 Corinthians 11:2). Revelation 21:1-2, 9 depict the New Jerusalem, which is a monumental symbol of the bride of Christ in her pristine glory. The city contains a flowing river, the tree of life, and it is made of gold, pearl, and precious stone (Revelation 21:11, 18, 21; 22:1-2, NKJV). The Garden of Eden contained these exact same elements (Genesis 2:9-12, NLT and NET Bible). In the end, the Garden becomes a city.
2. Revelation 7:9, ESV.

takes His glorious bride into marital union, and the *bride*—a virgin—becomes the *wife* of the Lamb.[3] This woman who has been hidden in the Son from eternity past becomes one with her Lord for all eternity.[4]

> *For he chose us in him before the creation of the world to be holy and blameless in his sight....* *(Ephesians 1:4, NIV)*

> *For the creation waits with eager longing for the revealing of the sons of God. (Romans 8:19, ESV)*

> *...The king has brought me into his chambers.... (Song of Solomon 1:4, NKJV)*

> *...so that he might present the church to himself in splendor, without spot or wrinkle or any such thing, that she might be holy and without blemish. ..."Therefore a man shall leave his father and mother and hold fast to his wife, and the two shall become one flesh." This mystery is profound, and I am saying that it refers to Christ and the church. (Ephesians 5:27, 31-32, ESV)*

The wife of the Lamb is fully revealed and brought into complete union with Christ, her bridegroom. She brilliantly bears His image and perfectly exercises His authority. Her name is ekklesia, and she is the mystery hidden in God from before the foundation of the world.[5]

And you, dear Christian, are part of her.

The three persons of the divine community consummate their plan of expanding their fellowship and extending their heavenly kingdom fully to earth. Heaven and earth have

---

3. Revelation 21:9. A bride is an unmarried virgin who is betrothed. A wife has consummated the union in marriage.
4. See Frank Viola, *From Eternity to Here*, Part 1 for details and biblical references.
5. Ephesians 5:28-32. I develop these themes in detail in episode #43, "Who Is This Woman? God's Ultimate Passion," on the Christ is All podcast at frankviola.org/thechristisallpodcast.

been completely restored, and they are inseparably joined.[6] Jesus Christ and His beloved wife experience unhindered eternal union. The Son returns all things He inherited to His Father, and God becomes *All* in *All*.[7]

6. Isaiah 65:17 and 66:22 prophesy a new heaven and a new earth. Revelation 21 explains the reality. 2 Peter 3:13 also references the new heaven and earth; however, Peter is not describing a scenario where the old earth will be completely destroyed. Instead, he speaks about the corrupting elements of decay and death being removed, and the earth being renewed and manifested, just as the children of God will be manifested at Christ's royal appearance (Romans 8; 1 Corinthians 15; 1 John 2; Colossians 3). N.T. Wright offers an explanation in *The Resurrection of the Son of God*, 462-466.

7. 1 Corinthians 15:28. In the beginning, God was *All*. But in the end, He will be *All* in *All*. No one knows what this will look like, but we know that what we do in this present life will in some way go forward into the new heavens and new earth. Therefore, our labor here is not in vain. 1 Corinthians 15:58.

EPILOGUE

I heard a loud voice out of heaven saying, "Behold, God's dwelling is with people, and he will dwell with them, and they will be his people, and God himself will be with them as their God. He will wipe away every tear from their eyes. Death will be no more; neither will there be mourning, nor crying, nor pain, any more. The first things have passed away." (Revelation 21:3-4)

THE STORY YOU JUST READ is the epic saga of God's eternal purpose. It's the story of Jesus Christ—this world's true Lord—and how the living God has established His kingdom in and through His beloved Son to the visible universe. The New Testament contains the drama of God's grand mission, which centers on the rejoining of heaven and earth, just as it was united in the Garden and later in the Man, Jesus of Nazareth.

This theme—the kingdom of the heavens coming to God's good earth—is what your Bible is all about.[1] If you are a follower of Jesus the King, you are part of His glorious bride—the ekklesia—the assembly of the living God. Therefore, this story is also *your* story.

---

1. For a detailed treatment of God's eternal purpose, see my books *From Eternity to Here* and *Insurgence*. *From Eternity to Here* explores the eternal purpose from the perspectives of the bride of Christ, the house of God, the body of Christ, and the family of God. *Insurgence* explores God's timeless purpose from the perspective of God's kingdom. These two books are a supplement to the book you're reading now.

WHAT NOW?

THE NEXT PAGE OF CHURCH HISTORY

You have heard me teach things that have been confirmed by many reliable witnesses. Now teach these truths to other trustworthy people who will be able to pass them on to others. (2 Timothy 2:2, NLT)

THE STORY OF THE NEW TESTAMENT CHURCH is a glorious paradox. It's a combination of unmatched wonder alongside a persistent train wreck.[1] The saga is both exuberant and harrowing. It depicts the sublime within the malign.

Beginning with the Twelve, the apostolic workers whom Jesus called, trained, and sent out preached the world-transforming gospel of the kingdom throughout the Roman Empire. The good news of the kingdom came first to the Jews, then to people of all nations, largely through the efforts of Paul and his co-workers.

Individual lives were changed and outposts of God's kingdom were established throughout the Mediterranean world. Miracles were performed to demonstrate the inbreaking of the kingdom. People were healed and delivered. Yet in the midst of these amazing events and the creation of beautiful kingdom communities, there were disasters, incredible suffering, and spectacular failures. The ekklesias faced opposition from the Jews who did not accept Jesus as the Messiah as well as from the Greeks and Romans who saw their refusal to worship the emperor as treason.

The ekklesias were also torn apart by heresies from within. They were constantly plagued by outside opposition and internal conflicts. And yet, despite all of it, the kingdom

---

1. I owe this metaphor to Tim Oslovich who shared this observation with me on the phone on 3/1/24 after reading the unpublished manuscript of this book.

of God continued to survive and expand. In this regard, the body of Christ replayed the life and ministry of its head, Jesus Christ.

During His earthly ministry, Jesus brought God's kingdom to earth for the first time. Lives were transformed, people were healed and delivered, and a beautiful kingdom community was established, made up of twelve men and around seven women. Yet every step of the way, the ministry of Jesus was plagued with external opposition, great suffering, and internal conflicts, including denial and betrayal from some of His closest followers. But in spite of it, the kingdom of God survived and expanded.

It's been two millennia since the ekklesia first appeared on the planet, and throughout that time, it has continued its pattern of peerless wonder alongside a persistent train wreck. From the first century until now, the church has been a mixture of glory and gore, triumph and tragedy, success and suffering.[2]

But the next page of church history is blank.

Before I get to that, I want to pull out one thread from our story. The church in Century One and the church today are so radically different that they hardly seem to share the same universe.[3] Since the Protestant Reformation, theologians have left us with the impression that the first-century Christians were persons of great doctrine and theology. But the truth is that with rare exception, the people who made up the primitive churches

2. For details, see Andrew Miller, *Miller's Church History* (Addison, IL: Bible Truth Publishers, reprint edition 1980); Philip Jenkins, *The Lost History of Christianity: The Thousand-Year Golden Age of the Church and How It Died* (New York, NY: HarperOne, 2008); Leonard Verduin, *The Reformers and Their Stepchildren* (Grand Rapids, MI: Eerdmans, 1964); Peter Hoover, *The Secret of the Strength: What Would the Anabaptists Tell This Generation?* (Shippensburg, PA: Benchmark Press, 1997).

3. In addition to *The Normal Christian Church Life* by Watchman Nee and *God's Spiritual House* by T. Austin-Sparks (previously cited), other seminal works that explain how the first-century church functioned are Emil Brunner, *The Misunderstanding of the Church* (London: Lutterworth Press, 1952); Elton Trueblood, *The Incendiary Fellowship* (New York, NY: Harper & Row, 1967); *The Yoke of Christ and Other Sermons* (New York, NY: Harper & Brothers, 1958); Ernest Loosley, *When the Church Was Very Young* (Worthing: George Allen & Unwin, 1935); Jon Zens, *58-0: How Christ Leads Through the One Anothers* (Omaha, NE: Ekklesia Press, 2013); *Jesus is Family: His Life Together* (Oak Glen, CA: Quoir, 2017); *Elusive Community: Why Do We Avoid What We Were Created For?* (Oak Glen, CA: Quoir, 2020); *We Are Christ on Earth: The Visible Expression of Jesus in Space and Time* (Oak Glen, CA: Quoir, 2021).

could not read or write. They weren't people who graduated from the finest seminaries on the planet. (Seminaries didn't even exist until over a thousand years later.)

Most of what they knew was the Lord Jesus Christ who indwelt them by the Holy Spirit. But they had something else that many Christians today don't possess—a face-to-face community of spiritual brothers and sisters who stood with them through thick and thin. The gospel of the kingdom that was preached in Century One gave both Jews and Greeks a dimension of life that no one else on the planet had.

The Antioch line of church planting, a pattern that dominates the story, contains several incredible features. Two wandering men enter a town bare-fisted. They preach the explosive gospel of the kingdom in the synagogues to Jews and God-fearers. They also preach in the marketplace to Gentile pagans, including slaves, free people, and the upper strata of society.[4]

Their message is as subversive as it is riveting. They tell the story of Jesus of Nazareth in light of the Hebrew narrative, boldly declaring that He is the promised Messiah and this world's true Lord. Jesus is also the center of creation and God's timeless purpose, and He is establishing a heavenly kingdom right here on this earth.[5] One scholar rightly describes how Paul and his co-workers understood the biblical story saying:

> *This Story is a tale as large as the universe and yet as small as an individual human being. It is, however, not a Story about everything, not even about all of human history. It is a Story that focuses on God's relationship to humankind, from the beginning of the human race in Adam to its climax. ...For Paul, Christ is the central and most crucial character in the human drama, and everything Paul says about all other aspects of the Story is colored and affected by this conviction. ...In Paul's view, one is always in danger of saying too little about Jesus Christ, not too much.*[6]

A nucleus of people responds to the eruptive message, and a group of Christ-followers is born.[7]

---

4. They were prepared to take ground from the enemy and participate in the restoration of the nations, removing fallen humans from his grasp and returning them to the living God.

5. Paul of Tarsus was one of the men who proclaimed this titanic message.

6. Ben Witherington III, *Paul's Narrative Thought World*, 2-3.

7. Paul's most productive years were between A.D. 47 and 57 during which he raised up kingdom communities in four Roman provinces and wrote numerous life-changing letters that survive today. Paul Barnett, *Paul: Missionary of Jesus*, 199.

Christ-followers share life together as a family.

The first instinct of the Christians is to meet, and to meet often. Their gatherings are held before sunup or after sundown because so many of them come from the class of laborers and artisans. Sometimes they gather during the afternoon siesta. Women and men learn to sing together, and eventually, they write their own songs. They meet informally in private homes and public spaces.

While they have certain practices and traditions, they are devoid of empty religious rituals. Consequently, they are not a religion. They have no temples, shrines, sacrifices, altars, cult statues, or special priesthood.[8] Instead, they live as an extended household—an alternative family in the world.[9] They are profoundly impacted by the fact that the Lord Jesus Christ has come to indwell them. And because the God who created the universe lives inside them, they have unspeakable joy.[10]

Christ-followers love boldly like no others.

The Christians also do something that's exotically rare in the Roman Empire. They begin to love each other and care for one another's needs, even to the point of laying down their lives for each other. The early wanderers—the apostles of God—declare the message of Christ and His glorious kingdom. They herald the message in city after city, town after town, being expelled from many of them due to the radical nature of the message.

With rare exception, they only stay with the new kingdom communities they found a short period of time, often three to six months.[11] They then leave them alone to the Holy

8. Wayne Meeks, *The First Urban Christians*, 140; J.G. Davies, *The Secular Use of Church Buildings* (New York, NY: The Seabury Press, 1968), 2. The Christians had no special priesthood or temples because all believers in Christ are called priests and comprise God's temple. 1 Peter 2:4-5, 9; Revelation 1:5-6; 20:6; 1 Corinthians 3:16-17; 6:15-20; 2 Corinthians 6:14-18; Ephesians 2:19-22. For more on how the early Christians were a "priestly people" with no normative priests as in other religions, see Nijay Gupta, *Strange Religion*, chap. 9.

9. The first-century ekklesia was an extended family, usually revolving around a single household. The members lived and worked in close proximity with one another and saw one another daily. They shared life together. Roger Gehring, *House Church and Mission*, 240. See Acts 2:46 and Hebrews 3:13 for examples.

10. "Though you have not seen him, you love him. Though you do not now see him, you believe in him and rejoice with joy that is inexpressible and filled with glory" (1 Peter 1:8 ESV).

11. Richard Plummer, et al., *Paul's Missionary Methods*, 223-224.

Spirit, trusting the foundation they laid, believing it to be gold, silver, and precious stone. Thus, it is able to endure the fires of hell.[12] And fire does fall, both from the Jewish community and the pagans who surround them.

Again, these apostolic workers only spend an average of three to six months[13] with the new believing communities, only to leave them alone for a year or more. And they survived. But how? What on earth did those men preach in such a short period of time? The answer: They proclaimed the titanic, earthshaking gospel of the kingdom—a gospel that utterly transforms people. And it causes them to endure fire.[14]

That gospel brought the lost a spiritual reality so glorious, so powerful, and so incredible that it shook the empire to its foundations. But the tragedy is that most Christians today have never heard or experienced that gospel. *And that gospel gave the new believers an indwelling Lord.*[15] Indeed, the overriding power of the New Testament church rests upon an indwelling Christ. But that's not all.

Christian workers train others whom God has called to His work.

As we have seen, when Paul of Tarsus became older, he duplicated the ministry of Christ by training workers in Ephesus just as Jesus trained workers in Galilee. Paul trained eight men, with a ninth added shortly afterward (Epaphras). All of them were Gentiles except Aristarchus and Sopater. The seasoned apostle from Tarsus believed that if his work was

---

12. 1 Corinthians 3:10ff. Again, while this text applies especially to the day of judgment, it has application for all workers in the present. If a church is built on imperishable material, it will endure fiery testing (1 Peter 1:7, etc.).

13. Roland Allen, *Missionary Methods*, 84-85. The exceptions were Corinth (eighteen months) and Ephesus (around three years). I am of course speaking of the ministry of Paul (along with his co-workers Barnabas and then Silas). The apostolic workers kept in touch with the church as much as they could through letters, some of which made it into our New Testament (86-87).

14. I detail this explosive gospel in my book *Insurgence*.

15. Allen rightly talks about the power of an indwelling Spirit as the secret to Paul's ministry. Roland Allen, *Missionary Methods*, 148-149. I'll add that Paul no doubt taught the new believers how to live by the indwelling life of Christ through the Holy Spirit. For an introduction to this topic, see the Christ is All podcast at frankviola.org/thechristisallpodcast, episode #37, "Living by the Indwelling Life of Christ."

made of imperishable materials it would continue after his lifetime. So he passed the torch on to others. And indeed, his labor has been carried on, even to this day.

In this regard, I pray that the seed of this book would fall into the hands of some young people who are called to God's work[16]—people who burn with a passion for God's eternal purpose, who are possessed with the desire to make Jesus Christ visible again on this earth, and who are willing to sacrifice everything for that goal.

The leaders I've mentioned throughout this book were giants who once walked the earth.[17] Today, the earth needs a new breed of Christian workers who stand in their lineage—firebrands on the planet, making the world take note and forcing hell to retreat.

It needs workers who know and have experienced the titanic gospel of the kingdom—workers who are willing to experience the life of the body of Christ as simple believers rather than having an ambition to be "leaders"—workers humble enough to be trained by older workers who have a rich heritage, who know the Lord deeply, who have experienced the self-emptying work of the cross countless times, who have been through blood up to the horse's bridle, and who know by experience what it takes to raise up the house of God.[18]

Yes, the next page of church history is blank. I don't know what will be written upon it, but I hope there are some serious followers of Jesus reading these words who are willing to take the torch and continue writing this glorious story.[19] *The need of the hour is for a group of people who burn for Christ to accept responsibility for that blank page and seize the torch.* This is absolutely necessary if we will see the next stage of divine restoration and recovery.

So with the untold story of the New Testament church in mind, what story will *you* be writing on that page?

---

16. While this book is written to people of all ages, I am using the phrase "young people" here because my burden is for the next generation. The next generation will carry the torch of God's work into the future. Jesus trained workers younger than Himself and so did Paul. If you're someone who considers yourself older or more seasoned, I hope you will join me in honoring the divine call to the next generation. And pass this book on to them.

17. For details, see my article "When Giants Walked the Earth (The Real Apostolic Succession)" at frankviola.org/giants.

18. For details, see my article "Where Are the Workers?" at frankviola.org/wherearetheworkers.

19. For more on how the torch of God's work has been passed on from generation to generation, see Frank Viola, "Passing the Torch," at frankviola.org/torch.

KINGDOM STRATEGY

And this gospel of the kingdom will be preached in the whole world as a testimony to all nations, and then the end will come. (Matthew 24:14, NIV)

PAUL'S STRATEGY IN MINISTRY involved careful planning, but it wasn't disconnected from the supernatural guidance he received from the Lord. The apostle's stratagems were a blending of several elements: vision and calling (the big picture), tactical planning and specific guidance of the Spirit (the details).[1] The following four principles have to do with the kingdom of God and the apostolic patterns that are woven into the story you just read. Each principle sheds light on the New Testament as well as God's mission today.

Paul's fourfold pattern for kingdom advancement.

1) Paul intentionally brought the gospel of the kingdom to populated cities in the Roman Empire.[2] His purpose appears to have been to plant strong discipleship communities

---

1. The leading of the Spirit and wise planning are not mutually exclusive. For further details on Paul's apostolic strategies, see Eckhard Schnabel, *Early Christian Mission*, 2:1294-1475; James D.G. Dunn, *Beginning from Jerusalem*, 555-557; Paul Barnett, *Paul: Missionary of Jesus*, 214. (These authors use the term "missionary" instead of "apostolic," but it's essentially the same thing.)

2. Meeks points out that Paul divided the world into city, wilderness, and sea (2 Corinthians 11:26). He argues (persuasively) that Christianity was an urban movement. Wayne Meeks, *The First Urban Christians*, 9-10. Paul sought to bring the gospel to metropolitan centers that served as "strategic cities" in the Roman Empire. Eckhard Schnabel, *Paul the Missionary*, 280ff. This explains how and why we got the term "pagan." The word was used by the early Christian apologists to group non-Christians into a convenient package. At its root, a "pagan" was a country dweller, an inhabitant of the *pagus* or rural district. Because Christianity primarily spread in the cities, the country bumpkins (or "pagans") were regarded as those who believed in the old gods. Joan Taylor, *Christians and the Holy Places: The Myth of Jewish-Christian Origins* (Oxford: Clarendon Press, 1993), 301. The same applies to the word "heathen." Heathens were those who lived out in the "heath" (uncultivated lands outside the city). By contrast, the Christians lived in the cities (with few exceptions). Eckhard Schnabel, *Paul the Missionary*, 219-220; James D.G. Dunn, *The Acts of the Apostles*, 225. In his apostolic travels, Paul "followed the commercial routes of world trade" and "his mission initially embraced

through whom the gospel would naturally spread throughout those cities and beyond.[3] For this reason, if the gospel had penetrated a city enough for a kingdom community to be born, Paul considered the entire city and province to be evangelized.[4]

2) Paul would preach the gospel to the Jew first, then to the Gentile.[5] While the apostle's specific commission was to the Gentiles, his heart was with his own people (the Jews).

Brothers, my heart's desire and my prayer to God is for Israel, that they may be saved. (Romans 10:1)

The gospel, therefore, was to be preached to the Jew first, just as Jesus did.[6] Consequently, Paul would typically seek to preach in cities with a decent-sized Jewish population, beginning in the synagogue.[7] If a synagogue wasn't present, he would seek out a clean place (like a river) where Jews and God-fearers worshipped. (This took place in Philippi.)

3) Paul sought to convert a well-to-do person who owned a home.[8] After being converted to Christ, that person (being the head of a household) would serve as the host for

---

urban centers." Roger Gehring, *House Church and Mission*, 179. While the cities were mostly evangelized by the Christians, the countrysides were nearly untouched. Since the majority of the empire was made up of the countrysides, by A.D. 400 the empire was predominantly non-Christian. But the Christians during that time controlled the leadership positions, power, and media. Ramsay MacMullen, *Christianizing the Roman Empire: A.D. 100-400* (New Haven, CT: Yale University Press, 1984), 83.

3. John Stott, *The Message of Romans*, 382; Ben Witherington III, *Paul's Letter to the Romans*, 357. Paul was an urban church planter. For the most part, he bypassed the rural areas and ignored the small communities and sleepy little towns. Instead, he went directly to the major urban areas. He appears to have spent a lot of time in and around coastal cities in the Mediterranean, probably because travel was easier and the populations were larger. The more urban areas in the *pax Romana* (Roman peace) better prepared people for the gospel given their ethnic diversity and unconventional nature. Richard Plummer, et al., *Paul's Missionary Methods*, 20, 180-181.

4. Romans 15:19, 23. See the explanation by Roland Allen, *Missionary Methods*, 13.

5. Romans 1:16; 2:9-10; Acts 1:8; 13:46.

6. James D.G. Dunn, *Beginning from Jerusalem*, 547-549; Paul Barnett, *Paul: Missionary of Jesus*, 100-102.

7. James D.G. Dunn, *The Acts of the Apostles*, 225; *Beginning from Jerusalem*, 557-563.

8. Roger Gehring, *House Church and Mission*, 167-171, 185-187; James D.G. Dunn, *Beginning from Jerusalem*, 571. In the first century, only people who were well-to-do could afford a house. See Jeffrey Weima, *1-2 Thessalonians*, 27-28. "Well-to-do" doesn't mean "rich." The rich lived in villas. According to Robert Banks, we have no evidence that the first-century Christians had villas. The Christians hadn't penetrated that

Paul's operations.[9] From that home, Paul would raise up a new kingdom community in the city. The house would be the place where the ekklesia gathered.[10] This strategy corresponds to Jesus' instructions to His disciples about finding a man of peace (Luke 10:5ff.).[11] As one scholar put it,

It was typical of the Pauline missional approach in any given city to initially target individuals from higher social levels. In this way Paul was able to win homeowners, along with their entire

---

stratum of society until the second and third century. Personal correspondence with Robert Banks, 9/19/21. David deSilva agrees, pointing out that villas were usually owned by the uber rich. Personal correspondence with deSilva, 3/11/22. For the classic design of a villa, see Ben Witherington III, *A Week in the Fall of Jerusalem*, 70. While the early Christians weren't rich, some of them had means. Examples are Priscilla and Aquila, who hosted believers and churches in different cities and had enough money to travel (which was expensive in that day). They had a home in Corinth in the early days (Acts 18:26, NIV), Ephesus (1 Corinthians 16:19), and Rome (Romans 16:5). There is also Lydia in Philippi (Acts 16:40); Gaius Titius Justice in Corinth later (Romans 16:23); Jason in Thessalonica (Acts 17:5-7); Philemon in Colossae (Philemon 1:2); Nympha in Hierapolis (Colossians 4:15). These were all well-to-do. Very few Christians lived in their own homes in the first century. Instead, the vast majority of believers rented small *insulae* (tenement apartments) in urban areas. This was in accordance with the structure of Roman society. Roger Gehring, *House Church and Mission*, 147. Because of the spatial requirements that Christians needed, they likely gathered in peristyle houses. David Balch, et al., *Early Christian Families in Context*, 42. A peristyle home featured an interior open space or garden that was surrounded by roofed colonnades on three or four of its sides. The entrances to living, sleeping, and kitchen spaces would be found all along the perimeter of the colonnade. As previously pointed out, Luke (in Acts) liked to report the conversions of people of status and means.

9. In the New Testament, "household" was a code word for well-to-do. Personal correspondence with Jeffrey Weima, 2/10/22. "Early Christianity was a household movement. It sought the conversion of heads of households, whose dependents followed them into the faith." John Byron, *A Week in the Life of a Slave*, 24. "[M]ost scholars are in agreement: the fact that early Christian communities met in homes is of great socio-historical, ecclesiological, and missional significance." Roger Gehring, *House Church and Mission*, 1.

10. According to Keener, "Homes rather than 'church' buildings were where the Christians met for the first three centuries of the church's existence." Craig Keener, "Lessons on Acts," Session 21. See also *Ante Pacem*, chaps. 5 and 166. According to McKnight, Christians wouldn't meet in basilicas until the time of Constantine. Scot McKnight, *Reading Romans Backwards*, 10.

11. "…the house and household were the immediate mission objective; the house fellowship was the starting and gathering point for the final objective, which was reaching the entire town or city." Roger Gehring, *House Church and Mission*, 54. The "wealthiest member and the largest house" provided a "regular venue for 'the whole church' in different centres." James D.G. Dunn, *Jesus, Paul, and the Gospels*, 168.

households, for the gospel and to set up a base of operations in their house for local and regional mission.[12]

4) Paul continually moved west as he preached the gospel of the kingdom.[13] If you examine all his apostolic journeys, you'll note that he traveled from Syrian Antioch, to Galatia, to Greece, to Roman Asia, to Rome, to Spain.[14] As I've argued in *Insurgence*, Paul was seeking to reclaim the nations for God. He was tracing the Gentile nations that rebelled against the Creator in Genesis 10 until he came to "the end of the earth" in his day. His goal was to bring in what he called "the fullness of the Gentiles."[15]

Why did Paul and the other apostles risk their lives and suffer untold horrors to bring the gospel to the world?

The common evangelical answer is to save individuals from hell. There's no question that the gospel brings life to individual souls, eternal life in the present age and the age to come. However, as I've argued in *From Eternity to Here*, the mission of God goes far beyond the salvation of individual souls from eternal judgment.

God has an eternal purpose that reaches from before humans fell and were in need of salvation. God's timeless purpose is to secure a body for the Son, a house for the Father, a bride for the Son, and a family for the Father—all through the Holy Spirit. Put another way, the ageless purpose of God is to expand the fellowship and communion of the triune God eternally.[16]

---

12. Roger Gehring, *House Church and Mission*, 187.

13. Richard Plummer, et al., *Paul's Missionary Methods*, 43.

14. For details on the journey motif in Luke-Acts, see Floyd Filson, "The Journey Motif in Luke-Acts," in W. Ward Gasque & Ralph Martin, eds., *Apostolic History and the Gospel, Biblical and Historical Essays Presented to F.F. Bruce* (Exeter: The Paternoster Press, 1970), 68-77. For further information on travel, money, letters, and people in Paul's day, see E.P. Sanders, *Paul: The Apostle's Life, Letters, and Thought*, chap. 4.

15. Frank Viola, *Insurgence*, 351-361; James D.G. Dunn, *Beginning from Jerusalem*, 541-546; Michael Heiser, *The Unseen Realm*, 298-306.

16. This explains why salvation in the New Testament is a community-creating event, not simply an individualistic experience. Joseph Hellerman, *When the Church Was a Family*, 120ff.; Stanley Grenz, *Theology for the Community of God* (Grand Rapids, MI: Eerdmans, 2000). To be "added to the Lord" was to be "added to the church" (Acts 2:41, 47; 5:14; 11:24, ESV). Keener rightly notes, "As far in the future as we look, we will

Evangelism, discipleship, and the forming of ekklesias are never separated in the New Testament.[17] This epic idea is wrapped up in the phrase *the kingdom of God*—the central message of Jesus. The kingdom of God is the joining together of heaven and earth, just as it was in the beginning (and as it will be in the end).[18]

Paul and the other apostles sought to bring the gospel message to all who never heard it.[19] That gospel wasn't only about salvation from eternal judgment. It was primarily about fulfilling God's eternal purpose, which in a fallen world begins (not ends) with salvation. The apostolic mission, therefore, was to establish kingdom communities throughout the Roman Empire that would fulfill God's eternal purpose.[20]

Those kingdom communities—ekklesias—were colonies of heaven on earth. Through them, God was reclaiming the nations that had fallen under the grip of evil powers. Paul's church planting trips, therefore, were designed to "establish a new kind of kingdom on

---

always be His servants before His face, not being *Him* (Revelation 22:3-4). But the shape of the New Jerusalem (Revelation 21:3, 16, 22)—a cube like the Old Testament Holiest Place—connotes perfect indwelling, without distraction, forever and ever!" Personal correspondence with Craig Keener, 12/4/23.

17. Eckhard Schnabel, *Early Christian Mission*, 1:356-357. Schnabel rightly says, "Missionary work and church must not be separated, since the very goal and purpose of missionary work is the creation of a community of disciples" (356). In *Discipleship in Crisis*, I make the case that Jesus' word to the Twelve in Matthew 28 to "make disciples of all nations" was fulfilled through the apostolic planting of ekklesias. (A free copy of this eBook is available at frankviola.org/discipleship.) Disciples are made within the context of the ekklesia, not apart from it. The ekklesia is the believer's native habitat.

18. Genesis chapters 1 and 2 and Revelation chapters 21 and 22. The Garden of Eden was the intersection of the divine realm (heaven) and the human realm (earth). It reappears again at the end of Revelation, only this time is has become a city. Genesis chapters 1 and 2 and Revelation chapters 21 and 22 are the only chapters in the Bible where there is no sin, corruption, or marks of the Fall. For this reason, they give us a clear window into God's eternal purpose.

19. One of Paul's specific strategies was to pioneer the gospel in virgin territories (Romans 15:20).

20. In the words of Roland Allen, "Paul did not go about as a missionary preacher merely to convert individuals: he went to establish churches from which the light might radiate throughout the whole country round." Roland Allen, *Missionary Methods*, 81. Paul was not just an evangelist; he planted churches and visited them. He also wrote letters to them. And when he couldn't visit them, he sent his co-workers in his place. Mark Fairchild, "The Last Apostle," documentary film. For a full examination of how Paul proclaimed the gospel throughout his ministry, along with his extra-local shepherding responsibilities, see Eckhard Schnabel, *New Testament Theology*, 333-653.

earth as it is in heaven."[21] *In other words, they were to produce the ekklesia of God.*[22] As one philosopher famously said, "He who has a why to live can bear almost any how."[23] In this chapter, I have presented the "why" of the story.

21. N.T. Wright, *Paul: A Biography*, 106-107.

22. This is the final answer to the Lord's prayer in Matthew 6:10. I explain and develop all of these themes in my books *From Eternity to Here* and *Insurgence*.

23. Friedrich Nietzsche, *Twilight of the Idols* (originally published in 1889) in the section entitled, "Skirmishes of an Untimely Man." Of course, I disagree with Nietzsche's overall philosophy, but this quote is fitting.

OBSERVATIONS WORTH CONSIDERING

The past is a foreign country, they do things differently there.[1]

THROUGHOUT THE UNTOLD STORY of the first-century church, some remarkable patterns emerge. Here are twelve that stand out. After you read each observation, ask yourself this question: *Could this be an enduring principle that we would be wise to follow today?*

Observation 1: Apostolic workers labor together.[2] The Twelve, Peter and John, Paul and Barnabas, Paul and Silas, and the men Paul trained were often grouped in pairs as they co-worked.[3] And even though the workers (Paul, Peter, John, etc.) were called to different spheres of ministry, they still co-labored on some level, "watering" one another's fields.[4]

1. L.P. Hartley, *The Go Between* (New York, NY: NYRB Classics, 2002), 1.
2. For details, see Frank Viola, *Finding Organic Church*, 43-45.
3. The New Testament calls more than twenty people "apostles." For a list of them, see Frank Viola, *Finding Organic Church*, chap. 11. Sometimes apostolic workers had a falling out, but they later reconciled. For instance, Paul and Barnabas parted ways in A.D. 50, but five years later, Paul paid tribute to Barnabas as a like-minded servant of Christ (1 Corinthians 9:6). Paul and Mark also had a falling out in A.D. 50, but twelve years later, Paul commends Mark (Colossians 4:10). And near the end of his life, the apostle stated that Mark was helpful to him in the ministry (2 Timothy 4:11). In addition, while apostolic workers were called to different spheres, they also labored together. For example, Silas labored with Paul on the second apostolic journey, but he also helped Peter years later (1 Peter 5:12, NIV). And John labored in Ephesus years after Paul planted the ekklesia there.
4. According to Galatians 2:7-8 (NLT), Peter was an apostle to the Jews and Paul was an apostle to the Gentiles. Yet later in the story, Peter is writing to Gentile believers in "Paul's pond." 1 Peter 1:1 includes the Christians in the Roman province of Asia (that would include Ephesus, Colossae, etc.) as well as the Roman province of Galatia (that would include the four churches in Galatia that Paul planted). Peter also worked with Silas (Paul's co-worker on the second apostolic journey) as well as Mark, the man who accompanied Paul on his first apostolic journey (1 Peter 5:12-13). Later in the story, John moved to Ephesus and wrote to the believers there. He also wrote to the church in Ephesus (Revelation 2:1ff.). I call this principle "cross-watering." Meaning, the apostles watered in fields they didn't plant. The metaphor comes from 1 Corinthians

Observation 2: One way that church planting (founding kingdom communities) was accomplished is by a group of apostles working together to raise up an ekklesia; and then later, that same ekklesia transplanting itself into many other cities, thus establishing new assemblies (this has been called the Jerusalem line).[5]

Observation 3: Another way of church planting is where an ekklesia sends out workers who have been called, prepared, and sent to plant new assemblies in other cities. Those workers leave the assemblies to the Holy Spirit (this has been called the Antioch line).[6] Later, the apostles return to re-center the church and navigate it through crises.[7]

Observation 4: Yet another way of church planting is where a seasoned worker trains younger workers in a city while he raises up a new church (and his apprentices observe). The seasoned worker then sends out his apprentices to plant new assemblies in other cities (this has been called the Ephesian line).[8]

3:6-9. Barnett remarks that in time, the "missionary agreement" in Galatians 2 became less important, perhaps because so few Jews were responding to the gospel message. Therefore, Peter and John redirected their attention to the Gentiles. Paul Barnett, *Bethlehem to Patmos,* 215. Paul never understood his mission in terms of limiting him to only evangelizing the Gentiles. His five synagogue beatings confirm this. Ben Witherington III, *Conflict and Community in Corinth,* 452, n. 50. Note that the apostolic workers didn't inappropriately intrude into one another's fields. They knew each other personally and supported one another's ministries. However, unlike the other apostles, Paul preferred not to build on anyone else's foundation (Romans 15:20; 2 Corinthians 10:13-16). In this respect, Paul was a trailblazer, a pioneer, and a church planter into virgin territory. He didn't appreciate those who didn't build well on his foundation, and he didn't want to be guilty of doing the same. 1 Corinthians 3:10. F.F. Bruce, *Romans,* 248.

5. The Jerusalem "line," the Antioch "line," etc. refer to the consistent patterns of God's work that we see throughout the entire New Testament narrative. Unless we look at the story chronologically, as I've presented in this book, those "lines" or "patterns" are difficult to detect. For details, see Frank Viola, *Finding Organic Church,* 26-35.

6. Watchman Nee was the first person to introduce me to the Jerusalem line and the Antioch line in his remarkable book, *The Normal Christian Church Life.*

7. The first-century apostles left the new churches totally at sea for long periods of time. The churches either relied on the Holy Spirit or they sunk. The apostles didn't erect a clergy to run things in their absence. In some of the churches, they acknowledged elders, but this came later, sometimes years. And the elders didn't control or dominate the churches. The churches were dependent on an indwelling Lord to keep and sustain them. Extra local apostolic workers would return to the churches they established to re-center and encourage them. They would also connect with them through other means of communication (letters, etc.), especially if they were experiencing a crisis. If the apostle built with gold, silver, and precious stone, the church would survive in the midst of crisis (1 Corinthians 3:11ff.).

8. For details, see Frank Viola, *Finding Organic Church,* 35-40.

Observation 5: Still one more way of church planting is where an apostolic worker sends members of different assemblies to one city to raise up a brand-new church (this has been called the Roman line).[9]

Observation 6: Apostles who are touching the center of God's heart and fulfilling His eternal purpose will attract detractors, and they will often encounter one or more persons (a "thorn in the flesh") who will work overtime to destroy them and their ministries. Paul had an unnamed person, most likely a convert from among the Pharisees, who headed up the circumcision party in Jerusalem and followed Paul's work in an effort to undermine it. Peter's nemesis was Simon Magus, who in later traditions created heartache for Peter in Rome.[10]

Observation 7: Virtually all the churches in the first century were raised up and/or helped by a traveling apostolic worker who had first been *called* by God to the apostolic ministry, *prepared* by being a simple believer in an authentic ekklesia, and then *sent* out by the church or a seasoned worker.[11]

Observation 8: Apostolic workers, like Paul, often revisited the churches they planted.[12] When a worker couldn't visit a church, the worker would send a co-worker or an apprentice in his place.[13]

Observation 9: God's people dominate the first-century story. The apostolic ministry exists for the local assembly and not the other way around. The same is true for local overseers. For this reason, whenever Paul would write a letter to a church, he would address the entire assembly rather than its elders.[14]

---

9. For details, see Frank Viola, *Finding Organic Church,* 40-43. Gene Edwards was the first to introduce me to the Ephesian line and the Roman line in a private meeting in June 1998.

10. J.D. Douglas, et al., eds., *New Bible Dictionary,* 1116. The historical accuracy of this tradition is uncertain.

11. For details, see Frank Viola, *Finding Organic Church,* chap. 3.

12. This was Paul's "regular practice." I. Howard Marshall, *Acts,* 241.

13. Paul would often write the church an epistle as well. For specifics on how an apostolic worker in the first century cared for a church, see Frank Viola, *Finding Organic Church,* chap. 23; Robert Banks, *Paul's Idea of Community,* chaps. 15-18.

14. With respect to Paul's letters to the churches, Philippians is the only epistle where leaders are addressed in the opening. But they are mentioned fleetingly after the whole church is addressed (Philippians 1:1). The rest of the letter is directed to the entire assembly, as are Paul's other epistles to churches.

Observation 10: A local ekklesia will experience crises from within and from without. Apostolic workers exist to help the church survive the crises they face. Virtually every letter in the New Testament was written by an apostle to a local assembly that was undergoing adversity or turmoil of some kind.[15]

Observation 11: God's people will sometimes misunderstand what an apostolic worker speaks and writes.[16] At times, this will create tension between the church and its worker.[17]

Observation 12: God's eternal purpose is fulfilled by kingdom communities (ekklesias) that express God's image and exercise His authority as shared-life communities who individually and collectively live by the indwelling life of Christ.[18]

---

15. There are very few exceptions. Even the letters written to individuals such as the epistles to Timothy, Titus, Philemon, and Gaius addressed significant crises.

16. This was a common pattern in Paul's ministry. 2 Thessalonians 2:1 and 2 Corinthians 1:15-16 are just two examples. It was also true in the ministry of Jesus (John 21:20-23). I've addressed this problem in my book *48 Laws of Spiritual Power*, Law 16.

17. Paul's turbulent relationship with the Corinthian assembly is a prime illustration.

18. For details on how a local ekklesia manifests God's eternal purpose, see Frank Viola, *Reimagining Church*, chap. 7.

ACKNOWLEDGMENTS

WHEN I WAS a young Christian in my teens, I came across a little book that speculated when Paul wrote his various letters within the story told in Acts. I don't recall the name of the book or the author, but the concept electrified me. After reading it, I marked the places in my Bible where Paul allegedly authored his epistles within the Acts narrative. Years later, I was introduced to the work of F.F. Bruce, perhaps the most brilliant New Testament scholar of the twentieth century. Bruce produced a collection of remarkable works that meshed the story in Acts with the rest of the New Testament, specifically Paul's letters. (He even produced a translation of Paul's letters in chronological order.)

Then in May 1998, I met Gene Edwards at a conference where we both spoke back to back.[1] Not long after we met, he challenged me to build my own chronological model of the first-century church, something he had done himself when he was a young man.[2] Since I already had an interest in finding out what occurred in Century One due to the influences of F.F. Bruce and the other author whose name and book escape me, I accepted the challenge and produced the first edition of this work.[3]

During my research, I discovered Donald Guthrie's book *The Apostles,* which sought to put together the entire story of the first-century church chronologically from Pentecost to Patmos.[4] Sometime later, I found another work that set out to do the same thing—Paul Barnett's *Bethlehem to Patmos.*[5] As far as I know, these are the only two books written by scholars that seek to reconstruct the entire story of the early church similar to the way that

---

1. The message I delivered at that conference is available at frankviola.org/thechristisallpodcast. It's episode #42 of the Christ is All podcast, "A City Whose Builder and Maker is God."

2. He issued the same challenge to some other men who were present in a meeting. I also give Edwards credit for inspiring the "blank page" metaphor in the "What Now?" chapter.

3. The first edition, published in 2005, was poorly written and full of errors. I wrote it in a hurry and didn't have access to a fraction of the resources that are available to me today. In addition, no scholar reviewed it before publication. Therefore, this heavily revised and expanded edition begged to be written.

4. Donald Guthrie, *The Apostles.* This book was cited earlier. It was published in 1975 and has been out of print for many years.

5. *Bethlehem to Patmos: The New Testament Story* (Sydney: Hodder & Stoughton Australia, 1989).

I've done in this work. Both books, however, are outdated and contain minimal sourcing. Yet I regard them as a solid beginning.[6]

For this reason, I decided to take on the mammoth task of reconstructing the entire saga of the first-century church afresh with full documentation. Destiny Image Publishers was gracious enough to publish the first version back in 2005. But I'm especially grateful that they were eager to publish this new revised and expanded edition, which is far more comprehensive, accurate, and up to date.

I want to credit the late James Rutz for giving me the title, *The Untold Story of the New Testament Church*. He did so during a phone conversation we had in the early 2000s. Special thanks also goes to the following scholars: Craig Keener, David deSilva, Jeffrey Weima, Alan Bandy, Eckhard Schnabel, Paul Barnett, Mark Fairchild, Mark Wilson, Darrell Bock, Robert Banks, Michael Brown, N.T. Wright, Craig Blomberg, Ben Witherington III, Clinton Arnold, Scot McKnight, Nijay Gupta, Joel Green, and James D.G. Dunn. Each of them answered countless questions over the years about various pieces of the first-century narrative.[7]

In addition, I'm grateful to Glenn Seleen, Steve Kolk, Jack McCarty, Taylor Englund, Laura Callarman, Rosten Callarman, Mark Bushfield, Matt Adams, and Matthew Winters for helping me with some of the research. I also want to acknowledge Curt Shirley for creating the maps, and Amanda Cook, Lynsey Barry, Jon Zens, Brooke Redwine Turbyfill, Mara Eller, Tim Oslovich along with the Destiny Image team for editing the revised manuscript. Finally, thanks to my agent Greg Daniel for his advice and encouragement. Without the contributions from all of these people, this book would not exist.

---

6. Guthrie's book has no documentation at all, except for a short bibliography at the end. Barnett's book was republished in 2013, but the content is virtually the same as the 1989 version.

7. Some of our correspondences were over the phone, others via email, and some in person.

ABOUT THE AUTHOR

FRANK VIOLA is a bestselling author, conference speaker, blogger, and podcaster. His ministry is designed to help serious followers of Jesus know their Lord more deeply so they can experience real transformation and make a lasting impact.

His blog (frankviola.org) contains over 1,000 articles and is regularly ranked in the top five of all Christian blogs on the Web. His podcast "Christ is All" reached #1 in Canada and #2 in the USA on Apple podcasts with more than 2 million downloads. His more recent "Insurgence podcast" features numerous conversation partners and has been ranked #9 on Apple podcasts with 600,000+ downloads.

Viola is best known for his groundbreaking books: *Insurgence: Reclaiming the Gospel of the Kingdom*, *48 Laws of Spiritual Power*, *From Eternity to Here*, and *God's Favorite Place on Earth*. Currently, nine of his more than fifteen books have been bestsellers.

LEARN THE STORY

FRANK SPEAKS IN conferences and seminars on the topics treated in his books, including this one. He also holds premium masterminds for people in ministry. His spoken ministry is different from his written work, and many consider it to be more powerful.

If you would like to book him to speak at your conference, church, seminary, Bible school, or discipleship training center, go to frankviola.org/events for details. Samples also appear on the page.

If you are in ministry and you're interested in Frank's high-level mastermind for Christian leaders, visit MinistryMind.org and apply.

In all of these venues and resources, Frank enlarges on the electrifying story you've just read.

THERE IS MORE

WE PLAN TO release "The Untold Story of the New Testament Church" podcast sometime in 2025. The podcast is an audio supplement to this book.

Go to **TheUntoldStory.me** for information.

For a deep dive into Paul's epistles, check out the master classes on The Deeper Christian Life Network.

The master classes include recorded conference messages by Frank that present Paul's letters in 3D. They combine a right-brained, creative approach with a verse-by-verse exposition of each epistle. The master classes go beyond the brief treatment given to each New Testament letter in this book.

For details and samples, go to **thedeeperchristianlife.com/classes**.

BIBLIOGRAPHY

THE FOLLOWING BIBLIOGRAPHY contains most of the volumes used in the research for this book. A small number of the works cited in the footnotes are not listed here, including journal articles.

Aageson, James. *After Paul: The Apostle's Legacy in Early Christianity.* Waco, TX: Baylor University Press, 2023.

Alexander, David, and Pat Alexander, eds. *Handbook to the Bible*, fifth edition. Grand Rapids, MI: Zondervan, 2009.

Allen, Garrick. *Words Are Not Enough: Paratexts, Manuscripts, and the Real New Testament.* Grand Rapids, MI: Eerdmans, 2024.

Allen, Roland. *Missionary Methods: St. Paul's or Ours?* Grand Rapids, MI: Eerdmans, 1962.

Angela, Alberto. *A Day in the Life of Ancient Rome.* New York, NY: Europa Editions, 2009.

Arnold, Clinton. *Ephesians: Power and Magic.* Eugene, OR: Wipf & Stock, 1989.

———. *Ephesians: Zondervan Exegetical Commentary on the New Testament.* Grand Rapids, MI: Zondervan, 2010.

———, ed. *Zondervan Illustrated Bible Backgrounds Commentary*, 5 vols. Grand Rapids, MI: Zondervan, 2002-2019.

Balch, David, and Carolyn Osiek. *Early Christian Families in Context: An Interdisciplinary Dialogue.* Grand Rapids, MI: Eerdmans, 2003.

Ball, Charles Ferguson. *The Life and Times of the Apostle Paul.* Wheaton, IL: Tyndale, 1996.

Bandy, Alan. *An Illustrated Guide to the Apostle Paul: His Life, Ministry, and Missionary Journeys.* Grand Rapids, MI: Baker Books, 2021.

Banks, Robert. *Paul's Idea of Community: Spirit and Culture in the Early House Churches.* Grand Rapids, MI: Baker Academic, 2020.

———. *Going to Church in the First Century.* Beaumont, TX: Christian Books Publishing House, 1980.

Barclay, John. *Jews in the Mediterranean Diaspora: From Alexander to Trajan (323 BCE – 117 CE).* Edinburgh: T & T Clark, 1996.

———. *Pauline Churches and Diaspora Jews.* Grand Rapids, MI: Eerdmans, 2016.

Barnett, Paul. *A Short Book about Paul: The Servant of Jesus*. Eugene, OR: Cascade Books, 2019.

———. *Bethlehem to Patmos: The New Testament Story*. Sydney: Hodder & Stoughton, Australia, 1989.

———. *Finding the Historical Christ*. Grand Rapids, MI: Eerdmans, 2009.

———. *From Jerusalem to Illyricum: Earliest Christianity through the Eyes of Paul*. Eugene, OR: Cascade Books, 2022.

———. *Jesus & the Rise of Early Christianity: A History of New Testament Times*. Downers Grove, IL: InterVarsity Press, 1999.

———. *Paul: Missionary of Jesus*. Grand Rapids, MI: Eerdmans, 2008.

———. *The Birth of Christianity: The First Twenty Years*. Grand Rapids, MI: Eerdmans, 2005.

———. *The Message of 2 Corinthians: Power in Weakness*. Downers Grove, IL: InterVarsity Press, 1988.

———. *The Second Epistle to the Corinthians*, NICNT. Grand Rapids, MI: Eerdmans, 1997.

Barr, David. *New Testament Story: An Introduction*. New York, NY: Wadsworth Publishing Company, 1995.

Bauckham, Richard. *Gospel Women: Studies of the Named Women in the Gospels*. Grand Rapids, MI: Eerdmans, 2002.

———. *Jesus and the Eyewitnesses: The Gospels as Eyewitness Testimony*, second edition. Grand Rapids, MI: Eerdmans, 2017.

Bauer, David. *The Book of Acts as Story: A Narrative-Critical Study*. Grand Rapids, MI: Baker Academic, 2021.

Beale, G.K. *The Temple and the Church's Mission: A Biblical Theology of the Dwelling Place of God*. Downers Grove, IL: InterVarsity Press, 2004.

Beers, Holly. *A Week in the Life of a Greco-Roman Woman*. Downers Grove, IL: InterVarsity Press, 2019.

Beitzel, Barry, ed. *Lexham Geographic Commentary on Acts through Revelation*. Bellingham, WA: Lexham Press, 2019.

———. *Lexham Geographic Commentary on the Gospels*. Bellingham, WA: Lexham Press, 2017.

Bernier, Jonathan. *Rethinking the Dates of the New Testament: The Evidence for Early Composition*. Grand Rapids, MI: Baker Academic, 2022.

Bilezikian, Gilbert. *Community 101: Reclaiming the Local Church as Community of Oneness*. Grand Rapids, MI: Zondervan, 1997.

Bird, Michael. *A Bird's-Eye View of Luke and Acts: Context, Story, and Themes.* Downers Grove, IL: InterVarsity Press, 2023.

———. *Jesus Among the Gods: Early Christology in the Greco-Roman World.* Waco, TX: Baylor University Press, 2022.

Blaiklock, E.M. *Cities of the New Testament.* Grand Rapids, MI: Fleming Revell, 1965.

Blomberg, Craig, and Darlene Seal. *From Pentecost to Patmos: An Introduction to Acts Through Revelation,* second edition. Nashville, TN: B&H Academic, 2021.

Bock, Darrell. *Acts: Baker Exegetical Commentary on the New Testament.* Grand Rapids, MI: Baker Academic, 2007.

———. *Studying the Historical Jesus: A Guide to Sources and Methods.* Grand Rapids, MI: Baker Academic, 2002.

Boin, Douglas Ray. *Coming Out Christian in the Roman World: How the Followers of Jesus Made a Place in Caesar's Empire.* New York, NY: Bloomsbury, 2015.

Bowsher, Clive. *Life in the Son: Exploring Participation and Union with Christ in John's Gospel and Letters.* Downers Grove, IL: InterVarsity Press, 2023.

Branick, Vincent. *The House Church in the Writings of Paul.* Eugene, OR: Wipf & Stock, 1989.

Brown, Raymond. *The Message of Hebrews: Christ Above All.* Downers Grove, IL: InterVarsity Press, 1982.

Brown, Sherri, and Francis Moloney. *Interpreting the Gospel and Letters of John: An Introduction.* Grand Rapids, MI: Zondervan, 2017.

Bruce, F.F. *1 and 2 Corinthians.* London: Marshall, Morgan and Scott, 1971.

———. *1 & 2 Thessalonians,* WBC. Waco, TX: Word Books, 1982.

———. *A Mind for What Matters: Collected Essays.* Grand Rapids, MI: Eerdmans, 1990.

———. *Answers to Questions.* Grand Rapids, MI: Zondervan, 1973.

———. *In the Steps of the Apostle Paul.* Grand Rapids, MI: Kregel, 1995.

———. *Jesus and Paul: Places They Knew.* Nashville, TN: Thomas Nelson, 1983.

———. *New Testament Development of Old Testament Themes.* Grand Rapids, MI: Eerdmans, 1994.

———. *New Testament History.* New York, NY: Doubleday, 1983.

———. *Paul: Apostle of the Heart Set Free.* Grand Rapids, MI: Eerdmans, 1977.

———. *Peter, Stephen, James & John: Studies in Non-Pauline Christianity.* Grand Rapids, MI: Eerdmans, 1980.

———. *Philippians*, NIBC. Peabody, MA: Hendrickson, 1989.

———. *Romans*, revised edition, TNTC. Grand Rapids, MI: Eerdmans, 1985.

———. *The Book of the Acts*, revised edition, NICNT. Grand Rapids, MI: Eerdmans, 1988.

———. *The Canon of Scripture*. Downers Grove, IL: InterVarsity Press, 1988.

———. *The Defense of the Gospel in the New Testament*. Grand Rapids, MI: Eerdmans, 1977.

———. *The Epistles of John*. Grand Rapids, MI: Eerdmans, 1970.

———. *The Epistles to the Colossians, to Philemon, and to the Ephesians*, NICNT. Grand Rapids, MI: Eerdmans, 1984.

———. *The Epistle to the Galatians*, NIGTC. Grand Rapids, MI: Eerdmans, 2013.

———. *The Epistle to the Hebrews*, revised edition, NICNT. Grand Rapids, MI: Eerdmans, 1990.

———. *The Gospel & Epistles of John*. Grand Rapids, MI: Eerdmans, 1983.

———. *The Letters of Paul: An Expanded Paraphrase*. Grand Rapids, MI: Eerdmans, 1965.

———. *The Message of the New Testament*. Grand Rapids, MI: Eerdmans, 1973.

———. *The Pauline Circle*. Grand Rapids, MI: Eerdmans, 1985.

———. *The Spreading Flame: The Rise and Progress of Christianity from Its First Beginnings to the Conversion of the English*. Grand Rapids, MI: Eerdmans, 1958.

———. *The Time is Fulfilled*. Grand Rapids, MI: Eerdmans, 1995.

Burge, Gary. *A Week in the Life of a Roman Centurion*. Downers Grove, IL: InterVarsity Press, 2015.

———. *Jesus and the Jewish Festivals: Uncover the Ancient Culture, Discover Hidden Meanings*. Grand Rapids, MI: Zondervan, 2012.

———, Lynn Cohick, and Gene Green. *The New Testament in Antiquity: A Survey of the New Testament Within Its Cultural Contexts*. Grand Rapids, MI: Zondervan, 1995.

Burnett, D. Clint. *Paul and Imperial Divine Honors: Christ, Caesar, and the Gospel*. Grand Rapids, MI: Eerdmans, 2024.

Byron, John. *A Week in the Life of a Slave*. Downers Grove, IL: InterVarsity Press, 2019.

Campbell, Constantine. *The Letter to the Ephesians*, PNTC. Grand Rapids, MI: Eerdmans, 2023.

Campbell, Douglas. *Paul: An Apostle's Journey*. Grand Rapids, MI: Eerdmans, 2018.

Capes, David, Rodney Reeves, and E. Randolph Richards. *Rediscovering Paul: An Introduction to His World, Letters and Theology*, second edition. Downers Grove, IL: InterVarsity Press, 2017.

Carey, Holly. *Women Who Do: Female Disciples in the Gospels.* Grand Rapids, MI: Eerdmans, 2023.

Casson, Lionel. *Everyday Life in Ancient Rome.* Baltimore, MD: John Hopkins University Press, 1998.

———. *Travel in the Ancient World.* Baltimore, MD: John Hopkins University Press, 1994.

Cohick, Lynn. *Women in the World of the Earliest Christians: Illuminating Ancient Ways of Life.* Grand Rapids, MI: Baker Academic, 2009.

Conybeare, W.J., and J.S. Howson. *The Life & Epistles of St. Paul.* Grand Rapids, MI: Eerdmans, 1966.

Corbishley, Mike. *The Romans?* New York, NY: Peter Bedrick Books, 2001.

Cranfield, C.E.B. *Romans: A Shorter Commentary.* Grand Rapids, MI: Eerdmans, 1985.

Davids, Peter. *The First Epistle of Peter*, NICNT. Grand Rapids, MI: Eerdmans, 1990.

Dempster, Stephen. *The Return of the Kingdom: A Biblical Theology of God's Reign.* Downers Grove, IL: InterVarsity Press, 2024.

deSilva, David. *A Week in the Life of Ephesus.* Downers Grove, IL: InterVarsity Press, 2020.

———. *An Introduction to the New Testament: Contexts, Methods & Ministry Formation*, second edition. Downers Grove, IL: InterVarsity Press, 2018.

———. *Discovering Revelation: Content, Interpretation, Reception.* Grand Rapids, MI: Baker Academic, 2021.

———. *Ephesians*, NCBC. New York, NY: Cambridge University Press, 2022.

———. *Honor, Patronage, Kinship & Purity: Unlocking New Testament Culture.* Downers Grove, IL: InterVarsity Press, 2000.

———. *Paul and the Macedonians: The Life and Letters of Paul.* Nashville, TN: Abingdon Press, 2001.

———. *Perseverance in Gratitude: A Socio-rhetorical Commentary on the Epistle "to the Hebrews."* Grand Rapids, MI: Eerdmans, 2000.

———. *The Letter to the Galatians*, NICNT. Grand Rapids, MI: Eerdmans, 2018.

———. *Unholy Allegiances: Heeding Revelation's Warning.* Peabody MA: Hendrickson, 2013.

Dodd, C.H. *The Founder of Christianity.* New York, NY: The Macmillan Company, 1970.

Donfried, Karl. *The Romans Debate.* Grand Rapids, MI: Baker Academic, 1991.

Douglas, J.D., and N. Hillyer, eds. *New Bible Dictionary*, second edition. Downers Grove, IL: InterVarsity Press, 1982.

Drane, John. *Early Christians: Life in the First Years of the Church*. San Francisco, CA: Harper & Row, 1982.

———. *Paul: An Illustrated Documentary on the Life and Writings of a Key Figure in the Beginnings of Christianity*. San Francisco, CA: Harper & Row, 1976.

———. *Paul: Libertine or Legalist?* London: SPCK, 1975.

Dunn, James D.G. *Beginning from Jerusalem*. Grand Rapids, MI: Eerdmans, 2009.

———. *Jesus, Paul, and the Gospels*. Grand Rapids, MI: Eerdmans, 2011.

———. *Jesus Remembered*. Grand Rapids, MI: Eerdmans, 2003.

———. *Neither Jew Nor Greek: A Contested Identity*. Grand Rapids, MI: Eerdmans, 2015.

———. *Romans 9–16*, WBC. Logos edition. Dallas, TX: Word Books, 1988.

———. *The Acts of the Apostles*. Grand Rapids, MI: Eerdmans, 2016.

———. *The Parting of the Ways: Between Christianity and Judaism and Their Significance for the Character of Christianity*, second edition. Hymns Ancient & Modern Ltd. Norwich: Canterbury Press, 2006.

———. *The Theology of Paul the Apostle*. Grand Rapids, MI: Eerdmans, 1998.

———. *Unity and Diversity in the New Testament: An Inquiry into the Character of Earliest Christianity*. Philadelphia, PA: Westminster Press, 1977.

Elder, Nicholas. *Gospel Media: Reading, Writing, and Circulating Jesus Traditions*. Grand Rapids, MI: Eerdmans, 2024.

Engelbert, Omer. *The Lives of the Saints*. New York, NY: Barnes and Noble, 1951.

Evans, Craig, and Stanley Porter, eds. *Dictionary of New Testament Background*. Downers Grove, IL: InterVarsity Press, 2000.

Fairchild, Mark. *Christian Origins in Ephesus & Asia Minor*, second edition. Peabody, MA: Hendrickson, 2017.

Fant, Clyde, and Mitchell Reddish. *A Guide to Biblical Sites in Greece and Turkey*. Oxford: Oxford University Press, 2003.

Fee, Gordon. *Paul's Letter to the Philippians*, NICNT. Grand Rapids, MI: Eerdmans, 1995.

———. *The First Epistle to the Corinthians*, NICNT. Grand Rapids, MI: Eerdmans, 1987.

Ferguson, Everett. *Backgrounds of Early Christianity*. Grand Rapids, MI: Eerdmans, 2003.

Finegan, Jack. *Handbook of Biblical Chronology*. Peabody, MA: Hendrickson, 2015.

Finger, Reta Halteman. *Of Widows and Meals: Communal Meals in the Book of Acts*. Grand Rapids, MI: Eerdmans, 2007.

———. *Roman House Churches for Today: A Practical Guide for Small Groups.* Grand Rapids, MI: Eerdmans, 2007.

Fox, Robin Lane. *Pagans and Christians in the Mediterranean World from the Second Century AD to the Conversion of Constantine.* New York, NY: Alfred A. Knopf, 1986.

Foxe, John. *Foxe's Christian Martyrs of the World.* Westwood, NJ: Barbour and Company, 1985.

France, R.T. *The Gospel of Matthew*, NICNT. Grand Rapids, MI: Eerdmans, 2007.

Frank, Harry Thomas. *Atlas of the Bible Lands.* Long Island City, NY: Hammond Incorporated, 1977.

Garnsey, Peter, and Richard Saller. *The Roman Empire: Economy, Society and Culture*, second edition. Oakland, CA: University of California, 2014.

Gehring, Roger. *House Church and Mission: The Importance of Household Structures in Early Christianity.* Peabody, MA: Hendrickson, 2004.

Giles, Kevin. *Jesus and the Father: Modern Evangelicals Reinventing the Doctrine of the Trinity.* Grand Rapids, MI: Zondervan, 2006.

———. *What on Earth is the Church? An Exploration in New Testament Theology.* Downers Grove, IL: InterVarsity Press, 2005.

Goldingay, John. *Reading Jesus's Bible: How the New Testament Helps Us Understand the Old Testament.* Grand Rapids, MI: Eerdmans, 2017.

Goodenough, Simon. *Citizens of Rome.* London: Crown Publishers, 1979.

Grant, Michael. *Paul in the Roman World: The Conflict at Corinth.* Louisville, KY: Westminster John Knox Press, 2001.

Gray, Patrick. *Paul as a Problem in History and Culture: The Apostle and His Critics through the Centuries.* Grand Rapids, MI: Baker Academic, 2016.

Green, Gene. *The Letters to the Thessalonians.* Grand Rapids, MI: Eerdmans, 2002.

Green, Joel, and Lee Martin McDonald. *The World of the New Testament.* Grand Rapids, MI: Baker, 2013.

Green, Joel, Jeannine Brown, and Nicholas Perrin, eds. *Dictionary of Jesus and the Gospels*, second edition. Downers Grove, IL: InterVarsity Press, 2013.

Green, Michael. *2 Peter and Jude*, TNTC. Grand Rapids, MI: Eerdmans, 1987.

———. *Evangelism: Learning from the Past.* Grand Rapids, MI: Eerdmans, 2023.

Grenz, Stanley. *Theology for the Community of God.* Grand Rapids, MI: Eerdmans, 2000.

Grindheim, Sigurd. *The Letter to the Hebrews*, PNTC. Grand Rapids, MI: Eerdmans, 2023.

Grudem, Wayne. *1 Peter: An Introduction and Commentary*, TNTC. Grand Rapids, MI: Eerdmans, 1988.

Gundry, Robert. *A Survey of the New Testament*, third edition. Grand Rapids, MI: Zondervan, 1994.

———. *Matthew: A Commentary on His Handbook for a Mixed Church Under Persecution*, second edition. Grand Rapids, MI: Eerdmans, 1994.

Gunther, John. *Paul: Messenger and Exile: A Study in the Chronology of His Life and Letters*. Valley Forge, PA: Judson Press, 1972.

Gupta, Nijay. *1 & 2 Thessalonians*, CINT. Grand Rapids, MI: Zondervan, 2019.

———. *Strange Religion: How the First Christians Were Weird, Dangerous, and Compelling*. Grand Rapids, MI: Brazos Press, 2024.

———. *Tell Her Story: How Women Led, Taught, and Ministered in the Early Church*. Downers Grove, IL: InterVarsity Press, 2023.

Guthrie, Donald. *New Testament Introduction*, revised edition. Downers Grove, IL: InterVarsity Press, 1990.

———. *The Apostles*. Grand Rapids, MI: Zondervan, 1975.

———. *The Pastoral Epistles: An Introduction and Commentary*, revised edition, TNTC. Grand Rapids, MI: Eerdmans, 1990.

Hanson, J.W. *An Urban Geography of the Roman World, 100 BC to AD 300*. Oxford: Archaeopress, 2016.

Harrington, Daniel. *The Gospel of Matthew*, Sacra Pagina. Collegeville, MN: Liturgical Press, 1991.

Harris, William. *Ancient Literacy*. Cambridge, MA: Harvard University Press, 1991.

Hawthorne, Gerald, and Ralph Martin, eds. *Dictionary of Paul and His Letters*. Downers Grove, IL: InterVarsity Press, 2009.

Heilig, Christoph. *The Apostle and the Empire: Paul's Implicit and Explicit Criticism of Rome*. Grand Rapids, MI: Eerdmans, 2022.

Heiser, Michael. *The Unseen Realm: Recovering the Supernatural Worldview of the Bible*. Bellingham, WA: Lexham Press, 2015.

Hellerman, Joseph. *The Ancient Church as Family*. Minneapolis, MN: Fortress Press, 2001.

———. *When the Church Was a Family: Recapturing Jesus' Vision for Authentic Christian Community*. Nashville, TN: B&H Publishing, 2009.

Hemer, Colin. *The Book of Acts in the Setting of Hellenistic History*. Winona Lake, IN: Eisen-brauns, 1990.

Hengel, Martin. *Acts and the History of Earliest Christianity*. Minneapolis, MN: Fortress Press, 1980.

———, and Anna Maria Schwemer. *Paul Between Damascus and Antioch: The Unknown Years*. Louisville, KY: Westminster John Knox Press, 1997.

———. *The Pre-Christian Paul*. Philadelphia, PA: Trinity Press International, 1991.

Hoehner, Harold. *Chronological Aspects of the Life of Christ*. Grand Rapids, MI: Zondervan, 1977.

Horsley, Richard. *Jesus and Empire: The Kingdom of God and the New World Disorder*. Minneapolis, MN: Fortress Press, 2003.

———. *Paul and Politics: Ekklesia, Israel, Imperium, Interpretation*. Harrisburg, PA: Trinity Press International, 2000.

———, and Neil Asher Silberman. *The Message and the Kingdom: How Jesus and Paul Ignited a Revolution and Transformed the Ancient World*. New York, NY: Grosset/Putnam, 1997.

Hutchinson, Robert. *The Dawn of Christianity: How God Used Simple Fishermen, Soldiers, and Prostitutes to Transform the World*. Nashville, TN: Nelson Books, 2017.

Hylen, Susan. *Finding Phoebe: What New Testament Women Were Really Like*. Grand Rapids, MI: Eerdmans, 2023.

Jackson, Andrew. *The Christian Saints of Turkey: A Guide Inside the Early Church in Asia Minor*. Oakland, CA: Nomadic Publishing, 2016.

Jeffers, James. *The Greco-Roman World of the New Testament Era: Exploring the Background of Early Christianity*. Downers Grove, IL: InterVarsity Press, 1999.

Jewett, Robert. *A Chronology of Paul's Life*. Minneapolis, MN: Fortress Press, 1979.

Johnson, Andy. *1 & 2 Thessalonians*. Grand Rapids, MI: Eerdmans, 2016.

Judge, Edwin. *The Social Pattern of the Christian Groups in the First Century*. Wheaton, IL: The Tyndale Press, 1960.

Keener, Craig. *1–2 Corinthians*, NCBC. New York, NY: Cambridge University Press, 2005.

———. *1 Peter: A Commentary*. Grand Rapids, MI: Baker Academic, 2021.

———. *Acts: An Exegetical Commentary*. 4 vols. Grand Rapids, MI: Baker Academic, 2012-2015.

———. *Acts*. NCBC. New York, NY: Cambridge University Press, 2018.

———. *Christobiography: Memory, History, and the Reliability of the Gospels.* Grand Rapids, MI: Eerdmans, 2025.

———. *Galatians,* NCBC. New York, NY: Cambridge University Press, 2020.

———, Joseph Dodson, and Caryn Reeder. *Journeys of the Apostle Paul.* Bellingham, WA: Lexham Press, 2019.

———, and John Walton. *NIV Cultural Backgrounds Study Bible.* Grand Rapids, MI: Zondervan, 2016.

———. *Romans: A New Covenant Commentary,* NCCS. Eugene, OR: Cascade Books, 2009.

———. *The Gospel of John: A Commentary.* 2 vols. Peabody, MA: Hendrickson, 2003.

———. *The Gospel of Matthew: A Socio-Rhetorical Commentary.* Grand Rapids, MI: Eerdmans, 2009.

———. *The Historical Jesus of the Gospels.* Grand Rapids, MI: Eerdmans, 2009.

———. *The IVP Bible Background Commentary: New Testament,* second edition. Downers Grove, IL: InterVarsity Press, 2014.

Kierspel, Lars. *Charts on the Life, Letters, and Theology of Paul.* Grand Rapids, MI: Kregel Academic, 2012.

Kistemaker, Simon. *Exposition of the Acts of the Apostles,* Logos edition. Grand Rapids, MI: Baker, 1990.

Klink III, Edward. *The Beginning and End of All Things: A Biblical Theology of Creation and New Creation.* Downers Grove, IL: InterVarsity Press, 2023.

Knight, George. *The Pastoral Epistles: A Commentary on the Greek Text,* NIGTC. Grand Rapids, MI: Eerdmans, 1992.

Korb, Scott. *Life in Year One: What the World Was Like in First-Century Palestine.* New York, NY: Riverhead, 2010.

Ladd, George. *A Theology of the New Testament,* revised edition. Grand Rapids, MI: Eerdmans, 1993.

Laird, Benjamin. *Creating the Canon: Composition, Controversy, and the Authority of the New Testament.* Downers Grove, IL: InterVarsity Press, 2023.

Lampe, Peter. *From Paul to Valentinus: Christians at Rome in the First Two Centuries.* Minneapolis, MN: Fortress Press, 2003.

Leitzmann, Hans. *A History of the Early Church,* 2 vols. London: Lutterworth Press, 1961.

Levine, Amy-Jill, and Ben Witherington III. *The Gospel of Luke,* NCBC. New York, NY: Cambridge University Press, 2018.

Licona, Michael. *Jesus, Contradicted: Why the Gospels Tell the Same Story Differently.* Grand Rapids, MI: Zondervan, 2024.

Lightfoot, J.B. *The Acts of the Apostles.* Downers Grove, IL: InterVarsity Press, 2014.

Liversidge, Joan. *Everyday Life in the Roman Empire.* New York, NY: G.P. Putnam's Sons, 1976.

Lohfink, Gerhard. *Jesus and Community: The Social Dimensions of Christian Faith.* Minneapolis, MN: Fortress Press, 1984.

Lockyer, Herbert, ed. *Nelson's Illustrated Bible Dictionary.* Nashville, TN: Thomas Nelson, 1986.

Longenecker, Bruce. *In Stone and Story: Early Christianity in the Roman World.* Grand Rapids, MI: Baker Academic, 2020.

———. *The Lost Letters of Pergamum.* Grand Rapids, MI: Baker Academic, 2003.

———. *The New Cambridge Companion to St. Paul.* New York, NY: Cambridge University Press, 2020.

———, and Todd Still. *Thinking Through Paul: A Survey of His Life, Letters and Theology.* Grand Rapids, MI: Zondervan, 2014.

Longenecker, Richard. *Community Formation in the Early Church and in the Church Today.* Peabody, MA: Hendrickson, 2002.

———. *Galatians,* WBC. Grand Rapids, MI: Zondervan, 1990.

———. *Luke-Acts,* revised edition, EBC. Grand Rapids, MI: Zondervan, 2007.

———. *Paul, Apostle of Liberty,* second edition. Grand Rapids, MI: Eerdmans, 2015.

———. *The Epistle to the Romans,* NIGTC. Grand Rapids, MI: Eerdmans, 2016.

———. *The Ministry and Message of Paul.* Grand Rapids, MI: Zondervan, 1971.

Lucas, R.C. *The Message of Colossians & Philemon: Fullness and Freedom.* Downers Grove, IL: InterVarsity Press, 1980.

Ludemann, Gerd. *Paul, Apostle to the Gentiles: Studies in Chronology.* Minneapolis, MN: Fortress Press, 1984.

Macaulay, David. *City: A Story of Roman Planning and Construction.* New York, NY: Houghton Mifflin, 1974.

Malherbe, Abraham. *Social Aspects of Early Christianity.* Minneapolis, MN: Fortress Press, 2003.

Malina, Bruce. *The New Testament World: Insights from Cultural Anthropology.* Louisville, KY: Westminster John Knox Press, 2001.

———, and John Pilch. *Social-Science Commentary on the Book of Acts*. Minneapolis, MN: Fortress Press, 2008.

———, and Richard Rohrbaugh. *Social-Science Commentary on the Gospel of John*. Minneapolis, MN: Fortress Press, 1998.

———, and John Pilch. *Social-Science Commentary on the Letters of Paul*. Minneapolis, MN: Fortress Press, 2006.

———, and Richard Rohrbaugh. *Social-Science Commentary on the Synoptic Gospels*. Minneapolis, MN: Fortress Press, 1992.

Marshall, David. *Footprints of Paul: A Modern Traveler Follows the Trail of Christ's Greatest Champion*. Pittsburgh, PA: Autumn House, 1995.

Marshall, I. Howard. *Acts: An Introduction and Commentary*, TNTC. Grand Rapids, MI: Eerdmans, 1980.

———. *The Epistles of John*, NICNT. Grand Rapids, MI: Eerdmans, 1978.

Martin, Ralph, and Peter Davids, eds. *Dictionary of the Later New Testament & Its Development*. Downers Grove, IL: InterVarsity Press, 1997.

McKnight, Scot. *Junia is Not Alone*. Englewood, CO: Patheos Press, 2011.

———. *Reading Romans Backwards: A Gospel of Peace in the Midst of Empire*. Waco, TX: Baylor University Press, 2019.

———. *The Letter of James*, NICNT. Grand Rapids, MI: Eerdmans, 2011.

———. *The Letter to the Colossians*, NICNT. Grand Rapids, MI: Eerdmans, 2018.

Meeks, Wayne, ed. *Library of Early Christianity*, 8 vols. Philadelphia, PA: Westminster Press, 1985-1988.

———. *The First Urban Christians: The Social World of the Apostle Paul*. New Haven, CT: Yale University Press, 1983.

———. *The Moral World of the First Christians*. Louisville, KY: Westminster John Knox Press, 1986.

Meinardus, Otto F.A. *St. John of Patmos and the Seven Churches of the Apocalypse*. Athens, Greece: Lycabettus Press, 1974.

———. *St. Paul in Ephesus and the Cities of Galatia and Cyprus*. Athens, Greece: Lycabettus Press, 1973.

———. *St. Paul in Greece*. Athens, Greece: Lycabettus Press, 1994.

———. *St. Paul's Last Journey*. New Rochelle, NY: Caratzas Brothers Publishing, 1978.

Mitchell, Alan. *Hebrews*, Sacra Pagina. Collegeville, MN: Liturgical Press, 2007.

Moo, Douglas. *Epistle to the Romans*, NICNT. Grand Rapids, MI: Eerdmans, 1996.

———. *James*, TNTC. Grand Rapids, MI: Eerdmans, 1985.

Morgan, G. Campbell. *The Analyzed Bible*. Grand Rapids, MI: Fleming Revell, 1964.

Morris, Leon. *1 and 2 Thessalonians*, revised edition, TNTC. Grand Rapids, MI: Eerdmans, 1984.

———. *1 Corinthians: An Introduction and Commentary*, revised edition, TNTC. Grand Rapids, MI: Eerdmans, 1988.

———. *Luke: An Introduction and Commentary*, revised edition, TNTC. Grand Rapids, MI: Eerdmans, 1988.

———. *The First and Second Epistles to the Thessalonians*, revised edition, NICNT. Grand Rapids, MI: Eerdmans, 1991.

Morton, H.V. *In the Steps of St. Paul*. Cambridge, MA: Da Capo Press, 2002.

Mounce, William. *Pastoral Epistles*, WBC. Nashville, TN: Thomas Nelson, 2000.

Murphy-O'Connor, Jerome. *Paul: A Critical Life*. Oxford, NY: Clarendon Press, 1998.

———. *Paul: His Story*. Oxford: Oxford University Press, 2004.

———. *Paul the Letter-Writer: His World, His Options, His Skills*. Collegeville, MN: Liturgical Press, 1994.

———. *St. Paul's Corinth*. Collegeville, MN: The Liturgical Press, 2002.

Nee, Watchman. *Further Talks on the Church Life*. Anaheim, CA: Living Stream Ministry, 1974.

———. *The Normal Christian Church Life*. Anaheim, CA: Living Stream Ministry, 1980.

Novenson, Matthew. *Paul Then and Now*. Grand Rapids, MI: Eerdmans, 2022.

Oakes, Peter. *Empire, Economics, and the New Testament*. Grand Rapids, MI: Eerdmans, 2020.

———. *The Chronology of the Life of Paul*. Eugene, OR: Epworth, 2016.

Painter, John. *1, 2, and 3 John*, Sacra Pagina. Collegeville, MN: Liturgical Press, 2002.

Papandrea, James. *A Week in the Life of Rome*. Downers Grove, IL: InterVarsity Press, 2019.

Peeler, Amy. *Hebrews*. Grand Rapids, MI: Eerdmans, 2024.

Perrin, Nicholas, and Richard Hays. *Jesus, Paul, and the People of God: A Theological Dialogue with N.T. Wright*. Downers Grove, IL: InterVarsity Press, 2011.

Pitre, Brant. *Jesus and Divine Christology*. Grand Rapids, MI: Eerdmans, 2024.

Plummer, Richard, and John Mark Terry. *Paul's Missionary Methods: In His Time and Ours*. Downers Grove, IL: InterVarsity Press, 2012.

Pollock, John. *The Man Who Shook the World*. Wheaton, IL: Victor Books, 1972.

Porter, Stanley. *Paul in Acts*. Peabody, MA: Hendrickson, 2000.

Ramsay, William. *St. Paul the Traveler and Roman Citizen*, revised and updated by Mark Wilson. Grand Rapids, MI: Kregel, 2001.

———. *The Church in the Roman Empire*. New York, NY: G.P. Putnam's Sons, 1893.

Rapske, Brian. *The Book of Acts and Paul in Roman Custody*. Grand Rapids, MI: Eerdmans, 2004.

Rhoads, David. *Israel in Revolution 6-74 C.E.: A Political History Based on the Writings of Josephus*. Minneapolis, MN: Fortress Press, 1976.

Riesner, Rainer. *Paul's Early Period: Chronology, Mission Strategy, Theology*. Grand Rapids, MI: Eerdmans, 1998.

Robinson, John A.T. *Redating the New Testament*. London: SCM Press, 1976.

Roetzel, Calvin. *The Letters of Paul: Conversations in Context*. Louisville, KY: Westminster John Knox Press, 1982.

———. *The World That Shaped the New Testament*. Louisville, KY: Westminster John Knox Press, 2002.

Rose Publishing. *Rose Chronological Guide to the Bible*. Peabody, MA: Rose Publishing, 2019.

Rowe, C. Kavin. *Studies in Luke, Acts, and Paul*. Grand Rapids, MI: Eerdmans, 2024.

Ruden, Sarah. *Paul Among the People: The Apostle Reinterpreted and Reimagined in His Own Time*. New York, NY: Image, 2010.

Saller, Richard. *The Roman Empire: Economy, Society, and Culture*. Oakland, CA: Berkeley, 2015.

Sanders, E.P. *Paul: The Apostle's Life, Letters, and Thought*. Minneapolis, MN: Fortress Press, 2015.

Schmidt, Thomas. *The Apostles After Acts: A Sequel*. Eugene, OR: Cascade Books, 2013.

Schnabel, Eckhard. *Acts: Zondervan Exegetical Commentary on the New Testament*. Grand Rapids, MI: Zondervan, 2012.

———. *Early Christian Mission*, 2 vols. Downers Grove, IL: InterVarsity Press, 2004.

———. *Jesus in Jerusalem: The Last Days*. Grand Rapids, MI: Eerdmans, 2018.

———. *New Testament Theology*. Grand Rapids, MI: Baker Academic, 2023.

———. *Paul the Missionary: Realities, Strategies, and Methods*. Downers Grove, IL: InterVarsity Press, 2008.

Schreiner, Thomas. *1, 2 Peter, Jude*, NAC. Nashville, TN: Broadman & Holman Publishers, 2003.

———. *Galatians: Zondervan Exegetical Commentary on the New Testament*. Grand Rapids, MI: Zondervan, 2010.

———. *Paul, Apostle of God's Glory in Christ: A Pauline Theology*, second edition. Downers Grove, IL: InterVarsity Press, 2020.

Scroggie, W. Graham. *The Unfolding Drama of Redemption*. Grand Rapids, MI: Kregel, 1957.

———. *Scroggie's Bible Handbook*. Old Tappan, NJ: Fleming Revell, 1989.

Shenk, David, and Ervin Stutzman. *Creating Communities of the Kingdom: New Testament Models of Church Planting*. Scottdale, PA: Herald, 1988.

Shepherd, Michael. *An Introduction to the Making and Meaning of the Bible*. Grand Rapids, MI: Eerdmans, 2024.

Sievers, Joseph, and Amy-Jill Levine. *The Pharisees*. Grand Rapids, MI: Eerdmans, 2021.

Smallwood, E. Mary. *The Jews Under Roman Rule*. Leiden, Netherlands: Brill, 2014.

Smith, Christopher. *After Chapters & Verses: Engaging the Bible in the Coming Generations*. Colorado Springs, CO: Biblica Publishing, 2010.

———. *The Beauty Behind the Mask: Rediscovering the Books of the Bible*. Toronto: Clements Publishing, 2007.

Smith, David. *The Life and Letters of St. Paul*. New York, NY: Harper Brothers, 1950.

Smith, E. Elbert. *Church Planting by the Book*. Fort Washington, PA: CLC Publications, 2015.

Smith, F. LaGard. *The Narrated Bible in Chronological Order*. Irvine, CA: Harvest House, 1999.

Smith, M.A. *From Christ to Constantine*. Downers Grove, IL: InterVarsity Press, 1973.

Snyder, Howard. *The Community of the King*. Downers Grove, IL: InterVarsity Press, 1977.

Stambaugh, John, and David Balch. *The New Testament in Its Social Environment*. Louisville, KY: Westminster John Knox Press, 1986.

Stark, Rodney. *The Rise of Christianity: How the Obscure, Marginal Jesus Movement Became the Dominant Force in the Western World in a Few Centuries*. San Francisco, CA: Harper Collins, 1997.

Sterling, Gregory. *Shaping the Past to Define the Present: Luke-Acts and Apologetic Historiography*. Grand Rapids, MI: Eerdmans, 2023.

Stott, John. *Basic Introduction to the New Testament*. Grand Rapids, MI: Eerdmans, 2017.

———. *The Letters of John: An Introduction and Commentary*, revised edition, TNTC. Grand Rapids, MI: Eerdmans, 1988.

———. *The Message of 1 & 2 Thessalonians: The Gospel & the End Time*. Downers Grove, IL: Inter-Varsity Press, 1991.

———. *The Message of 1 Timothy & Titus: Guard the Gospel*. Downers Grove, IL: InterVarsity Press, 1996.

———. *The Message of 2 Timothy: Guard the Gospel*. Downers Grove, IL: InterVarsity Press, 1973.

———. *The Message of Acts: The Spirit, the Church & the World*. Downers Grove, IL: InterVarsity Press, 1990.

———. *The Message of Ephesians: God's New Society*. Downers Grove, IL: InterVarsity Press, 1979.

———. *The Message of Galatians: Only One Way*. Downers Grove, IL: InterVarsity Press, 1968.

———. *The Message of Romans: Good News for the World*. Downers Grove, IL: InterVarsity Press, 1994.

Stowers, Stanley. *Letter Writing in Greco-Roman Antiquity*. Louisville, KY: Westminster John Knox Press, 1986.

Strange, James Riley. *Excavating the Land of Jesus: How Archaeologists Study the People of the Gospels*. Grand Rapids, MI: Eerdmans, 2023.

Strauss, Mark. *Four Portraits, One Jesus*. Grand Rapids, MI: Zondervan, 2020.

Strom, Mark. *Reframing Paul: Conversations in Grace & Community*. Downers Grove, IL: InterVarsity Press, 2000.

Sweet, Leonard, and Frank Viola. *Jesus: A Theography*. Nashville, TN: Thomas Nelson, 2012.

Tasker, R.V.C. *John: An Introduction and Commentary*, TNTC, revised edition. Grand Rapids, MI: Eerdmans, 1960.

Theissen, Gerd. *Social Reality and the Early Christians: Theology, Ethics, and the World of the New Testament*. Minneapolis, MN: Fortress Press, 1992.

Thiselton, Anthony. *Discovering Romans: Content, Interpretation, Reception*. Grand Rapids, MI: Eerdmans, 2016.

Tidball, Derek. *The Social Context of the New Testament: Sociological Analysis*. Grand Rapids, MI: Zondervan, 1984.

Towner, Philip. *The Letters to Timothy and Titus*, NICNT. Grand Rapids, MI: Eerdmans, 2006.

VanderKam, James. *An Introduction to Early Judaism*, second edition. Grand Rapids, MI: Eerdmans, 2022.

Viola, Frank. *48 Laws of Spiritual Power*. Carol Stream, IL: Tyndale, 2022.

———. *Insurgence: Reclaiming the Gospel of the Kingdom*. Grand Rapids, MI: Baker, 2018.

———. *Finding Organic Church: A Comprehensive Guide to Starting and Sustaining Authentic Christian Communities*. Colorado Springs, CO: David C. Cook, 2009.

———. *From Eternity to Here: Rediscovering the Ageless Purpose of God*. Colorado Springs, CO: David C. Cook, 2009.

———. *God's Favorite Place on Earth*. Colorado Springs, CO: David C. Cook, 2013.

———. *Reimagining Church: Pursuing the Dream of Organic Christianity*. Colorado Springs, CO: David C. Cook, 2008.

———, and Mary DeMuth, *The Day I Met Jesus: The Revealing Diaries of Five Women from the Gospels*. Grand Rapids, MI: Baker, 2015.

Walker, Peter. *In the Steps of Paul: An Illustrated Guide to the Apostle's Life and Journeys*. Grand Rapids, MI: Zondervan, 2008.

Wanamaker, Charles. *The Epistle to the Thessalonians*, NIGTC. Grand Rapids, MI: Eerdmans, 1990.

Weima, Jeffrey. *1-2 Thessalonians: Baker Exegetical Commentary on the New Testament*. Grand Rapids, MI: Baker Academic, 2014.

———. *Paul the Ancient Letter Writer: An Introduction to Epistolary Analysis*. Grand Rapids, MI: Baker Academic, 2016.

———. *The Sermons to the Seven Churches of Revelation: A Commentary and Guide*. Grand Rapids, MI: Baker Academic, 2021.

Weiss, Johannes. *Earliest Christianity: A History of the Period A.D. 30-150*, vol 1. New York, NY: Harper & Brothers, 1959.

White, Jefferson. *Evidence and Paul's Journeys: An Historical Investigation into the Travels of the Apostle Paul*. Hilliard, OH: Parsagard Press, 2001.

Wilson, Mark. *Biblical Turkey: A Guide to the Jewish and Christian Sites of Asia Minor*, revised edition. Istanbul: Ege, 2020.

Winter, Bruce. *After Paul Left Corinth: The Influence of Secular Ethics and Social Change*. Grand Rapids, MI: Eerdmans, 2000.

———. *Roman Wives, Roman Widows: The Appearance of New Women and the Pauline Communities*. Grand Rapids, MI: Eerdmans, 2003.

———. *Seek the Welfare of the City: Christians as Benefactors and Citizens*. Grand Rapids, MI: Eerdmans, 1994.

———, et al., eds. *The Book of Acts in Its First Century Setting*. 6 vols. Grand Rapids, MI: Eerdmans, 1993-2004.

Witherington III, Ben. *1 and 2 Thessalonians: A Socio-Rhetorical Commentary*. Grand Rapids, MI: Eerdmans, 2006.

———. *A Week in the Life of Corinth*. Downers Grove, IL: InterVarsity Press, 2012.

———. *A Week in the Fall of Jerusalem*. Downers Grove, IL: InterVarsity Press, 2017.

———. *Conflict and Community in Corinth: A Socio-Rhetorical Commentary on 1 and 2 Corinthians*. Grand Rapids, MI: Eerdmans, 1995.

———, and Ann Witherington. *Corinthian Leather: The Fourth Art West Adventure*. Eugene, OR: Pickwick, 2011.

———. *Friends and Finances in Philippi: The Letter of Paul to the Philippians*. Harrisburg, PA: Trinity Press International, 1994.

———. *Grace in Galatia: A Commentary on Paul's Letter to the Galatians*. Grand Rapids, MI: Eerdmans, 1998.

———, ed. *History, Literature and Society in the Book of Acts*. New York, NY: Cambridge University Press, 1996.

———. *Invitation to the New Testament: First Things*, second edition. New York, NY: Oxford University Press, 2017.

———. *Letters and Homilies for Hellenized Christians: A Socio-Rhetorical Commentary*, 3 vols. Downers Grove, IL: InterVarsity Press, 2006-2007.

———. *New Testament History: A Narrative Account*. Grand Rapids, MI: Baker, 2003.

———. *Paul's Letter to the Philippians: A Socio-Rhetorical Commentary*. Grand Rapids, MI: Eerdmans, 2011.

———. *Paul's Letter to the Romans: A Socio-Rhetorical Commentary*. Grand Rapids, MI: Eerdmans, 2004.

———. *Paul's Narrative Thought World: The Tapestry and Tragedy of Triumph*. Louisville, KY: Westminster John Knox Press, 1994.

———. *Revelation,* NCBC. New York, NY: Cambridge University Press, 2003.

———. *The Acts of the Apostles: A Socio-Rhetorical Commentary.* Grand Rapids, MI: Eerdmans, 1998.

———. *The Gospel of Mark: A Socio-Rhetorical Commentary.* Grand Rapids, MI: Eerdmans, 2001.

———. *The Indelible Image, Volume I: The Theological and Ethical Thought World of the New Testament (The Individual Witnesses).* Downers Grove, IL: InterVarsity Press, 2009.

———. *The Indelible Image, Volume II: The Theological and Ethical Thought World of the New Testament (The Collective Witness).* Downers Grove, IL: InterVarsity Press, 2010.

———. *The Letters to Philemon, the Colossians, and the Ephesians: A Socio-Rhetorical Commentary on the Captivity Letters.* Grand Rapids, MI: Eerdmans, 2007.

———. *The New Testament Story.* Grand Rapids, MI: Eerdmans, 2004.

———. *The Paul Quest: The Renewed Search for the Jew of Tarsus.* Downers Grove, IL: InterVarsity Press, 1998.

———. *Women in the Earliest Churches.* New York, NY: Cambridge University Press, 1988.

Worth, Roland. *The Seven Cities of the Apocalypse and Greco-Asian Culture.* Mahwah, NJ: Paulist Press, 1999.

Wright, N.T. *Acts for Everyone: Parts One and Two.* Louisville, KY: Westminster John Knox Press, 2008.

———. *How God Became King: The Forgotten Story of the Gospels.* New York, NY: HarperOne, 2012.

———. *Interpreting Jesus: Essays on the Gospels.* Grand Rapids, MI: Zondervan, 2020.

———. *Interpreting Paul: Essays on the Apostle and His Letters.* Grand Rapids, MI: Zondervan, 2020.

———. *Interpreting Scripture: Essays on the Bible and Hermeneutics.* Grand Rapids, MI: Zondervan, 2020.

———. *Jesus and the Victory of God.* Minneapolis, MN: Fortress Press, 1996.

———. *Luke for Everyone.* Louisville, KY: Westminster John Knox Press, 2004.

———. *Mark for Everyone.* Louisville, KY: Westminster John Knox Press, 2004.

———. *Matthew for Everyone: Part Two.* Louisville, KY: Westminster John Knox Press, 2004.

———. *Paul: A Biography.* New York, NY: HarperOne, 2018.

———. *Paul and the Faithfulness of God.* 2 vols. Minneapolis, MN: Fortress Press, 2013.

———. *Paul for Everyone: 2 Corinthians.* Louisville, KY: Westminster John Knox Press, 2008.

———. *Paul for Everyone: Galatians and Thessalonians*. Louisville, KY: Westminster John Knox Press, 2004.

———. *Paul for Everyone: The Prison Letters*. Louisville, KY: Westminster John Knox Press, 2004.

———. *Paul: In Fresh Perspective*. Minneapolis, MN: Fortress Press, 2009.

———. *Pauline Perspectives: Essays on Paul, 1978-2013*. Minneapolis, MN: Fortress Press, 2013.

———. *Revelation for Everyone*, advanced reader copy. Louisville, KY: Westminster John Knox Press, 2011.

———. *Simply Jesus: A New Vision of Who He Was, What He Did, and Why He Matters*. New York, NY: HarperOne, 2011.

———. *The Challenge of Jesus: Rediscovering Who Jesus Was and Is*. Downers Grove, IL: InterVarsity Press, 1999.

———. *The Early Christian Letters for Everyone*. Louisville, KY: Westminster John Knox Press, 2011.

———. *The New Testament and the People of God*. Minneapolis, MN: Fortress Press, 1992.

———, and Michael Bird. *The New Testament in Its World: An Introduction to the History, Literature, and Theology of the First Christians*. Grand Rapids, MI: Zondervan, 2019.

Zetterholm, Magnus. *The Formation of Christianity in Antioch: A Social-Scientific Approach to the Separation Between Judaism and Christianity*. New York, NY: Routledge, 2003.

ALSO BY FRANK VIOLA

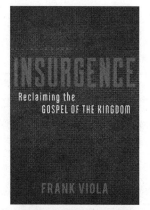

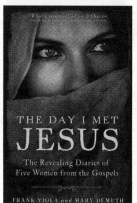

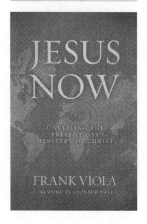

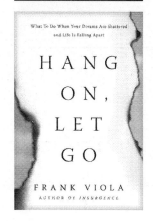

Want to Delve Deeper?

Check out Frank Viola's discipleship course, *Learning How to Live by the Indwelling Life of Christ*: a ten-part audio program with workbook and action plans.

For details, go to TheDeeperJourney.com

CHECK OUT THE CHRIST IS ALL PODCAST

frankviola.org/cia

CHECK OUT THE INSURGENCE PODCAST

frankviola.org/insurgencepodcast

COMING SOON

THE UNTOLD STORY OF THE NEW TESTAMENT CHURCH PODCAST

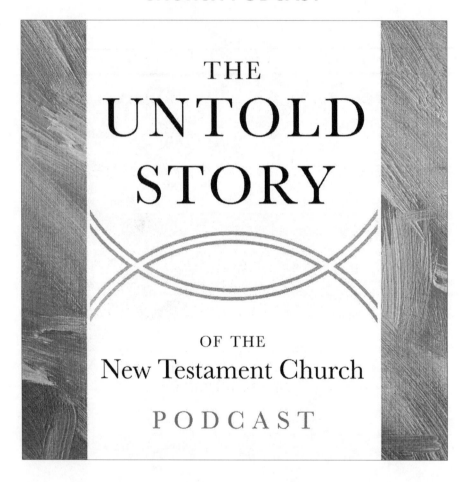

theuntoldstory.me

Follow

FRANK VIOLA

at Beyond Evangelical

Blog: frankviola.org

JOIN

THE DEEPER CHRISTIAN LIFE NETWORK

An online community for virtual mentoring and connection into the deeper things of God.

THEDEEPERCHRISTIANLIFE.COM

In the Right Hands, This Book Will Change Lives!

Most of the people who need this message will not be looking for this book. To change their lives, you need to **put a copy of this book in their hands.**

Our ministry is constantly seeking methods to find the people who need this anointed message to change their lives. **Will you help us reach these people?**

Extend this ministry by sowing three, five, ten, or *even more* books today and change people's lives for the better! Your generosity will be part of catalyzing the Great Awakening that many have been prophesying and praying for.